The TRAGIC HISTORY *of the* SEA

The
TRAGIC HISTORY
of the SEA

EDITED AND TRANSLATED BY

C. R. Boxer

FOREWORD AND ADDITIONAL TRANSLATION BY

Josiah Blackmore

UNIVERSITY OF MINNESOTA PRESS

Minneapolis / London

First University of Minnesota Press edition, 2001

Published by the University of Minnesota Press
111 Third Avenue South, Suite 290
Minneapolis, MN 55401-2520
http://www.upress.umn.edu

ISBN: 0-8166-3890-X

A Cataloging-in-Publication record for this book is available
from the Library of Congress.

Printed in the United States of America on acid-free paper

The University of Minnesota is an equal-opportunity
educator and employer.

12 11 10 09 08 07 06 05 04 03 02 01   10 9 8 7 6 5 4 3 2 1

CONTENTS

FOREWORD

A Shipwrecks Legacy

Josiah Blackmore

"Everything," writes Diogo do Couto, "was against them." He is recounting how a Portuguese ship suffered a storm at sea in the waning years of the sixteenth century. "All this night," Couto continues,

> they passed in great trouble and distress, for everything they could see represented death. For beneath them they saw a ship full of water, and above them the Heavens conspired against all, for the sky was shrouded with the deepest gloom and darkness. The air moaned on every side as if it was calling out "death, death"; and as if the water which was entering beneath them was not sufficient, that which the Heavens poured on them from above seemed as if it would drown them in another deluge. Within the ship nothing was heard but sighs, groans, shrieks, moans, and prayers to God for mercy, as it seemed that He was wroth with all of them for the sins of some who were in the ship.[1]

The passengers of the homeward-bound Indiaman *São Thomé* wallow in the embrace of a maritime circle of hell, the first anguished moment in a journey of loss, hunger, hardship, and privation. As the ship begins to sink at sea, the overcrowded lifeboats are unable to accommodate everyone and many perish in the dark depths. What awaits the survivors of the wreck is an expedition on blistered foot through a region of Africa, a trek so arduous that Couto is led to exclaim, "how fortunate may we consider those who remained in the ship, whose troubles were all ended in a moment! And how wretched these who thought themselves more fortunate in escaping from it!"[2]

The story of the wreck of the *São Thomé* is but one of several shipwreck tales written in Portugal in the sixteenth and seventeenth centuries during the mercantile frenzy known as the *carreira da Índia* (India route), the sea route between Portugal and the subcontinent traveled by ships carrying merchants, aristocrats, missionaries, sailors, Inquisitors, botanists, and statesmen as they pursued the material spoils of empire in the form of tantalizing Indian riches.[3] This trading route was notoriously dangerous and came to be known to a great degree by the wrecks of the ships that occurred in its waters; "on account of this staggering wealth," José Saramago observes in a 1972 essay, "people died in all possible ways."[4] The survivors of those wrecks often returned to Portugal to tell their stories in print or act as informants for others to do so. We refer to this collective storytelling enterprise as the Portuguese literature or narrative of shipwreck: the dramas of despair recounting the dangers and terrors of the high seas and the fate of castaways in distant lands.

Originally appearing as printed pamphlets, the shipwreck narratives were rescued for posterity by eighteenth-century editor Bernardo Gomes de Brito, who published a two-volume anthology of twelve narratives entitled *História Trágico-Marítima* (1735-36), or "The Tragic History of the Sea." Gomes de Brito thus marked the arrival once and for all of shipwreck and its textual incarnation as a kind of cultural institution in Portugal and, more widely, in Europe, the compelling and often gory details being available to anyone who could read Portuguese. Two hundred years after the publication of Gomes de Brito's volumes (plus a number of third "apocryphal" volumes containing other narratives), Charles Ralph Boxer, the preeminent historian of Portuguese and Dutch overseas expansion, took an interest in the tales. Through his masterful translator's pen, six of the shipwreck stories lived again.[5] Like his predecessor, Boxer published his work in two volumes: the first, *The Tragic History of the Sea*, appeared in 1959, and the second, *Further Selections from the Tragic History of the Sea*, in 1968.[6] Although Boxer wasn't the first to publish English translations of the shipwreck narratives, his versions nonetheless conferred a new authority on the stories for students of history and literature, especially for those working in the Anglophone world.[7] The Portuguese shipwreck narrative enterprise claims no equal in the Iberian tradition and few parallels outside of it. Now, decades later, Boxer's translations of the shipwreck narratives see the light of day once more. This book contains the entire text of Boxer's two volumes, brought together under the uniform title *The Tragic History of the Sea*. And with this reissue comes again a question critics have wrestled with over the years: what are we to make of these texts?

On one level, we can of course read the shipwreck tales for their sheer emotive appeal, for the exhilaration to be experienced as we participate, vicariously and safely, in the drastic and disastrous turns of fate, in existence and survival pushed to the limits. This very quality helps explain the power of these narratives to engage readers across the centuries. It underlies their universality and even makes it possible to consider them as "classics" in the sense that they can always be the same, and forever new. Yet, from a critical perspective, the shipwreck accounts have elicited a range of readings over time. They are either records of heroism, or the testimony of its opposite; they represent the suffering necessary for empire, or signal empire's decline. Some scholars have found literary or textual qualities of the highest merit in these works while others consider them of negligible worth.

It was Boxer who first sketched a glimpse of the rocky critical road traveled by the *História Trágico-Marítima*,[8] and I would like to revisit a few moments in its history here. We begin with Luís de Camões (1524?-1580), perhaps the most famous reader of the story of Manuel de Sousa Sepúlveda and the loss of the *S. João*; he included it in his *Os Lusíadas* (The Lusiads, 1572), the ten-canto poem about expansionist Portugal's past and prophetic future that resides at the center of the Portuguese canon. For Camões, this shipwreck tale stands as an emblem of the dire cost of empire, and represents not so much a tragic heroism as it does the conviction that empire contains disaster at its core, that it is built on the seeds of its own undoing. Years later, in the dedication of his anthology to D. João V, Gomes de Brito underscores the narratives as singular and constituent moments of Portuguese history. He declares that by his act of editorial dedication the stories are inducted into the monarchic and institutional consolidation of the past. This, Gomes de Brito claims, mitigates—even overturns—the horror of shipwreck by subsuming it within the otherwise glorious march of national history. In like spirit, Manuel de Sá, in his Inquisitorial license printed in the first volume of the *História Trágico-Marítima*, enjoins readers to "glory [in] the heroism of those magnanimous spirits."

Camões's and Gomes de Brito's understanding of shipwreck as first and foremost a historical circumstance was lasting and influential. Shipwreck can admit one to the historical archive. This historical inflection of the shipwreck stories lasts to our day—and for obvious reasons. Generally, shipwreck is contextualized within the history of empire and is related negatively to it. In the first monographic study of the *História Trágico-Marítima* and its circumstances, James Duffy reads the narratives as evidence of the decline of empire in the East, observing that "the eighteen narratives of shipwreck are simultaneously the negation of a heroic concept and the affirmation of a national decline. It is this candid picture, not the dramatic or epic mural, which is the significance of the *História trágico-marítima*."[9] Boxer reiterates the anti-heroic or anti-epic nature of the tales, remarking that "they give us the seamy side of the Portuguese 'conquest, navigation, and commerce,'" but also recognizes their value as literary and ethnographic documents.[10]

The literary treatment of the shipwreck narratives presents a similar history of varied assessment. Ramalho Ortigão, one of the founders of Portuguese realism, enthuses in 1876: "the most extraordinary work in Portugal written in prose is the *História trágico-marítima*," complemented on the poetic side by nothing other than *Os Lusíadas*.[11] Not only is shipwreck narrative on a canonical par with Camões, it is the highest expression of realist writing, a model of exteriority in which sentiment finds no place, as Ortigão overstatedly claims about the narrative of Sepúlveda and the wreck of the *S. João*. Albino Forjaz de Sampaio follows Ortigão's thinking somewhat when he notes the "literary brilliance, historical interest, and purity of language" he sees in the narratives, "model moments of good and legitimate Portuguese prose," which, because of their uniqueness to Portugal, boast a "patriotic value."[12]

If Sampaio's exuberance is heir to Ortigão's, so is João Gaspar Simões's reading of shipwreck literature through the lens of realism. In his book on the Portuguese novel, Gaspar Simões counts shipwreck narrative as one of the possible realist sources of modern Portuguese fiction while at the same time noting the problems it presents to generic classification; the narratives are a "confusion between a commemorative document, descriptive memory, travel account, a draft or direct annotation of facts, [and a] literary creation in the strict sense."[13] This generic uncertainty is reiterated by other critics, who alternately see shipwreck narrative as belonging properly to novels of chivalry, epic and anti-epic texts, travel literature, or chronistic writing.

Duffy eschews the "literary merits" of the narratives, noting that they "do not seem to warrant a more evolved literary treatment than they have already received" (which was relatively little at the time he was writing).[14] This sentiment is implicitly echoed in many of the standard histories of Portuguese literature that mention the narratives in passing or omit them altogether. Only recently has the *História Trágico-Marítima* begun to enjoy a critical renaissance in literary studies, thus overcoming Duffy's pronouncement of 1955.[15]

The resistance of the shipwreck narratives to easy categorization, generic distinctions, or clear-cut historical lessons is precisely what underlies their scholarly appeal. Approaching them anew, we need to revel more in their messiness. Many scholars, for example, continue to regard shipwreck narrative as a form of travel writing, but this category is too broad to offer the problematic readings these narratives demand; during the era of Iberian maritime expansion and conquest, the majority of texts produced were, in one form or another, travel literature.

Instead, a much more productive engagement with the narratives is possible if we consider them within the discursive production of early modern imperialism and colonialism, a production in which the texts of Portuguese and Spanish explorers were key.[16] We must reassess the shipwreck text in relation to the imperialist, textual agenda of early modern Iberia by recognizing that shipwreck narrative is primarily a product of the historiographic culture of expansion while at the same time it works against this culture as a kind of counterhistoriography by troubling the hegemonic vision of empire. Collectively, the shipwreck narratives disrupt the master historiographic narrative of imperialism in its cultural, political, and economic valences, upsetting the imperative of order and the unifying paradigms of "discovery" or "conquest" textuality. The shipwreck texts resist the writings of figures like Gomes Eanes de Zurara, who redacted the chronicles of the first Portuguese military movement into Africa in the fifteenth century, or the letters, diaries, and histories of Christopher Columbus, Pero Vaz de Caminha, Hernán Cortés, Bernal Díaz del Castillo, João de Barros, or Fernão Lopes de Castanheda. The closest—and only—Castilian congener of the narratives is *Los naufragios* of Álvar Núñez Cabeza de Vaca (1542 and 1555), a text that only gestures toward the more disruptive writing that will be elaborated by the Portuguese authors. Cabeza de Vaca's account remains within the mold of conquest writing and the textual relations of authority characteristic of it.[17] Hence, the "mainstream" texts that consolidate and perpetuate power, given their links to the political and hermeneutic prerogative of the crown, find a sustained contravention in the work of the shipwreck authors. The shipwreck experience and its textualization work against the tenets of the official historiographic edifice by demonstrating that the radically altered circumstances of shipwreck do not allow for the wholesale survival of the ideologies underlying expansionist campaigns.

When this edition of *The Tragic History of the Sea* was in development, Charles Ralph Boxer died in England at the age of 96, leaving behind a life's work of more than 350 books, articles, translations, and reviews. Obituaries in newspapers in Europe and North America acknowledged Boxer's formidable scholarly achievements and prolific output, pursuing as he did what amounted to three separate careers: first, he was an officer in the British military, then served as a professor at King's College, London, and then, on retirement from English academic life, he enjoyed a career in several universities in the United States (Indiana, Michigan, Missouri at St. Louis, Virginia, and Yale). These obituaries also give an idea of the intrigue and romance Boxer had lived as a military officer in the Far East, and some of them award him the enthralling epithet of "British spy." Boxer's own life was clearly filled with the adventure of faraway places, foreign languages, and the abiding presence of the sea. This volume is published, in part, as a tribute to his life and work.

I offer in this book a new translation of the most well known shipwreck narrative of them all: the wreck of the *S. João* and the death of Manuel de Sousa Sepúlveda and his family in east Africa in 1552. Boxer did not include this narrative in his volumes, no doubt because Theal's and Ley's versions had been published some years before; these translations are now long out of print. This narrative was celebrated and retold by a host of writers throughout Europe in the years following its appearance.[18] I present this new translation to contribute in a modest way to Boxer's remarkable translation project.

This book owes a great debt to the interest and sustained initiative of Richard Morrison of the University of Minnesota Press, who shepherded it quickly and enthusiastically into production. Thanks to him, the shipwreck survivors arrive at the shore again.

NOTES

1. "Narrative of the Shipwreck of the Great Ship *São Thomé*," in *The Tragic History of the Sea*, 57-58.

2. Ibid., 93.

3. For more on the *carreira da Índia*, see Boxer's "Introduction" to *The Tragic History of the Sea*.

4. José Saramago, "A morte familiar," in Neves Águas, ed., *História Trágico-Marítima* (Lisbon: Afrodite, 1972), 2: cvii.

5. Boxer's translations are based on versions of Portuguese originals that vary from the versions in Gomes de Brito's compilation; see Boxer's introductions to individual narratives for further details.

6. C. R. Boxer, ed. and trans., *The Tragic History of the Sea, 1589–1622: Narratives of the shipwrecks of the Portuguese East Indiamen* São Thomé *(1589)*, Santo Alberto *(1593)*, São João Baptista *(1622)*, *and the journeys of the survivors in South East Africa*, Second Series 112 of the Hakluyt Society (Cambridge, England: Cambridge University Press, 1959; Millwood, N.Y.: Kraus Reprint, 1986); C. R. Boxer, ed. and trans., *Further Selections from the Tragic History of the Sea, 1559–1565: Narratives of the shipwrecks of the Portuguese East Indiamen* Aguia and Garça *(1559)*, São Paulo *(1561)* *and the misadventures of the Brazil-ship* Santo António *(1565)*, Second Series 132 of the Hakluyt Society (Cambridge, England: Cambridge University Press, 1968). Also see Boxer's article "Some Second Thoughts on 'The Tragic History of the Sea, 1550-1650,'" *Annual Talk/Annual Report and Statement of Accounts for 1978. The Hakluyt Society* (1978): 1–9.

7. Prior to Boxer, English translations of some of the narratives were published in Charles David Ley, trans., *Portuguese Voyages, 1498–1663*, Everyman's Library 986 (London: J. M. Dent; New York: E. P. Dutton, 1947), and George McCall Theal, ed. and trans., *Records of South-Eastern Africa Collected in Various Libraries and Archive Departments in Europe*, 9 vols. (London: Government of the Cape Colony, 1898–1903).

8. "An Introduction to the *História Trágico-Marítima*," in *Miscelânea de estudos em honra do prof. Hernâni Cidade* (Lisbon: Universidade de Lisboa, 1957), 89-99; reprinted in C. R. Boxer, *From Lisbon to Goa, 1500–1750: Studies in Portuguese Maritime Enterprise* (London: Variorum, 1984).

9. *Shipwreck and Empire: Being an Account of Portuguese Maritime Disasters in a Century of Decline* (Cambridge, Mass.: Harvard University Press, 1955), 47.

10. *The Tragic History of the Sea*, vii.

11. *As praias de Portugal: guia do banhista e do viajante* (Porto: Magalhães & Moniz, 1876), 19.

12. *História da literatura portuguesa ilustrada* (Paris and Lisbon: Aillaud e Bertrand, 1929–32), 3: 352–53.

13. *História do romance português* (Lisbon: Estúdios Cor, 1967), 1: 189. With regard to the English tradition, Edward Said observes, "The prototypical modern realistic novel is *Robinson Crusoe*, and certainly not accidentally it is about a European who creates a fiefdom for himself on a distant, non-European island" (*Culture and Imperialism* [New York: Vintage, 1993], xii). Perhaps it is also no accident that *Robinson Crusoe* is a shipwreck story.

14. *Shipwreck and Empire*, v.

15. See the introductory study in Giulia Lanciani, *Sucessos e naufrágios das naus portuguesas* (Lisbon: Caminho, 1997); also see Maria Alzira Seixo and Alberto Carvalho, eds., *A "História Trágico-Marítima": análises e perspectivas* (Lisbon: Cosmos, 1996).

16. For elaboration on this and other aspects of the shipwreck narratives, see Josiah Blackmore, *Manifest Perdition* (Minneapolis: University of Minnesota Press, 2002).

17. For the "discourse of failure" in Cabeza de Vaca, see chapter 3 of Beatriz Pastor Bodmer, *The Armature of Conquest: Spanish Accounts of the Discovery of America, 1492–1589*, trans. Lydia Longstreth Hunt (Stanford: Stanford University Press, 1992). Of necessary consultation also is chapter 1 of José Rabasa, *Writing Violence on the Northern Frontier: The Historiography of Sixteenth-Century New Mexico and Florida and the Legacy of Conquest* (Durham: Duke University Press, 2000).

18. For a survey of the Sepúlveda story in European texts, see Roberto Barchiesi, "Un tema portoghese: il naufragio di Sepúlveda e la sua diffusione," *Annali dell'Istituto Universitario Orientale, Sezione Romanza* 18 (1976): 193–231, and J. Cândido Martins, *Naufrágio de Sepúlveda: texto e intertexto* (Lisbon: Replicação, 1997), 54–168.

ACCOUNT *of the*
VERY REMARKABLE LOSS
of the GREAT GALLEON S. JOÃO

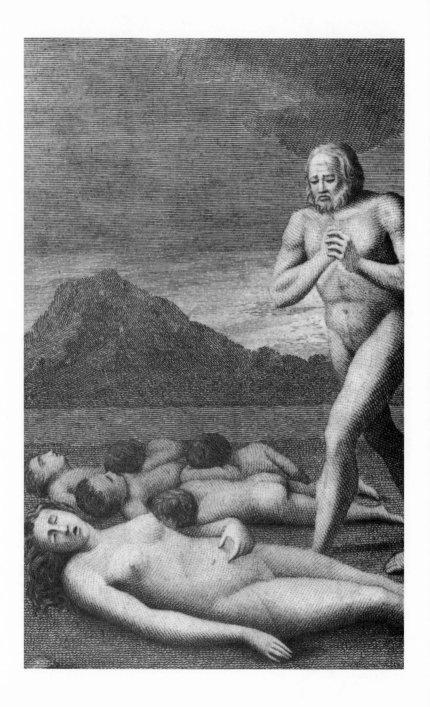

ACCOUNT *of the* VERY REMARKABLE LOSS *of the* GREAT GALLEON S. JOÃO

which narrates the great hardships and pitiful trials
visited on Captain Manuel de Sousa Sepúlveda,
and the lamentable end that he, his wife, and children met,
along with all the others, in the land of Natal
where they wrecked on June 24, 1552.

TRANSLATED BY

Josiah Blackmore

PROLOGUE

The matter narrated in this shipwreck should make men very
much fear God's punishments and become good Christians, and
bring the fear of God before their eyes so His commandments
will not be broken. For Manuel de Sousa was a noble *fidalgo*[1]
and a worthy gentleman, and during his time in India he spent
more than fifty thousand *cruzados* in feeding many people and in
doing good deeds for many others. He would end his life among
the Kaffirs,[2] as would his wife and children, in such misery and
want that he lacked food, drink, and clothing. He suffered so
many hardships before his death that they seem incredible except
to those who experienced them, including one Álvaro Fernandes,
boatswain's mate of the galleon, who told me this story in great

detail. I happened across him here in Mozambique in the year fifteen hundred and fifty-four.

And since this seemed to me a story which would stand as a good example and warning to all, I wrote the account of the trials and death of this *fidalgo* and his company so that those who wander over the sea may commend themselves to God and Our Lady, who intercedes on behalf of us all. Amen.

SHIPWRECK OF THE GREAT GALLEON *S. JOÃO*
IN THE LAND OF NATAL IN THE YEAR 1552

On the third of February in the year fifty-two, Manuel de Sousa (may God forgive him) left Cochin on this galleon to make his unfortunate voyage. He left so late because he had gone to Quilon to pick up cargo. But since there was so little pepper there—he acquired about four thousand *quintais*[3]—he went to Cochin to take on more, ending up with seven thousand *quintais*. This task was beset by many problems due to the war in Malabar. With this cargo he left for Portugal, though he could have taken twelve thousand *quintais* in all. Even with little pepper, this did not mean the ship was not very burdened with other merchandise. Ships so overladen must take extreme cautions since they run great risks.

Manuel de Sousa sighted the Cape's shoreline on the thirteenth of April, at thirty-two degrees. They sailed close in, because for many days after leaving India they were delayed from reaching the Cape due to the poor condition of their sails. This was one of the causes—indeed, the main one—of their destruction. The pilot André Vaz was making his way toward Cape Agulhas, but Captain Manuel de Sousa asked him to keep closer to land. The pilot did so in order to comply with the captain's wishes. This is why they headed toward Natal. When Natal came into sight the wind blew favorably, and they sailed along the coast, taking constant soundings, until they sighted Cape Agulhas. The winds were such that one day they blew east, and the other they blew west. It was already March[4] eleventh and they were north-southwest, with the Cape of Good Hope twenty-five leagues away, when they were hit by a wind from the west and west-northwest accompanied by many lightning bolts. It was nearing nightfall when the captain called the master and the pilot and asked what they should do in such weather, which was hitting them on the prow. Both responded: head for shore.

The reasons they gave for this were that the ship was very large and long, and laden with crates and merchandise. They had no sails other than those already on the yards, as the other set of sails had been through a storm on the Equator and was torn and could not be trusted. If they stood off, and if the weather grew worse and they had to run before it to make land, the winds might carry away the only sails they had. This would endanger their journey and their salvation, as there were no other sails on board. The ones they had were in such a state that just as much time was spent patching them as in sailing with them.

One of the reasons they had not already rounded the Cape by this time was the time spent in striking the sails in order to repair them. So the best thing to do was make for land with the foremast sails half-furled, because if they used only the foresail, old as it was, the wind would certainly tear it from the yard, given the enormous bulk of the ship. This way, the sails would work together. As they were heading for shore about one hundred thirty leagues from the Cape, the wind shifted so fiercely to the northeast and east-northeast that they were obliged to turn again south by southwest. Heavy seas from west and east swamped the galleon with so much water that with each roll she seemed to be on her way to the bottom.

Three days passed in this manner, at the end of which the wind calmed. The sea was still so heavy and the ship labored so much that it lost three pintles from the rudder, that is, the part of it on which the entire perdition or salvation of a ship depends. But no one knew this, only the ship's carpenter who went to check on the rudder and found the parts missing. Then he went to the master, Cristóvão Fernandes da Cunha, "the Short," and told him this in secret. As a responsible official and good man, the master said that this information should not be communicated to the captain or any other person to avoid inciting terror and fear in everyone. The carpenter obeyed.

While in this debilitated condition, the wind again failed them from the east-southeast, and the storm broke out in all its fury. Then it seemed to please God to make an end of them, as later happened. Heading again for shore under the same sails, the ship refused the helm, which caused it to heel and run toward leeward. The savage wind tore the mainsail off the main yard. When they found themselves without the sail and knowing there was no other, they ran to take in the foresail with all diligence since they preferred the risk of the sea hitting the ship abeam to being left with no sail at all. The foresail was not yet fully lowered when the ship was hit abeam so forcefully by three enormous waves that the violent rolling caused the rigging and the beams on the port side to explode into pieces, leaving nothing more than the three forestays.

Finding the rigging destroyed and no shrouds on that side of the mast, the crew grabbed some hawsers to make backstays. While they were doing this the sea was so heavy that it seemed a useless task and that it would be a better idea to cut down the mast and relieve the ship's labors. The wind and the sea were so fierce that it was impossible to do anything, and no one could keep a footing. The crew, axes in hand, began chopping at the mast when all of a sudden it snapped above the pulleys as if it had been felled by a single stroke. The wind hurled it and its sails into the sea on the starboard side as if they were very light; then they cut the rigging and sail on the other side and everything plunged into the ocean. With mast and yard gone, from the remaining stump of the mast they made another one from a section of spar, nailing it down and securing it with lines as best they could. On this they attached a yard for a stormsail and made another yard (from another piece of spar) for a mainsail. Some old sails were attached to this mainyard; the same was done for the foremast. This arrangement was so makeshift and so shaky that any strong wind would have destroyed it.

Once this was done, they set sail with the wind from the south-southwest. Since the rudder was missing its three main pintles, the ship could only be steered with great difficulty, and the sheets had to augment the rudder in steerage of the vessel. The wind grew stronger and the ship ran toward leeward, responding neither to the helm nor to the sheets. Then, the wind tore off the mainsail and the stormsail. Once again, seeing themselves without sails, the crew resorted to the foresail when the ship began to heave and labor. A wave broke the rotten rudder in two and carried away half of it, leaving the pintles in the sternpost gudgeons. This just shows how much the rudder and sails need to be cared for because of the many trials awaiting ships on this route.

Those who understand the sea well, or who give thought to what has just been described, will understand the affliction of Manuel de Sousa (with his wife and the other people on board) when he found himself on a ship off the Cape of Good Hope without rudder, without mast, and without sails—and without materials to make new ones.

At this point the vessel was laboring so hard and shipping so much water that the best way to keep it from sinking was to cut down the foremast, which was causing her to break open. As the crew was preparing to do this, a wave struck the ship so violently that it uprooted the mast and threw it into the sea. All the crew had to do after this was cut the shrouds. When the mast fell it struck the bowsprit, knocking it from its fastenings and lodging it almost entirely within the ship. All of these events were foreshadowings of even greater hardships yet to come. No amount of diligence would save this company from their sins. Still no land had been sighted since leaving the Cape, which was now fifteen or twenty leagues distant.

Now lacking mast, rudder, and sails, the ship began to head toward shore. Helpless, Manuel de Sousa and his men decided that all they could do was repair the rudder and make some sails from the textiles on board. They then might be able to reach Mozambique. So right away everyone was assigned a task: some worked on fixing the rudder, others on the mast, and others on making sails. Ten days were spent in this work.

When the rudder was finished it proved useless since it was

too narrow and too short. But, nonetheless, they hoisted the sails they had in the hope they might be saved. They tried the new rudder, but the ship refused to be steered by it since its measurements were different from the first one the sea had taken away. But by now land had been sighted. This was on June 8. The ship was near the coast; the sea and the wind were driving it toward land. The only thing left to do was let the ship run ashore and pray to God it would not sink. By God's miraculous help the ship, leaking badly, remained afloat on the waves of the sea.

Manuel de Sousa, finding himself and his ship so close to land in such a helpless situation, sought the opinions of his officers. The only way to save their lives, they reasoned, was to allow themselves to be carried along until they sounded a depth of ten fathoms, and then drop the longboats. They immediately launched a small boat with a few men to scout out the best landing-point for longboats along the beach. Once everyone had disembarked on the boats, what provisions and weapons that could then be recovered from the ship would be taken. Any other items they might salvage from the galleon would cause further loss, as the Kaffirs would certainly rob them of such things.

This was the plan. And so they went at the mercy of the sea and the wind, rolling now to this side, now to that. The ship could not be steered, and there were more than fifteen spans of water below deck. Closer to land they took a sounding and found the water to be still quite deep, so on they went. Some time later the small boat returned to the ship, its crew reporting that not far from there was a beach suitable for landing if they could reach it. Everywhere else there were ragged rocks and sheer cliffs, and no possibility of finding safety. Truly, men ought to think on this, for it causes great fear! So the galleon ran ashore in the land of the Kaffirs, which, dangerous as it was, would be their only means of salvation. And it is here where you will see the many hardships awaiting Manuel de Sousa, his wife, and his children.

When the small boat returned, everyone prepared to make for the beach at the place identified by the scouts as the best for landing. As the water was already at seven fathoms, they dropped an anchor. After this, they diligently took the necessary measures to launch the longboat. The first thing they did (once the lifeboat was away) was cast an anchor on land. The wind was more favorable, and the galleon was two crossbow-shots from the shore. On seeing that nothing could be done to save his sinking galleon, Manuel de Sousa summoned the master and pilot and told them the first thing they needed to do was get him, his wife, and children to land, along with twenty others to guard them. After this, they were to retrieve the weapons, provisions, and gun-powder from the ship, as well as some cambric cloth in the event they could trade it for food. They decided to make a fort there out of barrels and build a rough caravel out of wood from the ship in order to send a message to Sofala. But since it was already written on high that this captain, his family, and all of his company would meet their end, anything they might try to accomplish would be overturned by fate. For just as soon as the plans were made for the fort, the wind began to blow with great fury and the sea swells increased, driving the galleon against the coast and making it impossible to carry out their plan.

By this time Manuel de Sousa, his wife, and children, along with some thirty others, were on land. Everyone else was still on the galleon. To say that the captain (along with his wife and the thirty others) faced danger when disembarking is, of course, needless, but as I wish to tell the true and pitiful story, I will say that on the third run to the shore, the boat sunk. Some died then, including Bento Rodrigues's son. Until that point the larger lifeboat had not yet gone to shore, since, with the rough seas, no one would send it. The small boat escaped those first two times because it was lighter.

The master, pilot, and everyone else still on board saw that the galleon was responding to the landline, and realized that the sea line had been cut because they had been anchored for two days over a foul bottom. On the morning of the third day they saw that this was so, and the pilot said to them, as the wind rose and the ship began to touch ground: "Brethren, before the ship splits open and sinks to the bottom, anyone who wants to go with me in the longboat can." Then he embarked, helping the master, who was old and failing in spirit because of his age, to embark also. About forty people boarded the boat, all with great effort since the wind was so strong. The sea was so heavy against the coast that it smashed the lifeboat to pieces on the beach. God ordained that no one from that boatload would die—quite a miracle, since before reaching the beach the sea capsized the vessel.

The captain, who had gone ashore the day before, was walking along the beach encouraging everyone, bringing as many as he could to sit by the fire he had lit since the cold was tremendous. Better than five hundred people were still on the ship: two hundred Portuguese, including Duarte Fernandes, the quartermaster and the boatswain—all the others were slaves. As the ship was already repeatedly striking the ground, they decided to let out the landline by hand and allow the ship to go directly to the beach. They did not want to cut it because the undertow might draw them back to sea. Soon after the ship went aground she broke in two, one half from the mast forward and the other from the mast to the stern. In about one hour these two pieces became four. The decks were broken open, so the merchandise and crates came to the surface. Many of those on board struggled to cling to the boxes and pieces of wood in order to get to land. More than forty Portuguese and seventy slaves died this way. The rest came to land as God pleased: some on top of the waves, and some under, and many were wounded by the nails and wood. In about four hours the galleon was completely destroyed. Not a single piece of it any longer than a couple of feet could be found. The sea delivered all the pieces onto the beach in a great fury. They say that all of the merchandise on board—the king's, and that belonging to others—was worth a thousand pieces of gold. Since the discovery of India no ship had left its ports so richly burdened. With the ship in pieces, Captain Manuel de Sousa realized he would not be able to build the smaller boat as he had intended, since there was no lifeboat or indeed anything out of which he could construct a crude caravel. So he had to think of something else.

The captain and his company, on seeing that there was no

way of building another boat, sought the counsel of the officers and noblemen in the complement (these were Pantaleão de Sá, Tristão de Sousa, Amador de Sousa, and Diogo Mendes Dourado de Setúbal). Since there was sufficient water it was decided that they should remain on the shore for a few days until the sick got better. There, they made a fortification out of chests and barrels and remained for twelve days, during which time no blacks came from the country to speak to them. During the first three days nine Kaffirs appeared on a hill where they stood for two hours without attempting to speak to us. Then they left, as if frightened. Two days later it was decided that a man along with a Kaffir from the galleon should be sent inland to see if there were any blacks willing to talk with them in order to trade for food. These two men searched for two days without finding a living soul, only some uninhabited straw huts from which they surmised that the blacks had fled in fear. As they were returning to camp they came across some dwellings shot through with arrows. This, they say, is the Kaffirs' sign of war.

Three days later, while the company still occupied the place on the beach to which they had escaped from the galleon, seven or eight Kaffirs appeared on a hill and they had a cow with them. Using hand signals, the Christians got them to come down. The captain and four men went to speak with them, and after they assured them they would not be harmed, the blacks said (through gestures) that they wanted iron. So the captain ordered half a dozen nails to be brought and showed them to the blacks, who delighted in seeing them. The blacks came closer to our people and began to negotiate the price of the cow. Just as an agreement was reached five Kaffirs appeared on another hill and began shouting in their language not to trade the cow for nails. The Kaffirs left us without saying a word, taking the cow with them. The captain refused to take the cow from them even though he very much needed it for his wife and children.

Thus the captain was beset with worry and vigilance, arising three or four times each night to keep the watch, a difficult task. Twelve days passed in this manner until the sick convalesced. At the end of this time, the captain saw that everyone was fit enough to walk and called a council. Before discussing the situation he addressed everyone: "Friends and gentlemen: You clearly see the state we are in because of our sins. I truly believe mine alone are enough to account for our dire travails. But God is so merciful that He granted us a great favor by not allowing us to sink with our ship, inundated as it was by water below-deck. It will please Him Who was served in rescuing us from that danger to deliver us to a land of Christians. To those who might die of hardships on this journey, may their souls find salvation. You well understand, gentlemen, that the days we spent here were necessary for the convalescence of our sick. And now, God be praised, they are well enough to walk, so I have called you together so we may decide what path we are to take in order to reach salvation. Our plan to build a boat, as you saw, was struck down since we could not salvage any materials from the ship to make it. So, gentlemen and brethren, as your lives are concerned as well as mine, it would not be right to do or decide on anything without everyone's consent. The one boon I ask of you is that you do not abandon me or leave me, if, on account of my wife and children, I am not able to walk as quickly as the best of you. Thus united will God in His great mercy help us."

After this speech was made and everyone had discussed the route they should take, all agreed that there was no alternative but to walk (maintaining order as best they could) along the shore in the direction of the river discovered by Lourenço Marques. With promises to their captain that they would not abandon him, the company immediately set out. The river was about one hundred eighty leagues away by coast, but they marched more than three hundred because of all the detours they took to ford all the rivers and cross all the marshes in their path. After this they returned to the sea. This took five and a half months.

From this beach, where they wrecked at thirty-one degrees on the seventh of June in fifty-two, the company began to march in the following order: Manuel de Sousa with his wife and children, along with eighty Portuguese and one hundred slaves; André Vaz, the pilot, was also in this company, and he marched in the vanguard carrying a banner with a crucifix on it. Some slaves carried D. Leonor, the captain's wife, on a litter. Directly behind came the master of the galleon, the sailors, and the women slaves. Pantaleão de Sá, with the other Portuguese and slaves (about two hundred people), marched in the rearguard. All together there were about five hundred people, one hundred eighty of whom were Portuguese. They walked in this manner for a month, experiencing many hardships and much hunger and thirst, for in all that time they had nothing to eat but the rice that was rescued from the galleon and some fruit from the jungle. They could find no other food in the land or anyone to sell them some. The great sterility they suffered cannot be believed or written.

In the entire month they must have walked a hundred leagues, but because of the detours they took to cross rivers they did not advance probably more than thirty leagues along the coast. Ten or twelve people had already been lost. One was an illegitimate son of Manuel de Sousa, ten or twelve years of age, who was left behind (since he was already so frail from starvation) along with the slave who was carrying him on his back. When Manuel de Sousa asked after his son and was told that he had been left half a league behind, he almost lost his mind. He thought his son was in the rear with his uncle Pantaleão de Sá, as he often was, and this is how he lost track of him. He immediately promised to pay five hundred *cruzados* to any two men who would turn back and search for him. But no one would accept the offer since it was almost night and people were afraid that tigers[5] and lions would eat anyone separated from the group. Manuel de Sousa was forced to keep moving and leave his son behind, but his father's eyes kept looking back. Here it is especially clear how many hardships this nobleman faced before his death. António de Sampaio, nephew of Lopo Vaz de Sampaio (who was governor of India), was also lost from sheer hunger and the labor of the march, along with five or six Portuguese and some slaves.

During this time there had been skirmishes, but the Kaffirs always got the worst of it; in one fight, the Kaffirs killed Diogo

Mendes Dourado, who fought well to the death like a valiant knight. The labor of keeping watch, overcoming hunger, and maintaining the march was so relentless that each day more people in the company grew weak. Not one day passed without one or two being left on the beaches or in the jungle from fatigue. These people were immediately eaten by tigers and snakes, of which there are many in the land. To see such people abandoned in those deserts was truly painful and heart-rending for all: he who fell behind would bid his companions of the march—his father, perhaps, or brothers, or friends—to go on, commending them to God. It was a cause of bitter suffering to witness relatives or friends being left behind without being able to help, since everyone knew that in a short time they would be eaten by wild animals. Just to hear of this causes sorrow; think how much more was felt by those who saw it, and lived it.

Beset by the greatest misfortunes, the march moved on. The company would go inland to look for food and to cross rivers, and would then return to the coast, now by climbing steep mountains, now by descending other, terrifically dangerous ones. As if these travails were not enough, the Kaffirs created many others. They went on like this for about two and a half months, and their hunger and thirst were so acute that on most days extraordinary things occurred. I will relate a few of the most remarkable.

It often happened that within the company a pint of water was sold for ten *cruzados*; a cauldron containing eight liters would fetch one hundred *cruzados*. As this sometimes caused disorder, the captain would send for a cauldron of water (since there was no larger container to be found), paying one hundred *cruzados* to whomever went to get it. He rationed out the water himself, and what he took for his wife and children cost him eight to ten *cruzados* per pint. He rationed the rest at the same price. Because of the money made in one day selling water there was always someone willing to put himself at risk on the next to go fetch more. In addition to this, everyone suffered such hunger that a great sum of money would be paid for any fish that might be found on the beach or any animal from the hills.

So they continued the daily grind of the march, negotiating the land as they found it and always confronted with the hardships I have mentioned. Three months must have passed as they searched for that river found by Lourenço Marques, which empties into Boa Paz, the water-supply point for ships. For many days they could find nothing to eat but the fruit they found by chance, or the bones they toasted. Frequently a goatskin was sold at camp for fifteen *cruzados*: if it was dry, it would be soaked in water, then eaten. When they marched along the beach, they would find sustenance in fish or other creatures surrendered by the sea. At the end of this time they encountered a Kaffir, chief of two villages, an old man who appeared to be of a generous disposition—and was, as the help he provided to them proved. He told the company not to leave but to remain with him, and he would provide for them as best he could.

The lack of food there, the Kaffir said, was not because the land could not yield a crop but because the Kaffirs are men who sow very little, eating nothing more than the wild animals they kill. The Kaffir king strongly enjoined Manuel de Sousa and his people to stay with him. He told them he was at war with another king (whose lands the company would soon cross if they moved forward) and asked for their help. He said that if they continued on, they would certainly be robbed by the other king, who was more powerful than he was. On account of the help he was hoping for from this company, and because of the experiences with Portuguese who had already been there (Lourenço Marques and António Caldeira), the Kaffir king did as much as he could to convince them not to leave. The two previous Portuguese had given this Kaffir the name Garcia de Sá, since he looked like Garcia de Sá, and, like him, was an old and generous man. There is no doubt that in all nations there are both good and bad men. He offered shelter to the Portuguese and honored them, doing all he could to keep them there and telling them they would be robbed by the other king with whom he was at war. The Portuguese remained there for six days considering what they had heard. But as it seemed to be already determined that Manuel de Sousa along with the greater part of his company would meet their end on this journey, they did not follow the counsel of the little king, who nonetheless attempted to make them see their mistake.

When the king saw that the captain still intended to leave, he asked for his help (and that of some of the captain's men) against another king they had already left behind. Manuel de Sousa and the Portuguese felt they could not refuse this request given the hospitality and shelter they had received. They also did not want to offend him since they were in his power and in that of his people. Manuel de Sousa asked his brother-in-law Pantaleão de Sá to gather twenty Portuguese men to help their friend the king. Pantaleão de Sá, twenty Portuguese, and five hundred Kaffirs with their captains turned back and went six leagues through the country they had already crossed. They fought the insurgent Kaffir and took all his livestock as the spoils of war, and brought it back to camp where Manuel de Sousa was waiting with the king. They spent five or six days doing this.

After Pantaleão de Sá came back from that war which was meant to help the little king and his people and had rested from that labor, the captain sought advice about their departure. The advice rendered was so poor that they resolved to march in search of the Lourenço Marques river, not knowing they had already reached it. This river supplies the water for Boa Paz in three tributaries—they were on the first—and all empty into the same estuary. And though they found a red cap, a sign that other Portuguese had previously been there, their ill fortune blinded them and they decided the only thing to do was move forward. They would have to cross the river, but this could only be done in canoes since it was so wide. The captain wanted to take seven or eight canoes he found secured in chains, but the king did not wish to give them to him because he wanted the company to stay, seeking all possible ways to keep the Portuguese from crossing. So the captain sent some men to see if the canoes could be taken. Two of those men returned and said it would be a difficult thing to do. The others, out of malice, remained behind, taking one of the canoes and going down river, abandoning their captain. The captain understood that there would be no hope of crossing the river without the king's consent. So he asked the king if he would allow the company to be transported to the other side of the river in the canoes, adding that he would pay his people well for this. To please the king, the captain gave him some of their weapons so that he might release them and arrange for the crossing.

The king went in person with them to the river. The Portuguese, fearful of treachery, begged Captain Manuel de Sousa to convince the king to go back to the village with his people, leaving behind only the blacks who would help them cross in the canoes when they so wished. As the little black king harbored no malice but instead wanted to do all he could to help, it was easy to persuade him to return. He left right away, which allowed them to cross as they pleased. At that point Manuel de Sousa sent thirty men with three muskets in the canoes to the other side. After these thirty had crossed, the captain, his wife, and children crossed also, and after them all the rest. Up to that point they had not been robbed, and, once on the other side, they arranged themselves again into an ordered marching column.

They must have walked about twenty leagues for five days in the direction of the second river when they reached the middle river. There, at sunset, they came across some other blacks who directed them toward the ocean. On the bank of the river they saw two large canoes and made camp on the beach, where they spent the night. The water in this river was brackish, and there was no fresh water anywhere near, only where they had already marched. During the night their thirst was so great it was unbearable. Manuel de Sousa wanted to send someone to search for water, but there was no one who would go for less than a hundred *cruzados* per cauldron. He ordered some men to go fetch water and paid them two hundred *cruzados* per cauldron, because otherwise there would have been no way of getting any water. And, as I said earlier, food was very scarce, so God determined that the water would have to serve as sustenance.

On the following day, still at camp, some blacks arrived in three canoes near nightfall. They told a black woman in the camp who was already beginning to understand a little of their language that a ship had arrived with men on it like the Portuguese, but had already departed. Manuel de Sousa asked them if they would take his company to the other side of the river. The blacks responded that it was already night (for Kaffirs do nothing at night), but they would take them on the following day, for pay. When day broke, the blacks came back with four canoes, and for the price of a few nails began to take people across the river. First the captain sent some men across to guard the pass. Then he himself embarked in a canoe with his wife and children, accompanied by the other three canoes filled with people. They would make their way to the other side where they would wait for the rest of the company. But as Manuel de Sousa's canoe went a slightly different way to avoid a sandbar, the captain thought he was being separated from the others in order to be robbed, since he had no interpreter along to inform him of the reason for the detour. It is also said that by that time the captain was not in his right mind because the burden of vigilance and work was heavier on him than on others. Thinking that the blacks were planning treachery, he put hand to sword and drew it against the rowers, saying, "Where are you taking me, you dogs?"

Seeing the naked sword, the blacks jumped into the water and were in danger of drowning. His wife and a few others with him told him not to do the blacks any harm because otherwise they would all be lost. Truly, anyone who saw Manuel de Sousa do this and who knew of his manners and gentleness would easily have said he was not in his right mind, as the captain was a wise and considerate man. From that point on he never again exercised command over his people as he had done until then. On reaching the other side he greatly complained about his head. Towels were applied to it as the company gathered together once more.

When everyone was on the other side of the river and ready to resume the march, they saw a band of Kaffirs and made ready to fight, thinking they were about to be robbed. The Kaffirs drew nearer and began to speak with our people, asking who they were and what they were seeking. They said they were shipwrecked Christians and asked the Kaffirs to guide them to a big river that lay ahead. They also said that if the Kaffirs had any food they should bring it out so it could be purchased. Through a Kaffir woman from Sofala the blacks said that if they wanted food they would have to go with them to where their king was, who would take them in. At that time there were still some one hundred and twenty in the company. D. Leonor was already among those traveling on foot. A noblewoman, young and delicate, she marched along those harsh and arduous paths like any robust man from the countryside, on many occasions consoling others in the company and helping to carry her children. This was the situation after no more slaves were left to carry her litter. It truly seems that Our Lord's grace was at work there, since without it a woman so fragile and so unaccustomed to hardships would not have been able to traverse such long and arduous trails, always suffering hunger and thirst. By now the company had already gone more than three hundred leagues because of the detours.

But back to the story. Once the captain and his company were given to understand that the king was near, they took the Kaffirs as guides and warily made their way to the place indicated, suffering a hunger and thirst only God could know. The king was a league away. When they arrived, the king sent word that they should not enter (the Kaffirs keep the king's residence concealed) but rather wait under some trees indicated to them where food would be sent. Manuel de Sousa obeyed, as someone in a foreign land might, not knowing as much about the Kaffirs as we do now given the experience of this wreck and that of the ship *S. Bento*. A hundred men armed with muskets could cross the whole of Kaffraria since the Kaffirs fear these things more than they do the Devil himself.

After retiring to the shade of the trees, they began to receive some food in exchange for nails. They remained there for five days, thinking they would stay until the next India ship arrived, as the blacks told them. Manuel de Sousa asked the Kaffir king for a hut so he could shelter himself with his wife and children. The Kaffir said he would give it to him, but that the others could not all remain there together because of the lack of food in that land. He, his wife, and children could stay, along with a few others, but the rest would be divided up and sent to other places in

his domain. He would provide food and shelter to them until the
next ship came. This was the malicious intention of the king, it
seemed, given what happened later. This shows that it is true
what they say that Kaffirs have a great fear of muskets since they
separated the Portuguese by sending them to various places in
order to rob them, even though there were only about five muskets among a hundred and twenty people. It was an easy job, as
the Portuguese were nearly dead from hunger. Not knowing how
much wiser it would have been not to disband, they surrendered
themselves to fate and did the bidding of that king who was
planning their perdition. They had always refused the advice of
the other little Kaffir king who had done nothing but speak to
them honestly and help them as best he could. From this men
must see how they can never say or accomplish anything based
on their will alone, but should put everything into the hands of
Our Lord.

When the Kaffir king decided, with the consent of Manuel
de Sousa, that the Portuguese were to be divided among various
villages and other places in order to receive food, he also said that
he had captains there who would each take charge of a number
of Portuguese in order to feed them. But this could not be
accomplished unless the Portuguese abandoned their arms as the
Kaffirs feared them so long as their weapons were in sight. He
would store the muskets in a hut, to be returned as soon as
another Portuguese ship arrived.

Since Manuel de Sousa was already quite sick and had lost
his judgment, he responded (as he would not have done were he
well) that he would speak with his people. But as the hour had
arrived in which he was to be robbed, he spoke with the other
Portuguese and told them he would not leave that place. One
way or the other, he said, they would find help, either by a ship
or by some other means God might devise. The river they were
on was the river discovered by Lourenço Marques, as his pilot
André Vaz said. Any who wished to move on could do so, but he
could not out of love for his wife and children. His wife was
already very debilitated from her immense hardships and she
could no longer walk, and there were no slaves to help her. He

was resolved to end his life with his family, whenever God was pleased that this should happen. He asked those who went on to send news if they came across a Portuguese ship. Those who wished to remain with him were welcome to do so, and wherever he might go, so would they. Furthermore, he said it was necessary for them to surrender their arms so the blacks would trust them and not think they were a roving band of thieves. This was the way to relieve their suffering from the hunger they had endured for so long.

So the judgment of Manuel de Sousa as well as those with him was that of people who were not in their right minds. For if they thought about it, they would have realized that the Kaffirs never got too close to them as long as they were carrying arms. So the captain ordered everyone to turn over their weapons even though their salvation resided in them, apart from God. This went against the will of some of the company and especially against that of D. Leonor. No one contradicted the captain except her, although it did no good. She said, "You surrender your arms, and I give myself up as lost along with all these people." The blacks gathered up the guns, and took them to the house of the king.

As soon as the Kaffirs saw the Portuguese without weapons (having already plotted this treachery), they immediately began to separate them and rob them, taking them into the jungle, each group to its own fate. Once they reached the appointed places they were stripped, without a shred of clothing being left to them. They were thrown out of the villages with the blows of many clubs. Manuel de Sousa was not in the groups treated like this, but remained with the king along with his wife, children, the pilot André Vaz, and some twenty others, since they had jewels, precious gems, and money. They say that the worth of all that wealth totaled more than a hundred thousand *cruzados*.

When Manuel de Sousa, his wife, and the twenty others were separated from everyone else, they were robbed of everything they had but were not stripped. And the king said the captain should leave in search of his company, for he did not wish to do him further harm, or lay hands on his person or that of his wife. When Manuel de Sousa heard this, he surely was reminded of the grave error he had made in surrendering the weapons. He was forced to do what he was told, as the situation was no longer in his hands.

The other ninety members of the company (including Pantaleão de Sá and three other noblemen), though they had been separated from one another, little by little began to regroup after being robbed and stripped by the Kaffirs to whom the king had delivered them. They were able to do this since they were not far from one another. So together, ill treated and miserable, without weapons, clothes, money to buy food, or their captain, they began to march. But now they did not look like men. With no one to lead them, they marched without order, along many paths. Some went through the jungle, and others through the mountains. They dispersed in all directions. Each man thought about nothing other than the best way to save his own life, whether among Kaffirs or Moors, since there was no one to offer counsel or gather them together for this purpose. They were wandering now as men completely lost, but I will stop speaking of them and return to Manuel de Sousa, his poor wife, and their children.

Manuel de Sousa, seeing himself robbed and dismissed by the king to search for his company, and finding himself without money, weapons, or people to wield them, still very much felt the affront that had been done to him even though he had not been right in the head for many days. So what then is to be thought of a very delicate woman, who finds herself amidst so many hardships and privations, the greatest one of all seeing her husband so ill-treated and unable to keep his command or care for his children? But, as a woman of good judgment, and with the opinions of the men still with her, they began to make their way into those jungles without any hope or conviction other than God.

At this time André Vaz (the pilot) was still in the company, as was the boatswain (who never left her), one or two Portuguese women, and some women slaves. As they made their way, it occurred to them that it would be a good idea to follow those ninety men who had been robbed and who had gone ahead of them, so for two days they followed their footprints. D. Leonor was now so weak, sad, and disconsolate on seeing her husband so ill and on finding herself separated from the others that she thought it would be impossible to rejoin them. To think on this breaks your heart! During their march the Kaffirs attacked Manuel de Sousa, his wife, and the few of their company who remained, stripping them completely. Seeing themselves in this plight, with two very young infants, they gave thanks to Our Lord.

It is said that D. Leonor would not allow herself to be stripped, defending her body by fists and blows since it was her nature to prefer being killed by the Kaffirs than to find herself naked in front of everyone. There can be no doubt that at that instant her life would have ended had it not been for Manuel de Sousa, who pleaded with her to let herself be stripped. He reminded her that they were born naked and that God wished her to be, too. One of the greatest hardships they suffered was seeing two small infants, their own children, crying and asking for food without their being able to give them any. Once naked, D. Leonor threw herself on the ground immediately and covered herself with her very long hair. She made a hole in the sand and buried herself in it up to her waist; she never again would rise from the sand. Manuel de Sousa asked an old nanny of hers for her torn shawl so that D. Leonor could cover herself with it, and the nanny gave it to him. Even so, D. Leonor never again rose from that place where she fell after finding herself naked.

I can truly say that I know of no one who could hear of this without great pity and sadness. To see a noble woman, daughter and wife of two honorable *fidalgos* so mistreated, and with such a lack of respect! When the men in the company beheld Manuel de Sousa and his wife naked, they retreated a bit, ashamed in finding their captain and D. Leonor thus. D. Leonor then said to André Vaz, the pilot: "You can all see what we have been brought to. We will not be able to move on, and will find our end here because of our sins. Leave here in order to be saved, and commend yourselves to God. If you should reach India, or in time, Portugal, relate how you left Manuel de Sousa, me, and my children." The others, seeing they could do nothing to cure their captain's fatigue or remedy the misery or want of his wife and children, went off into the jungle to search for a way to survive.

After André Vaz left Manuel de Sousa and his wife, Duarte Fernandes the boatswain and some women slaves remained behind with them. Three of these slaves survived and reached Goa where they told how they saw D. Leonor die. Manuel de Sousa, though he was not in his right wits, did not forget that his wife and children needed to eat. Limping from a wound in his leg inflicted by the Kaffirs, he went into the forest in this battered state to find some fruit for them. When he returned, he found D. Leonor weak from hunger and weeping; after the Kaffirs stripped her, she never again rose from the sand, and never stopped sobbing. He found one of his children dead, and buried him in the sand with his own two hands. The next day Manuel de Sousa returned to the jungle, again in search of fruit, and this time when he returned he found that D. Leonor and the other child had died. Five slave women were crying bitterly over them.

They say that when he found D. Leonor dead, Manuel de Sousa did nothing but send the slaves away and sit down beside her with his face in his hands for about half an hour, without crying or saying anything. His eyes remained fixed on her. He paid little attention to the child. Then, he rose and began to dig a grave in the sand with the help of the slave women. All the while, never speaking a word, he buried her and the child. Once this was done, he turned and followed the path he had taken when searching for fruit. Without saying anything to the slaves, he went into the jungle, never to be seen again. Wandering through that wilderness, he certainly must have been devoured by tigers and lions. Thus did husband and wife end their lives after plodding through the land of the Kaffirs, beset by so many hardships.

Those who escaped from this company, out of the people who remained with Manuel de Sousa when he was robbed as well as the ninety others who had walked on ahead of him, probably numbered about eight Portuguese and fourteen slaves, and three of the slave women who were with D. Leonor when she died. Among this group were Pantaleão de Sá, Tristão de Sousa, the

pilot André Vaz, Baltasar de Sequeira, Manuel de Castro, and
Álvaro Fernandes. As they made their way through the wilderness without hope of returning to Christian lands, a ship arrived
to that river in which a relative of Diogo de Mesquita was traveling to trade in ivory. When he heard the news that there were
Portuguese castaways in the land, he sent a search party after
them and ransomed them for beads. Each person cost two coins'
worth of beads, the items most valued by the blacks. If Manuel
de Sousa had been alive, he, too, would have been ransomed. But
it must have been for the good of his soul that this was not the
case, since it was God's will. The survivors reached Mozambique
on the twenty-fifth of May, fifteen hundred and fifty-three.[6]

Pantaleão de Sá, wandering aimlessly for a long time through
the lands of the Kaffirs, arrived at the Kaffir court exhausted
from hunger, nakedness, and the hardships of such a long trek.
At the entrance, he asked the courtiers to arrange for some kind
of help from the king. They turned down the request, explaining
that the king, for some time, had been suffering from a great illness. The illustrious Portuguese asked what the illness was, and
the courtiers said it was a leg wound, infected and unhealing to
a degree that they expected the king's death at any moment. He
listened attentively and requested that his arrival be communicated to the king. He said he was a physician and could perhaps
restore the king to health. Overjoyed, the courtiers related the
news to the king, who sent for him immediately. When
Pantaleão de Sá saw the wound, he remarked, "I am very confident you will soon recover." He then stepped outside to consider the situation he had put himself in. He certainly would not
escape with his life since he knew of no remedy, since he had
been trained to take lives rather than cure ailments in order to
save them.

Lost in these reflections, as one who no longer was concerned for himself and preferred to die once and for all rather
than many times, he urinated on the ground. Taking the mud
thus produced he went inside and applied it to the almost incur-
able sore. That day passed, and on the next, as the celebrated Sá
was expecting a death sentence rather than a reprieve for his

life—and much less a reprieve for the life of the king—the courtiers came outside in a considerable stir, wanting to carry him around on their shoulders. He asked them the cause of such sudden joy. They answered that the wound, because of the medication, had rid itself of the infection and that all that remained was clean and healthy flesh. The false physician went inside and saw that this was indeed the case. He ordered the treatment to be continued, and the king enjoyed a complete recovery in a few days' time. Because of this, and in addition to other honors, they placed Pantaleão de Sá on an altar and venerated him as a deity. The king asked him to stay at his court, offering him half his kingdom; if he did not wish this, the king would grant anything he desired. Pantaleão de Sá refused the offer, saying it was necessary to return to his own people. The king rewarded him magnificently with much gold and many gems, and ordered his people to accompany him to Mozambique.

TRANSLATOR'S NOTES

This translation is based on the Portuguese text in Giulia Lanciani, ed., *Sucessos e naufrágios das naus portuguesas* (Lisbon: Caminho, 1997), 183–213.

1. A gentleman or nobleman.

2. *Cafre* is translated throughout as "Kaffir." Although this term may offend modern sensibilities, it is the only accurate rendering of the Portuguese word.

3. The *quintal* (pl. *quintais*) was an "Indo-Portuguese weight of 130 lbs." (*The Tragic History of the Sea*, 280).

4. I.e., May.

5. *Tigres* (tigers) should be understood as "leopards" (Charles David Ley, trans., *Portuguese Voyages, 1498–1663*, Everyman's Library 986 [London: J. M. Dent; New York: E. P. Dutton, 1947], 249n1), no doubt because tigers are not native to Africa.

6. The three sixteenth-century pamphlet editions of the narrative all end here; only in Brito's *História Trágico-Marítima* version does the final episode about Pantaleão de Sá appear. For bibliographic comments on all these versions, see C. R. Boxer, "An Introduction to the *História Trágico-Marítima*" and "An Introduction to the 'História Trágico-Marítima' (1957): Some Corrections and Clarifications," reprinted in C. R. Boxer, *From Lisbon to Goa, 1500–1750: Studies in Portuguese Maritime Enterprise* (London: Variorum, 1984).

The TRAGIC HISTORY *of the* SEA

I. A Portuguese carrack of the sixteenth century
From a painting by the 'Master of Lourinhã'

THE
TRAGIC HISTORY
OF THE SEA
1589–1622

Narratives of the shipwrecks of the Portuguese
East Indiamen *São Thomé* (1589), *Santo Alberto* (1593),
São João Baptista (1622), and the journeys of the
survivors in South East Africa

EDITED FROM THE ORIGINAL PORTUGUESE

BY

C. R. BOXER

Camoens Professor of Portuguese, University of London,
King's College

PREFACE

In the years 1735–6, a dozen narratives (mostly reprints) of ship-wrecks and other maritime disasters were published in a collected two-volume edition at Lisbon by Bernardo Gomes de Brito, under the title of *História Trágico-Marítima,* or *Tragic History of the Sea.* The printing and publishing licences of these two volumes bear dates ranging between 8 March 1729 and 12 June 1736, so they were some seven years in the press. During this time, or possibly a little later, a third volume appeared, bearing no contemporary licences but containing about half a dozen narratives of similar origin, separately paginated, and collected together without any general title-page or introductory matter. The person or persons responsible for this clandestinely published third volume, which is much rarer than the other two, have never been identified; but it has always been regarded as forming a continuation of those two volumes, and is discussed by bibliographers and catalogued by booksellers under the same general title. The first two volumes include shipwrecks and maritime disasters from the loss of the *São João* off the coast of Natal in 1552, down to the capture of the *Santiago* by the Dutch off Saint Helena in 1602. The third volume usually contains reprints of six narratives originally published between 1625 and 1651, but it sometimes includes one or more original eighteenth-century relations, and no two of the copies which I have examined are exactly alike.

The bibliographical and editorial problems connected with the *História Trágico-Marítima* have been discussed in considerable detail elsewhere, and there is no need to go over the same ground here.[1] Suffice it to say that these narratives were eagerly read when

[1] J. Duffy, *Shipwreck and Empire. Being an account of Portuguese maritime disasters in a century of decline* (Harvard University Press, 1955); C. R. Boxer, 'An introduction to the *História Trágico-Marítima*', reprinted from the *Miscelânea de Estudos em honra do Professor Hernâni Cidade* (Lisboa, 1957).

they were first published individually in pamphlet form contemporaneously with the disasters they described. Such pamphlets were generally displayed hanging from a string or cord in the bookshop where they were offered for sale, hence the term *literatura de cordel*, or 'string literature', which is often applied to them. They soon went out of print and are nowadays exceedingly rare, some of them surviving in one or two copies only, and the original editions of others are untraceable. Gomes de Brito's collected edition was likewise well received, but it was a long time before these tragic tales of the sea achieved recognition as literary masterpieces. Not until 1904–7 was a second edition of the *História Trágico-Marítima* published, but nowadays this work is generally regarded as a fine example of classical Portuguese prose and is widely used in schools.

The original relations were either the work of survivors or were compiled by contemporary writers from their accounts. They are as a rule movingly and graphically written, if not always as grammatically as could be wished. The majority of the shipwrecks described in the pages of the *História Trágico-Marítima* befell homeward-bound East-Indiamen off the coast of Natal, and the survivors tried to march overland to the seasonal Portuguese trading-station at Delagoa Bay, or to the fort of São Caetano at Sofala. There is thus a basic similarity between these accounts, however much the details may differ. It may be added that the nature of the coastline, and more particularly that of the river mouths, has changed a good deal in certain districts since the sixteenth and seventeenth centuries. Much of the dense bush which then came down to the sea has been cleared away in many places; and allowance must also be made for the seasonal changes which dry up numerous streams at one time in the year and make them raging torrents at another. The going for the half-starved and barefooted castaways of nearly four centuries ago was incomparably harder than it would be for a fit and well-shod man today, as pointed out by Professor P. R. Kirby in his invaluable *Source book on the Wreck of the Grosvenor* (pp. 4–5).

There can be no two opinions about the historical value of the *História Trágico-Marítima*. Written almost invariably with the utmost frankness, these narratives bring vividly before us the dangers and discomforts of life aboard the crowded East-India carracks. The reasons for the loss of so many of these 'wooden mountains' and 'floating Babylons', as some contemporary critics called them, are clearly and unanimously stated by all those writers, and are discussed in the first part of the Introduction below. They give us the seamy side of the Portuguese 'conquest, navigation, and commerce', the obverse of which is so majestically perpetuated in the *Decadas* of João de Barros and the *Lusíadas* of Luís de Camões.

The other outstanding feature of most of these narratives is their value for the historical ethnography of the tribes of South East Africa. Their importance in this respect has long been recognized by South African historians and ethnographers, for these early Portuguese relations describe the South African Bantu (and, to a lesser extent, the Hottentots) at a time when they were still un-affected by close contact with white men, or at any rate by white rule. They likewise bring vividly before us the danger and hard-ships of the 'long march' through Kaffraria.

This also accounts for their inclusion in the truly monumental series translated and edited by George McCall Theal under the title of *Records of South-Eastern Africa* (9 vols., London, 1898–1903), although he provided no introductions or notes. He used the versions printed in the *História Trágico-Marítima*, whereas I have gone to the first editions where these are available; but I checked my translations with his, and, generally speaking, where I found the latter to be markedly superior, I amended my own accord-ingly. Theal's translation was avowedly a free rather than a literal one, but mine inclines the other way, in order to retain fidelity to the original even at the cost of awkwardness of expression. All translators owe a great debt to their predecessors in any particular field; and if I found a few places where my precursor had slipped up, there were many more where he had solved puzzles which baffled me.

The reason why I selected these three particular narratives out of ten which were relevant to South East Africa is because the first and the third are typical of what generally happened, whereas the second forms a shining exception. Taken together, they thus display all aspects of the eighteen different relations which make up the *Tragic History of the Sea*, and provide both the variety and the unity which is required in a work of this kind.

ACKNOWLEDGEMENTS

My debt to G. McCall Theal is acknowledged in the preface, but for help in the elucidation or clarification of passages which baffled both of us I am indebted to several kind friends and acquaintances. Dr R. C. Anderson, President of the Society for Nautical Research, Captain António Marques Esparteiro, of the Portuguese Navy, and Lieut-Commander G. P. B. Naish, R.N.V.R., were most helpful in the elucidation of various sixteenth-century Portuguese maritime terms. If some of these have been incorrectly rendered this must be ascribed to my landsman's ignorance—and in part, perhaps, to the obscurity of the originals. Professor Isaac Schapera of the London School of Economics kindly lent me his copy of H. A. Junod's invaluable pamphlet on the condition of the natives of South East Africa in the sixteenth century. Senhor Carlos de Azevedo, the distinguished Portuguese art-historian, kindly provided the photograph of the painting by the anonymous 'Master of Lourinhã' which forms the frontispiece, and obtained permission for its reproduction. The Librarian of the Houghton Library, University of Harvard, kindly supplied photostats of relevant documents among the papers of Dom António de Ataíde, and gave permission for their reproduction. My colleague, Senhor Luís de Sousa Rebello, helped to elucidate some of the more difficult Portuguese words, and the Hon. Secretary, Mr R. A. Skelton, found time amid his manifold occupations to be consistently helpful in his editorial capacity. Last not least, thanks are due to the editor and publisher of *Man* and to Dr W. G. N. van der Sleen of Naarden-Bussum, Holland, author of the article on 'Trade-wind beads' (*Man*, February 1956, pp. 27–9), for permission to reproduce two of the illustrations therein as Plate V of this work. The sketch maps were drawn by Mrs A. M. Huhtala.

CONTENTS

xi

ILLUSTRATIONS AND MAPS IN

The Tragic History of the Sea

Page numbers indicate placement of art in the original edition.

xiii

INTRODUCTION

A. The Carreira da India

THE *carreira da India* was the term used by the Portuguese for the round voyage made by their Indiamen between Lisbon and Goa in days of sail. It was generally considered by contemporaries to be 'without any doubt the greatest and most arduous of any that are known in the world',[1] although some would have excepted the annual voyage of the Manila galleon across the Pacific. In both cases the seasonal winds of the Tropics formed the determining factor, and the round voyage, including the stop-over at Goa or at Manila, took about a year and a half for the Portuguese ships and a year for the Spanish, under the most favourable conditions.

The SW monsoon, which normally begins on the west coast of India about the beginning of June, had the effect of virtually closing all harbours in this region from the end of May to the beginning of September, whereas the trading season lasted from this latter month to April. Once the Cape route to India had been opened, the Portuguese ships tried to leave Lisbon before Easter, so as to round the Cape of Good Hope in time to catch the tail-end of the SW monsoon winds off the East African coast, north of the equator, which would bring them to Goa in September or October. Similarly, they aimed at leaving Goa (or Cochin) with the NE monsoon about Christmas, so as to round the Cape before the stormy 'winter' weather set in there in May.

The ships used in the *carreira da India* were principally carracks and galleons, smaller vessels being only occasionally employed. The carrack, or *Náo* ('Great Ship'), was a type of merchant-ship used by the Venetians and Genoese in the later Middle Ages; but it was the Portuguese who brought it to its greatest and most spectacular development in the *Náo da carreira da India* during the

[1] A. Valignano, S.J., *Historia del principio y progresso de la Compañía de Jesús en las Indias Orientales* (ed. Rome, 1944), 9.

late sixteenth and early seventeenth centuries. Broadly speaking, a Portuguese East India carrack was a large merchant-ship, broad in the beam, with three or four flush decks, a high poop and fore-castle, but lightly gunned for her size, and often a sluggish sailer. Originally of about 400 tons burden, they eventually attained over 2,000 tons. These huge argosies were the largest vessels afloat at the turn of the sixteenth century, being rivalled only by the great Manila galleons, some of which attained comparable dimensions.[1] They excited the wonder of the Elizabethans in much the same way as the *Queen Mary* does with us. Richard Hakluyt records admiringly the measurements of the 1,600 ton *Madre de Deus*, captured by six English ships off the Azores in 1592 when home-ward-bound from India, and taken into Dartmouth. She was the wonder of the West Country, people flocking from all over Eng-land to see her. Even the gigantic *Sovereign of the Seas*, built for Charles I in 1637, was apparently surpassed in size by her Portu-guese contemporary, the *Santa Tereza*, built as a *Náo da carreira da India* at Oporto in the same year, and lost at the battle of the Downs in 1639.[2]

A galleon, on the other hand, was primarily a fighting-ship, and a lighter and handier vessel than a carrack as a general rule, but more heavily gunned, and with a less cumbersome form of poop and forecastle. The distinction between carrack and galleon in Portuguese and Spanish terminology was not always a hard and fast one, and in the course of the seventeenth century it be-came very difficult to draw an exact line between the two types. Although galleons usually did not exceed 500–600 tons, whereas carracks were frequently over 1,000, yet galleons of 800–1,200 tons were not exactly uncommon. Some of these larger vessels were termed *Náos* and *Galeões* indiscriminately, even by the men who sailed in them. Prior to 1622, Portuguese carracks or *Náos* usually had four flush decks, but smaller types of three or even two decks occur, and these latter were sometimes called *navetas*. Here again is another fertile source of confusion, as the term *naveta*

---

[1] Cf. W. L. Schurz, *The Manila Galleon* (New York, 1939), 193–6.
[2] C. R. Boxer, *The Journal of Maarten Harpertszoon Tromp, Anno 1639* (Cam-bridge, 1930), 5, 216–17.

was also applied to small frigate-type India-built vessels which contemporary Dutch and English records call 'yachts' or 'frigates'. These frigates were, of course, much smaller vessels than the war-ships of the same name developed by the Dunkirk corsairs in the North Sea, and which later became a standard type in all Euro-pean navies. It may be added that the Portuguese and Spaniards very seldom used the word *carraca* to designate their carracks, but almost invariably called them *Náos* (*Naus* in modern Portuguese). Their Dutch and English contemporaries, on the other hand, equally invariably referred to such vessels as carracks, when they could distinguish them from galleons, and we are therefore justified in using the terms 'carrack' and *Náo* interchangeably to designate the same type of Great Ship.[1]

Some of the best and biggest Portuguese carracks were those built in India, where Cochin, Bassein (Baçaim), and, to a lesser extent, Damão, were all shipbuilding centres of importance where ships were built on contract—in the case of Cochin by contract with the local raja at the period with which we are dealing. Pride of place in this respect naturally went to the great royal arsenal and dockyard at Goa, which was probably the most highly organized industrial enterprise in India in the golden days of the Great Mogul.[2] The superiority of Indian teak over European pine, and even oak, as shipbuilding timber was fully recognized by the Por-tuguese. A royal order of 1585, repeated textually nine years later, emphasized the importance of building carracks for the *carreira* in India rather than in Europe, 'both because experience has shown that those which are built there last much longer than those built in this kingdom, as also because they are cheaper and stronger, and because timber for these carracks is increasingly hard to get here'.[3]

---

[1] Cf. E. E. de Barros, *Traçado e construção das Naus Portuguesas dos séculos XVI e XVII* (Lisboa, 1933); F. C. Bowen, *From Carrack to Clipper* (London, 1948); and articles by R. Morton Nance and L. Guilleux la Roërie on 'The Ship of the Renaissance' in *The Mariner's Mirror*, XLI (1955), 281–98; XLII (1956), 180–92; XLIII (1957), 179–93, for more technical details, illustrations, and sketches.

[2] W. H. Moreland, *From Akbar to Aurangzeb* (1923), 7.

[3] *Cartas régias* of 22.ii.1585 and 3.iii.1594, in *Archivo Portuguez Oriental*, III (Nova Goa, 1861), 46, 448–9.

B

Perhaps the most famous of these India-built carracks was the *Cinco Chagas* ('Five Wounds'), constructed at Goa by the viceroy Dom Constantino de Braganza in 1559–60. She served in the *carreira* for twenty-five years, making nine or ten round voyages apart from others, and was the flagship of five viceroys before ending her days as a hulk at Lisbon.[1] This was in marked contrast to the average Lisbon-built carrack which seldom made more than three or four round voyages or lasted for as long as a decade. For that matter, the English East India Company in the late eighteenth century did not normally allow a merchantman to undertake more than four round voyages. The India-built successor of the *Cinco Chagas* was less fortunate, being burnt and sunk on her maiden voyage after a heroic battle with the Earl of Cumberland's squadron off the Azores in 1594. Equally unfortunate was the India-built *São João Baptista* whose tragic end is the theme of the third narrative here translated

Experience having shown that ships of under 500 tons were more seaworthy and more economical than the unwieldy monsters of 1,000 tons or more, the Crown decreed in 1570 that thenceforth all the carracks constructed for use in the *carriera da India*, whether in Asia or in Europe, should not exceed 450 or be less than 300 tons.[2] Not much notice seems to have been taken of this instruction, at any rate in the India yards, although it was repeated in modified forms on later occasions, when it was ordered that carracks should have only three flush decks instead of four, but the tonnage limit was raised to 600 tons. Apart from the shipyard officials and building contractors, the ship's complements from captain to cabin-boy were interested in cramming a homeward-bound carrack with as much cargo as she could possibly hold, since their perquisites were correspondingly greater. Despite the obvious danger incurred by overloading a lubberly carrack, the majority of contractors, merchants, and seamen short-sightedly preferred to run this risk rather than have less cargo-space

---

, [1] Diogo do Couto, *Decada VII*, bk. 9, ch. XVII. Gomes de Solis, *Discursos* (1622), fol. 242, and *Alegacion* (1628), fols. 218–19, credits her with only eight round voyages, as do other contemporary writers.

[2] 'Regimento' of 1.iii.1570, in *APO*, v (Parte II, 1865), 723.

in smaller but more seaworthy ships. The folly of this practice was repeatedly pointed out by more sensible people, both ashore and afloat; but despite repeated legislation by the Crown against over-loading and over-ambitious shipbuilding, the vested interests concerned fought a successful rearguard action against the reformers for the best part of a century.[1] Equally ineffective was the legislation regarding the armament of these vessels. The standing-orders (*regimentos*) for this period envisaged that the East India carracks should mount a minimum of 28 guns, but in practice they seldom had more than 22 or 23, and too high a proportion of these were only eight-pounders.

Well aware of the superiority of India-built shipping, the Crown frequently legislated for the construction of carracks and galleons in India. From time to time, however, there was considerable discussion between the authorities at Lisbon and those at Goa as to whether it was cheaper to build ocean-going vessels in India or in Europe. Most of those best qualified to judge argued in favour of India-built shipping. In 1615, the Crown ordered the construction of two carracks yearly, both in Cochin if possible, since the local teak was allegedly superior to that of the North, but failing that, one in Cochin and the other in Bassein. The specie sent out annually from Portugal to defray the cost of these carracks was on no account to be diverted to any other use, however pressing, until such time as the *carreira* 'would be full of ships', when one a year would suffice.[2] Needless to say, this optimistic expectation was never fulfilled, and the costs of shipbuilding and repair at Goa rose sharply for reasons explained in a dispatch of 1631.

[1] The arguments of the reformers are given at length in João Pereira Corte-Real, *Discursos sobre la navegacion de las naos de la India de Portugal* (n.p., 1622; reprinted under the title of *Discursos y advertencias* in 1635); Duarte Gomes de Solis, *Discursos sobre los comercios de las dos Indias* (n.p., 1622; reprinted, Lisboa, 1943), and *Alegacion en favor de la Compañia de la India Oriental* (n.p., 1628; reprinted, Lisboa, 1955); all of which are conveniently summarized in Manuel Severim de Faria, *Noticias de Portugal* (Lisboa, 1655), 241–7. Cf. *Mariner's Mirror*, XXXVI (1940), 388–406.

[2] Dispatch of 23.ii.1615, in *APO*, VI (1875), 1074–6. For other legislation on this subject in the period 1585–1623, cf. *APO*, III (1861), 46, 71, 106, 184, 577, 579, 722–3; *APO*, VI, 848, 860, 1017, 1213, 1229, 1235; *APO*, I (Parte 2), 123.

'There are no longer here the contractors who used to repair and refit carracks in the old days, and whose prices were reasonable because they tendered in competition with each other. Nowadays it is clean contrary, because they all went bankrupt and have no capital, so that there are only two men left and these two have an understanding between themselves and submit their tenders jointly.'[1] But the hand of the Portuguese shipwright—and of his Indian assistant—had not lost its cunning, and the Goa yards continued to produce carracks and galleons which aroused the admiration of Dutch and English contemporaries, even though, as one of the latter observed, 'they are very long a-doing and issue at excessive rates'.[2]

At the period with which we are concerned, an average of four or five of these leviathans left Lisbon annually for Goa. As noted above, the round voyage was estimated to last about eighteen months, including a three or four months' stay in India to load the spices and other return cargo. On the outward voyage, land was often touched at Mozambique, but sometimes the carracks sailed direct from Lisbon to Goa. On the return voyage a stop was usually envisaged at St Helena, before the Dutch frequented that island and made it dangerous for the Portuguese to do so; but otherwise the Azores were normally the only place of call if the ship did not make a through run as she often did. The duration of the voyage varied greatly, but something between six and eight months in either direction was very common. The quickest outward voyage was probably that made by Captain João da Costa, who took only three months and twenty-seven days from Lisbon to Goa in 1645.[3] For the homeward run, an exceptionally favourable voyage was that of Dom Francisco da Gama, who left Goa on Christmas Day 1600 and dropped anchor in the Tagus on 26 May 1601, 'without having stopped anywhere or lowered the

[1] Papers of the Goa representatives of the Portuguese East India Company, 1629–1633 (hereafter referred to as Codex-Lynch), fol. 83.

[2] *Travels of Peter Mundy* (Hak. Soc. ed.), III, 59.

[3] Simão Ferreira Paes, *Recopilação das famosas armadas que para a India foram, 1496–1650* (Rio de Janeiro, 1937), 141. Frazão de Vasconcelos, *Pilotos das navegações portuguesas dos séculos XVI e XVII* (Lisboa, 1942), 30, gives the year as 1640, but from other evidence I think 1645 is the correct date.

main-yard during the whole voyage'.[1] A record round voyage was apparently that of Luis de Mendoça Furtado's two galleons in 1651–2. They took only four and a half months for the outward run and five for the homeward, 'a thing which never happened to any carrack', observed Severim de Faria,[2] forgetful of Dom Francisco's precedent.

An experienced pilot of the *carriera*, when asked what was the best season for the departure of the Indiamen from Lisbon, is alleged to have replied: 'The last day of February is time enough, but the first day of March is late.'[3] Most seamen thought that the first half of March was about the best time, but in practice the ships often left in the second half of March or in the first half of April. Departures later in April, or even early in May, were not unknown, but the ships involved almost invariably made *arribadas*, or abortive voyages, being compelled either to return to Lisbon or to 'winter' in Brazil. Delayed departures were chiefly due to administrative and financial difficulties at Lisbon, such as a shortage of ready money when most needed, and trouble in collecting crews. There was a so-called 'winter monsoon', which involved leaving Lisbon in September, so as to reach Mozambique in March, and Goa before the bar of the Mandovi was closed by the monsoon in May; but this was normally utilized only by advice-ships and the like.

Successful passages out of due season, though extremely rare, were occasionally made. The most spectacular instance was that of the viceroy Matthias de Albuquerque in 1590. His squadron of five carracks left Lisbon on May 8, and as evidence of his determination to reach India he had a representation of himself trampling on Fortune painted on his standard. His four consorts all lost their voyage, but thanks largely to the exceptional skill of his

---

[1] D. António de Ataide, 'Roteiros para varios pontos' (codex of 1631 in the collection of C. R. Boxer), fol. 39. The pilot's original journal for this voyage (to 11 May 1601) was printed by Frazão de Vasconcelos in *Anais da Academia Portuguesa da Historia*, VIII (1944), 247–85.

[2] Severim de Faria, *Noticias* (1655), 245, implies the year 1653–4, but from other sources 1651–2 is more likely. The Fleet of 1655 also took just under five months for the outward voyage.

[3] M. Faria y Sousa, *Asia Portuguesa*, III (1675), 367.

pilot-major, Vicente Rodrigues, his flagship *Bom Jesus* rounded the Cape and sighted the coast of India before being forced back to Mozambique, which she reached on 10 January 1591 in a very distressed condition, and with most of her complement dead. From here the viceroy proceeded to Goa which he reached in May, a year after his departure from Lisbon.[1] Less dramatic and less costly was the remarkable voyage made by the squadron of Joseph Pinto Pereira in 1632. Leaving Lisbon with three vessels on 4 June, he reached Goa on 28 October, having touched nowhere on the way, and having beaten off an attack by the Dutch East Indiaman *Leeuwarden* in the Indian Ocean. He lost only 33 or 34 men in his own ship, though it would seem that no more than 148 soldiers reached Goa out of 284 who had embarked in this fleet.[2]

Just as departures from Lisbon tended to take place later than was advisable, so did those from Goa. Instead of leaving at Christmas-tide, or at New Year, ships often left in February or March, or occasionally even in April, when the chance of subsequently weathering the storms in the latitude of the Cape was correspondingly reduced. As at Lisbon, these belated departures in contravention of reiterated royal orders to avoid them, were mainly due to administrative delays at Goa, or to waiting for a full cargo of pepper, which was not easily arranged at times when the petty rajas of the Malabar coast were at odds with the Portuguese. Shortage of ready cash to buy the pepper sufficiently in advance was another perennial cause of delay.

The timing of the departure was also affected to some extent by whether the passage was to be made through the Mozambique Channel, or well to the east of Madagascar. For the first twenty-five years after Vasco da Gama's pioneer voyage, both outward and homeward-bound Indiamen took the former course, despite the notorious unhealthiness of Mozambique island as a port of call. During the period 1525–79, homeward-bound Indiamen

---

[1] Diogo do Couto, *Decada XI* (ed. 1788), 66–7.

[2] C. R. Boxer, 'José Pinto Pereira, Vedor da Fazenda Geral da India', in *APH*, VII (1942), 79–80. For that matter, Vasco da Gama left on his pioneer voyage on June 8, but this precedent seems to have been forgotten.

were ordered to avoid the Mozambique Channel (though ships bound for Goa continued to use it), and to take a course which kept them well clear of Madagascar. This outer route was also used in the reverse direction by carracks which rounded the Cape after mid-July. As a disturbing number of homeward-bound Indiamen were lost with man and mouse on this outer passage, the viceroy Dom Francisco da Gama reintroduced the use of the Mozambique Channel route in 1597–8, when a successful voyage was made by the pilot-major, Gaspar Ferreira Reimão.[1] Thenceforward homeward-bound Indiamen took either the outer or the inner passage according to what month they left India. The concensus of expert opinion in 1615 was 'ships leaving from Goa up to the end of December should take the inside passage, since the voyage is safer; from the first of January onwards this voyage is riskier, and they should take the outer passage; all ships leaving from Cochin should take the outer passage'.[2]

The crew of a four-deck carrack might total over 200, but the number of foremast hands officially allowed at this period was generally 120, equally divided between sailors and grummets.[3] The Crown *regimentos* stressed that only experienced mariners should be entered as sailors for the India voyage, but these have never been too plentiful in Portugal. As early as the first decade of the sixteenth century, a captain found that his rustic crew could not distinguish between starboard and larboard until he tied a bunch of onions to one side of the ship and a bunch of garlic to

---

[1] Gaspar Ferreira Reimão, *Roteiro da Navegação e carreira da India, 1612* (ed. Lisboa, 1939), 43–5.

[2] Decision of a junta of pilots of the *carreira* at Lisbon, 18.iii.1615, in *Documentos remettidos da India ou Livros das Monções*, III (1885), 326–7. Cf. the decisions of similar juntas in 1635 and 1646, respectively, in Frazão de Vasconcelos, *Pilotos*, 79–84.

[3] *Grumetes*. They were apprentice seamen, not necessarily boys, though most of them were probably in their teens. They did all the hardest work aboard the ship and slept on the deck at the waist, between the mainmast and foremast. Cf. *Voyage of Pyrard de Laval* (Hak. Soc. ed.), II, 187, 189–90. At the end of the last century the word 'grummet' still survived in south-east England with the meaning of 'awkward boy' (R. S. Whiteway, *Rise of the Portuguese Power in India 1497–1550*, London, 1899, 44 *note*). In 1633 Dom António de Ataide gave the complement of a *náo da India* as 18 officers, 60 sailors, 60 grummets, 4 pages and 26 gunners (Ataide MSS, Harvard University, 1).

the other. Those makeshift seamen who survived a couple of India voyages presumably became 'old salts', but complaints abounded in the years 1570–1650 that tailors, cobblers, lackeys, ploughmen and 'ignorant boys' of all kinds were freely shipped as deep-sea mariners.[1] The viceroy Pero da Silva complained that when he left Lisbon in 1635, ninety youthful stowaways were found in his flagship, and even more in her consort, although thirty had been sent ashore just prior to sailing, mostly boys of six or seven years old, 'and even under, these being brought as merchandise, some to be made friars, etc.'[2].

The mortality on board the East India carracks was very heavy, for reasons explained below, and the recruitment of sailors for the *carreira* varied a good deal. In 1623 João Pereira Corte-Real complained that the India voyage was so unpopular that it was necessary to press-gang sailors and keep them in irons till the ship had sailed.[3] Yet in 1565 and again in 1630, we find that common sailors as well as officers were bribing officials at the India House in order to be entered for the voyage.[4] In 1634 the viceroy wrote to the home government that he realized they were short of money, but he could not believe that Portugal lacked men.[5] Nearly everyone else, however, complained that she did, and certainly her population of about a million could not cope with the demands of her maritime and commercial empire from the Maranhão to Macao. Portuguese coastal shipping in Asia was largely operated by Asian seamen, and even the great carracks which visited Japan might have only a few white men besides the captain, pilot, and

---

[1] *Regimento dos Escrivaens das Naos da carreira da India* (Lisboa, 1611 and 1640); Codex-Lynch, fols. 140-1, 161-2; António Vieira [alias António de Sousa de Macedo], *Arte de Furtar* (ed. Lisboa, 1744), 39–40, 79–81.

[2] Pero da Silva to the Crown, Goa, 17 February 1636, in Torre do Tombo, 'Livros das Monções,' Livro 33, fol. 261.

[3] Autograph marginal note by João Pereira Corte-Real in the writer's copy of the *Discursos* (1622). Cf. also *Arte de Furtar* (ed. 1744), 262–3.

[4] A. da Silva Rego, *Documentação para a história das missões do padroado português do Oriente. Índia*, IX (1953), 535; Codex-Lynch, fols. 140, 161. Pyrard de Laval also states that the sailors had to buy their places in his day (1609). Cf. Hak. Soc. ed., II, 185.

[5] Linhares's dispatch of 29.xi.1634, printed in the *Chronista de Tissuary*, III (Nova-Goa, 1868), 272.

master-gunner in their complements. In the Indian Ocean the captain was sometimes the only European on board, for even the pilots were often Muslim Gujeratis.[1]

Most sixteenth–seventeenth-century Portuguese, including the writers in the *História Trágico-Marítima*, bitterly criticized sailors as a class, and frequently denounced their clownishness, indiscipline, selfishness and brutality. Official correspondence took the same line, and indeed contempt for sailors and their profession was a characteristic of contemporary Spain and Portugal.[2] This knowledge cannot have helped their self-respect, and the poor pay they received (when they got any at all) and the hard life which they led doubtless helped to brutalize them. It is therefore surprising to read Pyrard de Laval's eulogistic account of the gentlemanly behaviour of the sailors of the *carreira da India* in his day, which he contrasted with the boorish behaviour of French mariners.[3] There may be something in Pyrard's testimony, particularly since in most respects he is highly critical of the Portuguese and of sailors in general; but the weight of contemporary evidence indicates that the life of the average Portuguese sailor in the *carreira* was nasty, brutish, and short. This does not alter the fact that there were a fair number of men who spent useful lives in that difficult and dangerous calling, and chief among these were the pilots.

The captain of an East India carrack was usually a landsman, and by royal regulations the pilot had sole charge of the ship's navigation. He was therefore a more important and influential person than his equivalent in a Dutch, English, or French Indiaman, where the captain or master was generally a capable navigator and had the last word in deciding a ship's course. The efficient functioning of the *carreira da India* thus depended largely on the pilots, and on the whole they lived up to their responsibilities.

---

[1] E. Sanceau, *Cartas de D. João de Castro* (Lisboa, 1954), 22, 44; C. R. Boxer, *The Christian Century in Japan 1549–1650* (Berkeley, 1951), 128, 279, for some typical examples which it would be easy to multiply.

[2] Tomé Pinheiro da Veiga, *Fastigimia* (Coimbra, 1911), 54–5; Gomes de Solis, *Alegacion* (1628), fols. 233, 261; M. Herrero Garcia, *Ideas de los Españoles del siglo XVII* (Madrid, 1928), 275–6; J. Duffy, *Shipwreck and Empire* (Cambridge, Mass., 1955), 93–5.

[3] *Voyage of Pyrard de Laval*, II, 186.

When we consider the few and elementary navigating instruments which were then available; the inaccurate and small-scale charts which were used; the insufficient knowledge of natural phenomena like magnetic variation and ocean currents; the complete lack of any weather forecast; the want of a reliable nautical timepiece, or method of calculating longitude; and finally the bad sailing qualities of most of the lubberly carracks, it seems nothing short of miraculous that their pilots sometimes reached Goa just when they anticipated after a voyage of over 200 days, perhaps without having sighted land after leaving the mouth of the Tagus.

Miraculous, nevertheless, it was not, although the piety of these pilots and the hostility of their critics often implied that it was. 'God takes them out and God brings them back', was a favourite saying of both parties in the *carreira da India* concerning the annual voyage of the carracks. This aphorism was quoted approvingly by Diogo do Couto in his condemnation of pilots who relied on their beautifully decorated but misleading charts, as opposed to those old tarpaulins who had worked their way up from cabin-boy to master-mariner in repeated voyages, and whose skill was based rather on their knowledge of the winds, tides, and other natural phenomena than on their grasp of theoretical navigation. Couto's criticisms were echoed by many of his contemporaries, and the complacent arrogance of the pilots of the *carreira* was indeed proverbial.[1]

In the final analysis, a successful voyage resulted from a combination of good fortune and the pilot's skill in navigation. That skill, as Diogo do Couto observed, was only attained by continuous and careful observation throughout a series of voyages. This practical experience formed the basis of the pilots' *roteiros* (*anglice* rutters) or written sailing-directions, many of which were models of their kind. They may be said to be the forerunners of the Eng-

---

[1] Diogo do Couto, *Decada X*, Livro vii, 123–4 of the 1788 ed., and *Dialogo do Soldado Pratico Portuguez* (Lisboa, 1799), II, 8–12, 99–101; A. da Silva Rego, *Documentacão*, VI (1951), 190, and IX, 14; D. Garcia de Silva y Figueroa, *Comentarios, 1614–1624* (ed. Madrid, 2 vols., 1903), I, 48 ff., 80, 109–12, 121; II, 528, 546–50; Fernão de Queiroz, S.J., *Temporal and Spiritual Conquest of Ceylon* (ed. S. G. Perera, Colombo, 1930), 1098–9; Linschoten, *Discours of Voyages* (London, 1598), 146–8, 166.

lish Admiralty Pilot Handbooks which are the standby of navigators at the present day. The first printed *roteiro* of the India voyage was only published in 1608,[1] but manuscript ones were in circulation at least a century earlier. Later editions, with certain variations, were published at irregular intervals throughout the seventeenth century by successive cosmographers-royal of the Portuguese Crown.

The standard *roteiro*, whether printed or manuscript, consisted of two parts. The first was a treatise on the theory of navigation, and contained such items as: (*a*) calendar and tables of the sun's declination; (*b*) rules for finding the latitude by observing the sun on the meridian; (*c*) explanation of the mariner's compass with notes on its variation; (*d*) rules for plotting a ship's track on the chart; (*e*) directions for determining latitude by the Pole Star; (*f*) a traverse table for the dead-reckoning of the course; (*g*) rules for calculating a ship's daily run, based on the measurement of $17\frac{1}{2}$ leagues to the geographical degree; (*h*) a brief summary of John of Holywood's medieval *Tractatus de Sphaera*. The second part consisted of sailing directions between Lisbon on the one hand and Goa, Cochin, and Malacca on the other, with an appendix on the regional variations of the compass-needle. For the period 1575–1612, the sailing-directions for the India voyage were chiefly based on those elaborated by Vicente Rodrigues of Lagos, who spent a lifetime in the *carreira* before being lost with the returning *Bom Jesus* in 1591.[2] From 1612 onwards they embodied many of the amendments introduced by another celebrated pilot, Gaspar Ferreira Reimão, whose *Roteiro* was printed in a very limited edition in that year, and who was directly concerned in two out of the three shipwrecks described below.[3]

In addition to his own practical experience and that embodied in the *roteiros*, the pilot also had a few simple navigating instru-

[1] Manuel de Figueiredo, *Hydrographia. Exame de Pilotos* (Lisboa, 1608). For subsequent editions see A. Fontoura da Costa, *A Marinharia dos Descobrimentos* (Lisboa, 1933), 414–19.

[2] His *roteiros* were included in Linschoten's *Itinerario* which was the vade-mecum of the Dutch and English pioneer navigators in the East during the first two decades of the seventeenth century. Cf. also Silva y Figueroa, *Comentarios*, I, 81.

[3] Cf. 39–40 *infra*.

ments, such as the mariner's compass, astrolabe, cross-staff and quadrant. He also had an hour-glass, and a portulan-type nautical chart (*carta de marear*), drawn on a consistent distance scale but not on a consistent projection. Since he had no means of ascertaining the longitude, the chart was of very limited value, and most of the instruments could not be used in stormy or cloudy weather. Even in fine weather, the best he could hope for was a fairly accurate calculation of his position from a combination of observed latitude and dead reckoning when he was out of sight of land. One gets the impression from the surviving ships' journals or *diarios do bordo*, that the pilots' chief reliance was on their astrolabe, their mariner's compass, and on their experience of the ocean currents, the varying species of birds they saw, the colour and run of the sea, the kinds of seaweed, the sort of sand they dredged up when they took soundings, and so forth. In other words, on a combination of latitude-sailing, dead reckoning, and, above all, on their knowledge of how to interpret nature's signs. The following extract from Gaspar Ferreira's journal of 17 January 1598 is typical: '. . . and I tell you that steering this course, as soon as you see large numbers of seagulls from 8° to between 9° and 10° latitude, that you are off the islands of Arro, and you will find gulf-weed and branches of seaweed. On seeing these signs together with men-of-war birds and wind in the east, you should try to work south-westwards and approach Cape Delgado, and although there is likewise gulf-weed off this coast, it is not found together with seagulls and men-of-war birds.'[1]

This keen observation of the sea and sky around him did not prevent the pilot from watching his compass-needle continually, as testified in a striking passage by an English contemporary:

'In this point of steeridge, the Spaniards and Portugalls doe exceed all that I have seene, I meane for their care, which is chiefest in navigation. And I wish in this . . . we should follow

[1] Quirino da Fonseca, *Diários da Navegação da Carreira da Índia nos anos de 1595, 1596, 1597, 1600 e 1603* (Lisboa, 1938), 82. For the navigational methods of other nations cf. D. W. Waters, *The Art of Navigation in Elizabethan & Early Stuart Times* (London, 1958); the table of 'Land indications from sea-birds' in H. Gatty, *Nature is your guide* (London, 1958), 205-8; C. V. Sölver and G. J. Marcus, 'Dead reckoning and the ocean voyages of the past', in *Mariner's Mirror*, XLIV (1958), 18-34.

their examples. In every ship of moment, upon the half-deck, or quarter-deck, they have a chair or seat; out of which whilst they navigate, the Pilot, or his *adiutants* (which are the same officers which in our shippes we terme, the Master and his Mates) never depart, day nor night, from the sight of the compasse; and have another before them; whereby they see what they doe, and are ever witnesses of the good or bad steeridge of all men that do take the helme.'[1]

The navigational hazards of the *carreira da India* did not deter many people of all classes from sailing to seek their fortune in the East. The Italian Jesuit Visitor, Alexander Valignano, who made the voyage himself in 1574, noted that: 'it is an astounding thing to see the facility and frequency with which the Portuguese embark for India. . . . Each year four or five carracks leave Lisbon full of them; and many embark as if they were going no further than a league from Lisbon, taking with them only a shirt and two loaves in the hand, and carrying a cheese and a jar of marmalade, without any other kind of provision.'[2]

The resultant overcrowding and lack of elementary hygiene were appalling. By the time the carracks reached the equator they were often floating pest-houses, and their occupants died like flies. They had to endure extreme heat in the Gulf of Guinea, where they were sometimes becalmed for weeks together, and bitter cold off the Cape of Good Hope. Tropical rain and seasonal storms wetted or chilled them to the bone, especially the large numbers who had no place to sleep but on the upper decks. The ration-scale was quite adequate, consisting chiefly of biscuit, salted meat, dried fish, wine, and water, but it was not always adhered to as the regulations demanded; and fruit and fresh vegetables were naturally lacking after the first few days. Only the priests, *fidalgos*, and merchants had even the narrowest and most confined quarters. Most of the seamen and soldiers slept on the crowded

[1] *The Observations of Sir Richard Hawkins, Knight, in his Voyage into the South Sea, A.D. 1593* (ed. 1622), 57 of the Argonaut Press edition (1933). Pyrard de Laval likewise noted that a Portuguese pilot 'never leaves his place upon the poop, ever observing his needle and compass; in this he has a second pilot [*sota-piloto*] to help him' (*Voyage*, II, 189).

[2] Valignano, *Historia* (ed. 1944), 16.

decks, as those who were entitled to berths and cabin-space almost invariably sold them to the wealthier passengers for their accommodation and goods. Cooking facilities were limited to two large sand-filled boxes in the waist on either side of the mainmast, which could only be used in daylight hours and favourable weather. Food soon became rancid, or else was so salty that it induced an intolerable thirst which could only be satisfied adequately in a rainstorm. The drinking-water speedily putrefied, and most people drank it strained through a handkerchief or something of that sort. Wine usually lasted better, and if a man did not take all or any portion of his daily ration thereof, he could sell the balance to which he was entitled on his arrival at Goa. Too often the daily drinking-ration was gulped down as soon as received, thus causing the heedless recipients to suffer agonies from thirst for the remainder of the day.[1]

The chronic overcrowding naturally facilitated the spread of dysentery and infectious diseases, while the rancid or salty nature of much of the rations fostered the ravages of scurvy. The worst single cause of mortality was probably the insanitary habits of most of the ignorant soldiers and passengers. Seldom was any effort made to keep the ship clean, or to enforce the use of the 'heads' for their intended purpose, the use of jars and other receptacles being preferred.[2] Sea-sick and impotent persons were often left wallowing in their own filth, with the result that the spread of fecal-borne disease was greatly accelerated, and the stench between decks was so foul that anyone coming down the hatchway was liable to swoon.[3] Cockroaches and rats abounded

---

[1] For conditions on board Portuguese Indiamen, cf. Silva Rego, *Documentação*, IX, 317–39; X, 46–52; Quirino da Fonseca, *Diários da Navegação, 1595–1603*; Valignano, *Historia*, 9–16; *Voyage of Pyrard de Laval*, II, 180–202; Silva y Figueroa, *Comentarios*, I, 1–126.

[2] A notable exception was Captain Francisco de Mello de Castro in the *Nossa Senhora do Bom Despacho*, 1629–30. He had the ship thoroughly inspected twice weekly, and wherever any filth was found he compelled those responsible to clean it up and docked them of their day's rations. Cf. p. 4 of the *HTM* version.

[3] Silva Rego, *Documentação*, V (1951), 208; Quirino da Fonseca, *Diários da Navegação, 1595–1603*, 44. Pyrard noted: 'The Spaniards, French, and Italians do the same; but the English and Hollanders are exceedingly scrupulous and cleanly' (*Travels*, II, 196).

and at times assumed the proportions of a plague of Egypt. Each carrack was supposed to carry a physician and a qualified surgeon, together with amply-stocked medicine-chests provided by the Crown. In practice, however, there was usually only an ignorant barber-surgeon aboard, as in the fleet of 1633, which carried 3,000 men in four ships.[1] Possibly this was not so bad as it sounds, since the favourite remedy of the Portuguese medical profession was frequent bleeding, and in this way the doctors probably killed more patients than they cured. It was nothing uncommon to bleed a man of six or seven pints in a few days, and in one ship four hundred invalids were bled in a single day. Owing to all these reasons, and the fact that the ship might often be six or seven months at sea before making landfall, the mortality in the *carreira* was naturally very heavy. It was a common thing for three or four hundred men to die on the outward voyage in a carrack whose passengers and crew totalled six or eight hundred.[2]

If overcrowding was the chief danger on the outward voyage, overloading was that on the homeward. The carracks took out to India chiefly soldiers and specie, together with a little coral and some assorted goods of no great value, such as 'Nuremburger-ware', glass-ware and trinkets. They were not deeply laden, and the water and wine casks served as ballast. Their return lading, on the other hand, comprised bulky cargoes of spices (principally pepper and cinnamon), saltpetre, indigo, hardwoods, furniture, silks, and cotton piece-goods. Diamonds became an important item after the opening of new mines in Golconda, but these were in a different category. The holds were filled to capacity with the spices and saltpetre, while crates and packages of the other commodities were piled so high on the decks that a man could only

---

[1] Papers of D. António de Ataide (Harvard University, 1); Codex-Lynch, fol. 162; *Arte de Furtar* (ed. 1744), 263–4; Luís Pina, 'Na rota do Imperio. A medicina embarcada nos séculos XVI e XVII' (*Arquivo Historico de Portugal*, IV (1939), 283–323).

[2] Valignano, *Historia*, 16; Quirino da Fonseca, *Diários da Navegação 1595–1603*, xxiv–xxvii; Severim de Faria, *Noticias* (1655), 242. Pedro Barreto de Rezende, writing as paymaster at Goa on 20 November 1634, stated that out of 5,228 soldiers embarked at Lisbon for India in the years 1629–34, only 2,495 reached Goa alive— a loss of over fifty per cent (document in the writer's collection).

make his way from the prow to the poop by clambering over mounds of baggage and merchandise.[1]

As indicated previously, virtually all deck-space above the holds was the perquisite of some officer or member of the crew, who could sell it to the highest bidder. These men were also allowed *caixas de liberdade*, or 'liberty-chests', of a standard measurement, in which they were permitted to bring home cinnamon (otherwise a royal monopoly) and certain other goods partly duty-free. The value and number of these *caixas de liberdade* were graduated in a sliding scale according to rank from captain-major to cabin-boy, the former originally being allowed four chests each and the latter one chest between three.[2] The more feckless members of the crew sold their berths, deck-space, and liberty-chests to the highest bidders, and took shelter in what holes and corners they could find. Worse still, the ships' officers often cleared out naval stores from the space assigned them, to make room for their own goods or for those of merchants who bribed them, the stores being left to rot on the deck. Repeated injunctions were issued by the Crown against these and similar malpractices which resulted in the dangerous overloading of homeward-bound carracks, but to little or no effect. It was frequently suggested to the Crown that the perquisites of liberty-chests and deck-space should be abolished, and officers and seamen paid adequate wages instead. An attempt to do this was made in 1647–8, but the innovation proved so unpopular that it had to be dropped in 1649, when the time-honoured system was restored with certain modifications.[3]

A sixteenth-century Portuguese moralist has some harsh things to say about those of his countrymen 'who go to the ends of the

---

[1] Sources quoted on p. 16, n.1, with the addition of Gomes de Solis, *Alegacion* (1628), fols. 4, 158, 174–7, 187–9, 236; Severim de Faria, *Noticias* (1655), 242. Similar overloading was also a feature of the Manila galleons (Schurz, *Manila Galleon*, 158–76, 183–6).

[2] The 1515 *Regimento* for the *caixas de liberdade* is summarized in my article in *The Harvard Library Bulletin*, v, 37–8. By the early seventeenth century the Captain-major of an India voyage was allowed fifteen such chests. Cf. Appendix (*d*) below for the allowances *c.* 1620. A similar system prevailed in the Manila galleons (Schurz, *Manila Galleon*, 176–7).

[3] Arquivo Histórico Ultramarino, Lisboa, 'Consultas Mixtas', Cod. 14, fols. 22–4, 'consulta' of 2.iii.1647; Simão Ferreira Paes, *Recopilação*, 143–5, 147–8.

earth in search of riches, but do not take a step for the love of Christ'.[1] Similar sentiments occur in many other writers, and indeed virtually all Europeans who went out to the East, then and for long afterwards, went either to gain worldly wealth for themselves or else to gain souls for the kingdom of heaven. This juxtaposition of God and Mammon was inevitably a marked feature of the India voyage and is reflected in the numerous accounts of daily life on board.[2]

The missionaries' letters are full of complaints regarding the traditionally brutal and licentious soldiery who formed the majority of the passengers in the outward-bound carracks. They also comment sometimes on the neglect of the sick and impotent, and the want of religious devotion, save in times of storm and stress when outward manifestations of contrition seldom left anything to be desired. 'If you want to learn how to pray, go to sea', was a proverbial expression by 1564,[3] and the tendency of passengers and crew to invoke hysterically the aid of the Saints and the Virgin Mary in times of crisis, instead of making more practical efforts to save the ship, is a feature of most narratives in the *História Trágico-Marítima*, and was remarked by many foreign observers.[4] On such occasions it was the practice for those in peril to make vows of alms or other benefactions to their favourite shrine or saint if they reached their destination in safety. The purser's standing-orders enjoined him to remind such devout penitents of the great hospital of All Saints at Lisbon, where their thank-offerings would be put to good practical use in relieving the sick.[5]

A great deal depended on the captain's ability to enforce discipline and 'fair shares' in the crowded carrack, and when the captain was efficient the hardships of the voyage were rendered

[1] Fr Heitor Pinto, O.P., *Imagem da vida christã* (2 vols., 1563–72), IV, 208, of the 1940 reprint. Cf. also Silva Rego, *Documentação*, III, 351, 378.

[2] In addition to the classic accounts of Linschoten (1589) and Pyrard de Laval (1610), which are available in the Hakluyt Society editions, I have made special use of the following: Silva y Figueroa, *Comentarios*, I, 1–126; II, 499–558, 604–20; Quirino da Fonseca, *Diários da Navegação, 1595–1603, passim.*

[3] Silva Rego, *Documentação*, IX, 333.

[4] E.g. *Memoirs of William Hickey* (4 vols., London, n.d.), III, 8, 21.

[5] *Regimento dos Escrivaens das Naos da carreira da India*, 1611 and 1640. Cf. also Silva y Figueroa, *Comentarios*, II, 618.

C

more endurable. The missionaries pay tribute to the co-operation they received from many of these officers, and they themselves often did useful work in nursing the sick and in composing the quarrels which arose among prickly *fidalgos* and surly soldiers cooped up so closely together for so long. Cards were a frequent cause of strife, but though card-playing and gambling were officially discouraged whenever they were not prohibited, games of chance inevitably formed the principal antidote to boredom. The missionaries also frowned on the circulation of the romances of chivalry then so popular with the Iberian reading public. They flung these overboard when they had the chance, and substituted devotional treatises in their stead.[1] The tedium of a six or seven months' voyage without sighting land does not seem to have been enlivened by amateur theatricals, as long voyages sometimes were in Spanish and English vessels, where we have records of ships' companies playing Lope de Vega and Shakespeare, respectively. Fishing for sharks and catching sea-birds formed occasional diversions, and crossing the line was celebrated with the traditional horse-play. The mariners were well aware that work was the best cure for sea-sickness, and their hard life generally kept them fitter than the rest of those on board.[2]

Women went out to India in larger numbers than is generally realized, although there were never more than about fifteen or twenty in a carrack which might have six or eight hundred men. Their presence on board seems usually to have been a source of embarrassment or of scandal to the missionary writers, who seldom mention them sympathetically. Those who gave least trouble were respectable married women with their husbands, but the presence of prostitutes on board frequently resulted in unedifying scenes. Originally, the ships' officers seem to have been the chief offenders in bringing ladies of easy virtue out to India. Dom João de Castro wrote disgustedly after the arrival of the *Santo Espirito* at Goa in 1546: 'all the officers had mistresses, and were at odds with the captain . . . it should be ordained that any master, pilot, or other ship's officer who brings out a mistress, or takes one during the

[1] Silva Rego, *Documentação*, IX, 335–6.
[2] Silva Rego, *Documentação*, IX, 57; Silva y Figueroa, *Comentarios*, I, 85–6.

voyage, should suffer capital punishment, for this is the principal cause of all the disasters and broils which occur in the carracks.'[1]

Dom João's drastic remedy was not adopted, but the Crown on the whole persistently discouraged women of any kind from going to India, despite periodic urging from reformers that married women should be encouraged, or at least permitted, to go out with their husbands. An exception was made in favour of the *orfãs d'El-Rei*, or Crown orphans. These were respectable girls of marriageable age, provided with dowries in the form of colonial government posts for whoever would marry them after their arrival in India. There were seldom more than a dozen of these sent out in any one year, often only two or three, and sometimes none at all. The system was not a great success, and it is said that most of those who reached Goa and got married, either died or miscarried in childbirth. As time went on fewer white women went out to India, and in places like Muscat, Malacca, and Macao there were seldom more than one or two women to be found who had been born in Portugal.[2] White (or half-caste) women were not such a problem on the return voyage, as they were then invariably accompanied by their husbands or male relatives; but the presence of slave-girls periodically aroused the Crown's conscience, and some rather futile legislation was enacted against their being brought back to Lisbon under any circumstances.[3]

If the missionaries sometimes complained that life on shipboard was most unedifying, this was certainly not the fault of the Crown. The *regimentos* all laid great emphasis on the fear of the Lord being the beginning of wisdom and essential for a prosperous voyage.

[1] E. Sanceau, *Cartas de João de Castro*, 241–2. Cf. also Silva Rego, *Documentação*, III, 231–2; IV, 154; VI, 55; IX, 4, 60, 72, 315–16, 328, 446.

[2] For the *orfãs del-Rei* cf. Silva Rego, *Documentação*, III, 420, 500; IX, 4, 60, 72, 315–16. Germano da Silva Correia, *Historia da Colonização Portuguesa na India* (4 vols., 1948–52), has much new information from archival sources about white women going out to Goa, but the work is badly arranged and has no index. For frequency of deaths in childbirth see Fernão de Queiroz, S.J., *Temporal and Spiritual Conquest of Ceylon*, 1059; Gomes de Solis, *Alegacion*, 167–8; Fr Agostinho de Santa Maria, O.S.A., *Historia do Convento de Santa Monica de Goa* (Lisboa, 1699), 260–1.

[3] *Regimento dos Escrivaens das Naos da carreira da India*, 1611 and 1640; *APO*, VI, ocs. 51 and 468.

Profane swearers and blasphemers were threatened with condign punishment, even first-offenders being mulcted of all their wages.[1] For the first century of the *carreira*, mass was said on Sundays and Holy-days (weather permitting), but almost invariably without consecration of the elements and communion, being termed *missa seca*, or 'dry mass'. The first recorded full mass in a Portuguese Indiaman was that celebrated on 8 December 1608, by the Franciscan chaplain of the carrack *Santo António*.[2] The regular chaplains on board the Indiamen were usually Franciscan friars, although sometimes a Jesuit acted in this capacity on the outward voyage. The Religious on board usually organized processions and services on suitable occasions, but the most impressive ceremony may well have been the morning prayer described as follows by Pyrard:

'At break of day all the ship's boys chant a sea-orison or prayer, which is for all sorts and conditions of men on board, each in his particular office, with special mention also of the ship, and all her apparel in order, making apt reference in the case of each article to every stage and thing in the story of the Passion: so that this prayer lasts a full hour: it is said with a loud voice.'[3]

It is interesting to compare this with the contemporary Spanish practice after evening prayer (the Ave Maria), when a seaman came up the hatchway and rang a bell and intoned in a most lugubrious voice: 'Death is certain, the hour uncertain, the judge severe. Woe unto thee who art slothful! do that thou couldst wish thou hadst done when thou diest.' He then rang the bell again, and withdrew below, whereupon all the passengers and crew 'repenting for their sins went to rest in the deepest silence'.[4]

---

[1] *Regimento dos Escrivaens das Naos da carreira da Índia*, 1611 and 1640.

[2] *Voyage of Pyrard de Laval*, II, 187, 197; Frazão de Vasconcelos, 'A primeira missa no mar', in *Anais da Marinha* (Lisboa, 1957), 29–33; D. M. Gomes dos Santos, S.J., 'A missa a bordo das naus da India', in *Las Ciencias*, año XVII, núm. 4, 729–61 (Madrid, 1952).

[3] *Voyage of Pyrard de Laval*, II, 197. Cf. also Silva Rego, *Documentação*, IX, 321: 'the pilot, as is customary, recited very beautiful stanzas in honour of Our Lady and St James'.

[4] Fr Domingo Fernandez Navarrete, O.P., *Tratados Historicos, Politicos, Ethicos* (Madrid, 1676), 293. This source should be added to those used by A. Gschaedler 'Religious aspects of the Spanish voyages in the Pacific during the sixteenth century and the early part of the seventeenth', in *The Americas*, IV (1948), 302–15.

Hard though the conditions on board usually were, they did not necessarily form an unrelieved catalogue of horrors. If the food was usually rancid, the water putrid, the wine sour and all provisions in short supply, there were instances when they were adequate in both quantity and quality. An outward-bound Jesuit in 1564 wrote that when the missionaries asked their wealthier fellow-passengers for contributions on behalf of the sick: 'they gave us at once hens, mutton, raisins, almonds, comfits, fine white biscuit, and finally we had fresh bread every day in the ship, and whatever was necessary for the weakest was freely forthcoming.'[1] A sailor giving evidence at Goa in 1630, concerning the rottenness and insufficiency of the rations aboard the two outward-bound carracks of that year, contrasted them with those received in a voyage two years previously. The *Nossa Senhora do Rosario* had taken seven months to reach Goa in 1628, whereas the carracks of 1630 had taken only five, yet in the *Rosario* 'there was more than sufficient and to spare of good food and wine' throughout the whole voyage.[2]

Such instances of good living were admittedly exceptional; but even the familiar hardships of the *carreira da India* bred a certain amount of contempt once they were safely—if temporarily—past. This was particularly true of the sailors, who had their full share of the traditional hardihood and fecklessness of their kind. As a sixteenth-century voyager noted, apropos of the behaviour of his shipmates during a storm in the Indian Ocean: 'there was nobody, however brave and boastful, who did not then wish himself to be one of the lowest animals ashore . . . but men at sea behave very like women in child-bed, who swear in the extremity of their agonizing labour pains that if they survive them they will never lie with a man again. So likewise in these terrible and fearful storms, there is no one who does not swear that (if he lives) he will never go to sea again. But when the danger is over, it is gone and forgotten, and everything is dancing, strumming, and joking.'[3]

[1] Silva Rego, *Documentação*, IX, 320. This was admittedly in the early stages of the voyage, but the *Santo António* and her three consorts reached Goa with a total of only 24 or 25 dead between them.
[2] Codex-Lynch, fol. 148.
[3] Narrative of the loss of the *São Paulo* (1561), in *HTM*, I, 405. Admittedly, this

One of the most picturesque aspects of the *carreira da India* was the colourful scene off the bar of the river Mandovi when the carracks arrived there, or when they left 'Golden Goa' for Lisbon. On such occasions, numerous small craft came out to meet them or to see them off, bringing supplies of fresh food, fruits, and vegetables, and people playing on all kinds of musical instruments. Pyrard comments that 'it is one of the prettiest sights in the world', and Don Garcia de Silva y Figueroa was especially impressed by the Jesuits' *manchua*, 'painted in many colours and with its awning of crimson silk'.[1] The efficiency of the hospitals for the reception of the sick at Goa and at Mozambique was also favourably mentioned by several voyagers.[2]

During the century covered by the narratives of maritime disaster collected in the *História Trágico-Marítima* (1550–1650), the losses from shipwreck at times reached alarming proportions, particularly during the years 1585–92, 1620–3, and 1647–50. Unfortunately, the estimates of shipping casualties in the *carreira da India* do not always distinguish between shipwreck, foundering in the open sea, or casualties through other causes such as enemy action. No two contemporary lists entirely agree with each other, but a comparison of all the available sources leaves no doubt that losses were staggeringly heavy. Figueiredo Falcão, writing in 1612 with the archives of the *Casa da India* at his disposal, estimated that whereas only thirty-one Indiamen had been wrecked between 1500 and 1579, no fewer than thirty-five were wrecked in the thirty years between 1580 and 1610.[3] Gomes de Solis, who likewise had access to the official records at the India House in 1622–8, stated that out of seventeen carracks which left Lisbon for Goa in 1590–2, only two returned in safety. He also alleged that of thirty-

phrase does not occur in the original edition of 1565, and may be an interpolation of Gomes de Brito, but the same comparison is to be found elsewhere. Cf. *A Voyage round the World by Dr. John Francis Gemelli Careri* (reprinted from Churchill's *Voyages*, London, 1744), 468. The original Italian edition was published at Naples in 1701.

[1] *Voyage of Pyrard de Laval*, II, 276; Silva y Figueroa, *Comentarios*, I, 124.

[2] Silva Rego, *Documentação*, IX, 214, 327; *Voyage of Pyrard de Laval*, II, 3–15; Silva y Figueroa, *Comentarios*, I, 125–6.

[3] Luis de Figueiredo Falcão, *Livro em que se contém toda a fazenda* (ed. Lisboa 1859), 195.

three ships which left Lisbon in 1607–8 only three returned safely; and that twelve carracks of the *carreira* were lost in 1622–8, apart from the disastrous shipwreck of the Portuguese High Seas Fleet in the Bay of Biscay.[1] Quirino da Fonseca estimates the total losses for the century 1550–1650 at 112, but Duffy thinks it was nearer 130 and he is probably right. Some of these vessels were lost by enemy action or other causes, but the majority were either wrecked on the coast of East Africa or else foundered in the Indian Ocean with all hands.[2]

As indicated above, the great majority of shipwrecks occurred on the homeward passage before the carracks could round the Cape of Good Hope. Wrecks on the outward voyage, or after the Cape had been rounded on the homeward voyage, were much less frequent. The reasons for the loss of so many overladen carracks in the Indian Ocean, and especially off the coast of Natal, have also been discussed above, and need only be recapitulated here. They were mainly due to wilful overloading by the officers, passengers and crew, and to the superficial and inadequate careening carried out during the ship's stay at Goa. Contributory causes were inefficient stowage of the cargo; leaving Goa too late in the season; the crankiness of the top-heavy four-decked carracks;[3] ships in a fleet parting company so as to reach Lisbon first and get a better market for their 'private trade'; the mulish obstinacy of some of the pilots;[4] and the inexperience of some gentlemen-commanders.

If the Crown proved unable to stop these and other abuses, it

---

[1] Gomes de Solis, *Discursos* (1622), fol. 152; and *Alegacion* (1628), fol. 180. His figures for the years 1607–8 are demonstrably wrong, 33 being probably a misprint for 13. Even so, the losses for those two years were very heavy.

[2] Quirino da Fonseca, *Ementa Histórica das Naus Portuguesas* (Lisboa, 1926), 724–732; J. Duffy, *Shipwreck and Empire*, 62–3.

[3] 'God pardon the man who built her and erected so many and such high upper works upon so small a keel', wrote Gaspar Ferreira Reimão of the carrack *São Martinho* on his voyage to India in 1597 (Quirino da Fonseca, *Diários da Navegação*, 19).

[4] 'They wanted to make me believe that they saw the shoals and urged me to cast the lead, which I refused to do', wrote João Ramos, pilot of the homeward-bound *Nossa Senhora da Conceição* in his journal, 12.ii.1600 (Quirino da Fonseca, *Diários da Navegação*, 137).

was not for want of trying. The standing-orders (*regimentos*) for the voyage contained the most stringent injunctions against overloading, improper stowage of cargo, abuse of *gasalhados* (berth and deck space), the enlistment of unqualified mariners, or their substitution by inexperienced men. Mindful of the hazards to navigation which resulted when the pilot was not on speaking terms with his colleagues, the *regimentos* ordained that they should be severely punished if they failed to consult each other amicably. We know of at least one case where two inimical pilots were forced to take an oath to be friendly.[1] Minute instructions were given about the proper disposal of cargo space, the care of the armament and ship's stores, and even a forerunner of the Plimsoll Line was designed to prevent overloading. The Crown wrote to Goa in 1589 and again in 1597 that if the existing regulations were inadequate they would be revised, but that the real trouble was their lax enforcement by the local officials, in so far as these worthies made any attempt to enforce them at all.[2] Printed copies of the revised regulations were issued to all ships leaving Lisbon for the East, but it was many years before any lasting improvement in the conduct of the *carreira da India* was effected.[3]

After 1650 the shipwreck-rate dropped steeply, and by the eighteenth century a voyage to Goa in a Portuguese Indiaman was probably no more hazardous than a voyage to Bombay in an English one, or to Batavia in a Dutch ship. The reasons for this sudden improvement require further research, but perhaps the hanging of a couple of ship's officers who had misconducted themselves in the loss of the galleons *Santo Milagre* and *São Lourenço*, in 1647 and 1649 respectively, may have had something to do with it.[4] It is also evident that the regulations against overloading must have been at long last enforced; and it is likely that as fewer ships were now sent out to India yearly, there was not such difficulty in manning with trained seamen those that did go.

---

[1] Frazão de Vasconcelos. *Pilotos*, 78.　　　　[2] *APO*, III, 184, 722–3.

[3] The only two printed copies I have seen are dated 1611 and 1640, respectively, but doubtless manuscript copies must have been in use from the dawn of the sixteenth century.

[4] At any rate this was the hope expressed by Padre António Cardim, S.J., in his 1651 *Relaçam* of the loss of the *São Lourenço*, subsequently reprinted in *HTM*, III.

Whatever the reasons, the sudden fall in the shipwreck-rate after 1650 is as obvious as its sudden rise in 1585–92.

The reader of the *História Trágico-Marítima* may wonder how any Portuguese Indiamen survived the voyage at all, if the conditions so graphically depicted in that immortal work were the general rule in the *carreira da India* about the turn of the sixteenth century. The answer is, of course, that there was always a sufficiently large minority of honest, competent, and indeed outstanding seamen, to prevent the *carreira* from breaking down completely. These men worthily upheld the honour of the Portuguese pioneers 'in the oceans none had sailed before',[1] but which, since 1600, were being sailed with greater success by their Dutch, English, and French heirs. A few instances will exemplify what I mean.

Not all of the blue-blooded *fidalgos* who were given commands afloat were unwilling or unable to learn anything about the mariner's 'art, craft, and mystery'. Dom António de Ataíde (1567–1647), a scion of one of the noblest families of Portugal, first saw service afloat in 1582, but he always maintained the keenest interest in the theory and practice of nautical science. He was one of the prize pupils of the talented (and crypto-Jewish) cosmographer-royal, João Baptista Lavanha, and preserved for posterity some solar tables of his which would otherwise be lost. Whenever Dom António went to sea, he kept a careful journal in which he noted everything of interest, and compared his practical experience with the theoretical knowledge he had gained ashore. As Captain-major of the India voyage in 1611–12, he collected copies and originals of as many pilots' journals of the *carreira* as he could find, by way of checking the daily journal which he kept with such meticulous accuracy himself. Thanks to this combination of theory and practice, he was able to boast twenty years later 'these were the first ships which made the round voyage without ever parting company'.

Contrary to the practice of many Portuguese pilots who made a point of keeping their observations and calculations to themselves, often refusing to allow anyone else to take the altitude of the

[1] 'por mares nunca de antes navegados', Camões, *Lusíadas* (1572), Canto I, v. I.

sun, Dom António encouraged all competent seamen to do so whenever the weather permitted, including an English pilot who was a prisoner aboard his flagship on the return voyage. Apart from being an excellent navigator by the highest standards of the time, Dom António made a close study of other matters affecting the *carreira*, such as shipbuilding, naval gunnery, the improvement of nautical charts, and the training of seamen. He was responsible for raising the first regiment of marines in Portugal, and the second of its kind in Europe, being preceded only by the Spanish *Tercio de la Armada*. There was no branch of the sea-service which escaped his close and intelligent attention, as evidenced by the great mass of naval papers which he accumulated, studied, and annotated during his long life, and which still await the research worker in the libraries of Lisbon, London, Harvard, and Rio de Janeiro.[1]

João Pereira Corte-Real (*c.* 1580–1641) was not a direct descendant of the illustrious navigator who gave the Land of Labrador its name, but the fact that he took this genealogically unauthorized surname shows clearly where his interests lay. He belonged to the minor gentry, and apparently made his first voyage to India in 1603, where he served for the next nine years. After returning home, he went out again as captain of the galleon *Santo António* which left for Goa in the fleet of 1615. He made an exceptionally quick passage, but the return voyage was even more memorable as he had to contend with one of the very rare cases of mutiny against the Crown. This he did in a most drastic manner, personally stabbing one of the ringleaders to death and hanging two others out of hand, an act of rough and ready justice which was commended and rewarded by the King. He made another couple of prosperous India voyages, and in 1625 claimed that he had rounded the Cape of Good Hope eight times and worked his way up the promotion ladder from simple soldier to admiral of the Portuguese Crown. Like Dom António de Ataide,

---

[1] C. R. Boxer, 'Um roteirista desconhecido do século XVII, Dom António de Ataide', in *Arquivo Histórico da Marinha* (Lisboa, ·1934), I, 189–200; *idem*, 'The naval and colonial papers of Dom António de Ataide', in *Harvard Library Bulletin*, V (1951), 24–50.

he had made himself an expert navigator, and he wrote in 1622 that he was 'the only person of his quality whom a liking and attraction for the sea, together with zeal for the King's service', had induced to take (and to pass) the professional examination for the pilots of the *carreira*. He also invented a 'solar navigating instrument' of some kind, but no clear description of this has survived.

Corte-Real was a great memorialist, like so many of his contemporaries, and he deluged the Crown with suggestions for the reform of the *carreira da India*, but only two of these memorials achieved the dignity and publicity of print. The essence of his proposals was that the carrack-type of Indiaman should be abandoned in favour of the handier galleon-type, and that officers and crew should all receive adequate wages and no longer be allowed to sell deck and berth space, or to have liberty-chests of partly duty-free goods. Although many of those whom the Crown consulted on this matter agreed with him, only half-hearted and unsuccessful attempts to implement them were made during his lifetime and for long afterwards, as indicated above. The controversy over carracks versus galleons finally lapsed when both ceased to be built as distinctive types. By the end of the century the Portuguese *Náo da carreira da India* pretty well resembled the average English, Dutch, or French East Indiaman in design and build.[1]

António da Costa de Lemos was the son of a master in the *carreira da India*, and followed in his father's footsteps by making his first voyage to Goa in 1620, as an ordinary seaman at the age of nineteen. He continued in the *carreira*, save for a few short intervals of service in the Atlantic, until his death in 1651, having worked his way up to captain of the India-built galleon *Santo António de Mazagão*. During his thirty years of almost continuous sea service, he filled at one time or another every responsible post on board an Indiaman, including master's-mate, boatswain, master, second pilot, pilot, gunner, master-gunner, and purser—

[1] C. R. Boxer, 'Admiral João Pereira Corte-Real and the construction of Portuguese East Indiamen in the early seventeenth century', in *Mariner's Mirror*, XXVI (1940), 338-406.

always to the entire satisfaction of his superiors. He was never involved in any of the numerous shipwrecks which occurred in the *carreira* during this period, and it was obviously due to men like him that Portugal still remained a maritime power of some importance despite the grievous losses she suffered at sea.[1]

A distinguished naval historian who was also an experienced navigator once wrote that in days of sail nobody made a really good voyage without a certain amount of good luck. António da Costa de Lemos was obviously one of the lucky ones, be it said without any reflection on his proven professional competence. Few others who embarked for India at Lisbon in those disastrous years can have had much hope of returning, not once nor twice, but several times. Most of them must have realized that their chances were but even at the best. The bell of the pilots' church on the height of Chagas which announced the Indiaman's departure likewise tolled for the many aboard her who would not return:

> *Tlão ... Tlão ...*
> *Tlão ... Tlão ...*
> *Pelos que vão,*
> *Tlão ... Tlão ...*
> *Tlão ... Tlão ...*
> *E não voltarão.*
> *Tlão ... Tlão ...*[2]

B. *The Writers and their Narratives*

(i) *Diogo do Couto and the loss of the* São Thomé

It was the proud boast of Padre António Vieira, the great Portuguese Jesuit whose life roughly coincided with the seventeenth century, that the saga of the Portuguese discoveries and conquests

---

[1] Frazão de Vasconcelos, *Pilotos*, 5–14. The same was true of the *carrera* of the Manila galleons across the Pacific Ocean, where, wrote W. L. Schurz, 'a few seasoned pilots were the mainstay of the navigation' (*Manila Galleon*, 205).

[2] The Church of Chagas (= The Wounds of Christ) was founded in 1542 by the pilots and master-mariners of the *carreira da India*, and retained its close association with them for very nearly three hundred years.

had silenced all other histories.[1] This is a pardonable exaggeration; but it remains true that it is this aspect of Portuguese history which has attracted the majority of writers, both national and foreign. Fortunately for posterity, Portugal produced a remarkable pleiad of able and conscientious chroniclers who recorded the deeds and misdeeds of their countrymen both fully and frankly on the whole. Unhappily not all of their work has survived, while governmental and ecclesiastical censorship inevitably affected what was published in their lifetime. But these or similar drawbacks have been the bane of historians since Herodotus, and are not confined to any one nation or epoch. Contrarywise, we must remember that if their official position imposed certain restrictions on their freedom of expression, it also gave them access to numerous documents which otherwise they would not have seen and many of which have long since perished. The debt that modern scholarship owes to these old Portuguese chroniclers is duly acknowledged in many volumes of the Hakluyt Society, and to none is our obligation greater than to Diogo do Couto.[2]

Born about 1542 or 1543—the exact year is uncertain—the youthful Couto entered the royal household as a page to King John III's younger brother, the scholarly *Infante* Dom Luís. Thanks to the munificence of this prince, Couto received an excellent education not only at the Court in the company of Dom Luís, but at the Jesuit College of Santo Antão and the Dominican Convent of Bemfica. It has been observed that Renaissance learning came late to Portugal and left early; but its brief flowering produced some teachers at these two institutions who could hardly be bettered in their day and generation. They found an eager pupil in the young Couto, who, in addition to becoming well-read in

[1] 'Esta história era o silêncio de todas as histórias' (*História do Futuro*, ed. A Sergio and H. Cidade, Lisboa, 1953, 18).

[2] What follows is mainly based on my essay, 'Three historians of Portuguese Asia: Barros, Couto, and Bocarro,' reprinted from the *Boletim do Instituto Português de Hongkong*, 1 (Macao, 1948), 15–44, and the sources there quoted. More recent assessments of Couto's work will be found in the papers by J. B. Harrison, 'Five Portuguese historians,' and I. A. Macgregor, 'Some aspects of Portuguese historical writing of the sixteenth and seventeenth centuries on South East Asia,' included in the forthcoming volume on 'Historical Writing on the Peoples of Asia,' edited by the London School of Oriental and African Studies.

Latin, Italian, and Spanish literature, showed special aptitude for
the study of mathematics and geography. The erudition displayed
in his published work is at times almost suffocating; but his fondness for quoting classical tags and authorities unnecessarily is
partly atoned for by his frequent allusions to Iberian folk-litera-
ture, which his predecessor as the official chronicler of the Portuguese expansion, João de Barros (*c.* 1496–1570), would have
scorned as beneath the dignity of Clio. This difference in style
between Barros and Couto is not the only one, for the former took
Livy and the latter Tacitus as their respective models, but it serves
to bring out another important difference between them.

Barros, though a bastard, apparently came of noble stock on
both sides, and the accident of his birth proved no handicap to
him in his career as an official and as a writer. Couto, on the other
hand, was born of humble if honest parents, and this did prove a
handicap to him after the death of his princely patron in 1555.
For all his ostentatious parade of learning he was a man of the
people, nor was he allowed to forget it. Consequently a strong
undercurrent of mordant criticism pervades his work, which is
wholly absent from that of Barros. Almost alone among the
writers of his age, Couto protested openly against aristocratic
birth being given preference over acquired merit and experience,
when claims for services rendered to the Crown were being considered. In fact, Couto's caustic criticism of the failings of his
countrymen in general and of his own social superiors in particular is something quite unprecedented. In his *Diálogo do Soldado
Prático* (*Dialogue of the veteran soldier*) it frequently verges on sheer
vituperation.[1]

Whereas Barros never went further from Portugal than the Gulf
of Guinea, Couto spent fifty years of his life in India, for the first
ten years as a soldier (1559–69), and subsequently as a government
official, private citizen, and keeper of the archives at Goa. Unlike
another early chronicler of India, Fernão Lopes de Castanheda,
he never went east of Cape Comorin, but he saw a good deal of
active service along the west coast of India, and crossed swords

[1] *Dialogo do soldado pratico* (ed. Caetano do Amaral, Lisboa, 1790); *O soldado
prático* (ed. M. Rodrigues Lapa, Lisboa, 1937).

with tough fighters like the Turks in the Red Sea and the Persian Gulf. On his temporary return to Portugal in 1569, he wintered at Mozambique with his friend Luís de Camões, with whose 'arm for battle wrought' and 'mind, the Muses' own',[1] he clearly had much in common. His stay in Portugal was short, and after a brief visit to the Court at Almerim he returned in 1571 to India, where he spent the remainder of his long life until his death at Goa in 1616—the same year in which Shakespeare and Cervantes died. Couto thus saw Golden Goa decline from its noonday splendour into its sunset glow, after the arrival of the Dutch and the English in Eastern seas. His half-century in Asia also witnessed the fall of the Hindu empire of Vijayanagar, the apogee of the Muslim empire of the Great Mogul, and the unification of Japan under the military dictatorship of the Tokugawa.

He seems early to have meditated the continuation of João de Barros's great work on the history of the 'deeds done by the Portuguese in the discovery and conquest of the seas and lands of the East', collectively known as the *Decadas*, only three volumes of which had appeared in print before their author's death. In spite of open and covert opposition, both at Goa and at Lisbon, Couto eventually got himself nominated as the official chronicler and keeper of the records at Goa, with the title of *Chronista e Guarda-Mor da Torre do Tombo do Estado da India*, in 1595–1604—for it took several years before the local viceroys handed over to him all the state papers as they had been ordered to do by the Crown. Couto started work on his continuation of the *Decadas* in the 1590's, though he had collected some of the material long before. He began with a *Decada X*, covering the period of King Philip II of Castile's accession to the Portuguese Crown in 1580, out of gratitude to this monarch who had appointed him to the post he coveted in despite of hostile intriguers. The completed draft was sent home in 1600, but three years earlier Couto had forwarded the manuscript of a *Decada IV*, taking up the story where Barros had left off, on which he was working at the same time. Other

---

[1] '. . . braço às armas feito . . . mente às Musas dada' (*Lusíadas*, Canto X, v. 155). I have followed Leonard Bacon's translation (*The Lusiads of Luiz de Camões*, New York, 1950).

codices followed in rapid succession, despite a series of accidents, thefts, piracies (both literary and naval), and untoward mishaps which delayed the publication of most of them for many years and recall the Latin aphorism *habent sua fata libelli*.[1]

If his personal enemies failed in the long run to prevent his appointment as colonial chronicler, or to do more than unconscionably delay the publication of his *Decadas*, they were successful in blocking his application for admission into the Military Order of Christ. In December 1607, Couto wrote to his patron Dom Francisco da Gama: 'I am now sixty-four, and if they give me something it will be at the time when I may be buried in the church of St Francis, on the ashes of my books, papers, and notes, which I will order to be burnt before I die, lest another should profit from the sweat of my toil, and others should be given the rewards which are denied to me. I do not ask His Majesty to make me a *fidalgo*, nor to give me the Habit of Christ, because there are so many of them nowadays that it will be more distinctive to be known as the man who has not got a Habit, whereas once António Fernandes was known as "he of the Habit" . . . and I repeat to your worship that if I am neither honoured nor rewarded, I will grind everything to dust, and leave on my sepulchre the inscription of Fabricius, *Ingrata patria ossa mea non pocedebis*'.

Despite the inadequacy of official recognition of his efforts after the death of King Philip II (I of Portugal), and the 'great vexation' with which Couto consequently continued his *Decadas*, the old man plodded away with remarkable if querulous pertinacity. Add to this lengthy series written and re-written under the alternating tropical sun and monsoon rains of Goa, another imposing array of works on a wide variety of subjects (a polemical tract against a Dominican narrative of Abyssinia; an unfinished commentary on Camões's *Lusíadas*; a poetical *Miscellany*; a treatise on the maritime trade of Asia, etc., etc.), and it will be granted that Couto's was indeed the pen of a ready writer.

As a pioneer historian of the Orient, Diogo do Couto ranks

---

[1] Only *Decadas IV–VII* appeared during his lifetime (4 vols., Lisboa, 1602–16). *Decada VIII* was printed in 1673; part of *Decada XII* in 1645; *Decada IX* in 1736; *Decada X* in the collected edition of all the foregoing in 1778–88.

with João de Barros, and, as with his predecessor, some of his most interesting works were precisely those which have been stolen or lost. Just as Barros's compendious *Geography* and *Commerce* of Asia disappeared after his death, so Couto's complementary work on the interport trade of Asia, containing a wealth of information from native sources, went the way of his missing *Decadas* after his death. Though neither of the two chroniclers went so far as to learn any Asian language, they both did their best to secure qualified interpreters. Whereas Barros bought educated Chinese and Arabic-speaking slaves to translate works in those two languages for him, we find Couto consorting with Sinhalese princes, Mogul ambassadors, Ethiopian Jesuits, learned Brahmans and Banyans. Even the captive Kunji Ali, awaiting his judicial murder in Goa jail, was called on to contribute material for the *Decadas*.

Nor did old age wither Couto's activity of mind and body, though he complained increasingly of ill-health. In 1608 he volunteered to go to the court of Bijapur, disguised as a horse-coper with four horses for sale, with the idea of inducing the Adil Shah, 'who is a nitwit, whoremonger, actor, and effeminate as a woman', to place himself under Portuguese protection against the Great Mogul. Although, like Barros, he was sometimes betrayed by his ignorance of Sanskrit and fondness for fanciful etymology into making erroneous identifications, such as the ascription of a Chinese origin to the Sinhalese, his uncommon zeal for historical research (as then understood) led him to make some interesting discoveries as well.

Yule pointed out long ago that Couto was the first to realize the identity of the story of Barlaam and Josaphat (the 'Golden Legend' of medieval Christianity) with the life of Gautama Buddha—although, as a good Roman Catholic, he naturally claims that Sakya Muni was evolved from Saint Josaphat, instead of the other way round.[1] Couto made this discovery through questioning an old *yogi* in the famous Kanhari caves near Bombay; but this was no mere chance, since the similarity of the Golden Legend

[1] H. Yule and H. Cordier [eds.], *The Book of Ser Marco Polo* (3 vols., London, 1903–20), II, 325.

D

to the life of Buddha had struck him long before, and he had
formed the habit of questioning learned Hindus about it. He is
the first European to give us a summary (inevitably rather meagre
and inaccurate) of the Sinhalese chronicle *Rajávalia*, which he
obtained from some exiled native princes at Goa. He gives us
descriptions of the Kanhari caves, and of Elephanta island in
Bombay harbour, which the visitor to those historic spots can
profitably consult today. He also has an interesting account of
Adam's Peak in Ceylon, contradicting what he scornfully terms
'the fictions of Marco Polo, Nicolo de Conti, and other Venetians', with information derived from Sinhalese 'who were very
old and conversant with the affairs of that island, and with its
rites and customs, and they told us what is in their writings'.

As regards South East Asia, Couto has an interesting narrative
of the rise of Malacca and its subsequent Islamization. He places
these events in the last quarter of the fourteenth century, thus
anticipating the conclusions of the English Orientalist, Blagden.
He is the earliest European writer to allude to the Malays of
Malacca possessing a pre-Arabic script, and he provides details
about the capture of Johore Lama in 1587 which are not available elsewhere and were probably derived from his great friend,
Dom Paulo de Lima, who was the Portuguese commander. His
account of the Moluccas is confessedly derived from that of
Gabriel Rebello's 'Informação' of 1561-9, since he tells us that
he could find no documents in the archives at Goa to tell him
what had happened there previously. A recently deceased scholar
who made a special study of the Portuguese chroniclers and their
references to South East Asia states that Couto's *Decadas* are in
this respect 'of great but unequal value'. This itself is a sufficient
indication that the virtues outweigh the deficiencies.[1]

As regards the Far East, Couto referred his readers to the published accounts of the Jesuit missionaries who, as he said, had
learnt Chinese and Japanese and could supplement their own
knowledge from the study of the native historical records. As

---

[1] I. A. Macgregor's forthcoming paper cited on p. 31, n. 2 above; *idem*, 'Papers
on Johore Lama and the Portuguese in Malaya, 1511-1641,' in *Journal of the Malay
Branch of the Royal Asiatic Society*, XXVIII, pt. II (May, 1955), *passim*.

evidence of the range of his inquiring mind, however, I may mention that he secured a copy of the globe made by the celebrated Will Adams in Japan, which, from his account of it, formed a unique synthesis of Japanese and European cartography.[1]

Want of space forbids further consideration of Couto as a pioneer Orientalist, but it is germane to our present theme to note that he did not neglect South East Africa. While writing in 1611 about Will Adams and the *Liefde* in Japan, and denouncing the Dominican friar Luis Urreta's recently published *Historia Eclesiastica, politica, natural, y moral de los grandes y remotos reynos de la Ethiopia* (Valencia, 1610), he found time to compile a biography of Dom Paulo de Lima, at the request of the latter's half-sister. It was from this as yet unpublished work that Gomes de Brito extracted the narrative of the loss of the *São Thomé* and the subsequent tribulations of the survivors, which is printed on pp. 155–213 of the second volume of the *História Trágico-Marítima* (1736).

The version printed by Gomes de Brito is virtually identical with chapters xxxii–xli of Couto's *Life of Dom Paulo de Lima Pereira*, which was still in manuscript in the year 1736, but which was published in full twenty-nine years later, with a laudatory foreword by the celebrated Portuguese bibliographer, Diogo Barbosa Machado.[2] The *Life of Dom Paulo de Lima* was, in its turn, originally compiled by Couto from the references to Dom Paulo in his as yet unpublished *Decadas*, the *São Thomé* episode having been taken from the draft of his eleventh *Decada*, on which he was then working but which was subsequently lost, stolen, or strayed. Neither Gomes de Brito nor the editor of the 1765 *Vida de Dom Paulo de Lima* have printed Diogo do Couto's original dedication to Dona Ana de Lima Pereira, which explained how he came to

[1] *Decada XII*, bk. 5, ch. 11. An English translation of the relevant passage will be found on p. lxxxvii of D. Ferguson's introduction to *The Travels of Pedro Teixeira* (Hak. Soc. ed., London, 1902).

[2] *Vida de Dom Paulo de Lima Pereira, Capitam-mór de Armadas do Estado da India, donde por seu valor, e esforço nas batalhas de mar, e terra, de que sempre conseguio gloriosas victorias, foy chamado o Hercules portuguez* (Lisboa, 1765). Reprinted with a shorter title in Mello d'Azevedo's *Bibliotheca de Classicos Portuguezes*, xxxv (Lisboa, 1903).

write the work, and which I reproduce in part from an eighteenth-century copy in the British Museum Library.[1]

'To the Lady Dona Ana de Lima Pereira. The entreaties of a lady like yourself to whom I owe so much, have such force (you being the sister of one of my best friends) that when Dom António de Ataide[2] gave me your ladyship's message, in which you ordered me to help you in this matter, I at once dropped everything else and started on this work, in which I did not do more than I had already done, simply summarizing from my books the deeds of this valorous captain, Dom Paulo de Lima, your ladyship's brother, in which I served him well, for it seems that he foresaw that your ladyship would have to ask me for this in which I now serve you . . . Goa, the 10 November 1611.'

As Dom António de Ataide had only reached Goa from Lisbon on 12 September 1611, and Couto's dedication is dated two months later, it is clear that he had compiled the *Vida* in eight weeks by patching together the relevant extracts from his unpublished *Decadas*. That the account of the loss of the *São Thomé* and of the events leading to the death of Dom Paulo was 'lifted' bodily from his original *Decada XI*, is also clear from a perusal of the narrative itself, which abounds in expressions such as 'as we wrote in our sixth *Decada*', and 'of which we have already given an account in the ninth *Decada*', and 'as related in the tenth *Decada*'. In other words, the printed versions of 1736 and 1765 directly derive from the *Vida* hurriedly compiled at Goa in 1611,

---

[1] Add. MS 28487. 'Summario de todas as cousas que socederão a Dom Paulo de Lima Pereira do dia que entrou na India té sua perdiçam e morte. Dirigido à Senhora Dona Ana de Lima Pereira sua irmãa molher de Dom Antonio dataide filho do segundo conde de Castanheira. Por Diogo do Couto Chronista e guarda mor da torre do tombo da India.' As noted by the Conde de Tovar, *Catálogo dos manuscritos Portugueses no Museu Británico* (Lisboa, 1932), 229–30, this codex includes some material which is omitted in the editions of 1765 and 1903. The 'papel de Diogo do Couto,' to which he refers, was published by me in the *Congresso do Mundo Português. Publicações*, VII, tomo I, 454–5 (Lisboa, 1940). This codex purports to have been copied from the original.

[2] Dom António de Ataide (1567–1647), Captain-major of the India voyage, 1611–12; Commander-in-Chief of the Portuguese Fleet, 1618–21; ambassador to Vienna, 1629; governor of Portugal, 1631–3; married to D. Ana de Lima Pereira, half-sister of Dom Paulo, who was her father's illegitimate son by an unmarried woman.

and which was, in so far as the *São Thomé* episode is concerned, taken from Couto's lost *Decada XI*. In default of this missing original, the editors of the collected edition of 1777–88 compiled a summary *Decada XI*, chapters I–IV of which contain a digest of the 1736 (or 1765) version.

In an appendix to the *Vida* which is only preserved in the British Museum eighteenth-century copy, Couto alludes to a portrait of Dom Paulo de Lima as he appeared when disembarking at Johore in 1587, wearing a scarlet surcoat over his armour of chain-mail, but unfortunately this has not survived. Couto also alluded to his friend João Pereira Corte-Real being inspired by the sight of this picture to make some sonnets in praise of Dom Paulo, and this in turn inspired Couto to invoke 'the muse whom I have neglected so many years'. He was not satisfied with his effort and added 'if the book about Dom Paulo is printed, please print João Pereira's sonnet, which is very good, but not mine, which I only wrote for you to see'. None of the sonnets was included when the *Vida* was belatedly published in 1765, but their omission is no great loss since they do not reach even the mediocre standard of most such effusions.[1]

Contrary to what many modern authors, including H. A. Junod and S. R. Welch, affirm, Diogo do Couto was *not* aboard the *São Thomé* in 1589. The man of that name who figures in the narrative was a young sailor who had been involved in the loss of the *Santiago* four years previously. He should not be confused with the cantankerous old chronicler, whose name, incidentally, was a fairly common one. But though he was not a participant of this disaster, Couto naturally got his information from some of the survivors. Chief among these were probably the *sota-piloto*, Gaspar Ferreira Reimão, who is mentioned on p. 13 above, and Dom Paulo de Lima's widow, the indomitable lady to whom he repeatedly refers with such respectful affection. If his narrative is not (as is usually asserted) a first-hand source, it is at any rate an

---

[1] For João Pereira Corte-Real, see pp. 28–9 above. His sonnets are not included in the B.M. copy, which only contains an equally lame one ascribed to Manuel de Faria e Sousa, but they are to be found in a manuscript copy of Couto's *Decadas VIII* and *IX*, in the library of the Torre do Tombo, Lisboa (MS 613).

excellent second-hand one, and the most trustworthy version available owing to the disappearance of Gaspar Ferreira Reimão's unpublished eyewitness account.[1]

The haste with which Couto compiled his *Vida* of Dom Paulo de Lima in 1611, may explain the obscurity of some passages and the unintelligibility of others. Copyists' and printers' errors likewise help to muddle portions of it, to say nothing of Couto's straggling sentences, which are apt to run on far too long at the best of times. While attempting to keep the translation as literal as conveniently possible, I have, like Theal, cut up Couto's sentences, re-arranged his paragraphs, and amended his erratic punctuation where this seemed to be necessary. I have collated the 1736 text with that of the *Vida* of 1765 and the British Museum MS copy, but since the original manuscript of 1611 has disappeared, some obscure and doubtful readings still remain unresolved. The most confusing part is unfortunately one of the most important, namely Couto's description of the tribes of Kaffraria.

We can only guess why Couto's narrative was not printed in his lifetime or in that of the long-lived Dom António de Ataide. A possible reason is that Dom António and his wife were rather disappointed at Couto's outspokenness in describing the moral collapse of his hero and their relative, Dom Paulo de Lima Pereira, during the wreck of the *São Thomé* and later, when he failed to provide the leadership which was clearly expected from him. A slight indication of this is that Dom António subsequently tried his hand at writing a biography of his brother-in-law, but this has remained unpublished and I cannot say how far it is based on Couto's own account.[2] Be this as it may, Couto's

[1] 'Tratado dos grandes trabalhos que passaram os portuguezes que se salvaram do espantoso naufragio que fez a nau São Thomé que vinha para o reino o anno de 1589. Feito por Gaspar Ferreira, sota piloto da mesma nau, anno de 1590.' Manuscript of fifty-seven leaves, forming lot 39 in the Castel-Melhor sale of March 1879. Subsequently acquired by the Biblioteca Nacional, Lisboa, it could not be found here in 1932. Couto, of course, may have used this, since it was written at Goa.

[2] 'Historia de Dom Paulo de Lima, escripta por Dom Antonio de Ataide. Dedicada a D. Lourenço de Lima, Bisconde de Villa Nova da Cerveira: de Guimarães, 14 . . . de 1616' (Bibliotheca Publica, Evora, Cod. CXVI-1-24).

boldness in telling plain but unpalatable truths (*verdades chãs* he calls them in his *Soldado Prático*) was quite remarkable for an official chronicler. He gave great offence by this practice, and the delays in publishing some of his *Decadas* and the theft or suppression of others, were partly explicable on these grounds, as I have indicated above.

Couto was no more patient than modern authors in bearing with publishers' delays and slow sales. Writing to his patron, Dom Francisco da Gama, in 1608 he complained of the intolerable delay in printing his *Decadas*, 'which above all things I want to see finished'. He further asked that serving soldiers might be allowed to purchase his books against stoppages from their pay, 'for thus they will circulate throughout the ships of the fleet, and incite men to imitate former glories. And I will thereby be enabled to collect money to pay for the printing of my books; for if those already printed are not sold, I can hardly finance the remainder. Moreover, I confess to your worship that of three hundred copies [of *Decada IV*] which the padre[1] sent me, I did not sell more than thirty, while I gave away forty. And to cap everything, although I sent presentation copies to the viceroy, to the archbishop, and to every captain of a fortress, none of them gave me in return so much as a jar of marmalade. I tell you this, that you may see how bad is this occupation nowadays. It seems that they realized that I would not accept any gift from them, but withal they did not want to try and see'.[2]

What became of the original manuscript of Couto's *Vida de Dom Paulo de Lima* after Dom António de Ataide brought it home in 1612, I cannot say. From the copy of the certificate signed by Dr António das Povoas at Lisbon on 15 August 1636, which is preserved in the British Museum eighteenth-century version (Add. MS 28487), we know that the original was then in Lisbon, though in whose possession is not stated. The original codex does not figure among the voluminous papers of Dom António de

---

[1] Fr Adeodato da Trindade, O.E.S.A., Couto's brother-in-law, who helped to prepare the *Decadas* for publication at Lisbon, where he acted as the chronicler's representative.

[2] Autograph letter dated 28 December 1608, printed in A. Baião [ed.], *Diogo do Couto. Décadas. Seleccão, prefácio e notas* (Lisboa, 1947), lxxv–lxxxix.

Ataide, which passed to the Castel-Melhor family by inheritance and were dispersed in the great sale of 1879. While it may yet turn up in some forgotten corner of a library in Portugal, it is perhaps more likely to have perished in the great earthquake and fire of 1 November 1755, as the version printed ten years later was evidently a copy.

(ii) *João Baptista Lavanha and the loss of the* Santo Alberto

If Diogo do Couto was dissatisfied with the degree of official recognition accorded him during his lifetime, João Baptista Lavanha had little or nothing to complain of on that score. Born about the year 1550, of parents of crypto-Jewish (*Christão-novo*) stock, he first comes to notice as a protégé of King Sebastian. This ill-fated monarch sent him to Rome at an unascertained date in order to develop the mathematical abilities which he had displayed at an early age, and on his return he was employed as a mathematician at court. King Philip II not only continued his predecessor's patronage of Lavanha but increased it, nominating the young Portuguese as professor of 'cosmography, geography, and topography' of the Academy at Madrid in 1582. Five years later he was appointed Chief-Engineer (*Engenheiro-Mór*) of the kingdom of Portugal, but he does not seem to have gone to Lisbon until 1591. In that year we find him functioning in the Portuguese capital as 'chief mathematician and cosmographer-royal' of that kingdom, and it was in the latter capacity that he edited in 1597 the narrative of the loss of the *Santo Alberto*.

He returned to Madrid in 1599, and two years later he was sent on a mission of historical research to Flanders. In 1604 he was back in Spain with the Court at Valladolid, and two years later was engaged on some engineering works connected with the rivers Douro, Esgueva, and Pisuerga, exact details of which are lacking. In 1610–11 he carried out a celebrated cadastral survey of Aragon, which resulted in the magnificently engraved map of 1615 that was executed under his supervision in his own house. He also found time to edit the unpublished *Decada IV* of João de Barros from such relevant papers of the great Portuguese chronicler as had survived, in recognition of which he was appointed chronicler-royal of Portugal three years later. During these years he had acted as tutor in mathematics to various members of the royal family, including the future King Philip IV, and he accompanied the latter's father on his state visit to Lisbon in 1619, of which he wrote the officially published account.

He was by now one of the most learned men in the Iberian Peninsula, and is praised as such by his friend, Lope de Vega, in several of the latter's works. His apotheosis (so to speak) came in 1623, when two of his daughters, despite their Jewish blood, were received into the recently founded Franciscan Nunnery at Madrid. The ceremony when they took the veil was attended by the King, the Queen, and other members of the royal family, while one of the sponsors was the Countess of Olivares, wife of the all-powerful favourite whose features are so familiar to us from the portraits of Velasquez. João Baptista Lavanha had already received a royal dispensation which enabled him to become a knight in the Order of Christ despite his Jewish origin, but the patronage extended to his daughters on this occasion was an even more striking proof of the exceptional regard in which he was held. Further marks of royal gratification and esteem would doubtless have been forthcoming but for his death on 31 March 1624.[1]

The range and depth of Lavanha's learning are amply attested by the variety and number of the works which he left behind him, both published and unpublished. They include a *Regimento Nautico*, or *Handbook of Navigation*, which went through two editions (1595 and 1606) in his lifetime; a treatise on shipbuilding, and another on latitude and longitude; half a dozen genealogical works, several of them very extensive, and a chronicle of the reign of King Sebastian. Mathematician, engineer, architect, genealogist, and chronicler, he certainly played many parts even in an age when specialization was regarded as unbecoming for a gentleman.

[1] The foregoing is mainly from A. Cortesão, *Cartografia e cartógrafos portugueses dos séculos XV e XVI* (2 vols., Lisboa, 1935), II, 294-361, which provides the only satisfactory study of Lavanha's life and works. Cf. also *Ementas de habilitações de ordens militares nos princípios do século XVII* (ed. Bibliotheca Nacional, Lisboa, 1931), 79; article by F. P. Mendes da Luz, in *Garcia de Orta*, III (Lisboa, 1955), 63-77.

The original edition of the *Naufragio da Nao* Santo Alberto (1597) is dedicated to the heir-apparent of the Luso-Spanish empire, the first truly world empire on which the sun never set; and as Gomes de Brito has suppressed this dedication, I give here the translation of the original.

'To the Prince Our Lord.

Sire.

The Portuguese who were saved from the shipwreck of the Great Ship *Santo Alberto* in the year 1593 discovered a great part of savage Kaffraria. They made their way through it and opened a new route, travelling along which with unexpected ease, they reached the Bay of the Holy Spirit (*Spirito Santo*) the principal port for its trade and the most southerly of that region. And since the narrative of this journey may be of great help to those who are shipwrecked on that coast (which God grant may not happen) the governors of this kingdom[1] entrusted me with the compilation thereof. It is this which in this volume comes to Your Highness's hands as earnest of another greater one, which I am now finishing, of the description and history of all the states of His Majesty (to which Your Highness will succeed after the long years of his life), and of the genealogies of the kings and princes thereof.[2] A work which will receive the price of the greatness of the subject, and much more through being dedicated to Your Highness, whence it is likewise communicated to this one. If Your Highness will deign to look at it (great reward for so small a present) you will see the dangerous hardships which these your vassals suffer in the lengthy India voyage. Where fighting continually with infidels, they risk and lose their lives; and when, after shedding much of their blood they retain them and return to enjoy them in their country together with the deserved fruit of their victories, the sea deprives them thereof, infuriated at the dar-

[1] The five governors of Portugal were the archbishop of Lisbon, the counts of Portalegre, Santa Cruz, and Sabugal, and the *Escrivão da Puridade*, Miguel de Moura.

[2] This seems to be the manuscript work listed by Barbosa Machado, *Biblioteca Lusitana*, under the title of 'Livro Historico, y Genealogico de la Monarchia de España,' which was, however, still unfinished at the time of Lavanha's death.

ing with which they sail it; and in its rage it wrecks their great ships and drives them ashore as it did with this one. However, the Portuguese resist everything and pass through everything with courageous and cheerful hearts, for the honour of God and for the service of His Majesty and of Your Highness—happy and solid empire that is ruled with such clemency that it deserves to be obeyed with this love and goodwill! God prosper it for Your Highness whose life may he guard and keep many years. From Lisbon, 19 August 1597.

João Baptista Lavanha.'

The original edition of 1597 is a small octavo, comprising four preliminary leaves, including the title-page, printing and publishing licences, publishing monopoly for eighteen years, dedication to the Infante, Dom Felipe (later King Philip II), and errata, followed by the text on pp. 1–152 (see Appendix IV). Apart from the reprint by Gomes de Brito in the *História Trágico-Marítima*, II (1736), pp. 215–313, there are at least two counterfeit eighteenth-century editions of this work. Both of them are quartos, but one edition has three preliminary leaves (including the title-page) and sixty-five pages of text, whereas the other comprises the title-page leaf and sixty-five pages of text. They can also be readily distinguished from the genuine 1597 edition since they both have a woodcut of a sinking ship on their respective title-pages, which also differ slightly from each other and from the original in wording. The genuine edition of 1597 is exceedingly rare, the only copies known to me being that in the British Museum (on which the present translation is based), and that in the late King Manuel's library now housed at the old Braganza palace in Villa Viçosa.[1] Apart from his suppression of the dedication and other preliminary matter, Gomes de Brito made only

---

[1] For a detailed bibliographical description see H. M. King Manuel, *Early Portuguese Books, 1489–1600* (London, 1935), III, 407, no. 255. I may add that the copies quoted by A. Cortesão, *Cartografia*, II, 337–8, and Anselmo, *Bibliografia das obras impressas em Portugal no século XVI* (Lisboa, 1926), nr. 1065, as being in the National Libraries at Madrid and Lisbon, respectively, are examples of the eighteenth-century counterfeit editions.

a few trifling changes from the 1597 edition in his 1736 reprint of the text.[1]

As Lavanha explains at the beginning of his account, his own narrative was primarily based on the journal kept by the pilot, Rodrigo Migueis, during the march, which he checked from the information given him by Nuno Velho Pereira, the leader of the castaways, and doubtless from the recollections of other survivors as well. His narrative, therefore, like Diogo do Couto's version of the loss of the *São Thomé*, if not exactly an eyewitness account, is at any rate as good a second-hand one as can possibly be expected.

(iii) *Francisco Vaz d'Almada and the loss of the* São João Baptista

In contrast to Diogo do Couto and João Baptista Lavanha, almost nothing is known about Francisco Vaz d' Almada. He tells us that he had served as a soldier for an unspecified number of years in India; and from incidental mention of him in the *Decada XIII* of António Bocarro, it can be gathered that most of his service was on the west coast of India, at any rate in the years 1612–14.[2] As a result of his experiences in South East Africa after the loss of the *São João Baptista*, Francisco Vaz d'Almada also wrote another and much shorter account of the dilapidated state of the fortress of Sofala, the oldest Portuguese settlement on the coast, founded in 1505, entitled: *Narrative of the fortress of Sofala, and of the great importance thereof, and notice of the neglect and abandonment in which it has been for many years; which I saw when coming to it after the shipwreck of the great ship* São João *in the year 1623*.[3] This was a four-page memorial printed in Spanish for submission to one of the government councils at Madrid, but I myself have never seen a copy.

Francisco Vaz d'Almada returned to Europe at some un-

[1] My remarks in this connection on pp. 24–5 of my above-quoted essay 'An Introduction to the *História Trágico-Marítima*' (Lisboa, 1957), are misleading and should be amended accordingly.

[2] António Bocarro, *Decada XIII* (Lisboa, 1876), 14, 222, 307, 310, 313.

[3] *Relación de la fortaleza de Çofala, y de la grande importancia d'ella, y advertencia del descuido y desamparo en que está ha muchos años; que vide viniendo á ella del naufragio de la nave San Juan en el año de 623.* Cf. Domingo Garcia Peres, *Catalogo razonado de los autores Portugueses que escribieron en Castellano* (Madrid, 1890), 25.

ascertained date between 1625 and 1630, the next mention of him which I can find being in November 1631, when he left the Tagus for Goa with two pinnaces, the *Nossa Senhora dos Remedios e Santiago* and the *Nossa Senhora de Nazaré e Santo António*, he himself embarking in the first named which was a Swedish-built vessel.[1] The sailing-directions for this particular 'winter monsoon' voyage were drawn up at a meeting of all the India and Brazil pilots who were then in Lisbon. Vaz d' Almada was advised to take a course well clear of the Cape of Good Hope, which would take him into the area bordering on the 'roaring forties', partly so as to avoid the risk of encountering the Dutch and English East Indiamen which frequented Saldanha Bay. It was envisaged that he should reach Mozambique by mid-March, so as to leave that island for India between 20 March and 1 April 1632, but he was ordered to try to make Bombay if unduly delayed.[2]

The voyage took a good deal longer than anticipated. The *Nazaré* contrived to reach Goa in May 1632, just before the bar of the Mandovi was closed by the monsoon, but the *Remedios* was not so lucky. She only reached Goa in September 1632, having been forced off her course in the Indian Ocean and compelled to winter at Muscat. Despite the length of the voyage it seems to have been an unusually healthy one for the period. At any rate, Gaspar Rodrigues, a contemporary pilot of the *carreira da India*, has the following marginal note in an unpublished and undated document of about 1635: 'I [went] in a Swedish ship, one of two commanded by Francisco Vaz d'Almada, and not a soul died on board.'[3]

---

[1] The date of departure is variously given by contemporary sources as 22, 23, and 26 November, respectively. Cf. next note.

[2] 'Roteiro que se deu por ordem do governo aos dous pataxos que partirão para a India em 26 de Novembro 1631 para o qual se juntarão todos os pilotos da Carreira da India e do Brasil,' on fols. 152–3 of a collection of *roteiros* compiled by Dom António de Ataide, and now in the writer's library.

[3] 'Eu em hum navio de Zuecia, Cabo de dous Francisco Vas Dalmada e não nos morreo pessoa' (autograph 'Resposta' of Gaspar Rodrigues in the writer's library). I have assumed from this laconic note that Gaspar Rodrigues sailed in the *Remedios*, but it is just as likely that he was in the *Nazaré*. Cf. B.M. Add. MS 20902, fol. 137. Cf. also the Viceroy's dispatch of 23.xi.1632, in *Boletim da Filmo-teca Ultramarina Portuguesa*, no. 8 (Lisboa, 1958), p. 29.

I have not come across any further reference to Francisco Vaz d'Almada; but in July 1644, a certain Dona Ines Imperial was granted a pension in kind 'on account of the services of her brother Francisco Vaz d' Almeida in India', which implies he was dead by that date, assuming that Almeida is a misprint for Almada.[1]

The original edition of the *Tratado do successo que teve a nao Sam Ioam Baptista* (Lisboa, 1625), is an octavo of forty-two leaves. There is an eighteenth-century counterfeit edition which is usually included in the third volume of the *História Trágico-Marítima*, and is a quarto with the following collation. Two unnumbered leaves comprising the title-page [1 recto] and the dedication [2 recto]. The text, with a separate heading *Naufragio/Da Nao S. João Baptista no Cabo de Boa/Esperança no anno de 1622*, follows on pp. 5–96, each leaf (save the last) being numbered on both sides. Although the original edition of 1625 is not such an excessively rare work as the *Naufragio do Santo Alberto* of 1597, I cannot recall having seen more than two or three copies offered for sale in the last thirty years, including that which I acquired in 1929.

The dedication to Diogo Soares was reproduced in the eighteenth-century counterfeit edition, but since it was omitted by Theal and contains some relevant particulars, I give a translation below.

'To Diogo Soares, Secretary of His Majesty's
Treasury Council &c., and in his absence to
Padre Manuel Gomes da Silveira.

The great desire that I had to send your worship the narrative of this affair obliged me to write it in ten days, before the departure of these ships which God preserve.[2] And I had neglected to write

---

[1] *Inventario dos Livros das Portarias do Reino* (Lisboa, 1909), I, 108.

[2] '... antes que estas nàos, que Deos salue, se partisse.' As only one carrack (the *São Thomé*) left Goa for Lisbon in 1624, the reference must be to the homeward-bound fleet of four carracks and two galleons which left the Mandovi on 4 March 1625, under Dom António Tello and João Pereira Corte-Real. One of the carracks had to be beached at St Helena after springing a leak off the Cape of Good Hope, and Tello's flagship foundered on the Cachopos shoals at the entry to the Tagus. The other four vessels were brought safely into port by João Pereira Corte-Real on 23 October, after narrowly escaping the Anglo-Dutch fleet under Wimbledon and Haulthain on its way to attack Cadiz.

it for so long, because Padre Fr Diogo dos Anjos, who was like-wise my comrade, had told me that he was writing a very copious treatise, relating in detail all the particulars of our journey. And when I finally asked him for it so that I could send a copy to your worship, he told me that he had not been able to do it since he had been continually ailing, and also on account of his religious duties. This was the reason which induced me to write this, de-spite the fact that it is very difficult for me to write even a lengthy letter, to say nothing of such reams of paper, particularly as I do not know the style in which such works should be written. I therefore ask your worship to examine it very closely before you show it to anybody, amending the style and anything else that you consider necessary, pardoning my faults as a friend. And when it is fit to be published, do whatever you like.

Francisco Vaz Dalmada.'

Despite the *carte blanche* given to Diogo Soares to edit the *Tratado* for the press, he seems to have sent it straight to the printer, for it bears all the marks of having been written in great haste and none of having been revised for publication. Vaz d'Almada's thoughts clearly outran his pen on several occasions, and some sentences are almost unintelligible. It was also very poorly printed, even by the lax standards of seventeenth-century Portuguese book-production, but it has the undeniable advantage over the two previous accounts of being written wholly and solely by an eyewitness. It also relates the longest journey ever made by Portuguese castaways in South East Africa, since the survivors had walked almost every step of the way from the Keiskama River (or thereabouts) to Sofala in the ten months which elapsed between the landfall of the *São João Baptista* on 30 September 1622, and Vaz d'Almada's arrival at Sofala on 28 July 1623. Last not least, the fight of the *São João Baptista* against two stronger Dutch East Indiamen must surely rank among the great epics of the sea. For nineteen days they fought it out in the icy 'roaring forties', with the Portuguese carrack in a half-sinking condition, her ill-clad defenders numbed with the bitter cold and unable to cook a single hot meal during all that time. Though the carrack was leaking heavily, totally dismasted, and at the mercy of the sea, the wind, and the Dutch guns, at the end of this period there were still those on board who opposed the suggestion for an honourable surrender; and in fact the carrack eventually contrived to reach the African coast with her flag and her honour—if nothing much else—intact.

TEXTS

RELAÇAÕ
DO ʒ
NAUFRAGIO
DA
NAO S. THOMÈ

Na Terra dos Fumos, no anno de 1589.

E dos grandes trabalhos que paſſou

D. PAULO DE LIMA

Nas terras da Cafraria athè ſua morte.

ESCRITA POR DIOGO DO COUTO
Guarda mòr da Torre do Tombo.

A rogo da Senhora D. *Anna de Lima irmãa do*
dito D. *Paulo de Lima no Anno de* 1611.

Tom. II.   V

NARRATIVE

OF THE

SHIPWRECK

OF THE

GREAT SHIP *SÃO THOMÉ*

In the Land of the Fumos, in the year 1589

And of the toil and tribulation undergone by

DOM PAULO DE LIMA

In the regions of Kaffraria until his death

WRITTEN BY DIOGO DO COUTO
Chief Custodian of the Torre do Tombo

*At the request of the Lady D. Anna de Lima sister of the said D. Paulo de
Lima in the year 1611*

SHIPWRECK OF THE GREAT SHIP
SÃO THOMÉ

In the Land of the Fumos, in the year 1589

THE great ship *São Thomé*, captain Estevão da Veiga, left Cochin in January 1589, when Manuel de Sousa Coutinho was governor of the State of India.[1] The captain took his course outside the shoals,[2] and steering for the island of Diogo Rodrigues,[3] which is in twenty degrees southern latitude, the south-east wind blew so hard that the seas ran very high and the ship drove before the wind. Owing to the flapping of the sails against the [fore]mast, she sprang a leak by the forechains, whereby the caulking oakum was squeezed out and she began to ship some water, but this was soon dealt with and very well repaired.

The wind moderating, they continued on their voyage as far as the latitude of the tip of the Island of São Lourenço,[4] in latitude

[1] Manuel de Sousa Coutinho held this office from 4 May 1588 to 15 May 1591, after a long and distinguished career in the East. Accused of large-scale peculation and of favouring Hindu soothsayers, he was recalled by the home government in March 1591, but perished with three of his sons and everyone else on board the ship *Bom Jesus* when she foundered on the shoals of Garajaos at the end of February 1592.

[2] Presumably the shoals of Pedro dos Banhos and of the Garajaos, as explained in the *Roteiro de Portugal pera a India* of Vicente Rodrigues, 14–15 of the 1615 Lisbon edition. Cf. also *John Huighen van Linschoten his discours of voyages into ye Easte & West Indies* (London, 1598), 316. 'Garajaos' were a species of seagull (*Lauris Dominicanus*). Cdte. Humberto Leitão argues that the relative positions of the shoals of Pedro (or Pero) dos Banhos and of Chagas in the sixteenth-century *roteiros* have become transposed on modern charts. Cf. his article: 'Identificação dos Baixos de Pero dos Banhos e das Chagas,' in *Studia. Revista semestral do Centro de Estudos Ultramarinos*, I (Lisboa, 1958), 118–22.

[3] In lat. 19° 41′ S, long. 63° 23′ E, nowadays a dependency of Mauritius. Presumably named after a pilot of Affonso de Albuquerque, who was knighted after the conquest of Goa, receiving the royal confirmation of this honour in 1528 (Sousa Viterbo, *Trabalhos Nauticos dos Portuguezes nos séculos XVI e XVII*, Lisboa, 1898, I, 270).

[4] Madagascar; so called because it was allegedly discovered on St Lawrence Day (10 August) 1506. Cf. Camões, *Lusíadas*, X, 137.

twenty-six degrees, and between ninety and one hundred leagues from land. Here the carrack began to ship water in a greater quantity than the first time, and by another and more dangerous place, which was at the stern, below the sleepers by the aftermost fashion-pieces, where it is more difficult to get at than in any other part. The officers dealt with this by clearing the cargo from that part of the ship, and found the water which was very violent, as it was expelling oakum from the seams and the lead plates which were nailed on top. All this was due to the caulking, for which reason many ships are lost, which is very carelessly done, and to which the officers pay little heed, as if so many lives and so many goods which are embarked in these great ships were not their responsibility.

Having found the leak, they saw that it was such a spout that if an officer put his hand in, the strength of the water forced it back. And as they could not get at it without cutting the fashion-pieces they did this against the advice of many; but having cut some they stopped again as that was the place in which the whole ship was held together, and they had no proper fastenings on board to repair it, for the most or all of these ships sail at the mercy of God, to save four *cruzados*.[1] With knives, large nails, and other things they stopped the leak as well as they could, plugging the space between the timbers and the riders with many little sacks of rice so as to make a sticky substance, placing a chest on the top to hold them down, so that the water could not push them out.[2]

This helped them to some extent, and the water began to be less in the pump, and so they pursued their course in fair weather to the latitude of thirty-two and a half degrees south, a hundred and fifty leagues from Alagoa Bay,[3] and eighty from the nearest part of the land of Natal. In this latitude the wind veered to WSW, it being already the 11th of March. They therefore took in all sail

---

[1] A Portuguese coin whose value was fixed at 400 *reis* in 1517, but which was mainly used in the East as a money of account. As such, it was often loosely equated with the ducat, the crown, and the Spanish silver *peso* or rial-of-eight, and its value in English money estimated at about four shillings.

[2] This rendering is entirely conjectural as the original is so obscurely worded as to be incomprehensible.

[3] Nowadays spelt Algoa Bay, Port Elizabeth being situated on its southern shore.

except the courses, and stood towards the north. With the labouring caused by the wind and sea, the leak sprang again in the same place so quickly that there were soon six spans of water in the hold. All the people were in great consternation and began to throw into the sea everything on the waist so that the hatches should be clear; they passed the whole of that night without rest and with the pump-handles in their hands. There were already another two spans of water in the hold which began to rise above the ballast and to cover the pipes and Blackwood[1] which floated about on top of the water from side to side, giving such blows on the ship's sides as made the whole ship tremble.

Since the water kept rising, the officers[2] fixed some yards above the fore and aft hatches, from which were suspended many kegs of six *almudes*[3] which could easily be hauled up and down, and all on board were allotted to work these, without distinction of persons, beginning with D. Paulo de Lima,[4] who was a passenger with his wife,[5] as also Bernardim de Carvalho,[6] the captain Estevão da Veiga,[7] Gregorio Botelho, father-in-law of Guterre de Monroy,[8] who was taking his daughter to her husband, and other gentlemen and Religious who were on board the ship. All worked day and night at the pumps and the pulleys of the kegs, without leaving them even to eat; for the padres went about the waist with biscuits, preserves, and water, consoling them all bodily as well as

[1] Probably the chests made at Cochin from *Dalbergia latifolia*. Cf. *Travels of Peter Mundy* (Hak. Soc. ed., III, I, 112 n.).

[2] Here and elsewhere the word 'officiaes' (officers) is used in the sense of caulkers, carpenters and other artificers.

[3] A measure for selling wine, there being 26 *almudes* to a pipe.

[4] Dom Paulo de Lima Pereira, illegitimate son of Dom António de Lima, was born in 1538, and had served in the East since 1558, his principal feat being the capture and sack of Johore Lama in 1587. His exploits are related at length in Couto's *Vida*, written in 1611 and first published in 1765, and also in I. A. Macgregor's article 'Johore Lama in the sixteenth century,' *Journal of the Malay Branch Royal Asiatic Society*, XXVIII, pt. 2 (May, 1955), 88–120.

[5] Dona Brites (Beatrice) de Montaroio, daughter of a wealthy resident of Ormuz.

[6] He had served in the relief of Colombo from the siege by Rajasinha I of Kandy in the previous year.

[7] He had been captain of the *São Thomé* on the outward voyage in 1588.

[8] One of a family of Spanish origin whose members (usually named Guterre) had served in the East from the time of Affonso de Albuquerque, when a Guterre de Monroy married the governor's niece and was the first captain of the city of Goa.

spiritually. Yet notwithstanding all this diligence, the water gained ever more rapidly, so that they resolved to seek the nearest land and run the ship ashore there. They therefore put about under the foresail and the spritsail, not daring to set the mainsail, since they could not let go of the pumps and pulleys; for any time that they did so would suffice to let them be submerged.

While they were steering towards land, it being already the 14th March, the hold became waterlogged, and the pumps became blocked with the pepper which went into the hold so that they ceased to work and the men became discouraged; but those nobles, Religious, and honourable gentlemen continuing to labour with great heart and soul, they encouraged the others to work, persuading them not to lay down the baling gear, because this alone preserved them. The officers spent that day in clearing the pumps, fitting the pump-cisterns with tinplate so that they would not become choked again.[1] And forasmuch as it was necessary to throw overboard everything they could, this duty was entrusted to certain persons, who cast into the sea all the riches and luxury-goods with which the ship was so richly laden, which had all been gained with such sweat by some and with such care by others.

On the next day, which was the 15th of the month, the orlop-deck became covered with water, the wind was from the SW, and from time to time brought violent rain-storms, which caused them additional distress. In short, everything was against them, until the ship refused to answer the helm and broached-to, without sails, since they were all torn, while those on board could not do anything else but man the pumps, for this was their only hope of salvation if one existed. All this night they passed in great trouble and distress, for everything they could see represented death. For beneath them they saw a ship full of water, and above them the Heavens conspired against all, for the sky was shrouded with the deepest gloom and darkness. The air moaned on every side as if it was calling out 'death, death'; and as if the water which was entering beneath them was not sufficient, that which the Heavens poured on them from above seemed as if it would drown them in another deluge. Within the ship nothing was heard but sighs,

---

[1] Another conjectural translation of a very obscure passage.

groans, shrieks, moans, and prayers to God for mercy, as it seemed that He was wroth with all of them for the sins of some who were in the ship.

When next day dawned, and they all saw themselves without any hope, they tried to launch the ship's boat into the sea, for which purpose it was necessary to leave the bailing-kegs in order to open the ship. Between the decks it seemed as if the evil spirits were busy, so great was the noise made by the things which were floating about and bumping against each other, and crashing from side to side, so that those who went down below fancied that they beheld a likeness of the last judgment. The officers and other men hastened to get the boat ready, to which they affixed the washboards and whatever else seemed necessary for the voyage. This was all done with great difficulty, owing to the violent rolling of the ship which was lying in a cross sea, whose waves entered by the entry-port which had been cut open so that everything could be thrown from it into the sea, and this was the reason why the ship became so waterlogged.

At this time they were steering NW,[1] for the pilot[2] calculated that he was very close to land; and in fact they were really so near that at sunset on this day a sailor declared that he saw it, and shouted from the masthead 'land! land!' And as the pilot did not know whether there were any reefs in that locality, on which if the ship should strike they would all be lost, he thought he had better haul off and steer NE, so as to approach in the daytime and save all the people, who passed the whole of that night in the greatest depression of spirits and the greatest bodily toil that can be imagined.

At first light on the next day they could not see land, and they launched the boat into the sea with great difficulty, because while it was still on the tackles in mid-air, the men threw themselves into it like maniacs, without Dom Paulo de Lima, who had placed himself therein with a drawn sword, being able to stop them, for he

[1] NNW in the *Vida* (p. 149 of the 1903 edition).

[2] Gaspar Gonçalves, who had been pilot of the *Santiago*, wrecked on the Baixos da India in 1585. Cf. below, p. 67, n. 4. His behaviour on both occasions was severely criticized by Linschoten, *Discours of Voyages* (1598), 146–8, 166, and by Gomes de Solis, *Discursos* (1622), fol. 155.

wished to prevent the sailors going off in it and leaving him. But despite the vicious cuts and stabs which he mercilessly gave many of them, so many people crowded into it that it was in imminent danger of foundering on reaching the sea. With great difficulty Dom Paulo de Lima induced some of them to climb up out of it, by promising to save therein as many people as it could hold. The boat being finally lowered, it went round to the stern of the ship in order to take from the gallery the women who were there, with the Religious and the gentlemen; and as the ship was pitching so heavily that they were afraid she might swamp the boat, it was kept at a little distance. Orders were given that the women should be tied to pieces of muslin and thus lowered into the boat, which came closer to take them in, often after many a ducking, and with great trouble, grief and misery to all.

In the ship this work was directed by Bernardim de Carvalho, upon whom fell that duty as well as all other responsibilities; for Dom Paulo de Lima, being a good Christian and fearing God, thought that this disaster was caused by his sins; whereby he was so cast down that he did not seem to be the same man who in such great risks and perils as those in which he previously found himself had never lost a bit of his strength and courage, which now completely failed him.

In this manner were embarked: the wife of the said Dom Paulo; Dona Mariana, wife of Guterre de Monroy; and Dona Joanna de Mendoça, widow of Gonçalo Gomes de Azevedo, who was going to the kingdom to enter a convent, being disenchanted with the world, although still young and able to enjoy it, a very virtuous lady, who gave to all an admirable example during the whole of this journey, as we shall have occasion to relate. She had with her a daughter less than two years old, whom she held in her arms, with her eyes raised to Heaven imploring God for mercy; and in order to lower her into the boat, it was necessary to take the child from her and hand it to her nurse. After these, there embarked the Fathers, and Bernardim de Carvalho, and last of all the master and the boatswain, who were busy getting some kegs of biscuit and water that they threw into the boat, which was now quite full and accordingly put off.

Dona Joanna de Mendoça, seeing that her daughter was left in the ship in the arms of her nurse who held her up to view with great weeping and wailing, displayed such grief and spoke so heartrendingly that she moved them all to come closer to the ship and beg the child of the nurse. They told her to tie it to a piece of muslin and lower it into the boat, which she refused to do, saying that unless they took her in also she would not give up the child. Nor could they persuade her otherwise, however much her mistress besought her with tears and entreaties which might have moved a tiger had the child been in its clutches.

Because this caused some delay, and the girl was hard-hearted, and the ship was rolling most terribly, they were forced to put off the boat that it might not be swamped, which they did with great pity for the wretched mother, whose eyes were fixed upon her child with that tenderness which all are wont to show when they look upon those they dearly love. And seeing that she was forced to leave her, though she would much rather have remained clasping her in her arms than have abandoned her to those cruel waves which seemed ready to engulf her, she turned her back upon the ship, and lifting her eyes to Heaven offered to God her tender child in sacrifice, like another Isaac, begging God's mercy for herself, because her child was innocent and she knew that He would have her in safe keeping. This spectacle did not fail to cause deep sorrow in all who were in that condition, in which each one had sore need of another's pity, if there were any hearts free to feel for ills other than their own.[1]

The boat having put off a little, they remained waiting in the offing for Friar Nicolau do Rozario, of the Order of Preachers, who refused to embark in the boat without first confessing all those who remained in the ship; for he did not wish that so many people who were deprived of all corporal consolations should also lack those of the soul. He thus confessed and consoled all with great charity, weeping with them over their sad condition, and

[1] Fr João dos Santos, O.P., *Ethiopia Oriental* (Evora, 1609), II, 63, states that the wretched mother 'repeatedly begged those in the skiff to go and fetch her child, which none of them wished to do, but on the contrary they rebuked her for her importunities', and this callous behaviour is more in keeping with what subsequently happened.

absolving them generally and individually. And since it was not possible for the boat to approach and take him off by force, for he was resolved to remain in the ship for the consolation of those people, Dom Paulo de Lima spoke to him so efficaciously, and was so warmly seconded by all those who were in the boat, that he was finally persuaded to throw himself into the sea and swim out to the boat, wherein he was very warmly received by all on account of his great virtue and the example which he gave throughout the voyage, for which he was much loved and respected by all.[1] And after he was taken in, they steered for the land.

Those in the ship, seeing the departure of the boat, and having no further hope but in God and their own efforts, made some rafts as best they could, which were already alongside the ship when the boat put off. But as God Our Lord had chosen those people to perish in that place, all the rafts foundered, as did two *manchuas*[2] which were [being towed?] at the stern of the ship. It is certain that this must have been a punishment from God, for all the people in this ship might very easily have been saved if those in the boat had not cared only for themselves alone. For they could well first have prepared some large rafts, on which all might have taken refuge, with water and provisions, and been guided by the boat to land, which was so near that it was sighted next day. There would have been ample time for this, as the ship remained afloat for twenty-four hours without pumping, during which time as many rafts as necessary could have been prepared, for there were yards, masts, and spars, and more than sufficient timber.

For the loss of the ship *Santiago* on the Baixo da India (as re-

---

[1] Fr Nicolau do Rozario was a native of Pedrogão in the diocese of Coimbra and entered the Dominican Order in 1575. Having survived the loss of the *São Thomé* and the subsequent hardships of the journey to Sofala, he worked as a missionary among the Kaffirs of Zambesia until he was martyred near Sena in 1592. Cf. João dos Santos, O.P., *Ethiopia Oriental* (1609), I, bk. 2, ch. XVIII, and II, bk. 2, ch. IX; George Cardoso, *Agiologio Lusitano* (Lisboa, 1652), I, 473–4, 478.

[2] 'Manchuas or small vessels of recreation, used by the Portugals here [Macao] as also at Goa, pretty handsome things resembling little frigates; many curiously carved, guilded and painted, with little beak-heads' (I have modernized the spelling in this quotation from Peter Mundy, *Travels*, III, pt. I, p. 205). Cf. also *Hobson-Jobson* (ed. 1903), 549–50; Dalgado, *Glossário Luso-Asiático*, II, 19–20.

lated above in the tenth Decade)[1] occurred in much more difficult circumstances, yet many rafts were made, some of which
reached land without help from the skiff or the boat, the passage
lasting eight days. But the persons in this ship who could have
commanded some respect, and who might have been able to
arrange this, were firstly Dom Paulo de Lima, who had lost his
hitherto unvanquished courage at seeing himself with his wife in
such straits, and secondly Bernardim de Carvalho, a very honourable gentleman and a very good knight, but of so mild a disposition that seeing great disorder among all the sea-officers he overlooked many things of which he strongly disapproved, that all
might not be lost. For these seamen, on an occasion like this,
respect nothing, nor were they afterwards punished for the ex-
cesses which they had committed in these voyages.[2]

To return to the boat. As soon as it set out, the officers found it
so overburdened, being so heavily laden that it was nearly under
water, that they insisted that some persons should be thrown into
the sea to save the rest. To this those gentlemen consented, leaving
the selection of them to the officers, who at once threw six people
into the sea.[3] These were lifted into the air and thrown overboard,
where they were swallowed by the cruel waves and never reap-
peared. This pitiful sacrifice so horrified those who witnessed it
that they were in a maze, not realizing what they saw, or regarding
it as something seen in a dream. And even after these six persons
had been thrown overboard, there were still one hundred and four
people left in the boat.

Continuing on their course, they could not make any progress,

[1] This is one of several proofs that Couto took this narrative straight from his own
(since lost) *Decada XI*. The loss of the *Santiago* on the *baixos da India* in the Mozambique Channel in 1585 created a great sensation at the time. For the principal
accounts of this disaster including that in Couto's *Decada X*, bk. 7, ch. III, see my
essay 'An introduction to the *História Trágico-Marítima*,' 18–21. For the nomenclature and location of the *baixos da India* (also known as the *baixos da Judia*) whence
the actual English terminology 'Bassas da India,' cf. A. Fontoura da Costa, *A
Marinharia dos Descobrimentos* (2nd ed., Lisboa, 1939), 322 *n*. (436), and his edition
of the 1612 *Roteiro* of Gaspar Ferreira Reimão, (Lisboa, 1939), 22–3.

[2] Cf. Introduction, p. 11, and next note but one below.

[3] Fr João dos Santos, O.P., *Ethiopia Oriental* (1609), pt. 2, fol. 63v, says this was
done to 'many' by Captain Estevão da Veiga's order.

for the current drove them from the land out to sea, the men being unable to row, from exhaustion after their labours, and the boat being unmanageable from its weight. At midnight they found themselves out at sea a good distance from the ship, and taking to their oars they rowed towards it. They saw many lights in it, which were burning candles, for those in the ship passed the whole night in processions and litanies, commending themselves to God Our Lord with such loud cries and clamours that they could be heard in the boat.

When day dawned the boat drew near to the ship, and they spoke with those on board, encouraging them to make rafts, and offering to wait and accompany them. Those in the ship replied with loud cries and wails, begging for mercy in voices so heartfelt and pitiful as to inspire fear and terror, for the half-light of early dawn made the scene more awful and appalling. When it was broad daylight, several persons tried to reach the ship to get some matchlocks and provisions, for which purpose three or four sailors swam out to her. On climbing aboard, they found the deck already under water, and all the people as if out of their minds with fear of the death which they expected. Withal they had placed on the top-gallant-poop a beautiful altar-picture of Our Lady, round which were gathered all the slave-women, who with dishevelled hair were piteously wailing and begging that Lady for mercy.

The nurse of Dona Joanna was standing in front of them all with the baby in her arms, which she never put down, the child's tender age not allowing her to realize her danger; and even had she done so, in her innocence it would have troubled her little, for there is nothing which makes death seem so terrible as doubt of salvation. The sailors threw into the sea some kegs of water and biscuit, and one of wine, that were taken into the boat, which tried to approach the ship, to be lightened of still more persons, as it was not fit for navigation. The sailors returned without bringing Dona Joanna's baby, for most of these men are inhuman and cruel by nature.[1]

[1] Criticism which repeatedly occurs in these accounts. Cf. pp. 11, 84, 196, 225, etc.

As those in the boat could not get near enough to the ship to send away more people, they drew off, and let the officers have their way. These threw overboard some more persons, including Diogo Fernandes, a good man but a very timid one, who had just relinquished the post of Factor of Ceylon; a soldier named Diogo de Seixas; Diogo Duarte, a merchant; and Diogo Lopes Bayão, who was for many years in the Balagate,[1] where the Idalxà[2] gave him an income of three thousand *cruzados*, since he was a clever and scheming man who exported horses from Goa to that place, and who kept him informed of everything. He was even suspected of being doubtful in the faith, for which reason he was sent to Portugal (of which we gave a lengthy account in our tenth Decade),[3] for it was he who contrived the plot to lure Çufucão[4] to the mainland, whom the Idalxà wished to have in his power in order to kill him, because the kingdom was rightly his; and on this occasion [the Adil Shah] succeeded through the machinations of this Diogo Lopes, and commanded his eyes to be put out. This Diogo Lopes, when he was seized to be thrown overboard, handed to Friar Nicolau a little bag of jewels, said to be worth ten or twelve thousand *cruzados*, asking him, if he were saved, to deliver it to his agents at Goa if he went thither, or to his heirs at home if God should bring him to Portugal. Several slaves were thrown overboard with these men, all of whom were at once swallowed by those cruel waves. This abominable cruelty was done by the hands of the sea-officers, which God permitted that

[1] Balaghaut (*bhālāghāt* in Maratha-Konkani), the country 'above the passes', i.e. beyond the Western Ghauts, here applied to the kingdom of Bijapur.

[2] Adil Shah. The title by which the Portuguese distinguished the Sultans of the Muslim dynasty of Bijapur, 1490–1686. Cf. *Hobson-Jobson*, 431–2; Dalgado, *Glossário Luso-Asiático*, ii, 462–3. A seventeenth-century Englishman wrote this title as 'Idle Shaw'!

[3] *Decada X*, bk. 4. ch. x. The Inquisitors' dispatch of 9.xii.1588, announcing the remission of Diogo Lopes Baião as a prisoner in the *São Thomé*, is printed in A. Baião, *A Inquisição de Goa. Correspondencia dos Inquisidores da India, 1569–1630* (Coimbra, 1930), 122.

[4] Çufucão may be a corruption of either Yusuf-Khan, or (perhaps more likely) of the title *Sufu-Khan*. For a similar story of this otherwise unidentified claimant to the throne of Bijapur occupied by Sultan Ibrahim II, 1580–1627, see Pyrard de Laval, *Voyage*, Hak. Soc. ed., ii, 137–8. Cf. also P. Pissurlencar (ed.), *Regimentos das fortalezas da India* (Bastorá, 1951), 108–9.

they should pay for very shortly, since all or most of them died very miserably on shore in the bush.

The boat now began to row towards the land, and when they were some distance from the ship at ten o'clock in the morning, they saw it give a great lurch, and then founder immediately afterwards, disappearing under the water in sight of all as quick as a flash of lightning. They were left astounded, like men in a dream, at thus seeing a great ship, in which they had so recently been voyaging, so heavily laden with riches and merchandise almost beyond computation, now devoured by the waves and sunk under the water, heaping up riches in the depths of the sea from all those things which belonged to those in her and to others in India, acquired by such means as God knows, for which reason He often permits as little enjoyment of them as He did of these.

Although this sight was a very terrible one for them all, it was even more painful and fearful for the wretched Dona Joanna de Mendoça, for she saw that her beloved baby daughter and tender darling would be the prey of some sea-monster that might perhaps devour her while she was still alive; but as she had already offered everything in sacrifice to God, she spoke with Him in her heart about her sorrows, nor could He have failed to help her with some spiritual consolation, as could be gathered from the exemplary patience, virtue, and resignation which she showed on this occasion.

A sail was set in the boat, and with the wind from the east they steered for the nearest land on the course they had set, which they sighted on the evening of the 20th March.[1] They approached it with great rejoicing (if such could be in hearts which had just lately suffered such sorrows), and as it was nightfall they took in the sail, that they might not run ashore on a place where they would all be drowned, since God had brought them thus far.

Certainly the loss of this ship and the death of the people that had remained in her is a matter to be deeply pondered over, for in many ways it was very clearly a judgment of God. If that evening when the sailor said he saw land it had been sighted in the morn-

[1] Apparently somewhere near Santa Lucia Bay in Lower Zululand (Amatonga-land). Cf. sketch-map, fig. 2.

ing, or if the pilot had not changed course during the night, then all those people most certainly would not have perished; for they were only eight leagues from land at the most, and the ship remained afloat more than long enough to have allowed the first boatload of people to be landed ashore and the boat to return for the remainder. They could even have done still better by remaining in the ship until she ran ashore, for even if she had struck two leagues from land, this would have been close enough to have saved all the people in the boat, or even on rafts without the boat, which everyone would have made with a glad heart in sight of land, and thus they could all have been saved. But sin blinded their eyes, so that they could not realize this, and those were lost who were destined to be so.

The next day in the morning they came very close to the shore, and anchored where the waves broke, for all the bottom was clear there. Several sailors were sent ashore to see if they could see any villages.[1] From the top of some sandhills they saw fires, and going in search of them they found some straw huts inhabited by Kaffirs. These fled at the sight of the sailors, but then realizing that they were Portuguese, from the dealings they had with them in the ivory trade which they carry on there every year, they soon returned to them very familiarly and went with them to the beach, but without understanding each other for none of them spoke our language. The wind was then blowing from the west, wherefore they all agreed to go along the coast to the river of Lourenço Marques. Reembarking the sailors,[2] they began their voyage, but the wind increased and the seas ran so high that they were forced to run ashore on that beach, in order to avoid having to do so later on another one which might be more dangerous.

Running the boat ashore, they all landed with some biscuit which they had with them, and they prepared their matchlocks

[1] Two sailors, one of whom was called António Gomes Cacho, according to João dos Santos, O.P., *Ethiopia Oriental*, pt. II, bk. 3, ch. III, who gives a fuller account of this incident. Cf. below, p. 91, n. 2.

[2] Actually, the occupants of the boat abandoned the two sailors, but these were well treated by the Kaffirs and caught up with the boat later, having meantime picked up a lot of ambergris in their walk along the shore (João dos Santos, O.P., op. et loc. cit.).

and arms for use in any emergency. They passed that night among some sandhills where they lit their fires, keeping very good watch. This was on the 22nd March, and the next day they set fire to the boat to get out the nails, which are much esteemed among the Kaffirs, in order to use them as trade-goods.[1] They made wallets of dimity for the journey, and several water-bags from some skins (which had been thrown into the boat by chance) so as to carry water for the road.

They then made a muster of those present, who were found to total ninety-eight persons, including women, of whom we will name those that we have knowledge of: The captain Estevão da Veiga, Dom Paulo de Lima, Dona Beatris his wife, Gregorio Botelho and his daughter Dona Mariana wife of Guterre de Monroy, Dona Joanna de Mendoça widow of Gonçalo Gomes de Azevedo, Bernardim de Carvalho, Manuel Cabral da Veiga, Christovão Rabello Rodovalho, Nicolau da Silva, Diogo Lopes Leitão, a brother of the wife of Dom Paulo de Lima, Francisco Dorta, Factor of the ship, Antonio Caldeira son of Manuel Caldeira, shipping-contractor,[2] Friar Nicolau do Rozario of the Order of Preachers, Friar António, a Capuchin lay-brother,[3] Marcos Carneiro the ship's master, Gaspar Fernandes the pilot,[4] Diogo do Couto who had been wrecked in the ship *Santiago* on the Baixo da India,[5] and some other sailors and grummets.

The arms were found to consist of five matchlocks, as many swords, a keg of gunpowder, and some lunts. From the oars of the

[1] Santos (op. et loc. cit.) says the boat was run ashore and burnt at Inhaca island, for fear lest some of the castaways should try to steal a march on the others by sailing the boat to Sofala. Couto's version is obviously the correct one, since it took the castaways about a fortnight to march along the shore to Inhaca island.

[2] *Contador das Naos (HTM)*, *contractador das Naos (Vida)*; the latter being the correct reading. For Manuel Caldeira's contract to supply five carracks annually for the *carreira da India* in 1583–7, see Diogo do Couto, *Decada X*, bk. 4, ch. v; and bk. 10, ch. vi.

[3] In all probability Fr António da Magdalena, O.F.M., to whom we owe the earliest European account of the famous Khmer city of Angkor. See B. P. Groslier and C. R. Boxer, *L'Angkor et le Cambodge au XVIᵉ siècle d'après les sources portugaises et espagnoles* (Paris, 1958), 32–3, 49–51, 66–7, 82–4.

[4] A slip of Couto's pen for Gaspar Gonçalves, for whom see above, p. 58, n. 2.

[5] As indicated previously, this young sailor has been wrongly confused with the old chronicler of the same name by Theal, Welch, and other modern writers.

F

boat they made lance-hafts, with carpenters' gimlets for heads. The biscuit was divided among them all, in two or three handfuls each, the water-skins were filled, and this was their provision for the journey which they resolved to undertake.

On the 23rd March they started on their way, the Capuchin Friar António going in front with a crucifix held high. From the sails of the boat they had made two hammocks slung on some oars, in which the women might travel, and which were supposed to be carried by the sailors and grummets, to whom Dom Paulo de Lima promised a large sum of money. The wives of Dom Paulo and Guterre de Monroy wore white doublets, long breeches reaching to the ground,[1] and red caps; but Dona Joanna de Mendoça was dressed in the habit of St Francis, for as she was going home to become a nun in a convent of the Poor Clares, she wished to put on her habit so that if she died on the journey she might die in it, and thus fulfill her desires in part. And afterwards she accomplished this, for as there was no convent of the Poor Clares in India which she could enter, she retired to Our Lady of the Cape, in her habit which she never again took off, and built a little house or cell into which she withdrew, to be near the Capuchin friars who there lead holy lives, and herself no less so.[2] There she still lives in such retirement, abstinence, and prayer, that in no cloister could she do more, and her life and example are a consolation to this city of Goa.

Before we continue with the journey which these castaways made in Kaffraria, it seemed good to us to give a brief description of this region, because all the others are described in our ninth Decade,[3] where we dealt with the conquest of the gold-mines by the governor Francisco Barreto and Vasco Fernandes Homem.

[1] The baggy, zouave-like, and mosquito-proof trousers, fastened at the ankles, which were a noticeable feature of Indo-Portuguese dress. See the somewhat stilted engravings in Linschoten's *Itinerario*, and the more lively and colourful representations by Japanese artists in the *Namban-byōbu* ('Southern Barbarian folding-screens') of the *Keichō* period, 1596–1614.

[2] The Franciscan hermitage of Nossa Senhora do Cabo is now embodied in the official residence of the Governor-General of Portuguese India in this picturesque spot. The first convent of the Poor Clares in Portuguese Asia was that at Macao which was founded in 1633 and still exists.

[3] *Decada IX*, chs. XXI–XXII.

This we shall now do from this place where the boat ran ashore as far as Cape Correntes, which we reached in the other description of the kingdoms of Monomotapa and of all the rest of the interior and coast of this Lower Ethiopia.[1]

This region where this boat ran ashore is commonly called by our mariners 'Land of the Fumos', and thus it is called in our maritime charts. This name was given to it by the first of our people who passed that way, from the many smoking fires which they saw on land at night; but the native Kaffirs call it 'Land of the Macomates', from some Kaffirs so named who live along those shores.[2] This boat ran ashore in latitude $27\frac{1}{3}°$, near a river which is marked but unnamed in our charts, in latitude $27\frac{1}{2}°$, and which our people who sail from Mozambique to the river of Lourenço Marques for the ivory barter-trade call the river of Simão Dote, from a Portuguese of this name who went there in a *pangayo*.[3] This river is small, and only navigable by small craft, and it is about fifty leagues distant from the bay of Lourenço Marques to the south.[4]

[1] Cf. W. G. L. Randles, 'South East Africa as shown on selected printed maps of the 16th century' (*Imago Mundi*, XIII, 1956), for European ideas of the so-called 'empire' of Monomotapa (the Makalanga or Mokalanga tribal confederation) in Couto's day.

[2] S. R. Welch, *Portuguese Rule and Spanish Crown in South Africa* (Cape Town, 1950), 90, writes: 'the word for smoke in Portuguese is *fumo*, and the local Kaffir word for a petty chief was *mfumo*. This was indeed the land of petty chiefs but not of smoke.' On the other hand, H. A. Junod, 'The condition of the natives of South East Africa in the sixteenth century, according to the early Portuguese documents' (*The South African Journal of Science*, February 1914), accepts Couto's derivation as the correct one. In either case, the Land of the Fumos roughly coincided with the present Amatongaland (also written Tongaland), and was then inhabited by off-shoots of the Makalanga or Mokalanga tribes. Cf. I. H. Soga, *The South-Eastern Bantu*, 30.

[3] *Pangayo* (*pangaio*) was a small trading vessel of Swahili origin, varying in size from a sailing canoe to a two-masted barge. No iron was used in its construction, the planks (mostly formed by splitting the trunks of trees down the centre, and then trimming each block with an axe) being fastened to the timbers with wooden tree-nails. The sails were of matting, and the standing and running gear alike of coir, which was also used to sew or bind the various parts together. Cf. Theal, *The Beginning of South African History* (London, 1902), 111; *Hobson-Jobson*, 668; Dalgado, *Glossário Luso-Asiático*, II, 157–8; *Mariner's Mirror*, XXVII (1941), 261.

[4] S. R. Welch (*Portuguese Rule*, 90) identifies this river with the 'Mkusi [Um-kuzi] River in Amatongaland, which runs into St Lucia Bay'. He adds: 'if the

All this land of the Fumos belongs to the king called Viragune.[1] It extends for more than thirty leagues into the interior, and on the southern side is bounded with another called Mocalapapa,[2] which extends from the hinterland of the river Santa Luzia in latitude 28¼° to the first land of Natal, where it adjoins another kingdom, that of Vambe,[3] which runs southwards, whither our people also go for the ivory barter-trade. From this kingdom, which includes a great part of the land they call Natal, to the Cape of Good Hope there are no kings, but all is in the posses-

distance given were accurate it would indicate the Umfolosi [Umfolozi] River, half-way between Lourenço Marques and Durban. But no one could call it a small river, as it is now spanned by a bridge 3579 feet long.' The Evora version of the Perestrello chart of 1576 (which is the type of chart that Couto had in mind) does show a small unnamed indentation in lat. 27° 50′ S, north of the river (= bay) of Santa Lucia, but the Mkusi river does not come out on the coast at this point. Junod is no help here since he does not notice the contradiction between Couto's distance and latitude. On the assumption that the old chronicler's latitude was probably more nearly correct than his distance, I would suggest that the 'River of Simão Dote' and Perestrello's unnamed indentation may both be identical with the Sordwana river, 'a small and insignificant stream,' which enters the sea near the anchorage of the same name in lat. 27° 33′ S. Cf. the reproduction of the Evora chart in A. Fontoura da Costa [ed.], *Roteiro of the South and South-East Africa from the Cape of Good Hope to Cape Corrientes, 1576* (Lisboa, 1939); *Africa Pilot*, III (ed. 1954), 193; also the B.M. chart in Pl. IV above.

[1] H. A. Junod notes ('Condition of the natives,' 12) that Viragune is 'a name which does not sound much like Bantu'. S. R. Welch (*Portuguese Rule*, 91) locates this chief and his tribe, the above-mentioned Macomata, in the region round 'the bend of the Umfolosi River, where the English first met the formidable Zulu chief Panda, in his great kraal of Ulundi'.

[2] None of the authorities I have consulted has attempted to identify this tribe.

[3] The Vambe (elsewhere spelt Bambe) are identified by Theal, 'to a certainty', with the 'Abambo of Hlubi, Zizi, and other traditions, from whom Natal is still called Embo by the Bantu' (*Beginning of South African History*, 301). This identification is regarded as 'very doubtful' by H. A. Junod, for the reasons explained in his 'Condition of the natives,' 14 n. Whatever the exact names and locations of these various tribes were, Junod, Welch, and J. Soga (*The South-Eastern Bantu*, Johannesburg, 1930, 65, 84) all agree that the ethnic content of the population of sixteenth-century Amatongaland and Zululand was very similar to that of today, and that the language spoken was already the actual Zulu-Xosa. This disposes of Theal's contention that 'not a single tribe is mentioned of the same name as any one still existing now . . . [and] even if these names were accurate at the time, the communities that bore them have long since ceased to exist and never did anything to merit a place in history'.

sion of chiefs called Ancores,[1] who are heads and rulers of three, four, or five villages.

From the kingdom of Viragune, which comprises all that land of the Fumos, the kingdom of Inhaca[2] runs north-eastwards, reaching as far as the point of the bay of Lourenço Marques on the southern side, which is called the river of São Lourenço in our maritime charts, and is in latitude 25¾°.[3] It likewise includes two islands off the said point, one called Choambone, which is inhabited and has seven villages, and is about four leagues in extent, containing many cows, goats, and hens.[4] The other is called Setimuro and is uninhabited, and may be about two leagues in extent.[5] Here our people stay when they come for the ivory barter-trade, to be more secure from the Negroes of the Country, for the best trade is that with this Inhaca. This island has very good water, abundance of fish, and turtles, though their shells are worthless.

As we have now reached this bay, which is famous, and one of the principal of the continent called Africa by geographers, we shall describe it, that it may better appear what kings live around

[1] *Sic* in *HTM*; 'Ancozes' and 'Ancoses' in *Vida. Inkosi*, the Zulu-Xosa word for 'chief'.

[2] Nyaka. 'This tribe still exists though it has lost its independence, and "those of Nyaka" (*ba-ka-Nyaka*) still greet each other by saying: "*Shawan, Nyaka;*" "I greet you, Nyaka" ' (H. A. Junod, 'Condition of the natives,' 11). Also written Inyaka. Cf. H. P. Junod, 'Os indígenas de Moçambique no século XVI,' 48.

[3] The south-eastern corner of the Bay of Lourenço Marques is nowadays known as the Bahia de Machangulo. This is probably Couto's 'Rio de São Lourenço', as 'river' and 'bay' were often interchangeable on old Portuguese maps and charts. The nomenclature of the Bay of Lourenço Marques is rather confusing but illustrates this particular point. Originally called 'Rio da Lagoa' or 'River of the Lake' by its unidentified discoverer *c.* 1500–2, some forty-five years later it began to be termed the River (or Bay) of Lourenço Marques, in consequence of a pilot of that name having developed the barter-trade in ivory in this region. The English name, Delagoa Bay, thus derives from the original nomenclature used prior to 1545. Cf. Perestrello-Fontoura, *Roteiro* (ed. 1939), 87–95; Caetano Montez, *Descobrimento e fundação de Lourenço Marques* (Lourenço Marques, 1948), 13–15, 18–23.

[4] The present-day Ilha do Inhaca, or Inyaka Island.

[5] The present-day Ilha dos Portugueses, Island of the Portuguese, formerly called Ilha dos Elefantes, Island of the Elephants, which name is still commemorated by the Ponta dos Elefantes at its western extremity. Couto's 'Setimuro' is evidently derived from the Tonga word for the island, *Xitimúli*, which is still used at the present day (C. Montez, *Lourenço Marques*, 33).

it. Let us suppose a butterfly, with two points, the one of the Inhaca as aforesaid, and the other on the northern side, where lies the kingdom of Manhiça of which we shall shortly speak. The distance from one point to the other will be about six leagues,[1] and the depth from the mouth inwards fourteen fathoms.

In the middle of the bay is an island, which our people call the island of Birds, because of the great number there, as large as geese, and so plump that their grease is used for the lamps and binnacles of ships.[2] The wing of this butterfly on the southern side is a river which runs to the south-west, upon both sides of which extends the kingdom of Belingane, and so the river is called.[3] The wing on the north side is the river Manhiça, which flows straight through it, and from which the kingdom takes its name.[4]

This river is the largest of those which discharge here, and is one of those that we said in our eighth Decade,[5] in the description of the kingdom of Monomotapa, flows out of the Great Lake, together with the Nile and others. It enters the region which is commonly called Bahia Fermosa, which is in fact the river Espirito

[1] Both the *HTM* and *Vida* versions have 'e será distancia de huma boca a outra de seis legoas,' which is nonsense as it stands, and I have assumed that *boca* is a misprint for *ponta*.

[2] Perhaps the Ilha Xefina Grande, a low, sandy island about three and a quarter miles from the north-western shore is meant. There are no islands in the middle of the bay. Cf. *Africa Pilot*, III (1954), 200, and Admiralty Chart No. 644.

[3] H. A. Junod identifies this with the Maputo River, and adds: 'No doubt this is Buyingane, name of a chief who was located near the mouth of the river and who was conquered by the Maputju, but whose clan still exists in the same conditions as that of Nyaka. The country is still called Ka Buyingane' ('Condition of the natives', 12 n.). Cf. H. P. Junod, 'Os indígenas de Moçambique no século XVI,' 48–9.

[4] 'As regards the Manyisa [Manhiça] River, there is no doubt about its identification. It is the Nkomati [Incomati, Inkomati, etc.] of today; but natives do not call it by that name in this part of its course. . . . They may have termed it "*nambu wa ka Manyisa*," viz., the river flowing in the Manyisa country, and the chroniclers have mistaken this expression for the name of the river itself. . . . *Manhiça* is well known up to this day, and the "*ba-ka-Manyisa*" form one of the most numerous clans of the Ba-Ronga' (H. A. Junod, 'Condition of the natives', 11–12). Cf. also H. P. Junod, 'Os indígenas de Moçambique no século XVI,' 50.

[5] '. . . na nossa Oitava Decada' in both *HTM* and *Vida*. This is a slip of the pen or a misprint for *Nona Decada*, as Couto's description of Monomotapa and South East Africa is in *Decada IX*, chs. XXI–XXII.

Santo.[1] Here the Portuguese make their barter-trade in ivory, and have a factory, which they occupy during the four months of the year that the monsoon lasts.

The head of this butterfly divides into two antennae,[2] which are two rivers, that in the same way branching out from the head run into that lake [? Bay], which is the body of this butterfly. On the antenna to the north lies the kingdom of Rumo,[3] which was where Manuel de Sousa de Sepulveda, when he passed that way with his wife, delivered up his arms, as we wrote in our sixth Decade, and where she and her children died, and where the said Manuel de Sousa disappeared, entering the bush maddened with grief at seeing his wife and children dead, and where it seems that he was devoured by wild beasts.[4]

A few years ago that king ordered this bush to be cleared and the ground to be cultivated, in the course of which the native Kaffirs say that they found two richly bejewelled rings, which the king has, and shows to this day to the Portuguese who go to trade

---

[1] The Rio do Espirito Santo has kept its name down the centuries and the modern city and harbour of Lourenço Marques lie close within its mouth on the northern bank. The name Bahia Fermosa seems to have been dropped relatively early, but is another instance of the way in which the Portuguese regarded 'river' and 'bay' as being interchangeable.

[2] 'O cabo desta borboleta que se divide em duas farpas,' in both *HTM* and *Vida*. As *cabo* can mean either 'head', 'end', or 'tail', and *farpa* can mean either 'antenna', 'dart', or 'streamer', Couto's butterfly metaphor is singularly confusing and inept. I for one cannot make head or tail of it, and neither can any Portuguese with whom I have discussed it. The translation which follows is therefore given with all reserve, as I have opted for *cabo* as 'head', whereas Theal translated it as 'end' or 'tail' in his version.

[3] Rumo (*HTM*), Bumo (*Vida*), also written *Fumo* and *Vumo* elsewhere. H. A. Junod ('Condition of the natives', 10) identifies this with 'Mpfumo, the most celebrated of the Delagoa little kingdoms which ceased to exist as an independent clan after the war of 1894'. Cf. also H. P. Junod, 'Os indígenas de Moçambique no século XVI,' 49.

[4] Cf. *Decada VI*, bk. 9. chs. XXI–XXII. Much more famous is the *Historia da muy notavel perda do Galeão grande sam João*, first published about 1558, and subsequently reprinted many times, and translated into the principal European languages. It was the most popular of all the narratives included in the *História Trágico-Marítima*, and has some striking affinities with the wreck of the East Indiaman *Grosvenor*, which went ashore at almost exactly the same place in 1782. Cf. C. R. Boxer, 'An introduction to the *História Trágico-Marítima*,' 6–10, 48–9; and P. R. Kirby, *A Source Book on the Wreck of the Grosvenor* (Cape Town, 1953).

there. We heard this from several people, who assured us that they saw these rings, which in all probability are those of the said Manuel de Sousa, who was wearing them on his fingers.

The other antenna at the head of the butterfly on the southern side is a kingdom called Anzete;[1] and you must know that among these Kaffirs as soon as one succeeds to the kingdom he is called by the name of that kingdom. This kingdom borders on some great mountain ranges, extending for over twenty leagues, so rugged, impenetrable, and strong by nature, that they cannot be entered except by several very difficult passes. On their heights are several very large plains, which belong to a chief named Monhim-peca,[2] who never under any circumstances descends from the mountains or holds communication with his neighbours, for they are all alike very great thieves.

In these mountains there are very many elephants, and this chief has great caverns full of their tusks, but he never wants to trade them with the Portuguese, fearing that if he sent them down from the mountains they would be stolen by his neighbours. This Kaffir lives on the summit in great security, and without depending on anybody, for the land on these heights yields him all the necessities of life. The people of these mountains speak the same language as their neighbours the Vumos and Anzetes,[3] and they are usually all, both men and women, of such great stature that they look like giants.

These two rivers which form the antennae at the head of the butterfly unite after two days' journey where they flow through the highlands, to form another river which flows from Anzete to Vumo, and cuts that antenna through the middle. Upon this river lives a king called Angomanes,[4] whose kingdom extends

[1] H. A. Junod ('Condition of the natives', 12, 16) identifies the Anzete with the Tembe clan; S. R. Welch (*Portuguese Rule*, 92) with the Maputo.

[2] Neither H. A. Junod nor S. R. Welch attempts to identify this chief, tribe, or clan, who presumably lived somewhere in the Lebombo hills, or Swazi highlands. The Swazi did not then exist as a distinct tribe. Cf. J. H. Soga, *The South-Eastern Bantu*, 358–9.

[3] Mpfumo and Tembe clans, according to H. A. Junod, op. cit., 16.

[4] Ngomana, the name of a chief of the Mazwaya clan who formerly lived in the Lebombo hills, according to H. A. Junod, op. cit., 12. S. R. Welch states that Couto's Angomane is to be identified with Amangwane, one of the names by

towards the west; and this river runs along the foot of some mountains, upon whose skirts are several villages. And a Portuguese
told us that sailing up this river in a vessel to trade he came upon
the people of these villages, who were fishing in some small boats,
and he noticed that when they wanted anything from the land
they moved their boats to a place where they could be heard, and
gave certain pipes and whistles, upon which the villagers brought
all that they required, for they understand each other by these
noises, although they have their own language, and one very different from that of all those other kingdoms.

To return to the mouth of the river Espirito Santo, which is the
face of this butterfly, between it and the river of Manhiça there
runs a creek towards the south-west, and cuts off that point, making it an island, to which our people gave the name of Honey.[1]
From here the coast runs straight to the river of Kings (which our
people now call river of Gold),[2] in latitude 25°, on the western
side of which lies a kingdom called Inhàpula,[3] and on the other
side that of Manuça, which is a vassal of the former.[4]

From here the coast curves inwards to Cape Correntes,[5] so
much so that it makes a very deep roadstead not marked on our
charts, which looks like a great gulf to the ships from Mozambique which cross it on their way to the river of Lourenço
Marques. Along this bay live certain Kaffirs called Mocrangas,

which the Swazis of today call themselves (*Portuguese Rule*, 92). Cf. also H. P.
Junod, 'Os indígenas de Moçambique no século XVI,' 50.

[1] *Mel*. One of the actual Xefina Islands?

[2] Rio dos Reis (Vaz Dourado, 1571); Rio do Ouro (Perestrello, 1575). The
Limpopo River in lat. 25° 12′ S.

[3] Inhapule, also written Inhampura, 'is evidently *Nyapure*, the name by which
Natives still designate the country round the mouth of the Limpopo. As is the case
with Nyaka, the tribe no longer exists as independent, but the clan of Nyapure is
still living, "those of Nyapure," and they are saluted thus: "Good morning,
Nyapure," ' (H. A. Junod, 'Condition of the natives,' 14–15.)

[4] 'The same can be said of Manuça. "Those of Manuça" have lost their self-
governing condition, but people bearing that family or clan name are met with on
the eastern border of the Limpopo.' H. A. Junod, op. et loc. cit.; H. P. Junod,
'Os indígenas de Moçambique no século XVI,' 51.

[5] Cabo das Correntes, in lat. 24° 07′ S, the western extremity of the southern end
of the Mozambique Channel; the name is usually given in the hispanified form of
Cape Corrientes on most English maps and charts.

who are great thieves.[1] In the middle of it there is marked on our sea-charts a river in latitude 23⅘°, called Bazaruta, but it does not exist, nor is there one of that name along the whole coast. There are only the islands of Bazaruta, in latitude 21½°, opposite the point called São Sebastião in our charts, which is in latitude 22⅓°, of which we have already given an account in the ninth Decade, in the foregoing description of the whole of Kaffraria.[2]

In the hinterland of this bay of the Mocrangas there are two kingdoms, that of Manuça, already mentioned, which lies in the aforesaid region, and the other of Inhaboze, which extends to a great river called Inharingue,[3] below Cape Correntes. This is the one we have just mentioned as called Bazaruta on the sea-charts, but it is nearer to Cape Correntes than is indicated thereon. Upon the western side of this river is the kingdom of Panda,[4] next to that of Inhabuze, which borders with the kingdom of Monhibene,[5] that runs northwards from it along that river, and borders in its turn with another kingdom called Javara,[6] which is situated

[1] Mokalanga or Makalanga, a group which had originally emigrated from what is now south Rhodesia. Cf. H. A. Junod, op. et loc. cit.; H. P. Junod, 'Os indígenas de Moçambique no século XVI', 9; J. H. Soga, *The South-Eastern Bantu*, 30, 65, 71.

[2] *Decada IX*, ch. XXI, although neither of these places is described in the mutilated form in which Couto's *Decada IX* has come down to us. For a modern description of Cabo de São Sebastião and the Ilhas dos Bazarutos see *Africa Pilot*, III (1954), 220–2.

[3] The Inhaboze [Inyabuse] still exist in the region described by Couto but have lost their self-governing condition. The river Inharingue is the actual Inyarrime [Inharrime] lagoon, in the midst of the country of the so-called Ba-Chopi (H. A. Junod, 'Condition of the natives,' 15).

[4] 'Panda, still called by that name in the Portuguese orthography, but in reality Pande, is settled further North, directly westwards of Inhambane' (H. A. Junod, op. et loc. cit.). Cf. also A. Cabral, *Raças, usos e costumes dos indígenas do districto de Inhambane* (Lourenço Marques, 1910), 48–50, 72–3.

[5] 'Monhibene alone is unknown to my [Native] informants' (H. A. Junod, op. et loc. cit.), but S. R. Welch (*Portuguese Rule*, 100) identifies it with Morrumbane, an important centre of Portuguese administration. Cf. also A. Cabral, *Districto de Inhambane*, 40–3; and H. P. Junod, 'Os indígenas de Moçambique no século XVI,' 51.

[6] 'Javara is either *Zavalla* or *Zavora* (H. A. Junod, op. et loc. cit.). S. R. Welch prefers the form *Zavara*, and the *Africa Pilot*, III (1954), 213, *Zavora*. Cf. also A. Cabral, *Districto de Inhambane*, 52–5.

further inland up this river. On the opposite side are two other kingdoms: that of Gamba nearer the sea, and that of Mocumba in the interior.[1]

All these kingdoms here described are well known to the Portuguese who come from Mozambique for the barter-trade in ivory there. Upon which we will here say no more of them; and although it would not be out of place likewise to describe the barbarous customs and laws of these Kaffirs, I will not do so here, because it is foreign to my purpose, and I only wish to relate what happened to the people of this wreck on their journey until they reached the river of Lourenço Marques.

Our castaways, having set forth upon their journey as already stated, travelled along the shore very slowly, on account of the women, eating some of the little biscuit which they had with them, and drinking some of the little water in the skins, for most of it had leaked through the seams. In this way, with frequent halts, they went along till nightfall, when they withdrew to some sandhills where they took shelter, seeking, as they did all through this journey, a separate place for the women. There they made their fires and slept upon the hard sand, having no other pillow or coverlets but the sky. Next day they resumed their journey, being already without food or water, and they caught some crabs upon the shore, which they roasted and ate. The women were already very exhausted, and Dona Joanna de Mendoça was the most wretched of them all; for of the other two, one had her husband and the other her father, who helped and comforted them as best they could. This lady alone was unprotected and sorrowful, for there was not among all those people a single one bound to her by any tie, who could help her in such necessity.

But as God our Lord had His eyes upon her, since she had given Him her whole heart, He moved Bernardim de Carvalho,

---

[1] 'Gamba, the Mokalanga invader who was baptized by Padre Gonçalo da Silveira, S.J. [in 1561], is certainly the *Gwambe* clan, whose chief Khugunu (Cogune) is one of the most important among the Chopi. Mocumba is probably *Nkumbi*, his neighbour, and these two clans seem to inhabit exactly the same tract of country where the Portuguese found them in the sixteenth century' (H. A. Junod, op. et loc. cit.). Cf. H. P. Junod, 'Os indígenas de Moçambique no século XVI,' 9, 51.

a very virtuous gentleman,[1] to take pity on her. Seeing her weary
and alone, he drew near and gave his hand to assist her, with all
the respect due to a woman so dead to the things of this world,
that on the very day she stepped ashore she put on the habit of
Saint Francis, and cut off her beautiful hair, sacrificing it to God
and leaving it in those parts to be scattered where the wind listed.
And thus during all the time the journey lasted, she gave such an
example that all were lost in admiration. And this gentleman
served her with such love and respect, seeing her mortification,
that forgetting his own hardships, he thought only of hers, so that
no father or brother could have done more.

Thus they went on their way with great toil to the women,
whose feet were already blistered and wounded, which forced
them to go so slowly that on the third day's march some persons
wished to push on ahead, not daring to travel so leisurely and in
want of everything, with nothing to eat but crabs and some wild
fruit from the bush, and a few small things which they obtained
by barter from the Kaffirs.[2]

The confusion caused by those who wished to press on was
appeased by the captain and Dom Paulo de Lima, who spoke to
them with very obliging words and persuaded them to go slowly,
assuring them that God would help them. Hence from that time
forward they kept better order, for they divided into two parties,
Dom Paulo de Lima being in front with half the people and the
arms, while Captain Estevão da Veiga went behind with the rest.
The women went in the middle, and they were in such a state
that they cut everyone else to the heart, and thus they all went
along slowly with them.

Already on the fifth day they were followed by some Kaffirs,
numbering about three hundred, who seemed to have cast their
eyes upon some caps and other trifles which they saw. They gradually drew nearer and nearer, until they were emboldened to get in
front of our people and attack them, shouting their war-cries and

---

[1] Cf. above, p. 56, n. 6.
[2] S. R. Welch (*Portuguese Rule*, 92) erroneously states that this contretemps took
place after some weeks' journey, whereas it really happened on the third day, as
explicitly stated by Couto.

brandishing their weapons, which they call *Pemberar*.[1] The captain
and Dom Paulo de Lima, seeing their determination, formed into
one body, placing those with matchlocks and lances on the outside and the women in the centre. They advanced towards the
Kaffirs, who came on with loud cries and shouts, charging
them and hurling many fire-hardened sticks, which they call
fimbos,[2] and which would fell an ox if they struck it, but from
which none of our people received any hurt. The matchlocks
being fired upon them, they were so terrified on hearing the discharge that they all threw themselves together on the ground,
and then bounding like monkeys upon all-fours they fled into
the bush. Our people being thus rid of them, pursued their
journey.

On the same day there came out to meet them through some
passes in the mountains[3] another band of Kaffirs, among whom
there was one very old man with a white beard clad in a tiger's
skin, and with him a Kaffir woman who seemed to be his wife.
Coming very familiarly up to our people, they made signs that
they should follow them, which they did, thinking that he was
the chief of some village. They led them by the same path they had
used in coming, which they followed with some difficulty, it being
rather rugged, until they reached a village which was on the edge
of a lake more than a league in length. The Kaffir offered them
refuge, which they accepted, remaining there for what was left of
the day and for the whole night without any molestation. The
Kaffir women of the village gathered to see the white women, as
something marvellous, and all night they gave them many enter-
tainments and dances, which they would gladly have excused, as
the noise prevented them from sleeping and they had great need of
some rest.

[1] Unidentified. The *HTM* version says this attack took place on the 'second' day,
which I have corrected to 'fifth' from the *Vida*.

[2] Unidentified, as it can hardly be a corruption of *ntsimbi*, 'iron', with the
secondary meaning of 'ornament'. Cf. P. R. Kirby, *Wreck of the Grosvenor*, 95, 133.

[3] The nearest mountains were the Lebombo Hills, but as this range must have
been about forty or fifty miles away, I presume that the reference must be to the
coastal hills, which are from 200 to 400 feet high in this area, according to the
Africa Pilot, III (1954), 195.

Here they brought them hens, goats, raw and cooked fish, and lumps of millet-flour, of which they made cakes, bartering everything for pieces of nails and some shirts which our men stripped off their bodies for this purpose. They stayed here until next day in that rustic bliss, and the pilot took the altitude of the sun and found the lake to be situated in 26½° South.[1]

This is a freshwater lake, but the tide enters it by a little river which can be forded knee-deep at low water. The sea breaks violently at its mouth, and therefore the water of the lake is rather brackish, but there are many wells in that locality from which they drink. This day was Palm Sunday, and because of the great hospitality they received there they gave this river the name of Plenty. The next day they returned to seek the shore, where they found some staves of casks, the handle of a saw, some pieces of planks, and other driftwood. The Kaffirs who accompanied our people told them that those things had belonged to some Portuguese who came ashore there ; and therefore everyone thought that they must have been from one of the rafts of the ship *Santiago*, which the current had brought there, for several were made, but only two were ever heard of again.[2] The greatest hardship that our people suffered in this journey along the shore was thirst, which tormented them so much that they went back again into the bush, even though it might prove more toilsome.

The day after they left the river of Plenty, they came upon another small stream, which flowed into another lake not smaller than the last. They forded this at low tide, and the pilot next day measured the altitude of the sun there, finding it to be in 26¼°. Thenceforward they were penetrating the territory of the king of Manhiça [= Inhaca], of which we spoke in our description above.[3]

[1] S. R. Welch (*Portuguese Rule*, 93) identifies this lake with a large swamp near the mouth of the Maputo River, but from the context it would seem that the party had not penetrated so far inland, and were only a day's march from the coast. Perhaps Lake Fiti is meant, which is at any rate in the latitude given.

[2] Cf. above, p. 62, n. 1.

[3] By some quirk, both the *HTM* and *Vida* versions here and henceforward regularly confuse 'Manhiça' with 'Inhaca' in their respective texts. As Manhiça was north and Inhaca south of the Bay of Lourenço Marques, this makes the castaways' itinerary unintelligible in Couto's text as it stands. I have therefore followed Theal, Junod, and Welch in making the necessary transpositions.

He had already been informed of their approach, and sent several of his people to accompany them, who made much of them; and they were extremely pleased on finding a Kaffir who spoke Portuguese very well, and who told them that less than ten days previously a *naveta*[1] had left the river of Lourenço Marques for Mozambique, commanded by a certain Jeronimo Leitão and carrying much ivory.[2]

With this joyful news they reached the village, and sat down at the entrance of it under the shade of a beautiful tree. All the villagers, both men and women, came out to see our people, being astonished at the sight of the [white] women for they had never seen any before. The Kaffir women, seeing them so weary and distressed, made signs of compassion, and drawing near caressed and fondled them, offering the use of their huts and desiring even to take them there at once.

It was not long before the king arrived, accompanied by many people. He was naked, except for a cloth which covered his lower parts and a hooded cloak of green cloth which the royal standard bearer, Dom Jorge de Menezes, had sent him from Mozambique, being captain there.[3] Dom Paulo, the captain, and all the others rose up and received him with great courtesy, and he embraced them with a very joyful countenance, and sat down with them at the foot of the tree. Our people related their misfortune to him, and the hardships of the journey, and said how glad they all were at having reached his village, because they knew what a friend he was to the Portuguese and they hoped to find in him the remedy for their needs. The king listened to them very kindly, and answered them very good-naturedly, condoling

---

[1] A vague term usually applied (as here) to small sailing ships of under two or three hundred tons, but occasionally to larger vessels of twice that size.

[2] Jeronimo Leitão, a famous Portuguese pioneer trader on the South East African coast, who rejoiced in the Kaffir sobriquet of Inyale-fua. So influential was he in the Delagoa Bay region that the English interlopers under Captain Benjamin Wood who visited this Bay in March–June 1597, tried to pass themselves off as his associates. Cf. Gabriel Pereira, *Roteiros Portuguezes* (1898), 77–84; C. Montez, *Lourenço Marques*, 37, 155–60.

[3] Dom Jorge de Menezes, *Alferes-Mór do Reino*, assumed the captaincy of Mozambique in 1586.

with them and offering them everything which his kingdom contained.[1]

It seemed to them that they ought to make this man a present, because these people always have their eyes on your hands to see if you have brought anything to give them. Searching among themselves for something to give him, they found a piece of cloth worked in gold which Dona Mariana was using as a wrapper, a copper bowl (a thing which they highly esteem), and a piece of rough iron, all of which they presented to him, asking him to excuse them, for they had only saved their persons, as he saw, and even this piece of cloth had been taken from that woman. They threw it over his shoulders, and he was so proud of it that he eyed himself on every side and laughed with glee among his Kaffirs, counting this the day of his greatest triumph.

He at once gave orders to his people to bring them something to eat, and they returned directly with two baskets of a kind of pulse which they call *Ameixoeira*,[2] and a goat. He asked them to stay in that village, saying that he would provide for them as well as he could until the trading-ship came next year. He advised them not to risk travelling overland, for along the bay where they would have to pass there lived some Kaffirs who were great thieves, who would rob and kill them. He added that his father had warned Manuel de Sousa de Sepulveda of this when he had passed that way, and he was lost through not following this advice.[3] He further told our people that if they did not think themselves safe in that village, he would order them to be taken to an island where they would still find the huts in which the Portuguese lived when they came there for the ivory trade, and a small boat for their use; and he would order them to be provided with whatever they might need there.

[1] This Inhaca was the son and successor of a chief who had been named 'Garcia de Sá' by Lourenço Marques, on account of his real or fancied resemblance to the *fidalgo* of that name who was Governor of Portuguese India, 1548–9. Cf. Theal, *Beginning of South African History*, 218, 280, 286, 293.

[2] 'It is, if I am not mistaken, the Sorghum. The word *ameixoeira*, or *mexoeira*, nowadays designates the small grey kaffir corn in Lourenço Marques. The chroniclers seem to consider these names as indigenous, which I believe is a mistake' (H. A. Junod, 'Condition of the natives,' 20).

[3] This was perfectly true.

They looked upon this as a favour and accepted his advice, asking him to direct them to the island and to give them leave to go there next day. As soon as they had come to this hasty resolution the king withdrew, leaving some people to accompany them to the island. Our people left the village and went to pass the night outside with good watch and great fires. There they made cakes and cooked their meal, and the Kaffirs brought them hens, grains, beans, and other things for sale.

This was Maundy-Thursday, and therefore they did not wish to go further until Easter Day which fell on the 2nd April. On this day they began their journey with lighter hearts but not without hardship, for it rained so heavily that they suffered somewhat. On the second day of the octave[1] they came in sight of the bay of Espirito Santo, and as it was late they camped that night as well as they could. The next day they reached the sea, and the Kaffirs who were guiding them made signals to those of the island, which was nearby, and they soon came with two small canoes in which our people passed over to the island that day and the next. They journeyed about a league on the island, which they found all covered with beautiful trees and fine-looking pastures, where very fine cattle which belonged to the king were grazing. At the end of the island overlooking the bay they found some straw huts in which they took shelter.[2]

Next day at low tide, with the water to their waists, they passed from that island to the other, called Setimino, of which we spoke elsewhere.[3] Here they found more than fifty thatched huts, constructed and left by the Portuguese traders, in which they took shelter as best they could. They also found two small vessels, which the ship's officers examined and considered fit for use in passing to the other side of the bay, which was so wide that the opposite shore could not be seen. They estimated that the larger of the two could accommodate sixty persons, and the smaller

[1] Tuesday of Easter week.

[2] This was the modern Inhaca Island, which Couto elsewhere (p. 71 above) calls Choambone.

[3] Cf. p. 71 above, where the more usual spelling of Setimuro is given. Later called Ilha dos Elefantes and nowadays Ilha dos Portugueses, it is connected with the Ilha do Inhaca by a sand flat which dries (*Africa Pilot*, III, 198).

G

fifteen. They all rejoiced at this, for they thought that once they were on the other side they would find it easier to get to Sofala. The carpenter therefore began to repair the boats, and they sent to the Inhaca some of the few pieces of silver which they had saved, asking him for leave to do so, which he granted, so they pushed forward with their preparations for the passage.

Everything being ready, on the 18th April they began to embark in both boats, thinking these would hold them all. As soon as they began to embark, however, the boats began to fill with water, so that those who were in them called out to be put ashore, because they were sinking. Thus they disembarked again, wet and disconsolate, and retired into their huts disillusioned with the remedy which they thought they had possessed.

All the sailors in a body now asked that the boats should be given to them, for they said they wished to venture in them, and would take a message to Inhambane, where they might be able to arrange for a *pangayo* to return for the others. Upon this an altercation arose, with shouts and insolence on the part of the sailors, who are very unruly in this India Voyage.[1] The gentlemen and soldiers did not wish the boats to be given, that they might not be deprived of them, and also that those men might not separate from the others, for the salvation of all depended upon keeping together. There were such heated arguments and disputes over this that it seemed an endless pandemonium, and nothing could be agreed or decided.

At this time Dom Paulo de Lima had retired into a hut with his wife, for as he had lost hope of reaching the other side, he did not wish to do anything else but commend himself to God, without caring what was going on outside or attending to anything else. The captain and Bernardim de Carvalho, with the other gentlemen, the master, and the pilot, knowing his condition, sought him out and begged him not to deprive them of his counsel, for they were all determined to obey his orders alone, and to remain in his company there or wherever else it might be. Dom Paulo de Lima, who had resolved to remain there, committing himself to the hands of God and whatever might be His will, begged them

[1] Cf. Introduction, p. 11.

to leave him alone, since he was old and weary, and finding himself with his wife in these straits, he was determined to lead a hermit's life there, passing the remainder of his days in penance for his sins. He added that they could make ready, and that he was certain that whoever landed on the other side, even if he went also, so soon as they reached the shore they would abandon him and push on. Rather than find himself subsequently alone with his wife on those bare and uninhabitable shores, he preferred to remain where he was and see what fate God had reserved for him. Those who wished to cross over could do so and good luck to them, but he himself only desired to consider the salvation of his soul, and as for his body any portion of the earth would suffice for it.

These words, which he did not speak without tears running down upon his venerable beard, so touched them all that they could not refrain from weeping with him, and thus between their tears and sobs, those persons for whom he might have the most respect begged him to be consoled and to remember that his was that great spirit which had so distinguished itself on the many occasions in which Our Lord God had shown him so many favours and given him so many victories. And as He had also endowed him not only with such courage but also with a lively and enlightened knowledge and judgement, in these straits, where they were more than ever necessary, he ought not to abandon himself to the hands of chance, for that would be tempting God Himself who had so highly gifted him; He, who had preserved him so far, would continue to do so until He had brought him to a Christian land, where he could better fulfil his desire. Therefore, they said, he should attend to the preservation of his life and that of his wife, for whose sake he should spare his own life, for if he died of sheer grief, as now seemed likely, an account would be demanded of him in the other life of his being the sole cause of leaving her unprotected among those brutes[1] and in danger of doing something desperate. All there present offered themselves and pledged their faith that never at any time or under any circumstances would they forsake him, but would follow his fortune; and wherever it should lead him, thither would they go also. They

[1] I.e. the Kaffirs.

said that he should examine his conscience and see if he was not risking his soul in thus giving himself up to death of his own free will. That would be tempting God, whom he seemed to distrust in this matter, when he certainly knew that His mercy was unbounded; and he should not let himself be vanquished by fortune, which he had trodden underfoot all his life.

After those gentlemen had told him these things, the ship's master, as leader of all the seamen, assured him on behalf of them all, that they would never leave him in whatever straits he might be, but would always follow him until they should lose their lives for him; adding that the strongest sailors offered to carry his wife in a litter, and to serve her throughout all the journey whithersoever it might lead, as was but just.

Upon this, Dom Paulo de Lima could not but yield and trust himself to the hands of them all. They then decided with his advice that half the people should cross in the first boatload, with Captain Estevão da Veiga, and that when they reached the other shore the boat should return for the rest, which was carried out forthwith. The captain and pilot embarked in the largest boat with forty-five persons, among whom were the boatswain's mate, the second pilot Diogo Lopes Leitão, Francisco Dorta the ship's factor, and António Caldeira, all the rest being sailors. In the smaller boat there embarked the master with fifteen persons, including his son, and Friar Nicolau do Rozario of the Order of Preachers, all the others being common people. Thirty-six persons remained on the island, comprising the gentlemen and knights who would not leave Dom Paulo, and with them were likewise the other ladies.

The boats, having pushed off from the shore, set sail and steered for the other side. At sunset they cast anchor off the land, one league eastwards of the river of Manhiça,[1] as they learnt from some Kaffirs whom they found there. The wind failing, they remained at anchor all night, and this was the great mistake of that voyage and the cause of their future hardships, all of which arose from sparing themselves a little labour. For had they taken to their oars, they might easily have gone closer inshore and sought for

[1] Incomati (Inkomati, Nkomati, Komati, etc.) River.

the river of Inhaca,[1] which was not more than a league behind them.

They remained at anchor there all night, and as soon as day dawned the wind began to blow from WSW, which was unfavourable for them returning to the river, and therefore they thought they would do better to sail along the coast to the river of Gold,[2] which was thirteen or fourteen leagues distant, and that when the wind changed they could return for those who remained on the island. Thus they ran along the coast which was very clean; but towards evening the wind lulled until it shifted to SSE, which is a contrary one on that coast. With this they drifted towards the shore, until they got into the breakers, so that those in the larger boat were compelled to put about, but the smaller one cast anchor. Her ropes, which were of fibre, gave way, so she set sail again, and remained a little while without making headway so that they found themselves in the trough of the waves. They therefore pushed off, and by better navigation, the diligence of the master, and the will of God, they luffed so effectually that they cleared the points, and in the morning had already reached the river of Inhaca.[3]

On going ashore, they heard that in the village where the king lived, twelve leagues up the stream, there were some Portuguese; so they joyfully took to their oars, and with some difficulty, for they were all very weak, they rowed up the river until after two days they reached the village. Here they were welcomed by Jeronimo Leitão and some companions, who had left the river of Lourenço Marques about a month previously, as we said above, with a *pangayo* laden with ivory which had been wrecked near the river of Gold, where they had been robbed, and whence they had made their way to the village of that Inhaca,[4] since he was acquainted with him. Upon this meeting, they embraced each other with many tears and much affection, relating their hardships to each other, and thence they were taken to the king who received them kindly, comforted them, and ordered them to be lodged.

[1] *Sic* in both the *HTM* and *Vida* versions. An obvious mistake for the Manhiça (Incomati) River.

[2] The Limpopo.

[3] *Sic* in both the *HTM* and *Vida* versions, for Manhiça (Incomati).

[4] Probably a mistake for *Inkosi*, 'chief'.

And as they did not know what had become of the captain's boat, the master decided, with the advice of Jeronimo Leitão, to send the canoe to Dom Paulo, so that he should learn what had happened, and not give way to despair. Three persons were chosen to go in the canoe, two of the company of Jeronimo Leitão, and one of that of the master. They also sent word to Dom Paulo that he should cross over to the other side at once, for the land was good, and he would be better off there until a vessel should come from Sofala, which they had just sent to ask for; as Jeronimo Leitão, at the same time as the canoe left, sent a lad of his and a Muslim sailor from the shipwrecked *naveta* with letters to the captain of that fortress, in which he related the loss of the ship, the misfortunes of the people who had escaped therefrom, and likewise those of his own vessel and people, asking him to send forthwith a *pangayo* in which they could leave. Thus we will leave these two parties and return to the people who had remained on the island.

These, seeing that the boats did not return in seven, eight, and ten days, did not know to what it was to be attributed, unless to the negligence of the captain. Dom Paulo felt it very deeply, and in his chagrin became very wrathful against him. Not knowing what resolution to take, he passed many days sunk in deep melancholy, as did they all. For they began to despair of the rescue which they had expected from the boats enabling them to leave the island, both because their provisions were running short and because some of them were falling sick. A month having almost past, and being still without news of the others they consulted among themselves as to what they should do. They decided that since no ship from Mozambique could be expected until a year had passed, they should travel by land round the bay; for it would be a lesser evil to risk the hardships of the journey, commending themselves to God, than to stay there and die of hunger and sickness.

Having come to this decision, they sent word to the Inhaca of their resolve, asking him to advise them, and to give them leave to depart. To this message he replied that he could not advise them to undertake such a journey, owing to the great risk which they would run that way, for now they were separated, although if they had been all together he might have advised it, though even then it would not have been without danger. He added that if their decision was due to want of provisions, he would order them to be provided as best he could, as he had always done; nevertheless, if they thought fit to undertake the journey they were welcome to do so, for he would not prevent them, since he did not wish it to be said that he had tried to detain them in his own country. With this reply our people were in suspense and at a loss, not knowing what to do.

At this time there arrived the canoe which had been sent by the master and Jeronimo Leitão, and when they saw it approaching from seaward they all ran to the beach as if it had brought their only hope of safety, and when the men disembarked they were hugged by all with tears of joy. Then they sought out Dom Paulo de Lima in his hut, and from them he learnt what had happened to the boats, and that nothing was known of Estevão da Veiga's; and they related all that had since befallen them, adding that the master and Jeronimo Leitão wished them to cross over to the other side, for not only was the king of the country a friend to the Portuguese, but it was well provided with everything.

Dom Paulo de Lima was delighted with this news and at once prepared to depart; but as the canoe would only hold fourteen persons, lots were drawn to see who should go and who should remain. For the first boatload, the lots fell upon himself and his wife, her brother, Manoel Cabral da Veiga, Christovão Rebello, and others amounting to the aforesaid number, leaving ashore for the second boatload, Bernardim de Carvalho, who was very ill, Gregorio Botelho, his daughter Dona Mariana, and with her Dona Joanna de Mendoça, who, having no husbands, always lodged together, and other persons. Leaving the shore, the canoe reached the mouth of the river Inhaca[1] that same day, and they journeyed up river for three days. On reaching the village they were warmly welcomed by the king and the Portuguese, and they were all lodged in poor huts with no furniture save a few mats, and some had only dry straw. When the question arose of sending

[1] *Sic* for Manhiça (Incomati).

back the canoe, none of them wished to go in it, since they were all very weak and beginning to fall sick with fever.

Those who remained on the island awaited the canoe for five or six days, and as it did not appear they went about as if in a maze, not knowing what to do, and having no one to counsel or encourage them. For Bernardim de Carvalho, who might have done so, was very ill with fever, and as all remedies were wanting and he had no other delicacy than *ameixoeira*-gruel and the hard ground to lie upon, nature grew weary and delivered him into the hands of death. In that hour he proved himself to be a very good Christian, by the great patience with which he endured it, and by the contrition which he showed for his sins. His death was deeply felt and bewailed by all, for he was a very amiable gentleman, of very accomplished parts and qualities, and in all their hardships took the heaviest share upon himself, helping everyone at all times in their greatest need, especially Dona Joanna de Mendoça, for, as we have said, seeing her alone, he approached her, and accompanied and served her throughout the whole journey with such respect, honour, and virtue, that it astonished everybody. This was particularly so on the island, for he would go into the bush to cut firewood for her, carrying it on his shoulders, and to the spring to get water. When they bartered for a hen, it was he who killed, plucked, and cooked it, after which it was eaten by Gregorio Botelho, his daughter Dona Mariana, and Dona Joanna de Mendoça, he being always left with the smallest piece, and even of this he would keep a morsel for Dona Joanna at night, or for the next day. According to the account of the rest of the company, he died of sheer hardship. And what is most to be lamented is that his death was as miserable as it could be, for he was covered with lice, bred upon his body by the dampness of the ground and the sweat of his labours. He was buried at the foot of a cross which our people had erected there, naked, in the naked earth, amid the mournful lamentation of all, especially of Dona Joanna de Mendoça, who felt it as if he had been her own father, because of all she owed to him and the loss he would be to her in her needs. She remained very disconsolate, with none to condole with her except Gregorio Botelho and his daughter Dona Mariana, with whom she lodged for the sake of propriety. Several other persons also died, including the boatswain's mate and the caulker.

Since they now had nothing left to barter for what they needed, they crossed over to the other island which was inhabited,[1] and sent a message to the Inhaca relating what had befallen them, and of the great need in which they were, asking him to command that they should be provided with what they required until the arrival of the trading *pangaio*, when he would be well paid for all. He sent to tell them that they should come to his village, when being at hand he would observe their needs and provide for them; for as long as they were so far off he could not know if they were being supplied according to his orders. Upon this they made ready to go there, although some of them argued against it, and so finally they remained where they were for the time being; and there we will also leave them, to return to the other boat in which was Captain Estevão da Veiga.[2]

We will now continue with this boat, which we left with a contrary wind that obliged them to put about; but that was of no avail, for they again found themselves among the breakers, from which they received much damage. Being thereby undeceived, they decided they would have to run the boat ashore before the moon set, for this was in the night, as afterwards they might be obliged to do so in a place where they might all perish. Therefore they ran ashore on a sandy beach, where they remained the rest of the night, alongside fires which they lit, and with two loaded matchlocks for any emergency.

Next day, as soon as it was light, they continued on their way towards the river of Gold,[3] already followed by many Kaffirs who soon gathered and who disturbed and molested them many times, until they grew so bold that they snatched the caps from their heads and the wallets from their backs, bounding about with the

---

[1] Ilha do Inhaca (Inyaka Island).

[2] Fr João dos Santos, O.P., *Ethiopia Oriental* (1609), pt. II, fol. 64, writes as if only one boatload left the island, but gives us two additional names to those listed by Couto on p. 67 above, viz; the second pilot, Gaspar Ferreira Reimão, and António Gomes Cacho, 'one of the two who had originally landed on the shore of Kaffraria'. Cf. p. 66 above.

[3] The Limpopo, from which they were only a few miles distant.

agility of apes, without our people being able to get rid of them, though they attacked them frequently. With this trouble and with great bodily fatigue they reached the river of Gold so exhausted that they could not take a step further, being at this time accompanied by a Kaffir called Inhatembe, of the king's household, a man known to the Portuguese and who had been to Mozambique. He guided them to the village, which they entered an hour after nightfall. Here dwelt the King Inhàpula, of whom we spoke in the description of this country,[1] who came out to meet them kindly, and ordered that they should all be lodged together in a large hut, giving them some provisions of that country to eat, but in exchange for pieces of nails.

Next day they went to visit the king, and gave him an account of their misfortunes, asking him for a faithful guide to accompany them to Inhambane, where they would find means of paying him. The king consoled them, and gave them the same Inhatembe, who had come with them, and who was a sheikh.[2] In return they gave him a grey hat, with which he was very pleased. They stayed there for three days, during which some of them fell ill with fever. As five or six of these grew rapidly worse, it was necessary to leave them there until they should recover well enough to proceed to Inhambane, for which they sent to ask leave of the king, which he gave them. Thus they started on their journey, most of them in such a state that they could hardly move, especially the ship's pilot, Gaspar Gonçalves, who was at the end of his tether. That day they reached a village of the sheikh who accompanied them, where they were very well treated and where they stayed the night.

Next day a Kaffir came to them post-haste with a message from King Inhàpula, that they must return to his village at once to remove a Portuguese who was dead, and take away the sick; for he could not look upon a corpse, lest the sun would be angry with him and hide itself and allow no rain to fall upon the earth, which would then yield no fruit or provisions all that year.[3] This they

---

[1] Inhapule, or Inyapula. Cf. above, p. 75, n. 3.

[2] *Xeque.* Presumably used here in the sense of 'headman', and possibly with the implication that he was a Muslim.

[3] 'This is one of the most curious taboos of these tribes. They believe that Heaven (rather than the sun) is offended if any one dying an unnatural death is buried in

said because seeing the Portuguese to be white and fair, they believed that they were children of the sun. Estevão da Veiga was much annoyed at this message, which made it necessary to send back some of those who were healthiest to do this job. These, on arriving, wished to bury the dead man, but the Kaffirs would not allow it, and in great haste made them almost drag the corpse out of the village, and carry the sick away upon their backs. They left the corpse in the bush, covered with a little earth; and the sick men told them that when the Kaffirs saw them with the fever, which had plunged them into a kind of lethargy in which they could not move their hands and feet, thinking they were dead, they applied fire to their feet to see if they would stir. Having left the dead man, they carried the sick with them to the village in which our people were.

Next day they crossed to the other side of the river of Gold, which is about a matchlock-shot in width. At its mouth the sea breaks in spray, and the river can only be navigated by very small craft. It is situated in latitude 25°.[1] On its bank they left two of their comrades who were already in their death agony, and from whom they parted with great pain and grief, remaining with them as long as they were conscious, to remind them of the things of the soul and to repeat to them the most holy name of Jesus. Oh how fortunate may we consider those who remained in the ship, whose troubles were all ended in a moment! And how wretched these who thought themselves more fortunate in escaping from it! For their hardships, dangers, perils, and finally their deaths, were only rendered more painful and severe.

I certainly feel that this alone justifies that philosopher who replied to one who asked him: 'What is death?' when he made answer: 'Death is an eternal dream, a terror of the rich, a parting of friends, an uncertain pilgrimage, a thief of men, an end of those

dry ground. It would be more correct to say: If anyone dies having not been lawfully incorporated with the tribe by special rites: children dying before the ceremony of "tying the cotton string," twins, and also strangers, as they may bear this objectionable character which irritates Heaven and brings the malediction on the land' (H. A. Junod, 'Condition of the natives, 24).

[1] The mouth of the Limpopo is in lat. 25° 13′ S, long. 33° 31′ E, (*Africa Pilot*, III, 211).

who live, and a beginning of those who die.'[1] For all these will be found in the castaways from this wreck. What greater dream and what greater terror of the rich than that which they now witnessed? One day so rich and happy, making their voyage in so strong and great a ship, so richly laden and full of precious things, and on the morrow to see her sink beneath their feet, burying all her treasures in the depths of the sea. What more lamentable separation of friends than what they now saw here, leaving these to end their lives upon those shores with no other consolation and company than the solitude of those savage sands? What more uncertain pilgrimage than this which they were making here, every hour being fraught with such risks and dangers? And finally all of them in such a wretched condition that if there had been lions and tigers on those sands, they would certainly have pitied them more than they did the slave Androclus, who was preserved for a long time by a lion in a cave in Africa, being lamed by a splinter in his foot, which the lion drew out, and licked the wound with his tongue until it was cured.[2]

These disasters, and others which occur every day in this India Voyage, might serve as warnings to men, especially to the *fidalgos* who are captains of fortresses, to moderate themselves and be content with what the good God gives them, and allow the poor to live; for God has not made the sun in the heaven and the water in the spring for the great ones of the earth alone. We repeat this so often in the course of our *Decades,* because we have been much scandalized by the great injustices and cruelties daily practised in those fortresses against the poor and lowly. But God is so just that though kings now neglect to punish, He does so with a hand which is all the heavier, by so much as His justice is greater than that of men.

To return to the castaways. After they had crossed the river of Gold, they reached the kingdom of Mamuça,[3] where they were very well received, and there they remained three days, during

[1] 'This seems to be a collection of scattered thoughts from Cicero and Seneca' (S. R. Welch, *Portuguese Rule*, 562).

[2] Couto has here reversed the roles in the classical story of the Roman slave Androclus and the lion.

[3] Manuça. Cf. above, p. 75, n. 4, and S. R. Welch, op. cit., p. 100.

which time five or six of their comrades died from the very bad water which was all they could find, and which was full of weeds and slime. The Negroes of the village insisted that their bodies should be taken away with such haste, that they dragged them along and threw them into a swamp. Among these was the pilot, Gaspar Gonçalves, who had escaped from the wreck of the ship *Santiago* on the Baixo da India only to perish in this region in the greatest misery that could be imagined.[1]

From this village the survivors set out again, accompanied by two sons of that king, who saved them from many dangers and treacherous acts which the Kaffirs had planned against them on the way. This day they left two more of their comrades laid out in the bush, for they could go no further from weakness and approaching death, taking leave of these friends with enough sorrow and tears. That night they reached the village of a Kaffir called Inhabuze, where they took shelter; and thence they went to the kingdom of Panda nearer to Cape Correntes, which the people of Mozambique commonly call Imbane. That king received them very well, and would not let them leave there until the fifth day, for it is an old custom of his to detain his friends there and show his love for them by banquets and rejoicings, as he did to these castaways; for that king is a great friend of the Portuguese on account of the trade and contact which he has with those of Mozambique.

From this village they set out again, accompanied by a son of the king, and on the 11th May, on which day fell the feast of Our Lord's Ascension, they reached another river as large as that of Gold, which is in latitude 24½°, and separates the kingdoms of Panda and Gamba.[2] Crossing to the other bank, they reached the city[3] of this king Gamba, which is about a league and a half from the river, and he, having heard of their arrival, ordered them

[1] According to Linschoten, Gomes de Solis, and other contemporaries, he met with no more than his just deserts, his gross misconduct having been primarily responsible for the loss of both the *Santiago* and the *São Thomé*. Cf. above, p. 58, n. 2.

[2] Presumably the chain of lakes and swampy river shown on some maps as the Inharrime, and described in the *Africa Pilot* (III, 212) as the Lagoa Inhapavala, with an outlet on the sea at Aguada da Boa Paz in lat. 24° 53' S, long. 34° 26' E.

[3] 'cidade', *sic* for kraal.

to be received and lodged very well. This king and his sons were Christians, baptized by Padre Gonçalo da Silveira of the Company of Jesus, who in the years 1560 and 1561 traversed those parts preaching the law of the Holy Gospel among those savages, and he gave the king the name of Bastião de Sá, both in memory of the King Dom Sebastião then reigning,[1] and of Bastião de Sá, who was Captain of Mozambique at that time. To his sons he gave the names of Pero de Sá and João de Sá, and he likewise baptized several other Kaffirs, who all took the sobriquet of Sá.

It being necessary for him to go to the kingdom of Monomotapa, where martyrdom awaited him,[2] he left there with Padre André Fernandes, a truly apostolic man, of great learning and sanctity, so that his superior, Padre Mestre Francisco,[3] was wont to say that he was a true Israelite. Padre André Fernandes stayed in this kingdom, giving a goodly example by his life, and hourly threatened with martyrdom, which his soul desired to suffer for Christ Our Lord, and which he never tried to avoid; but on the contrary, whenever he was warned that his death had been ordered, he awaited that hour with such consolation and joy that it seemed to him as if the beautiful and resplendent crown which is given to true martyrs in heaven had already fallen on his head.

This man, who may with justice be called a saint, from the innocence of his life, afterwards lived in this city of Goa for many years, giving a rare example of virtue, and here he died at the age of ninety.[4] He was one of those who had entered the Company of

[1] Born 1554, reigned 1557–78.

[2] There is an extensive literature on Gonçalo da Silveira, S.J. (23.ii.1526–15.iii.1561) and his martyrdom, for which see Streit-Dindinger, *Bibliotheca Missionum*, XV (1951), 474–80.

[3] St Francis Xavier.

[4] André Fernandes, born at Campo Maior in 1516, served as a soldier in the East before becoming a Jesuit at Ormuz in 1550. After a mission to Europe as Xavier's personal representative in 1553–7, he returned to the East in 1558, and worked among the Kaffirs of South East Africa in 1560–2, and later at Cape Comorin. He died at Goa, 22.iii.1598, and was thus not quite so old as Couto states. Cf. A. Valignano—J. Wicki, S.J., *Historia* (ed. 1944), 199 n., which corrects on this point the bio-bibliographical notice in Streit-Dindinger, *Bibliotheca Missionum*, XV, 484, where it is erroneously stated that he died at Cape Comorin in 1568.

Jesus in the time of the Blessed Padre Ignacio, its founder. Many things might be said of his virtues, life, and death, for we were familiar with him many years and admired him greatly. But as Padre Sebastião Gonçalves of the Company of Jesus, in his Compendium of the members of the Company who came to these parts, speaks more particularly of him and of Padre Gonçalo da Silveira,[1] we will leave him now to follow the fortune of these castaways until we have brought them safely to port.

From this kingdom of Gamba they set out on the 21st May, which was the eve of Pentecost, and reached the river Inhambane,[2] where they found a half-caste named Simão Lopes, a native of Sofala, who had fled to this place on account of matters concerning the Faith. He received them as best he could, since he was poor, and there were now only thirty persons left out of the forty-five who had set out. Here they learnt from Simão Lopes that no *pangayo* could come from Mozambique before November. Upon this they took counsel, and agreed to travel by land, the country where they were being very sickly, since it lay under the Tropic of Capricorn.[3]

After they had rested some days they set out again, and in four days they reached the river Boene, being very badly treated by the Kaffirs who robbed them on the way.[4] Having crossed to the other side, they went on to another river called Morambele, which was very deep, so they travelled a good distance up it to find a ford, and on the way they were finally robbed of the little they had

---

[1] Sebastião Gonçalves, S.J. (*c.* 1555–1619), served in India since 1593, and wrote a *Historia dos Religiosos da Companhia de Jesus nos reynos e provincias da India Oriental*, which, although completed about the year 1614, was only published at Lisbon in 1958. Cf. also J. Wicki, S.J., article on Gonçalves in the *Neue Zeitschrift für Missionswissenschaft*, VIII (1952), 261–9.

[2] Here again the bay of Inhambane (Inyambane) is probably meant, although there is a river of the same name which flows close to the western shore of the bay and enters the sea across two bars. The present-day Inhambane town is in lat. 23° 52′ S, long. 35° 25′ E.

[3] Inhambane is nowadays 'considered to be the most healthy port in Portuguese East Africa, but fever should be guarded against from November to May' (*Africa Pilot*, III, 218). Cf. also A. Cabral, *Districto de Inhambane* (1910).

[4] Boene. The present island and anchorage of that name are just south of Sofala, so either Couto is mistaken or the name was applied to some other locality which I cannot identify. Cf. *Africa Pilot*, III, 226, and sketch-map.

left.[1] Having crossed this river, they came to a village named Sane, which is on the point of the land called São Sebastião on the sea-charts.[2] Here they began to traverse the gulf of Sane, where the low tide ebbs so far that the sea is not visible for five or six leagues. They travelled across it very swiftly for the most part of the day, lest the tide might overtake them, and after covering more than five leagues they reached the other side where they rested.

Next morning they continued on their journey as far as a place called Inbaxe,[3] where they found a Portuguese with a *luzio*, which is a kind of boat used in those parts, with which he had come there to trade.[4] With him was the boatswain's mate of the ship, whom Estevão da Veiga had sent on ahead with a message to Sofala, to see if there was some way of obtaining a vessel to go and fetch Dom Paulo de Lima and those who were with him on the island. Here they remained all that day with great rejoicing, as they saw that they were approaching the land of their salvation. Then they crossed over to the island of Bazaruta,[5] where there was a native of Sofala named António Rodrigues, to get him to guide them to Sofala. This island is inhabited by Muslims, who treated them all very well.

[1] Morambele. There is a Morumbane marked on some maps on the north-west shore of the Bay of Inhambane, but this is much too far south to fit the river described by Couto. I have the impression that this part of the castaways' journey has been drastically abridged or telescoped by Couto, and can only suggest that the Rio Mejungo, about 15–20 miles south of Cape São Sebastião, is meant here. Cf. *Africa Pilot*, III, 219–20.

[2] Cabo São Sebastião, a steep bluff about 228 feet high, in lat. 22° 05' S, long. 35° 29' E (*Africa Pilot*, III, 220–1).

[3] S. R. Welch (*Portuguese Rule*, 101) identifies this as 'the small but busy port now called Vilanculos, where to-day Portuguese traders and their ships handle the agricultural produce of the local Amatonga tribes, much to their mutual benefit.' He may well be right, although the *Africa Pilot* ignores this port's existence, while admitting that the bay 'has not yet been examined' (III, 221).

[4] *Luzio*. Theal (*History of Africa South of the Zambesi*, III, 111) equates the *luzio* with the Arab-Swahili *sambuk*, but does not give any authority for this. I cannot find the *luzio* among the craft described by J. Hornell, 'A tentative classification of Arab sea-craft' (*Mariner's Mirror*, XXVIII, 11–40), but I suspect the name may have had something to do with the old Swahili port of Luziwa (or Uziwa) which was usually written 'Luzio' by the Portuguese, on the mainland near Lamu Island, in what is now Kenya.

[5] For the island group of this name (now spelt Bazaruto) see the *Africa Pilot*, III, 221–3. The locality is the site of the pearl fishery of Sofala, and pearls and mother-of-pearl are occasionally found.

By direction of António Rodrigues they embarked there for Sofala in a vessel which he procured, and they sailed over the thirty leagues distance to that fortress very quickly and without any difficulty. On the fourth day of the voyage they entered the river of Sofala, unknown to anyone, and disembarking, they went in procession to the Dominican Church of Our Lady of the Rosary, offering themselves to her with many tears, and giving her thanks for the favours which they had received from her during all that journey. Here the captain of the fortress and all the married men came to meet them, embracing them all with great affection, and each took one of them as his guest. Thus they were distributed among those householders, who received them very kindly, having their bodies washed and their hair cut, for they were almost like savages. They were so well provided with everything that in a few days they had completely recovered, and it seemed to them that they were in another world.[1]

The captain[2] had already bought a *pangayo* to send for Dom Paulo de Lima, for he had learnt of his shipwreck from a letter of Jeronimo Leitão. On the arrival of these people he made more haste, and ordered everything needful for the castaways to be embarked, including clothes, and cloth for their ransom. The *pangayo* then set sail, and in a few days reached Inhambane, where three of the sick men of the company of Estevão da Veiga were already dead, and the others soon recovered with the remedies which were brought them in the *pangayo*. Since it was not possible for them to proceed to the river Espirito Santo,[3] because the *pangayo* was small, Simão Lopes went overland with the cloth, beads, and other things, carried on the shoulders of Kaffirs, and the *pangayo* returned to Sofala with the sick they had found there.[4]

It was almost a month after Dom Paulo de Lima had passed

---

[1] Couto's account of the castaway's arrival at Sofala is confirmed by that of an eyewitness, Fr João dos Santos, O.P., *Ethiopia Oriental* (1609), pt. II, fol. 64.

[2] Of Sofala.

[3] Presumably a slip for the River Manhiça (Incomati), although of course the people at Sofala did not know that nobody was now left on Inhaca Island.

[4] Presumably the party which included Fr Nicolau do Rosario, O.P., and Fr António da Magdalena, O.F.M. Cap., whose arrival at Sofala 'a few days' after that of Estavão da Veiga's party is recorded by Fr João dos Santos, op. et loc. cit.

H

over to the other side of the river of Lourenço Marques, before anyone would take back the canoe for those who were left on the island,[1] for they were all very weak and ill. Dom Paulo, however, did everything that he could, and at last persuaded the ship's master and Jeronimo Leitão to send on this service those men who were fittest for it, when they chose three from among the rest. By dint of hard rowing they reached the island, where they found them all very depressed and despairing of ever being sent for; but they rejoiced greatly at the arrival of the canoe and prepared to embark in it. As it could not hold them all, great dissension arose, for those who would be left behind ran the risk of no one returning for them. But those who came with the canoe reassured them by promising and swearing that as soon as they had landed the others at the mouth of the river,[2] they would return for them, and for greater security they left one of their number as a hostage, which quieted those who remained.

Then Gregorio Botelho embarked with his daughter and Dona Joanna de Mendoça, and eight or ten others, and crossing the Bay they reached the other side the same day. Landing the people on the point at the mouth of the river Manhiça, they then returned for the others. Next day they reached the island, where they took them all in, none remaining but the dead, who remained there for ever. All the survivors were landed on the other side, where they found those of the first boatload still at the mouth of the river. They all got into the canoe together, for although it was small there was no risk of its capsizing in their going up the narrow river and hugging the bank.

Thus crowded and uncomfortable they reached the village, where our people of the company of Dom Paulo came to meet them, and there was a most joyful reunion. The king ordered that they should be lodged among the villagers, Dona Joanna de Mendoça always remaining in the company of Dona Mariana. After they had rested, they all assembled and discussed whether it would be well for them to proceed to Inhambane. Jeronimo Leitão, who knew the country best, advised them not to move from there until

[1] Ilha do Inhaca in the Bay of Lourenço Marques. Cf. above, p. 91.
[2] Manhiça (Incomati). Cf. above, p. 99.

the arrival of the *pangayo*, which would be in October, for he had already written to Sofala about this. It was his opinion that they ought not to risk travelling overland, for the Kaffirs who inhabited the country further on were great thieves and very cruel. Moreover, they were here on safe ground, where provisions would not be wanting, for the king and his vassals would supply them very well, with an eye to the expected arrival of the *pangayo*, knowing that they would be very well paid for all, since those Kaffirs never do anything from virtue.[1]

Upon hearing this man's opinion, they all resolved to remain, but as the land was sickly, being under the Tropic, as we said, some of them began to fall ill with malignant fevers, of which most of them, including the master, soon died. Their bodies were buried in the flowing river, for the Kaffirs would not allow them to be interred in their land.

As for Dom Paulo de Lima, it seems that his heart forboded that some great evil would befall him in that region, and he often asked Jeronimo Leitão to take him away from that village, and accompany him and guide him, making him offers and promises with great insistence, but as this man was unstable, he sometimes said 'yes' and sometimes 'no', always urging as obstacles the difficulties of the way and the danger from the Kaffirs. With his 'yes' and 'no' he kept Dom Paulo many days in a state of irresolution, without deciding one thing or another, from which he finally received such disgust, and fell into such a depression, that he took to his bed, or rather to the ground, for this was his real bed. As he was in his fifties, with no remedies, and the hard earth for comfortable mattresses and sheets, with none but spiritual consolation, for Friar Nicolau do Rozario was at his side to confess and comfort him at great length,[2] on the seventh day of his relapse he

---

[1] This is distinctly unfair, as most of the Kaffir kraals barely cultivated enough crops for their own sustenance, so when a troop of white people arrived to claim hospitality there was seldom enough to go round. In spite of this, the Kaffirs were often generous to their unexpected guests. Cf. H. A. Junod, 'Condition of the natives,' 19, 22.

[2] As noted above, Fr João dos Santos, O.P., *Ethiopia Oriental* (1609), fols. 63–4, explicitly states that Fr Nicolau do Rosario reached Sofala a few days after Estevão da Veiga's party arrived there. Both Couto and Santos wrote many years after

yielded his soul to God Our Lord, on the 2nd August, on which day the Franciscan friars celebrate the feast of Our Lady of Portiuncula, for which there is a most plenary indulgence, and for which feast this gentleman had a great devotion.[1] From the signs he gave of being a great Christian and a contrite penitant, with an exemplary patience, it is to be presumed that his soul ascended to enjoy in Glory that indulgence which will endure there as long as God endures, which will be for ever.

His death was the greatest sorrow that could be imagined for them all, both from seeing a gentleman of such good parts and qualities as nature had endowed him with, die in the greatest destitution ever seen, as from finding themselves bereft of such a counsellor, on whom they had all relied in their greatest hardships. For the sight of his authority, gravity, and remarkable patience rendered these hardships more tolerable and of less weight, and therefore he was bewailed as if he had been the father of them all.

Let us leave the extremities of grief to which his wife gave way, for it is better to pass over them, lest we should move those who read this our narrative to shed as many tears. But it may be imagined what would be the grief of a wife on losing such a husband; and still more so at that time when she had such need of him for her help and comfort, seeing herself so solitary and unprotected in a place where only God Our Lord could help her.

And your ladyship (Senhora Dona Anna de Lima) I well know that on reading this you cannot fail to shed pious tears, and with good reason for the loss of a brother well worthy of the love which you, Lady, always bore him, and for the destitution in which he died, and in which, Lady, you would have counted yourself very happy if you could have been at his side and given him some little solace by resting his head in your lap, so that at least he might have died with some consolation, and you not have been left with such

these events, but as Santos was at Sofala in 1589 and knew Fr Nicolau well, I conclude that his version is probably the correct one.

[1] For the history of this indulgence and its connection with the church of Portiuncula, one of three churches at or near Assisi which were repaired by St Francis, see *A Catholic Dictionary* (ed. 1951), 652.

sorrow. But, Lady, you may greatly console yourself by hearing that the signs he gave at the hour of his death (as I have said) can assure you of his salvation; and those he gave in life of his prudence, courage, and strength may make you glory in such a brother; and after your long years of life, your children, grandchildren, and descendants shall boast of his prowess and knightly deeds, for in my History he will live for ever, and even though not so exaltedly as he deserves, at least it will be as well as I could, and I greatly wish it was much better.[1]

The Inhaca,[2] lord of that country, was soon informed of his death, and hurriedly sent order that he should be removed from the village, upon which he was taken from the arms of his beloved wife, and carried almost on their shoulders out of the village. At the foot of two trees on the bank of the river they made him a grave, in which they laid him with no other shroud than the poor filthy shirt and drawers in which he had escaped, with no other funeral pomp than the many tears of his companions, and with no other standards and trophies of all his victories than the dry branches of all those trees, nor other gravestones and marble monuments than those sands which covered him like another Pompey on the shores of Egypt.

His wife, Dona Brites, remained some time in Kaffraria with the other survivors, enduring infinite hardships and want.[3] Afterwards, when they went to Mozambique, she caused the bones of her husband, Dom Paulo de Lima, to be dug up and took them in a bag with her to Goa, where she gave them burial in the church of St Francis in that city, in the little chapel of the Seraphic Father, which is on the right-hand side as one enters the main door. They are buried in the wall, with a copper tablet with his epitaph as follows: '*Canatale, Dabul, and Jor.* They will

[1] As late as 1645 D. Anna de Lima, Countess of Castro and of Castanheira, was still claiming from the Crown some rewards for the services of her half-brother who had died in 1589. Arquivo Histórico Ultramarino, Lisboa, 'Consultas Mixtas,' Cod. 13, fol. 248v.

[2] A mistake for Manhiça, or, possibly, *Inkosi* (chief).

[3] Fr João dos Santos, O.P., *Ethiopia Oriental*, pt. II, fols. 64–5, relates that the castaways left on the Incomati had to wait for a year until a ship was finally sent from Mozambique to bring back those who were still alive. Neither Santos nor Couto explain why a ship was not sent earlier from Sofala.

tell that here lies Dom Paulo de Lima, who died of hardships in Kaffraria in the year 1589.'[1]

Of all the notable acts of this lady, I cannot fail to praise this deed of bringing her husband's bones through the midst of Kaffraria until she embarked, which was heroic, and renders her worthy of exaltation.[2] Nor do I wish to pass over another matter worthy of note, which is that of all the people of this great ship, I do not think that one is alive today, save only these three women, herself, Dona Mariana the wife of Guterre de Monroy, and Dona Joanna de Mendoça, who is retired in a house of Our Lady of the Cape, clothed in the habit of Saint Francis, a lady of great virtue, on whom the eyes of all this city of Goa are fixed, because of her wonderful example, retirement, and virtuous way of life. And so I make an end of this brief narrative, which God grant may be to his great praise and glory.

[1] In ch. xxxII of the *Vida de Dom Paulo de Lima*, Diogo do Couto relates how when Dom Paulo prepared to embark on his ill-fated voyage at the end of 1588, he took with him the bones of his only son of the same name, who had died when five or six years old, 'so like his father in appearance that it was amazing to see. And thus he was so fond of him that when he died he was almost out of his mind, and they buried him in the church of St Francis at Goa, in the chapter next to the chapel, where they put up a grating hung with black velvet cloth. And when he took his bones from there, I at once secured this same sepulchre for my own burying-place, in return for some alms which I gave to the said padres. And this was but just, since I had been in life such a great friend of his, so it was right that I should inherit in death the sepulchre which he had made for himself and his descendants, whose first occupant was that tender and beautiful Adonis, his son Dom Paulo: and I myself now have thereon my gravestone with its inscription, expecting any day to take up my abode there, as the surest dwelling-place on this earth.' The church of St Francis of Assisi at Goa still stands, but all efforts to locate these tombs have been unsuccessful. Cf. *O Oriente Português*, xII (Nova Goa, 1915), 301–2; xIII (1916), 38–9. The wording of the inscription *Canatale, Dabul, and Jor* refers to Dom Paulo de Lima's spectacular victories over the Malabar corsair, Kunjali Marakkar, in 1565, off the Bijapur port of Dabul in 1581, and the taking of Johore Lama in 1587, all of which are narrated at length in the *Vida*.

[2] Couto discreetly glosses over the fact that Dona Brites married again, her second husband being Rodrigo Homem, a citizen of Oporto. She was given a China Voyage in May 1600, as a belated reward for the services of her first husband. Cf. Luciano Ribeiro [ed.], *Registo da Casa da India* (Lisboa, 1954), I, 338, nr. 1420; I. A. Macgregor in *JMBRAS*, xxvIII, pt. 2 (May, 1955), 120.

NAVFRAGIO
DA NAO S. ALBERTO,
E ITINERARIO DA GENTE,
QVE DELLE SE
SALVOV.

De Ioáo Baptiſta Lava-
nha Coſmographo mòr
de Sua Mageſtade.

DEDICADO AO PRINCEPE
DOM PHILIPPE
NOSSO SENHOR.

EM LISBOA.

Em cáſa de Alexandre de Siqueira.
ANNO M. D. XCVII.

Com Licença, & Privilegio.

SHIPWRECK

OF THE GREAT SHIP *SANTO ALBERTO*

AND ITINERARY OF THE PEOPLE
WHO WERE SAVED
FROM IT

By João Baptista Lavanha
Cosmographer Royal
of His Majesty

DEDICATED TO THE PRINCE
DOM PHILIP
OUR LORD

IN LISBON

In the House of Alexandre de Siqueira
ANNO M.D.XCVII

With Licence and Privilege

SHIPWRECK OF THE GREAT SHIP
SANTO ALBERTO

and itinerary of the people who were saved therefrom

THE account of the loss of the great ship *Santo Alberto* at the
Penedo das Fontes,[1] where the Land of Natal begins, and the
narrative of the hundred days' journey made by the Portuguese
who were saved therefrom to the river of Lourenço Marques,
where they embarked for Mozambique, are of great importance
for our voyages, and very useful as a warning in them. For this
shipwreck teaches how our navigators should behave in another
like case, what useful measures they should take therein, what are
the false and harmful ones that should be avoided, what precautions they should take to reduce the loss by sea and to render
the journey by land safer, how they should disembark with the
least danger, and the reason for the loss of this great ship, which is
the same as that for nearly all of them. The narrative of the journey
shows what route should be followed and what avoided, what
preparations should be made in view of its length and difficulty,
how to treat and deal with the Kaffirs, how the necessary trade
with them should be carried on, and their barbarous nature and
customs.

In order to spread the necessary knowledge of such novel and
important matters, I write this brief treatise, resuming therein a
voluminous notebook which the pilot of the said ship made
of this journey, which I have corrected and verified with the information which was subsequently given me by Nuno Velho

[1] G. M. Theal (*Beginning of South African History*, 296) identifies the Penedo das
Fontes ('Rock of the springs') with the two remarkable and prominent rocks known
as the Hole-in-the-Wall, close to the entrance of the Mapaka River in lat. 32° 02' S,
long. 29° 07' E. Cf. *Africa Pilot*, III, 163; P. R. Kirby, *Wreck of the Grosvenor*, 131,
194.

Pereira, who was the Captain-major of the Portuguese during this journey.[1]

The great ship *Santo Alberto*, then, left Cochin on the 21st January 1593, captain Julião de Faria Cerveira, pilot Rodrigo Migueis,[2] and master João Martins. In her there went passengers for Portugal: Dona Isabel Pereira, daughter of Francisco Pereira, Captain and *Tanadar-mór*[3] of the Island of Goa, a widow who had been the wife of Diogo de Melo Coutinho, Captain of Ceylon, and who was accompanied by her daughter Dona Luisa, a beautiful damsel of sixteen; and likewise Nuno Velho Pereira who had been Captain of Sofala, Francisco Pereira Velho his nephew, Francisco da Silva, João de Valadares de Sotomaior, Dom Francisco de Azevedo, Francisco Nunes Marinho, Gonçalo Mendes de Vasconcellos, António Moniz da Silva, Diogo Nunes Gramaxo, captain of the great ship *São Luís* of Malacca, which had been driven off her course to India,[4] António Godinho, Henrique Leite, and an Augustinian friar, Pedro da Cruz, a Dominican friar, Br Pantaleão, and many other passengers.

The ship pursuing her course, with favourable weather reached latitude 10° S, where her fatal misfortunes began, for here she sprang a leak, though only a small one, which did not prevent her from continuing on her course towards the southern tip of the

[1] Nuno Velho Pereira had distinguished himself in the epic defence of Chaul (1570), and on 27 October 1577 was granted the captaincy of Mozambique and Sofala as a reward for his services in the East. He held that post from 1583 to 1586, and commanded the *armada do Malabar* in 1591. Returning to Portugal in June 1594, in the Bassein-built carrack *Cinco Chagas*, which was attacked by the Earl of Cumberland's squadron off the Azores, he was the soul of the heroic defence made by this ship, and one of the thirteen survivors who were spared by the English. Eleven of these prisoners were landed at Flores, Nuno Velho being taken to England with Captain Braz Correia, whose ransom he paid as well as his own after a year's detention. On his return to Portugal he was granted 'some rewards' by the Crown, but I have not been able to ascertain what these were.

[2] Rodrigo Migueis had been second pilot (*sotapiloto*) of the *Santiago* when she was wrecked in the Mozambique Channel in 1585.

[3] In modern Hindustani *thānadār* means the chief of a police station, but the Portuguese used the hybrid form *Thanadar-Mór* of a senior official who combined certain military, administrative, and judicial functions. Cf. *Hobson-Jobson*, 896; Dalgado, *Glossário Luso-Asiático*, II, 351–3.

[4] Simão Ferreira Paes, *Recopilação*, 85, states that Gramaxo went out to India as a passenger in the *São Luís*, but with the grant of the captaincy for the return voyage.

island of St Lawrence [Madagascar]. However, on reaching latitude 27° S, a south wind arose which caused this water to increase;
and the wind blowing harder, and the ship sailing close-hauled
very near the wind, in order to steer clear of the said point, she gave
a great forward plunge, and sprang the bowsprit, which was soon
repaired. Sailing along in this way, without the pump giving
much trouble, they sighted the Land of Natal on the 21st March,
in latitude $31\frac{1}{2}°$, and coasting along it and taking the latitude next
day, they found themselves to be in latitude 32° S.

That same evening a westerly wind blew up from the land, with
which they stood out to sea with only the courses set, and in the
second watch, without any cause from wind or sea, the ship began
to leak very much, the water rising rapidly in the pump. Going
below to examine the water, they found that it was coming in by
the fashion-pieces of the stern under a floor-timber, which is a very
dangerous place, and one difficult to repair. It seemed to the captain and the officers that they might be able to do it by cutting
away a piece of the said floor-timber, which was done accordingly.
And although they found the leak and began to stop it (for which
good news the pilot and the master asked a reward[1] from Nuno
Velho Pereira, which he promised them), this improvement lasted
but a short time, for as the water found that place weakened, it
beat against it with greater force and entered the ship at an increasingly alarming rate.

Experience thus shows, both in the case of this ship as in that of
the *São Thomé*, which was a very similar one, that every means
should be tried to stop the leak save this one of cutting away
timber, for it is more necessary to strengthen than to weaken such
a place. Though it may appear a good plan, it afterwards makes
matters much worse, as happened in these two ships; for if they
had not cut away a floor-timber in the *Santo Alberto*, and a part of
the sleeper and the end of a fashion-piece in the *São Thomé*, the
water would not have gained so rapidly in either of them. And
with less water in the hold, and making more use of other emergency measures, the *Santo Alberto* might have been able to put

[1] *Alviçaras.* A gratification or tip given to anybody bringing or announcing good
news.

back to Mozambique, and the *São Thomé* to have run ashore instead of foundering so far from land.

The officers, seeing the dangerous condition of the ship, and that there were eighteen spans of water in her, determined to lighten her and put her stern to the wind. Both these measures were carried out forthwith, and the master opened the main hatch, through which they baled out the water with kegs, which greatly relieved the ship. On hearing this, some people who were enamoured of the baubles in their chests, which were brought up on deck, hesitated to cast them overboard, still hoping to save these and themselves as well. But when Nuno Velho Pereira promised that if God would bring him safely ashore he would give them instead forty-five *quintals*[1] of cloves which he had aboard the ship, this shadowy profit was so powerful that the deck was immediately cleared. The danger subsequently increasing, they threw overboard everything on the gun-deck and in the spice-holds, so that the sea was covered with untold riches, most of them thrown away by their very owners, to whom they were now as hateful and despicable as they were formerly beloved and esteemed.

When it was nearly dawn and the beginning of the next day, the water was coming in at such a rate that the chests could not be removed from the second deck, but they were broken open with hatchets and their contents flung overboard. But although there was a great scoop working in the main hatch-way and another in the [aft?, or fore?] hatch-way, and a third in the spice-holds, through which the water was drawn off in kegs, while the pumps were working at the same time, none of these measures availed to reduce it. They continued at this work all day, Nuno Velho Pereira, the captain, the gentlemen, and the soldiers working with great speed and diligence in some places, and the master with the seamen in others.

At nightfall the pumps became choked with pepper and were rendered useless. There were now twelve spans of water in the ship, whereby many people lost heart, and those who did not were

[1] *Quintal*. Indo-Portuguese weight 'which represented about 130 lbs., and may be thought of as somewhat larger than a hundredweight' (W. H. Moreland, *India at the death of Akbar*, London, 1920, 53). Sometimes anglo-indicized as *Kintal*.

so exhausted that there was no one to go down to the second deck and fill the kegs, although the salvation of the ship depended upon the continuation of this work. Nuno Velho Pereira therefore went down into the hold at great risk, being lowered by the cords of the pumps, and began to fill the kegs. The other gentlemen and soldiers, fired by this example, did the same, and they did not cease from this work all that night. At dawn of the following day they sighted land, as the pilot had promised the previous afternoon. This sudden sight gladdened them all, and filled them with rapture, as if the saving of their lives was not as doubtful on shore as in the ship, which the sea was engulfing with great fury.

On sighting land, they started to throw overboard everything on the forecastle, under the steerage, and on the poop. The ship being somewhat relieved by this, they set the topsails, the mainsail, and the spritsail, so as to reach the coast more rapidly, being still able to steer, as it would seem miraculously, for two decks were already waterlogged, and the chain-wales awash.

Nuno Velho, foreseeing the future need of arms and ammunition, without which they would assuredly be as lost on the land which they saw as on the sea where they were, advised the captain to command that all the arms, gunpowder, lead, and lunt that could be found should be got together. He likewise ordered António Moniz da Silva to collect as many matchlocks as he could and tie them together in a pipe, so that they might be saved therein. This was done, albeit with much trouble, by collecting what could be found on the quarter-deck, whence they were salvaged with difficulty when the pieces of the ship were washed ashore.

This precaution and foresight of Nuno Velho was of such importance that without it there would have been no salvation for all these Portuguese. For the Kaffirs were obliged by their fear and awe of these firearms to be friendly, to barter provisions with them, and to refrain from working their will upon them, these people being naturally inclined to robbery and treachery, as will be seen in the course of this narrative. Thus in similar misfortunes, and in the like disastrous circumstances, great attention should be paid to collecting and keeping the arms, cloth, and copper, for defence and barter, since this is so vital, and care should be taken to place everything on the top-gallant poop, that it may more easily be saved.

Being now close to land, by order of the master the carpenters began to cut away the masts, and in eight and a half fathoms the rudder struck the bottom and was displaced, and in eight fathoms the ship first touched the ground. They at once cut the shrouds, when the masts went by the board amid the loud and piteous clamour of all on board. When the masts fell overboard many people rashly jumped down on them, thinking this a sure means of escape from the wreck. But as they were still encumbered with part of the rigging, the impetuous waves which broke against the ship with great fury swept over them, and all those on them had their arms and legs broken and were drowned.

This disaster was recompensed by a benefit which was unexpected by the living (who saw this sad sight from the ship), which was due to the same masts, for the furious blows which terrified them, and which they greatly feared would overwhelm them, proved to be their salvation by pounding the ship and breaking her up in such wise that (after she had grounded between nine and ten o'clock on the morning of the 24th March, some 400 paces from the shore) she split in two, the top decks breaking loose from the two bottom ones. These last remained in the place where the ship struck, and the top portion drifted towards the land until very close to it.

On the prow were the Captain, the pilot, the master, with many other people, while all the rest were on the poop with Nuno Velho Pereira, who accompanied and encouraged Dona Isabel and Dona Luisa, and was their protection from the waves which burst in between the masts and the poop and broke in spray over the latter. He sheltered these ladies under a large camlet cloak and stood so as to receive the first shock, which was so furious (especially on the poop, to which the shrouds which encumbered the masts were still attached), that many men were compelled to lash themselves to some of the fixed timbers in order to avoid being washed overboard. Others, who knew how to swim, fearing that night would fall before the pieces of the ship which they were on should reach the shore, and that the masts would then either crush them or force them underneath so that they would be drowned, dived into the sea; and what with blows from the many pieces of wood which were floating about, and with the backwash of the huge waves which broke on the great and sharp rocks along the shore, many of them were drowned.

At nightfall the poop broke loose from the prow, to which it had hitherto been connected underneath the water, and being now likewise freed from the masts, it drifted straight on to the beach. But Nuno Velho, fearing lest the great currents on that coast, which flow south-west, should carry the poop away with them, when it was nearly low tide ordered one of his servants, a good soldier named Diogo Fernandes, to swim ashore and fasten there a rope, which, being attached to that piece of the ship, would render it secure from the currents.[1] The soldier did this with great courage and better goodwill, and most of the people who were on this poop now got ashore. About midnight the forecastle drifted athwart the poop, and using this latter as a bridge, those who were on the former were able to get ashore. At the beginning of the third watch Nuno Velho Pereira landed with the gentlemen and soldiers who accompanied him, as also Dona Isabel and Dona Luisa, who were hauled ashore by the rope while the tide was rising, and when it ebbed the poop was left high and dry and they landed dry-shod.

After they had greeted each other with tearful embraces, they gave many thanks to God Our Lord for the great mercies he had shown them on the day of His miraculous incarnation,[2] by delivering them from such a dangerous shipwreck, and saving them on that shore (whose latitude is $32\frac{1}{2}°$ South) which our people call the *Penedo das Fontes*, and the Negroes 'Tizombe'.[3] On counting

[1] The *Africa Pilot*, III, 164–5, notes of this stretch of the coast: 'any landing during north-easterly winds would be attended with the gravest risk, and, more often than not, would be impossible.' Even with south-westerly winds, 'landing should only be attempted in a case of emergency'.

[2] On 25 March.

[3] 'The pilot believed the latitude of the place to be 32° 30′ S., but this was certainly an error, because there was only one large river between it and the Umzimvubu, and if it had been correct the Bashee and the Umtata must have been crossed. The Portuguese maps were still so defective that the position of all but very prominent places upon them was uncertain. The wrecked crew of the *Santo Alberto*

their numbers, they found that there were 125 live Portuguese and 28 dead, with 160 live slaves and 34 dead. They spent the rest of the day in drying the clothes in which they had escaped around many fires which they soon made from the driftwood which came ashore, warming themselves from the bitter cold which they felt, and resting from their past labour and anguish.

Such was the loss of this great ship *Santo Alberto*, and such were the circumstances of its shipwreck, caused, not by the storms of the Cape of Good Hope (for she was lost before reaching it, in favourable weather), but by careening and overloading, through which this great ship and many others lie buried in the depths of the sea. Both these defects are due to the covetousness of contractors and navigators. The contractors, because it costs much less to careen a ship than to lay her aground, are delighted with the Italian invention, which though it is all right in the Levant, where galleys can ride out storms and tempests, and where one can put into port every eight days, in this our ocean its use is one of the causes of the loss of these great ships.[1]

For besides the rotting of the timber caused by being so long in the sea (even though cut at the proper season), it is unduly strained when the hull is heeled over for careening, with the great weight of such huge carracks.[2] When they are caulked in this way they do

believed the remarkable rock now known as the Hole-in-the-Wall, close to which they were, to be the Penedo das Fontes of [Bartolomeu] Dias, and the first river beyond, which was the Umtata of our day, to be the Rio do Infante of that explorer' (G. M. Theal, *Beginning*, 295–6). On the other hand, S. R. Welch (*Portuguese Rule*, 146) states that the wreck occurred 'on the coast of the Transkei in January [*sic*] 1593, somewhere near the mouth of the Bashee River', in lat. 32° 15′ S, long. 28° 35′ E. In this conflict of interpretation I prefer to follow Theal, since he had the assistance of 'Walter Stanford, Esquire, C.M.G., recently chief magistrate of Griqualand East', who was thoroughly acquainted with the region traversed by the castaways. Theal further notes that 'the great rock, which then, according to the journal, bore the name Tizombe, is now [1902] called Zinkali'. The Griquas, an extremely mixed people of basically Hottentot origin, did not arrive in this region until about 1860.

[1] The 'Italian invention' evidently refers to the practice of heaving the ship down on one side by strong purchase to her masts from a hulk or pontoon in the water, instead of laying her aground, or in dry dock.

[2] '... grande pezo de tamanhas Carracas.' This is one of the very rare instances of the term *carraca(s)*, carrack(s), by a Portuguese writer. Cf. Introduction, p. 3 above.

I

not take the oakum properly, being damp and badly dried. And afterwards during a voyage, when they are tossed by heavy seas and buffeted by strong winds, the caulking comes away and the open seams let in the water which sinks them. Experience has shown that before this prejudicial invention was in use, a ship could make ten or twelve voyages to India, whereas nowadays she cannot make two with it.[1]

This evil is increased by the artificers who undertake the work, or who do it under contract (which is a prejudicial system in any case). These, to save time when they cannot save on the materials, never finish anything properly, as should be done in a work of such importance, and thus they leave everything imperfect. If they discover in an old ship any defects or deficiencies which cannot be remedied without loss to themselves, they conceal them, and hide the damage in such a way that everything seems to be in good order, whereas the certainty of shipwreck lurks hidden underneath.

They also fell the timbers out of their due season, which is in the waning of the January moon, and thus cause them to be heavy, green, and unseasoned. For this reason, they warp, shrink, split, and become loose, thus casting the nails and caulking, so that the seams gape, and with the dampness of the water without, and the great heat of the pepper and spices within, the timbers grow rotten and unsound on the first voyage; hence one plank cut out of season suffices to cause the loss of a great ship. Such must have been the state of the *Santo Alberto*'s timbers, since her keel (the base and foundation of every ship) was so rotten that when the fury of the seas wrenched it from the spot where it was aground and washed it ashore (with several cannon which were still lying in it) Nuno Velho Pereira broke it into small pieces with a Bengal cane.

The navigators are no less blameworthy for this loss, although it affects them still more closely, since they adventure their lives in the ship. They lade her without properly distributing the cargo,

[1] This is an exaggeration, as even the long-lived *Chagas*, which apparently held the record in this respect, did not make more than eight or nine round voyages. Cf. above, p. 4.

putting the lighter merchandise in the lower part of the hold and the heavier on top, whereas it should be the other way round. To enrich themselves quickly, they overload the ship in such a way that they exceed her limited cargo capacity, which necessarily makes it impossible to steer her properly; and if any of the afore-said mishaps occur, she opens at the seams and goes down.[1] And this is so inevitable, that without it the other reasons may not always cause the loss of a ship, whereas this one alone suffices to do so. Experience shows that some old ships, repaired and patched up by careening, come safely home from India because they do not carry a full cargo, whereas new ships which are overloaded are lost.

[26 March] Our people being thus saved as above described from the wreck of the *Santo Alberto*, on the next day, the 26th March, the captain asked them to set to work to collect what arms and provisions they could find, which was immediately done. The master, boatswain, and all the seamen went to the pieces of the wreck, while the soldiers searched along the shore. These found three kegs of gunpowder, and the others twelve matchlocks, some shields and swords, three cauldrons, and a little rice. The gun-powder was entrusted to the gunners (the post of master-gunner being given to the most experienced), so that they could dry it and refine it with a keg of vinegar which was washed ashore. The pro-visions and arms were at once placed in the quarters of Nuno Velho Pereira, our people guarding everything with great care to secure themselves from the thefts and attacks of the Kaffirs. To the same end, they entrenched themselves as well as the time and the place permitted; and to shelter themselves they made tents of valu-able carpets of Cambay and Odiaz,[2] of rich quilts of ginghams,[3]

[1] Cf. above, pp. 17–18. Severim de Faria, writing in 1655, tells us that his friend Francisco Barreto, Bishop-elect of Cranganor, testified to the truth of this habitual overloading from personal experience (*Noticias*, 242).

[2] Though almost invariably written and printed like a place-name (Odia, Odiaz, Diaz, etc.), this is in fact an Indo-Portuguese word, *odiá* or *adiá*, meaning 'a present offered to a superior'. Cf. Dalgado, *Glossário Luso-Asiático*, I, 11.

[3] The word was used in various senses by the Portuguese, being apparently derived from the Malay *gin ggang*, 'striped', and applied to various cotton, and cotton-and-silk textiles. 'It is not certain whether Coromandel ginghams were, like Bengal ginghams, of mixed cotton-and-Tussur-silk, or whether they were cotton through-

cachas,[1] and mats from the Maldive Islands,[2] all of which had been laden in the ship for very different purposes; and in these they took refuge from the cold at night and from the sun by day.

[27 March] The next day, which was the 27th, they resolved to choose a Captain-major, for which purpose the soldiers nominated ten electors, who were the captain Julião de Faria, Francisco da Silva, João de Valadares, Francisco Pereira Velho, Gonçalo Mendes de Vasconcellos, Diogo Nunes Gramaxo, António Godinho, Francisco Nunes Marinho, Fr Pedro and Fr Pantaleão, while the seamen nominated the pilot and the master. These were unanimously given full power, and the rest obliged themselves by oath to approve whomsoever they might elect as leader and faithfully to obey him.

With one consent they elected Nuno Velho Pereira, on account of his nobility, prudence, courage, and experience. He declined the election, asking them all to give this responsibility to the captain, Julião de Faria,[3] who deserved it for his qualities and his good behaviour in the shipwreck; and he promised to help him with such counsel as might be desired and could be expected from his age. They refused to accept this excuse of Nuno Velho and that he might not make any other, they told him that if he would not accept this responsibility they were resolved to go their separate ways and pursue their journey disunited and in bands, how best they could. Since this resolution meant the total destruction of all these people, that it might not be carried out, putting the public good before his own peace and quiet, he accepted this nomination, and took the usual oath to fulfil his obligations, and all the rest likewise took a similar oath to obey him.

out. The important feature to traders was that they were woven with double-threaded warps and wefts, thus having a distinctive texture.' J. Irwin in *Journal of Indian Textile History*, II (1956), 41. Cf. also Dalgado, *Glossário Luso-Asiático*, I, 449.

[1] *Cachas, Catches.* 'Probably from Hindi *kach*, 'loincloth'. Cotton cloth of unknown description, woven mainly in Tinnevelly areas and exported to the Malay Archipelago and Persia' (J. Irwin, loc. cit.). Cf. also Dalgado, *Glossário Luso-Asiático*, I, 163–4.

[2] Presumably coir mats.

[3] He had come out to India in command of the carrack *São João* in the fleet of 1591.

As it was late and the tide was out, some of the seamen went with the master to the wreck, and they brought back six matchlocks, twelve pikes, and three bags of rice, all of which was delivered to Nuno Velho, who ordered it to be dried and divided with the rest equally among all. In order to see if they could find anything else of value, they set fire that night to the remains of the ship.

This should always be done in similar circumstances, that our people may make use of the nails for the barter-trade, and so that the Negroes can only obtain them from our hands, and thus their requisite value will be maintained. Whatsoever cannot be used should be thrown into the sea at a time when the Negroes are not looking, and in a place where they cannot salvage it. For if it is left on the shore, as this was, when the Kaffirs afterwards came to trade with cattle, seeing it there, they did not wish to sell their beasts but returned with them, believing that they would shortly be masters of the iron for which they were ready to barter their cows and sheep.

[28 March] At dawn the next day, Nuno Velho sent the captain to the beach, and the master with some men to the ship, where they found three muskets, four matchlocks, two bags of rice, a hogshead of meat, two of wine, four jars of bread, some olive-oil, and a large quantity of preserves. After dinner they found a chest of the Captain-major's containing many gold and silver pieces, and some small writing-boxes,[1] full of crystal rosaries. All this was handed to the captain, and he gave it to Nuno Velho, and it was put under guard by his orders, the provisions being served out to the people.

It being now late, the chief of that region, who had heard from some of his Kaffirs that our people were there, came with about sixty Negroes to visit the Captain-major. When he drew near, Nuno Velho got up and went a few steps to receive him, and the Negro, after welcoming him by saying 'Nanhatá, Nanhatá', as a sign of peace and friendship laid his hand on the Captain-major's

---

[1] *Escritorios.* For a description and illustration of a typical Luso-Japanese writing-box see J. Irwin, 'A Jacobean vogue for Oriental lacquer-ware', in *The Burlington Magazine* (June, 1953), 193–4.

beard and after stroking it kissed his own hand. All the other barbarians performed the same courtesy to our people, and ours to them. This Negro was called Luspance. He was fairly tall, well made, of a cheerful countenance, not very black, with a short beard, long moustaches, and appeared to be about forty-five years old.[1]

After Nuno Velho and the Negro had exchanged these courtesies they both sat down on a carpet, and two of our slaves near them, one belonging to Manuel Fernandes Girão, who understood the language of these Kaffirs and spoke that of Mozambique, and the other belonging to António Godinho, who knew this latter language and spoke our own; and thus they conversed through the medium of these two interpreters.

Nuno Velho asked this Kaffir what he thought of his soldiers. He replied that he thought highly of them, for their bodies were fashioned like his, and that they were the children of the sun (since they were white), but that he would be glad to know how they came there. Nuno Velho answered this question by saying that they were vassals of the most powerful king on earth, who was obeyed and paid tribute by the whole of India, where a viceroy of his dwelt to rule it. He was going from India to Portugal, his country, in a great ship which carried all these people, and as many more who had perished when the fury of the sea had opened the ship and cast them ashore on that beach, whereat all the Kaffirs were astonished.

This king then made them a present of two great sheep like those of Ormuz,[2] which were immediately killed and divided among the people. When the Negro saw them killed, he went with another of his Kaffirs to where they were being skinned and told them to pick up the refuse from their entrails, which he threw into the sea with his own hands, with some ceremonies and words

---

[1] H. A. Junod, 'Condition of the natives', 13, tentatively identifies the chief Luspance as Lusiphansi (?). G. M. Theal (*Beginning*, 297) notes: 'From this description it is evident that Luspance's clan was of mixed Bantu and Hottentot blood, the former, however, prevailing.'

[2] The fat-tailed sheep of Ormuz were famous, and were sometimes called 'sheep with five quarters' (Fr Gaspar de São Bernardino, O.F.M., *Itinerario da India por terra* (Lisboa, 1611), fol. 57).

of gratitude for bringing the Portuguese to his country, from whose loss he hoped to get great gain, wherefore he offered the sea this present, as to a friend.[1]

Having done this, he went back to Nuno Velho, who invited him to partake of some sweetmeats and wine, which he praised exceedingly, for it seemed to him a very good thing for the stomach, which felt warmed by it. When he was about to leave, the Captain-major gave him a brass bowl full of nails, and a gilded Chinese writing-box, with which the Negro was greatly pleased. On taking leave of him and the other Portuguese with the same ceremony as at their first meeting, he went away promising to send one of his men the next day to show them where to find water, of which our people already felt the need, drinking it hitherto from the pipes which had been washed ashore, although it was somewhat brackish from the mixture of salt water.

The dress of these Kaffirs was a mantle of calf-skins, with the hair on the outside, which they rub with grease to make soft.[2] They are shod with two or three soles of raw hide fastened together in a round shape, secured to the foot with thongs and with this they run with great speed.[3] They carry in their hand a thin stick to which is fastened the tail of an ape or of a fox,[4] with which they clean themselves and shade their eyes when observing. This dress is used by nearly all the Negroes of this Kaffraria, and the kings and chiefs wear hanging from their left ear a little copper bell, without a clapper, which they make after their fashion.

---

[1] 'This is exactly the rite which takes place in most of the sacrifices of South African Bantu. It is an invocation to the spirits of the ancestor, who are buried near the sea, and are more or less confounded with the impersonal power of the sea itself, this rite showing the transition between a purely ancestrolatric and a naturist sacrifice.' The man who threw the refuse into the sea was 'no doubt the priest of the family' (H. A. Junod, loc. cit., 23).

[2] Karosses of ox hide, they would be called nowadays.

[3] 'They had but one shoe, made of buffalo hide, which they wear on the right foot. It has not top leather, except over the toe, and is tied round the ankle with two strings from the heel. . . . Lewis says they wear one shoe and are very nimble; that he could not run half as fast' (P. R. Kirby (ed.), *Wreck of the Grosvenor* (1953), 36–7).

[4] More probably jackals' tails, as Theal notes. These sticks were presumably knobsticks or knoberries.

These and all the other Kaffirs are herdsmen and husbandmen, by which means they subsist. Their husbandry is millet, which is white, about the size of a peppercorn, and forms the ear of a plant which resembles a reed in shape and size. From this millet, ground between two stones or in wooden mortars, they make flour, and of this they make cakes, which they bake under the embers. Of the same grain they make wine,[1] mixing it with a lot of water, which after being fermented in a clay jar, cooled off, and turned sour, they drink with great gusto.

Their cattle are numerous, fat, tender, tasty, and large, the pastures being very fertile. Most of them are polled cows, in whose number and abundance their wealth consists. They also subsist on their milk and on the butter which they make from it.

They live together in small villages, in huts made of reed mats, which do not keep out the rain. These huts are round and low, and if any person dies in one of them, all the other huts and the whole village are pulled down, and they make others from the same material in another place, believing that in the village where their neighbour or relation died, everything will turn out unluckily.[2] And thus, to save themselves this trouble, when anyone falls ill they carry him into the bush, so that if he dies it may be outside their huts. They surround their huts with a fence, within which they keep their cattle.

They sleep in skins of animals, on the earth, in a narrow pit measuring six or seven spans long and one or two deep. They use vessels of clay dried in the sun, and also of wood carved with some iron hatchets, which resemble a wedge set in a piece of wood, and they also use these for clearing the bush. In war they make use of assegais; and they have gelded whelps about the shape and size of our large curs.

They are very brutish and worship nothing, and thus they would receive our holy Christian faith very easily. They believe that the sky is another world like this one in which we live, inhabited by another kind of people, who cause the thunder by

---

[1] 'Beer' would be more exact.

[2] 'This is the great law consequent to the taboo of death still observed in our days' (H. A. Junod, loc. cit., 24).

running and the rain by urinating.[1] Most of the inhabitants of this land from latitude 29° southwards are circumcised.[2] They are very sensual, and have as many wives as they can maintain, of whom they are jealous. They obey chiefs whom they call Ancosses.[3]

The language is almost the same in the whole of Kaffraria, the difference between them resembling that between the languages of Italy, or between the ordinary ones of Spain.[4] They seldom go far away from their villages, and thus they know and hear nothing except what concerns their neighbours. They are very covetous, and so long as they have not received payment they will serve, but if payment is made in advance no service is to be expected of them, for when they have received it they make off with it.

They value the most essential metals, such as iron and copper, and thus for very small pieces of either of these they will barter cattle, which is what they most prize, and with cattle they drive their trade and commerce, and cattle forms their treasure.[5] Gold and silver have no value among them, nor does there appear to be either of these two metals in the country, for our people saw no signs of them in the regions through which they passed.

The above is all they noticed of the dress, customs, ceremonies, and laws of these Kaffirs, nor can there be more to take note of among so barbarous a people.

The land is very abundant and most fertile, and the Portuguese saw of plants which they knew: marjoram, wormwood, ferns, watercress, penny-royal, mallows, garden-rosemary, rue, myrtle with large and tasty berries, brambles with fruit, rosemary, blites,

---

[1] 'This is almost the same superstition as that of the "balungwane" still met with amongst the Thonga-Shangaan; *balungwane*, little men who are said to inhabit heaven and look down to us. When they see a man walking on earth they sometimes discuss who he is. If not agreeing, they spit on the traveller; he looks to the sky to see where this unexpected drop of rain comes from; they then see his face, and thus they know him' (H. A. Junod, loc. cit., 23).

[2] Whether derived from the Arabs (Swahili) or not, the circumcision initiation, as it is now practised in South Africa, 'bears the Bantu character so strongly, that it can be said to have been thoroughly adapted to the circumstance and to the genius of these animistic tribes' (H. A. Junod, loc. cit., 18).

[3] *Inkosi, Izinkosi,* chief, headman, head and lord of three, four, five villages (H. A. Junod, loc. cit., 17).

[4] Castilian, Galician, Portuguese, etc., but excluding Basque and Catalan.

[5] Polygamy was founded on *lobola* (cattle marriage). H. A. Junod, loc. cit., 18

wild mint, and aloe shrubs so large and tall that they looked like trees, the stalks being four or five spans long and one wide, from the middle of which grew a stem with yellow flowers. There were likewise many other herbs which they had never seen save in those fields. The trees were very different from ours, and of those resembling these they only found olive-trees with some very small olives, wild olive-trees, jujube-trees, and fig-trees.

There are large and dense forests, in which they never met lions, tigers, or animals of this kind. Of poisonous reptiles, they only saw one huge viper, which they killed, and some snakes like our water-snakes, and small lizards: the others will be spoken of in their place. In the rivers, which are numerous, they descried fish. Anything else of importance will be mentioned in its due place, these present remarks being applicable to the whole of Kaffraria in general, being placed here so that the description of the journey which follows may be the better understood.

[29 March] To return to our narrative. On the morning of the next day, the 29th March, it seemed necessary to the Captain-major to select the requisite officers for the proper control of their little camp,[1] since without this nothing can be preserved for any length of time. Thus he gave the charge of arranging and sub-dividing it to Captain Julião de Faria Cerveira; Diogo Nunes Gramaxo was appointed purveyor, and the master, João Martins, as treasurer; and he ordered that they two and Friar Pedro should have charge of the objects of gold and silver and other things for bartering, and that on such occasions António Godinho should be present, he being a man of great experience in trading with the Kaffirs, with whom he had for long associated in the rivers of Cuama.[2]

Captain Julião de Faria then divided their camp into its chief parts, namely vanguard, main-body, and rearguard, distributing the soldiers in three parties for watch-keeping, of which Francisco da Silva, João de Valadares, and Francisco Pereira were appointed captains. He divided the seamen into another three parties, with

---

[1] *arraial*, a camp, often in the sense of entrenched camp; and hence by extension an army, a punitive column, or even a mining-settlement and the like.

[2] 'Rios de Cuama.' The Zambesi; the Zambesi delta and river valley.

the pilot, the master, and Custodio Gonçalves the boatswain, as their respective captains. The arms which had been previously collected and some which were found that day were served out to the soldiers in proper order. They totalled twelve pikes, twenty-seven matchlocks, five muskets, and several swords and shields.

Nuno Velho, foreseeing what would be required for so lengthy a journey, ordered the gunners that after refining the gunpowder they should place it in some bamboos, which had been found on the beach, and which had been used in the ship instead of buckets. These were covered with leather on the outside, to keep the powder from becoming damp. He ordered that little bags like wallets should be made to hold the copper of a cauldron and six kettles, which had been broken up into small pieces for bartering, and other larger sacks of the same pattern for the few provisions which had been saved from the ship.

No other goods having been salvaged except the aforesaid writing-boxes and the chest of Nuno Velho with seventeen pieces of gold and twenty-seven of silver, he generously presented them all to his soldiers, saying that he wished the gift was equal to the goodwill with which he gave it. And so he ordered the coins to be given to the purveyor and the treasurer, so that when they reached one of our ports the value of what remained after the journey might be divided among them all, as was afterwards done at Mozambique, where sixteen hundred *cruzados*, for which they were sold, were distributed among those who arrived there.

All these things having been arranged, our people provided themselves with water, which the Negroes showed them in two places, one along the beach in a pool where there was but little; and the other behind a hill in some pools on the bank of a stream.[1] This lack of water is general along the whole coast of Kaffraria, and not less wanting are springs in the interior, but streams of good water are abundant, which compensates for the want of that of the springs.

[31 March] On the last day of March they discussed what route they should follow, and the majority voted in favour of

[1] The Mapaka (Mapako) River, according to G. M. Theal, about ten miles west of the mouth of the Umtata.

travelling along the shore. But Nuno Velho, remembering the loss of the great ship *São Thomé* in the Land of the Fumos in 1589, an account of which, written by her second pilot, Gaspar Ferreira [Reimão], he had read in Goa, showed from this example and from those of the galleon *São João* and the great ship *São Bento*, which had been wrecked in those parts in 1552 and 1554 respectively,[1] the great hardships, difficulties, and dangers which they would have to undergo, and the hunger, thirst, and sicknesses which they would suffer in travelling along the coast of Kaffraria; and that their tribulations would far surpass those of their predecessors, since the place where they were was further away from Lourenço Marques, the nearest port on that coast which the Portuguese frequented for trade and barter.

Upon this prudent advice (as subsequent experience showed it to be) they all changed their minds, and resolved by common consent to pursue their journey through the hinterland, and avoid the inevitable hardships of the coast. This being settled, and the captain having arranged the people in their order of march, and assigned the soldiers to the stations they were to keep, there came the same Inkosi who had visited them before, and Nuno Velho asked him for some guides to lead them to the next Inkosi, his neighbour. He promised to provide them, and sent them at the time of their departure.

The Captain-major therefore ordered all to be ready to start the next day, which was the 1st April. During that night there was a false alarm, to which our soldiers responded with great zeal and good order by seizing their arms and taking up their appointed stations. When the scare had died down, and it was daylight, they began to march on their way, moving to a valley which was situated between two hills, marching in very good order. The guides came with their chief, Luspance, and they brought two cows and two sheep, which they bartered for three pieces of copper the size of a hand.

The cows, by order of Nuno Velho, were shot with a matchlock, as was usually done in front of the Negroes, in order to

---

[1] Both these accounts were reprinted in the first volume of the *HTM* and are available in English translation in G. M. Theal, *Records of South-Eastern Africa*, 1.

astonish and terrify them. For the same purpose, he ordered the muskets to be fired at some empty hogsheads, which were shattered with a loud noise. The Inkosi, overcome with fear, wanted to run away, but Nuno Velho took him by the arm and reassured him, and our people likewise did the same with the other Kaffirs. After they had all eaten together the Kaffirs withdrew, to return the next day when they were due to leave; but as it rained a lot that night they did not set out, since they had to dry the tents and clothing in the sun, which was very bright.

[3 April] On the next day, however, which was the 3rd April, at nine o'clock the Portuguese left that shore, some of them suffering from wounds received during the wreck, among them being Francisco Nunes Marinho who was badly hurt in the leg—and a little Negro with a broken leg who was left in charge of the Kaffirs, who, in return for the copper which was given them to nurse and maintain him, took him in and gave him hospitality with evident signs of goodwill. Thus were left the pieces of the ship on which they were saved, and beneath the waves the riches which they had amassed with such anxiety during a long time, now lost in a single day.

The captain and the pilot went in front with one of the guides, and the others with their king accompanied Nuno Velho. The pilot observed the direction of their route with a sundial, and found that it was NNE. The way was level, and over a pleasant plain covered with long grass, through which they travelled slowly, it being their first day's march. At three o'clock they reached a valley, through which flowed a beautiful stream that entered another river which further down the vale mixed its sweet water with the salt water of the sea. In this place the guide called a halt, which was the first of the journey; and our people took shelter along the stream in thick woods of different colours which were in the valley.

[4 April] The next day, searching along the river (which is the Infante)[1] for a ford whereby they could cross over to the other side, they came across two Negroes, whom Luspance, who was still

---

[1] As noted above, p. 114, n. 3, Theal identifies this river with the Umtata, the real Rio do Infante being the present-day Great Fish River in lat. 33° 31′ S.

accompanying our people, asked to act as guides to their chief, for which they would be well paid. The two Negroes agreed, and for this purpose were presented to the Captain-major, who put two crystal rosaries around their necks, with which they were satisfied. They then returned and showed our people the ford, which they crossed with the water to their knees, as it was low tide. In this river there were many hippopotami and numerous ducks.

When they reached the other bank the Negroes and the Inkosi Luspance, who had come thus far from the beach, took leave of them, and thereafter they followed the two new guides. These led them up a thickly wooded ridge, at the top of which they reached a delightful plain, bordered on both sides with hills covered with trees. The plain extended to the foot of a high circular hill, climbing up the slope of which fatigued our people very much. On reaching the summit, therefore, Nuno Velho sent to ask the guides whether it was far to the spot where they intended to halt; and on their replying that it was, and that they could not reach it that night, he ordered that they should go no further, but that the people should take shelter, which they did in a valley into which they descended, where there was plenty of firewood and a stream of very good water.

The direction in which they travelled during all that day and for many others was still NNE. They had marched about two leagues, and the Kaffirs declared that along this route they would always find habitations with provisions, water, and firewood. When the Negroes saw our people encamped, they asked leave of the Captain-major to return to their village that night, and said they would bring some cows next morning. He gave them leave, and promised that the cows would be well paid for.

[5 April] The two Kaffirs kept their word, and returned in the morning with eight cows, for which they were given pieces of copper worth about two *cruzados*. That day they journeyed through luxurious meadow-lands, filled with high grass, and crossed by many streams. At sunset they encamped on the thickly wooded bank of a stream, where they killed two of the cows which they had bought. The meat was equally divided among all, as was invariably done during the whole of this journey. In this place our people buried two muskets, by order of Nuno Velho, because they were very heavy, a great encumbrance, and little needed. They passed the night here in heavy rain, for it was then almost the beginning of winter in those southern regions, where the month of April corresponds with that of October in these our northern lands. An old Indian woman, the captain's slave, remained in this place, being unable to continue the journey.

[6 April] As our people were very wet, they did not travel far the next day, although it was easy going over level ground, with a few low hills, and abounding with pastures and water. Though the Negroes' village was near, according to what they said, the rain came on so heavily that our people went no further than the bank of a stream which was well supplied with firewood, and there they remained.

[7 April] On the following morning, the 7th April, after all the people had eaten (which they did at dawn so that they could travel all day), they began their march over a good level way. Coming in sight of some Negroes' huts which were those of the guides who accompanied them, these, fearing that our people would injure their crops of millet around the huts, left the track and led them along where there was no grain. The Captain-major seeing this, and asking and learning the reason for being side-tracked, ordered the column to halt, and made proclamation that no one should touch anything belonging to those Kaffirs, on pain of death. They, learning this from the interpreter, were astonished, and then returned laughing to the proper way. Our people encamped alongside their huts and bought a little millet from them for the slaves; and one of the Negroes went to visit his Inkosi who was not far off.

[8 April] Our people reached the village of this king the next day at eleven o'clock, after travelling over level ground with very rich and abundant pastures. He was already waiting for them on the track, accompanied by four Negroes. They were amazed at seeing white men, but being reassured by the Negroes who came with our people, they came closer to them. Their Inkosi approached the Captain-major, using the same ceremony as the other Inkosi, Luspance, and laying his hand upon the former's beard, finding it soft and smooth, and his own rough and woolly, he laughed heartily thereat. He went along with Nuno Velho, and his followers accompanied our people, who continued on their way leaving behind them the village from which the Negro ordered those cows to be bought, for which they gave him nine small pieces of copper.

At four in the afternoon they pitched their camp where there was firewood and water, and the Inkosi having taken his leave, they killed three cows which were equally divided among our people as usual. In the region through which they had travelled they found ducks, partridges, quails, doves, herons, sparrows, and crows. Four of our slaves remained in this place, three of them being Negroes and one a Malabari.

[9 April] The next day, the 9th April, after travelling a short distance they came to a village consisting of a few huts surrounded by a corral, in which there were about a hundred cows and a hundred and twenty very large sheep of the Ormuz breed.[1] Here lived an old patriarch with his sons and grandsons, who with great surprise and joy received our people, bringing them gourds full of milk which they put ready in haste. They bought four cows from him, for copper which was worth about four pence.

Continuing on their way, they met five Negroes, among whom was the brother of the Kaffir guide to whom the Inkosi Luspance had entrusted our people. He, hearing of his brother's coming, went to look for him, and presented him to the Captain-major, telling him of the relationship between them. Nuno Velho received him very kindly, and he welcomed him with their usual ceremony. This Negro was called Ubabu; he was of middling height, well made and proportioned, not very black, and of a cheerful appearance.

It being midday, Nuno Velho ordered the pilot to take the altitude of the sun with the astrolabe which was saved from the wreck, that they might know their actual position. The pilot did so, and found that they were in 32° 6' south latitude, by which reckoning, according to the way they had taken, they had

[1] Large-tailed sheep. Cf. above, p. 120, n. 2.

travelled ten leagues in eight days and a half, which they thought no small matter considering their encumbrances, not the least of these being Dona Isabel and her daughter Dona Luisa, whom the slaves of the Captain-major bore on their shoulders in *cachas*,[1] arranged like the hammocks of Brazil, which are called *machiras* in Zambesia.[2]

At four in the afternoon they reached a village of the Negro Ubabu, who made our people sit down near his hut, and with every mark of satisfaction showed them his cattle, which were very tame and domesticated. They comprised about two hundred cows, most of them polled, and those which were not were larger than the others. There was also a flock of two hundred large sheep. In order to show his pleasure at entertaining them, he sent for his wives, who were seven in number, and three daughters and several sons. He told the women to dance, and they, clapping their hands and singing, there rose up about sixty Negroes of the same village who were sitting around looking at our people, and these began to dance and jump to the same sound.

Nuno Velho declared himself pleased with the entertainment and asked the treasurer for some small crystal beads[3] threaded on silk, which he gave to the children (as he did all through the journey), and likewise three chessmen tied to three silk threads which he hung around the necks of the daughters of Ubabu, at which the brothers and father were much gratified and they promised Nuno Velho four cows in return. Then he and the rest then went and encamped near the same village, along the bank of a stream where firewood was not wanting.

[10 April] The next day the Negro was inflamed by covetousness which he had hitherto concealed; and besides putting off our people all morning with pretexts and pretences when they asked

---

[1] Loin-cloths. Cf. above, p. 118, n. 1.

[2] For more detailed descriptions of this hammock-litter, and discussion of the origin of the word *machira* (*machila*), see *Hobson-Jobson*, 596; Dalgado, *Glossário Luso-Asiático*, II, 5–7. Dalgado's contention that the word is of East African rather than Indian (as maintained by Yule and Burnell) origin, seems to me to be correct.

[3] '. . . continhas de cristal.' This seems to imply that they were different from the more common semi-opaque and cornelian beads, best described under the name of 'trade-wind beads' which are dealt with on p. 133, n. 4 below.

K

for the four cows he had promised, he demanded of Nuno Velho a cauldron as well, and, as if sulking because they would not give it him, he went and sat down outside his hut with his family. The Captain-major resolved to win this Negro with kindness, and thus, accompanied by fifteen arquebusiers and the interpreters, he went up to him, and with friendly words conducted him to his tent, where he treated him with sweets and wine. Discussing here once more the barter for the cows, the Negro demanded a brass candlestick which he had in his hand for three of them. At this, Nuno Velho lost patience with him and ordered the people to begin their march, saying that he would have punished this Kaffir if he did not remember the kindness of his brother (who was called Inhancosa),[1] and the obligation he was under to him.

This latter was absent, having gone to see his hut, which was some distance from the encampment, and when he returned and learnt what had happened, he interceded for his brother Ubabu, and to excuse him said that he must be mad. He offered to accompany Nuno Velho again as far as the track which ran behind a rise alongside his own huts. Having reached this place, he sent a little son of his for a cow, which he presented that evening. Here the people encamped on the thickly wooded bank of a river, and Inhancosa wished to depart, promising that he would return the next day; but Nuno Velho would not permit him to do so until he left another Negro as a hostage.

[11 April] The next day, which was Palm Sunday, they changed the order of march, the Captain-major moving to the van, because he walked slowly and most of the people could keep up with him. Guided by the Negro who had taken the place of Inhancosa, they passed near a village, from which at the summons of this Kaffir some people came to sell a cow, after they had camped where there was firewood and water. Our people kept the cattle which they bought where they could guard them; and when they encamped they placed them in the middle, and watched them carefully all night, so that the Kaffirs might not steal them. If the Kaffirs thought our people odd on account of the difference in colour and dress, their cattle were no less astonished, for they

[1] 'Evidently Nyana wenkosi, i.e. son of the chief' (G. M. Theal, *Beginning*, 298).

would run towards the Portuguese from a great distance, and then stop near them with their muzzles in the air, as if amazed at such a novelty. The Negroes were also watched (though secretly), that they might not leave after they were paid, it being their custom to run away as soon as anything is given them.

[12 April] The musketeers being tired with carrying their muskets, and these being unnecessary anyway, Nuno Velho Pereira and the captain thought it best that they should be thrown into that stream, which was done with the consent of all.[1] Thence they continued their march over a stony road (where some Negroes brought them milk in exchange for small pieces of nails), which made this day's journey a short one. When they were encamped, some other Kaffirs came and bartered three cows for copper worth about two *tostões*.[2] One of them offered to accompany our people, and Nuno Velho ordered the lid of a silver salt-cellar to be given him.

The dress of these Negroes is like that of those of Tizombe, but they wear in addition red beads in their ears. Nuno Velho asking the Kaffir to whom he gave the lid where these were obtained, he understood from his description that they were brought from the land of the Unhaca,[3] who is the king of the people living by the river of Lourenço Marques. These beads are made of clay of all colours, of the size of a coriander seed. They are made in India at Negapatam, whence they are brought to Mozambique, and thence they reach these Negroes through the Portuguese who barter them for ivory in the said river.[4]

[1] Kabel's *Military Fireworks* of 1619 states that 'the musket is in all respects to be used like the arquebus, save that in respect it carries a double bullet, and is much more weighty'.

[2] Sometimes anglicized as testoons. The *Tostão* was a coin worth 100 *reis*, or about 2½d. in Elizabethan money.

[3] Inhaca.

[4] These are the so-called 'trade-wind beads', six different categories of which are described by W. G. N. van der Sleen in *Man* (February 1956), 27-9, the majority being made of opaque glass, as these probably were. The exact provenance of most varieties is still uncertain, although it is known that the carnelian and onyx ones came from the mines in Cambay. Some of the opaque glass varieties were undoubtedly exported from Negapatam, on the Coromandel Coast of India, but they were not necessarily made there. To the literature cited in Van der Sleen's article should be added the voluminous discussion by G. P. Rouffaer, 'Waar kwamen de

[13 April] The next day, before they had struck their camp, there came the son of an Inkosi who lived close by, accompanied by twenty other Negroes, round whose neck Nuno Velho hung the key of a writing-box with a silver chain. The Kaffir showed that he was very pleased, and in the hope of getting something else said that his father had sent him to see such strange people, and that he would be glad if they would pass through his village, even if it were a little out of their way. Nuno Velho replied that they must keep to their course, but that they might meet upon the road. Upon which this Negro and his companions took their leave, and the other Negro with great dissimulation went off with them, taking the silver lid with him.

Our people were thus left without a guide, and the pilot[1] had to undertake that duty by order of the Captain-major. This he did and by means of the needle of the portable sun-dial[2] directed them NNE., as had hitherto been the route. Whenever afterwards a guide was wanting, the pilot performed this office, though he was often ill and suffered much pain; but he bore up against it with great courage (having shown no less resolution during the ship-wreck), in order to do his duty in guiding his companions over those regions never seen or visited by them or by any other Portuguese before.

Climbing a hill which was near the camping place, they came upon a good track, where many Negroes brought them a quantity of milk, of which they gave a leather bag full, containing half an *almude*,[3] for three or four pump nails. At sunset they reached a large river which the pilot thought to be one of three rivers which are marked in that latitude on the sea-chart, of which they had already passed the Infante, which was the first one and in which

---

raadselachtige moetisalah's (aggri-kralen) in de Timor-groep oorsponkelijk van daan?' in *Bijdragen Taal- Land en Volkenkunde Nederlandsch Oost-Indien*, dl. 50 (1898), 409–675. Similar varieties of these beads have been found as far apart as Zimbabwe and Timor.

[1] Rodrigo Migueis.

[2] *relogio do sol*. For a description of this instrument and its use, see L. de Morais e Sousa, *A siência náutica dos pilotos portugueses nos séculos XV e XVI* (2 vols., Lisboa, 1924), I, 114–16.

[3] Twenty-six *almudes* to a pipe of wine.

they saw hippopotami; and they thought from the latitude that this must be the third, called São Christovão, and that they had not come across the middle one because their journey led them inland, and it is not a very big one.[1]

This river was very deep, with a very strong current, but seeing that some cattle crossed it higher up than where they were, they forded it in that place, although with difficulty and fear, lest the current should carry away any of the weak and ill.[2] But they all reached the other side in safety, where they camped along the bank that night, and by the large fires which they made they warmed themselves and dried their clothing which was wet from the passage.

[14 April] The next day, they followed the route laid down by the pilot, which was a good way with villages along it, whence people came out to sell them milk and a fruit resembling our water-melons, which the Kaffirs call *mabure*.[3] At eleven o'clock, the sun being very hot, they all rested under the shade of some trees by a stream. Here there came a Negro accompanied by many others driving about a hundred cows before them. As this man seemed by his bearing and following to be of a higher rank than any of the chiefs previously met, Nuno Velho ordered a carpet to be spread outside the camp, where he received him; and after greeting each other according to the usual way of that country, the Negro enquired who were these Portuguese, where they came from, and whither they were going.

Nuno Velho replied that they were vassals of the powerful king of all the Spains, that he was their captain, that the sea (which the

---

[1] According to Theal's interpretation (*Records*, II, xxviii–xxix; *Beginning*, 298), this river was the Umzimvubu, nowadays called St John's River, in lat. 31° 38′ S. The Rio do Infante of Bartolomeu Dias and the sixteenth-century Portuguese charts is generally identified with the modern Great Fish River, and the São Christovão with the Keiskama. Cf. the outline of the South East African coast as charted by Perestrello in 1576 compared with the actual outline in square projection *apud* Perestrello-Costa, *Roteiro* (ed. 1939). As noted on p. 114, n. 3, above, I follow Theal in assuming that Nuno Velho Pereira's party had mistaken the Umtata for the Rio do Infante.

[2] They crossed the Umzimvubu (St John's) River, the largest in Kaffraria, 'at the ford now known as the Etyeni,' according to Theal (*Beginning*, 298–9).

[3] *mabure*. Not identified.

Negroes call *Manga*)[1] had cast them upon this land as they were homeward-bound in a great ship, and that they were travelling through it in order to reach the Inhaca's country, where they would find a ship which would carry them back to where they had started from. Nuno Velho asked him for guides and provisions, both of which this Negro supplied. The guides were two of his sons, with two other Negroes who accompanied them, and the provisions were two cows. Nuno Velho had deserved all this, for when the chief arrived Nuno Velho had hung round his neck a pestle which weighed about four *arrateis*[2] and also presented him with a kettle and some crystal beads,[3] and to three of his sons he gave three rosaries. This Negro seemed to be about eighty years old, he was called Vibo, and he was tall and very black. At two o'clock he took leave of the Captain-major, his two sons remaining with our people as guides.

They conducted the party over very level country, and at sunset they halted and encamped under some trees in a field near a village. Here the two brothers obtained leave to go away, leaving in their place the other two Negroes, who also took their leave on the following day as they dreaded the unpopulated wasteland.

[15 April] On the 15th April, being Maundy Thursday, they set out before sunrise, journeying over beautiful fields and abundant pastures. They crossed two streams, near one of which they remained an hour, and encamped at the next. Here they killed two cows which were sparingly divided, reserving the remaining two for the uninhabited land which they would have to cross

---

[1] 'They were correct in believing that the word *manga* (properly *isimanga*) referred to the sea, though literally it means a wonder' (Theal, op. et loc. cit.).

[2] *Arratel*, from the Arabic *ratl*, a pound weight. Sometimes anglo-indicized as 'rottle', 'rattle', etc. Cf. *Hobson-Jobson*, 770.

[3] *contas de cristal*. Perhaps the opaque glass trade-wind beads described above, p. 133, n. 4. On the other hand, J. B. Tavernier, writing about a century later, notes that the Dutch who had recently settled at the Cape of Good Hope imported 'beads of crystal and agate, which are cheap at Surat', to barter with the Hottentots for cattle (J. B. Tavernier, *Travels*, ed. V. Bell and W. Crooke, 2 vols., London, 1925, II, 303). Jean Mocquet, who was at Mozambique in 1608, also refers to 'beads of glass or amber, as well good as counterfeit', as useful merchandise along the East African coast (*Travels and Voyages performed by Mr. John Mocquet*, ed. London, 1696, 229).

during the next three days, according to what the Negroes told them.

When our people were settled in their encampment, several pious persons erected an altar between two rocks, on which they placed a crucifix with two lighted candles. Friar Pedro recited the Litany before it, and afterwards preached a sermon suitable to the occasion, which was heard with no less tears than it was preached with devotion.

[16 April] For the next three days they journeyed through un-inhabited country. On the first day, which was Good Friday, at eleven o'clock they came to a marsh where there was only a little water and less shade; but at four in the afternoon they crossed over a broad and swiftly-running river, with the water up to their knees, and camped on the other side. Since they had not much to eat, they availed themselves of some roots which they gathered on the way, resembling those found between Minho and Douro and there called *nozelhas*,[1] which were very sweet and about the size of small turnips.

As the slaves of Nuno Velho Pereira were now much ex-hausted from carrying Dona Isabel and Dona Luisa, he begged the master to induce some of the seamen to carry these ladies. The master got the pilot to help him with his influence, and they both finally succeeded in doing what was asked of them, by arranging with sixteen grummets to carry them as far as the river of Lourenço Marques, in exchange for the sum of a thousand *cruzados*, pro-mised and guaranteed by Nuno Velho; and he duly paid that amount on behalf of the ladies in Mozambique.

[17 April] On Easter Eve, very early and in a heavy dew, they climbed up a hill, and afterwards, when the sun was up, several others. This tired our people very much, as most of them were bare-footed, their shoes being already worn out, and a pair was worth ten *cruzados*. Thus climbing up and down (but always going in the same fixed direction), they took their siesta under the shade of a dense thicket, through which ran a stream which they crossed with the water to their ankles.

While they were resting here, a Negro appeared with two

[1] *nozelhas*. Not identified.

women. They sent the interpreter to him, who brought him to Nuno Velho, leaving the two Negresses at some distance from our people. He asked him to act as his guide and promised to pay him very well. But the Kaffir excused himself because of the women in his charge, saying that if he had been alone he would have done so. Nuno Velho having given him a nail, he retired well satisfied. Not so our people, finding themselves in that uninhabited region, through which they continued their journey till sunset, when they encamped at the foot of a hill where there was water and firewood.

[18 April] On Easter morning they climbed the hill, finding on it certain roots which resembled carrots in the leaf and in taste, and in the bush they found a fruit which was rather sour, and tasted like our unripe fruit, by means of which they felt their want of provisions less. They sheltered themselves from the heat in the shade of some trees on a height; and it being midday the pilot took the altitude of the sun, and checking this with the declination, he found their position to be in latitude 31°South. He immediately informed Nuno Velho Pereira and the rest of the company of this fact, and they all rejoiced at such good news. But their joy did not last long, for resuming their journey and climbing another hill in hope of discovering some village, they saw nothing but vast and uninhabited plains, which saddened and discouraged them.

They encamped that night where there was firewood and water available, and here they resolved that next morning they would send four men to a height which was southward of their haltingplace, and four others to another height to the northward, to see if they could discover any human habitation. In the meanwhile the camp would be shifted to a valley which seemed to be about half a league distant, where they could glimpse a large stream of water, and there they would await these explorers.

[19 April] In the early morning the appointed scouts set out in both directions, and when the sun was high the camp was removed to the place which had been decided on the night before. At ten o'clock the four men who had gone south returned without news of any habitation, and at eleven came the others (who were António Godinho, Gonçalo Mendes de Vasconcellos, Simão Mendes, and António Moniz) singing. When they reached the Captain-major they said that from the height whither he had sent them they had seen people, and many cattle grazing, in a valley which was not very far off.

They all rejoiced at these desired tidings, and when the heat of the day was past they began their journey up the bank of the stream, seeking a ford, which they found, and crossed over to the other side with the water up to their knees. Then they climbed a hill (on the slopes of which they killed a hare), resting three times on the way up, and from the top they saw the people and cattle which had been seen by the four scouts; and who, as it was now late, were gradually moving towards their village. It seemed advisable to Nuno Velho Pereira to send some men there, and he selected for this purpose the master with António Godinho and an interpreter, accompanied by three soldiers, who were Gonçalo Mendes, António Monteiro, and Simão Mendes.

These men set out forthwith, and the rest of the party, keeping under cover of some hillocks, went and encamped close to some rocks in a valley, that they might not be discovered by the Kaffirs and frighten them by their numbers. The master and his companions, after they had walked about a league and a half, it being already night, came to a hut, and standing at some distance from it, the interpreter called out and asked leave to approach. A Negro, who was inside with his wife and children at the fire, put it out, so that they might not be discovered if the caller was an enemy, and then, coming out, asked who was there, for he knew it was not a native of that region, by the different pronunciation of the words.

The interpreter replied that they were some men he would like to see and talk with. But the Kaffir, not trusting what he said, told him to approach alone and leave the others where they were. He did so, and when the two Negroes had conversed, and he in the hut learnt from the other that his companions came in peace, he said they could come. The interpreter called them, and they were kindly received by the Kaffir and his wife, being welcomed with milk and to the fire which was relit. The master gave the hostess a crystal rosary, which she thanked him for, and she was astonished to see that our people resembled the Negroes in everything save only in colour.

The husband for a piece of copper sold them a lamb, which they at once killed and roasted. As they were beginning to eat (with no lack of appetite), there came three Negroes, and then six more, and though they sat down and reassured our people, the supper did not taste so good as it would have done without them. Having finished it hastily and in dread, they took leave of the Kaffirs, saying that they wished to return to their captain and give him news of them, which they did on reaching the camp at the following dawn.

[20 April] All rejoiced at what had occurred, and still more at the certainty of there being a village, to profit from which they at once set out on the way thither, which was very good. At nine o'clock they halted at the foot of a hill, where there were three Kaffir huts close to a stream. These Kaffirs immediately brought milk, which they bartered for the usual little nails.

The chief of that region, named Inhancunha,[1] hearing that our people had arrived there, came to visit the Captain-major, by whom he was received and entertained on a carpet. He gave him a crystal rosary, a piece of coral, and the brass tip of a sunshade, with which the Negro was greatly delighted. He promised the guides which Nuno Velho asked him for and presented him with a cow, which with six others that were secured by barter that morning, were killed and divided among them all, as provision for two days. In the afternoon ten more were obtained in exchange for pieces of copper. At sunset Inhancunha took leave of Nuno Velho and went to wait for him in his village, which was on the top of the hill.

[21 April] The next day they did not continue their journey, so that the people might rest from their past toil; but they bartered for four more cows and much milk and millet. And as the neighbouring villages heard that our people had not yet gone, many

---

[1] Nyankunya, according to H. A. Junod ('Condition of the natives', 13), who adds that this tribe can no longer be identified, having probably disappeared in the Zulu raids of Chaka which devastated Natal and Zululand from 1812 to 1820.

Negroes and Negresses came to see them, and ten of the slaves remained with them, fearing to face another uninhabited region like the one they had just passed through.

Nuno Velho, knowing how important it was to keep what copper, iron, and cloth there was in the camp for the bartering of provisions and the payment of guides, and that it was necessary to keep some to present to the kings and chiefs of the country through which they passed, hearing that some men were buying provisions without order of the purveyor and treasurer, which altered the price thereof and diminished the articles needed for trading, ordered an inventory to be made of all the copper, iron, and cloth which they had. He compelled them all to declare on oath what they had, and to deliver it to the said officials, so that the afore-mentioned drawbacks could be avoided, everything might be equally divided, and by economizing in their use they might not be wanting when they were most needed.

[22 April] The next day after sunrise they climbed the hill, on top of which the Inkosi Inhancunha was waiting for them. From among the Kaffirs he had with him, he gave two to the Captain-major to act as guides, and three to herd and domesticate fourteen cows which our people were taking along. It was two o'clock when they descended the hill and reached a level country covered with great trees that bore a yellow fruit, about the size of white plums and rather bitter in taste. Of these they ate and carried away many, all off the same tree, and it was so laden with fruit that even then it looked as though none had been gathered. Having passed these trees and gone a little further, it was time to halt, so they let the cattle loose in a field full of long grass; and the people en-camped under the trees which surrounded it, water not being wanting from a stream which ran by them.

[23 April] The camp was moved from here next day, the 23rd April, the cattle being driven in front. They passed through many villages, whose inhabitants bartered milk and millet for a few small nails and crystal beads. They climbed some other hills, which tired our people very much, and at eleven o'clock they crossed a river with the water up to their thighs, and took their siesta on the other bank. The heat being somewhat abated, they resumed their journey over land which was not very level but was thickly populated, the soil being much richer and more fertile than that of the country they had previously traversed. The Negroes call it Ospidainhama,[1] and its woods contain many sweet smelling pinks, both pink and red, exactly resembling those of Portugal, except in the stalks, which were longer. At sunset they encamped near a small village where they had firewood and water, which latter was not lacking from the sky, for during the night there was a severe thunderstorm from the west, with heavy rain.

[24 April] Opposite this encampment there was a high hill, which they climbed early the following morning, and from which they descended into a plain dotted with villages. Over this they journeyed until eleven o'clock, when they reached a stream flowing among rocks containing caves, in the shade of which our people passed the heat of the day. Here many Negroes with their women and children came to see them from the villages, and entertained them with singing and dancing. They were nearly all sallow black, handsome and healthy looking, their dress being the same as that of the Tizombe Kaffirs, but they do not place the hand on the beard so often as those do. In exchange for a few small nails they gave a quantity of milk and millet cakes, which they call *sincoá*.[2] At sundown our people left this stream, and marching over the same plain they reached another, near which they encamped that night under some large trees without fruit. They now had twenty-two cows with them.

[25 April] They left this stream next day and began to climb a mountain, which was the first of this journey, and on the summit, which they reached at nine o'clock, there was a village. From here they descended to a plain, on which they marched along past many huts, until they reached a great stream containing

[1] Can this be the Umzikaba River? Theal does not attempt to identify this river but states that the castaways were now travelling 'over the high ground behind the present [1902] mission-station of Palmerton' in Pondoland. If this is correct, they must have been somewhere near that river. H. A. Junod, loc. cit., suggests that this may have been the name of a chief, Usipidanyama.

[2] 'For the millet cakes, probably on account of their being so different from European bread, they used the native term *isinkwa*, which the journalist wrote *sincoa*' (Theal, *Beginning*, 299).

numerous hippopotami. This river, according to what the Negroes affirmed, was the same that they had left in the morning, which wound twisting and turning through that region. Our people encamped close to it, and they bartered from the Negroes six cows for one large gimlet and some pieces of copper which weighed about a pound.

One of these Kaffirs talked apart with the interpreter, and the pilot seeing this, asked the latter what they were talking about. He replied that the Negro had told him not to follow the path they were then pursuing, since it was very old and fallen into disuse, and ran for a long way through many uninhabited mountains. He said that it would be better to take another way which ran along a mountain-range close by, and which was not so rugged and desolate as the one they were now on. The pilot thought that the path pointed out by the Negro was a good one, and more in the direction of his course, and he said as much to Nuno Velho, reporting to him all that had passed between the Negroes.

The Captain-major left the choice of the path to the pilot, and though they asked the Kaffirs for guides along it, promising liberal reward and payment, none would undertake the task, fearing the barren region which lay ahead. To prepare for the start of the journey next day, therefore, that night they killed two cows, which were divided among them all. The twenty-six which were left were now so tame that any Portuguese could tend them.

[26 April] At daybreak they began their journey towards the mountain (which the Negroes call Moxangala)[1] and in order to skirt it they went eastwards. It is very fertile and cool, and fresh water is so abundant that in the two days during which our people journeyed along it they crossed twenty-three streams, three of which were very large. They crossed several on this day before four o'clock in the afternoon, when they reached the foot of a height where they encamped. Four Negroes, who had come in the morning to see our people as something marvellous, accompanied them to this place. The most important of them, who was called Catine, presented a skin full of milk to the Captain-major, who paid him

[1] Theal, op. et loc. cit., identifies this with the Ingele mountain, on the borders of Pondoland and Griqualand East. Cf. also H. A. Junod, loc. cit.

for it with a chessman tied to a thread of white silk, which he hung round his neck.

These Kaffirs assured them that they were on the right road, and on Nuno Velho asking them to guide him, they promised to do so if the pay was equal to the hardship of traversing such uninhabited regions. They did not disagree about this, for they were shown a brass candlestick and declared themselves satisfied. They remained with our people that night, and sent two of their number to fetch some cows to barter on the next day.

[27 April] Marching then along this mountain side, they observed one of the Negroes who went for the cows, on a height without them, whereupon Catine fled away. Our people laid hands on the other, who was called Noribe, and he, finding himself a prisoner, cried out in fear and terror to the others, who consoled him from afar. He was quieted, however, by promises and gifts, one of these being the candlestick promised to his companion, and he finally consented to guide them thus bound. Our people followed him along the mountain side, and after passing the heat of the day in the shade of some rocks, among which ran a stream, they resumed their journey in the afternoon towards the north-east. At sunset they passed the end of the mountain, and reached a river which flowed very swiftly through a large wood. They encamped beside it and furnished themselves with the necessary provisions for two days.

[28 April] They crossed the river on some large stones which were in it, and journeying over level ground, they came to another mountain-range[1] which ran from the east to join that of Moxangala[2] which they had just passed. Between the two was a valley, which led directly north-east. Our people travelled the whole length of the valley, and then climbed the other range, on the summit of which the Negro guide escaped from the turban by which Nuno Velho led him tied, by clearing a little brook with a great bound and running away very swiftly.

Our people were thus left without a guide, and after descending

---

[1] 'Outra serra.' Perhaps 'range of hills' would be a better translation, but 'serra' is a very vague term, ranging from low hills to high mountains.

[2] Ingele mountain (?) Cf. penultimate note.

from where they were and climbing another hill, they lost the track they were following, as this hill was all of stone. From it they descried a plain with abundant pasture, and at the end thereof were two large hills between the two mountain ranges. As these hills were to the north-east, and as it seemed that the best way would pass between them, the pilot ordered that they should march straight towards them. This they did, and on the other side of the hills they found a stream flowing by a large rock, where they encamped without firewood, which was a great pity as there was a thunderstorm with rain that night.

[29 April] At dawn they crossed the stream by means of some boulders in it, the water reaching to their knees. The ground on the other side was level, and on both sides were high hills covered with large green trees. The said stream wound sinuously through all this district, so that our people crossed it five times this day. At eleven o'clock they rested from the heat in the shadow of some high rocks, and when it was cooler they continued on their journey. They finally encamped on a rocky place where there were some trees, for want of a better shelter, where they passed that night with much wind and rain.

[30 April] On the last day of April in the morning they climbed a hill which was near the camp, and on its summit followed level ground, after which they crossed a large stream flowing between two hills. Our people climbed one of them in the hope of discovering some human habitation, but they were very far from any such. Disappointed at not seeing one, they descended again by a path which they saw led down to a valley, where they encamped at three o'clock, because there was firewood and water.

[1 May] The next day, the 1st May, they entered a wood which was near the camp, so high, thick, and close overhead that though the day was very windy and rainy, as the night had been, within it they were as sheltered as if they had been in houses, and could not feel anything. They encamped by a stream which ran through it, resolved to go no farther that day, as the wind, rain, and cold forbade it.

At midday, however, there was an opportunity of taking the height of the sun, and the pilot found that they were in latitude

29° 53′ S. This news rejoiced Nuno Velho Pereira and the rest of the company, and alleviated their present hardships. The pilot also affirmed that they had passed the rugged and rocky part of the country, and that therefore the weak should feel encouraged to push on so as to reach the river of Lourenço Marques by the end of June, which was the time when the trading vessel was due to leave for Mozambique. Rodrigo Migueis based this opinion (and rightly so) on their present latitude being that of the end of the land of Natal, which is higher than that of any other part of the coast, and in consequence there is in this region intense cold at sea and still more violent thunderstorms.[1]

[2 May] These ceased on the morning of the next day, when the weather cleared, so they struck camp and left the wood, marching along a small ridge, from which they descended to level ground. Thence they reached some hillocks, and after passing these, our people rested on top of a hill, where they found some water, as well as in the valleys. Here they left a dying Portuguese named Alvaro da Ponte, who was very ill, and had been carried for the last three or four days on the shoulders of his companions, with great charity; but the recent cold spell reduced him to the last extremity, and Friar Pedro left him already speechless. There likewise remained here two male slaves, and a female slave of Dona Isabel, who were in the same condition.

With this comrade the less, our people resumed their journey after the heat of the day, through a very long valley where they found a large stream, near which they encamped, it being almost night. From this place the pilot, seeing that to the north and north-east lay great and high mountain-ranges covered with snow,[2] resolved to lead them ENE, which he did on the next day's march.

[3 May] This proved very laborious, as they had to climb first many hillocks and then a hill. Two men went to the top of this last, to see if they could see any habitation, but returned without

---

[1] 'This part of the country, being too cold in the winter season to be pleasant for the Bantu, they found uninhabited' (Theal, *Beginning*, 299).

[2] The Drakensberg, but 'north-east' should perhaps read 'north-west'. They were presumably the first Europeans to set eyes on this range.

tidings of any, although they said that they had seen four columns of smoke to the ENE. The people were somewhat cheered by this, thinking that these were signs of habitation in the direction in which they were journeying; but they could only have been caused by hunters, for the smoke from these Negro villages is so slight that it can hardly be seen in the hut where a fire is lit. Therefore keeping the same direction they encamped on low ground near a stream, where there was no lack of firewood, after having passed between two hills and descended into the valley through which it flowed.

[4 May] Next day, in a heavy fall of dew, they climbed a small hill, covered with such thick high grass that our people could not see each other, and were obliged to part their way through it. From this hill, after descending to the level ground, they came to the largest and deepest river which they had hitherto encountered, and it ran from north to south.[1] The pilot and a companion went down-stream along the bank, seeking for a ford, while two others went up-stream for the same purpose. But they could find no better place for crossing than that where the column had halted, for there was an islet in mid-stream just there, and the water, being divided into two channels, ran less strongly and deeply. They all therefore resolved to ford it at that place.

Two men first crossed over with pikes in their hands, the water coming up to their chests, and they then returned to where their companions were waiting, in order to show them the way. It was then arranged that the strongest should enter the water and extend pikes from one to the other, by which the weak and the women could cross as if holding on to a balustrade. The sick were very charitably carried across on the shoulders of their companions and in the hammocks of Dona Isabel, who with her daughter entered the river and crossed holding to the arms of Francisco da Silva and João de Valadares, and the Captain-major crossed over in the same way.

This passage occupied the whole day, and having reached the other bank (where the cattle were already, having crossed the river very easily) they made great fires, at which they warmed and dried

[1] The upper reaches of the Umzimvubu?

themselves. Pitching their tents under some great trees, they took shelter for that night, after having gathered in the bush during the afternoon many jujubes and myrtle-berries.

[5 May] There was a hill opposite the encampment, which they climbed when it was morning, and having passed this and others, they took their siesta in the shade of some trees, refreshing themselves with water-melons which they found there, which seemed to be all the more delicious with the sight of three Negroes whom our people perceived upon a height. Nuno Velho Pereira sent one of his slaves (who had by now learnt the language) to contact them; and he brought them back and presented them. They saluted by saying, 'Alala, Alala,'[1] a different salutation from that used by those met previously.

They gave the wished-for information of a village, saying that it was close by, and one of them went to fetch eight other companions whom he had left behind the hill. They all returned, and journeying in our people's company (the heat of the day being past), asked them, since it was late and they could not reach the village that night, if they would halt at their huts? This seemed good to the Captain-major, and thus the Negroes led them to a deep valley, covered with thorny bush; and as it did not look as if the place could be inhabited except by wild beasts, our people were upon their guard and prepared their arms, fearing some treachery there. Nevertheless they followed the Kaffirs, and between some high sharp rocks, past which a stream flowed, they saw six huts in which these savages lived with their wives. They encamped close to these, keeping their usual watch.

[6 May] The Negroes, seeing that they could not carry out their purpose, which was to steal some of the cattle and whatever else they could, (robbery and hunting being their livelihood in that wilderness), and fearing they might be discovered and punished, fled during that night with their wives, taking with them a little millet which was still in the ear, and leaving nothing in their huts but traps and snares for birds. It being broad daylight when it was discovered that they were missing (after seeking them that they

[1] 'The gleeful exclamation *Halala! Halala!* they mistook for a form of greeting' (Theal, *Beginning*, 299).

might show the way), Nuno Velho ordered the pilot to guide them, as he always did on such occasions.

He directed them to take their course to the east, and having travelled a long way without seeing any village, by order of the Captain-major some men went to two heights which lay to the east and north-east of the place where they were, but none of them could discover what they so ardently desired. The impatient among them now became insubordinate, denouncing this journey into the uninhabited interior, and clamouring to be led and guided to the sea. The pilot and the master pointed out that their actual eastward course was the nearest way to the sea, which being confirmed by Nuno Velho, appeased them. Striking the camp, and still keeping to the east, they debouched on to a regular path, along which they journeyed leisurely until night, when they encamped on a bank of a stream, where there was much high grass and very little firewood.

[7 May] The contrary was the case at their next halting-place, which was under a grove of great trees, without water, having journeyed all the morning along a good and continuous path, which they lost in the afternoon in a valley; but they found another a little before they encamped on a height, after having climbed others and seen two Negroes in the distance while they were resting at midday, who fled when they observed our people.

[8 May] This last stage brought them to the end of the uninhabited region, which they had traversed in fourteen days; and to shorten the journey for whoever subsequently passes this way through Kaffraria, they should travel ENE when they find themselves in latitude 30°, for in this direction they will have less of the wilderness to cross and will sooner reach the inhabited country. Our people entered this on the 8th May, and found it so abounding in provisions that they forgot the want they had felt of them in the wilderness—although they had never lacked cows to eat, and of the twenty-seven with which they entered the waste land they reached this place with twelve remaining.

At daybreak they continued their journey, in which they met four Negroes who with many others had seen our people long before and were watching them, not daring to approach for fear of the injury they might receive from such a numerous company. Therefore Nuno Velho sent António Godinho and António the interpreter to meet these four who showed themselves; and for some pieces of copper which were given to them, three remained where they were, while the other one went to fetch about fifty more who were hidden behind a hill. Then they all came to the camp, and the principal men among them conversing with Nuno Velho gave him great news of the fertility and population of that region.

When debating about the bartering of provisions where the path divided into two, leading to two villages, an argument arose among the Kaffirs as to which of them our people should visit first. Nuno Velho appeased them by giving to the leader of the four who were first met a *tambaqua*[1] ring which he took from the finger of Gonçalo Mendes de Vasconcellos, and by promising that he would buy cows from them all, beginning with those who were nearest, who were the fifty who had come at the call of one of the first four. Dancing and singing, they all guided our people in the same ENE direction, and with them they reached a valley with many trees and water, where they made their camp, as it was late and the village was about half a league further on.

It did not seem too far for the Negroes to come and see our people, bringing much millet, cakes made of the flour of a grain about the size and colour of our millet, which they call *ameixoeira*, beans, a vegetable called *Jugo*[2] which is of the size of small beans, as also milk and butter, all of which they exchanged for a few tacks and pieces of nails. Among these savages were some youths dressed in reed mats, which is the attire of young nobles before they bear arms or copulate with women, which activities they do not indulge in until the age of twenty-two and upwards. They are all healthy-looking, blacker than those met previously, more truthful, and they are not accompanied by dogs like the others were.

At two o'clock in the morning a Negro called Inhanze, son of

[1] An alloy of copper and zinc, derived from the Malay *tambága*, according to Dalgado, *Glossário Luso-Asiático*, II, 346.

[2] As noted previously (p. 82), *ameixoeira* is either the sorghum or else the small grey kaffir corn. H. A. Junod ('Condition of the natives', 20) says the *jugo* 'is a kind of pea', but does not carry the identification any further, and neither can I.

the king of that country,[1] came to visit the Captain-major on be-half of his father. He brought a cow as a present, with a very fairly-worded message, saying that the king being in one of his villages at a little distance from the camp had heard of his arrival, at which he was greatly pleased, and as it was late and time that he should rest from the toil of his journey, he did not come to visit him then, but would do so in the morning. Nuno Velho replied with words of thanks, and gave him a piece of copper the size of a hand and a large nail, with which Inhanze withdrew well satisfied.

[9–10 May] It seemed to Nuno Velho that to enable our people to recover from the fatigue of the journey and gain fresh strength for the next stage, as also to buy many cows, they would be well advised to rest for two days in the valley in which they were en-camped. On learning this, the Negroes of the vicinity brought for bartering a grain like canary-seed, which they call *Nechinim*[2] (and of which they make flour), sesame, millet, milk, butter, hens, and sheep—and all in such quantities that no cows were killed, and there was more than enough left over for the slaves, there being no one in the camp who would buy anything more. In these two days they also bartered for copper of small value twenty-four cows, which, with the twelve that were left to our people after crossing the wilderness, made thirty-six in all.

At eleven o'clock came the king of the country, called Mabom-borucassobelo,[3] accompanied by some fifty Negroes armed with assegais, and he also brought his mother. The Captain-major received them with due courtesy, all three seating themselves upon a carpet. The Kaffirs were astonished at the appearance of our people, and the king wished to hear the details of their shipwreck and peregrination, which were related by Nuno Velho Pereira,

[1] This implies that 'Inhanze', like 'Inhacosa' (p. 132 above), is a corruption of Nyana wenkosi', son of the chief.

[2] 'No doubt this is the actual Kaffir corn or millet' (H. A. Junod, loc. cit.). The origin of this word, elsewhere written *nachenim*, *nachami*, etc., which Junod could not trace but suspected was Indian, is derived by Dalgado, *Glossário Luso-Asiático*, II, 87, from the Konkani *nātçnó*.

[3] H. A. Junod ('Condition of the natives', 13) reproduces this name without comment, so presumably this was another clan which disappeared in Chaka's invasions of 1812–20.

being heard by the Negro and his followers with great amazement.

Nuno Velho Pereira then added that he had heard of this king's fame long before he had reached his land, which had induced him to travel this way in order to see him. The savage was very flattered at this, and his attendants saying that it would be fitting for our people to be well entertained and guided by him, since they had come from so great a distance to see him, he assented, and promised to provide guides and everything else that his villages afforded. Nuno Velho thanked him, placing a branch of coral tied to a silk string round his neck, giving him also the lid of a cauldron, and his mother some green speckled crystal beads.[1] As it was dinner time, they ate the meal with him, and at three o'clock they went away with all their company. Likewise, the pilot made this halt memorable by measuring the altitude of the pole, and found the latitude to be 29° 45'. Their having travelled ENE and East was the reason for the very little difference between this and his last observation.

[11 May] Four slaves (two Kaffirs, one Japanese, and a Javanese) remained in this valley, which our people named the Vale of Mercy, on account of the great mercy God Our Lord vouchsafed them by bringing them to the most fertile and abundant region of Kaffraria, after fourteen days in the wilderness. They left it on the 11th May with the guides whom the king gave to Nuno Velho according to his promise. On taking leave of him that morning the Captain-major hung round his neck the cover of a silver flagon tied to a white silk string, while the two Negroes received two pieces of copper and two nails.

The path led to the north-east and up a height which they climbed, going down from it by a stony surface, and in the valley they found three villages. Having passed these, as well as a rivulet and a hill where they bought two cows, when it was getting late they reached another hill which they descended through very thick scrub until they came to a range which ran from the north-

---

[1] 'contas de cristal goarnecidas de verde', literally 'crystal beads decorated [or mounted] in [or with] green'. I have followed Theal's translation, but with a good deal of hesitation. I presume that some form of the 'trade-wind beads' is meant. Cf. above, p. 133, n. 4.

east and joined this hill. Here they were overtaken by the night, which was very dark, and thus they did not reach the bottom where there was water, but encamped without it.

[12 May] The next day at ten o'clock they completed their descent of the hill. There was in the valley a good path to the north, along which our people went about half a league, shaded by trees bearing a very bitter fruit resembling *ferrobas*,[1] until they reached a stream which they forded with the water up to their thighs. This stream was the limit of the land of the Inkosi Mabomborucassobelo, and therefore, when they had crossed it, one of the guides went to summon the lord of the land in which they were, whose name was Mocongolo.[2] He came at once, bringing a cow for the Captain-major, showing himself very pleased to see him, and promising that he would furnish the provisions and guides which the two Negroes who accompanied our people asked from him in the name of their king.

This place being the end of their journey, our old guides departed, with two more pieces of copper and two crystal rosaries decorated in green,[3] with which they thought themselves so well paid that the new Negroes considered this excessive prodigality, and many of them immediately offered themselves as guides, coveting a like reward. When the two Negroes had gone, and Mocongolo had taken leave of Nuno Velho to await him in his village, leaving some Kaffirs to guide him thither, the column moved on and encamped on the bank of the most beautiful and freshest river which they had yet seen in all their journey. It flowed from west to east, through a valley between high rocks with large and spreading trees of different colours.

[13 May] Invited by the coolness of this stream our people remained there for a day, and on account of its beauty they named it the River of Beautiful Flowers. The Negroes call it Mutangalo.[4]

[14 May] They left it regretfully on the 14th May, with two

[1] Presumably *Alfarroba* (*Cerratonia Siliqua* Lin.), carob, St John's Bread, an edible fruit of the Algarve.
[2] Umkongelo, according to H. A. Junod, loc. cit., who assumes that this clan or tribe was among those destroyed or amalgamated in Chaka's razzias of 1812-20.
[3] Or 'mounted in green' (?). Cf. above, p. 152, n. 1.
[4] The actual Umzimkulu, according to Theal (*Beginning*, 299).

Negroes supplied by the Inkosi, who was not displeased with what Nuno Velho gave him. When they halted at eleven o'clock to rest from the heat under some trees, the wives of their guides came with two gourds of excellent butter, which they bartered for copper worth six *reis*. But Nuno Velho wished to reward them for the good will they had shown in bringing it, and gave them two half rosaries of crystal, with which they were extremely delighted and their husbands correspondingly grateful.

As there was no water in that place, and our people were in need of it, one of the Negroes went to fetch some from a spring which was at a little distance from the camp. This was the first spring-water which they had seen on their journey, having hitherto found excellent water only in the streams which they had passed. The midday heat being ended, which could be felt (although it was the winter-time) when the sun was not covered with clouds, our people journeyed by a good track, where three Negroes came to them with a gourd of very tasty white honeycomb, which the Captain-major bought and divided among them all as a novelty. A little before nightfall they encamped in a fresh valley which extended between great rocks. In it there were some fifteen villages, from which the Negroes came with many provisions, which they exchanged for the usual money in kind.

[15 May] Our people went round one of these rocks, which faced south-east, and having passed a stream that ran by it, they resumed their journey north-eastwards until ten o'clock, when they rested. There came here more than 150[1] Negroes and Negresses with provisions, of which they bartered six cows for the equivalent of three testoons, many cakes of millet, milk, butter, and honey. These Kaffirs were accompanied by their Inkosi named Gogambampolo,[2] who presented a cow to the Captain-major, as did also one of his sons who came with him, in return for which they received two pieces of copper and two large nails. Upon this they took their leave, and our people journeyed on over

[1] '550' by a misprint in the *HTM*, which accordingly led Theal astray in his translation.
[2] Unidentified.

a level plain covered with high grass, where they remained near a stream that night.

[16 May] In the morning of the next day, continuing their journey over the same plain, at ten o'clock they came to a small river, where there were about thirty hamlets on both sides. Many Negroes came out from them, rejoicing and singing at the sight of the Portuguese; and with great show of affection, for which they were well paid, they helped them to pass the river. The villages on the other bank were subject to another chief, who came at once to visit Nuno Velho, and presented him with a cow. In return he received a piece of coral, two bits of copper, and some crystal beads. Upon this he gave his people leave to bring what they had for sale (the Negroes not being in the habit of doing so without permission), but they delayed, and our people made such haste that they left this place without bartering anything. They encamped in another place where they found water, killing what cows were required for food, as they always did whenever it was necessary.

[17 May] As long as this good path lasted, our people did not stop, and thus they had journeyed two leagues by eleven o'clock. While they were resting then, they saw five Negroes on a hill, and one of the guides went to them, reassured them, and induced them to call their Inkosi who was hiding behind the hill with more than a hundred Kaffirs. The Negro came, accompanied by his people, all armed with assegais, and greeting Nuno Velho with his 'Alala! Alala!'[1] he bade him welcome to his land, in which, he said, he would be well entertained and shown the way.

As they wished to continue the journey, the Captain-major led the Inkosi by the hand, and his Negroes going ahead singing, they guided our people to a stream, which they did not cross, both because it was late and because the path ended on that bank. On the other bank was a green mountain range, and villages on both banks whence people came to barter quantities of provisions. Nuno Velho gave the Negro the usual treasures, which were a branch of coral, some beads, and two pieces of copper, in return for a cow which he presented to him. On being asked for two of

[1] Cf. above, p. 148, n. 1.

his men as guides, he gave them at once. One of these men affirmed that he had already been to the land of the Inhaca where he had seen Portuguese and the *pangaio*.[1]

Although this news was false, our people greatly rejoiced on hearing it, thinking that they were now in a region where they were known, and that the river of Lourenço Marques could not be very far away, since this Negro had been there, and it is a natural custom of the Kaffirs not to travel far from their villages. But they were mistaken, for they were still about a hundred leagues away, and this Negro had never been there.[2] However, it gave them new heart, and encouraged them to face the rest of the journey. They passed that night with more than the usual contentment in their camp, which they made by the said stream.

[18 May] Here they waited until nine o'clock next day for the Inkosi, who on his arrival arranged with Nuno Velho that the guides should be given three pieces of copper of the size of six fingers when they returned. The father of one of them also came and asked for something, saying that otherwise he would not let his son leave. Nuno Velho ordered a piece of copper and a small nail to be given him, upon which the Negro was willing to let his son go. This having been arranged, they struck their camp and set out, following a good and very straight path, crossed by a stream which our people forded, and then climbed a hill, where they rested during the heat of the day. Here there came many Negroes and Negresses from some villages on the skirts of the hill, bringing milk, butter, and millet-cakes; and the siesta being over they resumed their journey. An hour before sunset they halted under some large jujube trees laden with fruit, with which they refreshed themselves that evening, water not being wanting from a stream, in which there were many wild ducks.

[19 May] The cold and dew were so great that night that our people set out the next morning at eight o'clock. They crossed a large stream by means of stones, with the water up to their knees,

---

[1] Theal makes one of his few serious slips here, mistranslating *vira* 'had seen', as *viera*, 'had come'. For *pangaio* see above, p. 69, n. 3.

[2] This seems a completely gratuitous supposition, and probably did the Negro an injustice.

and following a good path, took their siesta near another stream, where they were surrounded by many villages, from which the Negroes came to barter millet-cakes and milk. They encamped that evening in a place where was an abundance of water and firewood; and when they were settled about a hundred and twenty Negroes came down a hill, accompanying one of great dignity, who the guides said was their king. Nuno Velho therefore received him as such upon a carpet, and told him, through the interpreter, how he had been shipwrecked and had travelled far through those lands, having always been well received by the rulers thereof, so that he hoped as much from him.

The king, who was called Gimbacucubaba,[1] replied that he was likewise a castaway and refugee from his own kingdom, which one of his neighbours had taken from him in warfare, killing many of his people, and forcing him to take refuge in this country which belonged to one of his relatives; and he regretted that he was not in his own kingdom to receive him as the other kings had done. The Captain-major expressed his sorrow for his misfortune, and his desire to help him in the recovery of his kingdom, at which all the Negroes gave a joyful cry. He then asked him about the causes of the war and against whom he had waged it. The king replied that one of the Inhaca's captains had taken his land and killed his people, and that since he was deprived of both, nothing further could be done in this matter.[2]

Nuno Velho promised to use his influence with the Inhaca, to induce him to restore him to his kingdom, out of consideration for the Portuguese, of whom he was a friend; and that his people might see how he would proceed in this business, he bade him send two of them in his company. The Negro accepted the offer, and being poor and in exile presented to Nuno Velho a gourd of milk, for which he gave him some beads and a branch of coral, that he esteemed very highly on their telling him it was good for

[1] Unidentified.

[2] By 'captain' is meant *induna*, commander of a Zulu war-party. Apropos of this, H. A. Junod notes: 'The Delagoa Natives were raiding as far as Zululand and further south in those times, while the reverse took place in the 19th century, after the rise of Chaka' ('Condition of the natives', 17).

the heart and the eyes. When it was nightfall he withdrew, and our people retired to their tents.

[20 May] They struck camp when it was daylight, and after marching a little distance they met the king Gimbacucubaba, who was waiting for them at the foot of a tree with three of his wives and many Negroes. The Captain-major sat down with him, and again asked him for the men, so that when he had obtained from the Inhaca the restoration of his kingdom (as he confidently hoped to do) they could bring him the news. The king thanked him for his good will, and taking aside two Negroes whom he had chosen for the journey, he conversed with them as if instructing them what they were to do. When it was dinner time he took leave of Nuno Velho, carrying a piece of *canequim*[1] that was given him, of which he made four cloths, that he and his wives put on as a new and strange gala costume, and as such they esteemed it.

While our people were halted here, there came several sick and crippled Kaffirs who asked the Captain-major to cure them, offering him sheep and goats which they brought. Desiring to cure their souls, even if he could do nothing for their bodily ills and infirmities, he therefore told them that only one God who was in heaven (pointing thither with his hand) had power to bestow health, as He alone gave life and withdrew it. And with the sign of the Holy Cross (a powerful means of working wonders greater than the cure of these heathen) he dismissed them, not taking any of their presents.

When the heat of the day was over, our people went on their way, passing through many villages, in which they were well received and entertained with songs. In one of these they saw many cattle coming out of a pen, among them two very large oxen, of which the first had three horns branching out of one about a span from the head, where all three curved downwards equally, one remaining in the middle; while the other ox had four horns, two

---

[1] 'A cheap coarse calico, dyed blue or black. . . . Chiefly woven at Broach and Navsari in Western India, and saleable in all the main Asian markets' (J. Irwin, in *Journal of Indian Textile History*, I (1955), 26). Cf. also Dalgado, *Glossário Luso-Asiático*, I, 202–3.

ordinary, and two under these which twisted round the ears. At sunset they encamped along a stream, having passed seven others in that afternoon's march.

[21, 22, 23 May] The nights in this country are very cold, and seemed still more so to our people for want of firewood. Therefore as soon as it was morning, in order to warm themselves by exercise they began to march through uninhabited country, as was likewise that which they traversed during the two following days. It was, however, a land of good pastures and covered with high trees, and so temperate that skirting a hill they passed many streams, and halted near one which twisted and turned through a wide plain. Here our people found partridges, but saw no more lizards, snakes, and beetles, as they had seen in the country previously passed through. On the 22nd they came to a mountain-range, and in order to cross it more easily the Negroes led them to the north-west. Then returning on the 23rd to the north-east, now climbing hills, now travelling along valleys and crossing streams, they encamped that night beside a brook with their cattle, of which they killed what was necessary for their provision, finding that they had thirty-nine cows at their halting-place.

[24 May] It rained in the morning of the next day, and while the rain thus prevented them from continuing their journey, Nuno Velho sent one André Martins of Alcochete[1] with an interpreter and one of the guides, to ask the lord of the country which they were entering for permission to pass through it. At ten o'clock they broke up their camp, and marching along the foot of a hill, under thorny trees, for nearly a league, they came to two Negro huts, near which they encamped again. Here they were joined by André Martins with the Inkosi, whom Nuno Velho received as he did the others, and pleased him by giving him some crystal beads, in return for which he promised guides and everything else that his country contained.

[25 May] But the next day when our people reached his villages (which were seven in number) where they encamped, he would give them nothing but milk, butter, and millet-cakes, not allowing cows to be bartered, because he was at war with one of his

---

[1] A small town on the south bank of the Tagus, just above Lisbon.

neighbours, and he did not wish his followers to sell provisions which he might need later. But coveting a porcelain bottle of the Captain-major's which he saw, he gave him a large ox in exchange for it, and with great delight seeing it shine and that the glaze would not rub off, he put it to his eyes and afterwards to those of his people, and to any other parts of the body in which they felt a pain, in the belief that it gave health. And when it was known in the villages that their Inkosi, called Uquine Inhana,[1] had this bottle, they all came to see it, performing the same ceremonies and superstitions.

[26 May] This crowd of Negroes was necessary to help our people on the 26th in crossing a very large river, which without their help would have been very difficult and dangerous, for it was very rapid and the water reached to their waists. On the other bank the Negro took his leave, giving them two guides, and not allowing those they had with them to go any farther, nor the two Negroes whom the exiled king Gimbacucubaba sent with Nuno Velho Pereira to bring back the answer from the Inhaca—these Kaffirs not allowing the Negroes of other regions to pass through their lands. When they had rested a little, they resumed their journey through an inhabited country, where many people came to see them and sell them provisions. And though it was only two o'clock in the afternoon, our people encamped where there was firewood and water, for the next was a long way ahead.

[27 May] They reached it the following day at ten o'clock, and it proved to be a river running from the north-east and to the south-west.[2] It was the widest and had the strongest current of any that they had yet seen on their journey; and if there were Negroes to help them in fording the last one, they were not wanting here, where they were more needed. For when our people reached the bank, there came the lord of the land, called Mutuadondom-matale,[3] with about thirty others; and one of them (for a nail which Nuno Velho Pereira ordered to be given him) crossed the

---

[1] Ukinyane, according to H. A. Junod ('Condition of the natives', 13).
[2] The Tugela, according to Theal and Junod.
[3] Unidentified by Theal and Junod.

river with the water to his chest, the current running so furiously that our people were doubtful if they could ford it.

The pilot therefore searched in the bush for some wood from which to make rafts, but all they found was so heavy and close-grained that it would not float in the water, but sank like a stone to the bottom. Hereupon Nuno Velho, hearing from the Inkosi that the river level would fall next day, being swollen from a recent thunderstorm, ordered them to encamp in that place, and asked the Negro, who wished to retire, to come back with his followers in the morning and help our people across.

These Negroes are more covetous and self-interested than those met earlier in the journey, and for the same amount of copper—of which they wear bracelets on their arms—for which the others gave three cows they would only give one, it not being so valuable among them, and they also value cloth, which the others did not want. It is therefore best to make great use of copper and iron for bartering provisions as far as this region, and to keep the cloth for bartering from here onwards, for this is what these Negroes demanded in exchange for cows.

Nuno Velho, seeing signs of covetousness in them, that it might not lead them into some excess ordered that the cows which had to be killed for the camp's provision should be shot with a match-lock as was usual in such cases, so that they should be frightened and intimidated by the noise of the discharge.[1] This had the desired result, for having killed a cow in this manner, the Kaffirs who were present were struck with amazement, and the Inkosi, who had already left, hearing the noise, returned in great haste to see what it was. Seeing his followers overcome with surprise at what to them was a great marvel, which they related to him, he asked Nuno Velho to order another to be killed, which being shot with an arquebus, collapsed immediately.

At this the Negro was no less amazed, and taking the arquebus in his hands he turned it over a thousand times, saying that since it killed cows, it would also kill men. The interpreter assured him that such was the case, and that it would kill anything from an elephant to a little bird, at which he was still more impressed, and

[1] Cf. above, pp. 126–7.

withdrew in great fear to his villages, accompanied by his followers who were equally frightened.

[28 May] The next day dawned so cloudy that our people feared it would rain and swell the river, but as the sun rose higher the clouds vanished, making the day clear and serene, so that they resolved to cross, more especially as from a mark they had placed the evening before they realized that the river level had dropped by a span and a half. The Negro having arrived with his followers, he chose ten of the biggest who began to carry the boys over on their shoulders. Francisco Pereira and Francisco da Silva with some other Negroes took Dona Isabel and her daughter in quilts on their shoulders, and the rest of the party followed them. The cattle crossed with difficulty, for not keeping their footing they were liable to be swept away by the current. But a Kaffir got a cow over by pulling at a cord fastened to its nostrils, which encouraged the others to get across to the other bank. Here they encamped, accounting the fording of this dangerous stream a good day's journey. The Negroes, who were well paid for their trouble, call this river Vchugel.[1]

[29 May] The next morning the Inkosi sent two Negroes as guides, according to his promise, and another to take his pay, which was two pieces of copper, back to him (and this man likewise did not return empty-handed); and as our people were only awaiting this to continue their journey, they set out at once, and with great fatigue, the path being very stony, they skirted a large range which lay to the north. They camped for the night by the bank of a stream at the foot of it, where there was good pasture and trees.

[30–1 May] Following in the same direction next morning, at eleven o'clock they met a Negro whom the Captain-major told to go and fetch his chief. It was not long before he came, with about forty others, all armed with assegais, shields and bucklers, which they make of hides. They were well received by our people, and Nuno Velho leading the chief by the hand while the others went skirmishing in front, they reached their villages, which were on the bank of a stream. Here they pitched their camp, but nothing

[1] The Tugela?

was brought for barter except a cow belonging to the local chieftain, because provisions were scarce that year owing to want of
rain. The cow therefore cost dear, as they gave for it a piece of a
broken astrolabe, two handles of a cauldron, and six pieces of
copper. Nor could the land be very fertile, for it was full of rugged
hills, great crags, and black-coloured rocks, and with only a few
thorny trees. The country which they traversed on the last day of
May was of the same kind, and our people encamped when they
found a suitable spot.

[1 June] There were two grummets in the camp suffering from
a bloody flux,[1] caused by drinking a lot of milk, and being unable
to keep up with their companions they remained in the camping-
place on the 1st June, confessed by Friar Pedro and entrusted to a
Negro, who in return for four pieces of copper promised to feed
them for the days they might live, which, judging from their weakness, would be very few.

The terrain being now better and the path less stony, our people
halted during the heat of the day near some villages. And since
the captain Julião de Faria felt ill, they remained there that night,
and bought a cow from the local chieftain in exchange for a
cauldron-handle, three pieces of copper, and a piece of Turkish
silver money of the size of a rial of eight.

[2 June] The captain feeling better next day, they set out with
the guides given them by the Inkosi of those villages, dismissing
those who had come there with our people. They climbed a
mountain-pass, and descended from it to a level and pleasant land,
where they met many Negroes and Negresses, who offered them
ears of millet to lay their hands on those parts of their bodies where
they suffered pain, hoping to be cured by those means. Our people
made the sign of the cross upon them, at which they were very
joyful and pleased, and placing themselves in front of the vanguard they went along singing after their fashion.

They encamped halfway down a hill, as it was getting late, and
just before nightfall two Negroes came to the camp with a cow,
which they presented to Nuno Velho from a widow, who had
been the wife of a chief. Nuno Velho Pereira showed the Kaffirs

---

[1] *Camaras de sangue.* Dysentery.

M

how much he appreciated this attention by sending them back to the widow with three pieces of copper and a bed-curtain of Chinese silk of various colours worked with gold.

[3 June] In the morning they finished descending the hill and crossed a stream which flowed at the foot of it, and with their faces to the north they began to climb another range, on the top of which the path turned to the north-east. Though the ground was stony and hurt the feet of those who were unshod, they walked on until it was very late, when they reached a spot which they chose for their camp, because there was water and firewood.

[4 June] They left here on the 4th, and passed several villages from which the Negroes came out with great rejoicing to embrace and kiss our people, treating them with the utmost familiarity; and taking their rosaries, they hung them round their own necks and kissed the cross upon them, as they saw our people do. And realizing the great esteem in which our people hold this holy sign, they asked if it was lawful for them to copulate with their wives after they had received it.[1] Conversing in this way, they all reached a great river, which the Kaffirs helped our people to cross with much pleasure and goodwill, for which they were paid with some crystal beads and strips of cloth, which they immediately tied round their heads.

It being now the time of the siesta, they halted by a field of millet which was already ripe, but they did not touch it, partly so as not to offend the Negroes, and partly because these latter were very liberal with what they had already harvested, disposing of it for a very low price, and cakes made of it, and butter and milk. After the heat of the day, and after crossing the river (where they found very large and sweet myrtle-berries), they travelled over a marshy plain covered with crops of millet, and irrigated with

---

[1] 'This is quite in keeping with the sexual taboos of Native initiation' (H. A. Junod, 'Condition of the natives', 24). The answer of the Portuguese is not stated, but it may, perhaps, be inferred from the anecdote of a Portuguese *fidalgo* at Damão, related by Dellon nearly a century later: 'One of my neighbours coming to visit me, and seeing a crucifix upon my pillow, said to me, "Monsieur, remember to cover this image, if by chance you take any woman into bed to you, and to take heed of it. . . ." ' (Dellon, *The History of the Inquisition as it is exercised at Goa*, London, 1688, 22–3).

water from a mountain-range opposite. When our people climbed this they debouched on to a large and thickly populated plateau, where the Inkosi of the villages came to meet them with about thirty Negroes.

The Captain-major received him, and after telling him the particulars of the shipwreck and journey, and asking him for what he needed, the Kaffir said that he was very sorry to hear of all these hardships, but that it was good to be alive, and that guides and provisions would not be wanting. In earnest of this promise he sent for two large oxen, four sheep, and a gourd of milk, for which he was paid with three pieces of copper, a cauldron-handle, a branch of coral, and a Turkish silver coin. Furthermore, Nuno Velho gave him another Chinese curtain, like the one he had sent to the widow, with which the Inkosi, who was called Panjana, was extremely pleased, and they all marched along together through his territory.

When the camp was pitched his people brought this Negro a large gourd of their wine called *pombe*, made from millet and full of cockroaches, which he gave Nuno Velho and the other Portuguese who were with him to drink.[1] They all pretended to like it in order to please and flatter him. And as it was now nearly night, he withdrew to his village, promising to return next day with the guides, and our people retired to their tents.

[5 June] The Negro was as good as his word, and detained our people in their camp until dinner time, bartering an ox for three pieces of copper and giving Nuno Velho another, in return for which he presented him with some crystal beads, a bloodstone, and a little balsam which they told him was a good remedy for the asthma from which he suffered.[2] And seeing the pilot with a

[1] 'Evidently the *byala* or *tjwala* of which the Natives are so fond all over South Africa. This [beer] is a food as well as a beverage' (H. A. Junod, 'Condition of the natives', 20).

[2] Oddly enough, the great Portuguese botanist and physician, Garcia d'Orta, does not deal with this in his famous *Coloquios dos simples e drogas e cousas mediçinais da India* (Goa, 1563), but his Spanish contemporary, Dr Nicolas Monardes of Seville, makes the most extravagant claims for the curative properties of balsam in his *Historia Medicinal de las cosas que se traen de nuestras Indias Occidentales que sirven en Medicina* (Seville, 1574), fols. 9–12.

small flask of Ormuz glass, he asked him for it, and gave him a large ox and a fine sheep in exchange. It being now past midday, they struck their camp, and journeyed on over a good and level path, the Inkosi, who would not part from them, being still in their company. Not until after they had encamped at sunset did he take leave of them and of the Captain-major, to whom he sent a calf and a sheep.

[6 June] The Negroes, fearing a tract of uninhabited country which lay ahead, did not come the next day—which was that of Pentecost—to guide our people as the chief had promised. For the same reason, there were some impatient Portuguese, who determined to press forward and separate themselves from the rest of the company. Nuno Velho, hearing of this the night before, and knowing that they would be lost if they carried out their wrong-headed plans, with his customary prudence appeased this disturbance.

Striking their camp early in the morning, they travelled, without guides, over good ground until eleven o'clock, when they halted on the bank of a stream. Here they were visited by many Negroes with their Inkosi, who was called Malangana, and who lived in some villages away from the path. Seeing our people, they came out, bringing a cow which they bartered for one piece of coral and two of copper. Nuno Velho asked the chief for guides, which he refused for the aforesaid reason of the country being uninhabited, but he pointed out the way, showing with his hand the direction in which they must go. The pilot at once took a bearing on this with his compass, and it was to the north-east. After the Negroes had gone, our people travelled in that direction until night, when they encamped in a wood.

[7–8 June] They travelled through the wilderness on the 7th, and at midday on the 8th they came to a richly verdured range of hills, which divided into two spurs, one running north and the other east, a great valley lying between them. At the entrance to this valley our people saw eight Negroes who were busy burning the grass, and an interpreter was sent to summon them. Several of them went to fetch their chief who came with twenty others. They were all bandits who lived in this range upon the proceeds of their robberies, and thus they were all armed with assegais and arrows. They pretended that their village was at a distance, and in order to carry out their purpose they led our people to a deep valley where there was neither firewood nor water.

Nuno Velho was leading one of these Negroes, and seeing that he was restless and looked as if he wanted to separate a cow from the herd, in order to steal it, he told the soldiers to be on their guard. And the pilot, who was in front, noticing the same disposition in those who accompanied him, turned back, and all the rest of the company with him. The Negroes, thinking their evil design was discovered, continued to dissimulate, and one of them, getting among the cows, tried to separate one from the rest; but he was punished for his daring by a blow on the head from the butt-end of a halberd, which felled him to the ground. Seeing this, the others fled at full speed, and this one after them. Our people finished their afternoon march without such bad company, and camped on the hillside when it was almost night, keeping a vigilant watch for fear of the Kaffirs.

[9 June] At daylight they continued their march along the range which ran towards the east, with their faces to the ENE. They were seen from the top by some Negroes of their last encampment, at whose cries many others assembled with assegais, and began to descend a hill towards the column. And lest they should be of the same kind as the robber Negroes and find our people in disorder, the latter halted, and after ranging themselves in battle formation, continued their march. The Negroes paused on seeing our people's resolution, and some of them came forward to a spot whence they could be heard, and asked who they were and what they were doing in their country.

The interpreter gave the usual answer, and being reassured by him and by Nuno Velho, they went and fetched their chief whom the Captain-major entertained, and dismissed with a rosary of crystal beads. These men having gone, when they had marched a little further they met about sixty others, of whom three came to the camp. The oldest of them, after hearing about our people's shipwreck and journey, cried aloud to the rest, 'Come, come and see these men who are children of the sun and go to seek him!'

Upon which all the rest, leaving their arms in charge of a comrade, ran down at full speed to see and welcome our people, with whom they then marched along until the hour of the siesta, which they took in the shade of a wood.

Thither some Negroes brought millet which they bartered for crystal beads and strips of coloured cloths for their heads. Their Inkosi also came to this halting-place, and Nuno Velho not receiving the welcome he expected from him, and detecting in him a desire to attack our people if he found them off their guard, warned the soldiers who accompanied him to prepare their arquebuses, and each to pick out a Negro at whom he would fire. Seeing this intention, the Kaffir dissimulated with his own, and the Captain-major ordered the march to be resumed, and that no notice should be taken of this Negro or of his village, which they passed by shortly afterwards. At sunset they encamped in a convenient spot which contained what they needed; and here they were visited by two Negroes from other villages, who, pleased with two pieces of copper which were given them, promised to return the next day to guide our people.

[10–11 June] They kept their word by appearing in the camp at daybreak, and under their guidance they climbed a range, and although they saw others from the top of it, the Kaffirs led them by paths which made the rough going easier. They encamped for the night at the foot of the last one, which they crossed the next day, going east and ESE. Having passed it, they resumed their course to the ENE, through very thick woods of high and shady trees, and descending a hill they found some Negro huts between great rocks at the bottom, near which they encamped.

[12 June] These Kaffirs were poor and had nothing save a little millet and some milk, which they gave them. Here among these Kaffirs, in a hut built slightly apart from theirs, our people left an old man of seventy-five named Alvaro Gonçalvez, the boatswain's father, who was very ill, and all his comrades were so exhausted that they could no longer carry him on their shoulders as they had done hitherto. His loving son wanted to stay with him, but not being allowed to, he left him copper to buy what he needed, and the names of the most necessary things written on a piece of paper, so that he could ask the Negroes for them. With general tears at such a sad parting, they dragged the son away from his father, who dismissed him with a blessing, and remained, having confessed himself, like a good Christian very resigned to the will of God.

This delayed our people in the camp until midday of the 12th, when the pilot took the sun, and found that they were in latitude 27° 27′. He therefore determined to travel east by north-east, in order to reach the seashore sooner, from which he calculated that he was now forty leagues distant. At two o'clock the chief of the villages came with guides, for whom Nuno Velho gave him four pieces of copper. Following them over good and level ground due eastwards (in which direction, these Negroes said, lay the village where their red beads were sold, which are those that come to the River of Lourenço Marques),[1] at sunset they reached a valley where they encamped.

[13 June] They left it on the 13th, the feast of Saint Anthony,[2] and at ten o'clock they saw many villages, from which numerous Kaffirs came out to see our people, and on reaching them greeted them by saying '*Nanhatá, Nanhatá,*' like those first met with.[3] Among them was their headman, who was living in that village by order of the Inkosi, who was away. He was well received by the Captain-major, and on being asked for some things needed for the journey, the Negro replied that it was six days travelling from there to the sea, and twelve days by another way if they went through the lands of the Inhaca, where they would have to ford a great river with the water up to their chests. This news delighted them all, knowing that they were so near the place where they hoped to find a ship.

During the time of the siesta, a son of the Inkosi came to visit Nuno Velho on behalf of his father; and having done so, returned

---

[1] Presumably the Indian red opaque glass beads which are the most numerous category of the trade-wind beads in East Africa. Cf. above, p. 133, n. 4.

[2] The most popular saint in the Portuguese calendar, where he is usually styled 'of Lisbon', although Italians prefer to designate him as 'of Padua'. Cf. R. Gallop, *Portugal. A book of folk-ways* (Cambridge, 1936), 139–42.

[3] Cf. above, p. 119.

immediately with a silver medal round his neck, which was taken from a goblet. Our people, after they had killed several cows for their ordinary provisions and bartered for millet, milk, butter and sheep, journeyed on with the same headman as guide, until they encamped when it was almost night near a stream, whence the Negro sent word to his Inkosi to come and see Nuno Velho in the morning.

[14 June] His village was a long way off, and thus it was nearly eleven o'clock when he came. Nuno Velho came out to receive him, accompanied by fifteen arquebusiers, while the Inkosi (who was called Gamabela) came with a hundred unarmed Negroes. Taking each other by the hand they sat down on a carpet, and the Captain-major told him how glad he was to see him, and to have reached his land, where he felt sure he would receive the necessary help to enable him to reach his desired destination. Gamabela replied that he did well to rejoice, for he was now near the sea, and to conclude his journey nothing should be wanting which he had or could do.

Then they exchanged presents, the Inkosi giving two cows, and Nuno Velho some mother-of-pearl beads, a piece of silver, seven pieces of copper, and a blood-stone. After this they discussed about guides, and Gamabela selected his headman who came with our people from the village and two other Negroes. All the people were pleased with their good treatment by this Kaffir, and he much more in so doing. He said to Nuno Velho that in return for the good will with which he had given everything he had been asked for, he would like some keepsake of him by which he might always remember him and the Portuguese who accompanied him. Nuno Velho replied that he would do as he asked, and would give him the most precious and valuable jewel in the world; and taking the cross off the rosary which he had round his neck, and removing his hat, he kissed it very devoutly with his eyes raised to heaven. After handing it to the Portuguese near him, who did the same thing, he gave it to the Inkosi, telling him that this was the sacred pledge of friendship which he would leave with him, bidding him show it the same reverence as he had seen our people do. The savage took it and reverently kissed it in the same way, and then put it to his eyes, as did all the other Negroes subsequently.

Nuno Velho, seeing the veneration which they showed to the most holy cross, bade a carpenter make a cross from a tree which stood close by (happily and fortunately grown in that Kaffraria, since from one of its branches was made the symbol of our salvation), which was soon made, eight spans in height. Holding it in his hands, Nuno Velho delivered it to Gamabela, telling him that upon that tree the author of life overcame death with his own death, and thus it was a cure for death, and health for the sick; and by virtue of that sign the great emperors had conquered and the Catholic kings now overcame their enemies; and as so excellent a gift he offered and gave it to him, that he might place it before his hut. And every morning, on coming out, he should reverence it by kissing it, and adore it on his knees; and when health was wanting to his subjects, or rain for his fields, he should confidently ask for it, for a God and Man who died upon the cross to redeem the world would grant it. With these words he delivered the true trophy and singular glory of Christendom to the Inkosi, who carried it over his shoulder, and taking leave of our people (with sorrowful tears for the pledge he was taking from them), and followed by about five hundred of his own, he went with it to his village, to do as Nuno Velho had told and asked him.

This was a triumph of the Holy Cross, worthy of being celebrated like those of Constantine and Heraclius, for if those most Christian and pious emperors liberated the True Cross from their enemies, the one from the Jews and the other from the Persians,[1] by which it was exalted, so this one (the image of that) was raised and hoisted by this honourable and virtuous gentleman in the midst of Kaffraria, the centre of heathendom, over which it is triumphing today. And since by clinging to this sweet wood the world was saved from its shipwreck, may it please God Our Lord

[1] This seems to be a garbled reference to (*a*) Constantine's vision of the luminous cross in the sky as he was preparing to fight Maxentius in A.D. 312; (*b*) his mother Helena's discovery of the True Cross at Jerusalem in 326, and (*c*) the recovery of the True Cross by the Byzantine emperor Heraclius from the Sassanian Persians in the year 627. Cf. *Catholic Dictionary* (ed. 1951), 234.

to enlighten the understanding of these heathen, so that clinging to this faithful cross which was left to them, they may be saved from the perdition and blindness in which they live.

[15 June] The tree of the Holy Cross having thus been planted in Kaffraria, from which may be expected most sweet fruits of salvation among those people, on the next day, which was the 15th, our people took leave of it. They left that place accompanied by Gamabela, who wanted to go with the Captain-major for the first stage, and by the guides whom he had selected. At ten o'clock they reached a hut, where the Inkosi took leave of Nuno Velho with sincere demonstrations of friendship. The Negro having gone, they continued their march through thorny trees and uninhabited country, in which there were many aloe shrubs, and at nightfall they encamped beside a very fresh river.

[16 June] At daybreak they resumed their journey, and travelled on until two o'clock when they came to some villages where there were no people, but many hens and many provisions. Nuno Velho placed a guard over them, so that none of these things should be taken, and their owners (who were on some neighbouring hills) being called by the guides and interpreters, some of them came down. They explained that they had fled from and deserted their homes on account of the war which they had with some of their neighbours, who had robbed them of all their cattle a few days before. Seeing that our people were not the enemies they feared, they all returned to their shacks, and provided a Negro who guided the column to a place where there was the necessary firewood and water for that night's encampment.

[17 June] The next day, which was the feast of the Most Holy Sacrament, our people journeyed over a very wide marshy plain, where there were good pastures and trees, and many more wild cattle, buffaloes, deer, hares, pigs, and elephants, which were grazing in large herds. These were the first animals of this kind which they had met in this long march, and they come down to those plains from a great range which crosses them from north to south.[1] Our people entered it by a valley, along which ran a

---

[1] The Lebombo Hills?

stream which they crossed many times, and near which they encamped.

[18 June] They struck their camp at daybreak, and marched until ten o'clock along the same valley and stream, amid extremely rank vegetation. It was covered with trees of different colours, in which were seen many green parrots with red beaks, partridges, turtle-doves, and other kinds of birds. They climbed a spur of the range from the south-western side, and on a level space at the top of it they met four Negroes who were engaged in hunting. These, hearing from the guides with what liberality our people bought provisions, at once went away, saying that they would go and fetch some from their village. However, the column did not wait for them and made no delay, except during the siesta, which they spent in a wood by the same stream.

On the other side was a hill, which they climbed when the heat was passed, and then followed an extensive plain, watered by the said stream. Here, besides the game which they saw the day before, were geese, ducks, thrushes, cranes, wild-fowl, and monkeys. In a large pool which the river formed at the place where our people spent the night, they saw many hippopotami, whose bellowing prevented them from sleeping quietly.

[19 June] They therefore arose later than usual the next day, on which they reached a marsh, that the guides said was near a village. They encamped by this for the night, and Nuno Velho sent one of the guides to tell the Inkosi of his arrival.

[20 June] Early next morning he sent António Godinho (with another Negro) to visit him, and he returned when his comrades had reached the other side of the marsh, very weary after dragging the cattle across with ropes, without which they got bogged. The tidings which he brought, however, made them forget all their past hardships. This news was that the Inkosi he had visited was one of the Inhaca's captains,[1] who had received him hospitably and promised to provide them with everything in his country until they reached the Inhaca, with whom he knew that the Portuguese were friends; and that the ship was not gone,[2] because a

[1] An Induna.
[2] I.e. the annual *pangayo*, or vessel engaged in the ivory-trade with Mozambique.

few days before some Negroes had passed through his village with ivory for the barter-trade.

Then there came one of this Inkosi's headmen to visit Nuno Velho on his behalf, bringing two kids and two hens; and after him came the Inkosi himself, whom Nuno Velho seated on his carpet. After he had confirmed the news brought by António Godinho, and shown great pleasure at the Captain-major's inquiries about the Inhaca, he presented him with two cows. Nuno Velho gave him in return the lid of a silver goblet, and four pieces of copper, and to a nephew whom he had with him three other pieces, hanging round his neck half of a small silver cup, with which they withdrew well pleased, since their village was a long way off. Our people remained still more pleased in their halting-place by the marsh, where the pilot took the latitude of the sun and found that they were in latitude 27° 20′ South, and at an estimated distance of thirty leagues from the port where the ship was.[1]

[21 June] When it was daylight, our people marched to the Negro's village, hoping to find good and faithful guides, but they proved to be bad and false. One of them was the Inkosi himself, who, wishing to vex and tire them that they might give him something more, led them by a roundabout way back to the marsh from which they had started. Nuno Velho showed himself angry and displeased, and asked him to return what he had given him, since he wanted no guides from him. The Kaffir, finding his vain hope deceived, took two more pieces of copper which they gave him, and, with three other Negroes who wished to accompany him, began to guide the column by a sandy path, along which there were wild palm trees, some bearing dates and others a fruit which they call *Macomas*[2] in Zambesia, which is of the size and appearance of grey pears. When it was night they encamped under some trees without water.

[22 June] Reaching some huts early next morning, the Inkosi took their owners with him and led our people astray from the path into a wood, so that he could separate some cows from the herd and make off with them. Having passed this wood and a stream, they entered another wood, but in all these places our

---

[1] Delagoa Bay or Lourenço Marques.   [2] Not identified.

people, warned by the Captain-major, were never off their guard. The Negro, who went in front with the interpreter, finding that he could not do what he intended, and the wood being thick so that he was not seen by those who followed, threw an assegai at his companion, and, missing his aim, fled. The interpreter caught hold of one of the Negroes from the huts who was near him, and shouted, whereon our people came up and likewise seized the companions of him who was already prisoner.

They now left the wood with them and returned to the path from which they had been led astray, and on asking them who the Inkosi was who had fled, they replied that he was a great thief named Bambe, whom they obeyed and followed out of fear. On Nuno Velho asking them if they would guide him to the Inhaca, they promised to do so, and said that he could kill them if they failed to bring him there. Nevertheless, with great caution they journeyed through a wood and crossed a marsh, on the other side of which was a good path that they followed until nightfall, when they encamped by a stream, firewood not being wanting from some large trees which were close by.

[23 June] This land is very boggy, and thus has many marshes. Having passed those already mentioned, on the morning of the 23rd they crossed another with great difficulty, for besides being very miry, it was so deep in the middle that they could not feel the bottom with a pike. They crossed this stretch, which was a short one, by cutting down tree-trunks, of which they made foot-bridges, and elsewhere helped themselves by grasping the many flags which grew in the marsh. When our people reached the other side, it was time to rest from their efforts and the heat, which they did in the shade of some trees.

Here Nuno Velho ordered one of the Negroes to be set free, so that he could go to his hut and give news of the rest, the Kaffir feeling well compensated for his captivity with a present of a strip of red *bretangil*[1] and a piece of copper. They travelled on with

---

[1] '*Bretangis* are a certain kind of callico, dyed blue, and of a dark violet' (*Travels and voyages by Mr. John Mocquet*, ed. 1696, 229). The origin of the word is uncertain, but Dalgado (*Glossário Luso-Asiático*, I, 120) defines *bertangil(s)* as cotton piece-goods (blue, black, red) exported from Gujerat (Cambay) to East Africa.

those who remained (who likewise marched along gladly in the expectation of a great reward) until sunset, when they reached another marsh, where they encamped. From here they could see to the south-west the mouth of a river, which is called the river of Santa Lucia in the sea-charts, almost in latitude 28°, and which they had already crossed the day before, at a place which gave no trouble and was far from the mouth.[1] In this river perished Fernando Alvarez Cabral, captain of the great ship *São Bento*, when trying to cross it in a canoe, and he is buried on the bank, at the foot of a hill which the waves that drowned him cannot reach.[2]

[24 June] Early next morning, which was the feast-day of Saint John the Baptist, they saw from a height some huts which were like our vineyard shacks, and not circular like those hitherto seen.[3] The Negroes from them, seeing our people, assembled to the number of about two hundred, and the interpreter went to speak with them. Learning from him that the strangers were Portuguese, they at once came to see the Captain-major, and assured him that he was in the country of the Inhaca, this being the village of one of his sisters, and that the trading-ship had not left. Our people were all delighted at such good news, and on reaching the huts, the Inhaca's sister (of whom the Negroes had spoken) came with her husband to visit Nuno Velho. He received them with due courtesy, and expressing his regret at not being able to stay some days with them, he gave them a black cloth and two pieces of copper. From this village the sea is visible, the sight of

[1] Either the actual Santa Lucia Bay (Lagoon), or, more probably, in view of the context, the Umkuzi (Mkusi) river which runs into it in about the latitude given here. Cf. above, p. 69, n. 4.

[2] As Theal and Junod have pointed out, the captain of the *São Bento* was drowned during the crossing of the Tugela, many miles to the south, which Manuel de Mesquita Perestrello mistakenly identified with the River Santa Lucia in his *Naufragio da Nao Sam Bento* (Coimbra, 1564), reprinted in the *HTM*, 1, whence the translation in G. M. Theal, *Records of South-Eastern Africa*, 1.

[3] 'The huts had already their present round form, the two present patterns having been duly noticed by the *Santo Alberto* crew: the bee-hive hut of the Zulu, and the hut provided with a wall and conical roof, which is met with first at Inhaca's sister's village and is the typical dwelling of the Thonga-Shangaan' (H. A. Junod, 'Condition of the natives', 19).

which excited our people as if it was something new, and it is on that part of the coast which is called the Dunes of Gold.[1]

As the heat of the day was now past, they resumed their journey with one of the Inhaca's Negroes, who had come to visit his sister on his behalf, the other guides being dismissed well paid. They travelled along a great beach of reddish sand,[2] which tired them in a little while, so they climbed to the top of the dunes where the going was easier, and at sunset reached a village which was on the bank of a river. The tide being out, they crossed it at once, and as it was now night they encamped on the far bank, where for some small pieces of cloth they bought millet, hens, and large and tasty fish called *Tainhas*.[3]

[25 June] Early next morning the river was much bigger and swollen by the high tide, forming an islet at its mouth, and thus it can only be forded at low tide. This is the river to which the Portuguese castaways from the great ship *São Thomé* gave the name of Plenty.[4] Striking the camp, they journeyed on behind the sand dunes, through a fresh and beautiful country, until midday, when they halted beside a village. Here the pilot took the altitude of the sun, and found their position to be in latitude 26° 45'. When the heat was past, they crossed a marsh, and then encamped under some large trees, which proved very handy in sheltering them from the rain that night.

[26 June] Next day they travelled over wide and extensive plains until 10 o'clock, when they reached a large and beautiful lake of fresh water about a league in length,[5] near which were two villages where they bought some hens. During their midday siesta the pilot took the altitude of the sun, and found that they were in

---

[1] Also translated as 'Meadows', 'Banks', and 'Downs', but as it was so named from the colour of the sand, I think 'Dunes', or 'Sand-dunes', more appropriate. Cf. below, p. 244. The coastal stretch between the Bay of Santa Lucia and Lake (Bay) Kosi.

[2] The *Africa Pilot*, III (ed. 1954), 192, notes of a part of this region: 'the sea, in the vicinity of this cliff, is sometimes much discoloured from the red soil eroding from its base.'

[3] Quabs?

[4] Cf. above, p. 80. There tentatively identified with Lake Fiti, but in the present instance perhaps they were nearer Lake Kosi.

[5] Lake Fiti?

latitude 26° 20'. Thence they marched along the shore of the lake, seeing many ducks, geese, and herons, and they encamped on a plain beyond it, as they were not able to reach the village before dark. Here they killed three cows for their ordinary provision, twenty-three still remaining.

As a Negro who passed by the encampment told them that the ship had not yet left the river, Nuno Velho decided to send three men with the guide to make sure of what all these Kaffirs said. These were António Godinho, Simão Mendes, and António Monteiro. Late at night the guide came back with a Negro sent by the Inhaca to visit Nuno Velho, who on approaching him made a deep bow, took off the cap he had on his head, and said, 'I kiss your worship's hands'—as befitted a Kaffir brought up among the Portuguese, who had remained in that land from the wreck of the galleon *São João*.[1] They were all delighted at his speech and courtesy, and Nuno Velho asking him who he belonged to, he replied to the king, who was very glad to see the Portuguese in his village and to hear from them[2] that Nuno Velho had arrived in his land; that he would have liked to visit him forthwith, but put it off because it was night; and that Nuno Velho should rest at ease meanwhile, since the ship[3] was still in the river.

This was the most joyful news which our Portuguese had heard in all their journey, for the ship being in the river, they all had hope of life and safety, which would have been doubtful if she had sailed; for then they would have been obliged either to cross the bay and journey overland to Sofala, or else to wait a year for another ship. Both of these courses presented great difficulties, for the journey to Sofala was long, and would take two months at least, which, after the three which they had been travelling already, would be a great deal considering the exhausted condition in which they all were. Whereas if they should decide to wait, the risk was even greater, for they would have to wait at least a year, at the end of which they would hardly be alive, as the country

[1] With Manuel de Sousa de Sepulveda in 1552. Cf. above, p. 73.
[2] Presumably from António Godinho and his companion.
[3] The *pangayo*, or ivory-trade ship.

was very unhealthy, the water bad, and provisions few. Therefore they had good reason to rejoice greatly that night, hearing for a certainty that the ship was not gone.

[27 June] At daylight one of the men whom Nuno Velho had sent to the king Inhaca returned with a long account of the ship, which agreed in every particular with what the envoy had said. And thus, although it was raining, they joyfully struck their camp and marched on to the Inhaca's village, from which many Negroes came out to meet our people, calling them *Matalotes, Matalotes*.[1] The Captain-major sent the king word of his arrival, and received an answer from him that he should go and await him under a tree close to his hut, while he was rising and dressing. Nuno Velho accordingly did so, taking with him eight arquebusiers, the purveyor, the treasurer, the pilot, and the interpreter, and sat down on some mats which the king had ordered to be spread under the tree.

The Inhaca came, with nothing on his head, girt with a cloth in the same way as the women wear their dress in India,[2] and covered with a large cloak. He was of gigantic stature, well built, with a cheerful and pleasant countenance. Drawing near to Nuno Velho, who had risen to his feet, he took him by the hand, and they both sat down together on the mat. He congratulated him on his arrival, and condoled with him on his shipwreck, for which Nuno Velho thanked him profusely, as also for what he did for Dom Paulo de Lima and for the castaways from the great ship *São Thomé*, when they passed that way.[3] Nuno Velho also asked him for a man to carry a letter to the captain of the ship. The king proved himself most obliging in everything, on account of the friendship his father had with the Portuguese, and forthwith summoned one of his Negroes, who carried the letter, accompanied by António Godinho, two other soldiers, and an interpreter.

The Captain-major then offered his present, which was a black

---

[1] 'Sailors', 'shipmates', 'comrades', any or all of which meanings this word has in Portuguese.

[2] Like a *sari*.

[3] Cf. above, pp. 81–2.

N

felt sun-hat,[1] a piece of Chinese cloth worked in silk and gold, two cows (one of them in calf), two silver chains taken from the master's whistle,[2] a medal, and a small silver bottle. As our people were uncomfortably situated, the king, who was delighted with the presents, ordered one of his Negroes to go and entertain them in a place near the huts, where there was firewood and water. Here the camp was forthwith pitched by captain Julião de Faria, who went there with all the ordinary people, leaving Nuno Velho and the officers and soldiers who accompanied him in conversation with the Inhaca.

It now seemed to be dinner-time, and the pilot said that it was eleven o'clock by the watch,[3] at which the king was a good deal surprised, and much more so when he was shown by the compass bearings the way which they had taken hitherto. And as it was now time, they arose and went hand-in-hand to the camp, where, after the king had visited Dona Isabel and her daughter, he dined with Nuno Velho in his tent. At two o'clock he took leave of them all with a good grace, promising to see them off the next day.

[28 June] He came accordingly early in the morning, dressed in a loose robe of cloth-in-grain trimmed with red velvet, the hat which they had given him on his head, the chains of the whistle round his neck, and his arms covered with brass bracelets. The usual courtesies having been exchanged between him and Nuno Velho, the latter gave him the whistle, fastening it to the chain from which it had been taken, and the master piping it, the king was very pleased with it, thinking that it would be a good thing in time of war. One of his sons was given a silver cup, but the father took it from him.

Being now ready to march, they took leave of the Inhaca and

---

[1] *Sombreiro.* This can mean either a broad-brimmed sun-hat, or an Asian state-umbrella. The latter meaning is the more usual one, but the former is probably intended here. See the examples given in *Hobson-Jobson,* 851, and Dalgado, *Glossário Luso-Asiático,* II, 314–16.

[2] A silver whistle hung round the neck and chest from a silver chain, as depicted in the frontispiece of the monthly numbers of the *Mariner's Mirror.*

[3] *Relogio.* Probably the *relogio do sol,* or small portable sundial mentioned on p. 134, n.2, above.

he of them, with affectionate embraces, and started on their way under the shade of the trees and past lakes of fresh water, marching until ten o'clock, when they halted to rest from the heat. Here there came to meet them ten of the local Negroes, with two sailors from the ship, and a native of Mozambique (who are there called *Topás*).[1] This man told Nuno Velho that when he was trading for ivory up the river he heard from the Kaffirs that there were some Portuguese with the Inhaca, whereupon he left everything to come and see them, with those sailors his companions. Nuno Velho rewarded them for their good will, by giving the *Topás* a silver bottle, and another to the two sailors; and as it was now time to continue their journey, they went on until evening, when they encamped where there was water.

[29 June] At nine o'clock on the next day, which was the feast of St Peter, they reached a village belonging to a son of the Inhaca, who, on receiving a message from Nuno Velho, at once came to visit him, and supplied a man at his request to carry another letter to the captain of the ship, and this emissary left very diligently with one of the two sailors. In return, Nuno Velho rewarded the chief with the foot of a silver cup, and a piece of Chinese cloth like that which he had given to his father, while he in return made him a present of a goat and a basket of *ameixoeira*.[2] This Kaffir was very like his father, and lived here apart from him, and out of his favour, on account of having sought his death, in order to succeed to the kingdom.[3] Through intercourse with the Portuguese he spoke some words of our language. The Captain-major took leave of him, and after resuming their journey when the siesta was over, they encamped near a marsh.

[30 June] In these lands of the Inhaca the sea makes a great bay some fifteen or twenty leagues in length, and in parts little less in

---

[1] *Topás* (*Topaz, Topass, Tupassi,* etc.). Term applied to dark-skinned or half-caste claimants of Portuguese ancestry. Cf. *Hobson-Jobson,* 933–4; Dalgado, *Glossário Luso-Asiático,* II, 381–2; C. R. Boxer, *The Topasses of Timor* (Amsterdam, 1947).

[2] Cf. above, p. 82, n. 2.

[3] On the practice of ritual king-murder in South East Africa see H. A. Wieschoff, *The Zimbabwe-Monomotapa culture in Southeast Africa* (Menasha, Wisconsin, 1941), 95–100. Cf. also J. H. Soga, *The South-Eastern Bantu,* 103–4.

width, into which flow four great rivers that the tide enters for about ten or twelve leagues. The first and southernmost of these is called the Melengane or Zembe,[1] and divides the lands of a king so called from those of the Inhaca. The second is called the Ansate, and by our people the Santo Espirito or river of Lourenço Marques, the man from whom the bay takes its name having been the first to open up the ivory trade here.[2] The third is called the Fumo, because it flows through the lands of a chief of that name.[3] The fourth and last, called the Manhiça, lies to the north, along which occurred the disaster of Manuel de Sousa de Sepulveda, the pitiful deaths of his wife Dona Leonor and of their children, and his own disappearance.[4] There also died Dom Paulo de Lima, but not the memory of his glorious exploits.[5]

In the mouth of this bay (which in parts is fourteen and fifteen fathoms deep), near its southern point, is a large island, three leagues in circumference, which divides the entrance into two passages, one on the north-east side measuring seven or eight leagues in width, and the other on the south side narrow and confined. Our people call it the island of the Inhaca, and the king keeps a quantity of cattle there, because of the abundant pastures.[6] One point of this island is made by the sea into a separate islet, which can be reached at low tide with the water to the knees. It is in latitude 25° 40′, and is called nowadays the island of the Portuguese, because of the many who lie buried there out of those who escaped from the loss of the great ship *São Thomé*.[7]

A ship from Mozambique visits this bay about every two years, in order to carry on the ivory trade, and one was there when our

[1] Either the Tembe or the Maputo is meant, but here as elsewhere, the Portuguese seem to confuse the two. Cf. above, p. 72, n. 3; and H. A. Junod, 'Condition of the natives', 12, n.; H. P. Junod, *Os indígenas de Moçambique*, 48–9.

[2] Probably the Maputo, but possibly the Tembe. Cf. last note.

[3] *Fumo, Mpfumo*, petty chief. Difficult to say which river is meant.

[4] The Incomati (Nkomati, Komati) River. Cf. p. 74, n. 4.

[5] Cf. above, pp. 101–3.

[6] Cf. above, p. 71. Couto's name of Choambone had apparently already been dropped.

[7] Still so called, having been previously termed Setimuro, and Ilha dos Elephantes. Cf. above, p. 71, n. 5.

Portuguese reached the lands of the Inhaca. And since according to what the Negroes said it was now the monsoon and time for its departure, and as Nuno Velho wanted to embark therein with all the other Portuguese who were with him, he wrote by the different messengers aforesaid to Manuel Malheiro, the captain of the ship, asking him to wait for them, and to send boats to the shore to carry them to the island. He received no reply until the last day of June, after our people had left the marsh where they had encamped the previous day and had nearly reached the shore, when they met a Kaffir sailor from the ship with two letters, one from the captain to Nuno Velho, and the other from the pilot to Rodrigo Migueis. These letters informed them that the men who had carried their letters had remained with Malheiro and his pilot, and that the boats would come next day to carry the people to the island.

When it was almost night the captain of the ship came in a boat, and was well received by Nuno Velho; and as the tide was ebbing, it was thought proper that he should return at once, taking with him Dona Isabel and her daughter, the steward Diogo Nunes Gramaxo, and the two friars, Fr Pedro and Fr Pantaleão. This was done accordingly, and their companions remained behind, well sheltered and supplied with provisions of that country, which were millet, *ameixoeira*, hens, fish, and shellfish.

[1 July] At break of day the same boat returned with another to convey to the island the rest of the company, who were already on the beach waiting for them. But as the tide was not suitable until three o'clock, and much time was spent in getting the cattle across, they got no further than the first island where they encamped for the night.

[2 July] When it was morning and low tide, our people crossed over to the other island, where the people of the Mozambique ship were lodged in shacks made to shelter them, wherein with great good will they received and entertained 117 Portuguese and 65 slaves who arrived there having survived the shipwreck and their wanderings. Their journey had lasted three months, during which they had travelled more than 300 leagues, although the distance in a straight line from the Penedo das Fontes, whence they had started, to this island is not 150 leagues.[1]

[3 July] The next day Nuno Velho wanted to know what provisions and water there were in the ship, and when he inquired this of the captain, the latter replied that the sailors had ninety *caçapos*[2] of millet, equal to about seven hundred *alqueires*,[3] and some beans and *ameixoeiras*, while the ship's tanks were full of water and held about twelve pipes. As this last was insufficient, by order of Nuno Velho they emptied fifteen jars that were full of honey (which is very good in that country) and filled them with water. He ordered that the sailors should be paid straight away for the millet and honey at the price which these were worth in Mozambique, and one came to 180 *cruzados* and the other to 96. There were also left over from the journey nineteen cows, which was a great help for their provisioning.

[9 July] This being ordered and carried out, and the ivory cargo having been very carefully and evenly stowed, so that it should make soft beds for our Portuguese, they all embarked on the 9th July, to await in the ship the change of the moon, which would be on the 12th, and with it the westerly winds for their voyage. They embarked thus early, because for the ship to get away it must be outside a sandbank which is near the island, and there await favourable weather; for if it is inside it cannot put to sea with the said westerly wind.

When they were all embarked to the number of 280 souls, the ship was so overloaded that the pilot, who was named Baptista

[1] As a matter of fact it is a good deal more. Allowing three English statute miles to the Portuguese league, the distance in a straight line from the Umtata to Inhaca island is over 450 miles. Whatever the distance travelled, the achievement was an outstanding one, and they had lost only eight Portuguese and ninety-five slaves *en route*, most of the latter by desertion. Theal's summary of 1902 still stands: 'This wonderful success was due to its being the best time of the year for travelling, to their being so strong and so well armed that no natives dared to attack them, to their being provided with means to purchase food, and to their having slaves who could make themselves understood by the Bantu along the route' (*Beginning*, 300). And, of course, to the model leadership of Nuno Velho Pereira.

[2] *Caçapos*. I cannot find this word in the dictionaries, save as an Indo-Portuguese term for a piece of artillery. But probably a native measure of some kind is intended here.

[3] *Alqueire* is a Portuguese dry measure of 1⅗ peck (English), or 13 litres.

MAPS AND ILLUSTRATIONS

COMMON TO BOTH VOLUMES

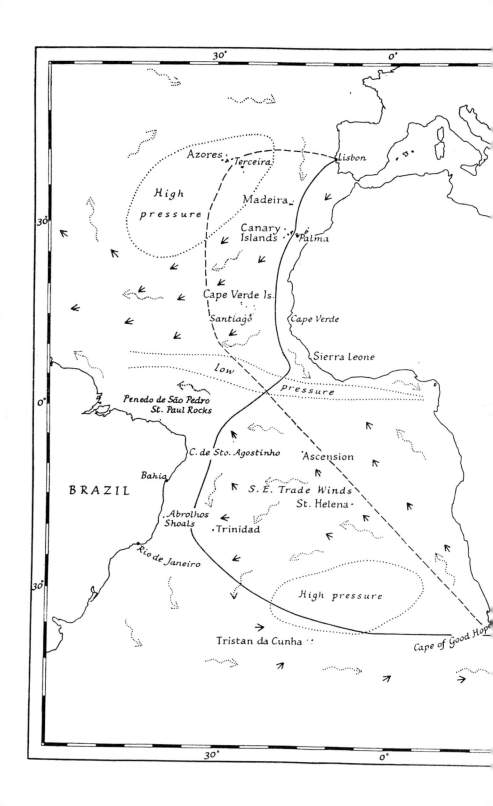

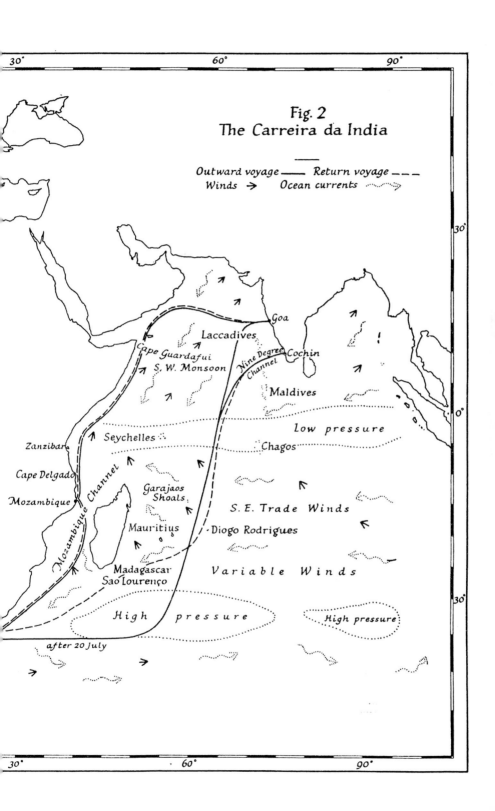

Fig. 2
The Carreira da India

South-east Africa and part of the Indian Ocean
From a map in Linschoten's *Itinerario* (1595)

MAPS AND ILLUSTRATIONS

FROM

The Tragic History of the Sea

Effigies Jacobi do Couto Regy apud Indos historiographi.

Exprimit effigies, quod solum in Cæsareuisum est
Historiam calamo tractat . et arma manu

Diogo do Couto
Frontispiece of his *Decada VII* (1616)

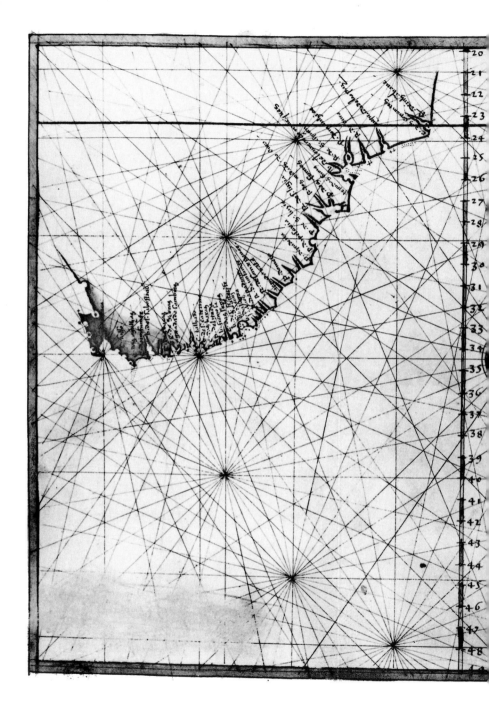

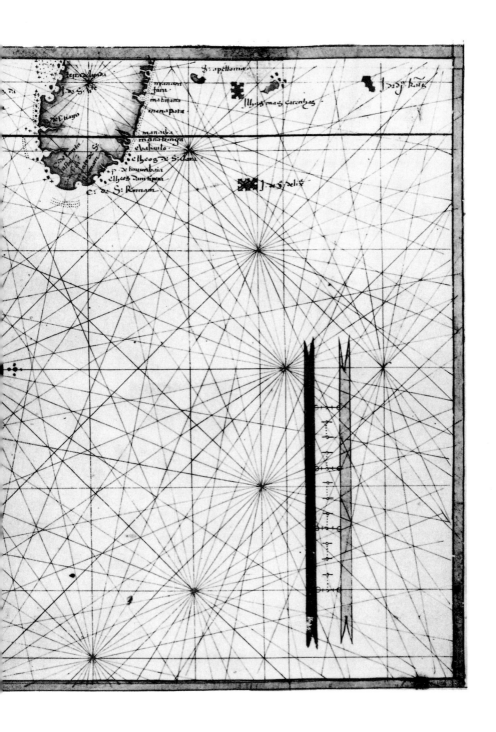

Perestrello's chart of South-east Africa and the Indian Ocean, 1576
B.M. Add. MS. 16932

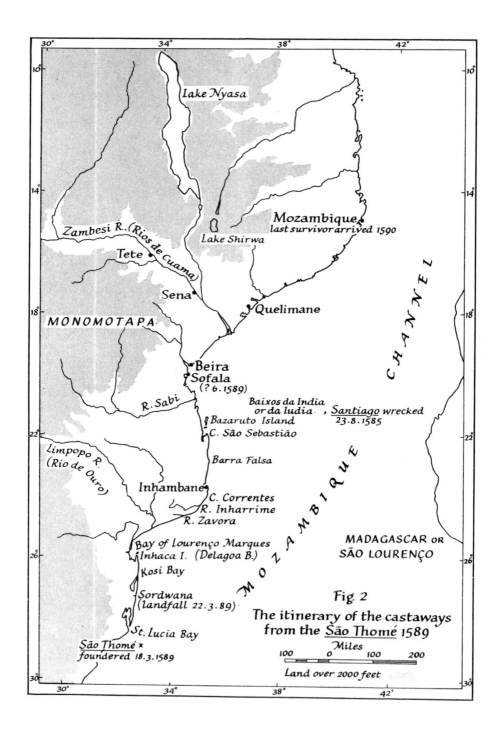

Fig 2

The itinerary of the castaways
from the São Thomé 1589

Land over 2000 feet

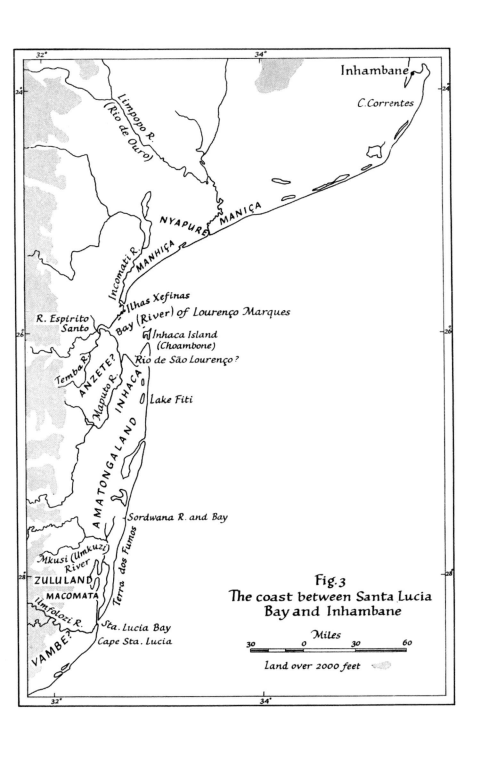

Inhambane

C. Correntes

Limpopo R. (Rio de Ouro)

NYAPURE MANIÇA

Incomati R.

MANHIÇA

Ilhas Xefinas

Bay (River) of Lourenço Marques

R. Espirito Santo

Inhaca Island (Choambone)

Temba R.

ANZETE?

Maputo R.

Rio de São Lourenço?

INHACA

Lake Fiti

AMATONGALAND

Sordwana R. and Bay

Terra dos Fumos

Mkusi (Umkuzi) River

ZULULAND

MACOMATA

Umfolozi R.

Sta. Lucia Bay

Cape Sta. Lucia

VAMBE?

Fig. 3
The coast between Santa Lucia
Bay and Inhambane

Miles

30   0   30   60

land over 2000 feet

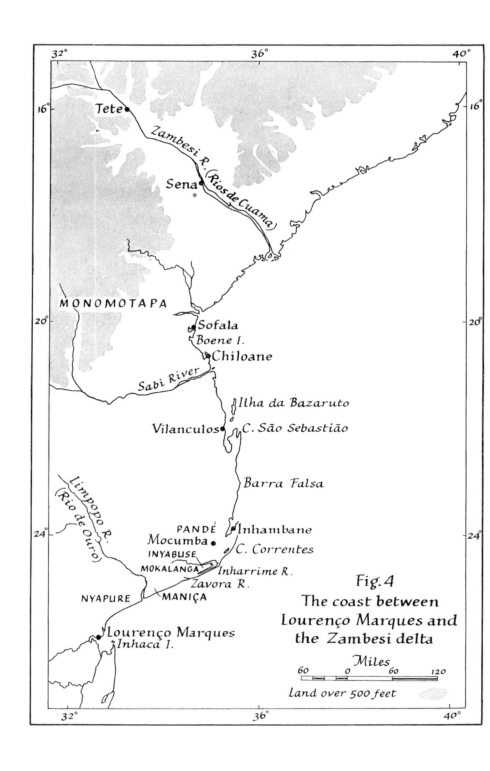

32°   36°   40°

16°   16°

Tete

Zambesi R. (Rios de Cuama)

Sena

MONOMOTAPA

20°   Sofala   20°
                      Boene I.
                      Chiloane

Sabi River

Ilha da Bazaruto

Vilanculos   C. São Sebastião

Barra Falsa

Limpopo R.
(Rio de Ouro)

24°   PANDÉ   Inhambane   24°
        Mocumba
        INYABUSE   C. Correntes
        MOKALANGA   Inharrime R.
                    Zavora R.   Fig. 4
    NYAPURE   MANIÇA   The coast between
                                 Lourenço Marques and
        Lourenço Marques   the Zambesi delta
          Inhaca I.

                                 Miles
                          60   0   60   120

                          land over 500 feet

32°   36°   40°

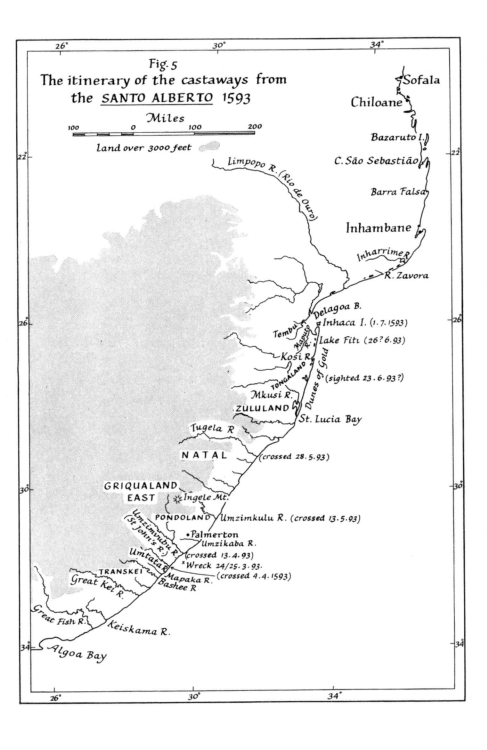

Fig. 5
The itinerary of the castaways from
the SANTO ALBERTO 1593

Miles

land over 3000 feet

Sofala

Chiloane

Bazaruto I.

C. São Sebastião

Barra Falsa

Inhambane

Inharrime R.

R. Zavora

Limpopo R. (Rio de Ouro)

Delagoa B.

Tembu R.

Maputo R.

Inhaca I. (1.7.1593)

Lake Fiti (26?6.93)

Kosi R.

(sighted 23.6.93?)

Dunes of Gold

TONGALAND

Mkusi R.

ZULULAND

St. Lucia Bay

Tugela R.

NATAL

(crossed 28.5.93)

GRIQUALAND
EAST

Ingele Mt.

PONDOLAND

Umzimkulu R. (crossed 13.5.93)

Umzimvubu R.
(St. John's R.)

•Palmerton

Umzikaba R.

(crossed 13.4.93)

Umtata R.

*Wreck 24/25.3.93.

Mapaka R.

(crossed 4.4.1593)

TRANSKEI

Bashee R.

Great Kei R.

Great Fish R.

Keiskama R.

Algoa Bay

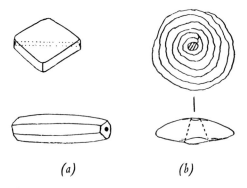

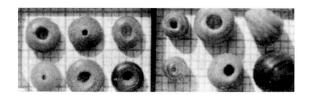

Trade-wind beads from East Africa beaches
(*a*) Lozenge-shaped carnelian beads, probably originating in Cambay. (*b, c*) Biconical perforated beads of opaque glass. (*d*) Spherical beads, wound from thin glass rods. Reproduced (by kind permission of the author and of the Editor of *Man*) from Dr. W. G. N. van der Sleen's note 'Trade-wind beads,' in *Man* (February 1956), pp. 27–9, figs. 2–3.

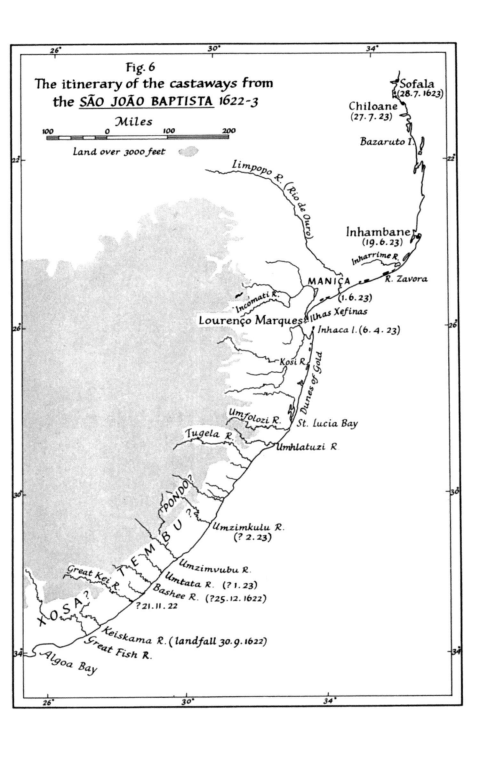

Fig. 6
The itinerary of the castaways from
the S̲Ā̲O̲ ̲J̲O̲Ā̲O̲ ̲B̲A̲P̲T̲I̲S̲T̲A̲ 1622-3

Miles

100   0   100   200

land over 3000 feet

Sofala
(28.7.1623)

Chiloane
(27.7.23)

Bazaruto I.

Inhambane
(19.6.23)

Inharrime R.

Limpopo R. (Rio de Ouro)

MANIÇA
(1.6.23)

R. Zavora

Incomati R.

Lourenço Marques Ilhas Xefinas

Inhaca I. (6.4.23)

Kosi R.

Dunes of Gold

Umfolozi R.

St. lucia Bay

Tugela R.

Umhlatuzi R.

"PONDO?"

T E M B U ?

Umzimkulu R.
(? 2.23)

Umzimvubu R.

Great Kei R.

Umtata R. (?1.23)

Bashee R. (?25.12.1622)

?21.11.22

X O S A ?

Keiskama R. (landfall 30.9.1622)

Great Fish R.

Algoa Bay

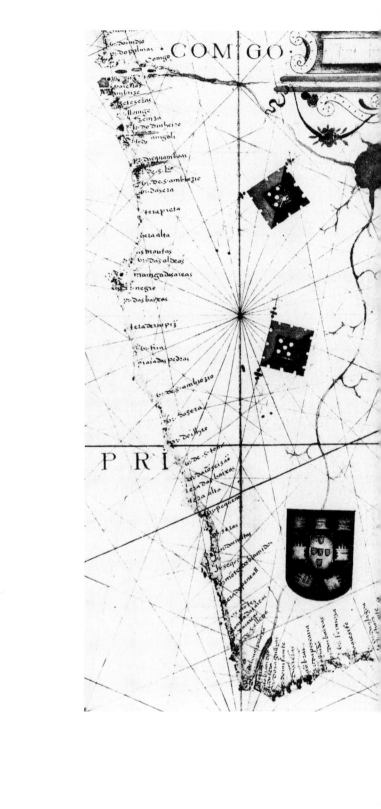

Southern Africa as known to the Portuguese, *c.* 1600
From Vaz Dourado's atlas of 1575. B.M. Add. MS. 31317, ff. 8v-9

MAPS AND ILLUSTRATIONS

FROM

Further Selections from the Tragic History of the Sea

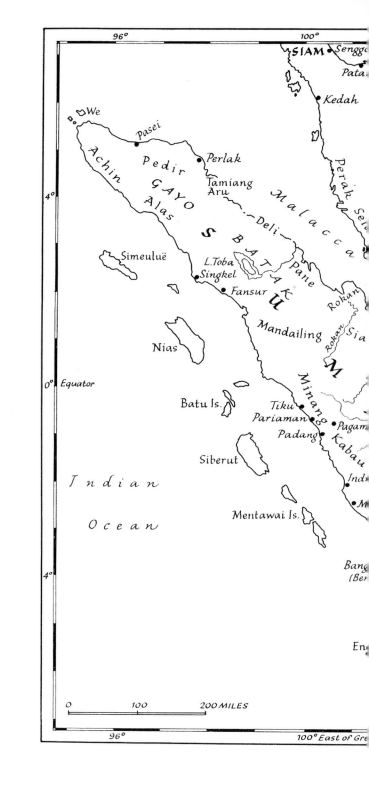

Fig. 1
Modern map of Sumatra and Malaya

Wreck of the *São Paulo*
From the original narrative of Manuel Álvares, S.J., 1561–2

The attack on the castaways
From the original narrative of Manuel Álvares, S.J., 1561–2

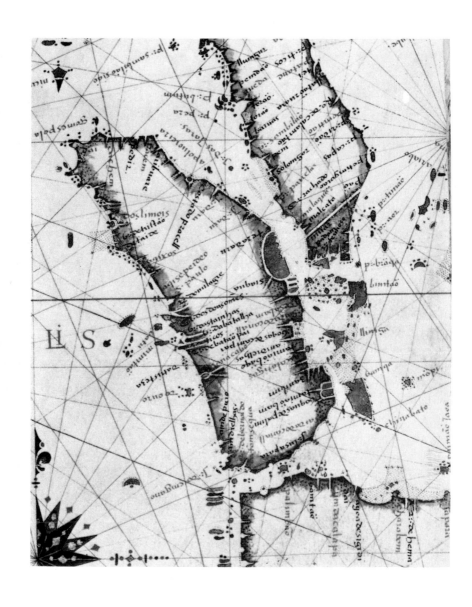

Vaz Dourado's chart of Sumatra, Java, and Malaya, 1575
(British Museum, Add. MS. 31317)

Martins and had been a sailor in the great ship *São Thomé*, said that he would not dare to navigate it as it was unmanageable, so that something must be done to remedy this excess. The Captain-major called a council, wherein it was decided to leave on shore the ship's sailors with their wives and families, who were Muslims, and as such would be better able to provide for themselves than the Portuguese. This resolution was carried out forthwith, and all the Muslims with their families and goods were disembarked, to the total of forty-five persons.[1] They offered no objection to this, on account of the liberal pay and compensation which Nuno Velho Pereira ordered to be given them, with which they hoped to make the journey overland to Mozambique more profitably and advantageously than they could have done by sea with the proceeds of their honey, which had been left on the beach, and their millet, which the Portuguese took with them.

The ship being thus lightened, after the change of the moon the wind still remained east as before, and thus they had to wait until the next moon. Some of the Portuguese, impatient with this delay, and with their cramped quarters in the ship and the scarcity of water, determined to go by land to Sofala, which was 160 leagues distant. Although Nuno Velho Pereira greatly regretted that they wished to part company from him, seeing their resolution and that it would make more room for those who remained, he gave them leave, and eight matchlocks, with all the necessary ammunition, fifty *cruzados* in silver specie, and a quantity of cloth. There went as captain of these Portuguese, who numbered twenty-eight, a soldier called Balthezar Pereira, nicknamed the *Reinol das forças*.[2] Having disembarked, they prepared two boats (which the ship had brought for ivory trading up-river) in which they crossed to the other side of the bay to the river Manhiça.[3] Making their way overland through that region they committed so many disorders

---

[1] It was a common practice for lascars to take their families with them on Indo-Portuguese ships.

[2] Literally 'the swashbuckling Griffin'—'Griffin' being the Anglo-Indian equivalent of the Portuguese *Reinol*. 'That is to say "man of the Kingdom", and the older hands mock them until they have made one or two voyages with them, and have learned the manners and customs of the Indies'. Cf. *Hobson-Jobson*, 759–60.

[3] Incomati.

that, although the way was a direct one and had been travelled by many Portuguese from the great ship *São Thomé* in regular stages, they were nearly all killed by the Kaffirs, and only two men of this company reached Sofala.[1]

[22 July] When the monsoon came, the ship, which was called *Nossa Senhora da Salvação*,[2] set sail on the 22nd July for Mozambique, and keeping inshore from Cape Correntes, there blew so great a gale from the south that our people thought themselves more surely lost than in the *Santo Alberto*. They threw many of the provisions into the sea, but after two days of this storm the weather became fine again, so that they reached Mozambique on the 6th August. Here they all disembarked and went in procession with the Dominican friars—who, being advised of their arrival, awaited them on the shore—to the Chapel of Nossa Senhora do Baluarte,[3] giving thanks to JESUS our Redeemer, and to the most holy Virgin his Mother, for the extraordinary favours and singular rewards received from their divine and liberal hands in this their shipwreck and journey.

END

[1] Deliberately ignoring the fact that only Portuguese were guilty of this misconduct, S. R. Welch pens the following travesty of history: 'But when Pereira left [*sic*], these Arabs and slaves changed their minds, and started out for Sofala by land instead of waiting to work as sailors. But lacking the wise guidance of their old leader, they behaved so badly, that most of them were killed by the Kaffirs on the way' (*Portuguese Rule*, 149). This monstrous distortion is typical of the man and his methods, for an exposure of which see C. R. Fuller's review of his work in *African Studies* (March, 1953), 31–2.

[2] 'Our Lady of Salvation', an apt name.

[3] 'Our Lady of the Bulwark (Bastion)', in the fortress of São Sebastião at the northern tip of the island, to whom the survivors from the *São João* likewise gave thanks. Cf. below, p. 271.

TRATADO

DO SVCCESSO QVE TEVE A NAO SAM IOAM BAPTISTA, E IORNA-
da, que fez a gente, que della escapou, desde trinta, & tres graos no Cabo de Boa Esperança, onde fez naufragio, até Zofala, vindo sempre marchando por terra.

A Diogo Soares Secretario do conselho da fazenda de sua Magestade, &c.

Auzente.

Ao padre Manoel Gomez da Silueira.

EM LISBOA.

Por Pedro Craesbeeck Impressor del Rei, anno 1625.

TREATISE

OF THE MISFORTUNE THAT BEFELL THE GREAT SHIP *SÃO JOÃO BAPTISTA*

And of the journey made by the people
who escaped from her, from latitude
33° where she was wrecked on the
coast of the Cape of Good Hope,
marching the whole way
overland to Sofala

*To Diogo Soares Secretary of His Majesty's
Council of the Exchequer*

in his absence

To Father Manuel Gomes da Silveira

*With licences of the Holy Inquisition, Ordinary
& the Palace*

IN LISBON

By Pedro Craesbeeck, the King's Printer, anno 1625

THE MISFORTUNE THAT BEFELL THE
GREAT SHIP SÃO JOÃO BAPTISTA

And of the journey made by the people who escaped from her.

ON the first day of March 1622, we left the bar of Goa with the flagship,[1] Captain-major Nuno Alvares Botelho,[2] and the great ship *São João* [*Baptista*],[3] Captain Pedro de Morais Sarmento.[4] After sailing fifteen or twenty days, on examining the pump we found fourteen or fifteen spans of water therein, which we endeavoured to clear out. But this proved impossible, the pumps of the ship being too small, since they had been made for a galleon and afterwards dismantled and enlarged, and only one of them was of any use. Using barrels as buckets we reduced the water to four spans, and continued on our voyage, enduring great heat until we reached latitude 25°S, and thereafter bitter cold.

[1] The carrack *Nossa Senhora do Paraiso*, which had left Lisbon on 31 March 1620, and wintered at Mombasa and at Bombay, before finally reaching Goa towards the end of 1621.

[2] Nuno Alvares Botelho had a most distinguished career in the East, particularly in fighting against the English in the Persian Gulf and Indian Ocean, and against the Achinese at Malacca, before his death in action against a Dutch ship at Jambi (Sumatra) in 1630. Cf. my article 'Anglo-Portuguese rivalry in the Persian Gulf, 1615–1635,' in E. Prestage [ed.], *Chapters in Anglo-Portuguese Relations* (Watford, 1935), 93–124.

[3] She had just been built at Goa by the acting master-shipwright, Diogo Luís, 'a pupil of Valentim Temudo, who is regarded as one of the greatest living shipwrights, and who is in no way inferior to his master Valentim Temudo, as he clearly proved in his building of the unlucky carrack *São João* [*Baptista*], which, if God had allowed it to reach Portugal and been seen for what it was, everyone would agree with what we say; apart from which he is a very good and true man, and of an upright conscience' (Letter of the administrators of the Companhia da India Oriental, Goa, January 1630, in Codex-Lynch fols. 106–7). For biographical details on Diogo Luís and Valentim Temudo see Sousa Viterbo, *Trabalhos Nauticos dos Portuguezes nos séculos XVI e XVII*, II, *Constructores Navaes* (Lisboa, 1900), 72–4, 93–5.

[4] He had been captain of the carrack *Santo Amaro*, lost when wintering at Mombasa in 1620.

On the 17th July we parted from the flagship in the night, because we could not see her poop-lantern; others say it was because the officers wanted to do so. For my part I can only tell you, as one who lost so much in losing the Captain-major's company, that I kept watch all night but never saw it.[1]

On Sunday the 19th July, in the morning, in latitude rather over 35° 30′ S we saw two great Dutch ships ahead,[2] and immediately made ready by clearing our ship for action, which we did with great difficulty, as she was much overburdened. Even so, we managed to give them two broadsides that afternoon, and we continued fighting with these two ships for the space of nineteen days until we reached latitude 42° S. We made bulwarks of the liberty-goods,[3] which proved a great help, since thereafter they killed very few of our people, whereas they killed twenty men in the first two days before we adopted this device. During nine of these days they fought with us from sunrise to sunset, and they finally reduced us to the most miserable condition that can be imagined; for they shot away our bowsprit close to the gammoning and the mainmast a yard and a half above the partners, and the foresail, and the rudder which was an old one, having belonged to a great ship that had been broken up at Goa and been left lying on the beach for two years, and so was rotten, for this is the usual way in which they fit out ships in this country. I say this because the want of a rudder caused our destruction, for it was in such a state that two shots sufficed to shatter it to pieces. Nor was this the only deficiency with which this ship left Goa, for she did

[1] The flagship, *Nossa Senhora do Paraiso*, after a difficult passage round the Cape, reached Lisbon on 9 November 1622.

[2] The *Mauritius* and the *Wapen van Rotterdam*, two Indiamen bound for Batavia, which had left the Cape on 13 June. Next day (20 June) these two Dutch Indiamen sighted five other Portuguese ships, but unfortunately the *São João Baptista* did not do so, nor did this squadron sight the homeward-bound carrick. These five sail were the outward-bound armada under the viceroy Dom Francisco da Gama, Conde da Vidigueira, which was subsequently intercepted and destroyed (save for one galleon) by the Anglo-Dutch 'Fleet of Defence' in the Mozambique Channel on 23–5 July. Cf. C. R. Boxer, *Dom Francisco da Gama, Conde da Vidigueira e a sua viagem para a India no ano de 1622. Combate naval de Moçambique em 23–25 de julho de 1622*, reprinted in a limited edition from the *Anais do Club Militar Naval* (May–June, 1930).

[3] *Fardos de liberdades*. Cf. above, p. 18, and Appendix (D) *infra*.

not carry sufficient gunpowder and armament for fighting, mounting only eighteen guns of very small calibre; but withal we fought
on until we had only two barrels of powder and twenty-eight
cartridges left.

Seeing that the ship was completely dismasted, and that the
spare spars were so riddled with shot that the least damaged had
nine holes in it, and that the ship was foundering through shot
which had struck us a fathom under water, while the rudder in
breaking wrenched away two of the gudgeons, leaving open their
bolt-holes, so that we were slowly sinking without being able to
overcome the leak or apply any remedy, although every soul on
board worked night and day at the pumps and scoops, the Religious tried to arrange some parley to distract the enemy, so that in
the meanwhile we might try to get the better of the water and plug
some of the leaks. And for that reason they asked me if I would
be willing to be one of the emissaries who would treat with the
Dutch for an honourable agreement. I had some sharp words
with them over this, telling them that those who wanted such an
agreement should go thither themselves, and that they were no
friends of mine who gave me such advice; and I went to the
station which the captain had assigned to me, so that I neither
saw any boat alongside, nor any Dutchmen, thus incurring the
hatred of many people in the ship. They afterwards asked Luís da
Fonseca and Manuel Peres to go and negotiate this agreement,
who went accordingly, but such severe and continual storms
supervened that we saw no more of the ship to which these two
men went.[1]

The other ship[2] followed us without attempting to board us,
and sent a boat to learn whether we had seen her consort, for they
had lost sight of her, and to ask us what we were going to do, in

---

[1] The *Mauritius*. Luís da Fonseca de Sampaio was one of the richest and most
active merchants at Goa. He was detained for five years as a prisoner at Batavia, but
became a leading alderman (*vereador*) of the senate or municipal council at Goa
after his release, and took a strongly anti-clerical stand in the controversy which
arose over the institution of the Augustinian nunnery of Santa Monica at Goa in
1632. Cf. Fr Agostinho de Santa Maria, O.P.A., *Historia da Fundação do Real Convento de Santa Monica da cidade de Goa* (Lisboa, 1699), 204 ff.

[2] *Wapen van Rotterdam.*

view of the fact that we were leaking so heavily and continuously while being totally dismasted and bereft of all resources. All our people being very miserable and discouraged, we told them that we knew nothing of their ship, and with this answer the boat returned whence it came. We were more wretched every moment, for we were suffering from the most notable storms and cold that ever men endured. It snowed very often, so that many slaves died of the cold, and we felt their loss greatly in working the pump and throwing things overboard, in which tasks we were all employed unceasingly and painfully, because the storms and the rolling of the ship prevented us from lighting the fires, thus making our hardships much worse.

Being in this state, we made a jury-mast of the mizzen-mast and placed it in the prow, with the outrigger for a bowsprit, and so went wherever the wind carried us. In this way the wind was often favourable for steering landwards but the ship drifted out to sea, for as we had no rudder nor means of steering, we could not point up into the wind but drove helplessly before it. All this occurred in latitude 42° S, with the last Dutch ship following us constantly. One night, as we were going seawards with her in stormy weather and dense darkness, we struck our jury-mast, praying to Our Lady of the Conception that she would allow our ship to go landward, and thus give the slip to the one that was pursuing us. And so it fell out, for at daybreak we were drifting landward, in which direction we continued for many days. The Dutch ships, as we now know, went seaward in quest of us as far as latitude 46° S. They eventually reached Jakarta in the condition which is notorious.[1]

It seemed to us, as I have said, that we were better off separated from the Dutch ships, on account of the continual storms and the leaks which opened again. Moreover, the people were all ex-

[1] It was indeed. When they finally reached the Straits of Sunda in October, the *Mauritius* had 242 dead, and 75 sick men left, while the *Wapen van Rotterdam* had lost 277 dead, and the 94 survivors were all very weak. The *Mauritius* was brought into Batavia a few days later, but the west monsoon burst before the *Rotterdam* could get through the straits, so 60 fresh men were placed aboard her and sailed her via the Straits of Bali to Amboina. (N. MacLeod, *De Oost-Indische Compagnie als zeemogendheid in Azië*, 2 vols., Rijswijk, 1927, I, 274-5.)

hausted by their hardships, for in addition to what I have related, they were employed in making a rudder, which was done on the deck. This idea had been put in the captain's head by the ship's carpenter, although it was absurd to think that one could be fixed in position during such weather in such latitudes, when it often happens that ships sheltering in bays and rivers fail to do so if the weather is the least unfavourable. Captain Pedro de Morais, though brave enough, was not very experienced, and he would not ask the advice of the ship's officers nor of the more experienced passengers, but followed that of an obstinate clown, refusing to make use of sweeps, which is the invariable resource of ships without a rudder. And finally, this rudder could never be shipped although it was suspended from the stern for fifteen days, awaiting a lull in the weather which would enable us to ship it; and one night the ropes with which it was bound parted and we lost it, which we considered a mercy from God, for it was damaging the ship by perpetually banging against her.

While this was being done, we expected hourly to go to the bottom, and had now no other hope than the salvation of our souls. The Religious who were passengers on board went about exhorting all the others to repent of their sins, making processions and scourging themselves nearly every day, nor was anyone else exempted therefrom, but rather they all joined in with many tears, both high and low alike. And in all these miseries we thought that it was a punishment from God that the enemy ships had separated from us, since it was an unprecedented thing that a dismasted and rudderless ship in such remote and stormy latitudes should be able to make any port at all. In which a miracle of the Virgin was manifestly displayed, as I have said above.

After the loss of the rudder two sweeps were made, very well contrived from the pieces of the masts and bowsprit which were left in the ship. In fact, no human resource was left untried, for as everyone was trying to save his own life they all worked without exception. When the sweeps were finished, as there were no jury-masts nor wood with which to make them, the ship was still unable to make progress, but after all these contrivances she remained a hulk at the mercy of the waves. For the enemy had demolished the greater part of the castles, leaving the nails and the wood splintered and jagged, so that with the violent pitching and rolling of the ship people were thrown against them and hurt, and for this reason they cut everything away.

In this confusion and extremity, on the 29th September, we found ourselves at daybreak two leagues from land, in latitude 33° 20′ S. Such was the joy of all on board, that we might have been off the bar of Lisbon, none thinking of the weary journey which we should have to travel nor of the hardships which awaited us in the future. There were no men of note killed on board ship during the fight, excepting João de Andrade Caminha and João de Lucena. Lopo de Sousa—may he be with God in heaven—and Captain Vidanha were stationed in the waist, where they fought bravely; and Lopo de Sousa lost three toes of his left foot, the foot being completely crushed, receiving at the same time a splinter in the hip, another in the belly, another in the face, and two in the head. Captain Vidanha received two splinter-wounds, one in the head and another in the belly. Thomé Coelho d'Almeida was stationed on the forecastle, and Rodrigo Affonso de Mello aft on the poop. I was in charge of the stern-chases, which the enemy attacked most frequently, for every time that they gave us a broadside after shooting away the bowsprit, they hit near the stern-chases under the gallery when firing at the rudder. I do not dwell here upon the manner in which we bore ourselves during this long fight, nor upon the hurt which the Dutch received, for I hope that they themselves will be the ones to spread it abroad.[1]

We could not get so close inshore that day as we wanted to, in order to anchor and disembark; but the next morning, which was the feast of St Jerome,[2] we found ourselves at daybreak lower down the coast and nearer the shore; and as the ship was unmanageable we feared that she might drift out to sea. And as we thought we saw a sandy beach and a good anchorage there (which we afterwards found was not so) we anchored in seven fathoms with two

[1] They certainly did. Cf. the previous note and W. Foster, *English Factories in India, 1622–23*, 210, 225.
[2] 30 September.

anchors. The captain then sent Rodrigo Affonso de Mello with fifteen arquebusiers to reconnoitre the shore and choose a good position from which to protect the landing. This he performed very carefully, as he did everything, and he sent us some sweet water and fragrant herbs, which gave us much pleasure. And in order not to omit anything noteworthy which occurred in this voyage, I will relate to your worship what follows.

On board this ship was a man called Manuel Domingues, who was boatswain's-mate, whom the captain had promoted to the post of master on the latter's death. This man became so proud, unruly, and insolent, that there were few people in the ship with whom he had not some quarrel. And as the majority of the sea-men were on his side, he became so brazen that he went to the captain and said, 'Sir, to-morrow morning you must get into the boat with thirty men, whom I have chosen for this purpose; we must take with us all the jewels, and land at a spot three leagues from here, where the chart shows a sandy beach, and we must traverse this land of Kaffraria as far as Cape Correntes. For travelling thus unencumbered, only thirty persons with our arms, we will be able to reach where I say; but it is idle to talk of going with a column of women and children for so great a distance over such rugged country.'

Pedro de Morais replied that he would do no such thing, for he did not wish God to punish him, and what account could he render to God and to men if he acted so cruelly? And he told him not to speak so insolently. The man replied that whether he were willing or no, they would seize him and place him in the boat. The captain seeing his damnable design, dissimulated for the time being; but realizing all the trouble, sorrow, and loss which would be caused by such evil counsel, he determined to kill him. This he accordingly did by stabbing him to death two days after the ship had anchored, although the master was by this time on his guard. His death caused sorrow to few and rejoicing to many.[1]

---

[1] Faria y Sousa comments acidulously that there were few pilots who were not equally obstinate and equally deserving of such a death—'raro el que dexa de ser tal y de merecer aquella muerte' (*Asia Portuguesa*, III, Lisboa, 1675, 358).

After this, the necessary provisions and weapons were landed, though with great difficulty, for it was a wild coast, so that every time the boat approached the shore to disembark something, it was necessary to anchor with a grapnel by the stern and wade ashore holding on to the line in order to keep head-on to the waves; so much so, that once when they did not anchor by the stern, eighteen persons were drowned in landing one boatload. This was the reason why we did not afterwards try to build a boat, for this coast is so stormy that we feared that after it was made we would not be able to launch it.[1]

On the 3rd October, while we were completing the landing of the things needed for our overland journey and building shacks to shelter us from the excessive cold of that region during the time we remained there, the men who kept watch raised the alarm that Negroes were approaching. We took up arms, and as they drew near to us they handed the assegais which they carried to their children until they were very close to us, when they squatted down on their haunches, clapping their hands and whistling softly, in such a way that they all kept in tune together, and many women who were with them began to dance. These Negroes are whiter than Mulattoes; they are stoutly-built men, and disfigure themselves with daubs of red ochre, charcoal, and ashes, with which they generally paint their faces, though they are really quite good-looking.[2]

On this first meeting they brought as a present a very fine large

[1] As Theal notes, the exact locality of the landfall of the *São João Baptista* cannot be given, but 'it must have been somewhere between the Fish and the Kei rivers' (*History and Ethnography of Africa South of the Zambesi, 1605–1795*, III, 1910, 68). If the Portuguese estimate of the latitude taken on 29 September was accurate, they must have landed somewhere near the mouth of the Keiskama river. Cf. below, p. 199, n. 3. This region is still known as the 'Wild Coast'.

[2] This was a more charitable verdict than that given by an English (?) traveller of 1800, who described their Griqua descendants as being 'a herd of wandering naked savages subsisting by plunder and the chase. Their bodies were daubed with red paint, their heads loaded with grease and shiny powder, with no covering but the filthy kaross over their shoulders, without knowledge, without morals or any trace of civilization, they were wholly abandoned to witchcraft, drunkenness and licentiousness' (*apud* W. Dower, *The early annals of Kokstad and Griqualand East*, Port Elizabeth, 1902, 4). These 1622 ancestors of the Griqua were pure Hottentots, the Bantu having not yet penetrated so far south.

ox and a leather bag of milk, which the king gave to Rodrigo Affonso de Mello, who was acting as captain at the time, Pedro de Morais being still aboard the ship. The courtesy which this king did to the aforesaid captain was to stroke his beard many times. After we had given some pieces of iron hoops and *bertangils*[1] as a return present to the king, he went to the ox and ordered it to be cut open alive at the navel, and he with most of those who were with him plunged their hands into the entrails of the ox while it was still alive and bellowing, smearing themselves with that filth. We realized that they performed all these ceremonies as a sign of good faith and friendship. They then cut up the ox into quarters and gave it to us, keeping for themselves the hide and entrails, which they placed on embers and devoured on the spot.[2]

During the month and six days that we remained in that place we could never understand a word these people said, for their speech is not like that of mankind, and when they want to say anything they make clicks with the mouth, one at the beginning, another in the middle, and another at the end; so that it may be deduced from these people that the earth is not all one, nor all mankind alike.

When we had entrenched ourselves on shore we made a church covered with canvas and hung inside with gold-embroidered Chinese coverlets and many other rich stuffs, so that it looked as if it were all sewn with gold. Here three masses were said every day, and we all went to confession and communion. When the seamen declared that it was impossible to build a vessel, Captain Pedro de Morais ordered the ship to be burnt, that the Kaffirs might not take the nails and make the rate of barter high for us.[3] He also ordered that all the jewels in the ship should be placed in a leather bag, sealed as they were in little packets, by the men to whom they had been entrusted, all this with authentic papers certifying that as the trouble of guarding them on the march was common to all, it likewise seemed but just that whatever reward

---

[1] Cf. above, p. 175, n. 1, for explanation.
[2] Cf. above, p. 121, n. 1, for a similar ceremony.
[3] Cf. above, p. 119.

and profit was derived from them should also be shared by all, each according to his part and conduct.[1]

During this time we bartered for cows, which we ate, though they were not as many as we needed. We kept those which seemed fit for work in a stockade, accustoming them to carry pack-saddles, which were very well made out of carpets, for there were not wanting workmen in the camp who knew how to make them. I, having reached land suffering from gout and scurvy,[2] realizing the long way I would have to go, endeavoured to take some exercise during this time. Carrying the best of my seven matchlocks I went out hunting, sometimes in the direction of the Cape of Good Hope and sometimes in that of Cape Correntes; and being the son of a hunter and reared to the chase, this was both healthy and pleasurable for me; so that at the end of the month and six days which we remained there, I had become so strong and fit that I can affirm there was no one in the camp in better condition than myself.

On the 6th November we set out from that land in latitude 33° S, in a column of march,[3] 279 persons divided into four bodies, the captains of which were Rodrigo Affonso de Mello, Thomé Coelho d'Almeida, António Godinho, and Sebastião de Morais. The company of Rodrigo Affonso de Mello and that of Sebastião de Morais marched in the van, Captain Pedro de Morais was in the centre with the baggage and the women, and Thomé Coelho and António Godinho brought up the rear. We had with us seventeen oxen laden with provisions and with the

[1] Some of these diamonds were eventually brought to Goa, where their disposal was the subject of a lawsuit between the royal treasury and the owners, judgement being finally given in favour of the latter (*Boletim da Filmoteca Ultramarina Portuguesa*, II (Lisboa, 1956), 528).

[2] *Mal de Loanda*, in the original. So called after the (then) notoriously unhealthy seaport and capital of Angola, or, more probably, from the prevalence of this disease among the slaves who were shipped thence for Brazil.

[3] *Arraial formado*, in the original. The latitude given here is that of the actual city and port of East London, but on p. 195 above, he implies that the landfall of the *São João Baptista* was somewhat lower down the coast than lat. 33° which would make it about the Keiskama river, as noted on p. 197, n. 1, above. Throughout this narrative Vaz d'Almada's identifications of places and times are few and vague, and I do not pretend to give more than the barest outline of the castaways' itinerary.

articles needed for barter, and four litters in which were Lopo de
Sousa, Beatriz Alvares wife of Luís da Fonseca, Dona Ursula,
widow of Domingos Cardoso de Mello, and the mother of Dona
Ursula.

This day was a very rainy one, and as things were not yet very
well arranged we marched for a league and then pitched camp on
the bank of a fresh-water river, where we passed a bad night on
account of the incessant rain. This land is intersected with rivers
of very good water, and firewood is available, but there is a lack
of fruit and provisions, though it seems as if the soil would yield
abundant crops of anything sown in it. The inhabitants thereof
live solely on shell-fish, some roots which look like truffles, and
the produce of the chase. They have no knowledge of any seed-
planting, or of any other kind of provisions. Even so, they are
vigorous and courageous, capable of performing remarkable feats
of strength and agility, for they will pursue a bull and hold it fast,
though these animals are of the most monstrous size imaginable.

The next day, the 7th November, we continued our journey,
keeping always close to the shore. When we had gone about three
leagues we made our camp in the afternoon on the bank of a
river, pitching our tents in a circle, within which we put the cows
at night, posting sentinels and making the rounds with great care
and vigilance. But this did not suffice to prevent the Kaffirs from
stealing all the cattle, though they did not get away scot-free. For
as these Kaffirs are great hunters they always have their hunting
dogs with them, and these cows are reared with the dogs who
guard them from the lions and tigers on this coast; and at their
approach these dogs rouse the cattle by barking, and thus they are
always together and mingle with each other, and even though they
are brute beasts they know and make much of each other. And as
the cows were leaving the land where they had been reared, they
lowed continually, as if in longing; and during the third watch the
Kaffirs came and let loose the dogs inside with low whistling and
shouts, and the cows when they heard them jumped through the
tents and fled with the dogs behind them. We followed, fighting
with the Kaffirs, and we killed the son of their king and many of
his company, and they wounded three of our men. This day was a

very sad one for us, for they carried off our cows which were laden with all our provisions, and which could have been used themselves for the same purpose.[1]

We had with us a Kaffir who turned up at the place where we landed, a native of the islands of Angoxa,[2] who was the only one that our Kaffir slaves could understand. He was a prisoner, because he had promised to come and guide us but later did not wish to do so, and thus we were obliged to take him along as a captive. This man told us that within twenty days as the Kaffirs travel, which would be about two months at our rate, we would reach a region where there were cows, but it was all a wilderness as far as that; as we afterwards found by experience, and it extended much further than he said. We continued our journey in orderly fashion, each one subsisting every day upon that which he could carry besides his arms and articles for barter, which were divided among all, so that everybody was very heavily laden. The dews were so heavy that we were generally wet until the sun dispersed them at noon; but this was a light hardship compared with the rains which generally afflicted us, and other greater miseries and hardships which we afterwards endured, and in which many lost their lives.

About the 21st of this month, on descending a very high range we reached a river which we crossed in the space of two days, and it was the first we crossed on rafts. We called it the Musk River,[3] as the captain ordered all the musk we had to be thrown into it, in order to lighten the burden of those who carried it. After two days' journey over very high stony ranges, we debouched on to a

[1] Theal states (*History of Africa South of the Zambesi*, III, 70) that the marauders who carried off the cattle were Bushmen, but he does not explain why. I presume they must really have been Hottentots, as they were evidently from the same group as those met on 3 October.

[2] A chain of islets and shoals between $3\frac{1}{2}$ and 8 miles offshore from the coast of Portuguese East Africa, in lat. 16° 49′ S, in the Mozambique Channel. Nowadays spelt Angoche.

[3] Possibly the Great Kei river, assuming that the castaways had started from the Keiskama river, or from near the present East London. As noted previously, Vaz d'Almada's dates and topographical identifications are too vague to allow anyone not intimately acquainted with the country to make more than the most tentative identifications. Cf. p. 199, n. 3.

beach of shingle and a river which we crossed on a raft that we made. On the opposite bank we found some Kaffir hunters, who sold us a little hippopotamus meat, which was a great relief to us. We called this river the Shrimp River,[1] because they sold us many there. Thence we journeyed over a range until we returned to the shingle beach, along which we marched with great difficulty.

Here a most pitiful incident occurred, and the time showed us a great cruelty, which was as follows. There was a young white girl in the company, daughter of an old Portuguese who died in the ship; he was a rich man and taking her to become a nun in Portugal. She was carried in a litter, but those who bore her for the sum of two thousand *cruzados* became exhausted, and as she had no one but her little brother to impress upon the captain the great cruelty of leaving a young and beautiful damsel to the lions and tigers in the wilderness, such compassion was not shown as so notable a case demanded. It is true that the captain made some efforts, taking up the litter on his own shoulders, as did likewise all the gentlemen in the company, to see if their example would move any of the others to do so, promising them a much larger sum than had previously been offered. But, in spite of all, no one could be found to do it, nor were we really able, on account of the great hunger which we then endured. She managed to walk until the next day, supported by two men, but being extremely weak she could only move very slowly. So we brought her along until she could not go a step further, and began to weep and wail that she was so unfortunate that for her sins, among so many people and where four litters were carried, there were none who would carry hers for any money, although it was the lightest in the company, she being so frail and small—with other pitiful words which she spoke very pathetically. She then asked for confession, and having finished this she said in a loud voice so that she might be heard: 'Father Friar Bernardo, I feel very sure that God will have mercy on my soul, for since He is pleased that I should suffer such misery and hardships at so tender an age, allowing me to be abandoned in a wilderness to the lions and tigers, with none to take pity on me, He will surely permit that it is all for my salvation.'

[1] Rio dos Camarões. Not identified.

Saying these words she lay down upon the ground, covering herself with a skirt of black taffeta that she wore, and every now and then as the people passed by she uncovered her face and said: 'Ah! cruel Portuguese, who have no pity on a poor young girl, a Portuguese like yourselves, and leave her to become food for beasts, may Our Lord bring you to your homes.' I, who was bringing up the rear, comforted her brother, who was with her, and asked him to go on, which he refused to do, sending word to the captain that he wanted to stay with his sister. The captain sent to tell me that I should on no account allow this, but bring him with me, as I did, comforting him the while; but his grief was so great that a few days later he likewise remained behind. Your worship can see what a pitiable incident this was. For my part I can only say that these and other similar sights caused me more sorrow than the hunger and hardships which I endured.

Journeying thus for three days, we came to a river where there was a sandy beach, and here we found some shell-fish, whereat we rejoiced greatly because of the extreme hunger from which we were suffering. We remained here one afternoon for the tide to finish ebbing so that we could cross over, but the delay was greater than we expected. The people being so famished, all began to eat some beans which they found along the river bank, which brought us all to the point of death, and had it not been for the quantity of bezoar stone which we had with us, not one would have escaped.[1] And in spite of this experience, famine brought us hourly into the same danger, driving us to eat every kind of herb and fruit which we found, and even the knowledge that they would do us harm was not enough to restrain us.

In the midst of this extremity we derived great benefit from the quantity of wild fig-trees which we found in this region, upon the stalks of which and upon a quantity of nettles we lived for many days. We remained by this river for two days, while recovering from the disaster which had befallen us, and when we set out

[1] For contemporary accounts of the allegedly curative properties of the bezoar-stone, particularly as an antidote against poison, see Garcia d'Orta, *Coloquios dos simples e drogas da India* (Goa, 1563), col. 45; Nicolas Monardes, *Libro que trata de dos medicinas excelentissimas contra todo veneno: que son la piedra Bezaar, y la yerua Escuerçonera* (Seville, 1574).

again our rearguard was followed by a few Kaffirs who had stolen two cauldrons from us. Since we did not punish them as their insolence deserved, they became so disdainful of us that they began to throw fire-hardened sticks at us. But they immediately paid for their daring insolence, for the ship's carpenter, who was the nearest, fired his matchlock at one of them, the shot breaking his arms and going through his chest. The Kaffirs, seeing the great hurt done them by a single one of our weapons, took to flight, and we proceeded on our way.

We were now reduced to such straits by hunger that we were compelled to eat unclean things cast up by the sea, such as starfish and jelly-fish; and our need was so great that anybody who had anything to eat would not share it even with a friend or relative who was dying before his eyes. In all these miseries, I came off better than most, praise be to God, for I carried the best matchlock in the company and was the best shot; and thus I never lacked game more or less, though I had great difficulty in seeking and finding it, this region being very bare of birds and beasts, so that I never had the chance of killing a large animal. I divided whatever I killed with those I thought proper, concealing the rest so that only these comrades knew of it. All this was necessary because of the hatred, ill-will, and dangers which otherwise might have arisen.

We continued our journey for several days until we reached a river in which there were many crabs, and which heavy rains prevented us from crossing. The next day in the morning a remarkable incident occurred, which was as follows. In the country which lay behind us, the captain Pedro de Morais had been told that Sebastião de Morais, captain of one of the groups and calling himself his kinsman, was trying to persuade the people whose captain he was (and who were mostly unruly youths) to go on ahead with him, taking the jewels from us, and push on separately, under the pretext that they wished to march faster. Pedro de Morais at once reacted to this by very secretly opening the bag and taking therefrom the eight packets of jewels which it contained, putting them in a wallet which he entrusted to the care of the ship's carpenter, Vicente Esteves, in whom he had implicit confidence; and he put in the bag which had contained the jewels, some stones of about the same weight as those he had removed. This was all done with such secrecy that very few persons knew about it.

It so happened that on the bank of this river where we were, and when we were all famished and extremely hungry, the carpenter's Negro slaves saw an extra wallet in his tent, which their master would entrust to no one. Thinking that it must contain rice, they conspired with the captain's Negroes and resolved to open it at night, which they did, taking out one of the packets of jewellery, thinking that each one contained a measure of rice, since we usually carried our rice in little packets of a measure apiece. Taking the packet out of the bag, they took it into the bush where they opened it, and finding that it contained jewellery they fled with it, fearing that they would be hanged for the theft.

In the morning the carpenter, seeing the wallet rifled, rushed to the captain, crying out that the jewellery was stolen. This jewellery being our salvation, we took up arms and hurried to the tent of captain Sebastião de Morais, where we saw the bag apparently full and fastened with the padlocks it originally had, so we thought the whole thing was a hoax. Captain Pedro de Morais in great vexation told us the aforesaid story, saying that there were now no jewels there,[1] and showing us where they had been we perceived the theft. Attaching full belief to the carpenter's story without attempting to verify it any further, the captain went to the tent of Sebastião de Morais and ordered him to be seized and his hands bound behind him, together with four men of his company, one of whom he put to cruel torture in his blind rage, although these poor men were quite innocent of what they were accused. The man whom they thus tortured severely was called João Carvalho, and the poor wretch called upon the Virgin Mary of the Conception to help him. She permitted that just at this time the identity of the real thieves was discovered, and if this had not happened so soon the captain would otherwise have had the men hung out of hand. Belatedly realizing the innocence of these four men, the

---

[1] This is another example of Vaz d'Almada's careless writing. As he himself states a few lines above, only one of the packets of diamonds was stolen, and, as explained on p. 199, n. 1, some of the remainder eventually reached Goa.

captain released them, still keeping their captain Sebastião de Morais a prisoner.

Then the captain summoned the chief men who were there, namely Rodrigo Affonso de Mello, captain Gregorio de Vidanha, Thomé Coelho d'Almeida, Vicente Lobo de Sequeira, António Godinho, and myself. He showed to each of us individually an accusation which he had drawn up against Sebastião de Morais, in which it was stated that he was an unruly and rebellious man, the head of a faction, a mutineer, and that it was feared he would be our destruction by inciting his partisans to go off with him after robbing us, which would leave our camp much enfeebled without those fighting men who were the best we had, with other incriminating charges of this kind. He told us that the peace of the camp demanded that this man should be killed, for his life might be the source of great troubles which his death would prevent. Then he called on these persons to vote on this matter, and they voted as seemed good to them. When it came to my turn and he put the case to me, I told him that I was no Crown Judge to sentence anyone to death, and that if he wished to order his execution he must find some other pretext to do so. He answered me in these words: 'What would you say to this if I had challenged him?' I held my peace, and he went to the shack of Lopo de Sousa to inform him about this matter, and after drawing up some papers,[1] he ordered the accused to be beheaded. This was done without anyone being able to save him, nor was any adequate reason given for this execution, which was naturally criticized, and in fact regarded as a great atrocity, particularly at a time when we had need of all our comrades, and the victim was a bold and resolute youth.

We continued our journey through these wastes, climbing and descending some very rugged ranges, and crossing many rivers which were full of hippopotami and other remarkable animals. Here we killed[2] the aforesaid Kaffir whom we had found at the place

---

[1] Despite all their hardships and the amount they had to carry, the castaways still seem to have had some paper, pens, and ink with them.

[2] *tomamos* in the original 1625 edition, which Gomes de Brito has corrected to *matámos* in the *HTM*.

where we disembarked and who said he came from Angoxa.[1] In return for what we gave him he had promised to accompany us and show us the way, and as he tried many times to escape we held him prisoner. Fearing lest he should tell the Kaffirs of our weak points, such as that our matchlocks could not be used when it rained (for he often asked about this from our Negroes, and he often saw that we tried to fire them but could not when they were wet), and because he would often tell us one thing and then the contrary, for all these reasons we resolved to put him to death.[2]

We continued our journey until about the 15th December, when we reached a river where we arrived half-dead with hunger, so that the sailors and grummets in the camp sold a measure of rice for 100 or 150 *pardaos*,[3] or even as much as 180. Some persons spent more than four thousand *pardaos* in this way, among whom were Dona Ursula, for her subsistence and that of her children, and Beatriz Alvares.[4] We were very sad, because we were losing many people, but none from sickness for the land was very healthy.

Here I was involved in an incident which I have sufficient confidence in your worship to tell you about, and also because it was well known to all. While we were still on the hill-side before we came down to the river, the captain bade me go forward about a league with fifteen arquebusiers to see if we could discover a village, for we had now reached the region where the Kaffir had told us that we would find cows. Having advanced about half a league along a river that was winding through a plain, I saw a hamlet of fifteen straw huts, and in order not to alarm the Kaffirs I ordered six men to advance and see if there was any kind of food that they would sell us. But they declined to obey, on the plea that there seemed to be many people in the village and that we would be too far off to help them if they got into difficulties. This vexed me, and after arguing angrily with them I chose the four best arque-

[1] Above, p. 201, n. 2.
[2] Vaz d'Almada's excuses for this example of 'killing no murder' are anything but convincing, and he himself was obviously not very happy about it.
[3] The gold *pardao* had a theoretical value of 360 *reis*, and the silver *pardao* of 300 *reis*.
[4] Presumably he means by promissory notes or IOU's, as in the prison-camps in the Far East in 1942–5.

busiers present, who were João Ribeiro, Cypriano Dias, Francisco Luís, and the ship's steward, with whom I descended the hill and crossed a valley which lay between us and the Negroes' kraal, in which there was a river then at high tide, and we forded it with the water to our chests.

Having reached the entrance of their enclosure, we asked them to sell us something to eat, speaking to them by signs, and putting our hands to our mouths; for by carelessness or forgetfulness we had not brought an interpreter with us to explain what we wanted, nor had we asked the captain for one, although these Kaffirs could understand the Negro slaves we had brought with us from India.[1] They were amazed at seeing us white and clothed, and the women and children made a great hullabaloo, calling to the people of another kraal which was in the bush. [We retired and] their husbands who were with them followed us closely, throwing fire-hardened sticks at us. Seeing the harm which they might do us, I ordered João Ribeiro to fire at them with his arquebus, which he immediately did, but it did not go off, and the Kaffirs grew more enraged, thinking that the making of the flame was witchcraft. Seeing the danger we were in, I took careful aim with my matchlock and killed three with a single shot, for I always fired with one [ordinary] bullet and three shaped like dice. These deaths caused great consternation among them, and the survivors broke off their pursuit of us.

I loaded the matchlock again, and we withdrew very slowly. When we reached the arm of the aforesaid river, we found it almost dry, and a fishgarth with two very large traps which we opened and found full of quabs.[2] At this moment we were joined by our comrades who had come downhill on hearing the report of the matchlock, and we all loaded ourselves with this fish, which was a great relief at that time. But we were rather nervous about what had happened to us, since the captain had enjoined us to be

[1] Theal notes that this was the first Bantu kraal which the castaways found, and that although the narrative provides no means of identifying it, it was probably on the Bashee river. This, however, does not seem very likely in view of what is recorded below, p. 218. As the reader will have observed, the Portuguese called both Hottentots, Bantu, and crossbreeds, *Cafres* (Kaffirs) indiscriminately.

[2] Theal notes that fish were the last food-resource of the Bantu of the south.

patient and not fall out with the Kaffirs, because he thought [that if we did] it would lead to the whole of Kaffraria being up in arms against us, which would end in our destruction. But it fell out exactly the opposite, for henceforward whenever we were obliged to kill some of them in different parts, the wife or child of the dead man immediately came from the same kraals to ask us for something.

On returning to where the captain was, I made him a fine present of quabs, with which he was very pleased, and when he was well satisfied with the sight of something so very desirable and estimable in a time of such great hunger, we told him what had happened to us. He was much upset at this, and I did not doubt that if anything untoward had happened as a result of this incident I would have paid dearly for it, for every transgression was most rigorously punished. Earlier this same day, as the captain was going down to the river he saw a Kaffir, who on being interrogated said that there were some cows and garden-plots further on. Then the captain asked Rodrigo Affonso de Mello to go with twenty men and see what was to be found. The Negro went with him, but afterwards told them to return, as it was getting late, promising to come the next day and guide them to the place he had spoken of. Rodrigo Affonso at once turned back, and passing by the village where we had killed the three Negroes he found them still unburied, and the Negroes pointed them out with great fear and trembling, to the amazement of Rodrigo Affonso, for he did not know what had happened. They told him that the dead were to blame, because they had begun the war, and so they had reported to their king; and they gave him some of the produce from their garden-plot, consisting of calabashes and green water-melons. Rodrigo Affonso gave them two little pieces of copper, which is the best article for barter in these parts, and went on his way back.

The next day the same Kaffir came again, and Rodrigo Affonso set off with him, and they travelled for a day and a night. Journeying further on, he met in a valley the son of the king of whom the Kaffir had spoken, accompanied by a hundred Kaffir warriors all well armed with iron assegais. These were on their way to visit our captain, and they brought the finest ox that ever I saw, without horns, and they made the captain a present of it. Next day they brought another four cows, which they sold us, saying that if we would wait for another eight days they would bring us for sale as many as we wished; but if we would not, then we should wait till the next day when they would bring us twenty cows for sale. We did so, but they never came.

As our people were growing steadily weaker, especially those who were carrying the litters, and the provisions were virtually finished, and we were now somewhat rested, we resolved to push on; since we gathered from what the Kaffir had told us, that the country ahead was well provided. Next day we went and slept near a swamp that had no frogs in it, which was a great disappointment to us. Our hunger was now intolerable, and all the dogs in the camp that could be killed were eaten. They make very good food (not speaking of times of famine) for often when I had cow's flesh and there was a fat dog to be had, I chose the latter in preference to the beef, and so did many others. The men who carried the litters now declined to do so any longer, as they were utterly exhausted, and when the captain tried to force some of them to do so, a sailor named Rezão fled from this place to the Kaffirs.

Journeying on for a few days we came to a river, where there was a village of fisher-folk upon a height on the side in the direction of the Cape [of Good Hope],[1] and we pitched our camp on the other bank. They brought us for sale a small quantity of dough made from some seeds smaller than mustard which come from a herb that sticks to one's clothes. It tasted very good to those who were able to get any of it.

Here all the men who carried the litters assembled in a body, saying that if no one in the camp could take a step for want of food, and many had already died from starvation, what could they do who carried the litters on their shoulders? They might well be ordered to be put to death, but they could carry them no further, even though they were given all the treasures in the world; and it seemed to them that they had done enough in carrying them for a month and a half, up hill and down dale, and they were

---

[1] A singularly clumsy way of saying 'on the southern bank'.

ready to forego all that had been promised them for their past labours—all this being said with a loud outcry and tears. Then the Religious intervened, telling the captain that he had no right to force anyone to undertake such deadly labour, that one man had already fled to the Kaffirs, and that each one of these poor men looked like a picture of death. The captain then assembled all the people, and in a loud voice ordered a proclamation to be made that he would give eight thousand *cruzados* to any four men who would carry Lopo de Sousa on their shoulders, and the same for any of the women who were in the litters, and he would immediately pay the money into their hands, each according to his share. But no one came forward to volunteer.

In this place, for my sins, I witnessed the greatest cruelties and the most grievous sights which ever occurred or can be imagined. For the women who were in the litters were asked if they could accompany us on foot, since there was no alternative, and for their sakes we had come very slowly and were very backward in our journey, and many of our company had died of pure hunger, and there was no one willing to carry them for any money. Moreover, in order to avoid greater evils, and upon the advice of a qualified Religious theologian, it had been decided not to wait for anyone who could not walk, for our numbers were decreasing. Therefore those who had strength to walk were given until next day to decide, and those who were to remain would be left, together with many others in the camp who were weak and ill, in the fishing-village which was opposite us.

Your worship can now imagine what this news meant to Beatriz Alvarez, who had with her four children, three of tender age, and to Dona Ursula, who had three little children, the eldest eleven years old, and her old mother, who would necessarily be left behind, her husband and father both being already dead—to say nothing of Lopo de Sousa, that honourable and valiant gentleman, who had fought as such on board the ship, and whose wounds were still open and who was suffering from dysentery. This to me was the greatest pain and sorrow of all, for we were brought up together in Lisbon and we had served in India at the same time.

P

All this night was passed wholly in tears and lamentations, those who were to go on taking leave of those who were to be left behind. It was the most pitiful sight ever witnessed, and whenever I think of it I cannot restrain my tears. It was learnt next day that Beatriz Alvarez would remain with two of her three boys and a girl of two years old, a lovely little creature. We took her youngest son with us, though against her will, that a whole generation might not perish there. There remained also the mother of Dona Ursula, Maria Colaça, and Lopo de Sousa, and three or four persons who were too weak to accompany us. They all confessed themselves with great sorrow and tears, so that really it seemed a cruel thing that we did not remain with them rather than suffer such a parting.

On the one hand we saw Beatriz Alvarez, a delicate and gently nurtured lady, with a little girl of two years on the breast of a Kaffir woman who remained with her and would never consent to abandon her, a little son of five years old, and another of seventeen. The latter showed the greatest courage and love, behaving in the noblest manner possible in such a situation; for his mother told him many times that she was half-dead, her old disease of the liver having made great progress, so that she could not live many days longer even if she had been surrounded with every comfort, and that his father had gone in one of those ships which had fought against us and might very well be dead,[1] and that he was a youth and should go with us. All the Religious likewise urged him with many arguments, telling him that he was not only risking his body but his soul by remaining in this

---

[1] Theal relates (*History of Africa South of the Zambesi*, III, 72) that Luís da Fonseca on his return to Goa from Batavia, fitted out a vessel to search the coast of Natal for his wife and children, but that no trace of them was ever found. He gives no authority for this statement, which I cannot find in any of the contemporary sources I have consulted, but it may well be true. Cf. A. Botelho de Sousa, *Subsídios*, III (1953), 500. The whole of Fonseca's family did not perish on this occasion, as a son of his was expelled from the Augustinian Order at Goa some eight or nine years later, having been previously admitted as a novice. This expulsion, which the Augustinian chronicler implies was due to the family being of Jewish descent, was naturally bitterly resented by the unhappy father, and led to his becoming an avowed opponent of the nunnery of Santa Monica as mentioned above, p. 192 n. 1.

heathen land, where he might be perverted by their evil customs and ceremonies. To all this he replied very courageously that Our Lord would have mercy on his soul, and that hitherto he had always regarded them as his friends, but now he thought differently about them, for what excuse could he subsequently make to men if he left his mother in the hands of savage Kaffirs?

On the other hand we saw Dona Ursula taking leave of her mother who was to remain. Your worship can imagine the sorrowful things that they said to each other, and the grief which they caused us. Everyone went to take leave of Lopo de Sousa, and he, seeing that I did not do so, ordered his litter to be carried to the tent where I was, and he spoke these words to me in a loud voice and with great spirit: 'How now, Senhor Francisco Vaz d'Almada! Are you not that friend who was brought up with me at school, and were we not always together in India? Why don't you speak to me now?' Your worship can imagine how I felt on seeing a gentleman whose particular servant I was in that sad state. I rose up and embraced him, saying: 'I confess my weakness, your worship, for I had not the courage to see one whom I love so much in such straits,' asking him to pardon me if I had offended him in this. He, whose face had hitherto been dry, could not restrain his tears at this, and he bade those who carried him go forward. I would have gone with him to the Kaffir kraal where he was to stay, but he would not suffer it, and covering his eyes with his hands he said: 'Go in peace, my friend, and remember my soul, if God brings you to a land where you can do so.' I confess that this was for me the greatest sorrow and grief that I had hitherto endured.

The captain gave him some articles of barter, such as many pieces of copper and brass, which are more valuable than anything else in those parts, and two cauldrons. Two men, named Gaspar Fixa and Pedro de Duenhas, secretly remained behind here.

We set out very sorrowfully, making our way over high hills, and that night we camped on the bank of a river where we found some little crabs, which was no small blessing for us. We continued our journey next day, and pitched our camp that night by a fresh river, along which, further up-river, were three or four villages, to which we sent a Kaffir interpreter to learn whether they had any cows, or anybody who could tell us where such were to be found. In the meantime we went hungrily looking for shell-fish on a stony bridge formed by the shore, and to cut wild fig-trees for food. At nightfall we returned to the tents which we had pitched previously, very pleased with ourselves at having cut many fig-trees to eat. Here we learnt that the interpreter had returned, bringing two Negroes with him, who said that if they were given a piece of copper and two men, they would take these latter to a place where there were cows, and if they carried copper they would bring cows in the morning.

The captain joyfully agreed, sending Fructuoso d'Andrade and Gaspar Dias, who took with them what the Kaffirs asked for, and we were greatly rejoiced, hoping that they would return with very good tidings, upon which the lives of all depended. It pleased God that the next day at ten o'clock the men came back rejoicing, bringing us a cow and the news that they had seen many villages and cows at all of them. Then the cow was ordered to be killed and divided, and it was eaten roasted. It was our habit not to reject anything but the large dung, for the smaller, and the hoofs, marrow of the horns, and hide, were all eaten. Your worship need not be amazed at this, for those who had eaten all the Whites and Negroes who had died found this much tastier food.

Then we went in search of the villages, taking as guides the Kaffirs who had come with the two Portuguese that had brought the cow. Not being able to reach them that day, though we travelled far, we slept that night in a valley where the long grass stood higher than a lance. Next day we rose early in the morning, and marched up a hillside through some very pleasant country. On meeting some Negroes we asked them about the villages, and they replied that if we walked fast we would reach them when the sun was in the meridian. Being eager and in want, though weak, we kept on climbing, and in the afternoon we reached the top of a range from which we had the most beautiful view that our eyes could desire, for many valleys lay before us intersected by rivers and smaller hills, in which were an infinite number of villages

with herds of cattle and garden-plots. At this sight we descended
the hillside very joyfully, and the Kaffirs came out to meet us on
our way bringing jars of milk and cows for sale. We would
not buy the cows then, but told them we would cross a river
which was visible from the summit and pitch our camp upon
a small hill, where we would remain for three or four days;
and therefore we bade them consult among themselves, and all
those who had any eatables which they wished to sell for that
money, which was pieces of brass and copper, should come and
meet us.

Crossing the river, we reached the above-mentioned place at
sunset and pitched our tents in orderly fashion. The captain then
sent António Borges, whose task it was to buy all the provisions,
with an escort of four matchlock-men to station himself at a distance from the camp, in order to prevent the Negroes from mixing
with us—a custom which we kept inviolably throughout our
whole journey. And so that your worship may realize what good
order prevailed among us, I tell you that we carried all the articles
of barter and things to be exchanged for provisions proportion-
ately divided among us, those who had fewer weapons carrying a
greater quantity, in such wise that there was no single person who
was exempt from these labours. Everything, however small, was
entered in a receipt book, and was expended by this António
Borges in his capacity of factor and purchaser. And if anyone else
tried to buy anything, he was very severely punished, even if the
purchase was made with something that had been concealed. This
was done to prevent the fluctuations of price which are caused by
there being many buyers. This man gave an account to the captain like a purser[1] of everything which he spent, and this was
done during the life of the captain, and by me after I had succeeded him, until the end, as will be related below.

Before the day was out we had bought four head of cattle, including a large bull that the captain asked me to kill with my
matchlock, because an enormous number of Negroes were assembled, and he wished to show them the strength and power of

[1] 'Com escrivão' in the text, which must be a misprint for 'como escrivão'.
(Theal, 'like a secretary').

the weapons we carried. This bull was feeding among the cows, and in order to astound the Negroes more, I told them to stand aside so that the weapon might not harm them. They paid little attention to this, and remained where they were. I approached to within about thirty paces of the bull, and gave a shout so that he raised his head, which was bent down while grazing, and when he did so I shot him in the forehead, so that he immediately fell dead. The Kaffirs, seeing the effect of the matchlock, took to flight. The captain sent to call them back, and they returned very timidly, their fear being greatly increased when they saw the bull dead, and put their fingers into the bullet hole in his forehead.

All these four head of cattle were killed that day, and equally divided among all the people, as was always done, by men appointed for that purpose. The next day we bought ten or twelve more, and killed another four, the share of each person amounting to three pounds, not including the hide and the entrails, for everything was divided. The captain wished the people to enjoy this plenty, to see if we would recover our health and strength, and he had four cows killed every day while we were here. But this plenty caused us all to suffer from dysentery, because we ate the meat half-raw, and thus we were little better off than before. It truly horrified us to see that we were dying from want of food, and that a surfeit likewise killed us. Here they also brought us for sale a great quantity of milk and some fruits of the colour and taste of cherries, but longer.

This was the place where we bartered a greater quantity of cattle together than at any other time in the whole journey; for besides the thirteen which were killed while we remained there, which was five days, we took the same number along with us at the end of that time. We then travelled along a high and very long range of hills, where the Negroes brought us for sale many calabashes of milk, and the aforesaid fruits, and we camped in the middle of this range, surrounded by villages with abundance of cattle and garden-plots, and with a river at the foot. Negroes coming the next day with cattle for sale, we bought ten or eleven head. Here the captain ordered a Negress to be hanged for stealing a

small piece of meat which did not weigh half a pound—an excessively cruel punishment.

Next day we climbed to the top of that range, which was very
high, in quest of a village where dwelt the king of that whole
district. We reached it in the afternoon, and it was the largest we
had yet seen. The king, who was blind, came to visit the captain,
and brought him as a present a little millet in a calabash. Though
old, he was a healthy-looking man. It is worthy of note that though
they are savages without any knowledge of the truth, they have
such a serious mien and are so respected by their subjects, that I
cannot exaggerate it. They rule and punish them in such a way
that they keep them quiet and obedient. They have their laws, and
they punish adulterers gallantly in the following manner: if a
woman is guilty of adultery towards her husband, and he can
prove it by witnesses, she is ordered to be put to death, together
with the adulterer if they can catch him, whose wives the ag-
grieved husband then marries.

When anyone wishes to marry, the king makes the match, so
that no marriage can take place unless he names the bride. It is
their custom when their sons are ten years old, to turn them into
the bush, where they clothe themselves from the waist downwards with the leaves of a tree like the palm, and rub themselves
with ashes till they look as if they were whitewashed. They all
keep together in a body, but they do not come to the village, their
mothers taking food to them in the bush. These boys have the
duty of dancing at weddings and feasts which it is customary to
hold, and they are paid with cows, calves, and goats where there
are any. When any one of them has got together in this way some
three or four head of cattle and has reached the age of over eighteen years, his father or mother goes to their king and tells him
that they have a son of a fitting age who by his own exertions has
gained so many head of cattle, and the said father or mother is
willing to help him by giving him something further, and they
request the king to give him a wife. The king then replies: 'Go
to such a place, and tell so-and-so to bring his daughter here.'
When they come, he arranges about the dowry which the husband
is obliged to pay his father-in-law, and the king's palms are

always greased in making these contracts. This is the custom as
far as Vnhaca Manganheira, which is the river of Lourenço
Marques.[1]

After the captain had been visited by this king, as he was
greater than any we had yet seen, he resolved to give him a
specially fine present, which was a small brass candlestick with a
nail fastened to the bottom so that it made a noise like a bell. It
was well cleaned and tied to a twisted silken thread, by which the
captain hung it round his neck. The king was greatly pleased
with it, and his people were astonished to see such an excellent
thing. Thence we continued our journey next day till we came
to the biggest river which we had yet seen, above which we slept.
The following day we marched along some very high hills near
the river, with the intention of seeing if we could find a ford, or
some place where it was narrow and flowed with less fury, so that
we could cross over on a raft.[2]

We had with us twenty cows, and though we killed one every
day, and each person's share thereof was a pound, we suffered
great pangs of hunger. The river being very broad, we marched
for two days along a range of hills by very dangerous and pre-
cipitous paths overhanging the stream, until we reached a water-
meadow above which were some villages, wherein we resolved to
buy some cows. The Negroes lay in ambush on the bank of the
river in a place where we were obliged to go for water, and they
stole from us two cauldrons which served to hold it. But they paid
for their insolence, for when we had bought two cows from them,
seeing that they brought no more for sale, and a Negro bringing

[1] These were evidently Bantu customs, and Theal considers that the tribe concerned belonged either to the Tembu or to the Xosa clan. He adds that probably
only the Tembu were west of the Umzimvubu in 1623, the Xosa more likely being
still to the east, though the latter claim to be the pioneers of the Bantu race in its
onward march (*History of Africa South of the Zambesi*, III, 76). For the Vnhaca
(Inhaca) of Lourenço Marques see above, p. 71. Cf. also J. H. Soga, *The South-
Eastern Bantu*, 71, 81, 84, 86, 87, 92, 102, for the migrations of the Xosa.

[2] Theal considers that this river was in all probability the Umzimvubu, 'though
it is not absolutely certain' (op. et loc. cit.). Personally I consider this identification
very doubtful, as many weeks later they had only reached the vicinity of the Mapaka
river where the *Santo Alberto* was wrecked. Cf. below, p. 228. I suggest it may have
been the Bashee river.

some stalks of millet for sale, which we often bought to eat because they were sweet, the captain ordered me to fire at him, which I did, wounding him in the breast with a shot, and so he fled up the hillside. Here the captain ordered one of our Kaffirs to be hanged, since he had deserted from us twice.

Having marched for another two days along the hillside by the river, we reached a place where it seemed to us to be narrower. Here the captain ordered a Mulatto of his who was a very good swimmer to see if he could cross the river; but he was swept away and drowned on entering the water, owing to the strong current which was like a whirlpool. Seeing the strength of the current we resolved to go further up-stream; and the next day we journeyed on through some very pleasant hills which we found full of villages, and we pitched our camp at midday. After this, continuing our march with the design aforesaid, we passed by a village which stood upon a height, and as we did so, the inhabitants brought us a large quantity of the aforementioned fruits, which they bartered to us for the tags of laces.

Two grummets who were very weak came straggling behind the rearguard with their matchlocks on their shoulders. Seeing them in this condition, and that they were separated from us, a few Negroes came out of the village and took their guns away from them. Thomé Coelho and I, and some other soldiers in the rearguard came to the rescue, and entering the village we killed every living soul we found there.[1] We seized fourteen steers which we found penned up there, and brought them back with us. We pitched the camp below this village on the other side of a rivulet, near some other kraals, with great order and vigilance.

Early next day they sent us two old Negroes to make peace and friendship, but the captain showed himself much offended, saying that he was going on his way without harming anyone when they robbed him, and he threatened to be revenged for the injury they had done him. They made their excuses, and pointed out that we had killed many of their people; and after a lot of argument they

[1] Including inoffensive women and children, apparently. A particularly foul atrocity as the Negroes who had taken the grummets' guns had not done the lads any bodily harm, nor did they know how to use these weapons.

brought back the matchlocks and paid us an indemnity of two
small cows, and they gave us another two in return for the assegais
which we had previously taken from them. We also returned to
them nine of the fourteen calves which we had seized, for we had
killed the other five that same night, one falling to the share of me
and my comrades, which we divided with our friends.

In the afternoon they brought us two more cows and a bull,
which we bought from them. As the bull was very fierce, the
captain ordered that he should be killed with swords, from which
he defended himself so well that they could not kill him, and he
tossed the captain and three or four others severely. He therefore
asked me to shoot the bull with my matchlock, but before I could
do so he gave me a severe wound and sent the matchlock flying.
Picking myself [and the gun] up I then shot him through the
shoulder-blades, and he fell down dead below a bank on which
I was standing, as was my invariable habit on such occasions.
This was a contrivance of mine, for they gave me the foreleg of
every bull that I shot, which under the circumstances was no
small advantage.

Thence we went to the bank of a river and camped near it in a
strong place on a hill, where we resolved to wait till the violence
of the current abated, which it did not do for about twenty-five
days, which we spent in this neighbourhood, always patrolling
the river bank.[1] During that time the following incidents occurred.
On Christmas Day in the morning the captain sent Thomé
Coelho d'Almeida with twenty men to climb a very high range
which ran alongside the river, and to go five or six leagues along
it in sight of the river to see if they could find any place to cross.
After being away for two days he returned with the news that
there was no better crossing place than that where we were, and
that we had better wait till the rains were over and then the river
would flow less furiously and have less water; and so we did. Here
the captain ordered two little Negroes, one belonging to Thomé
Coelho and the other to Dona Ursula, to be hanged, simply for
stealing two small pieces of meat. The eldest was not twelve years of
age, and everyone felt very sorry for them and criticized such cruelty.

[1] Thus they had to wait about a month before crossing this river, whatever it was.

We christened this river that of Famine, for we suffered here the worst hunger that we endured during the whole journey. In order to see if there were any means of crossing it, the captain promised a hundred *cruzados* to any person who would swim to the other side, taking a fishing line tied to another stronger one that could sustain a raft on which we could cross over, like we had already done in a previous river. As nobody would attempt it, a Negro of mine named Agostinho volunteered to do it without any reward, and he accomplished it easily, being a strong swimmer. But after the line had been passed across, it was broken by the violence of the current, so that it was clearly shown that we could not cross over as we wished until a few more days had elapsed. During this time we subsisted by placing ourselves in sight of some villages to see if they would sell us any cows, which they did more from fear than goodwill. For we went right into the kraals to buy, being so desperate that if they had not sold them to us voluntarily we would have taken them by force.

Here I went to a kraal with António Godinho, and after we had bought two more cows, seeing that there was nothing more to be done I set out to return to the camp, which was in sight of us. After I had gone a little way I looked back, and seeing that my comrades were not yet coming, I sat down to wait for them where they could see me. Behind me was some very high grass, through which a Kaffir crept stealthily towards me and seized me from behind, pinning me down on the matchlock with one hand on the butt and the other on the muzzle, so that I was between him and the matchlock. We struggled like this for a long time until finally I remembered that I carried a knife, and I unsheathed it, invoking Our Lady of the Conception, for I was utterly exhausted, the Kaffir being very strong. I stabbed him several times until he let go the matchlock, which I immediately took up and aimed, but when trying to fire it I fell down from sheer exhaustion, and was only able to do so when he was already a long way off. Even so, I hurt him badly, and I afterwards picked up his cloak of skins which he had wound round his arm, and left behind in his flight.

All these Kaffirs wear cloaks of very well-dressed skins, which hang below their hips. The skins are those of small animals with beautiful fur, and these furs vary according to the quality of the Kaffir who wears them, and they are very punctilious about this. They wear nothing but these capes and a politer skin which covers their privy parts. I saw a grave Kaffir with a cloak of sable skins, and when I asked him where these animals were to be found, he said that there were so many of them further inland, that nearly everyone there wore them.

I also found upon the ground two assegais and a little piece of wood of the thickness of a finger and about two and a half spans long, covered from the middle upwards with a monkey's tail. It is customary to carry a stick of this kind throughout almost the whole of Kaffraria as far as the river of Lourenço Marques, and they never converse without it, for they emphasize all their talk by gesticulating with this stick in their hand, and they call it their mouth, making gestures and grimaces.[1] My comrades who were approaching saw what had happened to me and hurried forward, thinking that I was hurt, and we returned together to the camp, where we were very eagerly awaited because of the cows which they saw we were bringing.

Two days later, when we were still in the same place, there arrived one of our Negroes who had remained behind with Lopo de Sousa. The captain went up to him before anyone had spoken a word to him, and seized him, saying: 'Oh, dog! Who killed the Portuguese? Confess it, or else I will order you to be hanged forthwith!' The Negro was stunned, and said that he was not guilty of their deaths, nor were any of our Negroes who had remained behind with him. We were astounded that the captain should ask such a question without having heard any tidings of those people, and we asked him who had brought him such news. He replied that for two days those people had been continually in his mind, and that his heart had invariably told him that the Negroes who had stayed with them had killed them— and this was why he had asked that question.

This Negro further stated that the local Kaffirs killed in one night Gaspar Ficha [Fixa], Pedro de Duenhas,[2] and the nephew

---

[1] Cf. above, p. 121, n. 4.   [2] Cf. above, p. 213.

of the boatswain Manuel Alvarez, in order to steal a cauldron from them; and that our Negroes, his companions, were in another kraal, lower down and separate from the Portuguese. Being asked about Lopo de Sousa, he replied that when he had left that place three days before he was speechless, and that he had undoubtedly died on the last day that he saw him. That Beatriz Alvares, wife of Luís da Fonseca, was very ill and had become a leper, so that she could not move, and that the others were almost dead with hunger and had not strength to walk. This was the reason why they had not accompanied him, and they were doubtless all dead by now. The captain ordered him to be searched, and finding on him some gold pieces and diamonds which he knew had belonged to the Portuguese who had stayed behind, he ordered that he should be closely watched, intending to have him killed during the night. But he did not wait until dark, for a little while after we saw two youths of his company approaching, and when he recognized them, fearing the truth would come to light, he fled.

When the aforesaid two youths arrived they were at once seized and put to the torture, when they confessed as follows. Three days after we had separated from Lopo de Sousa, a Kaffir king came to that kraal with forty cows, saying that it was he who had promised to bring them to the captain, for whom he asked. They told him that the captain had gone, having first waited for him, but seeing that he had not come at the promised time, he had set out. The Kaffir replied that the swollen state of some of the rivers had prevented him from coming any earlier, and he asked if it was possible for him to overtake us. They said it was not, for we had been gone many days, but that two parties of our people had been left there, one consisting of Portuguese and the other of Negroes, and that they had money with which they could buy some cows from them. The Kaffir replied that he was very glad to hear it, as it was for this purpose that he had brought the cows from such a distance. The Portuguese immediately bought three of them, and the Negroes four, and they asked the king not to go away with those that were left him, for when they had eaten what they had bought they would buy more. But he replied that as there was no good pasture there he would move around for six or seven days, and then return to sell them those which they might need.

During the king's absence the Portuguese party ate up the cows they had bought, and were left with none. Gaspar Fixa then went down to the other kraal where our Negroes were, who had still two cows left alive, and asked him to kill one of them and lend him half, promising that as soon as the Kaffirs returned he would buy sufficient to repay them. They made no difficulty in doing so, killing one of the cows and giving him what he asked for. Two days later the Kaffirs returned, and all provided themselves with cows. Then the Negroes claimed payment for what they had lent, and went to ask for it on a day when the Portuguese had killed a very small cow. Gaspar Fixa replied that they could see the slaughtered cow, and must realize that their share would be a small one in comparison with what they had lent, which was the reason why he did not give it to them then, but if they would wait two days, which was the time it would take to eat that cow, then he would give them half of the largest he had. The Negroes retorted that he should kill it immediately and repay them, to which Gaspar Fixa answered that then half of the meat would be wasted; and seeing that they would not be appeased by his arguments, and infuriated with their insolent boldness, he struck a Sinhalese nigger[1] who was the leader of the others, calling him a dog and other insulting names, on which they withdrew.

Gaspar Fixa and his comrades were little perturbed by this incident, and when they were asleep in their kraal at night our Negroes came with some assegais which they had picked up on the line of march from the Kaffirs whom we had shot. They sent one of their number ahead to ask for a light, so that the Portuguese might open the door for him, which they did, never thinking what might happen to them. The Negroes then all rushed in together and killed everyone they found in the straw hut except Lopo de Sousa, who was in the state I have described, and the dead were those whom I named above. These two Negroes also

---

[1] 'Negro Chingala'. *Chingala* was the Portuguese word for 'Sinhalese', and not a personal name as Theal mistranslates it. Cf. Dalgado, *Glossário Luso-Asiático*, I, 274–5.

affirmed that Beatriz Alvares was in the same condition as described by the first Negro fugitive. They further alleged that they themselves had not participated in this killing, and that the ringleader in the crime was already dead, having been killed by the other Negro who had now fled.

We were deeply distressed at this news, seeing it was touch and go that our own Negroes had not rebelled against us, and we gave thanks to God, beseeching his mercy. The captain ordered them to be hanged that very day, though they did not remain on the gallows until morning, because of the fearful hunger we then suffered, but they were secretly eaten by Negroes (and by others who were none such) of our camp, which was overlooked and allowed to pass. Often in the camp at night I saw many spit-fulls of meat, which smelt like most savoury pork; so that one day when I got up to go on guard-duty, my comrade Gregorio de Vidanha told me to go and see what meat our servants were roasting that smelt so appetizing. I went to look, and asking one of them what it was, he asked if I would like to eat some, for it was excellent and very strengthening. But realizing that it was human flesh, I went away, pretending not to understand. By this your worship can see to what straits we were reduced, all for my sins.

Two days later, while we were still in this same place, the captain ordered a Portuguese lad who was a servant of the boatswain to be hanged, because he had been detected bartering for some food with a piece of an iron hoop which he had taken from the wallet of the second pilot, and also because he had fled to the Kaffirs. He was a sturdy youth, who could have been useful to the company, and truly these excessive cruelties finished us off in the midst of so many hardships—for although great rigour is requisite in whoever controls seamen, it should not be carried to such excess. This poor wretch begged for burial, that he might not be eaten; but his petition availed him little, for the captain gave an opportunity to our servants, who were weak with hunger, by ordering them to throw him into the bush, and they took good care to give him the same burial as they had usually given to those who died.

The next day the captain ordered three persons to cross this ill-fated river, the passage of which cost us so dear, and to explore the opposite bank and see what kind of country it was, and whether there were any cattle, and if the Negroes knew anything about us. They did this very thoroughly, and returned two days later very pleased with themselves, asking the captain for a reward as the bearers of good tidings. He enquired of João Ribeiro, their leader, if he would like something worth three hundred *cruzados*. The latter answered no, but that he would rather be given for himself and his comrade the caulker, the hearts of all the cattle which might subsequently be killed in the camp, which the captain granted him. From this your worship can see how little we prized anything, however valuable it was, in comparison with food.

After this promise had been made him, he said that four leagues away on the other side of the river there were many villages with plenty of cows, that their inhabitants seemed to be friendly, and they wanted us to go thither that they might sell us some of their cattle, and that they had received him hospitably. This was great news for us, since we hitherto had no idea of what was to be found there, and also because we were keeping some cows to take with us to the other side for food, in case there were none there, and this fear was the cause of our making a rule which was a great hardship for us, because we ate much less on this account.

On receiving this news, we moved towards the river, passing by the village where, as I have said before, we had killed many people.[1] We found the Negroes of that locality up in arms against us, and they pursued our rearguard, hurling many stones and assegais; but it pleased God that none of the many which they hurled did us any harm. Here we found the raft which we had made when we were there for the first time, when we thought that the current might allow us to cross on it, and as we found this contrivance we crossed over easily enough. Before doing so, we ate our fill, killing the cows which, as I have said, we had been saving for use on the other side, since we were now assured that we would find some there. Having crossed the river, which took us two days, we journeyed up over a very rugged mountain-range which we judged to be more than three leagues high, for we began

[1] Cf. above, p. 219. n. 1.

our ascent about eleven o'clock and did not reach the top until night had fallen. Thence we descended into a kind of valley, where we found water, but it was impossible to cook any food, as it was very late.

The next day at dawn we set out in search of the villages, which we reached at noon. The Kaffirs living there brought us three very large old bulls, for they usually sold us these as soon as they became too old for breeding, and cows of the same sort, but withal we thought they did us a great favour. And since we had not yet shown them what use we could make of our firearms, the captain ordered me to shoot one of the bulls which we had bought from them. This I did, and when they saw that it was dead they displayed the usual amazement. We remained there that evening, eating it and waiting for them to bring others for sale. Seeing that they did not do so, we set out again in the morning, and they followed our rearguard as we were descending the mountain, where, as it was very steep, they could have done us much harm, from which God delivered us.

Proceeding on our way we passed through some kraals before noon, when we stopped to dine above a river. Here they brought us two oxen for sale, and one of them being very wild was shot and furnished our dinner. We slept that night above three kraals which were situated on a slope, and interrogating the people thereof they told us that we would find no villages during the next four days' journey, and that if we wanted any cattle we had better wait there for two days. To this we replied that we could not wait, and if they wished to sell us any they should come early in the morning, for we would set out as soon as it was day, which we did. When we had journeyed some part of the morning, a few Kaffirs well armed with assegais came out to meet us, thinking to attack us in some way. They sold us a cow which was very wild, and having received the price of it they fled, and the cow did the same. But we seized hold of one of the Kaffirs, and bound him, taking him with us a short distance to see if they would bring us back the cow they had taken. This they soon did, a very tall Kaffir coming with it and apologizing for the theft which his people had tried to practice on us.

Q

Continuing our journey over lower ranges of hills some three or four leagues distant from the shore, we reached a very beautiful river, where they brought us for sale quantities of fruits, like those new ones which we had eaten of before, without stones, but they were more plentiful here.[1] Recognizing afterwards the great harm which this fruit constantly caused us, the captain did his best to avoid it, issuing proclamations with severe penalties [against eating it]; but all in vain, owing to the great hunger we suffered.

Here we found a Javanese from the shipwrecked party of Nuno Velho Pereira, who was already very old and spoke [Portuguese] badly. With many tears he kissed the crucifixes which we wore and made the sign of the cross. I confess to your worship that it was a great joy to me to see in such remote regions and among such barbarous people a man who knew God and the instruments and figures of the passion of Christ. This man told us how Nuno Velho was wrecked upon a beach about a day's journey further down;[2] and as his eyes were much injured and he was wounded in the legs he had remained behind in that place. He warned us about many things which we should observe in dealing with the Kaffirs, telling us that after four days' journey we would find a Malabar nigger[3] who had likewise escaped from the same shipwreck, and another nine or ten days from there we would find a Kaffir named Jorge, of the same party. And in the same kraal where this Kaffir lived there was a Portuguese born in São Gonçalo de Amarante,[4] called Diogo, who was married and had children. As my comrade Gregorio de Vidanha was by now quite exhausted, he resolved to remain with this Javanese, that he

[1] Cf. above, p. 216. Theal translates these 'new ones' as 'apricots', but this does not seem to be very satisfactory, as they were originally said to resemble an elongated cherry.
[2] Near the Hole-in-the-Wall, and mouth of the Mapaka river. Cf. above, p. 114, n. 3. Since the Javanese lived so close to the spot where the *Santo Alberto* was wrecked in 1593, this would seem to dispose of Theal's suggestion that the castaways from the *São João Baptista* had reached the Umzimvubu before Christmas Day. Cf. above, p. 218, n. 2.
[3] 'Hum negro Malabar' in the original.
[4] In the Minho province of Portugal. Famous for finding husbands for old women—'casamenteiro das velhas'. Cf. R. Gallop, *Portugal. A book of folk-ways* (Cambridge, 1936), 131, 133, 136.

might not afterwards be left in some desolate bush country, as had frequently happened before. This was a grief and loss to us, he being such a man as I have previously described.[1]

The king of this region came to see the captain in a very dignified manner, bringing a beautiful sheep with five quarters[2] to sell to him, and he asked more for it than the price of a large cow. Seeing what little use a sheep would be to us in comparison with the cow which we might buy with the price demanded for it, we told him to order cows to be brought to us, for we did not want sheep. Upon this they brought three, and being resolved to practise some cheat or theft upon us, they sold us a cow, and when they had the price thereof in their hand they began to flee with the animal. But we captured one of them and would have killed him, had not the Javanese bade us desist, saying that he would soon bring back the cow, explaining that the Negroes had acted like this because they did not know us. He asked us not to annoy anybody and promised to bring back the cow forthwith, which he promptly did. Seeing what badly disposed people these were, we went on our way, leaving Gregorio de Vidanha in the hut of the said Javanese, with a sailor named Francisco Rodrigues Machado in his company. We gave them some things which were of value there, that they at once hid[3], in order to buy a milch-cow or something else on which they might subsist until the season of the millet harvest, which was now green.

Passing through this kraal we went on our way, likewise leaving here Cypriano Dias, whom they robbed in our sight. Then all the Kaffirs of this kraal assembled and came after us with loud shouts, molesting our rearguard by hurling many stones and assegais. Seeing the harm which they might do us as they were so numerous, I remained behind with eight companions, and when they approached I fired my matchlock at them and one falling down they all stopped, turned back, and followed us no more. The report of the gun so terrified these people that often when they followed us in this way two men would stand out and face them

---

[1] He has only mentioned him briefly. Cf. above, pp. 195, 206, 225.

[2] Large-tailed sheep of the so-called Ormuz breed. Cf. above, p. 120, n. 2.

[3] 'Esconderão.' Possibly a misprint for 'escolherão', 'chose' or 'selected'.

with slings, which they made for this purpose, and at the crack of these catapults they would throw themselves on the ground.

Thence we journeyed through a country in which there was great lack of provisions, until, after four days, on descending a mountain we came to a kraal where the vanguard, which reached it first, shouted and passed back the word that there was a Kanarese from Bardes,[1] on which we hurried forward, and when we had all arrived we saw that it was the Malabar of whom the aforesaid Javanese had told us. He met us with many signs of joy, saying: 'You are very welcome, my Christians,'[2] and he bade us remain there and he would negotiate for all that we required. He said these Kaffirs had known of our coming two days before, and they had been told that we ate men, which was why they were up in arms.

The next day, finding that this report was false, the king came to see us, very mournful, his father having recently died. He sold us four cows at the request of the Malabar, who took us to see his daughters. They were the most beautiful Negresses in those parts, and on our asking him how many wives he had, he answered two, by whom he had twenty children, twelve sons and eight daughters. We asked him why he did not come with us, as he was a Christian, but he retorted how could he bring his twenty children with him. Moreover, he was married to one of the king's sisters, and he had cattle from which he lived, and even if he wished to go his wives' relatives would not allow it. He added that it would not be advisable for us to have him in our company, because of the harm that might befall us on this account, but that he was a Christian and that God would have mercy on his soul. He asked us for some rosary beads which we at once gave him, and kissing the cross tearfully, he hung them round his neck.

Three of our servant-girls who were married to three of our Kaffirs remained here, two of them being Kaffirs and the other a Javanese. The next day we continued on our way, the Malabar accompanying us for a good distance; then with many embraces and signs of sorrow he told us that we had a long journey before

---

[1] The district on the mainland immediately north of the island of Goa.
[2] 'Minha Christandade', literally 'my Christendom', in the original.

us, over many high mountain-ranges, and so he left us. The Kaffirs of that kraal, which was a large one, did not do us any harm, and therefore we called it the Land of Friends.

We journeyed on for three days, during which we saw few people and no kraals; and at the end of this time one afternoon we spied a few sheep grazing in the distance. As it was now late, we went no further, but we sent some men to find out what was ahead, so that in the morning we might have recourse to our barter as usual. On their return, these scouts said that as it was so late they had seen nothing but many fires, and had heard the lowing of many cattle in different directions. In the morning we climbed up a range, and we saw many kraals in very rugged places out of the course we were following. But soon a Kaffir met us and told us that there were kraals in all directions, except that whence we had come, and he pointed out some which were on the way that we ought to follow. And as he went along with us we saw upon the side of a hill two large kraals with many cows and some sheep, and it seemed to us that these people were more civilized and well provided. Here they sold us a cow, but afterwards repented of having done so, and we, knowing this, shot it with a matchlock. They were upset at this, and an elder brother of the man who had sold it to us gave him a severe beating because he had not consulted them. These two kraals had garden-plots of millet and gourds, some of which they sold us, and we found the taste very good.

After dining there, we went and slept above a kraal where they sold us three cows, and this was the first place where we saw a hen, which they refused to sell us. Marching for two days through valleys where there were many garden-plots of millet, which was not yet ripe enough to eat, they came out to sell us some hens by the wayside. Reaching a village where they told us their Inkosi[1] (as they call a king in those parts) was, we traded for some hens, obtaining sufficient to allow one between every two persons. We stayed here that day, waiting for them to bring us cows, for we were in great want of them, and at last they sold us a little stale millet, some milk, and two cows. Next day we went down to a

[1] 'Anguose' in the original.

river, to which we gave the name 'River of Ants', for there were so many and such large ones there that we were helpless against them. Here we remained for two days, crossing the stream on the third with a raft that we made.

On the first day of February 1623 we began our journey from the other side of this river up a very high range of hills, in a very heavy downpour of rain which lasted for many days. We made our first camp while it was yet light on a hillside near two kraals, in which there was nothing but some gourds and a few hens, part of which we bought. Here they informed us that only a little further on we would find great plenty, whereat we rejoiced exceedingly, for we had nothing whatever to eat, and if we had lacked food for two days longer we would all have perished of hunger, if God had not succoured us.

Here remained behind a sailor named Motta, an Italian called Joseph Pedemassole, and a passenger who was crippled, and the son of Dona Ursula, the last a very grievous case. He was called Christovão de Mello, and was about eleven years old, of good education and understanding. He was so emaciated that he looked the picture of death, whereas he had resembled an angel before these hardships. When it was seen that this child could accompany us no further, his mother was sent on in front, and he remained behind as usual, as he could not walk so well. Seeing that he could march no further with us, he said that he wished to make confession, which he did. Then he begged the captain by the wounds of Christ to send for his mother that he might bid her farewell, to which the captain replied that this was not possible, as she was already far ahead. The child complained at this, saying: 'That is enough, sir! Why does your worship deny me this consolation?' The captain spoke loving words to him and led him by the hand until he could go no further, but remained as in a trance, and we all went weeping on our way. It is to be believed that if his mother had seen him, her heart would have burst with such a great sorrow, and therefore the captain prevented him from seeing her.

On the second day of February, Candlemas Day, after marching all the morning we dined in a beautiful wood, through which flowed a stream of water. Here they brought us seven goats for sale, with which we went on to see if we could reach some kraals where they told us there were plenty of provisions. But as the rain was very heavy we could not get so far, and we slept at a place where a few Kaffirs were waiting for us with baskets full of millet, which was bought and divided among us all. Each person received a cupful of millet, and a little piece of the six goats (which were likewise killed), and he who got the skin had the best share.

Next day we reached the kraals of the longed-for plenty, where they at once brought for sale many goats, cows, cakes as big as Flemish cheeses, and so much millet that afterwards we could not carry it all. Here the captain ordered eighteen goats and a cow to be killed, and each one of us received six pounds as his share. They also brought so many hens that each person had one, and the food was so plentiful that we would all have died if we had not been attacked by diarrhoea.

On the following day the Manamuze[1] of those places came to visit us, and he brought a very large bull as a present. The captain ordered me to kill it with my matchlock, so that they might hear it, for the chief had many men with him, and also that they might see what weapons we possessed. When they saw the bull fall dead, though I fired at it from a great distance, the king took to flight, so that we had to send and tell him that this was done to celebrate his arrival to see us, and that he should return, for otherwise the captain would have to go and fetch him. Hearing these arguments he came back, but in such a state that from black he had turned white. The captain hung round his neck the lock of a gilt writing-box, and gave him the handle of a cauldron. He valued these things highly, and withdrew with friendly words and a show of gratitude.

Then we divided the millet and the cakes which we had bought, and which formed two large heaps. After we had taken as much as each of us could carry, we set out; still leaving some, as we could not carry any more. We marched along on the tops of

---

[1] Theal translates as 'chief', which is obviously correct from the context, but does not explain what language this is.

the hills, on the slopes of which there were so many and such fine-looking kraals that it was admirable to see the great quantity of cattle which came out of them. They brought us along the way-side a lot of milk for sale, but it was all sour, for the Kaffirs do not drink it otherwise.

At midday we pitched our camp by a fresh river in a valley, and thither came many Kaffirs, all bringing something for sale. We did the usual barter-trade on the other side of the river apart from the tents, with men keeping guard. We did this here with greater precaution because more Kaffirs came than ever we had seen before, and their numbers were so great that many of them climbed up the trees merely to see us, especially on the top of three trees at the feet of which the bartering was carried on, because they sheltered us from the sun, so that I do not know how they did not break beneath so great a weight. Truly a fine picture could have been painted of that place and the concourse of people. We remained here until the afternoon, and afterwards we bought fifteen cows and many cakes, so that we were all more heavily laden.

A young woman—servant of Beatriz Alvares—stayed here with four other persons, surfeited with over-eating, but three of them subsequently rejoined us. Proceeding on our way, we went and slept in a burnt clearing, at the foot of which flowed a stream of good water that sufficed to assuage our thirst. The next day in the afternoon we camped in sight of two kraals which were upon a slope, and the Negroes brought all the cows they had to show us, but they would not sell us any. This did not worry us, since we were taking about twenty along with us. Journeying on next morning, we spent the heat of the day near a river which flowed through a water-meadow covered with trees, under which we rested.

Here we were met by the Kaffir of whom the Javanese had told us, and speaking in Portuguese he said: 'I kiss your worships' hands, I am also a Portuguese.' He told us how in a kraal further on, through which we would have to pass, there was a Portuguese named Diogo, a native of São Gonçalo de Amarante.[1] The captain then asked him if he [Diogo] would like to go with us,

[1] Above, p. 228.

but [the Negro] replied that the Kaffirs would not allow him, because he gave them rain when it was required, and he was already old and had children. As we laughed on hearing this, the Kaffir said he would show us Diogo's hut. Here we bought many hens, and cakes, milk, fresh butter, and some sugar-canes. This Kaffir asked us for a cloth blanket, which we immediately gave him, and with which he was delighted. Turning towards many Kaffirs who were standing nearby with their wives, he called out in a loud voice in their language: 'Kaffirs, inhabitants of this land, come and sell to the Portuguese who are now here, and who are the lords of the world and of the sea, all the things you have to eat (enumerating them by name), and avail yourselves of the treasures they bring with them; see how they eat off things which you wear as jewels in your ears and on your arms'. And he called them 'beasts' because they did not all immediately bring what they had.

When we had finished trading and eating, we began to form our order of march, but before we had completed this a Kaffir stole a small pot from us. However, we immediately seized hold of another Negro, whom Thomé Coelho wounded with a sword-cut on the head, and we held him fast. As we went on our way, they sent back to us what had been stolen, so we at once released our prisoner, and continued our journey up a range of hills. On reaching the summit we saw below us many kraals, among which was a very large one that was pointed out to us by the aforesaid Kaffir, who told us: 'That is the city where the Portuguese lives'.[1] When we got nearer the said kraal, we saw therein a thatched hut with a four-sided roof, something we had not seen before during our journey, for all the others were smaller and round. We urged the Kaffir to go and call the Portuguese, but he replied that we should not bother ourselves about him as he would not come.

Thence we went on through heavy rain and slept upon a height, and that night the Kaffir who had hitherto accompanied us went away. As he knew our arrangements he returned that same night through some scrub at the back of our camp, and raising the edge of a tent where he had seen an arquebus kept, he carried it off. He

[1] The sailor Diogo from Amarante. Cf. above, p. 228.

did this so stealthily that nobody noticed it, although we were all awake because of the rain which had poured without ceasing for two days and wet everything we had. When we found the arque-bus missing in the morning, we realized at once who had taken it. Although we wanted to push on, we were prevented from doing so by the incessant rain, and we stayed there another day, during which they brought us for sale some cakes, goats, and a beautiful bull. Seeing that the rain did not stop, but seemed rather to in-crease in fury, we resumed our march the next day until the after-noon, when we came to a large river, near which we camped on high ground, so that we had water and firewood near at hand. In order to dry ourselves we made large fires, which we kept up all night, and we placed the usual watches.

On the 12th February, when the first watch was relieved, the Kaffirs made an assault on us, attacking us on three sides. All the people sprang to arms, and seized their matchlocks, which were very wet, because it had rained unceasingly for three days. Seeing that they would not go off, I shouted to put them by the fire as they were, in order to dry out the gunpowder with which they were primed, and everyone did so. While we were thus waiting for them to dry, they almost drove us out of our camp, screaming such extraordinary war-cries and long-continued whistles that it seemed like hell. They killed Manuel Alvares and a gunner called Thin-gummy[1] Carvalho, both of whom died on the spot, and they seriously wounded sixty persons, of whom António Borges died next day. When the matchlocks were dry, we began to kill the Kaffirs, and the first to do so was a sailor named Manuel Gon-salves, who distinguished himself by firing the first shot. When the Kaffirs saw the heavy loss we were causing them, they took to flight, leaving a large trail of blood behind them. The Virgin Mary of the Conception was pleased that it should cease raining while we were fighting, which was a long time; and the moon shone forth so brightly that it was a great help to us in avoiding defeat. We kept watch all the rest of that night, moving the camp higher up to a stronger place; and we had suffered so severely that little would have sufficed to put an end to us.

[1] 'Fulano' in the original.

These Kaffirs fight in a better way than those previously met, for they use shields like targets of wild buffalo hide, which are very strong, and covering themselves therewith they hurl countless assegais, with which the camp was covered. We found so many of them next day, that there were 530 tipped with iron, besides many others from which the iron tips had been extracted and hidden in order to trade with.[1] Those of fire-hardened wood were so numerous that they could not be counted, and they did as much damage as the others. Early next morning we entrenched ourselves, and set about caring for the wounded, who were so many that not one of us escaped without hurt from an assegai or a stone. We made the best recoveries that ever I saw, for many were pierced through the breast from side to side, others through the thighs, and others had broken heads, but none of them died, although we had no dressing but cows' marrow. Captain Pedro de Morais had the inner side of his elbow pierced through.

We remained here for two days in which the carpenter, Vicente Esteves, made a raft like a boat, which was rowed with four oars. During this time the very Kaffirs who had attacked us came to sell us hens, cakes, and *pombe*, which is a wine that they make from millet.[2] We dissimulated, pretending not to know them, and bought from them what we needed. Other Kaffirs also came from the other side of the river to sell us the same things, crossing the river on pieces of wood, with a kind of pitchfork high above the water, from which their merchandise was suspended. These people asked us why we had killed so many of the others, and when we told them what had happened to us, they told us to cross over to the other side, as there were bad people on this. They said they would show us where we could cross the river three days later, for now the water was high and it would be lower then.

But before this time two persons crossed over on the raft, and afterwards Rodrigo Affonso, António Godinho, and Friar Bento

---

[1] A similar practice was noticed by the survivors of the *Grosvenor* after a skirmish with the natives on 10 August 1782: 'not choosing to lose the iron of the lance, they drew out the lance-staffs and sharpened the end, and threw these staffs at our people' (P. R. Kirby, *Source Book on the Wreck of the Grosvenor*, 37).

[2] Evidently the *byala* or *tiwala* (beer) mentioned on p. 165 above.

of the Order of St Francis, and others embarked upon it, and it capsized before they reached the bank. They were nearly drowned, and the father dropped his habit which he had stripped off and was carrying across. In it were lost a quantity of precious stones that had been given into his keeping, the proceeds of the sale of rice, for which people pledged diamonds, and other jewels which had been entrusted to him by many people, some of whom had stayed behind, and others had died. On the day indicated by the Kaffirs we crossed the river higher up, and we called it the River of Blood.[1] Four of our comrades remained here, and we saw elephants for the first time, one on each bank. The day after we had crossed over Father Manuel de Sousa died.

Thence we marched onwards for two days, keeping within two leagues of the shore, and at the end of that time we came to a river which looked like a lagoon and debouched on to the beach. Here we saw an elephant with a young one, and as the rearguard was coming along later they saw many elephants, which took no notice of us, nor in all this journey did they do us any harm at all.[2] Having crossed this river at the mouth, with the water up to our necks, we went on along the shore until we came to another river with many large rocks at the mouth, and we could not cross it because the water was too deep. Climbing up a steep hill, we saw some Kaffirs who said they would show us the ford, and for a few little pieces of copper they carried over the children and many persons who were sick. This people thenceforward are of a better type, and we called them the Naunetas, because when they met us they said 'Naunetas', which in their language means 'you are

[1] As they were apparently about two weeks' march from the region of the Mapaka—Umtata rivers where the Javanese castaway from the *Santo Alberto* lived (above, p. 228). I suggest, very tentatively, that this may have been the Umzimkulu river.

[2] The presence of elephants raises another puzzle. The castaways from the *Santo Alberto* first saw elephants not very far from the Lebombo Hills and long after they had crossed the Tugela. Cf. above, p. 172. According to Vaz d'Almada's account, the castaways from the *São João Baptista* can now only have been about fifteen days' march from near where the *Santo Alberto* was originally wrecked. Cf. above, p. 228. They must still have been far south of the Tugela, unless, as is possible, Vaz d'Almada's chronology is quite unreliable and he has telescoped the length of weeks into days.

welcome', and to this greeting the reply is 'Alaba', which means 'and you also'.[1] Here they sold us a great quantity of fish, and they helped us to carry the loads which our Negroes bore, singing and clapping their hands.

Thence we went and slept on the edge of the beach, where the king of the country, whom they call Manamuze,[2] came to see us. He was a youth, and came in a very dignified fashion with three brass collars round his neck, brass being valued above all else in those parts. On seeing him coming, the captain took him a little silver bell, which was incomparably more valuable to the king, and wearing his scarlet cloak he approached the spot where the king was waiting. They greeted each other, the Kaffir losing nothing of his high bearing; but when the captain saw his attitude he began to move his body so that the bell rang, at which they were all astonished, and the king could contain himself no longer. Taking the bell in his hand, he looked inside to see what it was that made it ring, and moving it and ringing it he laughed loudly the while, never taking his eyes off it all the time that he was there.

It is a remarkable thing how these brutes are respected in their way; and in their different generations and families they are so united that the sons never lose the places and kraals which are left them by their fathers. The eldest son inherits everything, the others calling him father and respecting him as such. Thieves are cruelly punished (though they are all thieves), and they have a jocund mode of justice which is as follows. If a Kaffir steals a kid or something trifling from another, the owner of the kid and his relatives can pass on the culprit what sentence they choose, which is usually that he be buried alive. Here they sold us a very large fat ox, and these they call *zembe*.

We marched for three more days into the interior until we came to a great river, which the Kaffirs showed us how to cross, with demonstrations of friendship. A sailor named Bernardo Jorge was left behind here. Thence we travelled for two days along the shore

[1] Cf. the greeting *Nanhatá* given by the chief Luspance to Nuno Velho on p. 119 above.

[2] Cf. above, p. 233.

until we reached another river, which was narrow at the mouth but very wide further up. As we were now in want of millet, we waited there for a day, and so many Kaffirs came bringing quantities of hens for sale that they covered the hills. I saw them bringing maimed people here on their backs in order to see us. Having crossed this river, which we called 'of the Crocodile' since we saw one swimming therein, we continued on our journey in the interior, keeping a league from the shore. Marching on for five days among friendly natives, we debouched at the mouth of a river, which seemed as if it could be forded; and remaining there for a day, they brought us some hens for sale.

There are numberless elephants in this region, and we heard them trumpeting all night long, but they never dared to come near us, on account of the many fires which we usually made. The Kaffirs told us to go further inland, for we could cross over the river then. We did so, and they showed us where the ford was and helped us in our passage of it. Dona Ursula was nearly drowned in this river, for the water reached to our beards, and as she was small it began to close over her. Since she could swim she thought she would be able to stem the current, and when it was seen that she was being carried downstream she was rescued only with difficulty. We called this river 'of the Islands', because there were several in mid-stream.

Thence we journeyed over some hills in quest of millet, of which we were in need, since we did not buy any at this river in order not to burden ourselves. At nightfall we reached some miserable kraals, where there was nothing to be had save gourds. After travelling another four or five days we reached another river, which was a good league in width, with many thick reeds along the banks, and we crossed it with the water up to our waists. Here and further back many persons were left behind with dysentery and other diseases, but I cannot recall their names as there were so many of them. All these ills were caused by the millet, which we ate whole and raw, and as we were not used to this food our stomachs were greatly weakened and debilitated by our eating many poisonous things. In the middle of this river is an island where we saw many hippopotami. We were almost the whole day crossing it, reaching the other bank in the afternoon, and there we slept.[1]

Next day we journeyed over some barren plains, and there came to meet us a Kaffir with a round brass ornament hung round his neck which covered all his breast, and he bade us go with him and he would lead us to a place where there were plenty of provisions. He led us along in a river with the water up to our knees, and it was shaded by trees so high and thick that during the two hours we were wading in it we did not see the sun. Having finished with this river, we travelled all that day without stopping, because we had no millet. We reached the kraals in the evening, and seeking to provide ourselves we found only one kind of food, which is the same as that which is given to canaries in Lisbon, and there called *alpiste*, and by the Kaffirs *amechueira*.[2] These people had lured us out of our way simply in order to see us, and they showed great surprise at the sight of us. They asked us the reason why we came through strange lands with our women and children, and when our Kaffirs told them, they twisted their fingers as if invoking curses upon whoever had caused our shipwreck.

Thence we travelled over a flat country inhabited by very poor people who nevertheless received us hospitably. After two days we reached a kraal near the shore, in which we found some fish, and the people showed themselves more compassionate than any we had yet met. For the women and children went down to the beach and threw many stones into the sea, uttering certain words which seemed like curses; and then turning their backs upon it they lifted up the skins which covered their backsides and exhibited their arses to the ocean. This is the worst form of insult which they have, and they did this because they had been told that the sea was the cause of our suffering so many hardships and of our wandering for five months through strange lands. This last was what surprised them most, as they usually never travel ten

[1] Could this river have been the Tugela? Assuming the River of Blood (above, p. 238) was the Umzikulu, and that Vaz d'Almada had forgotten how many days' march lay between them.

[2] The Kaffir-corn described on p. 82, n. 2, above.

leagues from the place where they were born, and they look upon
that as a far journey.[1]

From here we went back about a league into the interior,
traversing low sandy country, poorly supplied with provisions. At
the end of three days' march we came to the River of the Fishery,[2]
in which we found a lot of fish, and where the people made us
very welcome. At its mouth this river is narrow and has high
banks, but a league up-country it is more than three leagues broad,
and at low tide it is dry. The Kaffirs have countless fish-garths
here, which they call *gamboas*, made of wattles joined together,[3]
which the fish enter at high tide, and when it ebbs they are left
dry. As the tide was right out we crossed the river, many Kaffirs
going along with us, helping to carry our heaviest loads and singing very joyfully the while.

This day we took our dinner upon the seashore, and not finding
any fresh water there, we were very sad. However, we discovered
some in the salt water, for there was a spring the size of a conch-
shell in the sea, which bubbled up with such force that it spouted
up a span high above the salt water. When the tide went out it
was left on dry land, and we all quenched our thirst and cooked
our food there. We journeyed on for two days, keeping along the
shore of the Golden Dunes, which begin here.[4] At the end of this
time we were in great want, as we had only three cows left and
there was no water where we then were.

Here we met a Kaffir who told us that he would lead us to a
place where they would sell us plenty of millet, hens, and goats.

---

[1] Cf. above, p. 123.

[2] Rio da Pescaria. The identification of this river is another puzzle. Fontoura da
Costa in his 1939 edition of Manuel de Mesquita Perestrelo's *Roteiro* (1576),
identifies the Ponta da Pescaria with the modern Tugela Bluff in lat. 29° 13′ S,
which would identify this river with the Tugela. As, however, Vaz d'Almada
states below that the Medões do Ouro, or Golden Dunes, began after they had
crossed this river, it looks as if it must have been either the Umhlatuzi, or else the
Umfolozi, or one of the smaller rivers in between the two. Cf. *Africa Pilot*, III, 189.
Cf. above, pp. 176–7.

[3] 'Feitas des escadas juntas' in the original. *Escadas* means 'ladders', 'steps',
'stairs', or the like in Portuguese, but I have taken Theal's translation as making
better sense.

[4] Cf. penultimate note.

He guided us through a valley running inland, and leaving us near a large spring, he notified the neighbouring kraals, when they brought us plenty of hens and millet. Here the principal Kaffirs came to see us, wearing a novel sort of dress, consisting of large skin capes which came down to the tips of their toes. They were of a very grave and dignified mien, and they asked our captain to go past their kraals, wherein they would provide us with more food. We did so this same day, and as it was late we slept in a valley nearby. Next day we went to the kraals where we were well received, but we did not find what they had told us.

These Kaffirs saw me shoot a bird dead with my matchlock, at which they were greatly astonished, for it seemed witchcraft to them. While they were talking of it among themselves, there came up to the captain a man who had been crippled by a crocodile a long time before, and he showed him that the wound was an old one and asked him if he could heal it, promising to pay him very well if so. The captain cleverly replied that the wound had been inflicted a long time before, and therefore it could not be cured in a short time, and furthermore that he must give him something so that he might cure it with a good will, for without this nothing could be done. The Kaffir said that he was content, and sending for a bowl of millet he gave it to him, but the captain after taking it replied that he was not yet willing. The Kaffir then sent for three hens and gave them to him, asking if he was willing now? The captain answered 'yes', and the Kaffir observed that if he was not, he should not try to cure him, for he well knew that he could not be cured without a right good will.

The captain then treated him in the following manner. He took a brush which he carried and which had a small mirror at the back, and putting it before the Kaffir's eyes, the latter was astounded and called to the others who were there; but the captain told him not to move or speak, and when he had quieted down after seeing the mirror, the captain took the brush and brushed his wound, and anointing it with a little cow's fat he bound it up with a piece of *bertangil*.[1] Having done this, he told the Kaffir that after two moons he would be cured, but the wound

[1] Cf. above, p. 175, n. 1.

R

being so old it could not be healed quickly. The Kaffir felt very reassured and told the captain that he was only a poor man, otherwise he would have given him more. Other cripples immediately came forward, and they were all treated in the same way.

We marched along the shore for another two days and then we came to the River Santa Luzia,[1] where pieces of cloth are already valued, and we bartered them for millet and hens. We remained there one day, and crossed the river the next, when nine persons died from the cold. This river is two leagues wide, and as the water came up above our chests and the current was very strong we were half-dead by the time that we had got across it. Here an old sailor named Francisco Dias went out of his mind; he was maimed in both arms by two assegai wounds which the Kaffirs had given him in our late fight. We at once made large fires at which to warm ourselves, and the sailor recovered his reason when he became warm. We remained here till next day, trading for quantities of millet, cakes, and dough made of *ameichueira*,[2] which they usually eat raw, and we likewise did so. We bought two more cows, one of which I shot with my gun.

Thence we continued our journey along the shore of the Dunes of Gold, and this name was bestowed on it with good reason, for they look exactly like dunes, their earth being a golden colour and as fine as flour, but hard, and full of rivulets of water which course through these dunes and their water is yellow, of the same colour as the earth. And from what I saw further on in the lands of Cuama,[3] it seems to me that there must be gold here, for the earth resembles that from which quantities of gold-dust are extracted, and I am the more convinced of this because the earth is heavy. These dunes run along parallel to the shore and near to it, and they are about forty leagues long.[4]

[1] The entrance to Santa Lucia lake in lat. 28° 24′ S. Cf. above, p. 176.

[2] Cf. above, p. 82, n. 2.   [3] Zambesia. Cf. above, p. 124, n. 2.

[4] The reddish-coloured sand in this locality is mentioned in the *Africa Pilot*, III, 192. Perhaps the Portuguese name, Medões do Ouro, Golden Dunes, was originally derived from or suggested by the Arab term, 'Meadows (or Downs) of Gold', which seems to have been applied, at least in part, to where the land of Zanj marched with that of the Waq-Waqs, somewhere below Sofala. Cf. Masʿūdi's *Meadows of Gold and Mines of Gems* (compiled A.D. 956), as epitomized in E. Axelson, *South-East Africa, 1488–1530* (London, 1940), 2–3.

Marching onwards, we crossed a river where the Kaffirs robbed a sailor called António Martins, who had straggled behind the company in order to buy something secretly. Keeping along the shore, we came to another small river, in which the water reached to our knees, and we ate our dinner alongside it. The pilot being told to take the altitude of the sun, he found the latitude to be rather over 26° S, which caused us to rejoice, for we knew by this latitude that we were only twenty-six leagues (or a little more) from the river of Lourenço Marques, and we had thought that we were further off.[1] Here they brought us a dead buffalo for sale, at which our joy increased. We also met a Kaffir with a hat on his head and wearing a piece of cloth, who assured us that what the pilot had said was correct. We likewise saw other Kaffirs wearing cloths, and they told us that we could reach the Inhaca in four days' time. Here they do not know the river of Lourenço Marques, nor Cape Correntes, but only the Inhaca, who is a king living on an island at the mouth of the river of Lourenço Marques, as I shall relate hereafter.[2]

At this above-mentioned rivulet a child was left behind, the son of Luís da Fonseca and Beatriz Alvares. He was very emaciated, and had often stayed behind at some of the previous kraals, but the Kaffirs had always brought him along to us the next day, and we thought that the same thing would happen this time.[3]

We marched for another four days along the shore, at the end of which time a Kaffir came to meet us, accompanied by six others. He looked very much a gentleman, and was well adorned with a chain going many times round his neck, a fine piece of cloth round his waist, and both hands full of assegais, for this is the way in which their most important persons deck themselves out. And nothing in these people whom we met, from the remotest tribes in the place where we landed, surprised me more than what I shall now relate. They had so little knowledge of us, that they thought we were creatures born in the sea, and they asked us by signs to

[1] This was not a very accurate observation, as lat. 26° S runs through Inhaca island in the Bay of Lourenço Marques, and the castaways were now presumably somewhere in the vicinity of the Kosi river in lat. 26° 54′ S.

[2] Cf. also pp. 71–2 above.

[3] Either this or (more likely) another son did survive. Cf. above, p. 212, n. 1.

show our navels, which two sailors immediately did. They then asked us to breathe in and out, and when they saw us do this they nodded their heads, as if to say 'These are human beings like us'. All these Kaffirs as far as Sofala are circumcised, and I do not know who went thither and taught them this rite.[1]

This above-mentioned Kaffir was son of the Inhaca Sangane, the legitimate king and lord of the island in the river of Lourenço Marques, whom the Inhaca Manganheira had dispossessed.[2] He resided on the mainland with his followers, awaiting the death of this tyrant, who was very old, to return to his former possession, as I shall relate hereafter. He led us about a league into the interior to his kraals, where they sold us some goats. We asked him to lead us to his father, but he postponed this for a day, hoping that we would buy something more in his territory. Being eager to reach our destination, we would not remain there long, and when we set out again, he ordered the way to be shown us, realizing that nothing would induce us to stay longer. On this line of march we saw a large straw house, and before we reached it we could discern many figures without faces, fashioned like dogs, crocodiles, and men, all made of straw. On asking what they were, I was told that this was the house of a Kaffir who gave rain when their garden-plots needed it.[3] Witchcraft is their only form of government.

We ate our dinner in the shade of some trees, where they brought us a quantity of honey in the comb for sale. Here a Kaffir who spoke Portuguese came to meet us, bringing a message from the Inhaca Sangana, father of the Kaffir we had met before. The sight of this Kaffir was as joyful news to us, for we were reassured by him, and believed that what they had told us previously was true. He delivered his message, which was that the Inhaca bade us go to where he was, where nothing would be wanting for us, and he would give us a boat in which to cross to the other side of the river, and he would do all we wished. The captain, not trusting

[1] Cf. above, p. 123, n. 2, for a note on Bantu circumcision.
[2] Cf. above, p. 157, n. 2, and p. 181, n. 3.
[3] Presumably a witch-doctor's hut, rain-making being of course one of his principal functions.

to all this, sent a Portuguese to him carrying a present of some articles of copper. This man went and spoke with the Inhaca and many other Kaffirs there, after which he returned bringing the captain a bunch of bananas, at which we were delighted for they are good Indian fruit. This emissary said that the king seemed to be a good man, that he had no forces with which he could harm us, that he was waiting for us, and that his followers said that many Portuguese came there every year. In order to hasten our coming, he sent us a sailor from Mozambique, who had remained there from one of the ships which had visited the bay in past years.

Upon this we set out, and having marched for about a league along the edge of a marsh, we reached the place where the king resided, which was on a height between two small hills. As it was now night he did not speak to us, but sent his men to show us a place adjoining his kraals where we could pitch our tents. Next day the captain went to see him, and hung a gold chain with the insignia of the Order of Christ[1] round his neck, and gave him two *sarasas*, a kind of cotton-cloth worn by Indian women which is highly valued.[2] He received this with great dignity, and speaking but a few words told the captain not to worry for he would leave his lands well content, since he had no greater desire than to be a friend of the Portuguese. Thereupon the captain withdrew. This Negro is a great personage, and was always loyal to the Portuguese.

The next day he came to see us, and ordered goats, sheep, many hens, and *amechueira* to be brought us. But as he delayed showing us a boat which he said he had, we went straight to the beach, and after marching along it for two days we reached the river of Lourenço Marques, which we so greatly desired, on the 6th April

[1] The leading Portuguese military order of knighthood. Founded after the suppression of the Templars in 1319, the grand-mastership being incorporated in the Crown in 1522.

[2] A patterned cloth from Coromandel, much in demand in the Malay Archipelago as a waist-cloth, and for other uses in Japan, where the word was taken into the language. Mr J. Irwin notes that the pattern could be either painted or woven, and either in cotton or silk. He adds that the term may be derived from the Hindi *sarasa*, 'superior', and seems to have been used as the generic term for a sort of unsewn garment, rather than as an indication of style or pattern. Cf. Dalgado, *Glossário Luso-Asiático*, II, 293; J. Irwin in *Journal of Indian Textile History*, II, 42.

1623.[1] We did not recognize it until we actually reached it, for the above-mentioned island[2] lies very close to the mainland on the side of the Cape of Good Hope, and thus everything looked like a part of the mainland to us as we marched along.

When we had traversed the shore for about a quarter of a league we pitched our tents and fired [a salute of] three or four salvoes of matchlocks. As it was then night we lit our fires, and all with Fr Diogo dos Anjos, a Capuchin friar, and Fr Bento gave thanks to God for having brought us to a place where we were known and whither ships came from Mozambique. Next day we saw two dugout canoes with Negroes who spoke Portuguese very well, whereat we were still more pleased, for hitherto we had not seen a canoe or a boat of any sort. The captain sent to visit the king of the island, who was the Inhaca Manganheira aforesaid,[3] asking him to let us know whether he had a vessel in which we could go to Mozambique, and whether he had provisions upon which we could subsist for the month which we might have to remain there until a vessel could be got ready to take us over to the other side, so that we could reach it in good time to find the ship from Mozambique. The Inhaca replied that we should go to him and he would provide us with everything, sending us three small vessels in which to cross over to the island, which we immediately did.

When all our people had landed on the island, we marched in our usual order to the kraal where the king was. It was composed of large houses with palisaded courtyards, so that they looked like the dwelling-place of a warrior. He was seated on a mat, covered with a cinnamon-coloured serge cape, which seemed to be of English manufacture, and with a hat on his head. Seeing the captain he arose, but without moving forward, and gave him a hearty embrace. The captain took off the cape which the Inhaca wore, leaving him naked, and covered him with another one of black *capichuela*,[4] and hung round his neck a silver chain with a whistle, which had belonged to the boatswain Manuel Alvares,

---

[1] The Bay of Lourenço Marques (Delagoa Bay). Cf. above, p. 71, n. 3.
[2] Ilha do Inhaca, or Inhaca Island.   [3] Above, pp. 218, 246.
[4] Theal translates this as 'silk', and so it may have been, but I cannot find the word in any dictionary I have consulted.

a thing which he esteemed highly. This Negro looked very old and fat, whereas throughout the whole of Kaffraria I never saw a Kaffir who was round-shouldered or fat, but on the contrary they were all upstanding and lean. He bade us pitch our tents near the kraals, and next day they brought us for sale quantities of fish, hens and *amechueira*, and a few sheep.

The king came to see the captain and showed him the vessels which he had, which were small and badly damaged. When our carpenters saw them they said that they were only fit to take us over to the other side of the river [= bay], which was a distance of seven leagues; neither had they any stocks upon which to build larger vessels, and that it was no use waiting for the ship from Mozambique, which could not come until March of the following year, and therefore he should ask the Inhaca to order the vessels to be quickly repaired, for the Kaffirs are very dilatory. To this the captain replied: 'I think we should cross to the other side and march onwards to Inhambane, which is quite near, and we should not be more than a month at the most upon our way. We should not wait for a year in the lands of this Kaffir, who is a traitor, and who killed here two years ago a priest and three Portuguese to rob them, and therefore no *pangayo*[1] has come here for so long, nor is one likely to come soon, and in time he will gradually do the same to all of us.' All this had been told him by the other Inhaca on the other side, and so it had actually occurred.

Having spoken thus, the captain went to the Inhaca, and asked him to have the vessels repaired, for he was resolved to go on, and not to wait for the ships from Mozambique, which had not come there for two years, because of the treatment formerly received from him, and perhaps next year they would not come either. The Inhaca replied that it was true he had killed the priest and the Portuguese, but it was because they had killed his brother, and that if we did not trust him we should go to an island close by, which could be reached on foot at low tide, and there we would find water.[2] He added that he would order a fish-garth to be made for every two Portuguese so that we would have sufficient pro-

---

[1] Cf. above, p. 69, n. 3.
[2] Setimuro, or Ilha dos Portugueses. Cf. above, p. 71, n. 5.

visions, for Portuguese had often wintered there before, and they had never complained of him until now.

He said further that he would give us ten of his Kaffirs, and we might send two Portuguese with them to Inhambane to make known how we were waiting here for the ships to come. To this the captain replied that he was anxious to reach his destination quickly. The Kaffir reiterated that he should on no account undertake this journey, for the Mocrangas would kill him, as they had done to the people of Nuno Velho Pereira who could not find room in their vessel;[1] that the country beyond was very unhealthy; that his huts were full of ivory and amber which he could not dispose of if the Portuguese did not buy these from him; and that therefore it was in his own interest to treat us very well and not offend us; and that we should believe him.[2]

But the captain insisted on going, and told him so, begging him to order the vessels to be fitted out. After he had taken leave of him, we went to the aforesaid island,[3] which lies about a league distant, and there we remained while the ships were being repaired, which was until the 18th April. Rodrigo Affonso and I wanted to stay here, and we went to the captain and told him as much, saying that we did not dare to march any further overland, but would leave when a *pangayo* arrived. The captain rebuked our want of confidence, saying that he was amazed we should want to turn back from the journey when we were going in the right direction, and that we should not abandon him simply because it was said there were robbers further on; but if we did so in spite of everything, he would make a [formal written] protest against us. It seems that this gentleman foresaw what would happen.

Overborne by these arguments we embarked with the rest of the company in four boats, which could not carry us all at once, but had to make two trips. On this same day of our departure we reached an island on the other side of the same river [= bay] at midnight, where we landed and slept for the remainder of that night.

[1] Cf. above, pp. 185–6.

[2] All this was perfectly true, and the Portuguese had only themselves to blame, or rather the mulish obstinacy of Pedro de Morais, for the disasters which followed from their ignoring the Inhaca's advice.

[3] Setimuro, or Ilha dos Portugueses. Cf. above, p. 71, n. 5.

Next day at dawn Rodrigo Affonso de Mello, who was already ill, became much worse, but he could still speak plainly, and having made his confession he expired on another island which we reached that night. I assure your worship that nothing could have caused us greater grief, and the greatest share was mine as his servant, for besides being such a great gentleman he had an angelic disposition. I can say that it was due to him that we had surmounted all our hardships with relative ease, for he was always the first to fetch and carry firewood and water on his back, or to enter the sea in search of shell-fish, and when the others saw a person of such quality do this, they were encouraged to imitate him and not to lose heart. We buried him here in this island the next morning, and put a mark upon his grave.

Thence we followed an arm of this river [= bay] to another island belonging to a Negro called Melbomba,[1] where we disembarked and waited for the boats to return with the rest of the company who had remained on the island of the Inhaca,[2] which was until the 7th May. We all fell ill during this time on account of the unhealthiness of the locality and also because we ate much of our food raw. There died here Father Fr Bento, Manuel da Silva Alfanja, a gunner named Pascoal Henriques, a sailor called António Luís, and a grummet called João. When the remainder of the company arrived, most of them were also sick, and eight persons had died of those we had left with them, but as I do not know their names I cannot list them here. We left in this island, because they were very ill and could not accompany us, António Godinho de Lacerda, Gaspar Dias, ship's steward, Francisco da Costa, sailor, and a servant of the captain.

Crossing over to the mainland, we continued marching along the shore until we reached the lands of a king called the Manhisa,[3] who is the most powerful in these parts. On the 13th of the same month he came to see us on our way, where we were waiting for some of our people to recover, and as several of them grew worse

[1] This island and the one previously mentioned presumably belonged to the Xefina group off the north-western shore of the Bay of Lourenço Marques, near the mouth of the river Incomati.

[2] They had remained on Setimuro island really.

[3] Cf. above, p. 72, n. 4.

we left them with this king, who showed goodwill towards us; and generally when a ship comes to these parts it finds the best market in his country. He told us to travel inland, for the people were better, and he warned us that if we continued on the way we were going we would all be robbed and killed. As the captain never took advice from anybody, and relied solely on his own judgement, he acted unwisely in many things, besides which he was so partial to the seamen that he did nothing without their approval,[1] even though it might be some punishment which was inflicted on themselves. This was the reason why this matter was not remedied, and also because there were few men of gentle birth.

Dona Ursula remained here with her eldest son, whose name was António de Mello. There also stayed behind with her Iaques Enrique, two grummets, and a Negress belonging to Thomé Coelho. They carried this lady in a hammock made from pieces of cloth, with her son in her arms; and it was most pitiful to see a young and beautiful woman, whiter and fairer than a Fleming, the wife of a man so honourable as Domingos Cardoso de Mello, the Chief Justice of criminal cases in the State of India, and so rich, now in the power of Kaffirs, and shedding bitter tears. As we feared that she would not live long, we took her younger son with us, which added to her grief. The king took her with him, saying that she should want for nothing, and the captain promised to give him a *bar* of merchandise[2] if he treated her (and also the others) well.

As soon as the king left we set out, still keeping along the shore. The captain had been ill for some little time and was carried in a litter until we reached a river called Adoengres,[3] which was on the 16th of the same month. Here the captain, realizing his condition, and that he often spoke wanderingly, ordered that a

---

[1] Thus contradicting the assertion that he acted solely on his own judgement, without taking advice from anybody. In any event, it is obvious that Pedro de Morais was a singularly obstinate man.

[2] 'Um bar de fato.' The *bar* is here the Indo-Arabic *bahar*, a weight varying from 141 to 330 Kg., in accordance with the type of merchandise involved. Cf. Dalgado, *Glossário Luso-Asiático*, I, 78–9.

[3] This can hardly be the Incomati, but I cannot find any other sizeable stream between here and the Limpopo on such maps as I have consulted.

general election should be held to choose someone of merits and parts to take his place. Summoning the whole company, he declared that he was now no longer capable of leading them, and therefore they must consider what man among them could best do so, for they all knew each other well, and what each one was worth. He therefore placed this election in their hands, so that they should not subsequently complain of him, and when they had all voted he would do so likewise. They all voted for me, extolling my virtues, and the captain said that this was also his choice. Then Pedro de Morais sent for me, and told me that these people had elected me as their captain, and that he had voted likewise, and he hoped to God that I would lead them with more prudence than he had hitherto done, for as an onlooker I knew in what ways he had irked them. I replied that I would try to see if I could imitate him.

I immediately went to my tent, taking most of the people with me. I told them that I had accepted this post solely out of zeal for our common preservation. In order that none of them should complain of me at any time, I chose six of the principal persons present, without whose advice I would take no important step. They all approved of this, because captain Pedro de Morais never took counsel with anyone upon any matter whatever. The persons whom I thus chose were Father Fr Diogo dos Anjos, Thomé Coelho d'Almeida, gentleman, António Ferrão da Cunha, gentleman, Vicente Lobo de Sequeira, gentleman, André Velho Freire, and the pilot.

When this was done, the camp notary came with these six persons and notified me in the king's name that the precious stones in the wallet were in danger, for the Kaffirs had been following us for three days, and it was carried by one man whose sole duty was to look after it, and it might happen that farther on, where we were told that there were very warlike Kaffirs, they might defeat us and take it all from us, since it was all together in an unwieldy package. There was the more danger of this, as so many people were sick and could not manage the matchlocks, and the powder was useless as it had been wetted so often. [He said] that therefore I should order the wallet to be opened, in which there were seven packets of rough diamonds very well sealed, and divide those among such persons as I thought proper, taking a receipt from each one, declaring that he had in his possession the said packet of rough diamonds with so many wax seals and such and such arms; and that at no time could the person who carried it, if he should save it, claim more for doing so than what fell to his share, dividing it among all [the seven?] according to the merits of each one and that this should be done for the good of all and for the better security of the jewels.

As this was approved by most of the company, and was the best plan in case some misfortune should befall us, I sent for the wallet and ordered it to be opened in front of everybody. I then commanded that each of the seven packets of rough diamonds which it contained should be covered with leather, and making out the respective receipts, I entrusted the packages to the following persons: Thomé Coelho d'Almeida, Vicente Lobo de Sequeira, André Velho Freire, the pilot, Vicente Esteves master-carpenter, João Rodrigues [Leão], and myself. The receipts and other papers relating to this transaction were deposited in my hands.[1]

We had now been there two days, and we left at this place three of our comrades, one of them a gunner and the other two grummets. The Kaffirs brought us nothing whatever for sale, but on the contrary did us all the harm they could, refusing to show us where the river could be forded. I therefore sent one of our Negroes to sound it with a pole in his hand to find the passage, and that he might do it more willingly I gave him a golden chain; for here they were no longer our slaves, and it was necessary to keep them satisfied in order to prevent them fleeing to the local Negroes. He did this at once, sounding the stream in one part and another until he found the ford; and setting up sign-posts in it we crossed over with the water up to our beards.

As we were now entering the country of the robbers, we tried to march on as fast as we could. And so we did, fighting continually with them, which we did with great difficulty, being sick and

[1] Despite the hardships of their adventurous journey, they still seem to have been carrying pens, ink, and paper with them. Cf. above, p. 206, n. 1.

weak, for provisions were scarce and the Kaffirs would not sell us any.

We journeyed thus until we came to the river of Gold,[1] which is very deep and wide, and flows with such fury that more than eight leagues before we reached it we found huge trees torn up by the roots in such quantities that they covered the shore, so that very often we could not pass over them, and we soon realized we must be approaching some great river. The lord of all this region is a very old Negro, whom they call Hinhampuna.[2] We were greatly distressed at the sight of this river, for we thought it would be impossible to cross it. But before long we saw two dugout canoes coming down-stream, at the sight of which our fears diminished. Calling them over towards us, I sent to ask if they would carry us across, to which they replied 'yes', and said that they would come next day with more canoes in order to do so. I ordered a piece of *bertangil*[3] to be given them for their favourable answer, and they went away.

As we were waiting for them the next morning, the men who were on guard saw advancing upon our side of the river over two hundred Kaffirs very well armed with many assegais and arrows, and they were the first we had seen with these arms. I at once ranged everyone in order, and fired off several guns. They came towards us in a body, with their king in the middle. He was bravely dressed in the Portuguese fashion, with a doublet of *tafeçira*[4] inside out, a pair of baggy trousers back to front, and a hat upon his head. He came dressed like this to show that he had dealings with us, and that we might trust him, but his design was immediately perceived. He brought me a present of two

[1] The Limpopo.

[2] A misprint or misunderstanding for Inhampura (Nyapure), the name by which the natives still designate the country round the mouth of the Limpopo. Cf. above, p. 75, n. 3.

[3] See above, p. 175, n. 1, for explanation of this word.

[4] J. Irwin describes this material as a 'cheap striped cloth of mixed silk-and-cotton, patterned in the loom, much in demand by the slave traders, and also in the Malay Archipelago. Woven in the Cambay-Ahmedabad area and Sind' (*Journal of Indian Textile History*, I, 30). The quotations in Dalgado, *Glossário Luso-Asiático*, II, 336, show that the word was also applied to finer materials, but Irwin's definition is probably applicable in the present instance.

bunches of bananas, for which I paid him very well, giving him a *bertangil*.

Negotiating with him about sending us across in his boat, he said that he would do so if we paid him for it, upon which we settled for three *bertangils*. After this had been agreed upon he asked for two more. I at first refused this, but then said that because he was old and had come to see us, I would give him the other two pieces which he asked for. A little later he said that we must pay still more, whereupon I arose and withdrew to the tents, giving order that all were to be ready with their arms in their hands until after midday. Seeing that they did not withdraw, I sent him word that the Portuguese never allowed other people to stay alongside them, and that I told him this because it was growing late, and at night we might kill some of his followers with our guns, with which we kept watch all night. He returned answer that his people would go away at once, and that he alone would remain with four Kaffirs, waiting for the canoes to come next day, when he would give orders that we should be taken across, for he was our friend.

As soon as I saw his people going away, I ordered two shots to be fired over their heads, and when they heard the bullets whistling they threw themselves down on the ground, and sent to ask the meaning of this, for they did not wish to quarrel with us. I sent back a reply that it was an accident, as two guns went off when being unloaded and the bullets happened to go that way, where-upon they withdrew. The king stayed behind, as related above, and we kept strict guard all night, firing off our guns as each watch was relieved. In the morning, seeing how we had acted all the night, and that they could not do what they wanted without risk to themselves, the king took leave of me, saying that he would send straightaway two Kaffirs to arrange with me for our passage, and whatever they did he would agree to. This he did, sending the two Kaffirs, with whom I agreed for eight *bertangils*, which were not given them until after they had ferried us across. Two of our comrades died here.

During our passage of the river the Kaffirs had resolved to attack us in the following way. They had sent word to the Kaffirs on the other side to wait till half the company had crossed over and then to fall upon them, and they would do the same on their side. In order to accomplish this as the Kaffir king desired, they brought four small dugout canoes, intending that they should cross one by one, but I, perceiving their design, ordered the canoes to be lashed together in couples so that they might carry more people, and placed half of the best men in them, with orders that as soon as they reached the other side they should occupy a piece of high ground, which could be seen from where we were, and entrench themselves there while the others crossed over. I also ordered that two men with matchlocks should return in each of the two canoes, so that these could not make off.

While this was being done we remained with our matchlocks and lighted matches in our hands, so that we never gave them any chance of doing anything. It was an excellent idea to send two men in the canoes while the passage was being made, for if we had been divided we should have been lost. I crossed over last of all with eight comrades, and then the Kaffirs in the first canoe told me all their design, bidding me to be on our guard in the future, for that was the country of the worst Kaffirs in all Kaffraria, who would kill us simply for the sake of stealing the clothes that we wore, and they were very numerous. I thanked them for the warning, and gave them a piece of *bertangil*, and then pushed on as quickly as possible.

As soon as they knew that we had crossed the river, many Kaffirs came to attack us, with whom we fought all day. Our people were becoming disheartened, because they wounded us from afar with their arrows, so that very often we could not see who had injured us, for they shot at us from the bush and we were marching along the shore, and only a few of our men knew how to aim well with their matchlocks. Fearing that they would destroy us when they saw how weak we were, I decided to lie up in the bush during the day time and to march along the beach at night, for the sea ebbs a long way out there and this would leave us a good distance from the bush. And thus we marched by night when the tide was out, so that when the sea came in it might efface our tracks upon the sand.

On the eve of Pentecost, as we were marching by night, we saw many fires along the shore, from which we concealed ourselves, keeping very close to the sea; and we passed by them very quietly without being seen, pressing forward as quickly as we could until the third watch, when we took cover in the bush. We remained there keeping strict watch until it was night and the tide was half out, when we marched on in orderly fashion until the middle of the second watch, when we saw in front of us many fires which barred our way from the edge of the sea to the bush, so that we could not escape from them.

As we approached, the Mocaranga Muquulo, who was king of all that region, sent to tell us that we must not pass through his country at night, as it was not customary, and that he did not want to fight with us. I sent a reply that the Portuguese required no man's permission to go wherever they wanted. He then sent to tell me to beware of what I did and not to cause a war, for all the Portuguese who passed that way made him a present, as they did in other parts. On hearing this message all the company raised a loud clamour, saying that for the sake of two pieces of *bertangils* which we could easily pay him, I would destroy them all, for none of them were in a condition to fight.

Hearing this outcry, I summoned the persons aforesaid[1] so that we could decide together what we had better do. I told them that I thought it would be best to fight and pass through these Kaffirs by night, so that they could not perceive our weaknesses; that the guns inspired greater terror by night; and that if a disaster befell us we might more easily escape with the precious stones; but that if we waited till daylight as they desired, more enemies might come than were now before us, and they would see that we were weak and disheartened. To this they replied that most people were in such a state that they could not fight by day, let alone by night, and that if I insisted on doing so, only about ten or twelve men who were ashamed to do otherwise would fight, and that all the others would run away. That it might be that the Kaffirs would be contented with what we could give them and would withdraw, and thus we would avoid exposing ourselves to such a risk.

I insisted that we ought to pass, saying many times that if at the

---

[1] The members of the advisory council enumerated on p. 253 above.

River of Blood the Kaffirs had seen how few people were really fighting they would have killed us all; but as the darkness concealed this, they thought that we were all fighting, and therefore they fled. God knows how many there were who fought that night that I speak of.[1] They replied that I should not bother, for it was not advisable for us to pass by night, and this was the opinion of them all. When I saw that this was the opinion of the best men there, I said that they were witnesses that we remained against my judgement, and that they must give me such attestations to that effect as I thought necessary. It seemed as if my heart divined what afterwards occurred.

When I saw that we would have to remain there until morning, I sought out the strongest natural position which there was, upon a height; and ordering many camp-fires to be lit, I took all the packets of rough diamonds and had them buried secretly, commanding a large fire to be made over the place where they were buried. We spent the rest of the night with our arms in our hands, nobody going to sleep. Early in the morning the king himself came, with whom I agreed for nine *bertangils* and a scarlet cloak. He then asked for some silver pieces from the head-stall of a horse, which we likewise gave him; and he kept on asking for more and I gave him everything that he wanted, till, declaring himself satisfied, he took leave of us with demonstrations of friendship. When he had gone, and there was nobody in sight, I ordered the packets of diamonds to be dug up and returned them to those who had charge of them.

As we went marching along the shore, over a thousand Kaffirs sallied out of the bush and attacked our rearguard, which fought on its own and was soon defeated, all those therein being left very badly wounded and stripped bare with nothing left to cover their private parts. The remainder of the company, seeing this rout, fled into the bush without being able to hide anything, for the Kaffirs immediately fell upon them and stripped them, whereas if they had showed fight we should not have been defeated; and had they fired their matchlocks while we were reloading ours, we could have gone on fighting in this way and killing all the Kaffirs until

[1] Cf. above, p. 236.

they retreated, as others braver than these had done in our frequent combats.

Finding myself naked and with five deep arrow-wounds, one in the right temple, one through the chest, from which my breath escaped, one through the loins, whereby I urinated blood for twelve days and from which I could not extract the iron arrow-head, another in the left thigh, in which the iron also remained, and another in the right leg, which was bathed in blood, I resolved to go into the bush that they might tend me, and to see if they would give me something with which to cover myself. Being in this frame of mind, Thomé Coelho and the others sent to tell me that they would not go on without me, and that we should try to push on, as Inhambane must be near. I replied that I was good for nothing, and that they should go on and God help them. I asked a sailor named Tavares, who was also wounded in one leg, if he would like to go with me, and we would return if God gave us strength, for it could not be but that the Kaffirs would take pity on us on seeing our plight. He consented unwillingly, and we followed them for over a league until I could go no further, and there in an open field they all assembled with the things they had stolen from us. The king, recognizing me, ordered the arrow-heads to be extracted and my wounds to be dressed with a sort of oil which they have there called *mafura*, and when this was done they gave me an old sleeveless doublet, and a little of the food which they had robbed us of.

Here they divided all the treasures they had brought, setting more value on a clout than on priceless diamonds, all of which the king kept for himself, as two of our little Kaffirs, who were there with him, had told him that a diamond was the most precious thing of all, and that he would be given a *bertangil* for each one. When they had made this division they went away; and we, being left alone, returned to the shore to see if we could find any of our comrades, carrying a lighted lunt to make a fire at night.

When we had gone a little way we heard some whistling in the bush, and turning we saw two clothed Negroes, whom we at once recognized as ours. On speaking to them, they told us to wait and they would go and fetch João Rodrigues de Leão, who was in the bush. He soon came, and embraced me, saying that he had not been robbed, for he had hidden himself well; and taking off his coat he gave it to me, telling me that he had there intact the packet of diamonds with which I had entrusted him, bidding me to dispose of them as I pleased. I replied that since he had guarded them so well he should carry them as far as Inhambane, and there we would decide what to do. Thus we travelled on by night, for in the day these cursed Kaffirs would not have left us the miserable rags we wore. We were also joined by another of our comrades, a Frenchman named Salamão, whom I warmly welcomed because he could bleed me, for I could not move on account of the congealed blood from my wounds. He at once did this with a lancet which he carried.

Journeying for four days along the shore, we crossed a river[1] with the water up to our necks, which was ice cold, and did me great harm. Here we found the greater part of our people, who were glad because the Kaffirs gave them something to eat straightaway. Then André Velho Freire came to me and said that he had saved the packet of diamonds which I had entrusted to him, and asked my orders concerning it. I bade him carry it to Inhambane, and that there we would decide what to do. Thus we journeyed on through the lands of the Zavala, a shiekh or ruler who was our friend,[2] until we met an old Kaffir, the subject of a king named Aquetudo,[3] who as soon as he saw us refused to leave us, telling me that we must go through the territory of his king, where we would want for nothing; and so it proved from the time we met him until he led us to Inhambane.

That day he made us travel a long way in order to reach the place where the king was; and though we arrived at night he welcomed us very warmly, ordering us to be provided with everything needful while we remained there. He killed a cow for us, and came to see me three times every night, always bringing some-

---

[1] Evidently the Rio Inharrime.

[2] This district, bordering on the Rio Inharrime, is still called by the same name. See A. Cabral, *Raças, usos e costumes dos indígenas do districto de Inhambane* (Lourenço Marques, 1910), 52–5.

[3] Possibly a corruption of Nhacutô, name of a chief and district in this region. A. Cabral, *Districto de Inhambane*, 53.

thing to eat, and telling us not to worry any more as we were now in the country of the Portuguese, and he was like us, the only difference being that he was black. He kept us here four days, after which he accompanied us for a day upon our journey, and giving me two elephants' tusks he returned, leaving his eldest son to go with us to Inhambane, together with the old man aforesaid, who fed us all the way until our arrival there, which was on the 19th June. Here we were very well received, and had no lack of food that night.

Next day the pilot came to see me accompanied by Father Fr Diogo [dos Anjos], these two having reached the other side of the river a couple of days previously with the other people who were missing. They told me that the Innhapata and Matatima, two kings there,[1] were waiting for me, to distribute in my presence all those persons who were on the opposite bank, that I might afterwards pay them for all they should expend therein. I welcomed them, and told them that since I had only arrived the day before it would seem reasonable to arrange first about those who were on the Chamba side,[2] which was where I was, and that afterwards I would cross over and do as they said.

That same day there came to meet me a Christian Negro who lived here, named André, who served those kings as interpreter when the Portuguese came thither. He took me to his hut and I stayed there until I left for Inhambane [Sofala]. Next day the aforesaid king came to see me, with whom I arranged about accommodating the people in the huts of those Kaffirs who had most property. He thought this a good plan, but told me that it could not be done that day, because it was necessary to send for them, and he would return early the next day bringing them all with him. This he did, and when they were all assembled he asked me who would pay the expenses of lodging all those people? I told him that I would pay them, and he retorted laughingly that as I had not the wherewithal to buy a chicken, being still naked,

[1] Possibly the ancestors of two petty chiefs with similar-sounding names, Nhampata and Nhatitima, mentioned by A. Cabral, *Districto de Inhambane*, 46.

[2] From what is said immediately below, this was evidently the locality on the east side of the river Inhambane.

how could they trust me? To this I replied that the word of a Portuguese was worth more than all the riches of the Kaffirs; and after much talking on both sides, which is what they most prize, he made me promise to pay all the expense of their maintenance, and then the king said he would be my surety. I then distributed the Portuguese as the Christian Negro advised me, for calling [the Negroes] out by their names he said: 'To this Kaffir you may entrust some respectable man, for he is a good Negro and a rich one.' In this way were accommodated all those on the Chamba side, which is in the direction of Cape Correntes;[1] and then crossing over to the other side, where I was very well received, I did the same there.

This is a most beautiful river, half a league wide, and on the Chamba side there is good anchorage for ships of up to 300 tons burden. The middle is for the most part dry at low tide, and there is a quantity of shell-fish, of which the Kaffirs make use. The country itself is very healthy, and the best provided and cheapest that ever was seen, abounding in provisions such as millet, *ameichueira*, *jugos*, which are like grains,[2] *mungo*,[3] sesame, honey, butter, very fine oxen, one of which, however large, is valued at two *bertangils*, and many goats and sheep. The fish is the best I ever tasted in the whole of India, and so cheap that it is astonishing, for they will give a hundred very large quabs for a *bertangil*, or a *motava*[4] of beads, which is worth even less. The woods are all full of oranges and lemons, and there is abundance of timber from which ships may be built.

The articles of barter-trade in this region are much amber and ivory. The Dutch have often been there, and according to what the Matatima,[5] one of the kings, said to me, they wanted to trade there, and nearly every year when they passed by they sent boats ashore

---

[1] Cf. previous note.

[2] 'A kind of pea' according to H. A. Junod. Cf. above, p. 150, n. 2.

[3] *Phaseolus mungo*, Linn., a species of pulse, fed to horses as well as used for culinary purposes in India and East Africa. Cf. Dalgado, *Glossário Luso-Asiático*, II, 79–80.

[4] This word is still employed in Mozambique for a number of strings of beads used as currency.

[5] Nhatitima. Cf. above, p. 262, n. 1.

to barter for oranges and cows; but after one of their boats had been taken and the crew killed, they no longer sent them ashore, but the Kaffirs have gone out to the ships. I greatly fear that these enemies will occupy this port, from what I know of some of the people there, which I will not write here to avoid prolixity, and because I know that nothing will be done about it however much I write.[1] Here I was very kindly treated by these Kaffirs, especially the kings. Before I left, seven persons died and I believe it was through over-eating, for we arrived there very weak and debilitated, and afterwards in this plenty they took no heed of what might happen to them, and their names were as follows: Thomé Coelho d'Almeida, Vicente Esteves, João Gomes, João Gonsalves the *Balona*,[2] the master-gunner, and Bras Gonsalves.

Seeing that it was two years since a vessel had come there, and that there was a risk of one not coming that monsoon, the Motepe,[3] who is the Negro acting as interpreter, told me that when three months had passed and the Kaffirs saw there was no chance of our being able to repay what they had spent on us, they would all turn to me. Therefore I should go to Sofala, where, as I was so well known, I would be able to find someone who would lend me four *bahares* of merchandise,[4] with which I could return and ransom these people; and that he would speak to the kings, telling them that my going to Sofala would result in a ship coming with cloth to pay the expenses of the Portuguese.

I was then very ill, and told him that I dared not go, as I would soon die by the wayside. Then he went to see Father Fr Diogo [dos Anjos] to whom he related what had passed between us; and the padre strongly urged me to undertake the journey, bidding me to have no fear of dying on the way, for God would take special care to guard one employed in a matter so greatly to His service. I said I would do what he asked me, and that the Motepe should go and

[1] He did, however, present a memorial to the Crown on this subject which was duly printed. Cf. above, p. 46.

[2] 'A sort of band for men, which is now (!) scarcely in use; a large collar formerly used in Flanders', according to Michaelis' dictionary.

[3] The nearest word I can find to this is the Swahili *mtepe*, the double-ended sewn sailing vessels of Lamu and elsewhere, but I doubt if there is any connection here.

[4] See p. 252, n. 2, for explanation.

ask the kings to give me some Negroes to accompany me. He did so at once, but the kings laughed and said that I must not leave their territory as I was the security for all these people. However, this Negro put forward so many arguments that he finally convinced them, giving them some pieces of cloth which he lent me for this purpose, and for which I [subsequently] paid him six times their value.

Having leave to go, I arranged to take a Portuguese comrade with me in case of emergencies, and he was the best behaved there was in the company, and was named António Martins. After the kings had given me twenty Negroes to accompany me, I bade them all farewell with many tears. They were full of doubt that I would return for them, saying that from Sofala I would go to my home and leave them to perish there. Hearing this, I seized the hands of Father Diogo, and kissing them, I made a solemn vow to God in a loud voice, in which I promised to return for them unless death should prevent me, and they thereupon became more tranquil. I set out on the 2nd June with the aforesaid company,[1] leaving the jewels buried in a gourd, their existence being only known to the two persons who had brought them thither and to Father Diogo.

After marching all that day we crossed a river and slept on the opposite bank, where more Kaffirs joined our company, laden with ivory and amber to sell at Sofala. This continued throughout the rest of the journey, till at last I had more than a hundred Kaffirs with me, and they did this because of the respect that they have here for a Portuguese. I was very hospitably received everywhere upon the way, my chief regret upon this journey being the delays caused by the local rulers, for though these people are nearer to us than those of the Cape of Good Hope, they act much more astonished when they see a Portuguese.

After travelling fifteen days I reached the kraal of a greater chief than those I had hitherto seen, and who is called the Inhame.[2] He

---

[1] António Martins and the twenty Negro carriers. 'June' must be a mistake or a misprint for 'July', as he had only reached Inhambane on 19 June 1623. Cf. above, p. 262.

[2] This is also the Portuguese word for yam (sweet potato).

had twenty wives, and when I wished to set out the very next day he would not allow it, telling me that he had sent for his relations, who lived a long way off, to come and see me, for no Portuguese had ever passed that way before. And so it seemed from the concourse of people who flocked to see me, shouting, howling, and rejoicing. If I had not been in such a hurry to reach Sofala I would not have lost by this, because of the many things which they brought me, which all the company partook of, and even so a lot was left over, which they afterwards carried for use on those paths where there were no kraals.

A few days later we came to another king, who resides opposite the islands of Bazanito,[1] and whose name is Osanha. He received me in the same way, and thence I crossed a river which is dry at low tide and is more than three leagues wide. Having crossed this, I continued marching along the shore until the Eve of St James,[2] when I reached Molomone. Here begin the lands of a Mulatto named Luís Pereira, who lives in Sofala, and who is the most respected man in those parts. Before reaching this kraal, I heard that two of his sons were there, to whom I sent a note that I had ready to forward to Sofala a league before I reached it, in which I gave him an account of my approach and begged him for the love of God to send me a shirt and a pair of drawers, that I might cover my nakedness before appearing before them.

When this note was given to them, they sent what I asked for and a cloak as well, which served to cover me. They came to meet me on the road, where I embraced them with many tears. As I did not look like a living being, they made me lie down in a skiff, and when I asked them to send four Kaffirs with the hammock in which I had come to fetch my comrade whom I had left two leagues behind very ill, they did so at once. The next day they had a *luzio*[3] fitted out for me, so that I could go therein to Sofala. Seventeen of my Kaffirs had died up to now, the country being full of fetid swamps. Both I and my comrade were very ill, and after embarking we went and slept that night at Queluame,[4]

---

[1] *Sic* in the 1625 edition for Bazaruto. Cf. above, p. 76.　　　[2] 24 July 1623.
[3] Large boat, half-decked, of the sewn variety. Cf. above, p. 98, n. 4.
[4] Nowadays written Chiloane or Chiluane, at the mouth of Rio Ingomaimo.

which is also in Luís Pereira's lands, and where they killed a sheep for me and made great rejoicing.

Next day in the afternoon, being the 28th July, we reached Sofala, and when the married men and Luís Pereira saw our vessel coming up the river they went to the bank thereof, where the Kaffirs gave loud shouts: 'Muzungos, Muzungos'.[1] They then jumped on board and embraced me, and I, who could hardly walk, went with them to offer a prayer in the church, and asked them to have my comrade brought thither. He arrived in such a state that he at once asked for confession, and while confessing himself he gave up his soul to God. They buried him there forthwith, leaving me very disconsolate.

Luís Pereira ordered me to be taken to some houses and provided with everything necessary until the arrival of Dom Luís Lobo,[2] who was captain of the fortress; and as I was so ill they took me [first] to a house where I was anointed. After some days I began to recover, and I asked him to do me the favour of lending me gold with which to purchase four *bahares* of merchandise, and I would pay him whatever interest he wanted and pledge all the goods which he knew I had in India. I pointed out that besides risking nothing, he would be doing me a great favour, and show great charity to those who were left at Inhambane; for as Nuno da Cunha, who had been captain in those parts, was dead,[3] and there was but little merchandise, no *pangayo* would go thither,

---

[1] 'Whites', 'Europeans'. A. Cabral gives the forms 'Mulango' and 'Xungo' in *Districto de Inhambane*, 156. H. A. Junod ('Condition of the natives of Africa in the 16th century', 23) states that 'Balungo' is the name given to white people in Zulu and Utthonga, and thinks that the original meaning might have been 'people of heaven'.

[2] Came out to India in 1596, and served in the Cunhale campaign of 1599–1600. Captain of the galleon *São Martinho*, wrecked off Manar, Ceylon, in 1606, when bound for Malacca in the viceroy's expedition of that year. Captain of Cananor *c.* 1615–18; renounced the captaincy of Sofala in 1632; captain of the passage of São Lourenço near Goa, in 1635. He was also awarded the captaincies of Diu, Chaul, and Rachol at various times, but I do not know when he served in them.

[3] He had died at Sena on the Zambesi earlier in 1623, while serving for the second time as Captain-general of the Rivers of Cuama (Zambesi) and governor of Mozambique. He had a long and chequered career in the East, and was defeated by Thomas Best's squadron in the celebrated engagement of Suahli (Swally Hole) in 1612.

and they would be left to perish. He said that he would do all that I asked, provided I would pledge my property, which I immediately did.

Thinking that I was not in a fit state to endure such hardship, they warned me not to venture on this journey, reminding me of the condition I was in, and of the many mercies which God had vouchsafed me in delivering me so often when so many others had perished, and that since I was now in a Christian country I should remain there, for a man's first duty was to himself. To which I replied that, please God, no danger to my life should prevent me from doing my bounden duty, which was to go and fetch my comrades. Seeing my resolution, they wearied themselves no more with these arguments, and having purchased a large *luzio* from Luís Pereira for 120 *meticals*,[1] I placed therein the four *bahares* of cloth which I had bought, and taking with me a Portuguese companion who was a married man of that fortress, I left for Inhambane on the 15th August.

Through delaying at Queluane [Chiloane], I experienced much stormy weather, and miraculously arrived ten leagues beyond Inhambane. The Malemos,[2] thinking that we had not yet arrived there, wanted to go on, but I, who knew the country well, having so lately passed through it, said that it lay behind us. Going in that direction, three hours later we sighted the island at its mouth, and going up the river we arrived that evening at Inhambane. Here they all came to receive me with many tears, saying that they owed me everything and that I came to deliver them from the captivity of Pharaoh, for the Kaffirs would no longer give them anything to eat and drove them out of their huts, and if I had arrived ten days later they would all have perished beyond a doubt. But their gratitude did not last long.

When I had expended three *bahares* of merchandise in ransoming them, paying all and sundry for what they had spent, I wanted

---

[1] From the Arabic *mithqāl*, a unit of weight, used more particularly for precious metals, and also (as here) as the equivalent of a gold *cruzado*, worth 480 *reis*, or of the standard gold *dinar* weighing 66 gr. Cf. Dalgado, *Glossário Luso-Asiático*, II, 43–4.

[2] Arabic *mu'allim*. The master or, more commonly, the pilot of a native ship. Cf. Dalgado, *Glossário Luso-Asiático*, II, 16–17.

to go with the *bahar* that remained to the lands of the Quevendo to redeem all the jewels and valuables of which they had robbed us there, that the owners might repay me as this deserved. For as soon as I had reached Inhambane, I had sent a present to this King Quevendo, for it was he who had brought us thither after we were robbed, giving us food as I have related above.[1] This present consisted of two pieces of Pate cloth,[2] and half a *corge*[3] of *bertangils*, in gratitude for what he had done for us. He was so thankful for this that he forthwith ordered all his people to assemble, and killed many cows to celebrate worthily so great an honour. He sent me word that he was waiting for my arrival to accompany me to the place where we had been robbed, so that we could ransom everything they had taken from us.

But when I was preparing for this journey, leaving all our people free and with enough cloth to buy plenty of food during my absence, they objected to my going and complained to the kings of Inhambane. They asked them why they allowed me to take much cloth out of their country, whereas it ought to remain where we had received such hospitality. When the kings heard this, they sent me word that on no account could I leave that place except to go to Sofala, and that I should use the cloth which I had left in buying the produce of the country, which was amber and ivory. Then they resolved to rob me of what I had, and even undermined my hut one night.

Seeing that the whole company opposed me, I desisted from my intended journey, and sent word to the Quevendo that I could not go there, asking him to send a message to the place where the stolen goods were, that they might be brought hither, where I would redeem them, and that he should send his son with them. He replied that I should stay where I was, and that in fifteen days everything would arrive with his son, for he himself would go

[1] See pp. 261–2 above, where, however, the 'king' is called Aquetudo (Nhacutô?).

[2] Pate (Patte, Patta, etc.), one of the islands of the Lamu group on the coast of Kenya, formerly the seat of a Swahili Sultanate which was then a vassal or client state of the Portuguese Crown.

[3] Indo-Portuguese term for 'a score'. Cf. *Hobson-Jobson*, 255; Dalgado, *Glossário Luso-Asiático*, II, 309–11.

thither and negotiate their redemption. As soon as our people heard that I was going to wait for those Negroes, they all went to the vessel in which I had come and launched it out to sea, forcibly embarking me before the monsoon, for even the Padre[1] was against me. After compelling me to set sail, we were driven back again, because it was not the monsoon and that coast is very stormy.

When we finally set sail again, a great sea wind blew so violently that we were driven ashore twelve leagues from Inhambane, whence we marched to Molonone,[2] and there we embarked in some dugout canoes in which we reached Sofala. See, your worship, how they repaid me for fetching them at my own expense; for if I had declined to bring them from Inhambane, and had employed the cloth I spent upon them in buying amber, there is no doubt that I would have brought back over 15,000 *cruzados'* worth, as there was a great quantity, no cloth having been taken to that part for two years. Truly I marvel whenever I think that such men could be found in the world, who would let a stranger go and trade for what we had brought thither at the cost of so many and such great hardships, enduring such excessive hunger as I have related, rather than I who continually served them all without exception, and for whom I had shed so much blood, and to whom they owed great gratitude. God be praised in spite of all; but I wish that this should be kept in mind, so that henceforth men may see and consider for whom they should risk their lives and lose their goods.

From this fortress of Sofala we went to Mozambique, all except four of our comrades who had reached the former place with us: António Sigala, who was killed at Sofala; a sailor named Pedro de Torres who went absent because of a theft he had committed; a grummet who married and remained there; and Fructuoso d'Andrade, who fell into the sea when crossing the bar of this fortress. We arrived at Mozambique mustering the following persons: Padre Fr Diogo dos Anjos; António Ferrão da Cunha; Vicente Lobo de Sequeira; André Velho Freire; the pilot Domin-

[1] Fr. Diogo dos Anjos, O.F.M. Cap.
[2] Not identified, but perhaps in the vicinity of Cape S. Sebastião.

gos Fernandes, and the second pilot Francisco Alvares; Miguel Correa, purser; Pedro Diniz, cooper; João Rodrigues de Leão; João Ribeiro de Lucena; João Rodrigues, carpenter; Manuel Gonçalves; João Carvalho; João Tavares; António Gonsalves; Manuel Gonsalves Belem; Sebastião Rodrigues; Diogo de Azevedo; Salamão the Frenchman; Ventura de Mesquita; Fructuoso Coelho; a grummet whom they called the Candalatu;[1] Domingos Salgado; Belchior Rodrigues; João Coelho; Alvaro Luís and Luís Moreno.

On landing ashore we all went in procession to [the chapel of] Our Lady of the Bulwark,[2] carrying a wooden cross before us, and chanting the litanies with great devotion. After we had given thanks to God for all His many mercies in bringing us to this Christian land, Father Fr Diogo delivered a pious discourse, reminding us of the numerous hardships from which God had delivered us and of the obligation we were all under to lead exemplary lives thenceforth. After this, everyone went to seek a vessel in which to go to Goa. LAUS DEO

[1] I cannot explain this word.
[2] Nossa Senhora do Baluarte. This was the common practice of shipwrecked people who survived to reach this port. Cf. above, p. 186.

APPENDIXES

Appendixes (A) to (C) are taken from Luís de Figueiredo Falcão, *Livro em que se contém toda a fazenda e real patrimonio dos reinos de Portugal, India e Ilhas adjacentes* [*1612*], Lisboa, 1859, pp. 198–200 A. Appendix (D) is from vol. 1 of the papers of Dom António de Ataide in the Palha Collection, Library of Harvard University.

APPENDIX (A)

PAY AND ALLOWANCES OF THE COMPLEMENT OF A TYPICAL PORTUGUESE EAST INDIAMAN, c. 1600

The cost [in *milreis*] of the seamen of an East India carrack of 123 hands, calculated on the basis of eighteen months' wages and ten months' provisions, as follows:

Category	pay	'liberdades'	places	cabins, &c.	allowance in the India House	total
The Master	120$000	2 — 60$000	2 chests — 30$000	500$000	30$000	740$000
The Pilot	120$000	2 — 60$000	2 ,, — 30$000	340$000	30$000	580$000
The Boatswain	50$000	1 — 20$000	1 ,, — 15$000	300$000	20$000	405$000
Boatswain's Mate at 1$400 a month and 2$800 for quintalage[1]	28$000	1 — 12$000	1 ,, — 15$000	280$000	20$000	355$000
Second pilot @ 1$200 a month, and 2$800 for quintalage	24$000	1 — 30$000	1 ,, — 15$000	280$000	20$000	369$400
Rope-maker @ 1$000 a month, and 2$800 for quintalage	20$800	1 — 12$000	1 ,, — 15$000	180$000	15$000	242$800
Another rope-maker at the same rates	20$800	1 — 12$000	1 ,, — 15$000	180$000	15$000	242$800
Ship's carpenter at 1$600 a month, and 4$000 for quintalage	32$800	1 — 12$000	1 ,, — 15$000	150$000	15$000	224$800
Caulker at the same rate	32$800	1 — 12$000	1 ,, — 15$000	150$000	15$000	224$800
Carpenter's Mate, at the same rates, less berth	32$800	1 — 12$000	1 ,, — 15$000	60$000	10$000	129$800
Caulker's Mate	32$800	1 — 12$000	1 ,, — 15$000	60$000	10$000	129$800
Cooper @ 1$200 a month and 3$900 for quintalage	25$500	1 — 12$000	1 ,, — 15$000	60$000	10$000	122$500
Master-at-arms @ 1$200 a month	18$000	1 — 12$000	1 ,, — 15$000	200$000	15$000	260$000
Steward	18$000	1 — 12$000	1 ,, — 15$000	240$000	15$000	300$000
45 sailors @ 1$000 a month, and 2$800 for quintalage. Each worth 20$800. Total	936$000	45 — 540$000	45 — 675$000	900$000	675$000	3,726$000
48 grummets @ 666 a month, and 1$800 for quintalage. Each worth 13$248. Total	635$000	48 @ 8$000 — 384$000	48 fardels @ 10$ — 480$000	—	480$000	1,979$000
4 pages @ 444 a month, and 1$238 for quintalage. Each worth 9$238. Total	36$920	4 @ 5$300 — 21$200	4 ,, ,, — 20$000	—	20$000	98$120
Master-gunner @ 2$400	43$200	1 @ — 18$000	1 ,, ,, — 15$000	160$000	15$000	251$200
11 gunners @ about 1$ each a month, say 18$000 each one. Total	198$000	11 @ 12$000 — 132$000	11 ,, ,, @ 15$000 — 165$000	220$000	165$000	880$000
Grand Total	2,425$820	1,385$200	1,595$000	4,260$000	1,595$000	11,261$020

[1] *Quintalada*, or quintalage, the number of quintals (hundredweight) of spices which a person was entitled to ship home from Goa. Cf. João de Barros, *Decada I*, Book 8, ch. 3.

APPENDIX (B)

PROVISIONS OF AN OUTWARD-BOUND PORTUGUESE EAST INDIAMAN, c. 1600

The provisions which are necessary for the people who are usually on board an Indiaman of 550 tons, carrying 250 soldiers and 112 seamen, according to the dimensions thereof, are as follows:

Commodity	For all		For 250 soldiers	For 112 seamen
biscuit	1,074	quintals[1]	615	459
wines	115	pipes	72	43
meat	1,086	arrobas[2]	750	336
dried fish	150	dozen	104	46
olive-oil	31½	quartilhos[3]	19½	12
vinnegar	13	pipes	9	4
water	244	pipes (half of them iron-bound)	168	76
reserve	69	pipes	48	21
salt	2½	moios[4]	1½	1
sardines	130	arrobas	80	50
hoops	8	bundles	4	4
osiers	24	faggots	12	12
grains	14	alqueires[5]	8	6
almonds	10	alqueires	6	4
prunes	10	alqueires	6	4
lentils	10	alqueires	6	4
mustard	2	alqueires	1	1
garlic	724	ropes	500	224
onions	724	ropes	500	224
sugar	8	arrobas	4	4
honey	8	arrobas	4	4

[1] 1 quintal = 4 arrobas. [2] 1 arroba = 32 arratels or pounds avd.
[3] 4 quartilhos = 3 English pints. [4] 1 moio = 60 alqueires.
[5] 1 alqueire = 13 litres.

N.B. A more detailed ration-scale (for the year 1633) will be found in Vol. 1 of the papers of Dom António de Ataide in the Houghton Library, Harvard University.

Upper Deck

Middle Deck

Lower Deck

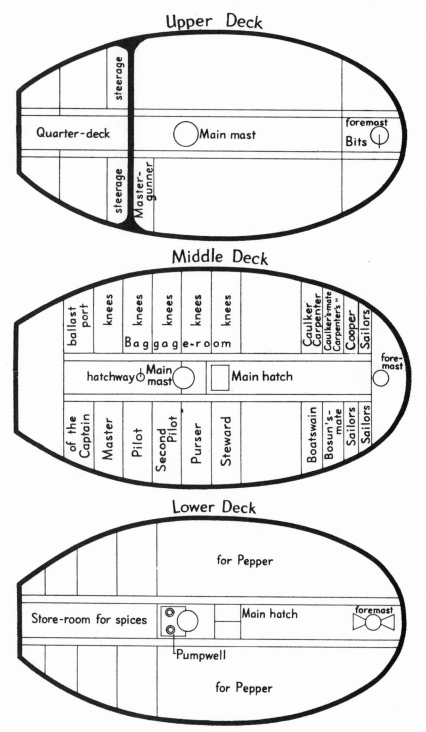

APPENDIX (D)

ALLOWANCE OF LIBERTY-CHESTS ON BOARD A PORTUGUESE EAST INDIAMAN, c. 1620

Category of Personnel	number of chests allowed[1]	value of each chest in milreis	free percentage on each chest	total amount duty-free in milreis	deducted for charity[2]	slave allowance
Captain-major of the voyage	15	300$000	20%	60$000	3$000	12, freight- & duty-free
Captain-major's servants (total, 12)	1 each	120$000	10%	12$000	1$200	
Captain	6	250$000	15%	37$000	2$500	
Captain's servants (total, 6)	1 each	120$000	10%	12$000	1$200	
Purser	2	200$000	15%	30$000	2$000	2, duty-free
Chaplain	1	120$000	10%	12$000	1$200	1, duty-free
Barber-surgeon	1	120$000	10%	12$000	1$200	
Pilot	2	200$000	15%	30$000	2$000	2, duty-free
Second Pilot	1	200$000	20%	40$000	2$000	2, freight- & duty-free[3]
Master	2	200$000	15%	30$000	2$000	2, duty-free
Boatswain	1	200$000	15%	30$000	2$000	
Boatswain's-mate	1	120$000	10%	12$000	1$200	
Caulker	1	120$000	10%	12$000	1$200	
Carpenter	1	120$000	10%	12$000	1$200	
Cooper	1	120$000	10%	12$000	1$200	
Master-at-arms	1	120$000	10%	12$000	1$200	
Steward	1	120$000	10%	12$000	1$200	
Rope-maker	1	120$000	10%	12$000	1$200	
Sailor	1	120$000	10%	12$000	1$200	
Grummet	1 fardel	80$000	10%	8$000	0$800	
Page	1 fardel	53$000	10%	5$000	0$533	
Gunner	1 chest	120$000	15%	18$000	1$200	

[1] By a royal decree of 20 February 1575, all such chests were to be made to standard measurements of 5 × 2½ × 2½ spans each. The fardel (fardo) was generally of forty-two pounds weight.

[2] Obra pia, lit. 'pious work'. Charitable establishments or endowments, such as the Misericordia, or the Hospital of All Saints.

[3] Cf. the alvará (royal decree) for Bento Gonçalves, sota-piloto of the carrack Nossa Senhora Conceição in 1623–5, published by Frazão de Vasconcellos, Pilotos das navegações Portuguesas séculos XVI e XVII, p. 19.

These words are explained in a footnote on their first occurrence in the text, but are repeated here for the convenience of the reader.

almude. A Portuguese measure for selling wine, there being 26 *almudes* to a pipe.

alqueire. A Portuguese dry measure of $1\frac{3}{5}$ peck (English), or 13 litres.

ameixoeira, ameichura, etc. Sometimes applied to sorghum, and sometimes to 'the small grey Kaffir corn'.

ancosse. Inkosi. Kaffir chief, or headman.

arratel. From the Arabic *ratl.* A pound weight (avd.).

bahar, bahare, bar, etc. A weight varying from 141 to 330 Kg., in accordance with the type of merchandise involved.

bertangil, bretangil, etc. Cotton piece-goods (blue, black, red) exported from Gujerat (Cambay) to East Africa.

canequim. A cheap coarse calico, dyed blue or black, chiefly woven at Broach and Navsari in Western India.

cruzado. Portuguese coin and money of account worth 400 *reis,* and roughly equivalent to four English shillings *c.* 1600.

ferroba (alfarroba). Carob, or St John's Bread. *Cerratonia Siliqua,* Linn.

fidalgo, 'filho d'algo.' 'Son of a somebody.' Gentleman, or nobleman.

luzio. Single-masted sewn vessel of Swahili origin, in all probability, but the term has not been properly identified. Cf. above, p. 98, n. 4.

milreis. Portuguese coin and money of account worth about ten English shillings *c.* 1600.

naveta. Vague term for a small sailing vessel. Cf. p. 81, n. 1.

pangaio, pangayo. 'A vessel like a barge, with one mat-sail of coconut-leaves. The barge is sewed together with the rinds of trees and pinned with wooden pins' (Hakluyt's *Voyages*, cited in *Mariner's Mirror*, XXVII (1941), 261).

pardao. The gold *pardao* was valued at 360 *reis* and the silver at 300.

quintal. Indo-Portuguese weight of 130 lbs. (avd.), slightly larger than a hundredweight.

roteiro. Rutter; sailing-directions.

Topas, Topaz, Tupassi, etc. Dark-skinned or half-caste claimants of Portuguese ancestry.

tostão(pl. *tostões*). Testoon. Worth 100 *reis* or about 2½d. in Elizabethan money. The *real* (plural *reis*) existed only as a money of account.

BIBLIOGRAPHY

(A) Texts translated in the present work

(i) DIOGO DO COUTO

Relação | do | Naufragio | da | Nao S. Thomè | Na Terra dos Fumos, no anno de 1589. | E dos grandes trabalhos que passou | D. Paulo de Lima | Nas terras da Cafraria athè sua morte. | [woodcut of a sinking ship and boatload of survivors] | *Escrita por Diogo do Couto | Guarda mòr da Torre do Tombo. | A rogo da Senhora D. Anna de Lima irmãa do | dito D. Paulo de Lima no Anno de 1611.*

On pp. 153–213 of the *História Trágico-Marítima*, Tomo II (Lisboa, 1736). 4to; signatures, Vij–Dij; 32 lines to a full page.

(ii) JOÃO BAPTISTA LAVANHA

Navfragio | Da Nao S. Alberto, | E Itinerario da gente, | qve delle se | salvov. | De Ioão Baptista Lava- | nha Cosmographo mòr | de Sua Magestade. | Dedicado ao Princepe | Dom Philippe | Nosso Senhor. | Em Lisboa. | Em casa de Alexandre de Siqueira. | Anno M.D.XCVII. | Com Licença, & Privilegio.

8vo. Four unnumbered preliminary leaves, comprising [fol. 1 *recto*] title-page; [fol. 1 *verso*] blank; [fol. 2 *recto*] Approbation of Fr Manuel Coelho, and licences to print and publish, dated 7 November 1596 and 17 April 1597; [fol. 2 *verso*] Royal privilege to the author, dated 28 November 1597; [fol. 3] Dedication to the Infante or Crown Prince dated 19 August 1597; [fol. 4 *verso*] *Erratas*. Text on fol. 1 [alias p. 1]–p. 152, numbered on both sides; 24 lines to a full page. Collation by signatures: *, 4 leaves; A–I, each 8 leaves; K, 4 leaves; total, 80 leaves.

Cf. *Early Portuguese Books, 1489–1600, in the Library of His Majesty the King of Portugal*, London, 1935, III, 407, item no. 255.

(iii) FRANCISCO VAZ DE ALMADA

Tratado | do svccesso qve | teve a Nao Sam | Ioam Baptista, e iorna- | da, que fez a gente, que della escapou, des- | de trinta, & tres graos no

281

Cabo de Boa | Esperança, onde fez naufragio, | até Zofala, vindo sempre | marchando por | terra. | A Diogo Soares Secretario do conselho da fa- | zenda de sua Magestade, &c. | Auzente. | Ao padre Manoel Gomez da Silueira. | [vignette] | *Com licença da S. Inquisiçam, Ordinario, & Paço. Em Lisboa. | Por Pedro Craesbeeck Impressor del Rei, anno 1625.* Small 4to. Two unnumbered leaves comprising [fol. 1] title-page, with the sale-price 'meyo tostam' on the *verso*; [fol. 2] dedication to Diogo Soares on the *recto*, and the first page of the text on the *verso*. Leaves 3–41, containing the rest of the text, numbered on the *recto*. At the end is an unnumbered leaf with colophon: *Em Lisboa. | Por Pedro Craesbeeck Im- | pressor del Rey an- | no Domini | 1625.* Total, 42 leaves; 33 lines to a full page.

Collation of text by signatures: B, 4 leaves—4 blank; C, 4 leaves—4 blank; D, 4 leaves—4 blank; E, 4 leaves—4 blank; F, 4 leaves—4 blank, including colophon leaf.

(B) Fuller titles of authorities quoted in the footnotes

Africa Pilot, III. *Comprising the Southern and Eastern coasts of Africa from Table Bay to Ras Hafun*. 11th edition. London, 1954. (Published by the Hydrographic Department, Admiralty.)

Anais da Academia Portuguesa da História. Lisboa, 1940–to date. (Cited as *APH*.)

Archivo Portuguez Oriental. 8 vols. Nova Goa, 1857–76. Edited by J. H. Cunha Rivara. (Cited as *APO*.)

Arte de Furtar, Espelho de Enganos, Theatro de Verdades, mostrador de horas minguadas, gazua geral dos Reynos de Portugal. Offerecida a ElRey Nosso Senhor D. João IV para que a emende. Composta no anno de 1652 pelo Padre Antonio Vieira. Amsterdam, 1744. (Despite the wording of the title, the work was, in all probability, originally composed by Dr António de Sousa de Macedo *c.* 1652, and printed clandestinely at Lisbon *c.* 1744.)

ATAIDE, Dom ANTÓNIO DE. 'Roteiros para varios pontos.' (MS codex of *c.* 1631, containing a number of Portuguese *roteiros* (rutters) and other nautical treatises, copied and annotated by Dom António de Ataide, in the present writer's collection.) Cf also CODEX-LYNCH.

Ataide MSS. 3 volumes of naval and colonial papers collected by D. António de Ataide, *c.* 1630–3, and now in the Houghton Library, Harvard University, U.S.A.

BARROS, EUGENIO ESTANISLAU DE. *Traçado e construção das Naus Portuguesas dos séculos XVI e XVII.* Lisboa, 1933.

BOTELHO DE SOUSA, ALFREDO DE. *Subsídios para a história militar marítima da India, 1585–1669.* I–IV. Lisboa, 1930–56. (In progress. These four volumes cover the years 1585–1650.)

BOXER, C. R. 'The naval and colonial papers of Dom António de Ataide, 1567–1647.' *Harvard Library Bulletin,* V (Winter 1951), 24–50.

——. 'An introduction to the *História Trágico-Marítima*,' reprint (56 pp.) from the *Miscelânea de Estudos em honra do Professor Hernâni Cidade,* Lisboa, 1957.

CABRAL, AUGUSTO. *Raças, Usos e Costumes dos indigenas do districto de Inhambane.* Lourenço Marques, 1910.

CASTRO, D. JOÃO DE. *Cartas de Dom João de Castro. Coligidas e anotadas por Elaine Sanceau.* Lisboa, 1954.

CODEX-LYNCH. (A collection of original papers relating to the Portuguese East India Company of 1628–33, including the correspondence of its representatives at Goa. Collected by Dom António de Ataide in 1633, sold at the Castel-Melhor sale in 1876, and donated by the late Sir Henry Lynch to the library of King's College, London University, in 1949.)

Comentarios de Don García de Silva y Figueroa de la embajada que de parte del Rey de España Don Felipe III hizo al Rey Xa Abas de Persia, 1614–1624. 2 vols. Madrid, 1903–5. (Published by the Socieded de Bibliófilos Españoles.)

CORTE-REAL. See PEREIRA CORTE-REAL.

CORTESÃO, ARMANDO. *Cartografia e cartógrafos portugueses dos séculos XV e XVI. Contribuição para um estudo completo.* 2 vols. Lisboa, 1935.

COUTO, DIOGO DO. *Decadas da Asia.* Lisboa, 1602–1788. (References to *Decadas IV–VIII* and *Decada XII* are from the original seventeenth-century editions, and those to other *Decadas* are from the collected edition of 14 vols., Lisboa, 1778–88.)

Couto, Diogo do. *Vida de Dom Paulo de Lima Pereira, Capitam-mór de Armadas do Estado da India, donde por seu valor, e esforço nas batalhas de mar, e terra, de que sempre conseguio gloriosas victorias, foy chamado o Hercules portuguez.* Lisboa, 1765. (References are to the reprinted *Vida de Dom Paulo de Lima Pereira* in the Bibliotheca de Classicos Portuguezes series edited by Mello de Azevedo, xxxv. Lisboa, 1903.)

——. *Observaçoes sobre as principaes causas da decadencia dos Portuguezes na Asia, escritas por Diogo do Couto, em forma de dialogo com o titulo de Soldado Pratico, publicadas de ordem da Academia Real das Sciencias de Lisboa por Antonio Caetano do Amaral.* Lisboa, 1790.

——. *O Soldado Prático. Texto restituído, prefácio e notas pelo prof. M. Rodrigues Lapa.* Lisboa, 1937.

Dalgado, Sebastião Rodolfo. *Glossário Luso-Asiático.* 2 vols. Coimbra, 1919–21.

Documentos remettidos da India ou Livros das Monções, 1605–1619. 5 vols. Lisboa, 1880–1935. (Published by the Academia das Ciências de Lisboa.)

Duffy, James. *Shipwreck and Empire. Being an account of Portuguese maritime disasters in a century of decline.* Harvard University Press, 1955.

Faria y Sousa, Manuel de. *Asia Portuguesa.* 3 vols. Lisboa, 1665–75.

Ferreira Paes, Simão. *Recopilação das famosas armadas que para a India foram, 1496–1650.* Rio de Janeiro, 1937. (Facsimile edition of the original MS of 1650.)

Ferreira Reimão, Gaspar. *Roteiro da Navegaçam e Carreira da India, com seus caminhos, & derrotas, sinaes, & aguageis, & differenças da agulha: tirado do que escreveo Vicente Rodrigues, & Dioguo Afonso Pilotos antigos. Agora nouamente acrescentado a viagem de Goa por dentro da São Lourenco, & Moçambique,& outras muitas cousas, & advertencias, por Guaspar Ferreira Reymão, cavaleiro do habito de Sanctiago, & Piloto mòr destes Reynos de Portugal.* Lisboa, 1612. (References are to the second edition, edited by A. Fontoura da Costa, Lisboa, 1939.)

Figueiredo Falcão, Luis de. *Livro em que se contém toda a*

Fazenda e Real Patrimonio dos Reinos de Portugal, India e Ilhas adjacentes e outros particularidades. Ordenado por Luis de Figueiredo Falcão Secretario de El-Rei Filippe II. Copiado fielmente do manuscripto original e impresso por ordem do governo de Sua Magestade Lisboa, 1859.

FONTOURA DA COSTA, ABEL. *A Marinharia dos Descobrimentos. Bibliografia Náutica Portuguesa até 1700.* Lisboa, 1933. (Cf. also under FERREIRA REIMÃO, above, and *Roteiro da Africa do Sul,* below.)

FRAZÃO DE VASCONCELOS, JOSÉ AUGUSTO AMARAL. *Pilotos das navegações portuguesas dos séculos XVI e XVII.* Lisboa, 1942.

GOMES DE SOLIS, DUARTE. *Discursos sobre los comercios de las dos Indias, donde se tratan materias importantes de Estado y Guerra.* n.p. Año M.DC.XXII. (New edition by M. Bensabat Amzalak, Lisboa, 1934.)

— —. *Alegacion en favor de la Compañía de la India Oriental y comercios vltramarinos, que de nuevo se instituyò en el Reyno de Portugal.* n.p. Año de M.DC.XXVIII. (New edition by M. Bensabat Amzalak, Lisboa, 1955.)

História Trágico-Marítima. Em que se escrevem chronologicamente os Naufragios que tiverão as Naos de Portugal, depois que se poz em exercicio a Navegação da India. Offerecido a Augusta Magestade do Muito Alto e Muito Poderoso Rey D. João V. Nosso Senhor. Por Bernardo Gomes de Brito. 2 vols. Lisboa, 1735–6. (For the third volume usually associated with these two, see the Introduction. The best modern edition is that edited by António Sergio in 3 vols., Lisboa, 1955–7. References to the *HTM* in these notes are to the edition of 1735–6, except where otherwise indicated.)

Hobson-Jobson. A glossary of colloquial Anglo-Indian words and phrases, and of kindred terms, etymological, historical, geographical and discursive. Edited by H. Yule, A. C. Burnell, and W. Crooke. London, 1903.

IRWIN, JOHN. 'Indian textile trade in the seventeenth century.' *Journal of Indian Textile History,* no. I (Ahmedabad, 1955), 5–3 3; no. II (1956), 24–42.

JUNOD, H. A. 'The condition of the natives in South-East Africa in the sixteenth century, according to the early Portuguese documents.' Reprint (25 pp.) of an article in *The South African Journal of Science*, February, 1914. (All my references are to the reprint.)

JUNOD, H. P. 'Os indígenas de Moçambique no século XVI e começo do XVII segundo os antigos documentos portugueses da época dos descobrimentos.' Reprint (88 pp.) from the quarterly periodical *Moçambique*, Lourenço Marques, 1939.

KIRBY, P. R. *A Source book on the Wreck of the Grosvenor East-Indiaman.* Cape Town, 1953. (Vol. 43 of the Van Riebeck Society's publications.)

LINSCHOTEN, J. H. van. *Iohn Hvighen van Linschoten his Discours of Voyages into ye Easte & West Indies.* London, 1598. (Includes his *Itinerario*.)

The Mariner's Mirror. The quarterly journal of the Society for Nautical Research. London, 1911–to date.

MONTEZ, CAETANO, *Descobrimento e fundação de Lourenço Marques 1500–1800.* Lourenço Marques, 1948.

PEREIRA CORTE-REAL, JOÃO. *Discursos sobre la nauegacion de las naos de la India de Portugal, por Iuan Pereyra Corte Real, Cauallero Portugues, para que V. Magestad sea servido de mandar ver.* n.p. [1622.] (Reprinted in 1635 with a different title beginning *Discursos y advertencias*. References are to the original edition of 1622.)

PERESTRELLO, MANUEL DE MESQUITA. See *Roteiro da África*.

QUEIROZ, FERNÃO DE, S.J. *The Temporal and Spiritual Conquest of Ceylon.* 3 vols. Colombo, 1930. (Translated and edited by S. G. Pereira, S.J., from the Portuguese text printed at Colombo in 1916. The original MS is dated 1687.)

QUIRINO DA FONSECA. *Os Portugueses no Mar. Memórias históricas e arqueológicas das naus de Portugal.* 1. *Ementa Histórica das naus portuguesas.* Lisboa, 1926. (No more published.)

— —. *Diários da Navegação da Carreira da Índia nos anos de 1595, 1596, 1597, 1600 e 1603. Manuscrito da Academia das Ciências de Lisboa publicado por ordem da mesma Academia.* Lisboa, 1938.

Regimento dos Escrivaens das Naos da Carreira da India. (These were evidently printed annually, but the only two editions I have ever seen are dated respectively 1611 (Harvard University) and 1640 (my own). The contents are identical, save that the 1640 edition has an extra leaf with a *despacho do Conselho da Fazenda* dated 23 December 1639.)

Roteiro da África do Sul e Sueste desde o Cabo de Boa Esperança até o das Correntes (1576). 'Roteiro' *of the South and South-East Africa, from the Cape of Good Hope to Cape Corrientes. Por Manuel de Mesquita Perestrello. Anotado por A. Fontoura da Costa.* Lisboa, 1939. (Text in Portuguese and English.)

SANCEAU, ELAINE. See CASTRO JOÃO DE.

SANTA MARIA, Fr AGOSTINHO DE, O.S.A. *Historia da Fundação do Real Convento de Santa Monica da Cidade de Goa, Corte do Estado da India, & do Imperio Lusitano do Oriente.* Lisboa, 1699.

SANTOS, Fr JOÃO DOS, O.P., *Ethiopia Oriental e varia historia de cousas notaveis do Oriente.* Evora, 1609.

SAÕ BERNARDINO, Fr GASPAR DE, O.F.M., *Itinerario da India por terra até este Reino de Portugal.* Lisboa, 1611.

SCHURZ, W. L. *The Manila Galleon.* New York, 1939.

SEVERIM DE FARIA, MANUEL. *Noticias de Portugal, offerecidas a ElRey N.S. Dom Ioão o IV. Declarãose as grandes commodidades que tem para crescer em gente, industria, comercio, riquezas, & forças militares por mar, & terra.* Lisboa, 1655.

SILVA REGO, ANTÓNIO DA. *Documentação para a história das missões do padroado português do Oriente. Índia.* I–II. Lisboa, 1950–1955. (In progress. Covers the years 1499–1572 so far.)

SOGA, J. H. *The South-Eastern Bantu. Abe-Nguni, Aba-mbo, Amalala.* Johannesburg, 1930.

THEAL, GEORGE MCCALL. *The Beginning of South African History.* London, 1902.

——. *Records of South-Eastern Africa.* 9 vols. London, 1898–1903.

——. *History and Ethnography of Africa South of the Zambesi,* 1505–1795. 3 vols. London, 1907–10.

Travels of Peter Mundy in Europe and Asia, 1608–1667. 5 vols. London, 1907–36. Edited for the Hakluyt Society, Series II, by R. C. Temple and L. M. Anstey.

VALIGNANO, ALESSANDRO, S.J. *Historia del principio y progresso de la Compañía de Jesús en las Indias Orientales, 1542–1564. Herausgegeben und erläutert von Josef Wicki, S.J.* Rome, 1944.

Voyage of François Pyrard of Laval to the East Indies, the Maldives, the Moluccas and Brazil. 3 vols in 2. London, 1887–90. (Edited for the Hakluyt Society, Series 1, by A. Gray and H. C. Bell from the French edition of 1619.)

WELCH, S. R. *Portuguese Rule and Spanish Crown in South Africa 1581–1640.* Cape Town, 1950. (To be used with caution, like all other works on South African history by the same writer.)

INDEX

All Portuguese personal (but not geographical) names are placed under the last surname: i.e., Pedro de Morais Sarmento is indexed under 'Sarmento, Pedro de Morais'. All ships' names are indexed under the word 'ships'.

u

FURTHER SELECTIONS *from*
the TRAGIC HISTORY *of the* SEA

I Portrait of Francisco Barreto
(British Museum, Sloane MS. 197)

FURTHER SELECTIONS FROM
THE TRAGIC HISTORY
OF THE SEA
1559-1565

Narratives of the shipwrecks of the Portuguese
East Indiamen *Aguia* and *Garça* (1559)
São Paulo (1561) and the misadventures
of the Brazil-ship *Santo António* (1565)

TRANSLATED AND EDITED FROM
THE ORIGINAL PORTUGUESE BY

C. R. BOXER

PREFACE

This is a companion volume to a work published by the Hakluyt Society eight years ago, *The Tragic History of the Sea, 1589–1622. Narratives of the shipwrecks of the Portuguese East Indiamen São Thomé* (1589), *Santo Alberto* (1593), *São João Baptista* (1622), *and the journeys of the survivors in South East Africa* (2nd series, vol. CXII, Cambridge, 1959). The three narratives translated in the present volume, like the three published in the previous one, are taken from the original editions of accounts which were subsequently included in the *História Trágico-Marítima*, or *Tragic History of the Sea*, edited by Bernardo Gomes de Brito at Lisbon in 1735–6. The present narratives have been selected for rather different reasons from those chosen for inclusion in the 1959 volume, which were all concerned with shipwrecks off the coast of South-east Africa and the subsequent trials and tribulations undergone by the survivors who managed to reach the shore.

The disasters narrated in this volume all occurred within a few years of each other in the middle of the sixteenth century, and none of them have been translated into English before. They are, however, typical of most of the narratives included in the *História Trágico-Marítima*, in that they clearly reveal two outstanding features of Lusitanian overseas expansion at this period—the characteristic improvidence of the Portuguese and their equally characteristic tenacity. As António Sergio has pointed out in his recent edition of the *HTM*, the three individuals who come out best as leaders from a comparison of all the protagonists in these stories of misadventures by sea and land are Francisco Barreto, Jorge d'Albuquerque Coelho, and Nuno Velho Pereira. The last-named featured in the 1959 volume, and the other two heroes are now presented to the English-reading public in this one.

ACKNOWLEDGEMENTS

I am indebted to the Trustees and Library staff of the National Maritime Museum, Greenwich, for permission to take photostats of the unique copy of the *Nao Sam Paulo* (Lisbon, 1565), which is one of the bibliographical treasures of that library; and to the Trustees of the British Museum for allowing me to photograph the portrait of Barreto, the Vaz Dourado chart and the woodcuts from the *Tratado das Batalhas*. My old friend and colleague, Professor Manoel Cardozo, Lima Librarian at the Catholic University of Washington, D.C., kindly supplied (free of charge) photostats of the exceedingly rare first edition of the *Naufrágio* of Jorge d'Albuquerque Coelho (Lisbon, 1601), which is one of the bibliographical plums of the Oliveira Lima collection. Dr Alexandre Eulálio Pimenta da Cunha, of the Instituto do Livro at the National Library, Rio de Janeiro, kindly obtained for me—and not for the first time—a Brazilian work which is not available in this country. Cdte. A. Teixeira da Mota and Mr Allan Pearsall saved me from making some errors in sixteenth-century nautical terminology, and such mistakes as remain are my own. The society is also indebted to Fr. G. Schurhammer S.J., and the Director of the Istituto Storico della Compagnia di Gesu at Rome, for kindly loaning two blocks of the original pen-and-ink sketches in Fr. Manuel Álvares S.J.'s original narrative of 1561-2 preserved in the Jesuit Archives. As with the previous volume, the Hon. Secretary, Mr R. A. Skelton, has been consistently helpful in his editorial capacity, and Miss Eila Campbell no less so in the same sense.

January 1967   C. R. B.

CONTENTS

ILLUSTRATIONS AND MAPS IN

Further Selections from the Tragic History of the Sea

Page numbers indicate placement of art in the original edition.

PLATES

IN TEXT

viii

ABBREVIATIONS

ABNRJ
Anais da Biblioteca Nacional do Rio de Janeiro.

HTM
História Trágico-Marítima. By Bernardo Gomes de Brito (2 vols., Lisbon, 1735-6).

HTM (ed. Sergio)
História Trágico-Marítima. By Bernardo Gomes de Brito. Edited by António Sergio (3 vols., Lisbon, 1955-7).

JMBRAS
Journal of the Malayan Branch of the Royal Asiatic Society.

MM
The Mariner's Mirror. The Quarterly Journal of the Society for Nautical Research.

THS, I
The Tragic History of the Sea, 1589-1622. Edited from the original Portuguese by C. R. BOXER (Hakluyt Society, 2nd series, vol. CXII, Cambridge, 1959).

INTRODUCTION

A. Diogo do Couto and the loss of the
Aguia *and* Garça

As several biographical sketches of Diogo do Couto are readily available in English, it is only necessary to remind the reader of this Portuguese soldier-chronicler's career in briefest outline. Couto was born at Lisbon in 1542 or 1543, and served as a page at court, where he received a good education in his youth. He embarked as a soldier for India in 1559, owing to the death of his father and of his patron, the *Infante* Dom Luís. After ten years' military service on the west coast of India, and (apparently) in the Persian Gulf and the Red Sea, Couto returned to Portugal in 1569–70, accompanied by his friend, Luís de Camões, on the second stage of the voyage from Moçambique to Lisbon. Unlike most of his comrades in arms, Couto evidently obtained speedy satisfaction for his claims for services rendered to the Crown, since he returned to India in the fleet of 1571. He spent the rest of his life at Goa, though he may have made short visits to some of the other Portuguese strongholds between Diu and Ceylon, in his succes-sive roles as a minor government official, a private citizen, and (from 1595 onwards) as chronicler and keeper of the archives in the Indo-Portuguese capital. He was a fecund writer who was active until within a few weeks of his death, which is foreshadowed in a petition of September 1616, stating that he is very ill and fears that 'he will expire with this moon'.[1] His death was reported by the viceroy in a despatch of the 30 December of the same year, though the exact date is not related and his tomb (which he had arranged for previously in the church of São Francisco) has never been found. The historical importance and the literary merits[2] of

[1] '...está muito mal e reçee que com esta luna se vâ...' (Historical Archives, Goa, 'Cartas, Patentes e Alvarás', vol. 4 [1616]).

[2] C. R. Boxer, *THS*, I, 30–42; J. H. Harrison, 'Five Portuguese Historians', in C. H. Philips (ed.), *Historians of India, Pakistan and Ceylon* (London, 1961), pp. 155–69; I. A. Macgregor, 'Some aspects of Portuguese historical writing of

2 2The Tragic History of the Sea

his work in general and of his *Décadas* in particular are fully discussed elsewhere and need not detain us here.

Couto's narrative of the misadventures of the *Aguia* and *Garça*
is given in his *Década VII* (Lisbon, 1616), Book 6, ch. III, and
ibid. Book 8, ch. I, XII and XIII. It was reproduced by Gomes
de Brito, with insignificant changes in wording and without the
slightest indication of its origin, as one of the six shipwreck
narratives in the first volume of his *História Trágico-Marítima*
(2 vols., Lisbon, 1735–6), pp. 219–52. Not content with concealing Couto's authorship of this account, Gomes de Brito
arbitrarily annexed thereto (on pp. 253–307) 'A Description of
the City of Colombo by Padre Manuel Barradas of the Company
of Jesus, sent to another Father of the same Company who was
living at Lisbon', thus implying that both accounts were the
work of Manuel Barradas, S.J., as can be seen from the wording
of the title-page reproduced on p. 24.

This Jesuit Father was a pioneer Indologist, and he states that
he was in Ceylon during the short-lived governorship of Dom
Francisco de Meneses Roxo (1613–14). On p. 284 of the 1735
edition, he alludes to the attempt of the English to found a factory
(or trading-agency) at Pulicat, which was thwarted by the death
of the Hindu King of Vellore in October 1614.[1] Despite the
wording of the title (clearly the work of Gomes de Brito), the
description of Colombo is limited to a few lines; and the subject-
matter is really an account of a journey made by Barradas to
Ceylon, the coast of Coromandel, and Malabar in 1614, and was
probably written at Cochin by the end of that year. Why Gomes
de Brito joined these two disparate accounts of Couto and Barradas together is anybody's guess. Since they really have nothing
whatever to do with each other, I have omitted Barradas's narrative here.[2]

the 16th and 17th centuries on South East Asia', in D. G. E. Hall (ed.), *Historians
of South East Asia* (London, 1961), pp. 186–89; A. F. G. Bell, *Diogo do Couto*
(Oxford, 1924).
[1] For the abortive English establishment at Pulicat see W. H. Moreland,
Relations of Golconda (London, 1931), p. xxiii.
[2] For Manuel Barradas, S. J. (1572–1614) and his work see R. Streit, *Bibliotheca Missionum*, v (Aachen, 1929), 214.

The disastrous voyage of the *Aguia* and *Garça* occurred in the same year that Couto came out to India, so obviously his account is not a first-hand one. Equally obviously, he must have met some of the participants at Goa in 1560 and subsequently, so it can be claimed as a good second-hand account. Moreover, as one of the first of many such maritime disasters during his long residence in India, it must have made a great impression on him at the time, even though he did not write this account until some forty years later.[1] In translating Couto's account, I have kept the paragraph-ing of the original *Década*, but modernized the spelling of proper names. I have also checked it with the Gomes de Brito text of 1735, and noted any divergences that call for comment.

This narrative of the *Aguia* and *Garça* affords an amusing instance of the tendency of editors and bibliographers to copy from each other without verifying their assertions. Gomes de Brito's arbitrary suppression of Couto's name and his mention of Barradas on the title-page of the 1735 version, misled subsequent commentators for over two centuries, from Barbosa Machado in 1752 to António Sergio in 1955.[2] Quirino da Fonseca, in his still useful chronological catalogue of Portuguese 'Great Ships' (*Náos, Naus*) published in 1926, made confusion worse confounded by alleging that there were basic differences between Couto's account of the *Aguia* and *Garça* in his *Década VII* and that given by Manuel Barradas, S.J. (whom Quirino erroneously terms 'Ber-nardes') in the *HTM* of 1735.[3] Reference to Quirino's footnotes for this unfounded allegation discloses that he only used two chapters of the *Década VII*, whereas Couto devotes four chapters to this theme; and these four chapters are, to all intents and

[1] Couto's preface to the printed edition (1616) of *Década VII* is dated Goa, 6 Nov-ember 1603. In it he explains that he had sent to Portugal an earlier draft, which was lost when 'the English' [actually, the Dutch] took the homeward-bound carrack *Santiago* off St Helena in March 1602. As the *Santiago* had left Goa on Christmas Day 1601, Couto presumably wrote his original *Década VII* in 1600–1.

[2] Diogo Barbosa Machado, *Bibliotheca Lusitana* (4 vols., Lisbon, 1741–59), vol. III, containing the notice on Manuel Barradas, being published in 1752; António Sergio (ed.), *História Trágico-Marítima* (3 vols., Lisbon, 1955–6), I, 168.

[3] Quirino da Fonseca, *Os Portugueses no Mar. Memorias Históricas e Arqueológicas das Naus de Portugal*, I [all published], *Ementa Histórica das Naus Portuguesas* (Lisbon, 1926), 344–6.

purposes, virtually identical with the narrative ascribed to Barradas and printed in the *HTM*, as the present writer pointed out in his *Introduction to the História Trágico-Marítima* in 1957. It may be hoped that henceforward Diogo do Couto, who was such a stickler for giving a man his due (*dar o seu ao seu dono*, as he says more than once in his *Décadas*), will receive the credit which is due to him in this connection.

Proof-reading of books published in Portugal during the six-teenth, seventeenth and eighteenth centuries seems to have been conspicuous by its absence; and in any event Diogo do Couto, writing at Goa, had no chance to correct the proofs of his books that were published half a world away in Lisbon. Gomes de Brito did not have the excuse of space and time to absolve him from careful proof-reading; but he does not seem to have taken much trouble over this—if indeed he took any trouble at all. Con-sequently, some obscurities and doubtful readings still remain, even after a careful comparison of the texts of 1616 and 1735. Generally speaking, I have followed the former for obvious reasons; but in instances where the *HTM* version gives a more sensible or satisfactory rendering I have not hesitated to follow this.

B. Henrique Dias and the loss of the São Paulo

The first edition of the *Voyage and Shipwreck of the Great Ship São Paulo* was published at Lisbon in April 1565. The title-page, while giving the names of the captain, the master, and the pilot of this ship, does not mention that of the author. The colophon begins: 'Here ends the shipwreck of the Great Ship *São Paulo*, written by a trustworthy man who was an eyewitness and partici-pant in all this', but it likewise does not mention his name. This first edition is exceedingly rare; and my translation has been made from the only copy which I have been able to trace, and which is now in the library of the National Maritime Museum, Greenwich.

This text of 1565 is less than one-quarter of the length of that printed by Gomes de Brito, who states that the 'Relation of the voyage and shipwreck of the Great Ship *São Paulo*' (*História Trágico-Marítima*, I, 351–479) was originally written by 'Henrique

Dias, servant of the lord Dom António, Prior of Crato', as can be seen from the wording of the title-page of the 1735 edition.[1] The name of Henrique Dias nowhere appears in the text of the 1565 edition, but in the *HTM* version which is attributed to him he gives us a few incidental notices about himself. From these we learn that he was a *Boticário* or apothecary (pharmacist, as we would say nowadays) by profession and that he had picked up some notions of theoretical and practical medicine 'through his friendship and familiarity with some excellent and famous doctors and outstanding surgeons of the King, when I was serving His Majesty the late King [Dom João III] in his pharmacy, where I was brought up in Almeirim, Lisbon, and Thomar, so that I acquired some knowledge and skill therein' (*HTM*, I, 365). He adds that he had embarked in the *São Paulo* after being appointed to the Crown post of apothecary in the Hospital of the Misericordia at Goa, and that he took a well-stocked medicine-chest with him, all of which he used up in ministering to the sick on board ship, 'for the medicine-chests which they issue to these Indiamen from the Storehouse at Lisbon contain only a few ointments, and those virtually useless'.[2] Henrique Dias was clearly a well educated man and his narrative, particularly the more extensive *HTM* version, is studded with classical and scriptural allusions, including Latin tags from Ovid, Horace, and the Spanish Humanist, Luis Vives.

[1] Dom António (1531–95), illegitimate son of the Infante Dom Luís, and unsuccessful claimant to the Portuguese throne in 1580. Diogo do Couto was also a member of Dom António's household for a time, but he does not mention Henrique Dias in his account of the *São Paulo*.

[2] For the charitable institution of the Santa Casa da Misericordia (Holy House of Mercy) at Goa and its hospital see J. F. Ferreira Martins, *Historia da Misericordia de Goa, 1520–1910* (3 vols., Nova Goa, 1910–14), and the corrections thereto made by G. Schurhammer, S. J., *Franz Xaver, sein Leben und seine Zeit*, II, *Asien, 1541–1552* (i) *Indien und Indonesien, 1531–1547* (Freiburg, 1963), 197–207. The contents of some of the regulation medicine-chests carried on board the *naus da carreira da India* have been published by me in A. da Silva Rego (ed.), *O Centro de Estudos Históricos Ultramarinos e as Comemorações Henriquinas* (Lisbon, 1961), pp. 62–6, and in *Studia*, VIII (1961), 120–30; by Luís de Pina, 'Na rota do Imperio. A Medicina embarcada nos séculos XVI e XVII', in *Arquivo Histórico de Portugal*, IV (Lisbon, 1939), 283–323; by Frazão de Vasconcelos, *Subsídios para a história da Carreira da India no tempo dos Filipes* (Lisbon, 1960), pp. 76–8, where references will be found to other such lists dating from the time of Magellan's voyage of circumnavigation onwards.

As Duffy has pointed out in his discussion of Dias' qualifica-tions as a writer: 'At the outset of his narrative he explains that a day-by-day listing of events will surely prove boring and that, instead, he will tell only the notable events of the voyage with the greatest brevity and let truth, rather than his own invention, orna-ment his tale. In spite of his intentions few incidents fail to bring to his mind a classical or scriptural parallel which the good pharmacist thoroughly labours. His story of the *São Paulo* is a lucid, petulant description by a cosmopolite suddenly exposed to the discomforts and terrors of the sea. His pretty classical conceits give way to a continual carping at the officers and conditions on shipboard, but in the end there remains only the fear and humility of a man who has escaped from death. In Dias' narrative, more than in any other, there is clearly traced the transformation of a personality.'[1]

This 'transformation' is not so evident in the 1565 edition, but I am inclined to believe that both these versions of the loss of the *São Paulo* were written by the same author, for the 1735 narrative in the *HTM* reads as if it was a greatly expanded version of the *editio princeps*. There are, of course, some striking differences, begin-ning with the omission of the author's name and occupation in the 1565 edition. The date of the departure from Belém in this edition is given as the 20 April 1560, and the next date mentioned in the text is the 23 April. In the 1735 version these dates appear as the 25 and 28 April, respectively; nor is there any question of a misprint, since in both texts the dates are given in words and not in figures. There are other differences of detail and emphasis, some of which are noted in my translation below;[2] but for the most part, the textual differences are mainly limited to the inclusion or ex-clusion of certain passages and pages. The narrative of the voyage down to the time of the shipwreck is very much shorter in the 1565 edition than in the 1735 version. Many details of the stay at Bahia (*HTM*, 1, 371–5) and the description of Sumatra (*HTM*, 1,

---

[1] J. Duffy, *Shipwreck and Empire. Being an account of Portuguese maritime disasters in a century of decline* (Harvard University Press, 1955), p. 31. Duffy did not know of the existence of the 1565 edition.

[2] E.g. pp. 63, 66, 68.

443–6) are omitted in the 1565 text. Most important of all, the story of the voyage in the South Atlantic, round the Cape of Good Hope and via the 'roaring forties' to due south of Sumatra, which occupies pp. 368–425 of the 1735 text, is reduced to a few lines on leaves 5 *verso*–6 *recto* of the 1565 edition.

Unfortunately, Gomes de Brito gives us no indication of where he obtained the text that he printed, nor does he make any mention of the 1565 edition, which in all probability was unknown to him as it was to Barbosa Machado and all other Portuguese biblio graphers. It is impossible to say, therefore, whether the 1565 edition is an abridged version of the original manuscript, or whether the 1735 edition is an expansion of the original with numerous inter polations and additions by Gomes de Brito. In 1957 I tentatively suggested that Henrique Dias wrote a much larger account of the wreck after the publication of the 1565 edition; and that this was the version (whether manuscript or another unrecorded edition) which Gomes de Brito utilized in the *HTM*. I now feel that this suggestion is very unlikely, as the wording of both the texts makes it clear that the original was written at Malacca between July and December 1561, while the author was waiting for an onward passage to Goa.[1] On balance, I am inclined to believe that Gomes de Brito had access to the original manuscript or a copy of the same, which he printed in full, probably with some interpolations and additions of his own. If this supposition is correct, it still remains to be explained why the printer or publisher of 1565 abridged the text so drastically, and why he sedulously removed all mention of the author's name and occupation. This is a prob lem that I do not pretend to solve; but it is one which will, I hope, attract the attention of a competent Portuguese bibliographer.

A feature which both the 1565 and the 1735 texts have in common is the outspoken admiration of the writer for the per sonality and character of the Jesuit Padre Manuel Álvares. This Jesuit, 'a notable painter' (*pintor insigne*), also wrote an account of the voyage of the *São Paulo* and the misadventures of the cast aways in Sumatra, which was resumed by António Franco, S.J.,

---

[1] P. 105 below. Cf. *HTM*, I, 476: 'And here in Malacca...the rest of us are awaiting the monsoon for India, which will be in December...'

8 *The Tragic History of the Sea*

in his *Imagem de Virtude em o noviciado da Companhia de Jesus no Real Collegio de Jesus de Coimbra*, vol. II, book 3, pp. 359–73 (Coimbra, 1719). Padre Manuel Álvares' account was first published in full, together with the reproduction of the charming little pen-and-ink sketches which illustrate the original in the Jesuit archives at Rome, by Frazão de Vasconcelos in 1948.[1] Other and shorter accounts were published by Diogo do Couto in 1616, and by Francisco de Sousa, S.J., in 1710.[2] None of these three accounts make any mention of Henrique Dias or of the edition of 1565, but I have used them all in the annotation of my own translation. A fourth account, which I have also utilized, was that compiled by the Jesuit chronicler Sebastião Gonçalves, who lived in India from 1593 till his death at Goa in 1619. It was included in his manu-script history of the Jesuit missions in Asia, completed in 1614, but only published within the last few years.[3]

Couto and Gonçalves both knew several survivors from the shipwreck of the *São Paulo*, four of whom were still alive at Goa when Gonçalves wrote the relevant portion of his chronicle in 1607, and whom he describes as follows: 'The first is Francisco Paes, whom Fortune (as they say) has always favoured. The second is Pero Barbosa, from whom worldly fortune has always averted her face; and although he is of gentle birth he is so poor that being employed as verger of the Cathedral at Goa, he begs at the doorways of the Religious Orders and of some leading families, who thus sustain him with their daily alms. The third, Francisco Fernandes, a grummet, who fell overboard but was saved and

[1] Frazão de Vasconcelos, *Naufrágio da nau 'S. Paulo' em um ilheu próximo de Samatra no ano de 1561. Narração inédita, escrita em Goa em 1562 pelo Padre Manuel Alvares, S.J.* (Lisbon, 1948). Another version of the same narrative, from a copy in the Ajuda Library, will be found in Padre Artur de Sá, *Documentação para a história das missões do padroado português no Oriente. Insulíndia*, II, *1550–1562* (Lisbon, 1955), 381–429. Manuel Álvares' letter was likewise written during the castaways' stay at Malacca (vide preceding note) but with a final paragraph added at Cochin, 5 January 1562. Frazão de Vasconcelos errs in ascribing it to Goa.

[2] Couto, *Década VII* (Lisbon, 1616), Livro 9, cap. XII; Francisco de Sousa, S.J., *Oriente Conquistado* (2 vols., Lisbon, 1710), I, 181–3.

[3] A. de Sá, *Documentação. Insulíndia*, II, 598–608, for the relevant passages; Sebastião Gonçalves, S.J., *História dos Religiosos da Companhia de Jesus nos reynos e provincias da India Oriental* (3 vols., Coimbra, 1957–62). Cf. also J. Wicki, S.J., article on Gonçalves in the *Neue Zeitschrift für Missionswissenschaft*, VIII (1952), 261–9.

lived to survive the shipwreck, was fortunate enough to become the Crier of the Auction-mart in the city of Goa, which office he still holds. The fourth is António da Fonseca, who was in the household of King D. João III, and likewise served in India, where he was well rewarded for his services. He was a married man of Baçaim [Bassein], where he served in the honourable municipal posts that the citizens are entitled to hold.[1] But finding himself later a widower, he said farewell to the world, and, in the year 1584 he entered the Company of Jesus, in which he lives at present as a good Religious.' Couto, writing in 1601–03, likewise mentions António da Fonseca S.J., and Francisco Paes, who was then *Provedor-Mór dos Contos* (Auditor-General).[2]

One of the most noteworthy features of Henrique Dias' narrative is his virulent criticism of pilots, sailors and mariners as a class, and he quotes with approval Luis Vives' definition of them as *Fex Maris* ('Dregs of the Sea').[3] This intense dislike of seamen is much more noticeable in the *HTM* version of 1735 than in the 1565 edition, as many of Dias' most scathing observations are in the lengthy section of the former (pp. 368–425) which is compressed to two pages in the latter. I have commented elsewhere on this dislike of and contempt for sailors as a class among Portuguese and Spaniards in general (*THS*, I, page 11), and the interested reader is also referred to Duffy's comments on the same subject in his *Shipwreck and Empire*, pp. 71–6, with which I entirely agree. In this connection, it should be said that Henrique Dias' severe criticism of the chief pilot of the *São Paulo*, António Dias, is offset to some extent, and perhaps entirely, by the praise of his nautical competence and skill given by Padre Manuel Álvares S.J., and

[1] For these municipal posts and the duties and privileges attached thereto, see C. R. Boxer, *Portuguese Society in the Tropics. The municipal councils of Goa, Macao, Bahia and Luanda, 1510–1800* (Wisconsin University Press, 1965), pp. 12–41.

[2] A. de Sá, *Documentação. Insulíndia*, II, 606–7; Couto, *Década VII*, Livro 9, cap. XVI. Francisco Paes was captain-major of the China–Japan voyage in 1585–6, and the log of his round voyage between Macao and Nagasaki was printed by Linschoten in his *Itinerario* of 1596. Cf. C. R. Boxer, *The Christian Century in Japan, 1549–1650* (California University Press, 1951), pp. 406–14; Ibidem, *The Great Ship from Amacon. Annals of Macao and the Old Japan Trade, 1555–1640* (Lisbon, 1959), pp. 46–7.

[3] *HTM*, I, 381.

other Jesuit writers who are mentioned below (pp. 62, 70). António Dias was certainly held in high regard by many of his contemporaries and he acquired the nickname of 'Sumatra' on account of the rutter and charts he made of this island as a result of his experiences in 1561.[1]

The quarrelsome band of castaways from the *São Paulo* who travelled along part of the south-west coast of Sumatra in that year were not, of course, ideally objective or intelligent observers of the Sumatran scene. But in a day of small mercies the heart is thankful for scraps, and the written sources of Sumatran history for this period are so few and far between that the glimpses of coastal Minangkabau which we get from the eyewitness accounts of Henrique Dias and Manuel Álvares, S.J., are no doubt welcome to modern historians of Indonesia.

The fecklessness and improvidence so characteristic of the Portuguese in Asia, as the best of their own writers, including Diogo do Couto and Francisco de Sousa, S.J., never ceased to deplore, is brought out repeatedly in the behaviour of the castaways from the *São Paulo*, particularly in the events culminating in the attack on them by the Minangkabauers described on pp. 101–3 below. The unfortunate D. Francisca Sardinha subsequently received most of the blame for unwittingly inciting the lust and greed of the Muslim assailants; but there was another factor which none of the Portuguese writers mentions, but which would seem to supply an even stronger motive for the treacherous assault. Before their arrival in this port, the castaways had had several hostile encounters with the natives at various places along the coast, in the last of which they had seized some ships after a determined resistance and executed in cold blood all of their prisoners save one man (pp. 92–3 below). It never seems to have occurred to them, or to those who subsequently wrote up the narrative of these events, that this man whose life they had spared must have told the Minangkabauers of the fate of their fellow Muslims. Even if he did not, some of their slaves must have done so, as these slaves

---

[1] Cf. the references to him by the Eurasian cartographer, Manuel Godinho de Eredia (1563–1623), as translated by J. V. Mills, 'Eredia's Description of Malacca, Meridional India and Cathay', in *JMBRAS*, VIII (1930), 67, 240, 264.

included Javanese, Malays and Gujaratis, all of them Muslims who spoke Malay and who moved about freely among the Minangkabauers in the days before the attack, when cordial relations outwardly prevailed between the Christian castaways and their Muslim hosts. Yet blindly oblivious of the provocation they had given by their piratical acts, even if some of these were done in self-defence as they claimed, the Portuguese, as all the eyewitness accounts make clear, behaved on this potentially hostile shore as if they were in the security of Lisbon without a care in the world.

The dissensions among the castaways more than once threatened to prove their undoing, and it is interesting to see that Diogo do Couto, whether wittingly or otherwise, glosses over the mutual mistrust which so often pervaded them and which is so glaringly apparent in the eyewitness accounts of Henrique Dias and Manuel Álvares, S.J. This fissiparous tendency is a reflection of the strongly individualistic nature of the Portuguese national character, and was deplored among others by the great Padre António Vieira, S.J., when he castigated 'our disunity, our jealousy, our pre-sumption, our carelessness and our perpetual concern for indi-vidual interests'.[1] On the credit side, we may recall that in one of their periodic bursts of co-operation and mutual assistance, the castaways constructed two boats out of the materials they had salvaged from the wreck, displaying great skill and ingenuity in doing so (pp. 79–80 below). The *casado* António Dias from São Tomé de Meliapor showed himself to be a courageous and un-selfish leader on more than one occasion; and the herculean master, João Luís, redeemed his previous selfishness (pp. 73, 84) by sacri-ficing his life in the defence of D. Francisca when her husband basely abandoned her (pp. 102–3 below).

In his annotated edition of the *HTM*, published at Lisbon in three volumes in 1955–6, António Sergio remarks that this text of the *São Paulo* is one of the worst in the whole collection and is

[1] '...Nós temos a nossa desunião, a nossa inveja, a nossa presunção, o nosso descuido e a nossa perpétua atenção ao particular', as Vieira wrote in his celebrated 'Papel Forte' of 1649. Padre A. da Silva Rego makes the same point, but more moderately, in his admirable survey of the Portuguese East-India voyages at this period, 'Viagens Portuguesas à India em meados do século XVI', in *Anais da Academia Portuguesa da História*, II series, V (1954), 115.

frequently obscure.[1] Unfortunately, the 1565 edition is no better
in this respect; but a careful comparison of both versions has sometimes enabled me to obtain a reasonable rendering of some doubtful
words or passages. In other instances, however, both texts are
equally faulty or obscure, and this drawback is inevitably reflected
in the wording of the corresponding parts of my translation. The
text of Manuel Álvares', S.J., relation, while better than either of
the two foregoing, is likewise not free from misprints and obscurities, but it has been useful as a check on those of 1565 and
1735.

C. Jorge d'Albuquerque Coelho and the misadventures of the Santo António

Jorge d'Albuquerque Coelho was born at Olinda, the chief town
of the recently settled captaincy of Pernambuco in north-eastern
Brazil, on 23 April 1539. His parents were the *donatário* (donatory,
or lord-proprietor) Duarte Coelho Pereira and his wife, Dona
Brites de Albuquerque. Duarte Coelho had a distinguished career
in the east, principally in South-east Asia between 1511 and 1530,
before investing the fortune that he had made there in the coloniza-
tion of Pernambuco in 1534–5. He was present at the capture of
Malacca in 1511, was twice ambassador to Siam, and had made
voyages to China, Indo-China, and Java, and participated in
numerous campaigns in Malayan waters including the capture of
Bintan in 1526. Apart from his warrior father, Jorge d'Albuquerque Coelho was related to the great conqueror Afonso de
Albuquerque through his mother, D. Brites, who was the niece
of Jorge de Albuquerque, twice captain of Malacca, 1514–16
and 1521–5.[2] Jorge d'Albuquerque Coelho thus came of stout
conquistador stock on both sides, a fact of which he was not
forgetful and one which coloured his own romantic and eventful
life.

[1] 'O texto do seu relato, tal como aparece na *História Trágico-Marítima*, é dos
mais imperfeitos, frequentemente obscuro' (*HTM*, ed. A. Sergio, II, 12).
[2] For details of the services of Duarte Coelho and Jorge de Albuquerque in Asia
see I. A. Macgregor, 'The Portuguese in Malaya', in *JMBRAS*, xxviii (1955),
17–20, 36–9.

Sent to Portugal as a boy with his elder brother, Duarte, Jorge d'Albuquerque (as we will henceforth call him) was educated at Lisbon, and the youths were still there when their father died in 1554. The founder of Pernambuco could claim with legitimate pride five years before his death that 'God, through His mercy and my excessive moil and toil, spending of money and shedding of blood, has been pleased to grant that [my captaincy] is better pacified, founded, populated, governed and administered in due form and justice than any of the others'. Although Pernambuco was one of the few Brazilian captaincies that had firmly taken root by this time, the pacification was not quite so complete as Duarte Coelho boasted. Several of the Amerindian tribes in this region were either unsubdued, or else periodically rose in rebellion against the settlers. It was to deal with one such rising that the brothers Duarte and Jorge d'Albuquerque were sent by the Crown to cope with a rebellion by the Cayté (or Caeté) tribes in the *sertão* (back-lands, or hinterland) of Pernambuco in the year 1560. Duarte, as the elder brother, had inherited the proprietorship of the captaincy on his father's death six years previously; but it was Jorge who was placed in command of the primitive columns composed of soldiers, settlers and slaves which harassed the hostile tribes—or 'dissidents' as they would be called nowadays—during the next five years.[1]

These arduous campaigns in the backlands, during which Jorge d'Albuquerque received a number of arrow-wounds, were concluded by the submission of the dissident tribes, or most of them, early in 1565. Partly on this account, but also because he was not on the best terms with some of the leading personalities in the captaincy, Jorge d'Albuquerque decided to return to Portugal. He set sail from the port of Recife in June of that year, after an abortive start in the previous month, in the ship *Santo António*. During the voyage, the ship was attacked and captured by French Huguenot pirates, and subsequently underwent the series of mis-

[1] A. Marchant, *From Barter to Slavery. The economic relations of Portuguese and Indians in the setttlement of Brazil, 1500–1580* (Baltimore, 1942), provides an admirable and well documented survey of the background to these wars between the Portu-guese settlers and the Amerindian tribes.

adventures at the hands of her captors and of the elements which are described on pp. 121–53 below. Jorge d'Albuquerque is said by Jabotão to have returned to Pernambuco in 1573, in order to act as the representative of his brother the lord-proprietor, who had meanwhile returned to Portugal, whither Jorge himself followed him in March 1576. One or both of these dates must be wrong, as Padre Amador Rebelo, S.J., the Jesuit tutor and writing-master of Dom Sebastião, states that Jorge d'Albuquerque Coelho was among the *fidalgos* who accompanied the young king on his madcap expedition to Ceuta and Tangier in August–October 1574. Padre Rebelo was a contemporary of Jorge d'Albuquerque and Dom Sebastião, whereas Friar Jabotão compiled his monumental *Orbe Serafico* two centuries later; so the Jesuit is obviously more likely to be right on this point than the Franciscan.[1]

Whatever the details of Jorge d'Albuquerque's services in 1565–76, it is certain that he was one of the *fidalgos* who enjoyed the good graces of his capricious king. He was given the post of *Enfermeiro-Mór*, or chief of the medical services, in Dom Sebastião's second expedition to Morocco which ended in disaster on the field of El-Ksar el-Kebir (4 August 1578). This post was probably more of an honorary one than anything else, as there is no reason to suppose that Jorge d'Albuquerque possessed any medical or surgical qualifications, and the rudimentary nursing services in the army were performed by Jesuits and friars, in so far as they existed at all.[2] Jorge d'Albuquerque also had a command in the regiment of *Aventureiros*, or Adventurers, which led the vanguard of the attack, and which for one fleeting moment looked as if it might win the battle with the *élan* of its initial onrush. It was also Jorge d'Albuquerque, who, when the king lost his head and forgot to give the signal for the attack, shouted to Dom Sebastião to do so, as otherwise the troops would be demoralized by the

---

[1] António de Santa Maria Jabotão, O.F.M., *Orbe Serafico novo brasilico* (Lisbon, 1761), Parte II, Livro I, cap. 5, pp. 108–20; Amador Rebelo, S.J., *Crónica de El-Rei Dom Sebastião*, ed. A. Ferreira de Serpa (Oporto, 1925), p. 38.

[2] The bishops of Coimbra and Oporto likewise held the post of *Enfermeiro-Mór* in Dom Sebastião's ramshackle army, and it is probable that they had more to do with the rudimentary medical and nursing services than had Jorge d'Albuquerque Coelho. Cf. Rebelo, *Crónica*, p. 161.

Moorish artillery bombardment. He was severely injured with numerous lance, sword, and bullet wounds during the battle; and he achieved lasting fame by offering his own charger to the king at a moment when the battle was lost and Dom Sebastião's own horse irremediably crippled, but when it seemed as if the monarch might still have a chance to escape in the prevailing confusion and turmoil. Dom Sebastião took the charger, which he had in vain tried to buy from Albuquerque some time before the war; but, instead of trying to escape on this exceptionally fine mount, he rode into where some of the fighting was still going on and was never seen alive again.[1]

Jorge d'Albuquerque miraculously survived not only his numerous severe wounds but the primitive surgical methods of the time, which he had to endure in his seven months' captivity in Fez, when 'more than twenty bones were removed from his body'. He was ransomed in 1579, as one of the first batch of eighty wealthy *fidalgos* who were released; but he had to walk with crutches or else supported by two retainers 'for nearly fourteen years', before he recovered sufficiently from his injuries to walk unaided. This physical disability did not, however, prevent him from marrying twice (1583 and 1587), and fathering two sons by his second wife and a daughter by his first during this period. His elder brother, Duarte, who was likewise captured by the Moors at El-Ksar el-Kebir, was released in 1581, but died in Morocco on the journey home. Jorge then became the third donatory or lord-proprietor of the captaincy of Pernambuco, where his mother was still living until her death in 1584, but he himself never returned to Brazil. He died sometime in the year 1601, shortly after the publication of the edition of the *Naufrágio* which is trans-lated below.[2] His two sons, Duarte de Albuquerque Coelho,

[1] The best account of this disastrous campaign and of D. Sebastião's end at El-Ksar el-Kebir is by J. M. Queiroz Veloso in Damião Peres (ed.), *História de Portugal. Edição Monumental*, v (Barcelos, 1933), 107–62. Those unable to read Portuguese may be referred to E. W. Bovill, *The Battle of Alcazar* (London, 1952), and M. E. Bishop, *A King for Portugal. The Madrigal Conspiracy, 1594–95* (Madison, 1964), pp. 144–9.

[2] The fullest biography of Jorge d'Albuquerque Coelho is still that published by Jabotão in his *Orbe Serafico* (1761), listed p. 14, n. 1, above. Jabotão made use of earlier works such as Jerónimo de Mendoça, *Jornada de Africa* (Lisbon, 1607),

who succeeded him as *donatário*, and Matthias de Albuquerque, both distinguished themselves as leaders of the defence of Per׳ nambuco against the Dutch in 1630-8, of which the former wrote a classic account, *Memorias Diarias de la guerra del Brasil* (Madrid, 1654).[1]

The *Naufrágio* which related Jorge d'Albuquerque's dramatic voyage in 1565 was first published in an edition of 1,000 copies at an unascertained date between that year and 1601, when a second edition was published, likewise of 1,000 copies.[2] Since no copy of the first edition has yet to come to light, nor is it recorded by Barbosa Machado or any of the standard bibliographers, I can׳ not say how far the text of 1601 was a mere reprint of the former. But we know from the publisher's prologue to the 1601 edition, that the *Prosopopéia* of Bento Teixeira (or Bento Teixeira Pinto, as he is often called) was printed for the first time as an appendix to the *Naufrágio* in this year, since it had been accidentally omitted from the first (or sixteenth׳century) edition. The *Prosopopéia* is a laudatory poem in praise of Jorge d'Albuquerque Coelho, which has attracted an amount of comment altogether disproportionate to its very slender poetical merits, since it was for centuries believed that Bento Teixeira was the first Brazilian poet and consequently the *Prosopopéia* the first Brazilian poem to appear in print. This confusion was perpetuated by (if it did not arise from) Gomes de Brito assuming that both the *Naufrágio* and the *Prosopopéia* had been written by Bento Teixeira, and publishing the former with a title׳page to this effect in his *HTM* of 1736. The error was com׳ pounded by Barbosa Machado in his classic *Bibliotheca Lusitana* (*in voce* Bento Teixeira Pinto), who stated that Bento Teixeira Pinto was a native of Pernambuco, and gave the great weight of his authority to the assertion that the *Naufrágio* and the *Prosopopéia*

and Miguel Leitão de Andrada, *Miscelânea* (Lisbon, 1629), though he evidently did not realize that there had been two editions of the *Naufrágio* (15?? and 1601) before Gomes de Brito published his version in the *HTM*, II (1736).

[1] C. R. Boxer, *The Dutch in Brazil, 1624-1654* (Oxford, 1957), pp. 297-8, for an assessment of the *Memorias Diarias*.

[2] See p. 117 below. It is interesting to note that the *Naufrágio* had two editions, each of 1,000 copies, as some authorities consider that at this period the average edition of a book in Western Europe did not exceed 300 copies. Cf. A. J. Saraiva, *História da Cultura em Portugal* (3 vols., Lisbon, 1950–62), II, 134–5.

were by the same author, although he had in his own library a copy of the 1601 edition.

It has been said: 'Give a mistake a start and there is no over/taking it', and this saying is certainly verified in the way that the erroneous attribution of the *Naufrágio* to Bento Teixeira has held its own through the ages. The present writer must plead guilty to committing in this connection the same bibliographical sin with which he has taxed others on p. 3 above, regarding the attribu/tion of the narrative of the loss of the *Aguia* and *Garça* to Manuel Barradas, S.J., instead of to Diogo do Couto. Misled by a super/ficial (and erroneous) observation of António Sergio on p. 112 of his edition of the *Naufrágio* (*HTM*, ed. Sergio, vol. 11, p. 112), I wrote in my 'Introduction to the *HTM*' of 1957: 'At one time the Brazilian historian, Francisco Adolfo Varnhagen, maintained that the pilot, Afonso Luís, was primarily responsible for this relation; but he adduced no convincing proof of this assertion which has been dropped from the later editions of the work where it was originally made. Most modern writers are inclined to attri/bute the *Naufrágio* to the pen of Bento Teixeira Pinto, and I like/wise feel that the traditional attribution should stand unless some new and convincing evidence can be adduced to disprove it.'[1]

Mea culpa, mea maxima culpa! When I wrote those lines, I had not seen a copy of the 1601 *Naufrágio*, nor had I checked all the editions of Varnhagen's *História Geral do Brasil*, but only two of them. I had not realized that Bento Teixeira's authorship of the *Naufrágio* had already been denied by other Brazilian scholars besides Varnhagen, including Capistrano de Abreu and José Honório Rodrigues.[2] All doubts were laid at rest by José António Gonsalves de Mello in a definitive essay, 'Bento Teixeira, autor da *Prosopopéia*' in his *Estudos Pernambucanos*, pp. 5–43 (Recife, 1960). Gonsalves de Mello showed conclusively that Bento Teixeira was born at Oporto in or about the year 1561, and that

[1] C.R.B., 'An Introduction to the História Trágico/Marítima', p. 18 of the reprint from the *Miscelânea de Estudos em honra do Prof. Hernâni Cidade* (Lisbon, 1957).
[2] F. A. Varnhagen, Visconde de Porto Seguro, *História Geral do Brasil antes de sua separação e independencia de Portugal* (3ª ed., São Paulo, n.d.), III, 121; José Honório Rodrigues, *Teoria da História do Brasil. Introdução Metodológica* (2ª ed., 2 vols., São Paulo, 1957), pp. 552–3.

he could not have participated in the voyage of the *Santo António* four years later, as the real author of the *Naufrágio* undoubtedly did. From the wording of the text on pp. 116–17 below, it seems quite clear that the pilot Afonso Luís, who was a passenger in the *Santo António*, wrote this narrative at the request of Jorge d'Albuquerque and that the pilot's narrative was then touched up for publication by a scholar named António de Castro, likewise at the request of Albuquerque. It is true that this attribution is not universely accepted, and Senhor Cândido Jucá (Filho) has argued that this passage is an interpolation and must be peremptorily rejected, but he adduces no convincing arguments in support of this assertion, which is therefore a mere conjecture.[1] The traditional attribution of the *Naufrágio* to Bento Teixeira (Pinto) is also retained in the standard bibliography of Rubens Borba de Moraes, *Bibliographia Brasiliana*, vol. II, p. 296 (Amsterdam and Rio de Janeiro, 1962). But Senhor Borba de Moraes, with whom I discussed this problem at São Paulo in 1963, told me that he had independently come to the same conclusion as myself, and that Varnhagen's original attribution was the correct one.

The only important differences between the 1601 text of the *Naufrágio* and the version printed by Gomes de Brito in 1736 (*HTM*, II, 1–59), are that this eighteenth-century editor has care-fully removed all indications that Afonso Luís wrote the original draft by substituting another 'Prologue to the Reader' for the 'Prologue' addressed to Jorge de Albuquerque by the editor-publisher António Ribeiro, and he also suppressed the original licences of the 1601 edition. Gomes de Brito has likewise omitted the lengthy passage on pp. A 3, *recto* and *verso* of the 1601 edition, corresponding to pp. 116–17 in the translation below, which make it clear that Afonso Luís and António de Castro (or Crasto) were the two authors concerned. Finally, by bodily removing the *Prosopopéia* from the 1736 edition, but by placing the name of Bento Teixeira Pinto on the title-page of the *Naufrágio* instead

---

[1] Cândido Jucá (Filho), 'Quem seja o autor do "Nufrágio"', in *Revista do Livro*, No. 7 (Rio de Janeiro, 1957), 83–8. I am indebted to Senhor Alexandre Eulálio Pimenta da Cunha, of the Instituto do Livro at the National Library, Rio, for kindly obtaining a copy of this article for me.

Gomes de Brito gave the reader no option but to believe that the *Naufrágio* was the work of the former. Why he did this, I have no idea; but it recalls his gratuitous deletion of Diogo do Couto's name in the narrative of the *Aguia* and *Garça* and his substitution by the Jesuit Manuel Barradas as the author.

As stated above, no copy of the sixteenth-century edition of the *Naufrágio* has yet to come to light, but since António Ribeiro states in the 1601 edition that he had originally intended to print the *Prosopopéia* with the first, this would imply that the *editio princeps* must have been printed after 1578, as the poem alludes to Jorge d'Albuquerque's deeds in the battle of El-Ksar el-Kebir. Moreover, it must have been printed before the year of 1592, as some of the woodcuts illustrating certain episodes in the voyage of the *Santo António*, and which are inserted in their proper places in the text of the 1601 edition, are also used to illustrate the 1592 edition of the *História da muy notável perda de Galeam grande Sam Joam*, with which they really have no connection. At a guess, therefore, the first edition may tentatively be ascribed to some time in the decade 1580–90. However that may be, the second edition of 1601 is also an exceedingly rare work. I have been able to trace only the following four copies, the first three of which I have actually seen.

(1) Ajuda Library, Lisbon.

(2) National Library, Rio de Janeiro.

(3) Lima Library, Catholic University of America, Washington, D.C.

(4) Library of the Faculty of Law, University of Recife, Pernambuco.

Varnhagen mentions a copy in the 'Biblioteca Publica de Lisboa', now the National Library, Lisbon, but I do not know if it is still there.

Almeida Garrett, the famous nineteenth-century Portuguese statesman, playwright, and Romantic author, claimed that Jorge d'Albuquerque's misadventures in the *Santo António* provided the main inspiration for one of the most famous Portuguese folk-ballads—the *Nau Catarineta*. This attribution has been both contested and supported, and the discussion still continues among

folklorists. All that need be said here is that, of the eighteen narra,
tives included in the original edition of the *História Trágica,
Marítima*, the misadventures of Jorge d'Albuquerque and his
companions in the *Santo António* are those which approximate
most closely to the sufferings of the captain and crew in the
Catarineta, who were likewise reduced by hunger to the verge of
cannibalism.[1]

The Luso,Brazilian chronicler, Loreto Couto, states with his
habitual baroque bombast that the fact of Jorge d'Albuquerque
Coelho having been born in Pernambuco was enough in itself
to shed eternal glory on that region.[2] But when we have dis,
counted such hyperbolic assertions, it remains true that the third
donatory of Pernambuco was an interesting and colourful charac,
ter in his own right. Whether or not his voyage of 1565 provided
the main inspiration for the ballad of the *Nau Catarineta*, his action
in giving his charger to the King at a critical moment in the battle
of El,Ksar el,Kebir certainly led many of his contemporaries to
believe that Dom Sebastião had in fact escaped from the stricken
field and would return one day to lead his nation to new heights
of glory. Jorge d'Albuquerque is therefore one of the persons
responsible for the development of this curious Messianic belief
among the Portuguese—a belief which flourished for nearly two
hundred years and which is not entirely extinct today in some of
the remoter regions of Brazil.[3]

[1] F. C. Pires de Lima, *A Nau Catarineta. Ensaio de Interpretação Histórica* (Oporto,
1954). One of the shorter versions of the *Nau Catarineta* is translated in Rodney
Gallop, *Portugal. A book of folk,ways* (Cambridge University Press, 1936), pp.
216–17.

[2] 'E ainda que Pernambuco não tivera produzido outro filho, bastaria este para
sua immortal gloria' (Domingos Loreto Couto, 'Desagravos do Brazil e Glorias
de Pernambuco', written *c.* 1757, and published in *ABNRJ*, XXIV, 325–7).

[3] Jorge d'Albuquerque's responsibility for helping to spread the belief that Dom
Sebastião had escaped on his (Albuquerque's) charger was pointed out by a hostile
Spanish critic who tried to prevent the publication of Duarte d'Albuquerque
Coelho's *Memorias Diarias* on these and other grounds *c.* 1645 (British Museum,
Add. MSS. 28461, fos. 95–102, published in *Documentação Ultramarina Portuguesa*, I,
Lisbon, 1960, 111–19). The anonymous critic was, however, wrong in his allega,
tion that no account of the battle of El,Ksar el,Kebir prior to Leitão de Andrade's
Miscelânea of 1629 made any mention of this incident. It figures prominently in the
Naufrágio and in the *Prosopopéia* of 1601 (and doubtless in the first edition of the

As Duffy has noted in his *Shipwreck and Empire* (p. 32), this account 'is the most avowedly religious one in the collection, with almost every action at sea translated in terms of God's infinite mercy or displeasure'. This emphasis may reflect Jorge d'Albu׳querque's own influence on the writer—whether Afonso Luís, António de Castro, or someone yet unidentified—for we know that he read the original draft and that he was a devoutly religious man. Not only did he patronize the Jesuits in Pernambuco, but he was directly responsible for introducing both the Franciscan friars and the Benedictine monks into his captaincy, endowing and encouraging their pioneer establishments.[1] Unfortunately, the writer's edifying sentiments are not always matched by clarity of exposition and grammatical correctness. Despite the claim that the original draft had been carefully revised and polished for publica׳tion by a distinguished scholar, the text as printed in the 1601 edition—and also as reprinted in 1736—is by no means free from obscurities and needless repetitions, some of which are unavoidably reflected in my own translation.

former), and is mentioned in Jerónimo de Mendoça's *Jornada de Africa* of 1607. It also occurs in Luís Coelho Barbuda, *Empresas Militares de Lusitanos* (Lisbon, 1624), p. 297.

[1] For details see Jabotão, *Orbe Serafico* (1761), Parte II, Livro I, 108–20.

TEXTS

RELAÇAÕ

DA
VIAGEM, E SUCCESSO
QUE TIVERAÕ AS NAOS
AGUIA, E GARÇA

Vindo da India para efte Reyno no Anno
de 1559.

COM HUMA DISCRIÇAÕ
da Cidade de Columbo,
PELO PADRE MANOEL BARRADAS
da Companhia de JESUS,

Enviada a outro Padre da mefma Companhia
morador em Lisboa.

Ee ij

NARRATIVE

OF THE

VOYAGE AND VICISSITUDES

WHICH BEFELL THE GREAT SHIPS
AGUIA AND *GARÇA*

Bound from India to this kingdom in the year
1559

WITH A DESCRIPTION
of the City of Colombo

BY THE FATHER MANOEL BARRADAS
of the Company of JESUS.[1]

*Sent to another Father of the same Company
living at Lisbon.*

---

[1] As noted in the introduction (pp. 2–4), the description of the city of Colombo by Father Manuel Barradas S.J. has nothing whatever to do with the description of the loss of the *Aguia* and *Garça* by Diogo do Couto, and it is therefore omitted from this translation.

VICISSITUDES
WHICH BEFELL THE GREAT SHIPS
AGUIA AND *GARÇA*[1]

Bound from India to this kingdom in the year 1559

WHEN the Viceroy D. Constantino de Bragança had taken charge of the government of India, the ex-governor, Francisco Barreto, remained for a time at Goa, in order to prepare for his departure to the kingdom. And as the great ship *Garça* in which the Viceroy D. Constantino had come in 1558, was a ship of 1,000 tons, the biggest which had hitherto been seen in the India Voyage,[2] and there was not enough cargo in Goa to provide her with a full lading, Francisco Barreto asked the viceroy to give her to João Rodrigues de Carvalho, so that he could go and complete her cargo [of pepper] at Cochin; and to give him instead the ship of João Rodrigues, which was smaller and already old on account of the many times she had wintered on her outward voyage before reaching India.[3] The viceroy willingly complied with this request, because it was advantageous for the ship and likewise gratified Francisco Barreto, who wanted to start from Goa. The great ship *Aguia* (which was also called *Patifa*) having been repaired, they

[1] This text is translated from the version given in Diogo do Couto's *Década VII*, which corresponds closely to that printed by Gomes de Brito in the *HTM*, I, 219–52. Cf. pp. 2 above and 158 below.

[2] Doubtfully true, as statements of this kind ('the biggest ever', 'the richest ever') were constantly being made about the galleons and carracks lost in the *Carreira da India*, just as they were about the Manila galleons lost in the Pacific crossing to Mexico in the sixteenth to eighteenth centuries. *Garça* is the Portuguese word for 'Heron', and not, in this instance, an obsolescent form of the word *Graça* (Grace), as it was sometimes. For this particular *Garça* and others of the same invocation see Frazão de Vasconcelos, 'As Naus *Garças*. Nota Histórica', in *O Mundo Português*, No. 94 (1941), 3–7 (Lisbon, 1941). D. Constantino de Bragança was viceroy of Portuguese India, September 1558 to September 1561, in succession to Francisco Barreto, who was governor, 1555–8.

[3] A distinct exaggeration, as she had only wintered twice at Moçambique in 1557–8, as can be deduced from Couto's own account in *Década VII*, Livro 5, caps. 2 and 5.

began to lade her with cargo and provisions for her voyage.[1] On 20 January of the year 1559, Francisco Barreto set sail from the bar of Goa, accompanied by many gentlemen and knights who were returning to ask for the rewards due for their services to the Crown, and to whom Francisco Barreto gave free board during the voyage. Those whose names we were able to ascertain are the following.[2]

Jerónimo Barreto Rolim, brother of Rui Barreto Rolim of Pampulha, first cousin of the Governor Francisco Barreto; Dom Diogo Lobo, nephew of Dom João Lobo, baron of Alvito; Dom Afonso Henriques, married in Baçaim, and a relative of Dom Jorge Henriques, lord of the manor of Alcaçovas; Dom Francisco de Moura, brother of Dom Rolim de Santarem; Dom Felipe de Castro, son of Dom Rodrigo Hombrinhos, those of the Torrão;[3] Manuel de Brito, the *Langará*;[4] Pedralvares de Mancellos, son of António de Mancellos who was killed in the second siege of Diu in the year 1546;[5] Manuel de Anhaia Coutinho, brother of Diogo de Anhaia Coutinho, natives of Santarem and closely related to Francisco Barreto. Bastião de Resende, illegitimate son of Garcia de Resende;[6] Diogo de Vasconcelos, foster-brother of the prince;[7] Francisco de Gouvea, and others of the king's servants whose names we did not learn.

[1] *Patifa*, the feminine form of *Patife*, which the dictionaries define somewhat loosely as; 'rascal; scoundrel; villain; scamp; lounger; good-for-nothing; a fish-porter'. *Aguia* means *Eagle*.

[2] This list of distinguished passengers is omitted in the *HTM* version.

[3] D. Felipe de Castro, son of D. Rodrigo de Castro, was granted the reversion of the captaincy of Damão in 1568, in reward for his previous services in India (L. Ribeiro, *Registo da Casa da Índia*. 2 vols., Lisbon, 1954, I, 165, nr. 710). *Hombrinhos* is presumably a nickname (?'narrow-shouldered', 'pigeon-chested', 'little men'?); and Torrão, south-east of Alcacer do Sal in the province of Alentejo is the place from which this family came.

[4] From Hindustani *Langra*, 'lame', 'cripple'. Cf. Dalgado, *Glossário Luso-Asiático*, I, 509.

[5] For the epic defence of Diu in 1546 against the army of the Sultan of Gujarat, see R. S. Whiteway, *The Rise of Portuguese Power in India, 1497–1550* (London, 1899), pp. 304–13; A. Baião (ed.), *História Quinhentista inédita do Segundo Cêrco de Dio* (Coimbra, 1927).

[6] Presumably Garcia de Resende, poet, diplomat, chronicler and court official (c. 1470–1536), friend and confidant of three successive Portuguese kings (D. João II, D. Manuel I, D. João III), chiefly famous as the compiler of the *Cancioneiro Geral* published in 1516.   [7] Not clear what prince is meant.

This great ship began her voyage with fair and favourable winds, and the others left Cochin at the same time, with D. Luís Fernandes de Vasconcelos[1] in the great ship *Galega*, with her consorts of the same convoy, which left towards the end of January. All these ships, both that of D. Luís Fernandes de Vasconcelos and that of Francisco Barreto, as well as the others which sailed from Cochin, were wafted on their voyage by easterly winds until after they had passed the southern tip of the island of St Laurence[2] and set their course for the Land of Natal. And when they arrived off the extremity thereof, which lies in $31°$ southern latitude, about 230 leagues from the Cape of Good Hope, they were struck by a very violent and widespread storm which overtook all of them, and damaged them so much that it was the entire cause of most of them being lost, some sooner and others later, according to the greater or lesser force with which it struck them, without their having sight of each other. Due to this storm, the winds were so strong and so contrary and the seas ran so high, and agitated and cross, that they were obliged to lie-to with great danger and diffi-culty. Worse still, these many days of trying[3] left them leaky and unmanageable, with their knees broken, their tree-nails twisted, and their strengthening-pieces torn apart, as happened to the great ship of Francisco Barreto, which we will deal with shortly. These ships spent the whole of the month of March endeavouring to double the Cape of Good Hope.

The great ships *Tigre*, *Castello* and *Rainha*, which had been in D. Constantino [de Bragança's] fleet, were able to round the Cape of Good Hope and to reach Portugal, either because their pilots were better navigators or because luckily God gave them better weather. But the others, which were the previous year's ships of

[1] D. Luís Fernandes de Vasconcelos, natural son of the archbishop of Lisbon, after a chequered maritime career was appointed governor-general of Brazil, but was intercepted off the Canaries and killed by French Calvinist corsairs from La Rochelle, when on his way there (12 September 1571). The French likewise killed in this fight, or subsequently threw overboard into the sea, thirteen Jesuits.

[2] Madagascar. For its discovery and naming by the Portuguese, see A. Kammerer, *La découverte de Madagascar par les Portugais et la cartographie de l'île* (Lisbon, 1950).

[3] 'The situation in which a ship lies nearly in the trough or hollow of the sea in a tempest, particularly when it blows contrary to her course' (W. Falconer, *A Universal Dictionary of the Marine*, ed. London, 1789, *in voce* 'Trying').

the fleet of D. Luís Fernandes de Vasconcelos, all of which had wintered [at Moçambique], were all shipwrecked in different regions.[1] The great ship *Framenga*, Captain António Mendes de Castro, even though she succeeded in doubling the Cape of Good Hope, was so badly battered that she was cast away on the island of São Thomé. The great ship *Garça* which was one of the fleet of the Viceroy Dom Constantino de Bragança and of which João Rodrigues de Carvalho was captain, was forced to lie a-hull for many days, until it was too late in the season for her to double the Cape; and since she was also leaking badly and there was insufficient drinking-water for those on board, she was forced to put back to Moçambique, which she accordingly did.

The *Patifa*, in which was the ex-Governor Francisco Barreto, encountered many contrary winds, which forced her to lie under bare poles for eighteen days, in the trough of the waves of cross-seas resembling high mountains, from the tops of which the ship often descended so far that it seemed she would never come up again. And with the heavy pitching and tossing of the ship, thirty-five of the knees were sprung by their throats, and there were twisted more than forty tree-nails as thick as the fleshy part of the arm, which made fast the knees to the ship's frame; and there were broken eighteen strengthening pieces which clamp the knees. All this damage added to the age and rottenness of the ship, made her spring so many leaks that she would certainly have gone to the bottom, had it not been for the courage and diligence with which Francisco Barreto made people work at the pumps and bail out the water which was pouring in through the numerous leaks. The gentlemen on board likewise participated with great care and assiduity in these tasks, Francisco Barreto being the foremost; whose presence and example encouraged everyone so much that it seemed they took in their stride a labour that only Portuguese could endure, in order to overcome the hardships which they suffered, without relinquishing the hand-ropes of the pumps by

[1] For the outward-bound ships of the fleets of 1557 and 1558, see Simão Ferreira Paes, *Recopilação das famosas armadas Portuguesas, 1496–1650* (ed. Rio de Janeiro, 1937), pp. 60–1. The *Rainha* and *Castello* reached Lisbon on 5 and 7 August 1559, and the *Tigre* on 11 August 1560, respectively (Luís de Figueiredo Falcão, *Livro em que se contem toda a Fazenda*, Lisbon, 1859, pp. 166–7).

day or night. On top of these exertions they had perforce to make another, which was the shifting of the pepper from some store-rooms to others, in order to try and stop the leaks in the latter; for they were afraid that if the pepper got into the pumps and clogged them, this would involve the final loss of the ship, since if they could not work the pumps all their excessive labour would be fruitless and in vain, through not being able to get rid of the water. Even as it was, the water increased gradually despite all their ceaseless pumping; and so much came in through the leaks that even if they stopped working the pumps for a very short time, they found that the water was three or four spans deeper than formerly. The ship passed four days in this way without their leaving off pumping continually by day and night. And because this toil was rendered still harder by the smoke from the galley-fire which blinded them, as at that time this pumping had to be done below the deck of the waist,[1] the gentlemen and the king's servants who were working at the pumps thought it a lesser evil to eat no cooked food at all, rather than have it cooked at the cost of so great an inconvenience. They therefore asked Francisco Barreto to make some other arrangement, for they could no longer endure to work at the pumps if they were suffocated by smoke from the galley. This he did, by having two pipes sawn in half, from which were made four fish-tubs that were placed in the waist, filled respectively with wine, water, biscuit, and also some comfits, with which they sustained themselves for three days, during which time they ate no cooked food at all. Having located the leaks which the ship was making, which numbered fifty-four in all, the officers (that is to say, the caulkers and the carpenters)[2] tried to stop them from inside the ship, since it was not possible to do so from outboard; and so they were stopped as far as possible by cutting away some of the knees, riders, and strengthening-pieces. But even though the ship now made less water, withal she was considerably weakened by the cutting away of the riders; and thus each time

---

[1] The site of the galley or galleys (there were sometimes two) was later shifted to the deck. Cf. *Voyage of Pyrard de Laval*, II(1), 192, 194.

[2] This is the sense in which the term 'officers' is subsequently used in this book. Cf. *THS*, I, 56, n. 2; *Voyage of Pyrard de Laval*, II(1), 192–3.

that she pitched or rolled, she shook so severely that all those who were in her thought that she was on the point of foundering and that their last hour had come, in which they were all going to perish miserably. For this reason, they had to frap the ship by passing several turns of a cable round the forepart and another cable round the stern quarter, tightening them with the capstan, so as to prevent her from coming apart at the seams and breaking up completely. And with all these makeshifts and devices the ship still continued to ship so much water that the gentlemen and knights aboard her never stopped working at both the pumps without their being able to expel and get rid of the water. There⁄fore Francisco Barreto, with the solemnly sworn advice of the ship's officers, ordered many of the merchants' goods to be thrown overboard, such as benzoin,[1] many hundredweights of which were thrown into the sea, and many fardels of indigo, and some chests of silks, and many valuable and rare Chinese goods.

It so happened that while they were thus engaged in throwing overboard these goods, they came across some fardels of indigo which formed part of a charitable gift that the king made each year by way of alms for the upkeep of the church of the monastery of Nossa Senhora da Graça at Lisbon.[2] And on their asking Francisco Barreto whether this lot of indigo should also be thrown into the sea, as they were doing with the other goods, he replied that it should not. He added that if matters reached the stage that the only hope of salvation lay in jettisoning his own merchandise, then that should be thrown overboard; but that he himself was prepared to carry ashore on his shoulders the merchandise belong⁄ing to Our Lady, in whose favour he trusted for the salvation and preservation of that ship.

As the leaks got steadily worse, and manning the pumps con⁄

---

[1] Benzoin or Benjamin, an aromatic resin (*Styrax benzoin*) from Sumatra and Siam, in great demand as an incense. Cf. Yule and Burnell, *Hobson⁄Jobson* (ed. 1903), pp. 86–7; S. R. Dalgado, *Glossário Luso⁄Asiático* (2 vols., Coimbra, 1919–21), I, 112–13, and the sources there quoted.

[2] An Augustinian establishment, 'a structure truly magnificent and plentifully endowed; the Church spacious, beautiful, and adorned with all imaginable cost, the monastry proportionable in all respects to its greatness' ([John Stevens], *The Ancient and Present State of Portugal*, London, 1706, p. 184).

tinuously did not suffice to prevent the vessel from shipping more water than the amount which was expelled, the pilot (named André Lopes)[1] fearing that she might founder at any moment as she was so leaky and battered, he decided, with the consent of Francisco Barreto, to set a course for the nearest land they could reach, which was more or less that of Natal (where Manuel de Sousa de Sepulveda had been cast away in the galleon *São João* on 24 June 1552 in 31° southern latitude),[2] considering that it was better to end their lives ashore than to become food for the fishes in the sea. And as they were thus steering for the land ahead, which was about fifty leagues away, Francisco Barreto called a council comprising the pilot, master, boatswain, assistant-pilot, and all the other ship's officers, and administering to them an oath upon a missal and a crucifix, on which they all placed their hands, he ordered them to say each one on the oath which he had taken, what they thought about the condition which the ship was in, and what they ought to do about it. To which the pilot, as the principal person, replied first, saying that he had been a mariner for fifty years and that he had made the India voyage many times, when he had often been in dire peril, but that he had never been in such great danger as this; since the ship was rotten and was making a tremendous amount of water through the open seams. And that if Our Lord in His mercy would bring them in sight of the land for which they were steering, this would be the greatest benefaction that any experienced seaman who had been in similar dangers could desire. The master and all the other ship's officers voted unanimously in exactly the same way.

Francisco Barreto, seeing the critical condition in which they were, made them all a brief speech, inspired by a heart which

---

[1] Nothing is known of this pilot beyond a brief mention of an undated *Roteiro* (Rutter) by him, cited by Barbosa Machado. Cf. Fontoura da Costa, *A Marinharia dos Descobrimentos* (ed. 1933), p. 483, nr, 63 M, where, however, the reference to the seventeenth century should be deleted.

[2] The loss of the great galleon *São João* in 1552, and the tragic fate of Manuel de Sepulveda and his beautiful and courageous young wife, was by far the most popular of the shipwreck narratives reprinted in the *HTM*, and numerous editions exist in several languages. Cf. C. R. Boxer, *An Introduction to the HTM*, pp. 6–10, 48; J. Duffy, *Shipwreck and Empire*, pp. 25–7, 44–6.

neither hardships could tire nor dangers could frighten into losing the smallest fraction of its courage (a speech like that which Aeneas made to his companions when they escaped from the destruction of Troy, scouring the Mediterranean in search of some region in Italy where they could found a settlement, at a time when they were dismayed and discouraged, as Virgil relates in his first book of the *Aenead*)[1] saying to them:

'Gentlemen and knights, friends and companions, you must not be downcast nor saddened at the thought of our making the land which lies ahead, because it could be that God is bringing us to a land where we will be able to conquer another new world and to discover a greater India than that which is already found.[2] For I have here gentlemen and knights for comrades, with whom I would dare to undertake any conquest or enterprise whatsoever, however arduous and difficult it might be. For what the experience of many who are here in this company has shown me, gives me the assurance and the confidence to have no fear or misgiving of anything in this world.'

Francisco Barreto said these words with as cheerful and serene a countenance as if he was enjoying himself in the orchards of the valley of Enxobregas,[3] and not on the point of being cast away in the land of the most brutish and barbarous people in the world. And withal these words inspired all his companions with new spirits and gave them new strength, so that they could carry on and press forward despite the hardships they endured, which were already great enough.

Having thus resolved to run ashore on the land of Natal, as the mercy which God usually grants to those who need His help is to show them that just when they least expect it then He gives it to

---

[1] All this section in brackets is omitted from the *HTM* version.

[2] A thinly veiled allusion to the allegedly gold-rich 'empire' (in reality, tribal confederation) of Monomotapa—a will-o-the-wisp which led many Portuguese to their deaths in the interior, including Francisco Barreto himself in the expedition up the Zambesi in 1573. Cf. W. G. L. Randles, *L'image du Sud-Est Africain dans la littérature européenne au XVIᵉ siècle* (Lisbon, 1959), especially pp. 101–6.

[3] Enxobregas, actually Xabregas, at the eastern end of Lisbon. The district alongside the river Tagus from here to Sacavem, was then dotted with *quintas* (country-houses) and regarded as the most fertile region in the immediate surroundings of the Portuguese capital.

them, so He did with these exhausted and afflicted voyagers, granting them the favour of moderating the winds and the waves (which up till then had been very high and rough), which resulted in the ship sailing better, pitching and rolling less, and shipping less water. The pilot and the other ship's officers seeing that the danger had lessened, were of the opinion that the course should be changed and set for Moçambique, where they hoped that God would bring them safely. And so it proved, for with the mild and favourable breezes, which they had from that time onwards, the ship continued on her voyage. But the gentlemen and passengers were continually with the pump-ropes in their hands, without letting them go for a single instant; because if they left off working both the pumps for however short a time, the water immediately increased by several spans and got the better of them. And in order that they should not be overcome by the water, they worked the pumps all the time.

Francisco Barreto, wishing to relieve the gentlemen of this heavy and ceaseless toil, summoned a foreman of the Kaffirs who came in this ship and supervised their work and was their overseer; and he promised him 100 *cruzados* if he with his companions could clear the pumps. The Kaffirs accepted this offer, and putting their chests to the work and their eyes on the promised reward, they cleared the pumps completely after a single day's work. Everyone was so pleased at this, that they gave three cheers[1] for the ship, just as if they had rounded the Cape of Good Hope or crossed the bar of Lisbon. And so they sailed to Moçambique, where they arrived at the beginning of April of the year 1559. And they found there the great ship *Garça* of João Rodrigues de Carvalho, which had arrived in a very battered condition the day before, in order to winter there.

As soon as Francisco Barreto reached Moçambique, he set about the repair of his ship and of that of João Rodrigues de Carvalho, which he did with great care and diligence, and with great expense of his own purse (something which neither captains nor governors nor viceroys are prepared to do nowadays). The trouble which he took over the repair of the ships did not prevent him from taking

[1] *Boa Viagem* in Portuguese.

great care of the gentlemen who went in his company, and of the other passengers and seamen in both these great ships. For all the time that he stayed in Moçambique (which lasted more than seven and a half months) he helped and supported them all most liberally, according to the quality and expenses of each one, for this was in keeping with his character and because he was one of the most generous gentlemen of his time. And likewise he realized that if he did not do this, all those men would perforce endure great hardships and short commons, since they were in a region where there was nobody to help them, nor anyone on whom they could rely, which was why he relieved them of their poverty, which was for them a second shipwreck, and one in which voyagers often risk their lives. And the generosity and liberality with which he treated these people produced two benefits: he helped both them and himself. For he so earned their gratitude by thus helping them, that he always could rely on them sub' sequently in the worst hardships which they had to endure, which were very many and very great; and with their help Our Lord delivered him from all the dangers that he underwent in this voyage. And thus he spent in the repair of the ships and in the maintenance of the people over 18,000 *cruzados* as we were told by several very reliable and trustworthy persons, who were participants in all these events, and who gave us all this information. In this way, Francisco Barreto, wishing to refit the ships in which he was to continue his voyage to the kingdom, began to give orders and make payments for this purpose, with the help of Bastião de Sá (who was then captain of Sofala and stationed at Moçam' bique),[1] who sent forthwith many officers, carpenters and sailors to the mainland in order to cut the timber needed for the repairs, where it was obtainable of a very good quality. And the ships were given a very good careening by being heaved down on one side in the river, and they were very well repaired as far as it could be done, humanly speaking, without laying them

---

[1] Bastião (Sebastião) de Sá was governor of Moçambique and Sofala in 1558–60. At this period the captaincy of Sofala and Moçambique was usually invested in the same individual, who spent most of his time at Moçambique, although Sofala was still nominally the senior post.

aground, which would have been done if the place had allowed of it.[1]

After the great ships had been very well repaired and refitted, they took on board their drinking-water and the needful provisions for their intended voyage. And when the time for their departure arrived, they both set sail with the easterly monsoon, on a Monday 17 November 1559. The two captains had agreed always to keep in sight of each other and never to part company, so that they could help each other in any crisis or emergency that might befall them. On the third day after they had left the bar, when they would have been about fifty leagues from Moçambique, the ship of Francisco Barreto began to make a lot of water, and on this account they had to clear both the pumps five times that day and as many again at night; and on the next day they could not pump out all the water though they worked the pumps continuously. Francisco Barreto therefore ordered a falcon-gun to be fired as a signal to the other ship that she should stand by him. And when they were within hailing distance, he ordered a sailor to tell the captain of the other ship that he was sailing badly because of the quantity of water which his vessel was shipping, and that he therefore asked him as a great favour not to abandon him, because he was bearing away for the Bazaruto Islands,[2] which are off the coast of Sofala, and he set as much sail as was possible with the contrary winds, since he could not put back to Moçambique as the easterly mon-soon had already begun with the winds which had wafted them from that port.

As the ship was sailing on this course, God granted them in His mercy that the pumps overcame the water, and thus they all decided that it would be better to alter their course and set it for the Cape of Good Hope. They continued in this way for two or three days, by which time they had got as far as the Cape of Correntes, opposite the southern tip of the island of St Laurence,

---

[1] For the deficiencies of Moçambique as a repair-station and port of call see my article 'Moçambique Island as a way-station for Portuguese East-Indiamen' in *MM*, XLVIII (1962), 3–18. For criticisms of careening methods in the *Carreira da India* see *THS*, I, 25, 55, 115–16.

[2] For the island group of this name see the *Africa Pilot*, III, 221–3.

which is in 25° southern latitude, nearly 200 leagues from Moçam⁄bique.[1] The ship was now making so much water that there was already a depth of three or four spans in the hold, without their being able to get rid of it. For this reason, Francisco Barreto was compelled by sheer necessity to fire off a falcon⁄gun as a signal to the ship of João Rodrigues Carvalho to bear down on him, as he would have to set course again for the Bazaruto Islands. João Rodrigues, hearing this signal ordered the pilot and master to follow the standard of our lord the king, as that ship was his, and she was in obvious peril and distress, since she had been forced to put back twice in the space of the eight days they had left Moçambique.

Neither the pilot nor the master nor the other officers [of the ship *Garça*] were willing to obey this order of the captain, João Rodrigues de Carvalho. On the contrary, they lodged the strongest protests and objections with him, insisting that he should continue his voyage to Portugal. They alleged that the other ship was bound to founder, and that there was no hope of her being saved; and that it was unreasonable that they should be lost with her; and that it was a lesser evil to lose one ship than two. And as the captain was alone and the others were many, force conquered right. And taking advantage of their majority opinion, they disregarded the captain's order and continued on their voyage to Portugal, deserting the other ship with Francisco Barreto on board, in the deliberate intention of abandoning her once for all.

On the next day, the people in Francisco Barreto's ship began to get the better of the water; and as the ship now sailed better, they tacked about and resumed their voyage to the Cape of Good Hope, placing all their hope in God alone, trusting that He would continue His goodness towards them. And knowing that at that season the winds are moderate in the latitude of the Cape, and the weather less stormy, they hoped they would be able (even if with great difficulty and by working the pumps continually) with the help of God to get as far as the island of St Helena, where they

---

[1] Cabo das Correntes in latitude 24° 07′ S., the western extremity of the southern end of the Moçambique channel; the name is usually given in the hispanified form of Cape Corrientes on most English maps and charts.

would wait for the great ships of the return voyage. They would then be able to tranship themselves, their merchandise and their guns, into one or two of these vessels and leave their own dis/mantled there. Francisco Barreto's great ship sailed with these intentions in the wake of the *Garça*, which had abandoned the former so heartlessly through no fault of the captain, and as the *Patifa*[1] was an excellent sailer she began to gain on the other, although she was also a very good one. But God ordained that the great ship of Francisco Barreto should overtake the *Garça* and be the means of saving those who were in her, as she was destined to be lost.

As soon as the great ship *Garça* sighted her consort she backed her fore/topsails and waited until the two ships were within hailing distance of each other, which was about three o'clock in the after/noon. When his flagship came up, Francisco Barreto sent a written protest to the captain and other officers of the *Garça*, notifying them in the name of our lord the king that they should follow his flagship and not abandon her, on pain of being declared traitors and rebels against the Crown, and on forfeiture of all their merchandise to the Crown, which was all drawn up in due form. To this representation, the officers of the *Garça* replied that they would follow the flagship, come what might.

As both ships continued their voyage in company, on the very next day after the delivery of the protest, almost at the hour of vespers, the great ship *Garça* fired a cannon/shot as a signal that she wanted assistance, which Francisco Barreto answered immedi/ately by launching his *manchua*.[2] And as he was not well enough to go in person (since he had been let blood that morning), he sent in his place Jerónimo Barreto Rolim, whom he empowered to settle any quarrels or disputes which might have arisen between the pilot, or the master, and the captain, so that he with his

---

[1] Couto is constantly and confusingly switching the name (*Aguia*) and nickname (*Patifa*) of this ship.

[2] 'Manchuas or small vessels of recreation, used by the Portugals here [Macao] as also at Goa, pretty handsome things resembling little frigates; many curiously carved, gilded and painted, with little beak/heads', as Peter Mundy described this type of Indo/Portuguese vessel in 1637. Cf. *THS*, I, 24, 61, n. 2, for this and other descriptions of *manchuas*.

prudence might compose them; and if it was some other matter, then he was likewise authorized to deal with that as the circum/ stances demanded. When Jerónimo Barreto reached the ship, he found they were all sorely afflicted, harassed and dismayed, sifting through the pepper in the store/rooms and trying to find the leak which was letting in a great deal of water—a fact which worried them greatly, as they feared it might be difficult to stop and would cause them much more trouble later on, as in fact it did, for this was the sole cause of the loss of the ship. With this news, Jerónimo Barreto Rolim returned to the ship of Francisco Barreto, to whom he gave an account of what had happened in the *Garça*, where they spent all the night keeping good watch and with both pumps continually working. As soon as it was daylight, the *Garça* launched a *manchua* with four sailors and the scrivener of the ship,[1] called João Rodrigues Pais, who came to the flagship of Francisco Barreto with a note from the captain of the *Garça* for him, which read as follows:

'Sir, it is very necessary for the service of God and of our lord the King that your worship should come here; and by the brevity of this note, you may guess what is happening here. I kiss your worship's hands.'

When Francisco Barreto read this note, he at once got into his *manchua*, accompanied by some of the gentlemen from his ship, and he went over to her consort, which was already in great difficulties owing to the quantity of water she was shipping, while the officers and crew were shifting the pepper in the store/rooms from one side to another in search of the leak, which task occupied them all that day; and Francisco Barreto returned to his ship with the gentlemen who had accompanied him, all of them very sad at seeing the wretched condition of the other one. And on entering his flagship, Francisco Barreto addressed all the gentlemen and knights on board her as follows: 'Gentlemen, that ship is in great

---

[1] *Escrivão da nao.* This functionary had a good deal more authority and status in a Portuguese ship than the English purser who filled some of the same functions in our own Indiamen. For the wide/ranging sphere of the *escrivão*, see Pyrard de Laval's description of his duties and prestige in *Voyage*, II(1), 187–8. Cf. also the note by A. Atye (*c.* 1581) in E. G. R. Taylor, *The Troublesome Voyage of Captain Edward Fenton, 1582–1583* (Hakluyt Society, 2nd series, vol. CXIII, Cambridge, 1959), p. 15.

difficulties and in imminent danger of being lost. Let us commend her to Our Lord, that in His mercy he may deign to save her.' And thus they all passed that night without sleeping, due to the parlous condition of both these ships, for that of Francisco Barreto was also making a lot of water; nor could they diminish it although they threw into the sea much merchandise belonging to private individuals and pepper belonging to the Crown, and 2,000 *quintals* of ebony,[1] of which they had laden a good quantity at Moçambique (this malpractice being the total destruction of the ships which winter there and one which should be forbidden on pain of the most rigorous penalties). Next day in the morning they fired a signal-shot from the *Garça*, to come and help them, which Francisco Barreto did not expect, for when they fired the gun he was already on his way (in his *manchua*) with some gentle-men and soldiers to see if he could help those of the *Garça* and had gone some distance from his own ship. The people in the *Garça* no longer had any hope of saving her, for she was shipping a great deal of water in a place which they could not stop nor get at properly, as it was below the aftermost fashion-pieces, a place which is irrepairable.

Francisco Barreto, the captain of the ship, and all the other officers, seeing the state she was in and that there was nothing else to do but abandon her, they agreed to tranship to the *Aguia* the women and children and all the other useless mouths, in the first place. After this, they would then tranship what provisions they could from the *Garça*, since there were not enough in the flagship for so many people. They therefore launched forthwith the ship's large boat, so that it could help the two *manchuas* which were already at sea, to evacuate the *Garça* quicker, both as regards people and provisions, which they immediately began to tranship, i.e. biscuit, rice, meat, and some casks of wine. This transfer was accomplished in three days, during all of which time Francisco Barreto remained aboard the great ship *Garça*, in order to prevent the confusion which usually occurs in such cases, and to supervise

---

[1] *Quintal.* Indo-Portuguese weight 'which represented about 150 lbs., and may be thought of as somewhat larger than a hundredweight' (W. H. Moreland, *India at the death of Akbar*, London, 1920, p. 53). Sometimes anglo-indianized as *Kintal.*

the work necessary to prevent her from foundering until everything needful for the forthcoming voyage had been taken out of her. And while this transhipment was being effected, Francisco Barreto stationed himself in the waist of the *Garça*, with a drawn sword in his hand, forbidding any passengers to take to the other ship any-thing more than they could carry in their sleeves or purses, in order to avoid overlading her, for she was likewise liable to founder with the quantity of water she was shipping. And so that this operation could be done as smoothly as it actually was, God vouchsafed a singular mercy to these people; which was that during all this time the sea was as calm and smooth as if it had been a river of sweet water. If it had not been like this, either nobody would have been saved, or else they would have been saved only with great difficulty.

After all the necessary provisions had been transhipped, Fran-cisco Barreto ordered the evacuation of all the men, himself remain-ing in the *Garça* to leave with the last boatload, in which went all the seamen, who numbered about eighty; and by this time the ship was waterlogged nearly up to the capstan-deck. And when the boat had got about a stone's-throw away from the *Garça*, those who were in her saw an ape[1] which had remained on the round-top during the time of the evacuation, persistently refusing to come down; but now that it saw itself alone, it clambered down the shrouds and perched on the gunwale, as if asking those in the boat to come back and fetch it. When Francisco Barreto saw this, he could not contain himself, being loath to leave a living thing on board the ship; and he twice ordered the sailors who were row-ing the boat to go back and fetch the ape, saying that he did not want it said in Portugal or wherever else this shipwreck might become known, that we had abandoned any living thing in the ship. To which all those in the boat replied that they insisted in the name of our Lord the king that he should not return to the

[1] *Bugio*. More likely a monkey (*macaco*), as the Portuguese, like other Europeans, seldom bothered to distinguish between apes and monkeys at this period. The chronicler, Duarte Nunes de Lião (1530–1608), noted that many of those imported into Portugal from Asia, Africa and Brazil, were subsequently re-exported to other European countries: 'From Portugal are exported, for the delight and amusement of other peoples, many apes [monkeys] of different kinds' (*apud* Sergio, ed., *HTM*, I, 182 n.).

ship, for she was on the point of sinking, and that if she sank the vortex of the water would carry the boat down with her, as they were all agreed. And so they pulled away from the ship, leaving the ape alone aboard her. It was about three o'clock in the after' noon when they got clear of her for good and all, and they could still see her afloat when night fell. Francisco Barreto and these seamen came aboard the *Aguia,* as did the captain of the *Garça,* João Rodrigues de Carvalho, all of them very sorrowful and fear' ful at seeing a great ship thus lost in fair weather, she being the largest and most richly laden hitherto seen in the India voyage.[1] And such was his sorrow and grief at the loss of those people's goods that it was necessary to console him in terms as if the loss had been his alone.[2] After all the people in the *Garça* had been saved, Francisco Barreto drew up a certificate worded as follows:

'The great ship *Garça* was lost after getting as far as the Cape of Correntes, in twenty'five degrees Southern latitude, and she foundered through shipping much water. I, together with the gentlemen and other people in my own ship, saved everyone in theirs, and we are now continuing our voyage to Portugal with the same difficulty. We ask for the love of God that all faithful Christians who may learn of this, through this boat reaching some place where there are Portuguese, to commend us in their prayers to Our Lord, that He may give us a good voyage and bring us safely to Portugal.'

This certificate was placed in a tube which was tightly closed and caulked, and they made a tall cross in the boat, to which they tied it, so as to keep it out of the water; and then they let the boat drive whither the waves would take it. God granted that it fetched up in the roadstead of Sofala, where Bastião de Sá was then captain, as they subsequently learnt when Francisco Barreto re' turned to winter at Moçambique for the second time.

Having done this and got on board the people from the great ship *Garça,* Francisco Barreto decided to make a muster of all

---

[1] A commonplace assertion, which reappears in most accounts in the *HTM.* Cf. p. 26, n. 2, above.

[2] The original is very clumsily worded and might refer to either Francisco Barreto or to Rodrigues de Carvalho, but I presume this latter is intended.

those in his ship, so as to organize and accommodate them in the best way; and he found that they amounted to 1,037 souls, between gentlemen, soldiers, seamen, slaves, women and children. And with all these people aboard, he set his course for the Cape of Good Hope, as the easterly winds were blowing, which are the only ones that avail for the voyage to Portugal. As the ship was sailing in this way, and shipping much water on her course for the Cape of Good Hope, with fine weather and following winds, she was suddenly struck head-on by such a violent and furious squall that it tore the mainsail in many places, on which account it was necessary to lower the mainyard, so as to patch and repair the sail. The ship was left driving under bare poles, and the pilots and officers of both the ships were astonished at a westerly wind blowing in the east monsoon, and they thought it would not last more than that day; but they were mistaken as it blew for another two.[1] When the pilots and the officers of the two ships saw this, they went in a body to Francisco Barreto and told him as follows.

That they had been familiar with the navigation of that India voyage for many years (especially Aires Fernandes, who was the pilot of the great ship *Garça*, whom Dom Constantino had brought with him from Portugal by dint of great honours and inducements, as he was already very old and retired from the service, having rounded the Cape of Good Hope thirty-four times),[2] and that they none of them could recall three days of continual westerly winds blowing during the east monsoon. This seemed to be rather a Divine dispensation than a natural pheno- menon, as if Our Lord wished to show them that He did not want that ship to be lost with so many souls therein. And that to attempt this voyage with the ship in its actual condition was sheer

[1] The *Africa Pilot*, III, 51, gives a table showing the monthly percentage frequency with which winds of force 4 or more blow from various directions in this region, those from a westerly direction in November varying from 1·7 (S.W.) to 0·2 (W. and N.W.) out of a total of 42·4. So although rare, they are not unknown. Cf. also *Journal of African History*, III (1962), 264–5.

[2] Aires Fernandes was a native of Terceira, and was followed in his career by his son, Luís Aires. Cf. António Cordeiro, S.J., *Historia Insulana* (Lisbon, 1717), p. 305. He also figures in the *Letters of John III, king of Portugal, 1521–1557* (ed. Ford, Cambridge, Mass., 1931), p. 183.

folly and more like tempting God than trusting in Him. Where´
fore they required and requested his worship in the name of Our
Lord that he should give orders to put back to Moçambique,
where He would provide some means of saving them through His
mercy, or do with them whatever seemed best to Him. When
Francisco Barreto saw this and heard their unanimous opinion,
he went up to them and had a formal declaration drafted to this
effect, signed by all the officers of both the ships. And so they
reversed their course and Our Lord was pleased to bring them
to Moçambique; but always working at the pumps, and so hard
that they would not have been able to endure this labour but
for the large number of extra hands among whom they could
divide the work.

When the great ship was already nearing Moçambique, she
met with another misfortune, not less dangerous than the water
which she was shipping. This was that when she was about fifty
leagues from the island of Moçambique and ten or twelve from
the mainland, coasting along with all sails set, a son of the pilot
who happened to be fishing from the top´gallant poop, gave a
loud shriek, screaming twice: 'Daddy! fathom and a half! fathom
and a half!' At this time Francisco Barreto was in his stern´
gallery; and when he heard what the pilot's son shouted, he
hurried out on to the quarter deck, where he found everything in
a state of utter confusion and disorder, with everyone having lost
their heads and not having the faintest idea what to do, as they
did not know what had caused such great uproar and turmoil.
At this point, the ship received a blow which shook her from stem
to stern, whereupon everyone fell so deeply silent that it seemed as
if there was not a living soul aboard. Seeing this, the pilot quickly
climbed to the round´top, so as to con the ship from there, and to
see if there was some sandbank ahead from which the ship should
be got clear (which he could not do from the chair because of the
sails, which were all set);[1] and in this manner he was able to con
the ship to windward away from the land, which was soon out of

---

[1] For the tributes paid by Pyrard de Laval and Richard Hawkins to the vigilance
of the Portuguese pilots in the *carreira da India*, which they exercised from a chair on
the quarter´deck or on the poop see *THS*, I, 14–15.

sight. The cause of the blow that the ship received, was that off this coast of Moçambique, some fifteen or twenty leagues to sea, ward, are some rocks which are covered by the sea to a depth of $1\frac{1}{2}$, or 2, or 3 fathoms, and which are not visible and are the type of rocks called Alfaques.[1] It seems that the ship passing by these struck one of them a glancing blow in the side of the hull, and this was the cause of that shock. If she had struck with the bow or the keel, she would have left her bones there, and the people would all have been drowned without any hope of being saved. When they were out of sight of land, they set their course for Moçambique, where they arrived on the 17 December 1559, having thus been exactly a month from the day they left this port until they returned to it.

As soon as Francisco Barreto reached Moçambique after his second abortive voyage, he resolved to return to India forthwith, so as to winter at Goa, and thus avoid staying at Moçambique for as many months as the first time he had wintered there. And like, wise because it was very expensive, and he had already spent most of his wealth, and did not have the money to maintain his status and the nobility of his character which was very generous, and liberal; and which he would be able to do at Goa more easily and at less expense to himself. And as the only vessel then available at that fortress was an old and unrigged *fusta*[2] belonging to the Crown, and as he was told there was a merchant[3] on the coast of Malindi who had a very good *fusta*, he hurriedly sent to buy this

[1] Probably an outlying portion of the Ilhas Primeiras, or Ilha das Primeira [!] as they are called in the *Africa Pilot*, III, 252, where they are described as 'a chain of islets and reefs which lie, at distances of 5 to 12 miles offshore, on the outer edge of a coral bank which fronts the coast between Ponta Almandia and Ponta Macalonga'. *Alfaque* is the same as *recife* in Portuguese—a reef or rocky shelf in the sea. If Couto's estimate of 10, 15, 20 leagues to seaward is correct, however, they may be some other reefs which I cannot identify.

[2] *Fusta*, a small single-masted vessel, rowed by anything from 10 to 35 pairs of oars, and sometimes mounting 3 or 4 small guns of the falcon-type, and carrying up to 30 soldiers besides the crew. Roughly corresponding to the English 'foist'. A typical *fusta* is illustrated in the original Dutch edition of Jan Huigen van Linschoten, *Itinerario* (Amsterdam, 1596), between leaves 46 and 47.

[3] *Chatim.* Corresponding to the Anglo-Indian *Chetty*, this Indo-Portuguese word was applied to 'a member of any of the trading castes in S. India, answering in every way to the *Banyans* of W. and N. India', *Hobson-Jobson*,

one from her owner. On this *fusta's* arrival, he had her beached, paid, and fitted-out; doing the same with the old one belonging to the Crown. When the two *fustas* had thus been made ready, he took one for himself and gave the command of the other to his cousin, Jerónimo Barreto Rolim, so that they should sail in com-pany along the coast of Malindi and then steer for Goa via the island of Socotra—which turned out otherwise, as he did it from Pate.

When the provisions had been taken aboard these *fustas* and while they were watering preparatory to sailing, João Rodrigues de Carvalho (ex-captain of the *Garça* which had been lost), wishing to go to India in that convoy, asked Jerónimo Barreto Rolim to take him in his *fusta*. Jerónimo Barreto was aghast at this suggestion, since he was terrified of sailing in the same vessel as João Rodrigues de Carvalho, as the latter was notoriously unlucky at sea and he had never yet embarked in a ship which had not subsequently been lost. Jerónimo Barreto Rolim therefore replied that he could not take him. It also seems that he used some expressions from which João Rodrigues de Carvalho inferred that he did not wish to have him on board owing to his ill fortune and little luck. João Rodrigues de Carvalho brooding about this, became so convinced that they didn't want to take him on this account that it caused his death. For the following night, when he was in bed in the house of Pero Mendes Moreira (who was the Factor and *Alcaide-Mór*[1] of Moçambique, with whom he was staying), he began to groan and sigh terribly. The two little boys of Pero Mendes Moreira, who were in the bed with him, one of them about three and the other four years old, said to him: 'Uncle' (for that was what the children called him), 'are you sighing and not sleeping because you have lost your ship?' The remarks that the innocent children made, so afflicted and over-came him that he died as a result. For when morning came, he

ed. 1903, pp. 189–90). By extension, the word was also applied by the Portuguese to their own merchants trading in India, sometimes in a derogatory or pejorative sense. Here, however, an Indian merchant is probably meant. Cf. also S. R. Dalgado, *Glossário Luso-Asiático*, I, 265–7, for the etymology from Dravidian and Sanskrit.

[1] A title of Moorish origin, corresponding here to castellan.

was found dead in the bed, with no other symptom to which his death could be attributed. Such is the strength and efficacy of grief and remorse, which in this case sufficed to suffocate his vital spirits and cause his death.

When the *fustas* had finished watering, Francisco Barreto em⁄ barked in his and Jerónimo Barreto Rolim in the other; and they left Moçambique at the beginning of March 1560, bound for the coast of Malindi in the little monsoon (so⁄called because of the dead calms which occur then).[1] The gentlemen whom Francisco Barreto took in his *fusta* were: Manuel Danaia Coutinho; Pedro Álvares de Mancelos, Francisco Álvares, Trustee for the Dead,[2] Francisco de Gouveia, and Thingammy[3] de Araujo, besides many other men who were beholden to Francisco Barreto; for the other gentlemen remained behind in Moçambique, intending to leave in the great monsoon (which is in August) in the ship *Patifa*.[4] Francisco Barreto touched at all the ports along the coast of Malindi, where he took in water and provisions. The first at which he called was Kilwa, which is in 6° southern latitude.[5] In this city (whose buildings showed that it used to be larger and more populous than it then was), he remained anchored for four days, during which time the king avoided seeing him.[6] Francisco Barreto was told that there were two monsters there, offspring of an ape and a Negress, who was said to be the wife of a Sheikh.

[1] 'The Coast of Malindi' corresponds to the Swahili Coast in the narrower sense of this term, i.e. to the coast of Tanganyika (Tanzania) and Kenya. The *Africa Pilot*, III, 58, gives a table of monthly wind frequencies for this region, adding: 'It is clear from the table that there are two seasonal winds, the north⁄easterly mon⁄ soon from December to February and the southerly to south⁄easterly monsoon from April to September.'

[2] 'Trustee for the Dead and Absent' was the more usual term.

[3] *Fulano* in the original Portuguese.

[4] *Aguia*. Cf. pp. 38, n. 1, above.

[5] Kilwa, or Kilwa Kisiwani as it is called nowadays, is actually in latitude 8° 57′ S., according to the *Africa Pilot*, III, 323–6. For Kilwa in the sixteenth century see J. Strandes, *The Portuguese Period in East Africa*, ed. J. S. Kirkman (Nairobi, 1961), pp. 54–66, 103–16, 336–9. The Portuguese had briefly occupied the place in 1505–12, but the extensive ruins which are nowadays ascribed to them are in fact Arab or Swahili.

[6] I have not been able to identify this Sultan from such likely sources as G. J. P. Freeman⁄Grenville, *Medieval History of the Coast of Tanganyika* (Berlin, 1962), the history of Kilwa at this period being very obscure.

Francisco Barreto tried very hard to get hold of them in order to take them to King Dom Sebastião; but as they belonged to the king of Kilwa, he refused to sell them. Francisco Barreto then decided to kidnap them; but as this plan was not kept secret enough, the king got wind of it, and he had the monsters hidden away until after Francisco Barreto had left.

After leaving this city, he called at that of Mombasa,[1] where he stayed for eight days, cleaning and repairing the *fustas*. As soon as he arrived, the king sent to greet him with a bountiful gift of refreshments, comprising cattle, sheep, chickens, honey, butter, dates, lemons, citrons and oranges, with which the island (which measures about seven leagues in circumference) is very fertile and well supplied. Francisco Barreto acknowledged this gift by sending another of many baubles, and valuable and rare pieces,[2] which he had brought along for this purpose, in which he showed how liberal and generous he was—for, as stated above, he was the most liberal gentleman of his time. So much so, that he was the living proof of the aphorism of Dom Antão de Noronha, sometime Viceroy of India,[3] who said that India could never enjoy prosperity save only while there were crazy captains who made fortunes during the tenure of their fortresses and subsequently squandered all their gains on maintaining the soldiers. This was what happened to Francisco Barreto, who having made a fortune of 80,000 *pardaus*[4] during his

---

[1] Mombasa was twice (1505 and 1528) sacked by the Portuguese, but they did not occupy it and make it their headquarters on the Swahili Coast until they began to build Fort Jesus there in 1593. Cf. Strandes–Kirkman, *The Portuguese Period in East Africa, passim*, and C. R. Boxer and Carlos de Azevedo, *Fort Jesus and the Portuguese in Mombasa, 1593–1729* (London, 1960).

[2] *peças ricas e curiosas*. The Portuguese *peça* has a wide range of meanings, but is probably here used in the sense of Indian piecegoods or textiles, which were among the most soughtafter commodities on the Swahili Coast.

[3] D. Antão de Noronha served for many years with distinction in Portuguese Asia, of which he was Governor from 3 September 1564 to 10 September 1568. He died at sea on the homeward voyage off the Cape of Good Hope in 1569.

[4] The gold *pardau* (probably the type meant here) was an Indian coin, originally from Vijayanagar, valued by the Portuguese at 360 *reis*. From 1548 onwards the Portuguese also struck at Goa (and for a time at Cochin) a gold *pardau sãotomé*, so called from the image of the Apostle St Thomas on it, likewise originally valued at 360 *reis*. There was also a silver *pardau*, theoretically valued at 300 *reis*, but which varied greatly in weight and consequently in intrinsic worth.

captaincy of Baçaim,[1] spent it all on paying the soldiers in the service of the Crown, so that he was already indebted to the tune of 28,000 *parduas* when he became governor of India. From this, and considering the condition in which India now is, we can readily conclude how many intelligent captains there are here nowadays.

And to continue with the voyage of Francisco Barreto: after he left Mombasa, he called successively at all the other ports and islands along the coast of Malindi, going on shore at this place to visit the king, and sending him a rich present, as he was a great friend of the Crown of Portugal and of the Portuguese in general.[2] After leaving Malindi he called at Pate,[3] where he found a topsail ship belonging to a merchant (*chatim*), which had taken in her cargo and was on the point of leaving for Chaul.[4] And as Fran⁄cisco Barreto's *fusta* was very crowded owing to the large number of people in her, he freighted this ship from her owner, and trans⁄ferred himself thereto with most of his men from the *fusta*. And from this city (which lies 3° northern latitude,[5] and 600 leagues from the river of Goa) he set sail for India; the voyage taking him forty days, whereas it is normally only twenty⁄five. During this passage across the Indian Ocean they suffered greatly from thirst, being often becalmed for long stretches. And if the voyage had lasted two days longer before reaching the coast of India, they

[1] Baçaim, nowadays commonly termed Bassein, a few miles north of Bombay. Acquired by the Portuguese in 1535, it was the headquarters of their 'Province of the North' until its capture by the Marathas after an epic defence in 1739. Francisco Barreto served as Captain of Baçaim in 1549–52.

[2] Malindi's friendship with the Portuguese, dating from the time of Vasco da Gama's pioneer voyage, was based mainly on its long⁄standing rivalry with the more powerful city⁄state of Mombasa. Cf. Strandes–Kirkman, *The Portuguese Period in East Africa, passim.*

[3] Pate (Patta), a Swahili city⁄state on the island of the same name in the Lamu group. In the seventeenth century it succeeded Mombasa as the centre of Muslim resistance to the Portuguese, and in the eighteenth century it disputed with Mombasa the hegemony of the coast. Cf. Strandes–Kirkman, *op. cit.*

[4] A seaport some 30 miles south of Bombay, held by the Portuguese from 1521 to 1740. Its architectural history and ruins have recently been intensively studied by Gritli von Mitterwallner, *Chaul. Eine unerforschte Stadt an der Westküste Indiens* (Berlin, 1964); a work which, for those who can read German, supersedes the otherwise still useful pioneer study of J. Gerson da Cunha, *Notes on the history and antiquities of Chaul and Bassein* (Bombay, 1876). For *chatim* see p. 45, n. 3 above.

[5] In latitude 2° 09' S., according to the *Africa Pilot*, III, 463.

would all have died from thirst, because they were already reduced
to one *almude*[1] of water, and they had not eaten rice for many days,
since there was no water wherewith to cook it. They had no
biscuit left, and they only had dates and coconuts to eat, sup-
plemented occasionally by roasted meat from a few sheep that
were carried in the ship's boat towed astern.

As they were sailing along enduring these hardships, they sighted
the coast of India one morning. And that very afternoon there came
out from a local river, the *catur*[2] of Roque Pinheiro, which had come
from the strait of Mecca,[3] whither the Viceroy Dom Constantino
had sent it, in company with Cristovão Pereira Homem, to
land at Massawa the Brother Fulgencio Freire of the Company of
Jesus with a message for the Bishop who was in Abyssinia.[4]

On sighting that ship, Roque Pinheiro bore up to her; and
learning that Francisco Barreto was there he came on board, and
threw himself at his feet with many tears, at seeing him now in
such a different state from that in which he had seen him a short
time before. After telling him how the corsair Cafar had taken
the ship of Cristovão Pereira Homem,[5] he provided Francisco
Barreto's ship with water, giving him all that he had, and
hurriedly returning to the land to fetch more, whereby he saved

[1] A measure for selling wine, 26 *almudes* making a pipe.

[2] A light rowing-vessel much used on the coast of Malabar in the sixteenth and
seventeenth centuries, sometimes provided with a mast and lateen sail. Some
authorities consider the English word 'cutter' as derived from *catur*, but the *N.E.D.*
and others reject this. See *Hobson-Jobson*, p. 175; Dalgado, *Glossário Luso-Asiático*, I,
239–40; *MM*, XLIV (1958), 203–4.

[3] Strait of Bab-el-Mandeb, at the entrance to the Red Sea.

[4] Andrés de Oviedo, S.J., titular bishop of Hieropolis and later patriarch of
Ethiopia, reached Abyssinia in 1557 with several other Jesuit missionaries. He was
unsuccessful in his efforts to persuade the emperor (or Negus) to acknowledge papal
supremacy, and after many vicissitudes, he died there in 1577. See Girma Beshah
and Merid Wolde Aregay, *The Question of the Union of the Churches in Luso-
Ethiopian Relations, 1500–1632* (Lisbon, 1964), pp. 53–68.

[5] The fight with the Turkish corsair, the death of Pereira Homem, the capture
of his ship and of Padre Fulgencio Freire, S.J., are narrated at length by Diogo do
Couto, *Década VII*, Livro 8, cap. 8, and in a letter of Padre Freire, S.J., written
from Mokka (Jiddah), 12 August 1560, published in C. Beccari, S.J., *Rerum
Aethiopicarum Scriptores Occidentales inediti* (15 vols., Rome, 1903–17), X (1910),
103–12. Freire was eventually ransomed at Cairo and returned via Rome to Lisbon,
dying on another voyage to India in 1571.

the lives of all those on board as by this time they had no water left at all. If they had not met this vessel just when they did, it is more than likely that day would have been the last one of their lives. On the morning of the next day, which was a Friday the 17 May 1560, they reached the bar of Goa, with their hands on their heads in desperation at the first signs of winter, whose onset is very violent in those regions, where it enters with a sword in the hand, and in fact the monsoon burst immediately afterwards.[1] On the next day, which was Saturday, after they had all disembarked, and Fran-cisco Barreto was lodged in the Franciscan monastery of Reis Magos in Bardes overlooking the bar of Goa[2], there raged such a violent storm of wind and rain that it seemed as if the end of the world had come and the Earth would be submerged in a second Deluge.

As soon as it was known in Goa that Francisco Barreto had reached the bar, he was at once visited by all the gentlemen and married men of Goa. He then embarked in a light *catur* and made his way to the city, to pay his respects to the Viceroy Dom Constantino, accompanied by all the gentry and citizens, who filled all the space from the quay to the fortress and the whole square in front of the latter. Making his way through that crowd of people, he reached the viceroy, who was waiting for him and greeted him with great joy and courtesy. They then went inside, where he rested and related what had happened to him on the voyage; after which they supped together with some gentlemen who were related to both of them, and he spent the night there. On the morning of the next day Francisco Barreto returned by river to Reis Magos, in order to fulfil a novena[3] which he had promised during his shipwreck, and he was accompanied by so

[1] In days of sail, the south-west monsoon had the effect of virtually closing all harbours on the west coast of India from about the end of May to the beginning of September.
[2] The Franciscan Church and College of Reis Magos on the north bank of the river Mandovi, opposite the present city of Panjim, was where the incoming viceroys usually took over the government from their predecessors, from the year 1571 onwards. This college, built in 1550 on the ruins of a Hindu temple, was demolished in the nineteenth century; but the Church and nearby fortress of the same name still survive, though somewhat altered from their original sixteenth-century structures.
[3] The dedication of a period of nine days to special prayer or devotion.

many of the nobility and gentry that it seemed as if the city had been evacuated. Dom Constantino, observing the great concourse of gentlemen and citizens who were seeing him off, said to those in his entourage: 'How grateful ought Francisco Barreto to be to God for making him so well beloved.'

While Francisco Barreto was completing his novena in the monastery of Reis Magos, the viceroy sent to visit him and presented him with a grant of 4,000 *pardaus* in the king's name, so as to help pay the expenses of his wintering at Goa. When this nine days' pilgrimage was over, Francisco Barreto went and lodged in the house of a citizen of Goa called Fernão Nunes, beyond the parish of Santa Luzia,[1] where he stayed until mid-December. During this time he remained on excellent terms with the viceroy, who sent to visit him again, and presented him with two very fine jennets, which he immediately gave away, one of them to his relative, Luís de Mello da Silva, and the other to his nephew, Dom Felipe de Meneses, son of his sister, Dona Brites de Vilhena, who was nicknamed 'The Dangerous', and her husband, Dom Henrique de Meneses.[2] And as Francisco Barreto had not got [the captaincy of] a great ship in which he could sail to Portugal, the viceroy gave him the great ship *São Gião*, which had wintered at Goa, and was beached at Panelim; where she was very well fitted out so that he could sail in her, the viceroy satisfying António de Sousa de Lamego concerning the captaincy of the ship.[3]

While Francisco Barreto is wintering at Goa and his great ship being prepared for the voyage, we will state what happened to the

---

[1] Santa Luzia was made a parish when the church of this invocation was built in 1544. Fernão Nunes is probably identical with the horse-trader of that name who wrote an eyewitness account of the Hindu empire of Vijayanagar at the height of its glory (c. 1535), first published by David Lopes, *Chronica dos Reis de Bisnaga* (Lisbon, 1897), and subsequently utilized by R. Sewell, *A Forgotten Empire: Vijayangar* (London, 1900), and all those who have concerned themselves with that kingdom.

[2] Couto does not explain why D. Brites de Vilhena was called *a perigosa*, but he tells us elsewhere in the same *Década* (Livro 5, cap. 11) that her husband, D. Henrique de Meneses, had been ambassador at Rome, whence 'he brought the Holy Inquisition to Portugal', in the year 1536.

[3] Most other authorities give the name of the captain of the *São Gião* as Luís Álvares de Sousa. Cf. Figueiredo Falcão, *Livro*, p. 167, and Simão Ferreira Paes, *Recopilação*, p. 62.

Patifa which was wintering at Moçambique after being forced back there for the second time.[1] As she was badly battered, Bastião de Sá, who had just finished his term as captain of Sofala, had her overhauled very thoroughly, so that he could leave in her for Goa with the main monsoon in August, together with the great ships which were then expected from Portugal. And when she was fitted out, Bastião de Sá had the water and provisions sent aboard, and when the time came he embarked in her with all his servants and the gentlemen who had come in her in Francisco Barreto's company, and who had wintered at Moçambique. The *Patifa* set sail on 11 August, and on the next day she began to ship so much water that she threatened to founder. And as she could not put back to Moçambique, she had to steer for Mombasa, where she was beached and broken up, everything in her being salvaged, both what belonged to the Crown and to private individuals. Bastião de Sá then embarked in a ship in which he sailed to India; but my informants could not tell me whether after wintering there, or in September.

Let us return to Francisco Barreto, whom we left wintering at Goa and fitting-out the great ship *São Gião* in which he was going to sail. When she had been overhauled and had begun to take in her lading, five great ships from Portugal reached the bar of Goa.[2] In one of them came Luís Fernandes de Vasconcelos, who had got to Moçambique after having been shipwrecked the previous year in the great ship *Galega*, and after wintering at the island of St Laurence, which he had reached in the ship's boat with sixty other survivors from the wreck.[3]

As soon as the viceroy learnt of his arrival, he at once sent a representative to visit him with a grant of 2,000 *pardaus*, a horse, and a nag. Dom Luís remained on very good terms with the

[1] Cf. p. 47 above.

[2] *Castelo, Drago, São Vicente, Cedro,* and *Rainha.* See p. 60 below for the departure of this fleet from Lisbon and the first stage of the voyage.

[3] For the wreck of the *Galega* and the equivocal behaviour of D. Luís Fernandes de Vasconcelos in this disaster, see the accounts in Couto, *Década VII, Livro 5,* cap. 11, and *ibid. Livro 8,* cap. 1; *HTM* (1, 311–49, of the 1735 edition), and the critical discussions by J. Duffy, *Shipwreck and Empire,* pp. 30–1, and C. R. Boxer, 'An introduction to the *HTM*', pp. 14–15.

Viceroy during the few days that he stayed at Goa, before embarking for Portugal in the great ship of Francisco Barreto, as he
was married with the latter's niece, Dona Branca de Vilhena,
daughter of Diogo Lopes de Sequeira who had been governor of
India,[1] and Dona Maria de Vilhena, his sister.

The great ship *São Gião* being finally rigged, laden, and ready,
with the provisions and water aboard, Francisco Barreto set sail
on the 20 December [1560], making a very prosperous voyage,
and messing at his table all the gentlemen who accompanied him,
namely: Dom Luís Fernandes de Vasconcelos; Dom João Pereira,
brother of the Count of Feira; Dom Duarte de Meneses, nicknamed 'Nosey', one of those from Penella;[2] Garcia Moniz
Barreto, native of the island of Madeira; Manuel Danaia Coutinho
and others whose names we could not learn. He reached Lisbon
on a Sunday, the 13 June 1561,[3] where he was received by all the
gentry with great joy and contentment, because they had given
him up for dead, as it was three years since he had left India the
first time. And accompanied by all this throng, they took him to
kiss the hand of the Queen [Regent] Dona Catarina, who was
then governing the kingdom of behalf of her grandson, the King
Dom Sebastião who was some seven years old.[4] She received him
with many honours, both on account of his quality and personal
worth, as because of the many services which he had rendered the
Crown of Portugal in India and in Africa.[5]

[1] From December 1518 to January 1522.

[2] 'O Narigão'. Hero of a skirmish at Punnaikâyal on the Fishery Coast,
described at length by Couto, *Década VII*, Livro 8, cap. xi. Penella, a small
castle-town in the Portuguese province of Beira, between Coimbra and Thomar.

[3] The *São Gião* reached Lisbon on the 8 June 1561, according to Figueiredo
Falcão, *Livro*, p. 167. *Gião* is an old form of the name *Julião* (Julian).

[4] D. Catarina de Austria (1507–78), daughter of Philip I and Joanna 'the Mad'
of Castile, and widow of King D. João III of Portugal. She acted as regent on
behalf of her infant grandson, the ill-fated D. Sebastião, from 1557 to 1563.

[5] Francisco Barreto subsequently served as captain-major of the galleys, and
participated in the Luso-Spanish expedition under D. Garcia de Toledo, viceroy
of Sicily, which occupied the Moroccan islet-fortress of Peñon de Vélez in 1564.
As noted previously (p. 33, n. 2, above), he was given command of the expedition
sent to discover and occupy the gold mines of Monomotapa in 1569, dying at
Sena on the Zambesi three years later, after experiencing many frustrations and
disappointments in Zambesia.

Nao sam Paulo.

¶ Viagem & naufragio da
Nao sam ſſßaulo que foy pera a Indía o anno
de mil ⁊ quinhentos ⁊ ſeſenta. Lapitão
Ruy de melo da camara. Meſtrê
Joam luys, ſßiloto An-
tonio Dias.

✠

Lom licença Impreſſo.

The Great Ship *São Paulo*

¶ Voyage and Shipwreck of the

Great Ship *São Paulo* which left for India in the year
fifteen hundred and sixty. Captain
Ruy de Melo da Camara, Master
João Luis, Pilot An⁄
tonio Dias

✠

Printed with Licence

VOYAGE AND SHIPWRECK OF THE
GREAT SHIP *SÃO PAULO*

Prologue

BEING about to write down the disastrous voyage of this great ship, it occurred to me how rash men are in their undertakings, chief among which, or one of the greatest, was confiding their lives to four planks lashed together, and to the discretion of the furious winds, with which they live in such wise that we can rightly say *quia ventus est vita mea*,[1] and thus they traverse the vast expanse of the watery element, encompassing the whole earth. This enterprise they undertake so unmindful of their consciences, and of what they are beholden to God, that where they should be most devout, which is in the worst dangers wherein they find themselves, there they are most negligent and careless, committing a thousand different sins, whereby they provoke the wrath of the Lord to descend on them, as it did on those who were aboard this great ship. And withal He is so merciful that He never strikes so harshly but that He recalls his ancient mercy, for the amendment of the guilty and as an example to those who would mock at them. All those who read the narratives of this history will be able to do this, and so it will help to amend each and every heart, placing their ultimate fate in Him, as being the beginning and end of all things. And in this narrative I will not relate anything other than what I actually saw, as briefly as possible, so that by avoiding a prolix story I will also avoid wearying the reader.

The Work Begins

This great ship was on the point of sailing from Santa Catarina de Ribamar[2] when one night a violent cross-wind severed one of the two cables which she had laid out to seawards, and we were within an ace of being driven ashore, because the ship was

---

[1] 'My life is like a wind'.
[2] Roadstead to the west of Lisbon, between Belém and the fort of São Julião. Site of a convent of the Franciscans of the Arrabida Province, founded in 1551.

anchored in only three and half fathoms. We were urgently compelled to ask help and aid by firing off our great guns all night, so that they could hear and help us with anchors and cables, as did all the officers of our lord the king at Belém,[1] with the boats of the other ships in our company. They worked throughout the night in making us fast and leaving us secure and out of danger. It is certain that the great care taken that night was the salvation of the ship and the reason why she was not beaten to pieces at the door of the house, which would to God she had been and thus the end of her. It seems that He did not wish this to happen because we did not deserve it, on account of the sins of many of us who were in the ship. For even though this would have involved losses both for the royal treasury as for private individuals, yet it would have subsequently saved us from so many days and months of weary voyaging, with the people exhausted and wasted away from most deadly diseases, famines, and the most frightful misadventures imaginable; for we saw and tasted death so many times and in such figures, guises, and manners, and finally we nearly all lost our lives in a place where no great ship of Christians, Muslims, or heathen had ever been.[2] And those of us who survived the fury and misfortune of this shipwreck, I think may be considered as the most unhappy of all, for most of us were and are the victims of such strange and extraordinary diseases that I doubt if our miserable existence can properly be termed life.

We left Belém on 20 April 1560 on a Saturday morning, the day before Low Sunday, and we sailed out to sea with a fresh north-east wind, being six great ships in company under the command of Dom Jorge de Sousa as captain-major in the *Rainha*. Our own ship *São Paulo* had been built in India, and she was very strong and like a firm rock in all the winds that blew, sailing wonderfully well with a following wind, when she skimmed over the sea; but as she was so heavy, she was an ill

[1] Bethlehem. Site of the famous Jeronimite monastery and the fortified Tower built by D. Manuel I; associated with the departure and return of the annual India Fleets since the first voyage of Vasco da Gama.

[2] Certainly not true of Gujarati, Sumatran and Javanese shipping, and doubt-fully true of Portuguese; though the last-named admittedly never frequented the western coast of Sumatra. Cf. p. 98, n. 1, below.

sailer when close-hauled, and difficult and hard to steer. We left so late in the season because the contrary winds would not let us clear the bar earlier, although we had been ready for a month, and this was one of the main reasons for our unfortunate voyage and perdition.[1]

On 23 April the wind changed and with it the pleasure that we all felt hitherto, and we had to ply off and on, in order to avoid being forced to put back to Lisbon. And the day before, all our ships had parted company, on account of the strong wind. *São Vicente* and the *Drago* sailed on ahead of the others and we had lost sight of them by the morning. The *Castelo* steered a course to the north-west, and we to the south-west, and the *Cedro* was left far astern as she listed badly and not being able to carry her sails she bore away for the coast of Barbary. And thus we continued with these tiresome contrary winds, tacking to and fro for five days, at the end of which time we had a favourable wind. On 27 April, on a Saturday morning, we sighted the islands of Deserta and Madeira, and in the afternoon that of Porto Santo, and we sailed along to windward of these islands, happy and relieved at thus making good progress.

On the morning of the 1 May when [nearly] becalmed, we sighted Palma, one of the Canary Islands, and we passed to the westward of it. And on the next day we saw one of the ships of our company, which came in our wake a long way astern of us. Everyone said it was the *Cedro* since she was alone, and thus we waited for her till the evening when we saluted her from afar, but we never got within hailing distance of her. And thus we con-

---

[1] There is a good deal of divergence on the date of departure, which is variously given as 15, 20 and 25 April 1560. In the *HTM* version the date is given as 25 April; but Simão Ferreira Paes (*Recopilação*) and Luís de Figueriedo Falcão (*Livro de toda a Fazenda*), two seventeenth-century officials who had access to the original records at the Casa da India (India House) at Lisbon, both give the date as 20 April. So does Padre Arboleda, S.J., who sailed in the *Castelo* and wrote a description of the voyage at Cochin, 15 January 1561 (Silva Rego, *Documentação. Índia*, VIII, 278, 284). There is more general agreement over the composition of this armada, which consisted of six carracks: *Nossa Senhora do Castelo, Rainha, Drago, Cedro, São Vicente, São Paulo*. Most other sources state that the flagship (*capitania*) was the *Castelo* and not the *Rainha*. For the fate of the other ships cf. Frazão de Vasconcelos, *Naufrágio da nau 'São Paulo'* (Lisbon, 1948), pp. 5–8.

tinued our voyage for three days on a southerly course. On 5 May the wind veered, being from the W. and W.S.W., with which we continued our voyage for fourteen days without squalls or thunderstorms; but from then on we had many sharp showers and dead calms, which brought us much vexation and toil.

On a Thursday, the 16 May, about four o'clock in the after' noon, we were sailing with a soft north'east wind, when we were assailed by a rainless thunderstorm,[1] so windy and so violent that the like had never been seen before in this latitude; for our master, who had sailed this way thirty'two times affirmed that this had never happened to him previously, and this was confirmed by many other veteran seamen of this voyage. Because it struck us without warning, all our sails were set, so that the ship nearly foundered; and it pleased God that the storm only lasted a short time, for if it had been longer we would all have ended our troubles there. The wind carried away the fore'topmast and sail, and broke the cap, leaving the sails torn and in shreds; and thus we ran along with the foresail at half'mast until the storm abated after a short while, when the blood returned to our veins and the hearts to our bodies. On the next day we found ourselves becalmed in 8° lat., and those who were charting our course estimated that we were forty leagues out to sea from the coast of Guinea.

If I were to write of our daily misfortunes and misadventures (for not a single day passed without them) this would be a lengthy process and would cause more weariness then pleasure to the reader. I will therefore limit myself to recording as briefly as possible the notable things that happened to us, both in our voyage as in our shipwreck, noting the dates on which they occurred. I will stick as closely to the truth as I can, for where my skill and my words fail, the truth is enough to ornament and embellish my narrative.

Since our pilot was a novice in this India voyage, and this was the first time that he had sailed from Portugal with this charge, as he had only been used to navigating here in the Indian Ocean,

---

[1] 'hũa travoada seca.' The *HTM* version has 'travoada cega', which I presume means a thunderstorm in which visibility was virtually nil, due to dark clouds or mist (*cega* = blind), but I have preferred the 1565 reading here.

which is merely a matter of consulting the rutter and casting the lead, as they term it here, he was more nervous than he need have been about the ship falling to leeward, thinking, as he explained, that he was well to the windward of Cape Santo Agostinho in Brazil, since the ship had not been able to double this cape in the previous year but had been forced to put back from there to Portugal.[1] For this reason he kept so close to the coast of Guinea that we were all in great danger of ending our lives there, for it was then the winter season in that region, and we had left Portugal so late that we encountered the full force of it here, with very strong sea winds and so many rain⁄squalls and thunderstorms that we kept tacking about to seaward and to landward for a good three months, while all the people became sick, whereby we endured great diseases and vexations.

On 19 May in the morning we sighted a small square⁄rigged ship five or six leagues distant, which seemed to us to be one of our company, and since she was so far ahead of us we could not hail her, and the other was also sailing on a southerly course.[2] By this time we had already two dozen people ill of fevers in our ship, and some of them with swellings in the groins. The first death occurred on the 23 of the said month: the fevers were so severe that anyone who fell ill immediately became delirious, in such wise

[1] As mentioned in the introduction, one of the main differences between the narrative of Henrique Dias and that of Manuel Álvares, S.J., is in their respective assessments of this pilot, the former being highly critical of him and the latter highly laudatory. In the *Imagem da Virtude* (1719) version of Álvares' voyage, the pilot António Dias is described as being 'a most skilful man in his profession and a great christian in his behaviour, as one who had learnt this from his familiarity with our pioneer Padres. For it was he who brought from Flanders to Portugal the holy Father Pierre Favre, companion of St Ignatius, and others. He also carried St Francis Xavier many times from the Moluccas to Malacca, and to Japan and China, being a great friend of the saint, and he did the same for other Fathers of great holiness' (*Apud* A. Sergio, ed., *HTM*, II, 106). If this is correct, then Henrique Dias' strictures on this pilot would seem to have been rather unfair, as António Dias was not merely experienced in Indonesian waters but in the Pacific and Atlantic Oceans as well. On the other hand, as Henrique states, the *São Paulo* with this pilot had lost her voyage in the previous year; and Diogo do Couto, who sailed for Goa in the same armada of 1559, likewise affirms that the *São Paulo* lost her voyage 'through bad navigation' (*Década VII*, Livro 8, cap. II).

[2] The 1565 text is hopelessly confused here and I have followed the *HTM* version, which makes more sense of this sentence.

that he spoke and raved a thousand follies and absurdities, some very laughable and others sad enough to cause tears. Some of the victims tried to throw themselves overboard in their delirium and had to be tied to each other to prevent them from doing so. It was certainly a most pitiable thing to see the poor soldiers who had been bled four or five times, lying on the deck of the ship exposed to the sun and the rain, for while we were in these latitudes hardly a day passed without continual thunderstorms.

On 8 June we had tremendous thunderstorms and heavy rain, while the seas ran so high and confusedly from the south that the ship laboured heavily and pitched so much from poop to prow that each time she fell it seemed to be as from a high tower and so that she would founder in the abyss; and she heeled by the stern to the captain's gallery, and by the prow with the forecastle and the bowsprit under the water. And with this tremendous pitching all her upper works were shaken apart, and the foremast was sprung above the cap; and we immediately made some running repairs, fishing it with four pieces, which answered the purpose very well.[1] And thus we sailed along with difficulty until 14 June, trying with the help of some gentle gales in the intervals of the thunderstorms, to get clear of the troublesome banks of Santa Anna without our being able to do so during the 35 days that we were on them. And every time we tacked towards the land the people became ill, and when we tacked seawards they got much better.

On 19 June just before nightfall, when we were reciting the Litany, the wind was blowing very strong and unfavourably, as always happened when we had a wind that did not serve, whereas whenever we had a favourable wind it was weak and scant. The seas were running very high, causing the ship to pitch heavily, and as the look-out man on the maintop was preparing to come down without due care and attention, the ship gave a sudden roll which threw the poor grummet off the maintop and he fell on one of the yardarms and from there into the sea, just at the feet of a man who was standing by the gunwale and was nearly knocked

[1] The *HTM* version adds that the mast was 'made in India of a single piece of wood and that everybody thought it was the best that there was on the waters of the sea'.

into the sea by the falling body, and who was injured in the leg by it. The victim's head was smashed to pieces on the yardarm where his brains were left embedded. He was a well set-up youth, and had just been married at Alfama.

Three days later another similar accident occurred, this time to the look-out man on the fore-top. But he was luckier, for though the ship was wallowing in the high seas in which she pitched and rolled heavily, he fell from the top into the sea, grazing one of the flukes of an anchor, and he had such presence of mind that he grasped a cord and they dragged him aboard all covered with blood. For the anchor had taken all the skin off the top of his head and it hung like a friar's hood from his occiput. It was a miracle that such a blow did not harm any part of his body and left him white as snow. He was examined very carefully and cured still better, and so he recovered completely from this very serious mishap.

I would never finish if I were to recount all the tribulations which we endured off the coast of Guinea during all the time that we were there. At times we had such dead calms and such boiling heat that the people swam alongside as if they had been off the Lisbon dockyard. Subsequently we had rain squalls and storms in such wise that besides rotting all the rigging our bodies likewise became infected, so that out of over 500 people in the ship only fifteen did not fall sick, and on one day there were 350 lying ill. Bleeding was done by the barber-surgeon, by the pilot, the second pilot, and a grummet, all of whom did it very well. And it happened once that when the master piped his whistle only one sailor and two grummets answered the call out of over a hundred seamen who were on board to work the ship. Our Lord always gave good health to the master, who was a great bearer of hardships.

What was of great help to the bodily and spiritual health of all these people were two Fathers of the Company of Jesus. One was a Portuguese named Manuel Álvares,[1] a very good scholar and

---

[1] Manuel Álvares, S.J., born in 1529, entered the Society of Jesus in 1549, and died at Goa in 1571. He was a fine painter (*insigne pintor*) and painted various pictures for the Colleges of Coimbra, Cochin, and Goa (Valignano–Wicki, S.J., *Historia del principio y progresso de la Compañía de Jesus en las Indias Orientales, 1542–1564*, Rome, 1944, p. 383 n.). Cf. A. Franco, S.J., *Imagem da Virtude*, II, 373.

preacher. The other was a Valencian named João Roxo,[1] very virtuous and zealous for the common good, who made clysters and applied them to the sick with his own hands, without ever leaving the galley, which was a great remedy for the health of all. Without these Religions, our tribulations, both spiritual and temporal, would have been doubled; for giving of their own and of what belonged to others which they had begged from some honourable men, they relieved many necessities. Among these generous givers were the captain and a certain João Gonçalves, a married man of Goa, who did a great deal of good to many people by distributing comfits which he had brought from the island of Madeira.[2] Five Portuguese and four slaves died from these diseases. And with these tribulations, we navigated these shoals from 7° latitude to 5°, during the space of sixty odd days,[3] until finally our Lord vouchsafed to deliver us from this place. During most of these nights we organized processions, in which the captain and the Fathers with the rest of us went barefoot, including all the boys, of whom there were about thirty from the age of twelve downwards, and we disciplined ourselves until Our Lord lifted his punitive hand from us.

And as we sailed along rather more pleased at having at last got clear of these shoals, although oppressed by the great heat, one night during the first watch, a man fell overboard and was left astern, since the ship was running before a fresh wind and the night was very dark and rainy. He was killed through his own greed, as he used to drink secretly without sharing anything with anyone who asked him for a drink from some water which he kept in a regulation-cask. He used to drink this outboard of the larboard side of the ship, and on this occasion a sheet of the foresail

---

[1] Juan Rojo (to give the Spanish form of his name), born in Valencia in 1529, entered the Society in 1549, came to Portugal in 1559, bound for the Angola mission, but transferred to the India mission in the following year at his own request. Alive at Goa in 1563, the date of his death being unknown (Valignano–Wicki, S.J., *Historia*, p. 383 n.).

[2] He was to play a prominent part later. Cf. pp. 91–92 below.

[3] '50 days' in *HTM*. Padre Arboleda, S.J., gives a very similar account of the *Castelo* being becalmed for over a month off the coast of Guinea, though she eventually rounded the Cape and reached India (*apud* Silva Rego, *Documentação. Índia*, VIII, 284–87; *ibid*. 'Viagens á Índia em meados do século XVI', pp. 87–90).

shook loose and knocked him into the sea. His name was Fernão Gonçalves.[1]

On 27 July Our Lord was pleased to make an end of these trials in order to begin with other and greater ones. And thus we found on this day that we had crossed the Line, and we shaped our course seawards for Cape Santo Agostinho. By this time many people had already recovered their health and others were con‑ valescing; but it was already too late to try to round the Cape of Good Hope, and there was a great shortage of water in the ship, and much of the gear had been rotted away by the rains of the continual thunderstorms off the coast of Guinea, and part had been swept overboard, and most of the people were much weakened and others were still sick and anxious to be cured. Moreover, even if we could have doubled the Cape, we could not have reached India this year, but would have had to winter at Moçambique. And thus everyone wanted to put into Brazil, which seemed good and necessary to all, and was approved by the advice of the fidalgos and the king's servants as well as the seamen, in order that we could there refresh the sick and take in fresh water, provisions, and many other things necessary for our voyage and navigation; since from these we could take our course better and more readily and reach India by the end of January. And thus we tacked about and steered for the coast of Brazil, in search of a good port where we could take refuge.

On the morning of 17 August, twenty‑six days after we had crossed the Line, we sighted the land of Brazil, and it proved to be the Bay of All Saints. We made directly for it, as it was the most convenient and right on our course, and there was the city of Salvador where we could supply ourselves with what was needful better than in any other port on that coast, since it was the residence of the governor, the bishop, the crown treasurer and the chief factor of our lord the king. The people certainly all rejoiced greatly thereat, being very pleased and delighted, just as if this was the end of their voyage and the rest from all their tribulations. And as we approached as close as we could with a north‑east wind, we began to signal our arrival by firing off our

[1] The *HTM* version narrates this incident but omits the man's name.

great guns, so that they should send a good pilot out to us who would guide us into the Bay. This they did, as soon as they heard us five or six leagues out to sea; and he went ahead, warning us against a shoal which was in the port. We anchored when it was nearly dark, this day being exactly four months since we had left Lisbon. We did not find the governor here, but we found news of him which doubled our pleasure, and which was that he had captured and razed to the ground the fort which the French had in Rio de Janeiro—a very strong and impregnable work. He came back a few days after our arrival, when the city and the people thereof received him most joyfully with mimes, ingenious theatri-cals, bull-fights and other celebrations.[1]

We stayed for forty-four days in this city of Salvador, taking in supplies and making ourselves ready. We made many thin cords, we repaired the rudder and other things needful; and all the sick recovered completely, being much stronger and fitter for any eventuality. We left there on a Wednesday the 2 October, at three o'clock in the afternoon, with a north-east wind which wafted us over the bar. And thus we continued our voyage, having left over a hundred men in Brazil who were bound for the discovery of the River of Gold whither the governor was then sending a captain. This turned out to be their good luck and fortune, although at the time we jeered at them and despised them, considering them to be gone on a wild-goose chase and silly fools.[2]

From here we took our course bound for that awe-inspiring Cape of Good Hope, traversing the most vast and immense gulf which there is in the whole sea and land, which is that from the

---

[1] For the expedition of Mem de Sá, governor-general of Brazil, to expel the French from Rio de Janeiro in 1560 cf. R. Southey, *History of Brazil*, 3 vols., London, 1810-19, I, 278-81. The French soon returned and another expedition had to be mounted in 1565; but only two years later the occupants of 'La France Antarctique' were expelled once for all.

[2] As things turned out, this expedition did not discover gold in any appreciable quantity, though it penetrated about 250 miles inland before being forced to turn back by the hostility of the Amerindians. It was commanded by Vasco Rodrigues de Caldas, and contemporary and modern references to it will be found in the letter of Padre Leonardo do Vale, S.J., dated Bahia, 29 June 1562, and in the other sources summarized by F. A. de Varnhagen, *História Geral do Brasil* (5 vols., 5th ed., São Paulo, 1948), I, 364, 377-8.

coast of Brazil to the opposite coast of Guinea and Ethiopia, lying in the great region of Africa, one of the three parts into which the ancients divided the terrestrial globe. And we met with such storms of winds, tempests, accidents, and tribulations, which we under' went day and night, penetrating this colossal expanse of the Ocean Sea, that to narrate them would require a vast tome and be very wearying for the reader, particularly as these miseries are the common lot of all those who seek their honour or their livelihood at sea. Thus it was that when we were in the position for doubling the Cape, there were great arguments between the captain, the pilot, and the master, with others who understood navigational problems, over whether it was better to make the voyage via the outer or the inner passage.[1] And they finally decided that it was best to take the outer passage, for reasons which then seemed best and most forceful to them. And this decision was the cause of the ship sailing so far away beyond India to end her days in a land which cost so dear to the wretched sailors and passengers on board, due to the cruel shipwreck which we suffered, which began on 20 January, on a very dismal, dark, and terrifying morning, when we sighted an island on about the latitude of the equator or a little below it, as we guessed, and we were bearing down on it from a distance of about seven or eight leagues. And as soon as we sighted it, anyone can imagine how nervous our hearts and souls felt after all the trials we had undergone and with the wind blowing with gale force from the west, and on a lee shore, and heavy showers and thunderstorms, for when one stopped

---

[1] I.e. via the Moçambique channel, or else to the east of the island of Madagascar. For a discussion of this problem, see *THS*, I, 8–9, and the sources there quoted. The *HTM* version here has a long disquisition on the ignorance and obstinacy of this particular pilot, 'with his decorated charts and gilded astrolabes, very different from other pilots, whose charts are all torn from constant use and their astrolabes covered with rust and verdigris. And thus, in their simplicity, Our Lord guides them to India and to Portugal, often (so it seems) because they are careful and aware of their own limitations, without going too far in anything; whereas this one spent all his time in contemplating the movements of the skies and the courses of the planets, all mere philosophy, in which it appears that he wanted to surpass Plato, Aristotle, and all the natural philosophers, although he was an ignorant clown and had not frequented nor graduated from the schools of Athens, until finally he ran us ashore and was the cause of so many misfortunes, calamities, and deaths. May God pardon those who in such critical cases deceive the Crown.'

another began with greater force and fury. The seas were very big and running so high that we nearly foundered owing to the hawse-holes which were still open, and which we had great difficulty in closing with coverlets and mattresses that we stuffed in them, as we had no time to do anything better. And our pilot, instead of tacking out to seawards on a southerly tack, continued on a northerly course until eleven o'clock, thinking to clear the island by holding on this course, which he could not do with the west wind. And if when he had sighted the island in the morning he had stood off on the other tack, he would have had more sea-room, and we could have sailed on and not been wrecked. But when he wanted to do this, it was too late, for it was blowing harder than ever and getting stronger all the time, and the ship was well among the many islands which lie offshore along the southern coast of Sumatra with its great bays. As we went thus sailing along on a southern tack, a sudden gust of wind struck us so heavily that we were unrigged in a trice, the partners of both masts being carried away at the same time together with all the shrouds, leaving all the sails torn and loose and we ourselves in manifest peril of our lives. And while we did not fail to work hard in this emergency, we first had recourse to the divine aid, and placed on the poop the banner of the holy relics, which our lady the queen gives to these great ships so that they can seek help therefrom in all their trials and tribulations, as we had done in all the past storms. And when this banner had been hoisted in position, everyone fell on their knees and prayed to it with many tears and sighs, imploring Our Lord for mercy and the pardon of our sins. Having done this, we tried everything possible to help ourselves, unpicking a hempen cable from which we made cords to take the place of shrouds and sustain the masts. We also worked at fixing a jury-sail for the foremast. And thus we lay a-hull all day, without sails, nor would any of the seamen do a hand's turn, because as soon as they had sighted land, most of them had given themselves up for lost. And the first one was the pilot, who for all his previous philosophizing now turned out to be absolutely use-less, and his heart failed him and he never said a word. Quite different was the behaviour of the second pilot, who was an outstanding seamen and sailor, who until the ship ran ashore and stuck fast, never lost his presence of mind nor ability to command.[1] In this way we lay a-hull during the rest of the day, off the shore, and comforting ourselves with the daylight.

At nightfall the wind began to abate somewhat, but the sea lost nothing of its rage and fury. As soon as the wind dropped, we had a succession of violent thunderstorms in the gloaming, and then a most dark and stormy night supervened, during which time each thunderstorm left us waterlogged in the trough of the waves which devoured and battered us to pieces. While we were in this state, and completely hopeless, thinking all our previous work in vain, the father took leave of the son, and brother from brother, and the messmate from his comrade, each one asking the other's forgive-ness, everybody making it up with everyone else during the whole night to the accompaniment of shrieks and cries. Miraculously, in a night like this with such a storm, and with our snouts towards the shore in the trough of the waves, we still did not run aground. And we passed over without seeing or knowing how, several shoals half a league long, on which the sea broke most terribly, which we subsequently were hardly able to negotiate in broad daylight, serene sky, and a favourable stern breeze, in a very small ship. At dawn we anchored with one cable off the shore, com-forting ourselves with the light of day, and commending ourselves to the mercy of God.

It was not long before morning came, the wind increasing with the daylight, though accompanied by continual thunderstorms which never stopped, and by violent downpours of rain. This forced us to lay out another and our only remaining anchor and a new hempen cable so that we could remain fast. When we paid out the cable it snapped at once, since all the bottom was of coral which cut like a razor. And thus we found ourselves drifting towards an island, one of sixteen or seventeen islands, islets, and large reefs which extend a long way out to sea. The main coast

---

[1] As noted above (p. 62), Manuel Álvares, S.J., gives a much more flattering account of the pilot's (António Dias) behaviour in this crisis, saying that he could not hear all of his confession, 'as he had to see to everything'. He also tells us the name of the second pilot, Pedro Álvares, which Henrique Dias omits to do.

lay at a distance of a full half-league from us, being marked by many bays whose points ran a long way out to sea. It was a terri-fying and awesome-looking land, from which vapours rose up in a thousand places, as it was all marshy and very thickly wooded with large trees. And drifting down on the islet, we cut the other cable, to see if with the wind which was dead astern we could enter a bay which lay athwart our bow; a very large and beautiful one, sheltered from all the winds; but we could not do this for want of our sails. And having cut the cable, we ended by drifting ashore on the islet, which was a very rocky and steep one, rounded like a castle made by the hand of man, and with a few trees on the top. The ship received three tremendous and frightful blows when she struck, but withal they did her no harm nor did she spring a leak, which proved what a strong and stout ship she was. And thus she listed and settled on the bottom on the starboard side, which was the one she always listed to; and she at once filled with water, with the whole of the forepart below water and the stern quarter above it all along the larboard side. We cut away the masts to prevent the ship breaking up completely, and they floated out to sea with the yards, all mixed up with the rigging. And so this miserable, pitiful, broken and torn great ship was wrecked on this obscure and uninhabited island, on Tuesday 21 January of the year 1561.[1]

As soon as the ship struck and began to list on the seaward side, some men, thinking that she would turn turtle and frightened of being trapped below, made themselves ready and swam ashore in the surge of the furious waves that were breaking on the island a league away.[2] And although they were strong swimmers, twelve

---

[1] The *HTM* version (ed. Sergio, II, 81) says the ship was wrecked on an islet 'just off the middle of the coast of Sumatra, a third of a degree below the Line'. Couto (*Década VII*, Livro 9, cap. XVI) says 'under the Line', 'debaixo da Equino-cial'. Padre Álvares, S.J., also implies it was on or just below the Equator. Fernão Vaz Dourado in his Atlas compiled at Goa in 1568, which is the first to indicate the site of the wreck, locates it just above the Equator, as does his subsequent map of 1575 (Plate V). Later maps, such as Linschoten's, derive from this prototype with minor variations.

[2] Above it is said that the islet (or island) was only half a league away. The *HTM* version is fuller and clearer in describing the actual wreck, to which Padre Álvares, S.J., also devotes more space. The *HTM* version gives the date of

or thirteen of the first were dashed to pieces, and others were severely hurt and very badly injured, so that some of them sub/ sequently died. And the loss would have been much heavier if the captain had not asserted himself and forbidden anyone to throw himself into the sea, giving them hope that with the help of God they might yet be saved. And at this moment they suc/ ceeded in launching the skiff which was on the deck, and the storm was rapidly moderating and the weather improving, as if it was no longer desirous of completely destroying us; because as it had beaten us, it now relented, and within a couple of hours was quiet and calm, as if there had never been a storm at all. And when they tried to get some bread out of the store/room they could not do it, because it was already full of water; but they got out some casks of gunpowder and shot and munitions, for our pro/ tection and defence. The captain stood by the side with a drawn sword in his hand, preventing anyone from getting into the skiff until all the women (who totalled thirty/three, including some slaves) and the children had been safely disembarked ashore, accompanied by their parents and by some trustworthy friends with a few weapons which could be procured for their guard and protection at such a time. And after they had all gone, the re/ mainder of the people were disembarked before nightfall, it being high tide, with the weapons that each person could carry. We camped beneath a grove of trees, assembling around the banner of the holy relics, where we spent the night together in a body.

It is certainly a most miserable thing to recount the behaviour of human nature, and still more so to weep for its covetousness and wretchedness. For the ship was still drifting towards the islet and had hardly struck before the seamen were pillaging chests, robbing cabins, and tying up bundles, bales, fardles and packages. And these were all taken ashore as if we were in our native land or in one of friends and neighbours, and as if there were safe and sure roads and pathways to traverse. And if the seamen were thus

the actual wreck as the 22 January, 'Day of the Blessed Saint Vincent', and Couto (*op. et loc. cit.*), implies that it was the 20 January, 'Day of the Blessed martyr Saint Sebastian'. Padre Álvares, S.J., agrees with this 1565 edition that it was the 21 January 1561.

occupied, neither were the landsmen idle, for they were breaking open barrels, chests, and boxes, which the sea washed ashore, while others were disciplining themselves and receiving absolution from the Father for their sins, and others were occupied in working for the common good. And thus we remained for a day and a night, keeping very good watch, sheltering in the depth of the wood under some trees which hid the sight of the ship from us. We did not dare to light a fire this day or the next, for fear of causing smoke and revealing our whereabouts; since we did not want to be found until we knew where we were, and whether the land was inhabited or not. It was now ten months since we had left Lisbon.

On the very first night there was a meeting of the captain, the Father, the pilot, the master, together with some of the most prudent and sensible persons, in order to take council as to what should be done for the good of all. This meeting started a muttering and excitement among the common people, who began to divide themselves into groups and gangs, thinking that their betters wished to make off in the skiff and abandon them, for which reason they at once mounted watch and ward over it. And what further deepened their suspicion was that they knew that the master and the second pilot in the loss of the *Algarvia*, had made off secretly in the ship's boat with the captain Francisco Nobre and some friends.[1] Some of them said that they would no longer recognize the captain; and thus these seamen were the cause of all these disputes and mutinies, some of them saying that we should kill the women and children and make our way along the land, and uttering a thousand other similar invectives against the women, as also against those who had allowed them to embark in Portugal. This was the state of affairs, with many arguments and disputes, at a time when we had such great need of asking God to save us; and thus we passed the time looking over our

[1] For the loss of the *Algarvia* (also called *Conceição*) on the Pero dos Banhos shoals in August 1555, and the misbehaviour of the captain and crew see my 'Introduction to the *História Trágico-Marítima*', pp. 11–13 and the sources there quoted. The *HTM* version of the loss of the *São Paulo* gives us the additional information that the second-pilot, Pedro Álvares, was a nephew of the master, João Luís.

shoulders and always keeping an eye on the skiff, eating cheese and olives and other things which were washed ashore, of which the beach was full, and we drank singular and delicious muscatel and Cretan wines.

And while things were still in this state of general confusion and mutual suspicions, at daybreak the next morning the Father Manuel Álvares convoked and assembled everyone together. And standing in front of an altar which he had made, with a retable of Our Lady, he began to make an admonitory speech, using very prudent words, worthy of such a pure man and so necessary at this time, saying:

'Most beloved brothers in Christ, let us recall that holy saying of the Gospel that a kingdom divided against itself cannot stand; and with concord small things grow into great, whereas with discord great things decline and diminish. I must remind you, brothers, that with all the other great ships which were wrecked in the region of the Cape of Good Hope, like the galleon [*São João Baptista*] and the *São Bento* and many others, one of the things which led to the total death and destruction of the survivors was the discord which prevailed among them—dividing themselves into gangs and bands, and handing over their weapons to their enemies and the enemies of our holy faith, so eager for our blood.[1] Let us not divide our forces, for *virtus unita fortior est*,[2] since we are all neighbours and all brothers, and we have been for so long companions in such a confined space, where we have endured so many misfortunes, penetrating the whole expanse of the Ocean, with all its perils and storms, such as other people have never endured before. Therefore I hope and believe in the great mercy of Christ and in his holy name and passion, that those of us who die here will all go to Heaven, as his knights and his martyrs, for

[1] For the wrecks of the *São João Baptista* (1552) and the *São Bento* (1554) off the coast of Natal, and the overland march of the survivors, cf. my 'Introduction to the *HTM*', pp. 6–11, and J. Duffy, *Shipwreck and Empire*, pp. 26–8, and the sources there quoted.

[2] *Virtus unita fortior est quam se ipsa dispersa* in the *HTM* version, which otherwise coincides pretty closely with that of 1565. Incidentally, Manuel Álvares, S.J., in his own account (p. 24) only gives the bare gist of this speech and none of the Latin phrases.

thus will Our Lord choose us for glory and for his better service and the glorification of his holy name. And he may yet bring us safely to the land of Christians, delivering us from our enemies with his strong arm, because if he is for us, *quis contra nos*? It is most necessary, dearest brothers, and most important, that we should all have a single head who will govern and rule the members, and whom we should obey, so that we will not be like a body without a soul. And to this end, I, as a Jesuit priest and clergyman, with the advice of all the principal men, considering what is most fit and proper for the common good, have elected and nominated as our captain and sovereign king over all, senhor Ruy de Melo da Camara, since it suffices that he is authorized to act as such by the hand of our lady the queen, and she having entrusted to him this ship and the people therein, as likewise has her grandson our lord the king,[1] both of whom estimate and prize him, under whose captaincy and banner we have served hitherto, and in which he has given proof of being an exceptional and most kindly captain, for which reason there is nobody else here who is better fitted to take this post nor better qualified to hold it. I beseech you all to believe that I do not tell you and advise you this, save only for the good of all; and on my soul and conscience as a religious of the Company of Jesus, I assure you that I esteem as highly the salvation and life of the soul of the meanest Christian slave among us as I do my own. You should already know this about me, since I am the spiritual father of you all, and you know whether I will tell you the truth or not, and that I will desire your salvation. And in order to expunge from your minds the slightest suspicion of me and of my words, which are pure and limpid, and said as by a father to his children, I swear to you that in so far as I am concerned, and I promise by my holy orders, that I will never leave this island unless we all go together.' Having ended this speech, he asked all those present in a loud voice whether they agreed with what he had said or not,

[1] The Dowager Queen-Regent, D. Catarina, widow of King D. João III, and her grandson, D. Sebastião, born in 1554 after his father's death. He came to the throne in 1557, on the death of his grandfather, and died unmarried and without issue in the disastrous battle of El-Ksar el-Kebir (Alcaçer-Quibir) in Morocco (4 August 1578). Cf. E. W. Bovill, *The Battle of Alcazar* (London, 1952).

telling them to give a clear and categorical answer. To which they all replied unanimously with one voice (shedding tears, as they had done during all the time of his speech) that Ruy de Melo da Camara should be their captain, and thus they swore and promised him, before that most holy image of Our Lady, to obey and carry out all his orders as their king and lord. When the Father heard this, he went down on his knees before anyone else, and swore obedience to the captain, and the captain embraced him and raised him up, like he did to everyone else, with many tears, one by one, as they vowed obedience to him. When this was finished, the captain swore on the holy gospels and on the image of Our Lady, that he would never leave nor set foot outside that island without taking the meanest of the company with him—which fell out very differently afterwards—and thus everyone remained quiet and relieved.

This done, the captain forthwith selected a certain Álvaro Freyre, a servant of the king, a man accustomed to endure hard-ships and a good swimmer,[1] to go out to the ship with all the others who knew how to swim and dive, in order to find and bring back food supplies and munitions, and whatever else was necessary for our remedy, sustenance, and defence. This was at once put into execution and carried out. On the other hand, the skiff manned by some others brought ashore everything that they could, while some people recovered and brought ashore what the swimmers fetched from the ship, while yet others went along the beaches salvaging whatever they could. Everything thus recovered was placed in a heap, while everyone worked equally hard irre-spective of rank and in spite of the scorching heat which burnt their bones.

It was also arranged forthwith that the master and the pilot with some other individuals would walk round the island, and see what they thought of it, and where would be the best place to live and pitch our camp and build our boats. They did not delay long,

[1] The *HTM* version has 'Álvaro Freire, a servant of the King, born in India of Portuguese parents, son of a certain Simão Álvares, who used to be the Royal Apothecary in these regions. He was a man accustomed to endure hardships and a beautiful swimmer' (*gentil nadador*).

but soon returned with the news that the island was uninhabited and very flat, all made of white coral,[1] about a league round in circuit, the interior being very thickly wooded with tall trees. There were many brown and black apes and many more white [? = grey] ones, which, when they became aware of us took refuge in the tops of the trees without our being able to knock them down. Subsequently, João Gonçalves and Bento Caldeira[2] killed a few with arquebus shots, which were given to the sick; but their flesh was foul and stinking, very difficult to digest and worse to taste. At night these apes descended from the trees and came into the camp to steal what food they could, without our ever being able to catch any, however hard we tried, thus verifying the adage that everyone is cock on his own dunghill.

On the morning of the 27th of the month, the captain went with seven or eight persons to reconnoitre the island and to see the place and site which the master and pilot said was the best and most suitable for the construction of our vessels. Having thoroughly examined the spot and been very satisfied with it, he summoned some of the people, including the carpenters with their axes, with which we cut down a lot of the bush on this side and cleared a good piece along the beach. And after it had been cleared and arranged as far as possible, we began to move our baggage from the first encampments to the new ones, which transfer was completed in three days. And thus we built our shacks made of branches and of planks from the ship, covered with some of the many textiles which the sea washed ashore, and which the rain rotted in a short time. And a few days later, necessity taught us to seek palm-leaves instead, which we found to be very good, this being a leaf shaped like a sword-lily, with which the people of these regions usually cover the roofs of their houses.

[1] *Mato branco* ('white wood' in the sense of white bush or jungle, in the 1565 text, which does not seem meaningful here; so I have followed the *HTM* version, which has *coral branco*).

[2] *HTM* version has here 'João Gonçalves, a married man of Goa, the oldest *lascarim* [veteran soldier] in India, and Bento Caldeira, a servant of the King and a very fine well set-up man, who had come out with the post of Factor of Baçaim' (ed. Sergio, II, 69). For these two men cf. also p. 65 above and pp. 91, 93, below.

The captain with his cronies, who numbered about thirty individuals, most of them prominent persons, made his quarters on
the seashore at the foot of a palm-tree. Next to this was placed the
storehouse of the provisions and munitions which we had been
able to salvage from the ship, and what was collected from various
individuals, which was mostly wine, olive-oil, olives, and cheeses,
all of which the captain entrusted to one of his confidants who was
solely responsible for issuing it. Next to the storehouse, they built
a small shack for the Fathers, and similarly many other shacks for
the rest of the people, seven or eight persons in each one. We had
six arquebuses, and many halberds, pikes and swords, which
were found in the chests washed up by the sea, and it seems they
had been embarked as trade-goods.[1] And as soon as we were all
settled in, we discussed what we must do next in order to save
ourselves, for which purpose the captain called a general council.
When the muster was made, it was found that we numbered
330 souls. Having ascertained this, it seemed that it would be very
difficult to build a vessel for so many people, and moreover we
had no more provisions than those which I mentioned and a little
manioc-flour from Brazil, which were kept for the workmen who
would have to do the boat-building, and this island was very
barren as was the shore of Sumatra opposite. It therefore seemed
very good and needful that we should break up the skiff and
rebuild it much bigger and send it to Sunda, manned by persons
of credit and confidence, in order to ask for help there, as that was
the nearest place which the Portuguese frequented for trade, and
some of them always wintered there.[2] But this project proved
abortive, owing to various differences of opinion which arose
about it. And thus it was decided to see if we could not get out of
the ship some part of the longboat, and all the yards, cables,
rigging and sails that we could, together with the planking, nails
and ironwork which we needed, and likewise cordage for oakum
—all of which was done with a great deal of difficulty.

[1] *Veniaga* in the 1565 text, which the *HTM* metamorphoses into *vingança*
(vengeance)! Cf. *HTM*, ed. Sergio, II, 84.

[2] Sunda, or Sunda Calapa (Kalapa), the region of western Java with its twin
ports, later known as Bantam and Jacatra. Cf. p. 104, n. 2, below, for further
discussion and the map of Java in the Vaz Dourado atlas of 1568.

This kind of work did not prevent us from undertaking other kinds, and sooner or later everything was fixed up, and every individual showed what he was worth, and what he could do. The pilot, who had formerly been a goldsmith, made two pairs of bellows from the materials of gilt leather hangings and boots. And thus we made a smithy, and the chief of the smiths was a gentle-man named Ruy de Melo, who had three smiths and four or five others to help him with the work. Eight of the grummets were chosen to make charcoal, which they did as good or better than that which is used at Lisbon. A certain António de Refoios was in charge of them.[1] Similarly, another twelve men were selected to saw some yards and masts, and to make some planks. And the master-gunner, Fernão Luís, made two large saws from some broadswords which had been salvaged, with which they were able to work very well and to make some fine planking. These men likewise had their captain, someone of quality and authority who provided them with what was needful; and all these workers had their regular ration of wine and olives for dinner and supper, besides shellfish and other things which were gathered for them. The captain acted as inspector of the watch, exercising general supervision over everybody, and all the rest of the people scattered in the bush and along the beaches, whence they fetched a lot of timber and enormous beams. Nobody was excused from working, nor did anyone try to avoid it, the men being occupied as related above and the women and children in wetting the cordage and picking oakum. Thanks to the efforts of a black Gujarati who was a slave of the master and a very skilful diver,[2] we got out from the bottom of the ship's hold, where the guns had been placed as ballast, eight *berços* and nine *camaras* and many cannon-balls, as

---

[1] Couto (*Década VII*, Livro 9, cap. xvi) calls him 'a very honourable knight who had come out with the post of captain of Quilon' in Malabar. He was killed later in the skirmish described on p. 102 below.

[2] The Portuguese made great use of Gujarati sailors, divers, and pilots, despite their longstanding antipathy to Muslims. To some extent their practice was followed by the Dutch. Gujarati divers sent from Batavia were mainly responsible for salvaging most of the treasure and guns in the outward-bound Dutch Indiaman *Batavia* wrecked off the coast of Western Australia in 1629 (H. Drake-Brockman, *Voyage to Disaster*, London, 1964, pp. 44 n., 150 n., 257).

also two falcons with another two *camaras* and a swivel-gun, and the five barrels of gunpowder mentioned above.[1] And with this artillery and with the people who were divided into squadrons, the guard of the camp was ordered and arranged.

We also made with great fervour and devotion a very beautiful and strong church roofed with palm-leaves, and with the walls inside decorated with hangings of Arras tapestry and Flanders cloths which had been salvaged from the ship, as also very striking adornments of velvet and satin which looked very fine and well made. These were blessed by Padre Manuel Álvares, who had authority to do this, and we celebrated mass daily, with a sermon on Sundays, and litanies every night. On Wednesdays and Fridays there were processions, in which many people disciplined themselves.

When the skiff (which did not go to Sunda as originally decided) had been enlarged, we also constructed a large vessel on a piece of the prow of the longboat as a keel, and this vessel was about the size of one of the caravels which bring corn to Lisbon from Alcácer.[2] It seemed to us that she would hold up to 260 persons for the other seventy odd would go in the skiff and in a gallevat[3] of the same size which had been built thanks to the industry and skill of the second pilot. And what had induced the people to bear patiently the immense toil they had in making this vessel, during all the burning heats, rains and storms, and above all the bitter hunger they endured, was the hope which they all shared that they would be able to embark and save themselves therein. Because if they had realized or suspected what was actually

[1] *Berço*, a small breech-loading gun firing a ball of up to 3 lbs. calibre; probably corresponding to the Elizabethan 'base', though this fired a shot of only 6 or 8 oz. The *Camara* was the separate or detachable 'chamber' which contained the charge of gunpowder, and was inserted in the breech of these primitive guns of small calibre. The falcon was likewise a small 2½ or 3 pounder gun.

[2] These caravels were presumably small coasting vessels of less than 100 tons, probably only about 50 or 60.

[3] *Galveta*. Originally a small Indo-Portuguese vessel, provided with sails and oars, which could only hold about ten men besides the rowers. Later there were larger types which could take up to 60 men besides 20 or 25 rowers and mounted a few small guns. Cf. the extensive notice in *Hobson-Jobson*, pp. 361–3, *in voce* 'Gallevat'.

going to happen, nobody would have done a hand's turn. And even as it was, they often kept dividing into gangs and bands, and wanted to stop working, which the Father prevented by his sermons and prudent words, wherewith he always succeeded in reducing them to concord and friendship. During all this time, the people were kept alive by some cheeses and olives and wine, which the sea cast up on the beach, together with some shellfish and some soaked lupines, and some land-crabs, of which we ate only the legs and the heads, for the bodies were exceedingly bitter. We also cooked some herbs in olive-oil, which thus extracted much of their venom and harmfulness, as also wild *palmitos*. And while these things lasted, they were a great help and alleviation to our hunger; but they were used up in a few days, and there was then nothing left which we could try out or rummage for. So we then decided to seek it on the opposite Sumatran shore, postponing all other work, as we could not fight and could only try to make peace with an enemy such as hunger.

We therefore went to look for food on the opposite shore, going along it southwards for a distance of six or seven leagues, where people went searching for some shellfish, spending five or six days up to their waists in water, and fishing for them at night by the light of lunts and candles; frying the fish which they caught, since it would not keep fresh from one day to another, owing to the great heat and humidity, and because we had no salt. And already at this time the land began to show us what it was, for people began to die. The first were a certain João Rodrigues, a native of Lisbon, and João Dias, who came with the daughter of António Pessoa, the comptroller of the exchequer, and thenceforward many others died. And on 13 February, when three of the sailors were searching for shellfish about three leagues to the north along the shore, they found a dugout-canoe with ten Blacks, five or six of whom were walking along the beach picking up nails from the wood of the ship and other things thrown up by the sea. And they spoke with them by signs, but could not make them understand anything, nor could they persuade them to return to the camp with them, despite the presents they gave them. One of the sailors came and told the captain, who at once went out to the canoe,

6

together with the pilot and a Javanese slave of the latter, both of whom spoke Malay fluently. The captain forbade anyone else to follow and told them all to stay on guard in the camp. It was extraordinary to see how the people, or most of them, passed from the other side, without anyone trying to stop them, though their captain did not want them to go like this, most of them swimming over with their pikes or their swords in their mouths, while others waded across the fording-place with the water up to their chests, thinking that there were many enemies about and fearing some ambush or deceit. Meanwhile, the captain found a league and a half away two of the Blacks sitting on the beach and conversing with our sailors by signs; for the other Blacks, not daring to approach, had already returned to the prau.[1] The captain sat down with the two, and asked them what land this was, and where they lived. They replied that this was an island about twelve leagues long, adjoining Sumatra, and that they lived and had their dwelling-place and settlement very near our camp. But they never, however much we begged and coaxed them, came to our camp, although they promised (on this occasion) to do so the next day, bringing some provisions of their land. And thus taking their departure with some pieces of cloth which the captain gave them, they went away to arouse the envy of their companions.

At dawn on the next day, the 14th of the month, there arrived off the point which I mentioned before, opposite the other of Sumatra, in front of our encampment, a launch with twenty Blacks, ten of whom were those which we had seen the previous day; and in order to reassure them we sent them two sailors as hostages, and they sent us two of their men in return. And all our people withdrew some distance away, except for the captain and the pilot, who stayed with them and asked them why they came and what they brought to sell. They replied that they had not brought anything, since they had not had any time to return to their land, but that they wanted to find out what sort of people we

---

[1] Same as the canoe (*almadia*, a dugout canoe) mentioned above. The word *prau* (*perahu, parao*, etc.), was the generic Malay or Javanese word for any sailing or rowing vessel, but was usually applied by Europeans to the smaller types of these craft, the larger sometimes being termed *juncos*.

were and where we were going. We told them about our misadventures, adding that we were Portuguese and were bound for
Malacca, and that we wanted to buy some provisions from them,
as also some kind of vessel, for which we would give a good price.
They promised to supply everything in abundance, both provisions and ship, but we could not persuade any of them to stay
with us while the others went to fetch what they had promised.
And so they took their leave with twenty red caps and a piece of
green cloth that we gave them. And the captain sent some people
to escort them to the launch and to bring back the sailors. But
these were a very bad sort of people, who were quite untrustworthy,
and we were deceived by them. And during the days that we
stayed here they killed and ate some of our men, without our ever
being able to catch any of them. And on the 19th of the month
there occurred such a furious storm that it smashed the great ship
to small pieces, without our being able to salvage anything therefrom, save only some wood and nails, ropes and cables, and a pipe
of pitch, which was great wealth and satisfaction for us at such
a time.

And when our large vessel was ready to be launched, the captain sent to summon all the people who were scattered along the
coast to the southward for distance of about eight or nine leagues,
so that they could help us with the launching. These people
arrived on the afternoon of 18 March, very sad and disgruntled,
numbering over seventy men all formed into a squadron. And
the reason for their grief was that going along the river of sweet
water, they had found the headless corpses of two of our men lying
on the beach, with their left hands missing, and all the calves of
their legs torn out. The bodies were also riddled with wounds
inflicted by many krisses and assegais, with which the Blacks had
killed them at daybreak, while they were looking for shellfish. Our
men also found on the way another sailor of this company who
had escaped by taking refuge in the bush.

On the next day, 19 March, the vessel being ready to be launched
into the sea, and gaily beflagged with many beautiful banners
which we had made for her, after Padre Manuel Álvares had said
mass therein, he blessed her and named her *Nossa Senhora da*

Salvação [*Our Lady of Salvation*]. And at the beginning of the flood-tide she went out to sea without any difficulty or danger, being as well built as she would have been in the dockyard at Lisbon, with which she gave us a most joyful sight, as she showed herself to be such an excellent result of our work, and, under God, she represented the sole hope of our salvation. And when she was anchored in about half a fathom of water, she fired all her guns, which greatly affected all our hearts and raised up our spirits anew from the depths of despair in which they had been plunged.

When everything was ready, both the large vessel, and the skiff and the gallevat, on the morning of 20 March, having taken on board all the cannon and casks of water, these ships left the en-campment for our original one, with the captain, officers and women on board, in order to embark the rest of the people there. And before they had all done so, while some people were still ashore, the big ship would not steer properly owing to the many people who were in her and for whom there was not sufficient room. And when anyone moved, she listed heavily and threatened to capsize. The reason for this was that in such a small ship they had made cabins and privies for Dona Francisca and the daughter of António Pereira and other women, wherein, with this pretext, they had stored many goods both well and ill gotten, which were valued more highly than the lives of men. And I will say no more about this, in order to avoid denouncing anyone, since I cannot tell the truth without giving offence to certain people. We all remained very bewildered and unhappy, for the time did not allow us to stay any longer in this place. When the master and the caulker, who were two very experienced seamen, saw this, they told the people that it was obvious they were much too crowded and that it would be exceedingly dangerous for them to sail in this condition; and that it would be much better for them to go by land and die there if necessary rather than at sea. They added that they themselves would rather do this, and would accompany any others who wished to make the journey by land. Some poor fools believed this assertion and rashly agreed to go, although the master and the caulker were telling a pack of lies, as was soon apparent.

Therefore at nightfall the ship was towed back into the roadstead, where all the shacks had already been burnt to ashes, for we had set fire to them before we left. When we got back, the captain made nearly all the people go ashore, as he also did, leaving on board a few private persons with the women. He lamented that he was a miserable wight for thus having laboured in vain to leave by sea, and for having to disembark the people to go by land, with whom he himself would likewise go. Padre Manuel Álvares thereupon retorted that since things had come to this pass, they should dismantle the store-room and the quarters made for Dona Francisca and the other women, which took up much space as far as the foot of the mast, and that they should then all go together in the ship as this critical time demanded, and that nobody should receive preferential treatment, but every effort should be made to save all their lives as far as possible; and that they should throw overboard a large jar which took up a lot of room in the ship, which belonged to the pilot and was full of olive-oil, though he said it contained water;[1] and that since we intended to coast along the shore looking for shellfish and other provisions, we would be able to obtain water, and meanwhile two pipes with a few barrels would be enough for a reserve, and that in this way there would be room on board for everyone. And that if, after all these measures had been taken there was still insufficient room, then they should hold another general discussion on what should best be done. To this the captain replied that it was a very good idea and that they ought to carry it out, and he went back to the ship with many of his cronies; and some other people, who divined what was afoot, likewise went back with him. Having boarded the ship, and late at night, he sent to call some of his friends (who were still on shore) together with the padres, these latter thinking that they were being summoned to attend a council meeting. And when the dawn broke, all the other people who were still on shore came down to the beach, expecting that they would be able to embark, or to see what had been decided on. But the captain shouted to them from the ship,

[1] Probably a 'Martaban jar', glazed vessels of a very large type which took two men to carry one when empty. Also called 'Pegu jars', and exported from Martaban in Pegu all over the East for many centuries. Cf. *Hobson-Jobson*, pp. 559–60.

which was some way off, that a hundred and fifty of them would have to go by land, and that there was absolutely no alternative. He promised that he would go and wait for them in the big bay eight or nine leagues to the southward, which some of them had already reached before, and there they would build another vessel if they found some kind of food supply. To this those on shore replied that he should land and organize them and appoint a captain to command them, and supply them with weapons to defend themselves, since they had none and needed some; and that he should take on board the children and the sick who were all ashore and who could not undertake the journey by land. The captain made answer that he had no time to disembark, and that as for the weapons he would give them what he could spare, as well as some provisions for the sick. When the people heard this and realized his evil intent, they asked him to give them one of the Fathers and either João Gonçalves or António Dias. And he, thinking that João Gonçalves would refuse, nominated António Dias, promising and assuring him, as likewise did Padre Álvares, that next day they would meet them all at the bay which I men/ tioned, where they would wait for them.[1] António Dias accepted this charge very willingly, like the most courageous man he was, very strong physically, and a man of upright life who had lived a long time in India and had once wintered at Sunda. He was a married man at São Tomé on the coast of Coromandel.[2] He at once jumped into the skiff with his astrolabe, pair of compasses and chart, for he knew well how to take the altitude of the sun, and the people asked him to bring them; for they thought it a joke about waiting in the bay for them, seeing that the others were pushing off. He was accompanied by Tomé Jorge, a stalwart youth born at Lagos, with an arquebus given him by the captain

[1] Padre Manuel Álvares, S.J., gives a much fuller account of this imbroglio, which differs in some particulars, but makes it equally clear that the captain was in fact trying to double/cross the castaways (ed. Frazão de Vasconcelos, pp. 34–7). Padre Álvares, S.J., likewise praises the behaviour of the *casado* António Dias.

[2] São Tomé de Meliapor (Mailapur) now a suburb of Madras, famous for the shrine of St Thomas the Apostle, on which there is a most extensive (and frequently controversial) literature. Cf. G. Schurhammer, S.J., *Franz Xaver, Sein Leben und seine Zeit*, ii, *1541–1552* (Freiburg, 1963), pp. 552–79.

and the Banner of the Holy Relics, as also by the Padre João Roxo, a Valencian, with a crucifix in his hands, and another Jesuit padre called Pero de Castro, a good and virtuous man, who had come with us from Brazil, being desirous of seeing India.[1] These were landed from the skiff on the Sumatra shore; while those people on the island were told to cross over by the fording-place, taking advantage of the low tide which would enable them to do so, and to assemble under the banner which would await them. And some of them tried to swim out to the vessels in order to be picked up by them, which those aboard refused to do although they could have done so; but on the contrary, they repulsed the swimmers with many blows of the hand and strokes of the flat of the sword when they reached them, throwing them back into the sea together with some others who were already hanging on to them, although they could have carried another sixty persons; and they left ashore many children and sick people without any con-solation at all, not even sharing with them the weapons which they had.[2] This was a very cruel, wretched and most lamentable deed, just like a second shipwreck, and formed the saddest parting that was ever seen; for wives were separated from their husbands ashore, and in other cases, fathers from sons, brothers from brothers, and friends from friends, according to the luck of each one; and all were left without the hope of seeing each other again, the tears, cries, and screams being so great that they reached to the heavens. And since I was one of those who was left on shore, and I do not wish to be branded as a slanderer, I will here pass over many ugly things which were done and which are greatly to be deplored.

We then all crossed over to the Sumatra shore by the fording-place to where the banner was awaiting us, and we all of us dumped what little baggage we had, so that we could travel

[1] Pedro de Castro had only arrived in Brazil from Portugal in December 1559.

[2] One of the men who was repulsed in this way, António Feio, subsequently challenged the captain, Rui de Melo da Camara, to a duel at Malacca; but the quarrel was composed by (? by the intervention of the local jesuits ?) before they actually crossed swords. Cf. Francisco de Sousa, S.J., *Oriente Conquistado* (2 vols., Lisbon, 1710), I, 183. One of the swimmers who did manage to get aboard was Francisco Paes, for whose subsequent career see pp. 8–9, n. 2, above.

lighter, but we took what arms we had with us. On Saturday, the eve of Palm Sunday, we began our journey southwards by land, in the direction of Sunda, headed by the padre carrying the crucifix. We then numbered 172 persons, including many people of quality. And of those who went by sea, there were about 98 or 102 persons in the big ship, eighteen in the gallevat, and fifteen in the skiff. These vessels put out to sea with the wind, and on this day and the next, which was Palm Sunday, they tacked back and forth off the island which they had just left. We went on our journey, and when we reached the river of sweet water, which some people had previously crossed by swimming, although at low tide, we determined to make some rafts, in addition to one that was already there, so that we could cross over to the other bank. But when some of our people dived in to swim across they found that they were in their depth the whole way, and so they reached the other side, shouting to us the news of such a manifest mercy as this was, and one with which Our Lord began to show us his greatness and pity.

When we had crossed over the river and got round a cape that jutted far out to sea, we saw the gallevat returning towards us, from which, with great danger, Pero Luís, a slave of the master, came swimming to see whether he could come and talk secretly with certain persons who had a lot at stake in the ships. On his arrival, great quarrels and disputes arose among us; because just before he arrived many people drew their swords and placed themselves on guard along the beach, forbidding anyone to go into the sea, and putting the points of their swords on the chests of those who came down to the water's edge. And they forbade the Black to come ashore, and said they would kill him if he tried. So standing in the water, he gave us a message from the captain, that if on the next day we should not find him at the bay which he had told us, then we should go on to some more islands which were over twenty leagues away. He was answered in terms that seemed good to those people [with the swords] and to the padre, and almost by force they made him swim back to the boat. That night we camped along the beach a good four leagues from where we had started, eating some white quirrel-monkeys which we found.

At dawn on the next day we began our march without any order or discipline, everyone trying to be first to reach the bay, which was a good five leagues distant and which everyone thought would be their salvation. We arrived there a little after midday, tired and exhausted by the difficult ground over which we had travelled, almost always with the water up to our chests, and over great reefs and rocks so sharp that our feet were cut open with a thousand wounds that penetrated to the quick, and for which we had no remedy other than tying them up with our clothes, and the pain made us forget to look for anything to eat. On reaching the roadstead and finding not a living soul there, whether on sea or on land, the people then realized the truth of what some of the more experienced in such matters had told them before—that they should not be in such a hurry, but should take things easier and slower, so as to husband their strength and make the journey less exhausting. But none of this good advice availed to make us rest in the noonday heat which burnt us alive, but we pressed on, madly anxious to round the cape in the hope of finding the others there. We arrived at sunset, quite exhausted and worn out, and we camped by a little brook, refreshing ourselves with the water and some soft *palmitos*, on which we fed to our hearts' content and thought ourselves exceedingly lucky therewith.[1] We decided to march thenceforward in a better order, both so as to be able to seek food supplies as likewise to preserve our lives from our enemies.

Having assembled next day in the morning, we confirmed and acknowledged António Dias as our captain, and we nominated an ensign to whom we entrusted the banner, and a judge who

[1] *Palmitos*. The celebrated botanist and physician, Garcia d'Orta, described this edible part of the palm⁄tree as follows in his *Coloquios dos Simples e Drogas da India* (Goa, 1563), Colloquy nr. 16: 'but first I want to tell you about a tasty food from this palm⁄tree, even though it is not very useful. It is the eye or inner rind of the palm together with the delicate young leaves, while still unfolded (which we call *palmitos*); and it tastes better than our *palmitos*, and rather like white and very tender chestnuts before the shell has fallen; but the *palmito* tastes better than this. Yet he who eats a *palmito* is really eating of a palm⁄tree, for it dries quickly; and the older the palm⁄tree the better the *palmito*.' In English, the young palm leaves, while still unfolded, with the succulent end of the stem from which they arise form what is usually termed 'the cabbage', but I have retained the word *palmito* in my translation. Cf. also *JMBRAS*, VIII (1930), 195.

would take cognizance of and settle our disputes, drawing up a declaration (*auto*) to this effect, which we all signed.[1] We then began our march in the following array: the ensign went in front with the banner of the Holy Relics, accompanied by fifty of the strongest and fittest men, armed with an arquebus, some pikes, and javelins of wood hardened by fire. A stone's-throw behind these came the Padres with the crucifix, accompanied by twenty men with another arquebus, and they helped along all the children and the sick with a steady pace. In the rearguard came the captain with a guidon and all the rest of the people. And in order to find something to eat, about fifty of the men went looking for shellfish along the beaches and reefs. We marched along in this formation, and on this day we passed through a very thick wood for the distance of about a league and a half. And when we had gone about six leagues and it was nearly nightfall, we camped alongside a river of clear sweet water, of which there are many in this region.

On this same day, the ships went and anchored among five clean islands, with no sandbanks or depths. Towards afternoon they set sail and entered a very large roadstead which lay ahead of them and which measured about twelve leagues across at the two extremities. When they had anchored, they sent ashore to get fresh water, which they found to be excellent. And late in the afternoon they saw a large sail out at sea, which came and anchored off the aforesaid islands, as if its occupants were familiar with the place and also wished to water there. And as soon as the captain sighted this ship, he ordered both the boats to prepare and clear for action. In the skiff he placed Ruy de Melo (he of Banda),[2] and

---

[1] It is extraordinary how often the Portuguese castaways in these shipwrecks when they had either lost nearly everything or abandoned so much in order to 'travel light', still contrived to produce ink and paper with which to draw up notarial documents. See *THS*, I, 206, 254. The same applies to their Spanish contemporaries. The present writer possesses some notarized documents drawn up by Luis Pérez Dasmariñas in January 1600, on a beach in Kwangtung province in South China, at a time when he and his shipwrecked companions had lost everything else save the clothes they stood up in, and when they had nothing to eat except shellfish.

[2] Ruy de Melo, gentleman of the royal household, and son of João de Melo de Faria, had already served in the East and had been granted the captaincy of the annual galleon leaving Goa for Banda to collect a cargo of nutmegs, the grant being

Christovão de Melo, son of Ruy de Melo who had been captain of Mina,[1] Ruy Gonçalves da Camara, João de Sousa, and other persons amounting to about twenty/three in all. In the gallevat went João Gonçalves, accompanied by Bento Caldeira, Baltasar Marinho, and his illegitimate brother, Lourenço Gomes de Abreu, a native of Monçao, with other men to the number of twenty/five. They were provided with some powder/pots [make/shift hand/grenades] made from old potsherds, and accompanied by a Chinese slave of the pilot, who spoke fluent Malay, which language is understood everywhere in these parts. The captain ordered them in God's name to go and find out from the new/comers who they were, and where we were, and if they would freight or sell us their ship, or another one, to go and get the rest of us—and if they refused to do this, then the ship was to be taken by force of arms, because there was nothing whatever left to eat in our own vessels, for since they had left the camp, the daily ration for each person was only seven lupines and five olives with half a coconut/shell of water. They were therefore all in imminent danger of death from starvation; but Our Lord, whose mercy never fails on such occasions, brought us this junk, and sub/sequently other vessels, so as to save those of us who were on land. For otherwise we would never have survived, and nobody would ever have known what had become of us, even if we had been a thousand men armed to the teeth.

Our men left at nightfall by the light of a bright moon which was shining, and they reached the junk at eleven o'clock, for she was lying more than three leagues from where our vessels were. The Blacks were already under arms when our interpreter asked them who they were, to which they never replied. And on being

dated Lisbon, 30 January 1560. Lucaino Ribeiro (ed.), *Registo da Casa da Índia* (2 vols., Lisbon, 1954), I, 129, nr. 560, and 138, nr. 597 (where the date is given as 25 January 1560). For the Crown's nutmeg monopoly and the Banda voyages see M. A. Meilink/Roelofsz, *Asian Trade and European Influence in the Indonesian Archipelago, 1500–1630* (The Hague, 1962), pp. 161–3, 167, 274.

[1] São Jorge da Mina on the Gold Coast in Guinea. Founded by Diogo de Azambuja by order of King D. João II in 1482 and taken by the Dutch in 1637. Better known to the Dutch and English as Elmina. For an exhaustive study of this old castle see A. W. Lawrence, *Trade Castles and Forts of West Africa* (London, 1963), pp. 103–79.

asked if they would sell us that ship and some provisions, they retorted that they were not merchants but warriors, and Achinese, as if they expected us to be frightened thereat, since all these peoples of Sumatra fear them like the very devils, and they have often waged war against the Portuguese in these parts.[1] Forthwith they discharged a hail of poisoned arrows, with which they wounded many of our men, and the boats were riddled with them. Our men replied by firing the *berços* at their hull, the skiff from one side and the gallevat on the other; and then rowing hard against the junk they boarded her by the stern, where they were greeted from above with such showers of arrows and javelins that they were forced to row away again owing to the great hurt they suffered, as the open boats were very exposed, and the junk being very high they could hardly reach up to the deck with their pikes. And having hauled off, they raked her severely with the guns, and they decided to cut away the prau that was being towed at her stern, in order to prevent the Achinese escaping therein. And boarding her again by the stern, they took the prau, and threw some of their powder-pots into the junk, but they did not explode. The Blacks fought like brave men, being quite fearless; and they replied with loud jeers to every salvo that we fired at them. At the fourth onset our men finally got aboard them, though they put up a very stiff resistance. The first man to board was a sailor named Bernardo da Fonseca, and after him João Gonçalves, who saved him from being killed by the Blacks, although he was very badly wounded. After these two, the rest of our men boarded the junk and overcame the defenders, most of whom jumped overboard, where they were drowned or were killed by our men who were in the boats; and five of them who were hiding under the deck were captured alive. Our casualties comprised ten wounded men in the gallevat and five in the skiff, all of them badly injured; and they were only saved from death by some anti-poison wood which the pilot gave them, which they at once chewed and so did not die.[2]

[1] For the longstanding Portuguese and Achinese rivalry cf. M. A. Meilink-Roelofsz, *Asian Trade and European Influence, 1500–1630*, pp. 136–46.

[2] Probably the *pao da cobra* extolled by Garcia d'Orta as an antidote against snake-bite in his *Coloquios* (Goa, 1563), Colloquy nr. 42. He also mentions that

As soon as the victory was won, which was about an hour after midnight, the leaders sent three men in the junk's prau with the news to the captain, who was already coming rowing to help them, for as he had heard the gunfire but did not see them, he thought they might have been taken; so that they all gave thanks to God at this news. The captain at once went in the prau to the junk, where he congratulated the captors; and leaving Pedro Álvares therein with what men were needed to bring the prize under sail into the roadstead, he returned with the wounded and the five Blacks who were bound. These last were forthwith put to the torture, but only one of them would speak and he told us that we were in the very place and region that we thought we were, which was the coast of Sumatra, and that they lived at a distance of three days' journey, and were going to lade a cargo of sago-flour, which is their principal food; and that they were taking to barter for it a lading of unhafted iron tools of various kinds, together with some red beads[1] and brass bracelets. We also found fourteen or fifteen sacks of rice, whereat we all rejoiced exceedingly, on account of the need we had for it. And out of revenge for the loss of our comrades whom they had killed in the camp and the way they had mutilated them, we cut off their heads one by one on board with an axe. They died with the greatest fortitude, one after the other; for as soon as one was beheaded and flung into the sea, the next man at once stepped forward and laid his head on the block. The only one whom we spared was their pilot, who knew the navigation of this coast and thus we had need of him.

On the morning of the next day, which was 1 April, the cap-tain sent the gallevat back to bring the good news to us who were coming by land of how they now had a ship big enough for all; and Bento Caldeira went in her, in order to accompany us by land. Meanwhile, we were marching along in the above order,

there was a similar species used in Malacca against poisoned arrow wounds, but adds that he had not seen this variety himself. Padre Manuel Álvares, S.J., gives a longer account of this fight and says that there was a fatal Portuguese casualty—a slave 'who was one of the first to board'.

[1] 'Trade-wind beads' evidently, for an account of which see *THS* I, 133 n, and the sources there quoted, to which should be added Diogo do Couto, *Década IX*, cap. 22, and the article in *JMBRAS*, XXXVIII (2), 87–124.

sometimes in great heat and at other times in heavy rain. We also traversed dense jungles and steep and dangerous rocks, but during all these hardships Our Lord vouchsafed us very great mercies; for we were able to catch with our hands and kill with blows so many fish, as well as lobsters and many other kinds of shellfish, besides coconuts and *palmitos*, that when we had finished the day's journey we spent the night in roasting and cooking. And on a Tuesday, 1 April, those who were going ahead came upon two crocodiles. One of them, as soon as it heard the sound of the marching people, made off into the jungle with a tremendous crashing noise, and the other turned back and made for the sea. This one was of such gigantic size and strength that it seemed incredible. It was over five *varas*[1] long and about as big as a tun, being covered on top with what looked like green shells, streaked with red veins in places and very colourful to behold. When it heard our people, it rushed out violently with a wonderful speed, and with its mouth wide open enough to have swallowed a large ox. Everyone got out of its way by taking refuge on the top of the rocks, and the crocodile went and fell in an opening between some high rocks, where it remained trapped and wedged in such wise that it could only move a very small part of its tail, with which it thrashed about, splashing up the water very high and very far. There it was killed with arquebus-shots and spear thrusts; and when it was skinned and divided among the people, it was found that half of it would suffice for us all. We made a joyful feast on this, as its roasted flesh tasted like that of a very good sheep, and we kept some of it for the next day.[2]

Marching along a beautiful beach on Wednesday, 2 April, between 11 and 12 o'clock in the morning we sighted the gallevat coming towards us. This threw us all into great confusion, which was remedied by a proclamation being made in the captain's name that nobody on pain of death should dare to cross a line which he

---

[1] The Portuguese yard. Nowadays equated with 1.096 m., but there were considerable regional variations in the sixteenth century.

[2] Francisco de Sousa, S.J., *Oriente Conquistado*, 1, 184, embellishes this story by saying that the crocodile voluntarily and miraculously gave itself up, without trying to escape or offering any resistance.

drew on the sand. And along this line he stationed fifteen or twenty armed men with orders to kill at once anyone who crossed it. This being done, the gallevat anchored a good way out to sea, as a heavy surf was breaking, and Bento Caldeira jumped in to swim ashore. He was not at first allowed to land, but told to deliver his message while standing in the surf. Finally, seeing how exhausted he was and what a long way he had swum, they let him come ashore; and he was followed by Bastião Álvares da Fonseca and Álvaro Freyre and various others. They told us what had happened, and that they had a junk with its prau, in which there would be room for us all. And after we had all spoken with each other and exchanged mutual congratulations between friends and acquaintances, we knelt down in front of the cross which the padre held in his hands, and we all gave many thanks to God and begged him for mercy with a loud voice, and Bento Caldeira said he would like to embark the sick in the gallevat, but we were not able to do so, since it could only be reached by swimming. And thus they withdrew with many lobsters and pieces of the crocodile which we gave them, as well as many coconuts and *palmitos* which they took on board, telling us that the next day we would reach the place where the ships were, and that meanwhile they would sail along in sight of us and keep us company.

Reverting to our march: we found ourselves this day in a sorry and agonizing plight; because after our start at dawn we never found any drinking water, and the sun was so hot that it roasted us. And in the vain hope of finding some soon, we kept on until two o'clock in the afternoon, when we reached a place where it seemed as if there might be some, since there were many clearings in the jungle there, but we never found it, however hard we tried. And while we were in this anguish and affliction, it so happened that a soldier cut open a green cane from one of the many that were hanging down from tall trees and bent over towards the ground (resembling the canes in Portugal and shaped like them but these are massive, very tough and strong, being used everywhere in these parts for cordage both by land and sea), and when he did so a trickle of water ran out. The soldier being extremely thirsty, put the cane to his mouth and found that this water was very good and sweet, so he drank his fill thereof. He told us of this unexpected discovery, whereupon we all did the same and we drank and refreshed ourselves to our hearts' content. And thus Our Lord helped us once again. Having taken our *sesta*, we went on our way, in which we spent the rest of the day and a good part of the night, since it was very difficult ground and we could not find any water, until just before eleven o'clock, when we found some among some rocks where we least expected it, and the gallevat anchored opposite us here. We caught here so many fish by moon-light in some pools, that we left a lot of them there—many very large quabs, tasty *choupas*, and innumerable lobsters. We spent more of that night in cooking and eating than in resting and sleeping. At daybreak on the Wednesday before Easter, the occupants of the gallevat took their leave of us, telling us that if we marched well we would meet the rest of our people that same day, and that meanwhile they might have need of them there. We then continued on our line of march, from which we never turned aside, being so anxious to reach our journey's end, and not believing anything save what we saw with our own eyes.

On Good Friday, 4 April, two launches came and anchored near where our ships were, but did not see them as the day had not yet quite dawned, and the captain at once sent the skiff and the gallevat against them. And when those opened fire with their prow-pieces, the Blacks immediately jumped overboard and swam to an island that was close by. These launches and another skiff were laden with very good provisions which they were taking elsewhere, for which most welcome alms they all gave great thanks to God, for there was such a quantity of provisions that there was hardly room to stow them. And at nine o'clock in the morning there arrived the other launch laden with the same sort of pro-visions. This vessel was likewise taken, and the Blacks jumped overboard into the sea where they were drowned. These launches were about the same size as the barks of Coina.[1]

[1] A. Sergio (ed. *HTM*, II, 98 n.) explains that these were boats which ferried passengers between Lisbon and the southern bank of the Tagus. The original word in the text is *lanchara*, probably derived from the Malay *lanchar-an*, 'quick, nimble'. See *JMBRAS*, VIII (1930), 159.

Our people in the ships were highly delighted at having secured so many vessels and provisions, and they were anxious to meet us as soon as possible. And the captain wishing to make the most of this good news, and to be the first to give it to the wretched people who were marching along the shore, in order to lighten the burden of their hardships, he at once started out to meet us, leaving the ships under the command of trustworthy and reliable persons. We met each other at four o'clock in the afternoon, with many tears of joy on both sides; and the captain embraced us one by one, begging pardon for his previous behaviour. This was a direct intervention of Providence, whereby all of us there would have been saved, had it not been for our own subsequent carelessness and over-confidence, which humiliated us as I will relate below.

Continuing on our way we met the other people who came with boats to fetch us. I will not describe the tears and embraces when we met; for the discreet reader will realize what they must have been like between persons who were closely united by ties of friendship and blood, and who had never expected to see each other again, and how each one of us told the other what had happened to him.

We stayed here preparing ourselves and taking on board fire-wood and water until Easter Day. The captain distributed the commanders and seamen in the different vessels, as likewise every-thing else including the necessary provisions. And thus we started on our voyage westwards, in search of a populous island called Mintão.[1] And at dawn on Monday, the first Octave of Easter, we found ourselves off this island. And after many squalls which scattered our vessels, [some of] which were so badly waterlogged that they nearly foundered, we all got together again and anchored at the mouth of the river.[2] Many of the Blacks at once came down to meet us, they being swarthy, upstanding people, smooth-skinned and well-dressed. Some of them got into dugout-canoes to come out and see us, but they did not dare to approach too closely. The

[1] Presumably one of the Mentawai islands, though I would not like to hazard which one.

[2] The text is very confused and it seems as if some words or sentences have been omitted here and in the *HTM* version. Padre Manuel Álvares', S.J., narrative is not much better, but at least he makes it clear that the river off which they anchored was not on the island, but on the mainland of Sumatra.

captain sent the skiff to the shore, and with it a Javanese slave of his to act as interpreter and to ask them in Malay what river and land that was. They asked for one of our people as a hostage, and when he was sent to them, a very fine-looking Black, who seemed to be one of the principal persons, came out to us. He told us that that was the river of 'Menencabo', where there was then living a son of the king of Campar.[1] When he learnt that we were Portuguese, he said that we could go up the river, and thus avoid anchoring off that very dangerous coast. He added that they were great friends of the Portuguese and drove a thriving trade with our people at Malacca, and that he would provide us with everything we needed. The captain, impressed by this speech, ordered us to sail up the river; although there were differences of opinion about the advisability of this action, since some people said that we ought not to trust these Blacks, while others said we should.

A hundred Blacks came to see us this day; and on Saturday morning, 12 April, there came to the flagship the Xabandar of the land, whose position is like that of a governor.[2] He was well accompanied, and made many proffers to the captain. He said that we could stay there in all security, for he was the sheikh of this land, and vassal of a king who was a great friend of the Portuguese. This king lived at a distance of a day or two's journey, and as a message about our arrival had already been sent to him, it

---

[1] Couto (*Década VII*, Livro 9, cap. XVI) states that the river was located 'three degrees below the Line' or thereabouts. I would tentatively locate it in or near Muko-muko. The Vaz Dourado maps of 1568 and 1575 (Plate V), though based in part on information derived from the castaways, place Indrapura too far south, but show 'Manacaboo' roughly where Muko-muko is. In the Linschoten map of Sumatra (p. 32 of the English 1598 edition) 'Manancabo' has been shifted still further south and below (instead of above) Indrapura ('Andrepuro'). For Campar, or Kampar, and its relations with Malacca, cf. M. A. Meilink-Roelofsz, *Asian Trade and European Influence, 1500–1630*, pp. 30, 52, 80, 142. For the kingdom of Minangkabau, cf. G. Ferrand, *Malaka, Le Malayu et Malayur* (Paris, 1918), pp. (99)–(130), and Meilink-Roelofsz, *op. cit.* under the entry in the index. Couto, *Década VII*, Livro 9, cap. XVI, states that at this period the Minangkabauers would sometimes bring to Malacca as much as 'six, seven, and eight *candils* of gold' at a time. The *candil* was a South Indian weight, often equated at about 500 lb., but varying much in different parts.

[2] *Shāh-Bandar*, a title of Persian origin, usually translated as 'harbour-master'. He often was head of the customs, and sometimes had judicial as well as administrative functions, exercising (as here) supervision over visiting foreigners.

would not be long before he came. We should therefore come some distance up the river, where we would be safer. The captain replied with due thanks and acknowledgements for all this, and said that he would do so. We immediately weighed anchor and went some way up the river, where we anchored close inshore and near the *Baleus*[1] of the king. On this day some of the Blacks came to barter with chickens and rice and other things.

On the Sunday following, 13th of the month, at two o'clock in the afternoon, the king came down the river, to the accompaniment of many kettle-drums, conch-shells, hunting-horns and little bells. He brought with him as many as eighty canoes filled with armed men, looking very fine with their krisses, most of them very valuable, and shields and assegais of gleaming iron. The king was saluted by our artillery on his arrival; and on landing he went to his *bandel*,[2] taking his seat on a high place which had been prepared for him, his principal men ranging themselves below him. And before the captain went to speak with him, he sent him a present by António Soares, page of the royal household; for it is a general rule in these regions that nobody can appear before the king with empty hands. The present consisted of four ells of scarlet cloth-in-grain, and four of crimson velvet, and as many more of satin of the same colour, and a piece of green velvet, and some very beautiful crystal glass cups, and a very costly mirror. The king was delighted with this and said that he had never expected to receive anything at all from some shipwrecked people. And on his asking what the captain was doing, they replied that he was eating. To which he retorted that when kings put in an appearance it was no time for captains to be eating—an unexpectedly pointed remark by a barbarian. After António Soares had returned, the captain

[1] From the Malay *Balai*, hall of audience, court of an official. Cf. Dalgado, *Glossário Luso-Asiático*, I, 361–4. As can be seen from the drawings made *in situ* by Manuel Álvares, S.J., these *Baleus* were merely thatched wooden sheds, open on all sides, with a platform raised some distance above the ground. The Padre also tells us that the junk stranded going over the bar and eventually broke up, though all the people and goods were safely landed. Neither the 1565 text nor the *HTM* version make any mention of this incident.

[2] Derived from *bandar*, a wharf, and applied by extension to the waterfront (or other) district where foreigners or traders were settled to form their own self-contained community. Cf. *Hobson-Jobson*, p. 58; Dalgado, *Glossário Luso-Asiático*, I, 91–3.

at once went ashore, accompanied by three or four persons dressed as finely as possible in the circumstances, in order to visit and speak with the king. This latter was a very gentlemanly looking youth, richly dressed, with a gold-decorated kris, and a very costly turban on his head. He entertained and paid much honour to our people, with every sign of pleasure, telling the captain through a Black who spoke excellent Portuguese, that he could ask him for what he wanted, for he would do everything for him, since he was a son of the king of Minangkabau, a brother in arms of the king of Portugal. He said that if the captain wanted to send some men overland to Malacca, that he would have them safely escorted there within the space of ten days and handed over to the captain inside that fortress. The captain thanked him for these assurances and related to him the story of our misadventures hitherto. The king professed great sympathy and replied that he was ready to help us in any way which we might require; and he gave leave to his people thenceforth to sell and barter provisions with us. He added that he would like us to sell him our artillery, which he was most eager to acquire, or that we would give it to him in exchange for some large ship in which we could all leave. The captain declined this proposal with fair words, saying that the artillery was not his but belonged to the king of Portugal; and that he had to hand it over to the viceroy of India who would return it to our king. He added that if His Highness was waging war with some of his neighbours, then we would go and fight there in his service. The king was satisfied with this answer and dismissed us, saying that his Bendara[1] would explain and arrange everything, and he asked us once again to bring in the artillery as he would very much like to see it.[2] And thenceforward the local people came and

[1] The *Bendhara's* functions varied somewhat at different times and places, but at Malacca and elsewhere he was the highest official in the land. 'A sort of Prime Minister, [he] was in the first place Chancellor and Lord of the Treasury, but also Chief Justice for all civil and criminal affairs. He could condemn people of all ranks to death; not even noblemen or persons of foreign nationality were outside his jurisdiction' (M. A. Meilink-Roelofsz, *Asian Trade and European Influence*, p. 41).

[2] The desire of Asian potentates to acquire European cannon was most marked throughout the sixteenth to eighteenth centuries from Persia to Japan, as attested in the Portuguese, Dutch, English and French records. Even where Asian rulers had gun-foundries of their own, they vastly preferred European guns, as exemplified by

bartered hens, capons, and rice, for knives, nails and other things, with which we were very pleased and felt as secure as if we had completed the voyage and were safely in Malacca. So many were the Blacks who came to barter with us, bringing a lot of rice, hens, capons, yams, figs, salt, mad-apples, pepper and other provisions, together with some gold-dust, and they showed themselves so friendly and mixed with us so freely, that we abandoned the good order and strict discipline which we had formerly maintained, so that nobody mounted guard or thought of maintaining a good watch. Moreover, everyone slept ashore and nobody in the boats, for they felt as safe as they would have done in Lisbon.[1]

Owing to this carelessness, over-confidence, and the feigned friendliness of the Blacks, we never took any notice of the numerous canoes which kept arriving from elsewhere in these four or five days, laden with men at arms who lay concealed under coconuts which covered them. During this time they plotted and resolved to make an end of us, most or nearly all of our people being on shore, as I said. And so likewise was Dona Francisca, who came to be with her husband when he had an attack of the stone, she being a very comely girl and a very lady-like one.[2] At dawn on 17 April, when it was raining hard and thundering still more so,

the Japanese official who told Richard Cocks in 1617 that the Shogun 'would rather have one cast in England than ten of those cast in Japan'. In the case of Indonesian rulers, this desire for cannon was accompanied by the belief that they had some kind of sacro-magical efficacy. Cf. the series of articles by the late K. Crucq in the *Tijdschrift voor Taal-Land-en Volkenkunde van het Kon. Genoots-chap van Kunsten en Wetenschappen*, vols. 70–81 (Batavia, 1930–41), on the 'holy cannon' at Batavia, Bantam, Surakarta, Japara, Macassar and elsewhere in Indonesia, and the article in *JMBRAS*, XXXVIII (2), 156–72.

[1] As Francisco de Sousa, S.J., rightly observed in his *Oriente Conquistado* (I, 185, of the 1710 edition): 'The people lived ashore in some large *bayleos*, with that lack of caution in the Portuguese which has so often been punished in the East, but never amended.'

[2] Francisco de Sousa, S.J. (*op. et loc. cit.*) adds with his usual caustic humour that D. Francisca 'was as finely dressed as if it was her wedding-day'. The natives were so aston-ished at her beauty and rich attire, that they forthwith conspired to kidnap her for their king. Diogo do Couto (*Década VII*, Livro 9, cap. XVI) also states that D. Francisca Sardinha 'was one of the most beautiful women of her time', and adds that her great beauty and rich attire was the unwitting cause of the disaster that followed. It was certainly not the only cause, though it may well have been contributory. Cf. p. 10 above.

the Moors[1] suddenly fell upon us with loud yells, and there must have been at least 2,000 of them. As they caught us asleep and absolutely unprepared, they killed many people before they could realize what was happening, so that more than fifty died on the spot; and many others escaped badly wounded, fleeing along the beach to the vessels, while some others formed themselves into a body and showed fight. About thirty of us had got together when we encountered a squadron of about 500 Blacks, who attacked us with loud cries as if confident of victory. We charged them to the shout of 'Santiago', though we had only two pikes and a few swords, most of which were broken, and with our capes and jerkins [instead of shields] on our arms, and we drove them back up the beach. Meanwhile our ship, the skiff, and the gallevat, with the captain and the others who had been able to get aboard, came down the river, bombarding the beach and rescuing those who were along it from out of the hands of the enemy who were trying to stop them embarking, in which exploit our people did highly courageous deeds. And seventy of our people were killed,[2] among whom were many persons of quality. We left behind there Dona Francisca, who was sleeping with her husband ashore, as I said above. He came in front of her defending himself with a broadsword, but he was surrounded by many of the enemy and killed, for which we reason we suspect that she will still be alive. And there were lost with her one of her brothers named António Rodrigues de Azevedo, and a girl who came with us from Brazil.[3]

[1] *Mouros*, generic term used by the Portuguese for Muslims from Morocco to Mindanao.

[2] *HTM* version gives the number of the dead as sixty, and Manuel Álvares, S.J., as 'fifty or more'. Cf. A. Franco, *Imagem da Virtude*, II, 370–1.

[3] Padre Álvares, who gives a much more detailed description of this debacle, makes it clear that D. Francisca's husband, Diogo Pereira de Vasconcelos, fled precipitately at the first alarm and was one of the first to get aboard the boats. Couto also agrees with Padre Álvares that the man who tried to save D. Francisca was the herculean master, João Luís, who kept her assailants at bay for some time with his broadsword until he was overwhelmed by numbers and killed. D. Francisca was then carried off into the interior, presumably to be presented to the local raja for his harem; though Padre Francisco de Sousa, S.J., alleges, without citing any authority, that 'the unfortunate Helen, seeing herself deprived of her liberty and of her husband, died of chagrin' (*Oriente Conquistado*, I, 185 of the 1710 edition). Padre Álvares also makes it clear that most of those who did escape owed their lives to the courage

We lost all our baggage on shore, and, what was worse for us, all or most of our provisions, which had been laid out to dry. Our total material losses must have been worth more than 10,000 *cruzados*. And having got over the bar by nine o'clock in the morning, we continued on our voyage, very sad and miserable, most of us stark naked and many badly wounded, ten or twelve of whom subsequently died. No tears were shed for the dead, because each of us had enough to weep about over himself, or to tell how he had escaped, and we did not really feel safe yet. And after many days during which we suffered countless storms, tribulations and misadventures, we fetched up off the port of Banda in Sunda on 27 April, without our knowing where we were.[1] And we were all exhausted by the work of rowing and other hardships. so we clamoured to Our Lord for mercy, which he never denied. And thus he permitted that on this day about twelve o'clock noon, a prau passed so close to us that the occupants could hear us talking Portuguese. In it was a Portuguese youth, and he at once realized that we must be the castaways he had heard of and was looking for. He went to the big ship where he told and showed us that we were off the port in front of Sunda, in sight of our great ships, of which Pero Barreto Rolim was captain-major.[2] He added that João Gonçalves had already arrived there with his companions; and the captain-major, knowing we were due, had sent him back with provisions to look for us. Anyone can imagine how extremely delighted we were with such unexpected news that we could hardly believe it. And the captain gave him as a

of António Dias, the previously mentioned (pp. 86, 89) *casado* of São Tomé, who was evidently the leader of the party in which Henrique Dias says he fought. For the career of D. Francisca's cowardly husband see G. Schurhammer, S.J., 'Doppelganger in Portugiesisch-Asien', in Hans Fläsche [ed.], *Aufsätze zur portugiesischen Kulturgeschichte*, 1 (Münster, 1960), 217.

[1] By 'Banda in Sunda' is obviously meant the port of Bantam. 'Many days' is an exaggeration. They put to sea after the debacle on 17 or 18 April and reached the offing of Bantam on 27 April, so they were only nine or ten days at sea. Padre Álvares, S.J., gives a much more detailed account of their sufferings in this interval.

[2] For the distinguished career of Pedro (Pero) Barreto Rolim, Captain-Major of the China–Japan voyage in 1562, see C. R. Boxer, *The Great Ship from Amacon, 1555–1640* (Lisbon, 1959), pp. 28–9, where, however, the date of the wreck of the *São Paulo* is misprinted 1562. Manuel Álvares, S.J., states that Ruy de Melo da Camara was related to him.

reward a piece of cloth-in-grain for a *cabaia*,[1] and he returned with the news of our arrival.

When he had gone and given this news to all our Portuguese there, both those ashore and those afloat, they all embarked in the ships' boats and in many praus that there were in the port, and with great happiness and rejoicing they came out to look for us, contending with each other as to who should arrive first. And late in the evening, when it was almost night, the flagship's boat reached us, closely followed by all the others; and not a few disputes and arguments arose because each one wished to take more refugees than the other, with words worthy of great love and pity, and still more of charity. There was no lack of tears when they saw our miserable and pitiable condition, and they consoled us with kind and tender words, and still more with favours and good works, like parents to their children, clothing us all in rich Chinese silks of very diverse and beautiful colours; so that it seemed to us as if we were enchanted or in a dream. They also lent money to most people so that they could go and earn their living. And they did all this irrespective of whether some of us had relatives there, but simply because we were their compatriots and could give them news of Portugal.

There were about 240 Portuguese there, of whom 160 were on the point of sailing for China, and the others were staying to winter in Sunda and Calapa, twelve leagues from there, where there was a king who was more friendly to us than any other in those parts, including the traitor of Minangkabau; and the Portuguese are accustomed to trade here regularly and go to China with their merchandize in the annual monsoon.

We stayed here in Sunda and in Calapa (where the Portuguese who live there were no less kind to us than those of Sunda) for twenty-six days, in order to rest and recuperate.[2] Ten or twelve of

---

[1] *Cabaia, cabaya*, originally applied by the Portuguese to the surcoat or long tunic worn by wealthy Arabs and Indians. Later applied to almost any form of dress in dishabille and widely used by the Dutch in Java. Cf. The extensive notices in *Hobson-Jobson*, pp. 137–8, and Dalgado, *Glossário Luso-Asiático*, I, 158–9.

[2] Sunda Calapa (Sunda Kalapa) is invariably identified by modern writers as the port which later was called successively Jakarta (Jacatra), Batavia, and now Jakarta again. Cf. the detailed note in A. Cortesão, *Suma Oriental of Tomé Pires*, I,

our men died here from over-eating, because their enfeebled stomachs could not take all the food they gorged. From here we left for Malacca, by order of the Captain-Major Pero Barreto, very well supplied and fitted out with everything we needed. Gonçalo Vaz de Carvalho, captain and owner of a great ship, gained outstanding honour in this respect, for he took all the sick aboard his ship and carried them to Malacca at his own expense, which cost him a great deal.[1] We reached Malacca, on the 25 July when the captain, *fronteiros*[2] and citizens immediately strove to show themselves no less hospitable than those of Sunda and Calapa, for they tried to outdo each other in favours and good works. João de Mendoça, who was then captain of the fortress, was particularly prominent in this respect, clothing and lodging all the poor people, and giving free meals at his table to 130 men during the time of his captaincy, helping others outside, and spending a lot from his own pocket.[3] And here in Malacca, owing to the unhealthi-ness of this place and the fact that some of us were already suffer-ing from infectious diseases and were exhausted and debilitated by our hardships, over twenty people died. The rest of us are awaiting here the monsoon for India, which will be in December. And some of our companions went in the fleet to China, while others stayed in Sunda and Calapa with their friends, relatives, and acquaintances.

172, and M. A. Meilink-Roelofsz, *Asian Trade and European Influence*, pp. 83, 113–14, 241. The Vaz Dourado map of 1568 also shows 'Cumdacalapa' as situated slightly to the east of 'bamtão', thus supporting this identification. However, both Henrique Dias and Padre Manuel Álvares, S.J., explicitly distinguish between Sunda and Capala as being neighbouring but different ports. I can only suggest, therefore, that at this time Bantam was (sometimes) called Sunda and Jacatra was called Calapa. Confusion is made worse confounded by the fact that Sunda was also the term for the westernmost region of Java.

[1] Manuel Álvares, S.J., is even more emphatic in his praise of the generosity and charity of Gonçalo Vaz de Carvalho, who was trading between Siam and Japan in 1563 (C. R. Boxer, *Great Ship from Amacon*, p. 29).

[2] Lit. 'frontiersmen' and usually applied to those who garrisoned the Moroccan strongholds of Ceuta, Tangier, Arzila and Mazagão etc. For their life at Malacca see I. A. Macgregor, 'Notes on the Portuguese in Malaya, 1511–1641', in *JMBRAS* xxviii (Singapore, 1955), 5–47.

[3] Confirmed by Padre Manuel Álvares, S.J. João de Mendoça was Governor of Portuguese India from the 29 February to the 3 September 1564. He was killed in the disastrous battle of El-Ksar el-Kebir, 4 August 1578. Couto (*Década VII*, Livro 10, ch. xix) likewise pays tribute to his generosity and honesty.

And in truth whosoever considers this matter well will not be astonished at these trials and tribulations, for Man was born for them, like the Holy Job said, 'as the bird is to fly'.[1] And much more so, do humans deserve them for their sins, as is said in the psalm *Beati quorum*.[2] Many and various are the punishments inflicted on the transgressor; and all these misfortunes and trials, and others different from these, are prophesied for all those who go to sea and plough the waves of the ocean, by the royal prophet David in his Psalm 106,[3] where speaking of this matter he says: 'They that go down to the sea in ships, that do business in great waters; these see the works of the Lord and his wonders in the deep. For he commandeth and raiseth the stormy wind, which lifteth up the waves thereof. They mount up to the heaven, they go down again to the depths; their soul is melted because of trouble. They reel to and fro, and stagger like a drunken man, and are at their wits' end. Then they cry unto the Lord in their trouble, and he bringeth them out of their distress. He maketh the storm a calm, so that the waves thereof are still. Then they are glad because they be quiet; so he bringeth them unto their desired haven.'

Since this is already so well proved and known, as this holy prophet tells us, all these miseries and many more are the lot of him who sails the sea. Wherefore experience teaches us that whoever can avoid a maritime life lives in greater tranquillity of spirit and avoids such strife. It is better to live ashore less desirous of riches than to traverse the sea in quest of such transitory and fleeting things. And let us live on land like good Christians, obeying the law of God within the fold of the Holy Mother Church of Rome, and multiplying the talents which the Lord entrusted to each one of us. For if we give him a good reckoning therefor, we shall deserve to hear from him in the port of Salvation that sweet voice: 'Well done thou good and faithful servant: thou hast been faithful over a few things, I will make thee ruler over many things: enter

---

[1] This seems to be a misremembered version of Job iv. 7 (Anglican Authorized Version): 'man is born unto trouble as the sparks fly upwards', possibly confused with Job ix. 26: 'as the eagle hasteth to the prey'.

[2] Psalm xxxii in the Anglican Authorized version (31 in the RC).

[3] Psalm cvii. 23–30 in the Anglican Authorized Version.

thou into the joy of thy lord'[1]—which is the glory that He in his goodness wishes to give us. Amen.

Here ends the Shipwreck of the Great Ship *São Paulo*, written by a trustworthy man who was an eyewitness and participant in all this. And it was printed in the house of the widow formerly wife of Germão Gaillhard.[2] On the eighth of the month of April. Year of M.D.LXV.

---

[1] Matthew, xxv. 21 in the Anglican Authorized Version.

[2] Germain Gaillard, a French printer who worked in Portugal from 1519 until his death in 1561, principally at Lisbon, but also at Coimbra in 1530–1. For a list of the books printed by him and by his widow and heirs, see A. J. Anselmo, *Bibliografia das obras impressas em Portugal no século XVI* (Lisbon, 1926), pp. 160–92.

NAVFRAGIO, QVE

PASSOV IORGE DALBVQVERQVE

Coelho, Capitão, & Gouernador de Paranaìmbuco.

Em Lisboa: Impreſſo com licença da Sancta Inquiſição: Por
Antonio Aluarez. Anno M. CCCCCCI.

Vendemſe em caſa de Antonio Ribeyro Libreyro; Em a rua noua.

SHIPWRECK SUFFERED BY
JORGE D'ALBUQUERQUE COELHO
Captain and Governor of Pernambuco

In Lisbon: Printed with the licence of the Holy Inquisition *by Antonio Alvarez. Anno M.CCCCCI.*

For sale in the house of Antonio Ribeiro, Bookseller;
In the Rua Nova.[1]

[1] António Alvarez, one of the most productive of the Lisbon printers, active between 1586 and 1606. His printing is more notable for its quantity than its quality. The present work, like many others from his press, contains a fair crop of misprints and the proof-reading was evidently careless. For a list of his works published before 1606 see: A. J. Anselmo, *Bibliografia das obras impressas em Portugal no século xvi* (Lisbon, 1926), pp. 1–15.

António Ribeiro, a Lisbon printer and bookseller, who flourished in the last quarter of the sixteenth century, a list of whose works during this period is given in Anselmo's *Bibliografia*, pp. 267–87. It is not clear why António Ribeiro had this book printed by António Alvarez, when the former had his own press and his productions were of a higher standard than those of his colleague.

LICENCES

I saw and examined this narrative of the shipwreck suffered by Jorge d'Albuquerque. It is a pious and Catholic treatise which contains nothing offensive to Christian ears. There is annexed to it a *Prosopopaea* written by Bento Teyexeyra and dedicated to the said Jorge d'Albuquerque. There is no reason why it should not be printed.   FREY MANOEL COELHO[1]

In view of the above information, this shipwreck with the Prosopopaea annexed to it may be printed. After they are printed, they must be returned to this Council for comparison with the original, and to be given the licence for publication. In Lisbon, 20 March, 1601.

Marcos Teyxeyra.   BERTHOLOMEU DAFONSECA

[1] Fr. Manuel Coelho, O.P., entered the Dominican Order in 1568, and soon became one of the most famous Portuguese theologians and preachers of his time. He was a prominent censor of books for the Inquisition, and as such he licensed the 1591 edition of Camões' *Lusíadas* and the 1614 edition of Fernão Mendes Pinto's *Peregrinaçam*. He died in 1622, full of years and honours.

TO THE LORD
IORGE D'ALBUQUERQUE COELHO

Sonnet

The Great Croesus was rich, but miserly;
Alexander liberal, but haughty;
Hannibal unassuming, but lecherous;
Scipio chaste, but very scornful;
Tully, affable but of low birth;
Caesar was illustrious, but vindictive.
We always find the loftiest heroes of Antiquity
prisoners to some vice or other.
But I see you as rich as Croesus,
and with the helping hand of Alexander,
and the humanity of another Hannibal, the purity
of another Scipio.
You have the intelligence and the majesty of Tully and Caesar;
without covetousness, without vice, without ambition,
without anger, without fear, and without cruelty.

PROLOGUE

To Jorge d'Albuquerque Coelho
Captain and Governor of Pernambuco
New Lusitania

ALTHOUGH the duty of a servant is, after all, enough to induce me to employ myself in things of your service for as long as my life lasts, withal the second obligation which binds me to you, which is formed by the favours which I continuously receive from Your Worship and the special love with which you make them—these are fresh inducements for me always to attempt arduous enterprises in your service. And just as the recollection of happy and pros-perous days, according to what some philosophers tell us, causes sadness and grief when we find ourselves in very different circum-stances, so, on the other hand, does the recollection of past toils and tribulations give us happiness and contentment when we are no longer enduring them, And forasmuch as Your Worship's exploits in all circumstances reflect credit on you, as for example in the campaign for the pacification of Pernambuco, where the council, the valour, and the strength of your youthful heart sufficed during the space of five consecutive years (in the government of the Queen-Dowager Dona Catarina of glorious memory)[1] to dominate and subjugate the most barbarous and indomitable nation that we have yet discovered, and you left that province conquered and pacified at the cost of much of your blood—for in a single assault on a stronghold of the enemy you were the main reason for the victory, although receiving nine arrow-wounds in the chest and the face. We see that you excelled in the same way in the unfortunate expedition to Africa, where it seems that For-tune, wishing to give such a frightful blow to Portuguese prestige, and which virtually all of us have reason to lament for ever, yet

---

[1] D. Catarina de Austria (1507–78), widow of D. João III of Portugal, who acted as regent from 1557 to 1563. For a detailed survey of Pernambuco at this period see J. F. de Almeida Prado, *Pernambuco e as capitanias do Norte, 1530–1630* (4 vols., São Paulo, 1941).

wished Your Worship alone to appear to such advantage that it seemed as if you were victorious. For in the most terrible struggle of the battle you give your horse to your king and fulfil the loyal duty of your blood and of your stalwart spirit, although wounded and pierced by so many bullets and spears for helping to defend his life.[1] Nor are your qualities less resplendent in time of peace, whether in political or in domestic and private concerns, revealing your quick intelligence, urbane conversation, and bountiful generosity. These are qualities which were seldom bestowed save only on true grandees, but we see them all reflected in Your Worship, as in a shining mirror. And so that you should have had an opportunity to display them by sea, you were likewise persecuted therein, in such wise that the tribulations of your ship-wreck aroused compassionate astonishment in many people. And lest the memory of it should be clean forgotten, and being desirous of rendering a small service to Your Worship, I took upon myself the responsibility of newly renewing this your shipwreck, so that the recollection thereof, while serving as an example of pious resolution to many people, should also cause you pleasure and joy in this tranquil time of your spirit. There are also some verses annexed to it, written by a more pious than poetic soul.[2] May Your Worship receive all this with that natural benevolence which you have always shown me in everything; for this will suffice to repay me for the trouble I have taken therein. May God keep and prosper Your Worship's life and estate for many and lengthy years, for his holy service. ANTONIO RIBEYRO[3]

[1] El-Ksar el-Kebir, 4 August 1578. Cf. p. 15 above.

[2] Bento Teixeira, author of the *Prosopopéia*. Cf. pp. 16–18 above.

[3] This dedication by the Lisbon printer, publisher and bookseller, António Ribeiro, was suppressed by Gomes de Brito in the *HTM* version of 1736. It was substituted by one addressed 'to the reader' allegedly by the author to whom Gomes de Brito wrongly ascribed the original—Bento Teixeira Pinto. Cf. introduction, p. 16 above.

Chapter the First

In the time when the Queen Dowager Catarina, grandmother of the King Dom Sebastião, was governing this kingdom of Portugal on behalf of her grandson, there came news from the captaincy of Pernambuco in Brazil, that most of the chiefs of the savage tribes in the said captaincy had risen in revolt against the Portuguese and had besieged most of the settlements and towns that there were in the said captaincy. For this reason, the said queen ordered Duarte Coelho d'Albuquerque, who had inherited the captaincy, to go and succour it. And realizing how necessary it was that he should take with him his brother, Jorge d'Albuquerque Coelho, he asked the queen to order his said brother to accompany him in the relief expedition for that captaincy in order to help him therein. This was duly done, as the said lady queen ordered that he should go and render this service in that crisis, for the honour which he would thereby do to God, and to the king her grandson, and to the common weal of this kingdom. And he arrived in the said captaincy in the year 1560, when he was twenty years old. And since he already had some experience of active service, both ashore and afloat, after his brother, Duarte Coelho d'Albuquerque, had taken possession of the captaincy and was serving as captain and governor thereof, he called a council, which was attended by some of the more senior Fathers of the Company [of Jesus] who were in the college that the said Fathers have in the town of Olinda, one of the principal towns which there is in the captaincy of Pernambuco, together with many honourable men of those who were eligible to hold municipal office; and they unanimously agreed that Jorge d'Albuquerque Coelho should be elected as general of the war and conqueror of the land of the said captaincy. As they told him that it was very fitting for the service of God and the king, and the welfare of the people of that captaincy, that he should accept and serve the said charge, he did so; and he adventured and risked his life to render this service to God and to our lord the king, and for the welfare of the people, and to do what the said lady queen, Dona Catarina, had ordered and com

(114)

manded him. And he began to wage war on the enemy in the said year of 1560, taking with him many of his soldiers and ser' vants whom he provided with food, drink, clothing and shoes, at his own cost. And he spent five years in conquering the said captaincy, enduring many and great hardships by night and day, in summer and winter, in the hills, deserts and woods. He and his soldiers and servants were wounded many times, fighting sometimes on foot and sometimes on horseback. And when he withdrew to any one of the settlements or towns where our Portu' guese live, and found he could not reach it before nightfall, then he camped at the foot of the trees in the most beautiful wood that he could find, and ordered shacks to be made of branches and palm leaves, in which his soldiers could shelter. And these leafy shacks he had made by the numerous slaves he took with him, who also served to reconnoitre the terrain and to mount guard over the encampment together with some of the soldiers. All this campaigning was carried out on such short commons and want of supplies, that often they had nothing to eat except land'crabs and manioc'flour, and the wild fruits of the field. And with these things, and the encouraging words which he gave his soldiers, he kept them satisfied and contented. And when he captured some stronghold or village from the savages, he surfeited the soldiers with many pigs, hens, and other local provisions which he found in the said villages. And as soon as he had taken one village, he immediately moved against the next and took it easily, since the defenders did not have time to prepare to resist. And with this diligence and the speed which he used in this campaign, he was able to conquer the region in five years, although it was so thickly populated by hostile tribes that when he arrived in the said cap' taincy on the orders of the queen, Dona Catarina, the Portuguese who lived in the town of Olinda did not dare to venture further into the interior than one or two leagues, nor further along the coast than three or four leagues. And after he had completed the conquest, they could safely go fifteen or twenty leagues into the interior, and sixty along the coast, which is the extent of the said captaincy's jurisdiction. And leaving the captaincy conquered, and the enemy subdued and pacified, after suing for peace which he granted them, he embarked and set sail for this kingdom in the ship *Santo António*, in which voyage there happened to him what is related in this shipwreck.

And in this campaign of conquest, there befell him many great, notable, and extraordinary things, of which his soldiers and ser/vants who accompanied him are good witnesses; as likewise also are the settlers of the said town of Olinda. And one of these things was that in the assault on one of the strongholds which he took, he received nine arrow wounds between his forehead and his navel.[1]

Jorge d'Albuquerque was now exhausted by the hardships he had undergone together with his brother, Duarte Coelho d'Albu/querque, in the exploration of the river São Francisco in the captaincy of Pernambuco in Brazil, as well as in the wars which had lasted for five years in the captaincy after the said exploration, during which time the whole captaincy had been on the verge of being lost, and everyone had suffered great hardships, hunger and mortality. Everything now being pacified, and being anxious to return to this kingdom, he embarked in a ship of two hundred tons, called the *Santo António*, which was lading in the port of the town of Olinda,[2] in the said captaincy, bound for this city of Lisbon, the Master being André Rodrigues and the pilot Álvaro Marinho, both of them experts in the art of navigation, and who had made many previous voyages.[3]

At this time there was also in that captaincy a man named

[1] A clumsy repetition of what has already been stated above, p. 115, typical of the author's confused style.

[2] Recife, the port of Olinda, was connected with the latter by a narrow spit of sand, some three miles long. As a result of the Dutch occupation in 1630–54, Recife displaced Olinda as the chief town in the captaincy of Pernambuco, though Olinda did not abandon its pretensions to paramountcy until nearly a century later. Jorge d'Albuquerque's pacification of the hinterland in 1560–5 was not so complete as is implied by the writer of the *Naufrágio*. Another large/scale punitive campaign against some of the rebellious Amerindian tribes had to be mounted by his brother, the donatory, in 1577–8, and there were other outbreaks later on. Cf. Gabriel Soares de Sousa, *Tratado Descriptivo do Brasil em 1587* (Rio de Janeiro, 1879), pp. 23–31.

[3] As noted in the introduction (pp. 18–19), the whole of the next section, which categorically ascribes the authorship of the original narrative to the passenger/pilot Afonso Luís, and the polishing of his draft to António de Castro, was omitted by Gomes de Brito from the *HTM* (and hence from all subsequent) version(s).

Afonso Luís, a pilot who was reputed to be a very good seaman and very skilful in the art of navigation. Knowing this, Jorge d'Albuquerque Coelho earnestly entreated the said Afonso Luís to embark with him in the ship which was bound from that captaincy to this kingdom, promising that he would show him all possible help and favour in the voyage, and asking him to keep a journal of everything that might happen therein. This he did, but there were so many and such noteworthy events, that he could only note down those which are written in this little book, which does not contain even a tenth part of what actually happened but which is limited to relating some of the more memorable episodes out of the many that occurred in this disastrous voyage, in which we can see the greatness of God's mercy which he vouchsafed to those who sailed in this ship, and which will suffice to console, strengthen and animate those sinners who may find themselves in similar difficulties. And after they reached this kingdom of Portugal, the said pilot, Afonso Luís, showed Jorge d'Albu-querque Coelho the diary which he had kept of everything that had happened in the voyage; and since it was not written in a good style nor in elegant and polished language, they asked a very honourable man named António de Crasto [Castro], who at that time was acting as tutor to the lord Dom Duarte,[1] and who was reputed to be a good Latinist and a good poet, to rearrange and rewrite in better style the events which were narrated in the said journal, which the said António de Crasto accordingly did in the way which you will see in this little book. And because the first printing was limited to an edition of one thousand copies, which are already all gone, it has been decided to make another edition of a thousand copies, each one of which declares and sets forth the truth as contained in this little book. Moreover, some extra sheets have been added at the end, which are bound up in the same book, and which were accidentally omitted from the first edition by an oversight.[2]

And the ship having taken in a full cargo, and Jorge d'Albu-

[1] Dom Duarte, to whom António de Castro was tutor, was the fifth Duke of Guimarães, 1541–76, a grandson of King Manuel I.
[2] The *Prosopopéia* of Bento Teixeira.

querque Coelho and everyone else having embarked, she set sail
from the said port with a fair stern wind on Wednesday the
16 May 1565.[1] They had hardly got clear of the bar when the
wind dropped, and then shifted to the opposite quarter, where it
blew so strongly that with the current of the tide which had just
begun to ebb, the ship was forced back and struck on a sandbank
at the entrance of the bar, where she remained aground for four
successive tides and would have been lost if the seas had been
heavier. And as assistance was speedily forthcoming from many
boats and other vessels, all the people and the greater part of the
large cargo were taken off. But even when lightened in this way
the ship could not be got off the bank on which she had grounded;
so they cut away her masts, and this enabled her to float off and
be got clear of the shallows. Being brought back into the port of
the town she was examined by workmen to see if she was fit to
make the voyage, and since they found that she had not been
seriously damaged, she was repaired and the cargo taken on board
again. And many of Jorge d'Albuquerque's friends, seeing that
he wished to re-embark in this ship, tried to prevent him and
urged him with many arguments not to sail in a ship which had
made such an unlucky start to her voyage, for this unfortunate
beginning augured very ill for what would occur in the next one.
And this was the common talk in the town, where all the citizens
told their friends to be careful not to sail in a ship which seemed
fated to have a thousand misfortunes on her voyage. And notwithstanding all this, neither Jorge d'Albuquerque nor his companions believed these prognostications; but on the contrary,
trusting in the mercy of Our Lord, and disregarding the vain and
empty opinions of common people, he and all his companions
re-embarked in the said ship and left the port of the town of
Olinda on Friday, 29 June, feast-day of Saint Peter and Saint
Paul, in the same year of 1565.

[1] Misprinted 'sessenta e seis' in the 1601 edition and corrected here from the
context and the *HTM* version.

Chapter II

For five days after we left the port we continued with the same favourable wind until 5 July, when it suddenly shifted and blew from the opposite quarter to the one we needed. This wind blew so hard and the ship was so overloaded that she could not bear her sails well, and we were compelled to begin throwing some of the cargo into the sea, hoping that this would make the ship more trim. But having thrown overboard as much as seemed to be making the ship labour, on the afternoon of the same day we were struck by such a heavy storm that the ship sprang a large leak, so that we were forced to give as many as six thousand discharges to the pump between night and day. And sailing with this continual leak we found ourselves on 6 July in the latitude of the Line, in heavy seas; and we were navigating in this way when a sudden gust of wind sprung our bowsprit. It seems that Our Lord thereby wished those in the ship to understand that we should go no further since we had met with so many setbacks in such a short time. When the passengers and crew saw the bowsprit sprung and the ship making a lot of water, it was decided that we should bear up for the Antilles; to which the pilot and the master replied that this could not be done, because the wind was contrary and would not serve, and with the weather as it was we could neither bear up for the Antilles nor return to the port we had left. Somewhat downcast at this reply, we continued on our voyage and on our course, since we had no other alternative. And when we reached 12° northern latitude, the wind which had brought us there dropped, and we drifted becalmed for nineteen days with frequent thunderstorms. And as soon as we had better weather, we resolved to make for the island of Cape Verde,[1] in the latitude of which we were, in order to stop our leak and to repair our sprung bowsprit. And when we were near the island and almost in sight of it, we

---

[1] The Cape Verde group contains several large islands, but as the text persistently refers to 'island' in the singular, it is probable that the one which is meant is that of Santiago, which was then the most populous and the seat of the capital (Ribeira Grande).

sighted out to seawards a French ship and a *zabra*[1] on 29 July, Feast-day of Saint Martha. And when the French sighted our ship, they followed her until three o'clock in the night, when they got within hailing distance of us and summoned us to strike. And perceiving that our people were making ready to defend themselves and fight, they did not venture to attack us forthwith, owing to the darkness of the night, but they followed in our wake so that they could board us in the morning. And on the next day, which was 30 July, we had such a violent thunderstorm just before dawn that we were forced to part company, since we could not see each other for the thick weather. And on the last day of July when we were steering for the island, we were struck by such a violent offshore wind that we could not fetch the island and were forced to continue our voyage, despite the great peril we were in with our heavy leak. And we sailed along in this weather until we reached the latitude of 37° North and were very near Newfoundland[2] as the ship ran quickly before the wind. And in this latitude of 37° North, we drifted becalmed for eight days, at the end of which, on the Feast-day of the execution of the Blessed St John the Baptist, 29 August, we had a strong and favourable wind, with which we resolved to set our course for the Islands [of the Azores], to stop our leaks, for in addition to the one which we already had, we had sprung another, so that we shipped so much water that we had to work the pump continuously night and day. By this time we were running short of both provisions and drinking-water in the ship, and we suffered greatly from hunger and thirst. And Jorge d'Albuquerque realizing the fix we were in, and knowing that there were no more provisions in the ship other than what he had brought for himself and his servants, ordered these supplies to be brought in front of everyone, and he divided them out equally in brotherly fashion among the whole ship's company, without accepting any payment, though everyone was anxious to pay him since this food was worth a lot.

[1] A vessel of Arab origin used in the Mediterranean and the Indian Ocean. 'A small beaked sailing vessel, galley rigged, but with broadside guns' (*MM*, II, 98, 103).

[2] The writer was badly out in his reckoning, as Newfoundland lies between 46° 36' and 51° 39' N. latitudes.

But he refused to take anything, which greatly pleased and consoled all those present, who lived on these provisions for some
days. But the Devil, who cannot bear to see anyone happy, sowed
strife and discord between the passengers and the crew of the ship,
which threatened us all with final ruin. But Our Lord in His
mercy wished that Jorge d'Albuquerque should learn of this, in
order to act as a mediator between them, which he did, and pacified them and made peace again, whereby we did not feel so much
the hardships which we were enduring.

Chapter III

As we were approaching the Islands [of the Azores] in the
calamitous condition which I have described, on a Monday, the
3 September, when the pilot calculated that they were in the offing,
we encountered a French pirate ship, well gunned and equipped,
as they usually are. And since our ship was defenceless and without guns, as our vessels usually are at this time, the master, the pilot
and the rest of the crew, seeing that we had virtually nothing
wherewith to defend ourselves, save only one falcon, one *berço*, and
the weapons which Jorge d'Albuquerque had brought for himself and his servants, they determined to surrender and yield themselves up to the French. At this point, Jorge d'Albuquerque spoke
up and said God forbid that the ship in which he sailed should
surrender without a fight or defending herself for as long as possible.
He therefore urged everyone to do their duty and to help him fight,
and not to surrender basely like weaklings and cowards; for if they,
or most of them, would help him to fight, then he trusted that with
the help of Our Lord they would be able to defend the ship with
the single falcon and the single *berço* which they had. And to this
end he made them an encouraging speech, in so far as the time
allowed, urging them with courageous words to help him. But as
the ship was so illprovided with weapons, and most of the people
in her were very poorspirited, Jorge d'Albuquerque could not
find anyone willing to help him defend the ship, save for seven
men who volunteered to do so. And thus with these alone, against
the opinion of all the others, he gave battle with the [two] guns,

arquebuses, and bows and arrows to the French. This fight lasted nearly three days without the French daring to board us, owing to the fierce resistance they encountered from our ship, although those who actually fought were so few, and the ship did not mount more than the *berço* and the falcon, which Jorge d'Albu⁄querque loaded, aimed and fired, since there was no gunner in the ship, nor did anyone know how to do this better than he. And the pilot, the master and the sailors, seeing that this struggle had lasted nearly three days, in which our ship and people had received much hurt from the French artillery and arquebuses, and that our gun⁄powder was running short, they demanded to Jorge d'Albu⁄querque in the name of God and of the king that he should allow them to surrender, since they could not defend themselves, and they did not want to be all killed, or drowned if the ship sunk. Those who were fighting retorted that they would never surrender so long as they had strength to resist. And the others seeing their determination (and apparently plotting together) suddenly lowered the sails and began to call out to the French to board the ship, since they had already surrendered. Jorge d'Albuquerque and the companions who were helping him, seeing such a sudden and unexpected development, wanted to kill the pilot and the master for making such a display of weakness and cowardice, but lack of time and the critical condition they were in prevented them from doing so. For no sooner had the ship struck (which was a Wednesday, 5 September) than seventeen Frenchmen boarded her over the stern quarter, armed with naked weapons, including swords, shields, pistols, and some of them with halberds. They took possession of the ship without anyone being able to stop them, and seeing the state it was in, they asked with what artillery and munitions we had defended ourselves for so many days and how many of us had fought. And finding that there were only the one *berço* and the one falcon in the ship, as stated above, they were greatly astonished, and still more so when they were told how few people had actually fought. And the French captain was in⁄formed that Jorge d'Albuquerque was the one who made them defend the ship all that time, which our people told him so as to throw all the blame on him. And the French captain came up to Jorge d'Albuquerque, and said to him with a proud and rueful countenance: 'What a rash heart you must have, that you tried to defend your ship with such a defective armament against one so well equipped as ours is, and which has sixty arquebusiers?' To which he retorted very confidently: 'By this you can see what a fool I was to embark in such an ill-equipped ship, for if she had the surplus of what you have, I truly believe that you and I would be in very different circumstances than those in which we are now. But I blame my sins for this, since it is on their account that Our Lord allowed me to embark in so ill-found and defenceless a ship as you see, and so that you can see me in the state that you do now. And you can also credit the good fortune which you enjoyed against me to the treachery of my companions, the pilot, the master, and the sailors, who turned against me. For if they had helped me as did these my soldier friends and comrades, then you would not be in this ship as a victor nor I as a vanquished.' The French captain, seeing the great confidence and conviction with which Jorge d'Albuquerque spoke, said to him: 'I am not surprised at your resolution, for this is something which every good soldier has, but I am surprised that you should try and defend a ship so ill-found as this one is, with so little equipment, and with fewer companions. But do not be downcast, for this is the fortune of War, which today favours some and tomorrow others. And since you are such a good soldier, I will treat you very well, as also those who helped you to fight, for this is what is due to a man who does his duty and behaves in a way befitting his quality.' The French ship which boarded ours carried nearly eighty men, among whom were many Englishmen and Scotsmen, and some Portuguese. She was as well fitted out as a warship could possibly be, for nearly all her men were armed with cold steel, and some of them with greaves, swords, daggers, shields, halberds and pistols for use in boarding, and arquebuses wherewith to shoot. Each one kept his weapons in his quarters, so that he could grab them at any time when he might need them. And the ship was dressed and pavisaded from stern to stern, with its dummy boarding nets, and the round-tops enclosed and protected very well, and the hull so paid and clean that it seemed as if the ship had just been painted and that was her first day at sea, whereas she had been cruising for many months and had already taken several prizes.

Chapter IV

When the French saw themselves masters of our ship and realized that she had a valuable cargo, they set their course for their own country. And the very next day, which was 6 September, we sighted the islands of Fayal and Pico and Graciosa. We sailed by them, and the French wanted to set us all ashore there and make off with the ship; but they did not do so, because it began to blow very hard and the seas ran high. Because of these draw-backs, they continued their voyage with a following wind, steering north-eastwards, having decided to take us with them to their country in our own ship, with which they were pleased since she was a new one. And the French captain and those of his men who were in her, being afraid of Jorge d'Albuquerque, locked him in a cabin every night with two or three of the soldiers who had helped him to fight; but they treated them well in the daytime, so much so that their captain would not eat without first inviting Jorge d'Albuquerque, whom he placed at the head of the table. And on their asking him one day to say grace after the Portuguese manner, he did so, making the sign of the cross over the food on the table. Some of the French who were seated there, rebuked him for making the sign of the cross, to which he replied that he would cling to that sign of the cross as long as he lived, and through it he hoped to be saved from all his enemies, and he would arm himself with it not once but many times. And on his blessing himself again they turned on him with great disgust, and if it had not been for the captain and two other French gentlemen who were with him, he would have been in great danger of being killed or thrown into the sea. And when Jorge d'Albuquerque realized they were Lutherans,[1] he asked the captain for leave not to go and eat with

---

[1] More likely, Calvinists. But the Portuguese, like the Spaniards, could seldom distinguish between these two types of Protestants. I have not been able to identify this particular ship or captain; but the Atlantic at this period swarmed with French corsairs, many of them Huguenots from La Rochelle.

them any more but to eat what they gave him in his own cabin. And although the captain showed himself annoyed at this, yet he gave him the desired permission and he even went and took his meals with Jorge d'Albuquerque sometimes. At this time the French began openly to proclaim themselves as Lutherans, taking all the rosaries and prayer-books which they found among us and throwing them into the sea. And in addition they wanted to ill-treat our people, but they did not do it, through the intercession of a Portuguese among them, who knew Jorge d'Albuquerque and had previously made a voyage with him; and through the mediation of this man we were not so badly treated by the French as we realized they would have liked to have done. Jorge d'Albuquerque, seeing that the French had decided to take us to France, revealed to the soldiers who had helped him in the fight that he was determined to rise against the French and kill them all if they would help him to do this. And they replied that they would do it if there was some hope of salvation thereby, but that the condition of their ship prevented any such attempt, as she was a very sluggish sailer and answered the helm stiffly, and above all was leaking badly; whereas the French ship, which would pursue us in such an eventuality, sailed better with her foresail alone than we with all our sails set; and as the two ships kept close company, almost within hailing distance, it would be impossible to effect such an exploit safely. To which Jorge d'Albuquerque replied with very brave and encouraging words, giving them arguments to show that it was possible to do what he wanted, telling them that if they killed the seventeen Frenchmen who were in the ship, they could defend themselves from the other ship with their weapons; and that they would then have these seventeen less to deal with, who would be greatly missed by their own side, as they were mostly persons of quality; and that when the others learnt that these were dead, they would become disheartened; and that the ships would not always be within hailing distance of each other; and that since they had resisted the French for nearly three days with so few weapons, they would be able to defend them-selves much better with more weapons, especially as these were the excellent arms of the enemy; and that once the seventeen had been disposed of, there was less for them to fear. Therefore he urged them to make up their minds, telling them that he trusted in the mercy of Our Lord, whose enemies the French were, since they were heretics and Lutherans, and that therefore He would aid them; and that they should not be afraid, for he would show them a ruse whereby it would be very easy to kill all the seventeen and kill them very quickly. And on their replying that they would help him, he revealed the ruse to them, which they all thought a very good one. Jorge d'Albuquerque impressed upon them all the need for secrecy, so vital in a matter on which depended nothing less than the lives of them all, and that they should be ready to act when it was necessary. And thus they sailed along with everyone waiting for the weather to give them an opportunity of putting his plan into action, and in these days the ship reached the latitude of 43°.[1]

Chapter V

In which the shipwreck begins

When both of these ships were in the latitude which I have mentioned, on a Wednesday, 12 September, they were struck by the greatest, the most extraordinary and hellish storm of wind from the south-east that ever yet was seen, as can be judged from what it did to us. For the favourable wind which we had hitherto, suddenly dropped, then veered sharply to the south-east and began to blow so violently that we were all frightened at the threatening storm, seeing the rage and fury with which it was beginning to blow. And in this fear we started to take such precautions as are usual in such a crisis, throwing the cargo overboard in order to save our lives. And thus we threw overboard everything which was on the upper-deck and between decks; and as the sea ran higher than ever with the increasing force of the storm, we cut away the topmasts and threw overboard all the sea-chests in which everyone kept his kit. And least anyone should find this difficult, Jorge d'Albuquerque was the first to throw overboard the chest

---

[1] In the latitude of Cape Finisterre, the north-west extremity of the Iberian peninsula.

in which he kept his clothes and other valuables. And seeing that all this did not suffice, and that the seas were getting so huge that they threatened to swamp us, we threw overboard our artillery and many chests of sugar and many sacks of cotton.

While we were labouring with these difficulties, a sea struck us by the poop which dismantled our rudder, so that within a very few days it dropped off astern, leaving the ship lying a-hull; and although we tried to shape a course and let her drive before the wind, all our attempts proved vain. Seeing ourselves in such deadly peril, without a rudder, and with such huge and heavy seas running, some or rather nearly all of us began to lose heart. And Jorge d'Albuquerque seeing us all so affected, and with such good reason, although he himself felt the same way as each and all of us, yet he began to encourage us with brave words, and gave orders to some people how they should try to find some ways of steering the ship, while the others should kneel and pray to Our Lord and Our Lady for deliverance from such trial and tribula- tion. By this time (which was about nine o'clock in the morning) there was no sign of the French ship; and those Frenchmen who were on board our ship, seeing the raging storm, the rudder loose, the ship lying a-hull, and the great confusion aboard her, became so frightened that they all jumped into the waist and came up to our people in a friendly way and said to them: 'We are all lost, none of us can escape, since the ship is rudderless and the seas so high.' And being thus numbed by fear they did whatever we ordered them, as if they had been the slaves, prisoners and servants of us all. We then rigged up a jury mast and sail abaft the fore- castle, to see if we could steer the ship by this means; but no sooner had we done so than a most extraordinary and unheard-of thing happened to us. For at ten o'clock in the morning the weather became so thick that it was as black as night, while the sea with the violent clashing of the waves against each other seemed to give light from the white of the foam. The sea and the wind made such a frightful noise that we could hardly hear each other shouting or make ourselves understood.

At this moment, a tremendous sea, much higher than the previous one, bore down directly on the ship, so black and dark

Woodcut of the *Santo António* losing foremast.
(From p. 23 of the 1601 edition of the *Naufrágio*

below and so white with foam above, that all those who saw it fully realized that it would bring us all to the end of our lives in a few seconds. This sea, crashing over the bow with a gust of wind, broke over the ship in such a manner that it swept away the fore⁄mast and sail, yard and shrouds, as well as the bowsprit, the beak⁄head, and the forecastle with five men inside it, besides three anchors which were stowed there, two on one side and one on the other. In addition to this, it smashed the half⁄deck in such a way that it killed a sailor underneath it, and broke the ship's boat into four or five pieces, and stove in all the pipes of water and other provisions which were still left. Moreover, this sea so damaged the ship from the bow to the mainmast that it left it level with the sea and waterlogged for about half an hour, with those people below deck having no idea where they were. And seeing them⁄selves in such mortal peril, they were all terrified and scared out of their wits, fearing and believing that their last hour had come. And with thisfear they all crowded round a Father of the Com⁄

pany of Jesus, named Álvaro de Lucena,[1] who was a passenger on board, and they made their respective confessions to him, in the briefest possible terms, as time did not permit of anything more. And after they had all made their confessions, and begged pardon of each other, they all fell on their knees, begging Our Lord for mercy and taking as their mediator Our Lady the Most Holy Virgin, Mother of the Son of God, Lady of Luz and of Guadalupe.[2] The sea and the wind waxed stronger hourly, and everything was so terrifying with the thunder claps and lightning flashes, that it seemed as if the end of the world had come. Jorge d'Albuquerque, seeing the miserable condition of himself and his companions, gathering strength from weakness (into which he had fallen at the unhappiness of seeing his friends and himself in the state which they were) began to encourage them in a loud voice, with these words: 'My friends and comrades, we deserve to be afflicted with much worse hardships than those which we are suffering now; because if we were to be punished according to the measure of our sins, then the sea would have already devoured us. But let us all trust in the mercy of that Lord whose compassion is infinite, that He will take pity on us for His own sake and will deliver us out of this tribulation. Let us help ourselves with the arms that are necessary in such a crisis, which are heartfelt repentance of our past sins, and the determination not to sin again, and this in the steadfast faith and hope in the goodness of

[1] *Sic* for Fabiano de Lucena, S.J., who, after an edifying career since 1556 as a Jesuit missionary to the Amerindians in Espiritu Santo and elsewhere in Brazil, returned to Portugal in the *Santo António*, on his own initiative when his plea to be allowed to leave the colony on the grounds of ill-health had been rejected by the father-provincial. He was dismissed from the Society after his arrival in Portugal for this act of insubordination. Cf. S. Leite, *História*, I, 236–7.

[2] Manifestations of the Virgin to whom Jorge d'Albuquerque Coelho was particularly devoted. For the cult of Nossa Senhora da Luz, cf. Fr. Roque do Soveral, *Historia do insigne apparecimento de Nossa Senhora da Luz, e suas obras maravilhosas* (Lisbon, 1610); Miguel Leitão de Andrada, *Miscellanea. Do Sitio de Nossa Senhora da Luz do Perdogão Grande, apparecimento de sua santa imagem*, etc. (Lisbon, 1629). The shrine of Our Lady of Guadalupe in Cáceres province was one of the most famous in Spain, and the meeting-place for the interview between Dom Sebastião and King Philip II in December 1576. Cf. E. W. Bovill, *The Battle of Alcazar*, pp. 53–61; A. Rodríguez Moñino, *Viaje a España del Rey Don Sebastián de Portugal, 1576–1577* (Madrid, 1956).

Woodcut of the *Santo António* losing main and mizzen masts
(From p. 27 of the 1601 edition of the *Naufrágio*)

Him who created us and redeemed us with His precious blood,
that He may vouchsafe us His mercy, not regarding our faults, for
He is capable of everything, being all-wise and all-powerful as
He is. Let us remember that never yet did anyone implore God
for mercy with a pure heart and be refused. Therefore let us all
ask Him for it, and meanwhile try to do everything we can to
save ourselves, some of us working at the pump, others bailing
out the water from the waist and between decks, so long as we
have life and hope that Our Lord will supply through His great
mercy and goodness what is wanting in our hands. And if it
should please Him to dispose of us otherwise, then let each one of
us accept this patiently, since He alone knows what is best for us.'
With these words and many others which he said, some people at
once went to man the pumps, while others bailed out the water
above and below decks. The French [prize crew] who were left
in our ship (for their own had disappeared at the beginning of the
storm), seeing themselves in this tribulation, fell on their knees and

raised their hands to call on God, which up till then they had not done; and they asked us Portuguese for pardon, saying that this storm had arisen because of their sins, begging us to pray to God for them, since they gave themselves up for lost, as the ship was in the state which we all saw.

While some of us were thus manning the pump, and others bailing out the water, and those who were not otherwise employed were on their knees praying to Our Lord to save them in their great distress, a third most enormous sea struck us with a gust of wind on the stern quarter. This carried away the mainmast, yard, sails, and shrouds, as also part of the poop and the cabins, together with the mizzen-mast and one of the leading Frenchmen.[1] Our men working at the pump were flung all over the waist, some of them breaking their arms and others their legs. Jorge d'Albuquerque received such a blow that his right hand was maimed for nearly a year; and one of his servants named António Moreira broke his arm and died of his injury a few days later. The others who were standing near him in the waist were covered by the sea for such a long time that they all thought they were drowned. So much water poured in from this sea, since the half-deck was already smashed, that the ship was left quite helpless for a considerable time, and there was so much water in the waist and the quarterdeck that it almost came up to our knees. And when Jorge d'Albuquerque told them to find out how much water the ship was making below decks, they found that with another three spans she would have been completely waterlogged. Everyone seeing themselves so overwhelmed with tribulations, which increased with every moment, so likewise did their plaintive cries increase as they implored Our Lord for mercy, with the grief which filled them at the prospect of imminent and certain death. Jorge d'Albuquerque, finding himself and his companions at the last gasp, and so bereft of help, strength and comfort, and seeing that some people were so faint-hearted, he went up to them and said: 'My friends and brothers, you have every reason to dread greatly the danger and tribulation in which we all are now, for you can see that human help no longer avails us. But this is just

[1] A French pilot, according to the casualty list given on pp. 155–56 below.

Woodcut of the miracle of Our Lady of Light
(From p. 29 of the 1601 edition of the *Naufrágio*)

what gives us a much greater motive to trust in the mercy of Our Lord, with which He usually helps those who completely aban￢ don all hope of human remedy. Wherefore I earnestly entreat you all, that trusting in Him like we ought to do as Christians that we are, we should implore Him to extend His helping hand to us, since we have no other recourse whatsoever. As for myself, I assure you that I hope that in His goodness He will save us from the danger in which we are, and that I will yet see myself safe on land, where I will recount this many times, so that the world will learn of the mercy that Our Lord vouchsafed towards us.'

As he finished saying this, they all saw a refulgent splendour in the middle of the heavily overcast sky above them, whereupon they all fell on their knees, saying in loud voices: 'Good Jesu help us! Good Jesu have mercy on us! Virgin Mother of God pray for us!' And each one with the most devout words of which he was capable commended himself and his comrades to Our Lady the Virgin, advocate of sinners. The sea was raging so terribly and fearfully that I believe it had never looked so awe-inspiring. The seas that broke over the ship were so huge that they opened the seams and threw in such a quantity of sand that it was amazing. And the people who were struck by the waves were so covered in sand that they were nearly blinded and could hardly see each other. For this reason they suspected that they must be over some sand-banks or shallows, for it seemed impossible that the waves could fling such a quantity of sand into the ship unless she was in shallow water. On the other hand, the storm was such, that we could well believe that this mass of sand which was thrown into the ship had been dredged up from the depths of the sea. The wind howled around the ship with such fury that nobody dared to appear on the deck, save only Jorge d'Albuquerque, the master, and two or three men who were making the sign of the cross while awaiting the seas which battered the ship as if they wished to break her open—and all this with such thunder and lightning that it seemed as if all the devils in hell were loose.

On top of these tribulations we met with another greater and unexpected one, which caused us much anxiety. This was that the mainmast when it was broken and went by the board in the storm, was caught by the masthead in the shrouds on the leeward side; and being held fast in this way, it drifted under the ship to the windward side, and with each successive wave, it was dashed against the ship like a battering-ram, and with such violence that it seemed as if it would smash in the hull. Seeing all these setbacks, we gave ourselves up for lost, feeling each blow that the mast gave against the ship as if it had been inflicted on each one of us. And with each new tribulation that occurred, we all raised our voices imploring God for mercy, and begging Him to deliver us from the deadly danger in which we were placed by our own mast. His infinite goodness was pleased to send some seas which dis-engaged the mast from the ship and thus freed us from that unexpected tribulation. Let anyone who reads this, judge how people in that state we were in must have felt, overwhelmed by so many trials and tribulations, in which we had no other alleviation than the tears and sighs with which we implored Our Lord to remember us. For there was no question of either eating or drinking, since it was three days that we had done either, for this was as long as the storm raged, although the height of it lasted for about nine hours. But during the whole of these three days, we were almost submerged by the sea, working the pump night and day, seeing death in front of us and expecting to meet it hourly. And we were still more certain of it when at the end of those three days we found ourselves without a rudder, without masts, nor sails, nor yards, nor shrouds, nor cables, nor anchors, nor boat, and without any drinking water and provisions. Including the Frenchmen, we numbered nearly fifty people, and the ship was leaking so badly in many places that it seemed as if she was foundering, and we were 240 leagues from land. This storm was so fierce that it struck us in 43° Northern latitude and left us in 47°, without masts or sails. One thing I can affirm, and that is that what little is written here is as different from what we actually endured as a painting is from real life.

Chapter VI

At the end of the three days which the storm lasted, when the weather began to improve, we rigged up a jury-mast in the fore-part of the ship, which we made from some bits of wood from the half-deck which the seas had smashed, and which measured about two or three *braças* in length. And from the three remaining oars of the ship's boat we made a yardarm, and from a small spare sail (which was the only we had left) we made a makeshift foresail, and from some pieces of cords tied to each other we made the shrouds. When this was rigged up, it seemed ridiculous for us to try to navigate such a large ship with so small a sail. By this time, since we had no provisions and our men were infuriated with the French, they wanted to turn on them; but Jorge d'Albuquerque learning of this, called them altogether and dissuaded them from this project with several arguments, the principal one being that we had no hope of being saved (under God) except for the French ship, wherein we could take refuge. For if she had weathered the storm then those in her would have to try and find our ship because of their compatriots who were with us; and if they did not find them alive, then they would kill us all. And he further

reminded us that we had no drinking-water, nor wine, nor provisions, save what we might hope the French would give us; and
if the French ship did not appear within the next four or five days,
then we could do what we liked with the Frenchmen aboard us
and he would be the first to attack them. While we were arguing
in this way, the French ship made her appearance; and as soon as
we sighted her, we began to make many fire signals, and she came
at once to our help, which was on 15 September. She had also
been badly battered but was not nearly so damaged as we were;
and when those on board her saw the condition we were in, they
were astounded. And learning that our men had wanted to turn
on the French and that Jorge d'Albuquerque had prevented them,
they thanked him warmly and told him that if he would like to
go with them they would very willingly take both him and three
other persons whom he could choose, and that they would set him
ashore in the first land they reached if he wanted to stay there. He
thanked them, but said he would be much more grateful if they
would take them all, for he would not go alone, as he was not the
sort of man to abandon his comrades in such distress; and that
whatsoever Our Lord had decreed was in store for his companions
he was likewise resolved to share with them. And he ended by
again asking the French, in the name of us all, to take us with
them and put us ashore on the first land they reached. The French
replied that they could not do this, but that they would only take
him and three others, which offer Jorge d'Albuquerque rejected,
saying that since that was the case, then he would rather endure
further sufferings with his Christian companions than escape
therefrom in the company of Lutherans and heretics who were
enemies of God. On the second day after the French had reached
us, the weather cleared up; and without having the slightest pity or
compunction for our distressed condition, they began hurriedly to
tranship as much of our cargo as they could out of what remained
after the storm, or had not been thrown overboard during the same.
And not satisfied with plundering the ship in this way, they began
to strip some of our people of the very clothes they wore, so that
whatever was left to us after the storm was now taken by the
French. Withal some of the French were more humane, and while

the others went about plundering as I said, these latter busied themselves in nursing our sick, of whom there were many from the hardships we had endured, and gave them something to eat, which our people devoured with the greatest joy, since they had not eaten for many days and were exhausted by what they had undergone in the storm. Having plundered the ship, the French then left us on a Monday, 17 September, without any compunc' tion whatsoever, although we begged them earnestly to take us with them and leave us ashore on the first land which they reached. Not only did they refuse to do this, but they would not even give us some of the bare necessities which we needed out of the super' fluous abundance which they had, such as shrouds, sails, and yards. And they sailed away, hoping that either our ship would soon founder or else that we would all die of hunger. And only after much importuning by us, when we reminded them of the distress in which they were leaving us, did they give us two sacks of biscuit, so discoloured with green, black and yellow, through being rotten and mouldy, that not one of us could eat it, extremely hungry though we were, for it was bitter as gall. And they also left us a little beer, which was more sour than vinegar, and which very few of our people dared to drink.

Chapter VII

Seeing ourselves deprived of the French, who had disappeared over the horizon, and being left to our own devices in the midst of so many miseries, wants and perils, we again began to commend ourselves to the good Jesus and Our Lady the Virgin Mother of God, Lady of Luz and Guadalupe, and to all the male and female saints that they would help us and deign to be our mediators. And with the great reverence required by the critical situation in which we were, we then fell on our knees to pray the psalm *Miserere mei Deus*, with the Litany. When this was finished, Jorge d'Albuquerque ordered a search to be made for any pro' visions that might yet remain in the ship; as a result of which they could not find any water, wine, or provisions, save only about two *canadas* of wine in a single flagon, and about a *canada* of *agua de flor* in a glass-phial,[1] and a few coconuts, and a very few handfulls of manioc-flour, and five or six slices of meat and mackerel. Having put all this together with what the French had left us, it seemed impossible that those meagre provisions would last as long as three days, considering that there were nearly forty of us. However, we kept it to divide in brotherly fashion between all of us until it was finished, and Our Lord should help us with His mercy in this our need and in the others which we endured. Jorge d'Albu-querque divided these provisions with his own hands among us all, giving each person a larger share than that which he took for himself—something which astonished us all, to see how little he ate and how hard he worked by night and day. And we realized that he felt more the sufferings of his companions, both the sick and the healthy, than those of his own person, since there was no possibility of his remedying them, however much he desired to do so in accordance with their needs.

Chapter VIII

Concerning a miracle that happened to us

On the day that the storm broke, Jorge d'Albuquerque, on the advice of some of his companions, ordered to be thrown into the sea a cross of gold, in which was inserted a fragment of the Holy Wood of the True Cross and many other relics, the said cross being tied with a twist of green silk to a very strong cord, with a large nail as a weight, the end of this cord being tied to the ship's poop. And after the storm was over, Jorge d'Albuquerque be-thought him of his reliquary, and he went to the poop to see if the cord with which it was tied was still there. He found that it had got tangled up with some nails[2] so he earnestly begged and en-treated Afonso Luís, the pilot who had embarked as a passenger, to allow himself to be lowered at a rope's end so that he could free the cord with which the reliquary was tied, which Afonso Luís

---

[1] *Canada*, a Portuguese measure for liquids, containing 4 *quartilhos* or three English pints. *Agua de flor*, distilled water with flowers, usually orange-blossoms.

[2] Protruding from the stern of the ship, presumably, though the text is not clear.

accordingly did. And having freed the cord, he told those on the poop to haul it up, and a man named Graviel Damil[1] hauling the whole length of the cord up inside the ship, the cross fell on the quarterdeck quite untied and free, wrapped up in a little piece of cotton. All of us were astounded on seeing this miracle, and we gave many thanks to Our Lord for comforting and encouraging us with so great a miracle, by which it seemed to us that He wished to show us that He would miraculously deliver us from shipwreck, just as He had delivered the Reliquary-Cross from such a storm. This cross besides being tied to the cord with a silken twist was originally held fast by the twist running through the ring of the said cross, and how it had come untied and yet come up on deck with the cord, Our Lord alone knows. Suffice it to say that when we got the cord and the nail up into the ship, the said cross just fell among us standing there, not tied to anything and with its ring broken, though the silken twist was still tied to the cord as it had been when thrown into the sea. While our people were in transports of joy over such a miracle, many of the Frenchmen who were in the ship gathered round to see what we were so pleased about; and although all our people kissed the relics in front of the French with great devotion, it seems that Our Lord did not allow the latter to see what they were actually doing; for I am convinced that if they had seen them they would have taken them, as they were of gold, which they covet so greatly. And not only did they not see them then, but they did not on any other of the days when Jorge d'Albuquerque had them on his person, for whereas they often felt him to see if he was carrying anything concealed, they never found them. For which we must give many thanks to Our Lord for this miracle, and for the others which He wrought on behalf of all of us during this shipwreck. We did not fail to note, those of us who were there, that perchance Our Lord wished to grant us this favour on account of the Wood of the Holy Cross, and because of the sign of the cross that Jorge d'Albuquerque had made when saying grace at the Frenchmen's

[1] Gabriel Damil in modern orthography. *HTM* has Daniel Damil here. Possibly identical with a Gabriel Damian who was *meirinho* (bailiff) of the captaincy in 1593.

table, on which account they wanted to kill him or to throw him overboard. It seems that Our Lord permitted that this cross with the Holy Wood and relics which were therein should not be lost but should be returned to the hand of the said Jorge d'Albu⁄ querque, since he had offered to die out of love for this holy sign of the cross, to which he always showed himself devoutly attached throughout the whole voyage. And he told us several times that he had always felt this way since childhood, and that this devotion was inherited by him, because in all the four shields of the arms which he bore by virtue of his descent from two paternal and two maternal grandparents, the cross figured in all of them, which are the arms of the Albuquerques, the Coelhos, from whom he is directly descended, the Pereiras and the Bulhões.[1]

Chapter IX

After having got together all the provisions which we found in the ship on the same day that the French left us, on the very next day Jorge d'Albuquerque ordered a sail to be made out of some table⁄ cloths and napkins that were found in the ship. These were sewn on to a little sail which had been left us from the French skiff; and out of two oars from the ship's boat we made a yard, and we made a jury⁄mast from the stump of the mainmast with a piece of wood two *braças*[2] in height, and some makeshift shrouds from the strands of the shrouds which we had left, and ropes made from the nets and lunts; since there was nothing else in the ship that we could use for this purpose, for the storm had carried away everything— shrouds, cables, ropes, anchors, boat, and anything else that we might otherwise have used. The rudder was suspended from the one iron pintle that was left, and we affixed to it some cords to serve as tiller⁄ropes so that we could use it thus for two or three days. And thereupon we resumed our voyage, taking Our Lady

---

[1] Cf. the arms of Jorge d'Albuquerque Coelho, reproduced on the title⁄page of the 1601 edition, and on p. 108 above.

[2] As noted elsewhere, *braça* is usually translated as 'fathom' and/or as the distance between the tips of the fingers of a grown man when his arms are fully outstretched. Leitão and Lopes, *Dicionáro*, p. 83, give the old Portuguese *braça* as equivalent to about 1 m. 76 cm.; and the modern to two yards or about 1 m. 83 cm.

Mother of God as our guide, roughly estimating our position by the sun at sunrise, since we had no astrolable that was usable nor any navigating instrument to help us, because the French had taken them all, save only a compass needle that was so damaged and worn that it was often out of order. Being in this condition, we estimated that we were about 236 leagues from Cape Finisterre in 45° Northern latitude,[1] for we had made good the rest owing to the north-west wind which had been blowing up to then. The toil which we had in manning the pump by day and night weakened us so much, that many people from sheer exhaustion with the pumping, fell down on the deck in a swoon from pure hunger and overwork. While we continued in this tribulation, Jorge d'Albuquerque asked a sailor named Domingos da Guarda, who was a great diver, to dive into the sea and see if he could find and stop the leaks of the ship underwater, since this could not be done inside the ship as they were very low down among the fore and aft fashion-pieces, and we had already cut away many of the riders in the forepart fashion-pieces to see if we could find the leaks. And he told him that if he could stop the principal leak, he would not only thereby save his own life and those of all his comrades, but that he (Jorge d'Albuquerque) would pay him very well for it. It was a most astounding thing, and one for which Our Lord is greatly to be praised, that on that very day, which was 23 September, the sea was as calm and smooth as if it had been a river. And when the sailor made ready to dive into the sea, all of us in the ship fell on our knees praying to Our Lord for His help and mercy, beseeching Him to deliver us from the danger in which we were of foundering, despite working the pump by night and day. Our Lord, being who He is, deigned to hear and took pity on us; for each of the three times that the diver went down he was able to stop the worst of the leaks—a feat which greatly encouraged and comforted us, since we realized that we would have some relief and alleviation from working continually at the pump. The sailor came up into the ship very pleased, and everyone joyfully embraced him, seeing how well he had done; and Jorge d'Albuquerque was as good as his word and gave him something with

[1] As noted above, p. 126, n. 1, Cape Finisterre is in just under 43° N. latitude.

which he was very well satisfied.[1] Having stopped these leaks, on the next day, which was 23 September,[2] we again had a N.N.W. wind, which blew so strongly and was accompanied with such high seas and bitter cold that we could hardly bear it, nor could we stand up in the ship owing to the way she pitched and rolled. The chains of the chain-wales being loose, they clashed together with such an infernal din that it seemed like a frightful smithy, so much so that we could hardly make each other hear. The seas began to run so high that they passed over the ship and drenched us with water, as she was so damaged. Our meagre provisions were used up within a few days among so many people, however carefully we rationed them. The daily ration itself was such a small one, that three coconuts were divided among nearly forty people, each person's share being only about the size of a *tostão*.[3] Of the beer, which was sourer than vinegar, there was issued twice daily enough to wet the palate and this in itself did not amount to a draught; but even so, it was so bitter that many people did not drink any of it at all. Thus we continued on our voyage whither the sea and the wind carried us, spending all our time in praying and in working the pump. Jorge d'Albuquerque, in addition to taking his fraternal share of all these labours, likewise had that of comforting and encouraging his companions, who were completely exhausted both physically and spiritually. He could only comfort them by reminding them of the holy death and passion of Our Lord Jesus Christ, and how much He had suffered for us, so that the recollection thereof should make it easier for them to bear the tribulations which they endured. He urged them that since they were awaiting their last hour without any hope of human help, that they should trust in the mercy of Our Lord, which was all that was left them, so that in His compassion He might dispose of them as seemed best for His service and the salvation of their souls. This he told us with such friendly,

[1] After they had reached Lisbon, presumably, unless Jorge d'Albuquerque had contrived to conceal more valuables besides the reliquary-cross from the French. Cf. p. 153, n. 2 below.

[2] *HTM* corrects to 24 September, which seems more likely, unless the previous mention is a misprint for 22 September.

[3] A small silver coin with a nominal value of 100 *reis* at this period.

kind, and pious words, that utterly exhausted as we were, we got up and returned to our work. And often when he was speaking to us about these and other things, tears of pity welled from his eyes at seeing us in the same danger as he was, but less on his account than on that of his companions. One thing that greatly astonished all of us, was the fact the Jorge d'Albuquerque, who had been unwell for most of the voyage, since he was already afflicted at the time of embarkation by some ills which the hard⁄ ships of the campaign had caused him, after we fought with the French and endured the storm, he never again complained of any indisposition, and we saw him so strong and healthy and working so continuously that he amazed and shamed us all. Besides all these things which I mentioned previously, he said that he had such faith and confidence in the mercy of Our Lord that he assured us, as if he was absolutely certain of it, that Our Lord would deliver us from that peril and that we would sight land; just as if we had already sighted it, or had a ship capable of bringing us thereto. Yet withal we were by now so exhausted that there was hardly anyone who could work at the pump. And he, seeing us in this state, despairing of life, without strength, and without provisions to eat, strode into the midst of his companions and said to them with a resolute mien: 'My friends and brothers, each one of you realizes the wretched state we are in, and how remote we are from any human help, since our ship has neither sails, nor masts, nor rudder, nor shrouds, nor anything which is needed to make her seaworthy. Moreover, we do not know where we are, nor whither we are bound, for we have no certainty whatever about these things. And worst of all, we have nothing whatever to eat, since our provisions are finished. I know full well that these are all things which you can see with your own eyes, and that they are so inimical to our lives, that any single one of them would be enough to daunt you, and even the bravest man there is; for they are things against which bodily strength and stoutness of heart are of no avail, being hunger, fury of the sea, a rotten and dismasted ship, and ignorance of our course. But if you will recall what you have already endured on this voyage, and if you remember that terrible storm which struck us, and the waves that washed over us, and how often the ship

was left waterlogged and submerged by the sea, and that you all
gave yourselves up for dead, seeing that all the elements appeared to
be conspiring against our lives—the water, the wind, the lightning,
until even our mast apparently tried to drown us: and if you have
forgotten nothing of all this, then you will clearly see how much
reason you have to trust in the greatness of the mercy of Our Lord
and to believe firmly in Him that He will save you. For most
assuredly should you feel that He who has delivered us from so
many tribulations up till now, will equally deliver you from those
which are to come. For if He had wished to drown you by natural
means, any one of the waves which you see now would suffice to
plunge you to the bottom of the sea. And who knows whether
these are not trials with which He wishes to test your Faith, and
so, in fact, are endearments of Our Lord? I am as certain as if I
had sighted land, that Our Lord intends to bring us there, so that
the people thereof may learn about this miracle which He has
vouchsafed us, lest it remain unknown. And the people who will
hear about this our shipwreck, will always thereafter praise and
glorify Our Lord and thankfully exalt His Holy Name; and the
more so, because He will not bring us to a landfall just anywhere,
but to the very city of Lisbon, where we shall be able to recount a
tale so extraordinary as is this one. And for us to feel sure and
confident that this will happen, it is only necessary to have faith
in the Lord, for He says in one of the Gospels: "If Ye have faith as
a grain of mustard‑seed, ye shall say unto this mountain 'Remove
hence to yonder place', and it shall remove."[1] Wherefore my
brothers, placed in this state of faith and confidence in the Lord,
let us hope that He will deliver us from the utmost depths of the
sea on this piece of wood.' He said these things and others like
them to his devout companions better than I can relate them here,
whereat we were all greatly comforted; and still more so at seeing
him always so blithe and with such a cheerful countenance that
it seemed as if he was exempt from the trials and tribulations which
beset us all. And he always went about comforting whoever
seemed to him to be weakest, without showing that he himself
felt the danger in which we were. But in reality nobody realized

[1] Matt. xvii. 20, in the Authorized Version.

it better than he did, for sometimes at night we found him in a corner away from everyone, praying tearfully to Our Lord, be-seeching Him to deign to save us; but by day he comforted and encouraged us all. We saw him display such valour and fortitude in these tribulations that he often roused our drooping spirits; and in this he certainly appeared to be the son of his father and the nephew of his uncle, the great Afonso d'Albuquerque, both of whom he seemed to resemble.[1]

Chapter X

The wind which we had was so strong that it tore some parts of our makeshift sails, which were made from the feeble material that I described above, so that it was necessary to mend them. And while we were patching and sewing them, the rudder finally came loose, breaking the sole pintle to which it was attached, while the ropes with which it was tied also frayed and snapped so it was left astern. The pilot, the master, and the rest of the crew, seeing themselves without rudder, masts, sails, shrouds, ship's-boat, and with all the above-mentioned provisions exhausted, and as far from land as they suspected, they collapsed in the waist through sheer grief and discouragement, thinking themselves to be completely lost, and seeing themselves deprived of all help, for even though the rudder served but ill in its makeshift form yet even as it was it had been a great comfort to us. Jorge d'Albu-querque, seeing such demoralization among the people, was over-whelmed with grief and sorrow because there were no provisions nor drink left, nor had we drunk any water or wine for several days, and the vinegar [beer], which was all we had wherewith to moisten our mouths, was reduced to the dregs. Nobody could work at the pump any more, nor had they the strength to stand upright on their own legs. He earnestly bethought himself of what he could do to comfort his comrades, and of a sudden he jumped up, as strong and gay as if he had just come from some feast, and he began to summon each one of them by name. Then taking two leaves out of his book of devotions that he had hidden from the French, in one of which was depicted Our Lord Jesus Christ

[1] Cf. introduction, p. 12 above.

crucified and in the other Our Lady, he nailed these to the foot of the mast so that everyone could see them, and addressed us all in a loud voice as follows: 'Now my dear comrades, let nobody weaken nor be dismayed, but let us look at these pictures, the sight of which must needs rejoice and comfort us, knowing how much He suffered for us; and since He is all-merciful and all-powerful, He will deliver us from this terrible danger and bring us safely home—and the more so, since we have as mediatrix and intercessor the Most Holy Virgin Mary Our Lady Queen of the Angels, through whose intercession, prayers and merit, I hope and trust that we will see ourselves delivered from this peril. And I tell you again that we will not make a chance landfall, but arrive directly off Lisbon, so that our safe arrival will spread the fame of the miracles which He has vouchsafed us. And you know, my friends, how sure I am about this, for I preferred to be with you here than in the French ship, because when they offered to take me I refused, as you see, but I preferred to keep you company and to be an eyewitness of the dangers we have endured and of the great mercies which God has vouchsafed you.' When he finished this speech, we all fell on our knees before the pictures of the crucified Christ and of our Lady, imploring their mercy in such loud and doleful voices that I have not the slightest doubt but that if any-one had heard us they could not have failed to help us, being deeply moved by our misfortunes, however barbarous or stony-hearted they might have been. For it was a most pitiful and sorrow-ful thing to see the condition in which we wretched people were, so wasted and disfigured by our hardships and tribulations that by this time we could hardly recognize each other. Jorge d'Albu-querque, although he gave no sign of it to anyone else, realizing that the wretched condition they were in gave but little hope of their lives being saved, drew up his last will and testament, which, together with many other important papers he placed in a small wooden cask, which he closed and caulked very well, with the intention of throwing it into the sea when they should all reach their last hour; so that when it was found with these papers inside it, people would learn how we had met our end. But he did this so secretly that none of us knew anything about it at the time.

Seeing ourselves without the rudder, we made a makeshift *espadela*[1] like a large oar, from planks and wood which we hacked from the ship. And all these things and some others we made shift with, we made with an old axe and a chisel; and the holes which should have been bored with gimblets we made with red-hot nails. Jorge d'Albuquerque was the prime inventor of all these make-shifts, and he was always one of the first to lend a hand with them. The *espadela* which we made to replace the rudder was of very little use, as we could hardly steer the ship with it. But by hauling aft the wretched little makeshift sheets that we had, and by using two oars on either side, the ship made some kind of way, helped by a spritsail which we made from two cloaks worn by a couple of our comrades. But all these devices were of no use in a strong wind or high sea, and we could only use them in a light breeze. By this time even Jorge d'Albuquerque could give us no comfort other than telling us that when September was over—and it was then the 27th of that month—our tribulations would be ended, and that with the month of October he hoped we would have a favourable breeze and the favour of the Good Jesus and of Our Lady the Virgin.

Chapter XI

On the 27th of this same month, which was the Feast-day of Saint Cosmé and Saint Damião, we began to throw into the sea the bodies of some persons who had died from sheer exhaustion, starvation, and weakness. So greatly were we suffering from hunger, that some of our comrades went up to Jorge d'Albu-querque and told him that they were only too well aware that people were dying from pure starvation, while those who were still alive had nothing whatever to eat; and that since this was so, would he give them leave to eat the bodies of those that died, since the living had no other resource left. When he heard this appalling request, Jorge d'Albuquerque was pierced to the soul and his eyes streamed with tears, on seeing the state to which their

[1] Probably like the huge steering oar in the shape of an elongated letter S fitted to the stern-post of the Douro wine-barges, as described by J. Guthrie, 'Bizarre craft of Portugal', in *MM*, xxxv (1949), 153, 177-78.

misery had brought them. And he told them very sorrowfully that their request was so utterly unreasonable that it would be a great sin and blindness to allow such a bestial desire. He added that he saw full well that overcome by their present need they had followed the advice of such a bad councillor as was hunger; but he urged them to consider carefully what they wanted to do, because he himself would never allow it so long as he was alive, and that after he was dead they could do what they liked and eat him first of all. Whoever reads this can easily judge what sort of men these must have been to contemplate such an unheard-of thing, which had only occurred in the siege of Jerusalem. Then Jorge d'Albuquerque began to comfort them with encouraging words to put their trust in God, in whose hand was their only hope of salvation. And the perverse enemy,[1] seeing that he could not deprive us of the hope which Jorge d'Albuquerque's words had given us, nor of the special trust in God with which each one of us now hoped we would be saved, wishing to undermine this trust like the enemy of our souls that he is, he began to employ a new and unexpected ruse against us, which was as follows. Seeing that neither the wildness of the waves nor the fury of the storm had availed to finish us off, he planted a hellish conviction in the hearts of some of our people, that since there was no hope of them being saved or delivered from that dire peril, we would all have to die anyway. Convinced by this evil counsel of the faithless foe, some of them decided that since there was no chance whatsoever of being saved, as we were deprived of all human aid and the hunger which we were suffering made life intolerable, in order to avoid prolonging the agony they would scuttle the ship, so as to go to the bottom more quickly and thus end their lives and their sufferings together. Our Lord in His goodness ordained that Jorge d'Albuquerque should discover these damnable plots and diabolical determinations, in order to prevent their being carried into effect, which he did. And he implored Our Lady of Grace to intercede with her only begotten Son so that he [Jorge d'Albu-querque] could remedy such a terrible evil, and another one which was no less and which he likewise found out about, namely that

---

[1] I.e. the Devil.

all of those who were left alive in the ship were divided into rival gangs and bands, although we were close to death, as I said, and without strength and without weapons, because there were none in the ship save only a few broken knives and bits of wood where- with to fight, and none of us could stand upright. It seems that the hunger from which they were suffering and the despair which they had conceived, had brought them to such a senseless piece of folly; and, above all, the devil, who wanted them to die in such a hellish way by killing each other when they were in such an ill condition—but, in the upshot, neither the devil, nor the sea, nor the fury of the storm could prevail. And Jorge d'Albuquerque, with a good deal of horror and sorrow, placed himself in the midst of them, and began to reprove them for the diabolical decision which they had made by resolving to drown themselves. He also rebuked them for wishing to fight each other when they were in such a pitiful state, which was a shameful thing. And when he found out what was causing this strife, it turned out to be nothing but tale-bearing which the devil had sown among them. For this reason he again begged them to live in peace like brothers, reminding them that they ought always to do this, since they were Christians; and that now above all times they should be deeply ashamed of harbouring any hatred for their neighbours; and that in the mortal peril in which they were, they should think of nothing save only imploring God for mercy and having steadfast faith in Jesus Christ, that in His infinite goodness He might bring them to the port of salvation. They should not lose heart, nor wish to kill themselves with their own hands, for if they did this then they would slay both body and soul—something which every Christian should greatly fear and shun. And whosoever in these tribulations or in others like them (if there were any such in the world) placed himself in the hands of the Lord, he would always receive more and greater mercies than he dared to hope for. And thus he felt confident that Our Lord would not only deliver them from the peril in which they were, but that He would bring them to Lisbon, as he had told them several times; wherefore he be- sought them to lay aside all hatred and ill-will, because if they nurtured any rancour they would disqualify themselves from

receiving the mercies which they expected from the Divine
Majesty. It pleased Our Lord that with these words and with
many others that Jorge d'Albuquerque said, he dissuaded them
entirely from their damnable intentions, and thus they escaped
from the diabolical snare which the devil had laid for them. This
was the most dangerous crisis in which we were hitherto involved, for
our bodies might have perished in the previous perils but our souls
would have been saved through the contrition which we all displayed; whereas on this occasion, both bodies and souls would
have perished through wantonly committing self-murder, despairing
of the mercy of Our Lord. On the morning of 29 September, Feast-
day of the Archangel St Michael, we sighted a ship, to which we
made signal and lighted fires, showing that we were desirous of being rescued, as she came quite close to us. But whoever they were,
they were so uncharitable that they took not the slightest notice of
us, although they could see what a miserable plight our wreck
of a ship was in.

Chapter XII

All of us were now in such a state that we could hardly get up
on our feet, exhausted as we were with hunger, thirst, and the
continual work which we had with pumping at hourly intervals;
for even though the diver had stopped the worst of the leaks, yet
we still continued to make so much water that the pump had to
be kept going constantly. Being in the miserable condition I have
said, owing to the wants, hunger, thirst, and toil which I have
described, without our knowing where we were, nor whither we
were bound, the mercy of Our Lord which never fails those who
call upon Him, helped us so generously that on a Monday,
2 October, without our expecting it, we miraculously found
ourselves between the Berlengas and the Rock of Cintra, opposite
Nossa Senhora da Pena, whose shrine we could see at midday,[1]
when a thick morning mist and fog lifted. And because when we

[1] The hermitage of Nossa Senhora da Pena, with an attached convent of
Jeronimite friars built by King Manuel I, on the Serra da Cintra. It was largely
supported by the alms of mariners given in fulfilment of vows made to the Virgin
when in distress at sea. Cf. G. Cardoso, *Agiologio Lusitano*, II (Lisbon, 1657), 478-9.

Woodcut of *Santo António's* landfall off Cintra
(From p. 59 of the 1601 edition of the *Naufrágio*)

first sighted the land we thought it might be Galicia and then we soon realized where we were, we rejoiced exceedingly, as anyone can imagine; although we were saddened by the thought that we had no boat in which to go ashore. And as the ship got closer to the shore, many people began to make ready boards and planks wherewith they could throw themselves into the sea when the ship struck, which she seemed bound to do, and well-nigh impossible for any of us to escape, as that part of the coast is very rocky and wild as everyone knows. And when we were busy making rafts on which to escape, by the advice of the pilot and the master, Jorge d'Albuquerque said to us: 'Ah Sirs! Are you not ashamed of yourselves? Have you so little faith and so little trust in the mercy of Our Lord, that having delivered you from such toils and tribulations, He will bring you in sight of land only to cast you away thereon? Don't you believe such a thing; for He who has brought you here and within sight of the house of Our Lady, will not allow us to perish but on the contrary we shall all be saved. For I hope that He will bring us to a place where we can all go ashore dry-shod, just as I sometimes assured you when we were out there on the watery abyss and far distant from the land which we now see.' At this juncture we sighted many ships, to which we made signals; and the extraordinary thing was that the more we signalled the further they bore away from us. Some of our people thought that they must be afraid of our ship, which looked to them like a phantom one, for never before had there been seen on the sea the remains of a ship so unseaworthy as ours was. On the next day, 3 October, vigil of the Blessed St Francis, we found ourselves at dawn just off the Rock of Cintra and the Praia da Rocha, and as our ship seemed to be just on the point of drifting ashore, a caravel bound for Pederneira[1] passed near us. And we begged them for the honour of the death and passion of Our Lord that they would help us, telling them of all our tribula-tions, and that in addition to the service they would thereby render to Our Lord, we would pay them very well if they would rescue us and take us with them and put us ashore wherever they wanted, since it was in their power to save us. And although we implored them to do this with all the earnestness that our situation required, they answered us that Jesus Christ might help us, since they could not afford to lose any time on their voyage, and so they sailed away without the slightest pity for us. When we saw them go, we were so discouraged that there was not a single person among us whose eyes were not filled with tears at the sight of such cruelty used to-wards us by men who were Portuguese and our compatriots. This was truly a most reprehensible act of cruelty and one which the Crown should order to be punished. And as we were thus on the point of drifting ashore, without any hope of saving ourselves owing to the rocks on which we were about to strike, the Divine Mercy saved us through a small bark which was bound for Atouguia.[2]

---

[1] At this time still a fishing and ship-building port of some importance, but which decayed to the verge of extinction in the 18th century, and is now only a part of the port and tourist resort of Nazaré. Cf. P. M. Laranjo Coelho, *A Pederneira. Apontamentos para a história dos seus mareantes, pescadores, calafates e das suas construções navais nos séculos XV a XVII* (Lisbon, 1924).

[2] Fishing-port and village near Peniche, opposite the Berlengas. A medieval port of some importance, but already silting up at this period.

When we sighted her we made signals and hailed her, falling with shrieks on our knees and imploring her crew in the name of Jesus Christ to help us. And when the bark got within a *berço's*-shot of us, they speedily came to our aid, like good neighbours and Christians. And as soon as the crew of the bark reached us, they were astounded on seeing our condition; and they told us that while they were still a long way off they had heard our summons to help them in the name of Jesus—something which was certainly very remarkable, because none of us was strong enough to shout loudly and yet our voices had been heard over such a long distance. There were in the bark a certain Rodrigo Álvares of Atouguia, who was the master and owner thereof, and Francisco Gonçalves of Aveiro, and João Rodrigues of Atouguia, and a lad who was the son of the said Francisco Gonçalves. All these men, on seeing us and the peril in which we were, they began to comfort and encourage us, telling us not to be afraid, for they would not abandon us even if they should run the risk of perishing themselves, and that they would do everything possible to bring us safely ashore, nor did they want any reward for their trouble since they wished to do this for the service of Our Lord; because it seemed that some miracle had brought them there, as they had been unable to make any progress during the last three days, whether ahead or astern, for they had been beating about in a vain endeavour to make headway. From this it seems that Our Lord did not wish them to leave that spot, but to make them wait for us there in order to bring us to land; and when we cried out to them, they heard us and came promptly to our help with a following breeze, which they had never had up till that moment. And on seeing how battered and unseaworthy our ship was, and we ourselves so gaunt from starvation, they were absolutely astounded. Pitying us greatly, they began to cry and forthwith gave us some of the bread, water, and fruit which they had on board for themselves. Some of our people could not eat anything on account of the excessive joy they felt at seeing land and in wanting to go ashore, while others could not do so on account of their palates being so affected by their hunger and sufferings. And it is certain that if we had been another two or three days at sea, not one of us

would have been left alive. For none of us could stand upright
after the toil of working the pump, and we had drunk neither wine
nor water for seventeen days. During most of this time our daily
ration consisted of only three or four small coconuts; and if they
were something larger, then three sufficed to be divided among all
of us, amounting to nearly forty persons all told. The owner of the
bark as soon as he had given us something to eat, gave us a cable
wherewith we got the ship off from under the lee of the Praia da
Rocha, and thus he towed us along the coast until we reached the
port of Cascais[1] at sunset. Some of our people disembarked here
in barks that immediately put off from the shore, while others went
on to Belém where we landed dry-shod. Both parties at once
began to fulfil their promised pilgrimages, giving many thanks to
Our Lord for the great and merciful favours which He had vouchsafed us. Jorge d'Albuquerque before he disembarked rewarded
the owner and crew of the bark for the good work they had done
in bringing us there.[2] And on the very night of our arrival the
ship was made fast to the stern of the bark, for we had nothing to
anchor with; and although the bark had only a little anchor, it
held both the bark and the ship all that night until the next day,
which was Thursday, 5 October. On this same day the Infante
Dom Henrique, cardinal in this kingdom of Portugal, who was
then in charge of the government,[3] sent a galley to tow the said
ship up-river, which it did, and the ship was laid up in front of
the Church of St Paul, which is now a parish.[4] And during the
time of a month or more that she lay there, an amazing number of

---

[1] Now a popular residential town and seaside resort near Estoril.

[2] Not explained how he did this, if the French had pillaged the ship so thoroughly
as previously alleged; but cf. p. 141, n. 1 above.

[3] The cardinal-infante, D. Henrique, last surviving son of D. Manuel, acted as
regent from the retirement of the queen-dowager, D. Catarina, in 1563, until his
grand-nephew, D. Sebastião, was declared of age and took over the government
from him in January 1568. After the death of the latter at El-Ksar el-Kebir, he
ascended the throne as the last king of the dynasty of Aviz, dying on his sixty-eighth
birthday (31 January 1580).

[4] The recently organized parish of St Paul, just outside the medieval walls, was
a district largely populated by sailors, shipwrights, and other maritime personnel
at this period. *Barlow's Journal, 1659–1705*, I (1934), 62, mentions the 'graving place
by St Polves [*sic*] Church' as still in use in 1661.

people came to see her, and they were all utterly astounded at seeing what a wreck she was, and they gave great thanks and praise to Our Lord for saving those who came in her from the deadly perils they had undergone. And it is likewise only right that anyone else who learns about the singular mercy which God vouchsafed us, should give Him many thanks and much praise for bringing us to safety in such a wreck of a ship, when we were over 240 leagues from land, with neither sails nor masts, nor indeed any of the gear needed to make a ship navigable, and the ship herself on the point of foundering. And in addition to all this, we suffered hunger and thirst, without having [almost] anything to eat or drink, sailing for twenty-two days like I said, during seventeen of which, none of us drank water nor wine, neither had we anything more to eat than our daily ration of three or four coconuts divided among the nearly forty persons that we were. I was prompted to write this description of our shipwreck by the desire of making widely known the tribulations which people endure on these voyages, and to show how strong withal is the weakness of our body, which if it could be told of the sufferings that it is able to endure, would certainly faint away at the thought of them. I was further impelled to write this account so that everybody should see clearly how much reason we have to hope and trust in the mercy of the Lord, which never fails anyone in their direst straits, provided only that we implore it with a pure heart, with which we must be prepared to receive it. And in order to make known the greatness of the mercy of Our Lord, and the miracles that He vouchsafes to sinners in His goodness, I sat down to write this compendium of our tribulations, that they may serve as a mirror, advice, and consola-tion for those who may subsequently find themselves in a similar situation, so that they can steadfastly maintain their faith and trust in the mercy of Our Lord to deliver and save them, as He did to us. And for all of which may the Lord be blessed and praised for evermore. Amen.

Chapter XIII

I can truthfully assure all those who may read this account, that I have not written here the half of all that happened to us, because when we were suffering these tribulations I had no intention nor opportunity of writing them down, nor when they were past could I bear to think of them.[1] This is merely the brief sum of what I can recollect of having suffered in this voyage; but praised be the name of Jesus, whose goodness and mercy brought me to safety. Those of us who reached land alive were the following. Jorge d'Albu-querque Coelho, who was the one who worked hardest and suffered the heaviest loss among all those who were involved in this shipwreck; the pilot Álvaro Marinho; the master André Rodrigues; Afonso Luís, a pilot, but not of our ship;[2] André Gonçalves; Domingos da Guarda; António da Costa; a man named Velho; a lad named António; Balthasar Álvares; a Jesuit father named Álvaro de Lucena;[3] a bastard son of Jerónimo d'Albuquerque;[4] Gabril Damil; Simão Gonçalves; Simeão Gonçalves; Gomes Leitão; two brothers called 'the Bastards'; a man called Velho, a master of making sugar;[5] Braz Álvares Pacheco; a female slave of Jorge d'Albuquerque called Antónia,

[1] This seems to be in flagrant contradiction to what is said above (pp. 117), assuming that Afonso Luís was the writer of this account, as is there stated.

[2] The author of this account, as stated on pp. 116–17 above. Cf. previous note.

[3] *Sic* for Fabiano de Lucena, S.J. Cf. p. 129, n. 1, above.

[4] Jerónimo de Albuquerque was the brother of D. Beatriz de Albuquerque, Jorge d'Albuquerque Coelho's mother, whom he had accompanied to the cap-taincy in 1535. The chronicler, Fr. Vicente do Salvador, describes him as being 'naturally of a mild and friendly disposition, and since he had many children by the daughters of the [Amerindian] chiefs, he treated the latter with consideration'. Presumably one of these half-breed sons is meant here. At the time of making his will (13 November 1584), he acknowledged a progeny of twenty-four between legitimate and illegitimate offspring, but his death did not occur till eight or nine years later. Cf. Rodolfo Garcia [ed.], *Primeira Visitação do Santo Oficio ás partes do Brasil. Denunciações de Pernambuco* (São Paulo, 1929), pp. xiv–xvi, for details of the children of this 'Pernambucan Adam', from whom many leading families trace their descent.

[5] *Mestre de fazer açúcar.* Corresponded to the overseer or manager of a sugar-plantation in the British West Indies in the seventeenth and eighteenth centuries.

and some other slaves.[1] The men who were swept overboard and drowned were: the boatswain Toribio Gonçalves; António Fernandes; António the son of [the above-mentioned?] Velho; Gaspar Mouco; a French pilot; Domingos Gonçalves; António Moreira. The others had died during the voyage from hunger, thirst, and hardship.[2] I only wish to relate one more incident, to show the terrible hardships which we had endured and the condition of those of us who survived this shipwreck. Jorge d'Albuquerque, having started on his pilgrimage from Belém to Nossa Senhora da Luz,[3] accompanied by some of us, took the road via Nossa Senhora da Ajuda.[4] Meanwhile, his friends and relations in the city being informed of his arrival, his cousin Dom Jerónimo de Moura,[5] son of Dom Manuel de Moura, and many other persons at once went out to meet him. On being told that he had already landed and where he was going and what route he was taking, they went after him. And on catching up with us as we were walking along in procession, Dom Jerónimo greeted us and asked us if we were those people who had been saved with Jorge d'Albuquerque. When we replied 'Yes', he asked us: 'Is Jorge d'Albuquerque going in front, or behind, or is he taking another route?' And Jorge d'Albuquerque, who was standing right in front of him, answered: 'Senhor, Jorge d'Albuquerque is not in front,

[1] As some twenty-one persons are listed above, and the total of survivors is twice given in the text as 'nearly forty', presumably the remaining twelve or fifteen must also have been slaves.

[2] The total number of persons who embarked at Recife is nowhere stated, but as the *Santo António* was a ship of 200 tons she could easily have carried over 100 people between passengers and crew. It is typical of the careless way in which this narrative was edited that António Moreira, here said to have been drowned, on p. 131 above is said to have died from injuries received in a storm.

[3] Cf. p. 129, n. 2 above for Jorge d'Albuquerque's devotion to Nossa Senhora da Luz. The Lisbon church and chapel of this invocation was founded in the parish of Carnide in 1463, and transferred to the Order of Christ in 1545.

[4] The present-day suburb of Ajuda is chiefly noteworthy for the former royal palace which houses a remarkable (but badly organized) library of books and manuscripts, the property of the ruling dynasty of Bragança prior to the revolution of 1910.

[5] Brother-in-law of Jorge d'Albuquerque Coelho, though this is not stated here, and one of the protectors of the notorious alchemist and adventurer, António de Gouveia, the 'Golden Padre' (*Padre do Ouro*). Cf. Pedro Calmon, *História do Brasil* (ed. 1961), I, 301–3; Serafim Leite, S.J., *História*, I, 482.

nor behind, nor is he taking another route.' Dom Jerónimo, thinking he was joking, was rather annoyed, and told him not to make jokes but to answer the question he had been asked. Jorge d'Albuquerque thereupon retorted: 'Senhor Dom Jerónimo, if you saw Jorge d'Albuquerque, would you recognize him?' He answered that he would. 'Well then, I am Jorge d'Albuquerque, and you are my cousin Dom Jerónimo, son of my aunt, Dona Isabel d'Albuquerque. And you can see from the state I am in, what I have been through.' And although they had both been brought up together, and it was not a full year since they had last seen each other, and although they had been familiar and intimate friends for a long time, Dom Jerónimo thought he looked so utterly different that he still did not recognize him. It was then necessary for Jorge d'Albuquerque to show him certain marks on his body, which finally convinced him, whereupon he embraced him with many tears, astounded at how greatly his appearance had altered; and so it was with all the rest of us. I was an eyewitness of all this, which is the reason I relate it here. And Our Lord be praised that I recovered sufficiently to write this, which I had frequently despaired of being able to do.[1] But it is only God who knows all, may He be blessed and praised for evermore. Amen.

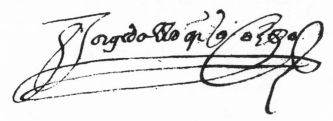

Autograph signature of Jorge d'Albuquerque Coelho
From a letter dated 26. xi. 1581 in the collection of C. R. Boxer

[1] Conclusive proof that Bento Teixeira Pinto could not be the author of this *Naufrágio*, as he was only four years old in 1565.

BIBLIOGRAPHY

(A) *Texts translated in the present work*

(i) DIOGO DO COUTO

Decada Setima | Da Asia | dos feitos que os portugueses fize⸗ | rão no descobrimento dos mares, & conquista das terras do Orien⸗ | te: em quanto gouernarão a India dom Pedro Mascarenhas, | Francisco Barreto, dom Constantino, o Conde do Re⸗ | dondo dom Francisco Coutinho, & Ioão | de Mendoça. | Composta por mandado dos | muito Catholicos, & inuenciueis Monarchas d'Espanha, & | Reys de Portugal dom Felipe de gloriosa memoria, o pri⸗ | meiro deste nome; & de seu filho dom Felipe nosso | senhor, o segundo do mesmo nome. | Por Diogo do Couto Chronista, | & guarda mor da torre do tombo do estado da India. | [woodcut of the royal arms of Portugal] *| Com licença do supremo conselho da santa & geral Inquisição dos reinos | de Portugal, & do Ordinario, & Paço. | Em Lisboa, por Pedro Craesbeeck. Anno 1616. | Com privilegio Real. Vendese na rua nova em casa de Mateus de Matos.*

Small folio, 10 preliminary unnumbered leaves + 247 leaves of text in two columns to a page.

The narrative of the misadventures of the *Aguia* and *Garça* is to be found Livro VI, capitulo 3, fols. 104 *recto* and *verso*; Livro VIII, capitulo 1, fols. 141–5; *ibid.* capitulos 12 and 13, fols. 164–71. This text corresponds (with a few very minor variations and trifling omissions) to that printed by Bernardo Gomes de Brito in the *História Trágico⸗Marítima*, Tomo I (Lisbon, 1735), pp. 219–52.

(ii) [HENRIQUE DIAS]

Nao sam Paulo | [woodcut of a ship within a decorated border] *| ¶ Viagem & naufragio da | Nao sam Paulo, que foy pera a India o anno | de mil & quinhentos & sesenta. Capitão | Ruy de melo da camara Mestre | Joam luys, Piloto An⸗ | tonio Dias | ✠ | Com licença Ympresso.*

Last six lines are in Gothic type.

'Quarto in eights', watermark and chain lines running as for quarto, but with eight leaves to a signature, comprising twenty-two unnumbered leaves in all, as follows: (*a*) (title-page)—Aiiij+ 4 unsigned leaves. (*b*) Aij, Biii–Bv, + 3 unsigned. C–Ciij + 3 unsigned. Civ might have had a signature originally, but the whole of the bottom line is in facsimile in this the only known and recorded copy, the bibliographical description of which has been kindly supplied by Mr J. Mundy of the National Maritime Museum, Greenwich. On the *verso* of the last leaf is the following colophon in gothic type:

¶ *Aqui se acaba o Naufragio da Nao sã Paulo feyto por |*
hum homem de credito que vio & passou tudo ysto. |
E foy impresso em casa da viuua, molher que |
foy de Germão Gallhard. Aos oyto do |
mes Dabril. Anno de M.D.Lxv.

The woodcut of the ship on the title-page does not specifically depict the *São Paulo* but was a printer's stock-in-trade, used previously in many other Portuguese books including the *Estoria de muy nobre Vespiano* (1496), the *Marco Paulo* (1502), and the *Historia da muy notavel perda do galeão grande sam João*, printed at an unascertained date between 1554 and 1565.

A greatly expanded version of this 1565 text, which is specifically ascribed to Henrique Dias, was printed by Gomes de Brito in the *História Trágico-Marítima*, Tomo I (Lisbon, 1735), 351–479.

(iii) ◄ *Naufragio, que* ► | *passov Iorge Dalbuqverqve | Coelho, Capitão, & Governador de Paranambuco.* | [woodcut in plain border with arms of Jorge d'A. C.] | ◄ *Em Lisboa: Impresso com licença da Sancta Inquisição: Por* ► | *Antonio Alvarez. Anno M. CCCCCCI.* | ◄ *Vendemse em casa de Antonio Ribeyro Libreyro: Em a rua nova* ►

Signatures: A–A5+ 3 unsigned leaves; B–B5+ 3 unsigned; C–C5+ 3 unsigned; D–D5+ 3 unsigned; E–E2+ 1 unsigned leaf.

The title-page is followed by five unnumbered preliminary pages, containing the licences, sonnet, and a prologue addressed to Jorge d'A. C. by Antonio Ribeyro. At the end of the prologue and at the bottom of the page is a medallion woodcut portrait (? of Jorge d'A.C. ?). This is followed by a full-page woodcut portrait of Don Alvaro de Baçán, the first Marquis of Santa Cruz (*d.* 1588), which was used in several previous publications and has no connection whatever with the text. There follows the text of the *Naufrágio* on 69 unnumbered pages, with woodcuts which are directly relevant to the text on pp. 23, 27, 29, 59. On the last page of the text [69] occurs the same medallion portrait as at the end of the prologue. Pp. 70–71 are a double-page spread repeating the four woodcuts on pp. 23, 27, 29, 59. As noted in the intro-duction, some of these woodcuts are also found in the 1592 edition of the shipwreck of the great galleon *São João* [in 1552], with which they have no connection, thus proving that they must have been originally engraved for the hitherto unlocated first edition of the *Naufrágio, c.* 1580–90. These four woodcuts of the mis-adventures of the *Santo António* in 1565 were likewise used to illustrate other seventeenth-century publications such as the *Tratado das Batalhas e successos do Galeão Sanctiago com os Olandeses na Ilha da Sancta Elena* (1604), with which they have no connection.

The four woodcuts on pp. 70–1 of the *Naufrágio* are followed by a blank unnumbered page, and then by a two-page prologue addressed to Jorge d'A. C. and signed *Bento Teyxeyra*, with a repetition of the woodcut on p. 59 of the *Naufrágio* underneath this signature. Then follows the text of the *Prosopopea,* | *Dirigida a Iorge Dalbuquerque* | *Coelho, Capitão, & Governador* | *de Peranam-buco, noua* | *Lusitania, &c.* on 33 unnumbered pp. followed by 1 p. with a *Soneta per* | *Eccos, ao mesmo Senhor Iorge* | *Dalbuquerque Coelho.* within an ornamented woodcut border, and a final blank leaf.

Bernardo Gomes de Brito reprinted this edition of 1601, sup-pressing the division into chapters and the bulk of the matter on pp. 5 and 6, which ascribe the authorship to Afonso Luís and António de Castro and mention the existence of a previous edition. Gomes de Brito substituted for António Ribeiro's pro-logue another one which he ascribed on his title-page to 'Bento Teixeira Pinto who was a participant in the said shipwreck'. Apart from these basic alterations and omissions, the text of the

Naufrágio as reprinted in the *História Trágico-Marítima*, Tomo II (Lisbon, 1736), 7–59, does not differ in any important respect from that of 1601.

(B) Fuller titles of selected authorities quoted in the footnotes

Africa Pilot, III. *Comprising the Southern and Eastern Coasts of Africa from Table Bay to Ras Hafun*. 11th edition. London, 1954. (Published by the Hydrographic Department, Admiralty.)

ALMEIDA PRADO, J. F. DE, *Pernambuco e as Capitanias do Norte do Brasil, 1530–1630*. 4 vols., São Paulo, 1941.

ÁLVARES, MANUEL, S. J. See under FRAZÃO DE VASCON-CELOS below.

Anais da Biblioteca Nacional do Rio de Janeiro. Rio de Janeiro, 1876 to date. (Published by the Biblioteca Nacional, Rio de Janeiro).

BARBOSA MACHADO, DIOGO. *Bibliotheca Lusitana. Historica, Critica, e Cronologica*. 4 vols., Lisbon, 1741–59. Reprinted 4 vols., Lisbon, 1930–5.

BOXER, C. R. 'An introduction to the *História Trágico-Marítima*', reprint (56 pp.) from the *Miscelânea de Estudos em honra do Professor Hernâni Cidade*, Lisbon, 1957.

——. 'Moçambique island and the *Carreira da India*', reprint (38 pp.) from *Studia. Revista Semestral*, VIII (Lisbon, 1961), 95–132.

——. 'Moçambique island as a way-station for Portuguese East-Indiamen.' *Mariner's Mirror*, XLVIII (London, 1962), 3–18. (See also under *Tragic History of the Sea* below.)

COUTO, DIOGO DO. *Décadas da Asia*, IV–VII. Lisbon, 1602–16. As there are several later editions (none of them entirely satisfactory) of this work, all my citations are from *Livro* (Book) and *capitulo* (chapter), and not page references.

DALGADO, SEBASTIÃO RODOLFO. *Glossário Luso-Asiático*. 2 vols Coimbra, 1919–21.

DUFFY, JAMES. *Shipwreck and Empire. Being an account of Portuguese maritime disasters in a century of decline*. Cambridge, Mass. 1955.

FALCONER, WILLIAM. *An Universal Dictionary of the Marine: or, a copious explanation of the technical terms and phrases employed in the . . . ship.* London, 1789. (For some inexplicable reason the pages are not numbered.)

FERREIRA PAES, SIMÃO. *Recopilação das famosas armadas que para a India foram, 1496–1650.* Rio de Janeiro, 1937. (Facsimile edition of the original MS. of 1650.)

FIGUEIREDO FALCÃO, LUÍS DE. *Livro em que se contém toda a Fazenda e Real Patrimonio dos Reinos de Portugal, India e Ilhas adjacentes e outros particularidades . . . Copiado fielmente do manúscripto original e impresso por ordem do governo de Sua Magestade.* Lisbon, 1859.

FONTOURA DA COSTA, ABEL. *A Marinharia dos descobrimentos. Bibliografia Náutica Portuguesa até 1700.* Lisbon, 1933; reprinted 1939.

FRAZÃO DE VASCONCELOS, JOSÉ AUGUSTO AMARAL. *Naúfrágio da Nau 'S. Paulo' em um ilheu próximo de Samatra, no ano de 1561. Narração inédita escrita em Goa em 1562 pelo Padre Manuel Álvares, S.J.* Lisbon, 1948. (This narrative was not written at Goa in 1562, as stated in the titlépage, but at Malacca in 1561.)

— —. *Subsídios para a história da carreira da Índia no tempo dos Filipes.* Lisbon, 1960.

GONSALVES DE MELLO, JOSÉ ANTONIO. *Estudos Pernambucanos. Crítica e problemas de algumas fontes da história de Pernambuco.* Recife, 1960.

História TrágicóMarítima. Em que se escrevem chronologicamente os Naufragios que tiverão as Naos de Portugal, depois que se poz em exercicio a Navegação da India. Por Bernardo Gomes de Brito. 2 vols., Lisbon, 1735–6. (References are to this edition save where '*HTM* (ed. Sergio)' is indicated, which refers to the 3́volume annotated edition by António Sergio, Lisbon, 1955–7.)

HobsońJobson. A glossary of colloquial Angló́Indian words and phrases and of kindred terms, etymological, historical, geographical and diścursive. Edited by H. Yule, A. C. Burnell and W. Crooke. London, 1903.

JABOTÃO, ANTONIO DE SANTA MARIA, O.F.M. *Orbe Serafico Novo Brasilico, descoberto, estabelecido, e cultivado . . . como Theatro glorioso, e Parte Primeira da Chronica dos frades menores da mais estreita e regular Observancia da Provincia do Brasil.* Lisbon, 1761. (A second edition, with some additional matter, was published by the Instituto Historico e Geographico Brasileiro, 5 vols., Rio de Janeiro, 1858–61.)

Journal of the Malay Branch of the Royal Asiatic Society. Singapore, 1878 to date. (Prior to 1923 it was named *Straits Branch.*)

LEITÃO, HUMBERTO and LOPES, J. VICENTE, *Dicionário da linguagem de Marinha antiga e actual.* Lisbon, 1963.

LEITE, SERAFIM, S.J. *História da Companhia de Jesus no Brasil.* 10 vols., Lisbon and Rio de Janeiro, 1938–50.

The Mariner's Mirror. The Quarterly Journal of the Society for Nautical Research. London, 1911 to date.

MEILINK-ROELOFSZ, MARIE ANTOINETTE PETRONELLA. *Asian Trade and European Influence in the Indonesian Archipelago between 1500 and about 1630.* The Hague, 1962.

PYRARD DE LAVAL. See under *Voyage* below.

QUIRINO DA FONSECA. *Os Portugueses no Mar. Memorias Históricas e Arqueológicas das Naus de Portugal. I. Ementa Histórica das Naus Portuguesas.* Lisbon, 1926. (No more published.)

RIBEIRO, LUCIANO (ed.). *Registo da Casa da Índia.* 2 vols.,Lisbon, 1954–5.

SÁ, ARTUR BASÍLIO DE. *Documentação para a história das missões do Padroado Português do Oriente. Insulíndia, 1506–1599.* 5 vols., Lisbon, 1954–8.

SCHURHAMMER, S.J., GEORG. *Franz Xaver, sein Leben und seine Zeit.* II. *Asien, 1541–1552* (i) *Indien und Indonesien, 1541–1547.* Freiburg, 1963. (Vol. I, published in 1955, has no relevance to the present work.)

SILVA REGO, ANTÓNIO DA. *Documentação para a história das missões do padroado português do Oriente. Índia, 1499–1582.* 12 vols., Lisbon, 1950– . (In progress.)

——. 'Viagens Portuguesas à Índia em meados do século XVI.' *Anais da Academia Portuguesa da História*, II Series, V (Lisbon, 1954), 77–142. (See also under *Studia* below.)

SOUSA, FRANCISCO DE, S.J. *Oriente Conquistado a Jesu Christo pelos Padres da Companhia de Jesus da Provincia de Goa*. 2 vols., Lisbon, 1710.

STRANDES, JUSTUS. *The Portuguese Period in East Africa. Translated from the German by Jean Wallwork and edited with topographical notes by J. S. Kirkman*. Nairobi, 1961.

Stuida. Revista Semestral. Lisbon, 1958 to date. (Edited by António da Silva Rego.)

The Tragic History of the Sea, 1589–1622. Narratives of the shipwrecks of the Portuguese East-Indiamen São Thomé (*1589*), Santo Alberto (*1593*), São João Baptista (*1622*), *and the journeys of the survivors in South East Africa. Edited from the original Portuguese by* C. R. Boxer, for the Hakluyt Society, Second Series, vol. CXII, Cambridge, 1959.

VALIGNANO, ALESSANDRO, S.J. *História del principio y progresso de la Compañía de Jesus en las Indias Orientales, 1542–1564. Herausgegeben und erläutert von Josef Wicki, S.J*. Rome, 1944.

Voyage of Francois Pyrard of Laval to the East Indies, the Maldives, the Moluccas and Brazil. 3 vols., in 2. Translated from the French edition of 1619, and edited by A. Gray and H. C. P. Bell for the Hakluyt Society, First Series, vols LXXVI–LXXVII, London, 1887–90.

INDEX

C. R. BOXER (1904–2000) was Camoens Professor of Portuguese at London University from 1947 to 1951 and from 1953 to 1967; he also served as professor of the History of the Far East at London University from 1951 to 1953. Author, translator, and editor of more than three hundred books and articles, he also held positions at several universities throughout the United States.

JOSIAH BLACKMORE is associate professor of Portuguese at the University of Toronto. He is the author of *Manifest Perdition*, also published by the University of Minnesota Press, and the coeditor (with Gregory S. Hutcheson) of *Queer Iberia: Sexualities, Cultures, and Crossings from the Middle Ages to the Renaissance.*